The Frontier Army
in the Settlement of the West

The Frontier Army
in the Settlement of the West

By Michael L. Tate

University of Oklahoma Press : Norman

ALSO BY MICHAEL L. TATE

The Indians of Texas: An Annotated Research Bibliography (Metuchen, N.J., 1986)

The Upstream People: An Annotated Research Bibliography of the Omaha Tribe (Metuchen, N.J., 1991)

Nebraska History: An Annotated Bibliography (Westport, Conn., 1995)

Library of Congress Cataloging-in-Publication Data

Tate, Michael L.
    The frontier army in the settlement of the West / by Michael L. Tate.
        p.   cm.
    Includes bibliographical references (p.   ) and index.
    ISBN 0–8061–3173–X (cloth : alk. paper)
    1. Frontier and pioneer life—West (U.S.)   2. West (U.S.)—History—19th
century.   3. United States.   Army—History—19th century.   4. United States.
Army—Military life—History—19th century.   I. Title.
    F596.T36   1999
    978'.02—dc21   99–36276
                                                                                      CIP

Text design by Gail Carter.

1 2 3 4 5 6 7 8 9 10

Contents

Illustrations

MAPS

Preface

Few American institutions have been more stereotyped than the frontier army of the nineteenth century. Pulp novels, movies, television, and the popular works of artists such as Frederic Remington and Charles Schreyvogel have conveyed the romantic image of the gallant and dashing cavalryman locked in continuous combat with feather-bedecked Indian warriors. Celebrated movie director John Ford contributed greatly to the longevity of this portrayal with his army trilogy *Fort Apache* (1948), *She Wore a Yellow Ribbon* (1949), and *Rio Grande* (1950), which remain immensely popular with audiences even today. Ford placed the military in the picturesque setting of Monument Valley, introduced elements of conflict with renegade Indians and unscrupulous whites, and presented rigidly typecast characters imitative of Captain Charles King's army novels of the late nineteenth century. His prize discovery, John Wayne, represented the tough, experienced ranking officer who drove his men through immense hardships but earned their respect and admiration. Ford's films also made important use of secondary characters such as Victor McLaglen, Ben Johnson, Harry Carey, Jr., and Ward Bond to convey the dutiful nature of frontier soldiers and their total commitment to the "regimental family."

Later movies such as Ralph Nelson's *Soldier Blue* (1970) and Arthur Penn's *Little Big Man* (1970) broke with Ford's tradition and instead cast the frontier army as a racist killing machine which happily murdered and mutilated peaceful Indian people at the behest of corrupt politicians and businessmen. Kevin Costner's critically acclaimed box office success *Dances With Wolves* (1990) evoked the same denunciation of frontier soldiers as a collection of insane officers and beastly enlisted men. Though these polarized perspectives drew upon historical events to document their cinematic portrayals, they missed a more crucial point. The army spent relatively little time in armed conflict with Native Americans. In truth, the overwhelming majority of its attention was devoted to performing tasks which played an even larger, holistic role in the development of the West. Among other things, the army conducted explorations; built roads; improved river transportation; offered nuclei for town building; served as "harbingers of civilization" with its schools, chapels, and hospitals open to civilian participation; undertook agricultural experiments; delivered federal mails; protected national parks; collected scientific data; created an artistic and cartographic record; published vital primary records of western life; provided stable revenues to attract settlers and businessmen; extended relief to destitute civilians; acted in concert with civilian officials to enforce the law; and frequently championed Indian rights. For all its virtues and faults, the "multipurpose army" served as the "right arm" of the federal government in its nineteenth-century expansionist policies, and it is in this larger context that the institution must be evaluated.

Francis Paul Prucha's 1953 book *Broadax and Bayonet* provided the most authoritative early account of the diverse accomplishments of the multipurpose army and clearly indicated that soldiers expended far more effort as laborers than they did as Indian fighters. By examining the northwestern region comprising Illinois, Wisconsin, Minnesota and Iowa between 1815 and 1860, Prucha found that the frontier army served as the nation's "orderly purveyor of civilization," and it "cannot be assigned a single position in the parade to the West; its presence was felt in all stages of the pioneering process."[1] In his 1969 work, *The Sword of the Republic: The United States Army on the Frontier, 1783–1846,* Prucha expanded the physical boundaries of his study to again document specific examples of the nonmartial role of the frontier army. He likewise broadened the list of multifaceted contributions to portray the officers and men as "agents of empire" who consciously strove for results beyond mere victories over Indian tribes.[2] These duties were no happenstance occurrences; they were the natural results of planned government policies to promote national sovereignty and accelerate settlement of the massive hinterland.

Although more concerned with documenting the frontier army's relationship with Indians, Robert Utley published two volumes which gave further validation to the importance of the diverse military roles. His *Frontiersmen in Blue: The United States Army and the Indian, 1848–1865* (1967), and *Frontier Regulars: The United States Army and the Indian, 1866–1891* (1973), shifted the setting away from Prucha's "prairie frontier" to the Great Plains and Far West. While quick to note the numerous shortcomings and outright failures of the army, Utley's overall assessment was positive.[3] He clearly sympathized with Albert Van Zant, formerly of the Sixth Cavalry, who wrote the following to the periodical *Winners of the West* in 1924: "Where today stands stately buildings and happy homes they voluntarily went into service for $13 a month and were not only soldiers but mechanics and laborers living in tents until quarters were built, cutting timber, building horse stables, wagon roads, bridges, telegraph lines, escorting wagon trains, U.S. mail, guarding highways, byways, people and flocks." Van Zant went on to lament that had these tasks been performed by civilians instead of soldiers, the former would have been heralded by fanfare, speeches, and banquets.[4]

Yet not everyone was so quick to accept the views offered by Prucha, Utley, and Van Zant. Historian Roger Nichols focused only on the brief period between 1800 and 1830, just as the army was establishing its initial presence in the Missouri River valley. Furthermore, instead of examining the full array of multipurpose duties, Nichols confined his investigation to the single subject of Indian and army relationships. In a well-argued, albeit narrow, case study, he concluded that "the demonstrated failure of the military to deal adequately with the Indians of the Missouri Valley prior to 1830 raises questions about the success of the soldiers with Indians in other parts of the West. While no one can say that the army always failed to achieve its goals, there is room for a healthy skepticism about claims that the military was 'an orderly purveyor of civilization.'"[5]

More encompassing were the arguments made by Leo E. Oliva, who examined the contributions of military posts to the settlement of western

Kansas, especially within the two decades following the Civil War. Yet, like Nichols, Oliva was primarily assessing the army's role in defeating the Indians, placing them permanently on reservations, and opening the vast region to white settlement. He pessimistically concluded that buffalo hunters and railroads probably had a greater impact on denying the Native Americans their domain than did all the military campaigns combined. Furthermore, none of the Santa Fe Trail forts built before the Civil War left a legacy important to overall settlement patterns within western Kansas. Even those constructed after 1865 contributed only minimally to rural and urban development. In summary, the major nonmilitary contribution of forts within that particular Plains region was primarily economic—first along the Santa Fe trade route and later within the counties that surrounded the posts and that maintained lucrative contracts with them.[6]

In his above-mentioned 1976 article, Oliva cautioned that the evidence was not conclusive, since examples were readily available to draw opposing views. The true test of the thesis could come only after the investigation of similar army performances in other regions throughout the entire expanse of the nineteenth century. Happily, the same author already had helped move the debate into a different realm of inquiry with a 1975 essay which reawakened interest in Francis Paul Prucha's original contentions. Rather than remaining focused on the Indian-army relationship, Oliva stressed the great range of practical contributions by the frontier army. Instead of visualizing rugged individualism triumphing over the wilderness, he held that only the federal government was powerful enough to meet many of these challenges. More important, according to Oliva, it was the army that was "*the* major institution of the federal government's partnership with the pioneers in the conquest of the continent."[7] The heart of his essay summarized mostly military contributions to exploration, road building, civilian relief efforts, and economic stimuli to settlement, but his brief "suggestions for further research" section echoed Prucha's earlier calls.

Oliva especially challenged historians and social scientists to quantify the economic significance of military installations: "The importance of the military market for early settlers, value of payrolls for civilian employees, investments by officers in various business endeavors, and the military partnership in community development (of towns and transportation networks) remain to be determined. The total impact of military contracts . . . needs to be assessed in relation to continental expansion and frontier growth. The economic relationship [*sic*] of the Army to livestock producers (cattle, horses, and mules), grain farmers, lumber suppliers, and transportation corporations are obvious areas for further research."[8]

This demand for systematic quantifiable detail to replace unreliable anecdotal evidence produced two classic studies within a decade. In 1983, Robert Frazer published *Forts and Supplies: The Role of the Army in the Economy of the Southwest, 1846–1861*. By assembling a vast array of statistical data, he proved beyond a shadow of a doubt that military spending was "the single most significant factor in the economic development of the Southwest" between the Mexican War and the Civil War.[9] After paying homage to both Prucha and Frazer, Darlis Miller carried the borderlands story almost to the end of the frontier period. Her massive *Soldiers and Settlers: Military Supply in the Southwest, 1861–1885* (1989) provided the definitive model for studying the diverse ways in which army payrolls and contracts powered regional economies.[10] Similar case studies for other frontier regions and time periods now beg to be written by other scholars who are willing to wade through a mountain of scattered financial records.

The level of sophistication attained by Frazer's and Miller's studies was advanced even further by Frank N. Schubert's *Buffalo Soldiers, Braves, and the Brass* (1993). The author demonstrated once and for all that post histories no longer had to remain as pedantic stories of daily drudgery punctuated by occasional Indian campaigns. Fort Robinson, located in the northwestern corner of Nebraska, provided the perfect example for a community study even beyond its glory days of the Sioux conflict of the mid-1870s. Schubert portrayed Fort Robinson as a "company town in which decisions regarding the nature and distribution of services emanated from a central authority."[11] Like mining communities and industrial centers which evidenced a controlling corporate relationship toward property and laborers, Fort Robinson dictated the fate not only of soldiers, but also of farmers, ranchers, mercantile owners, and a host of other civilians. By blending municipal records of Chadron and

Crawford with the standard military sources, Schubert wove a story of mutual dependency and benefit. He also demonstrated the significant dynamics of race relations between predominantly white civilians of the area and black regiments that frequently were stationed there. Even more important, he went beyond the economic dimensions of the story to delineate the whole range of social services that the army provided to civilians in its school, library, church, and hospital. His is a worthy model for all researchers who wish to undertake holistic approaches to western community studies.

The rise of the New Western History during the past decade has helped challenge many of the traditional views that Americans have held about the westward movement. Patricia Nelson Limerick's *The Legacy of Conquest: The Unbroken Past of the American West* (1987) judged the process in less than heroic terms as it identified a long procession of environmental exploitation, economic imperialism, racism, classism, and sexism. Furthermore, the author convincingly argued, the pattern did not end with conclusion of the frontier period, but continued into modern times. Richard White's *"It's Your Misfortune and None of My Own": A New History of the American West* (1991) argued the conquest and continuum themes even more convincingly, especially for the twentieth-century West.[12]

Yet, for all the ink that has been expended in this debate, a curious oversight still remains. A check of standard publications by and about the New Western Historians reveals an almost total neglect of the frontier army as an element in the westering story. When the military role is discussed, it is almost inevitably stylized in a negative way, mostly as destroyer of the Native American way of life, protector of corporate interests, or enemy of the working class. Thus the Sand Creek Massacre, soldier protection of corporate interests during labor strikes, and the army's removal of boomers from Oklahoma Territory appear briefly in these sources, but there is virtually no mention of the broader context of the multipurpose army.[13]

In a curious way, this neglect has led us almost full circle to the days when the frontier military was viewed in a one-dimensional way. While image makers such as Frederic Remington, Charles Schreyvogel, and John Ford helped create a heroic legacy for the bygone institution, the

New Western Historians merely turned the stereotype upside down and substituted a negative view more in keeping with modern cinematic portrayals in *Soldier Blue*, *Little Big Man*, and *Dances With Wolves*. Unfortunately, both images were flawed, because they failed to assess the *full* performance record of the army in all of its diverse roles.[14]

Precisely because so many historians have been content with the existing stereotype or because they have examined other dimensions of frontier military life, no one has yet tested Francis Paul Prucha's findings within the context of the entire West. I made a similar affirmation of this need in a 1980 essay entitled "The Multi-Purpose Army on the Frontier: A Call for Further Research," but no overview interpretation was forthcoming.[15] Now, I have attempted to address my own solicitation by writing this book, which takes up where the article left off. Because this is intended as a synthesis of the diverse roles of the frontier military, it relies heavily upon published sources—both primary and secondary—rather than on the endless collections of National Archives materials. Although I have profited from the evidence and conclusions advanced by many other researchers, I have in no way merely mimicked their efforts. I see my task as somewhat akin to Robert Utley's masterful studies of army and Indian relations—to take the large view and to place the findings within an interpretive framework. But rather than stressing the martial side of the story—with its emphasis on tactics, battles, and commanders—I have tried to stake out an important dimension of the "New Social History" as it applies to the frontier army.

Even though I have attempted to be thorough with the selection of individual multipurpose roles, I have purposely omitted three sizable topics that are germane to the broad study. First, I did not include a chapter on race relations on the frontier even though I originally intended to do so. Instead, I have included mention of the black regiments within each of the chapters as they pertain to specific issues. Second, I have not included the army's role in Alaska (even though it was considerable) or in Hawaii, because both those geographic locations better fit a different context of military participation. Third, I have not attempted to bring the story much beyond the beginning of the twentieth century. Even though many of the parallel themes of military contributions to western development can be seen in the early twentieth century, my effort focuses primarily on the frontier period of development in the western states and territories.[16]

Rather than providing the final word on this huge subject, this book performs three more manageable tasks. It provides the necessary synthesis to tie together the diverse topics into an understandable whole. It presents the most complete bibliography yet assembled on the multipurpose army concept. And I hope it suggests to other researchers how much still needs to be done with the individual dimensions of the army's role. Perhaps when the persistently romanticized images of John Ford give way to more accurate appraisals, modern generations will finally come to understand the wisdom of Col. Zachary Taylor's 1820 pronouncement that "the ax, pick, saw and trowel, has become more the implement of the American soldier than the cannon, musket or sword."[17] Until that understanding is achieved, the frontier army will remain a one-dimensional entity within the public consciousness and its true historical significance will be misperceived.

Acknowledgments

Twenty-five years ago, while still a graduate student, I came across a remarkable book which has excited and challenged me ever since. Francis Paul Prucha's *Broadax and Bayonet: The Role of the United States Army in the Development of the Northwest, 1815–1860* (1953) had already introduced a generation of historians to the multifaceted roles that the frontier army played during a significant phase of American development. Even at that early point in my academic career, I began to think in terms of crafting a companion volume that would examine Prucha's seminal thesis, expand his list of army activities, broaden the time period to include the entire nineteenth century, and embrace the expansive Trans-Mississippi West as a testing ground for the thesis.

At about that same time, I received an infusion of new ideas about the multipurpose army from a fellow graduate student who has remained a life-long friend. Frank N. "Mickey" Schubert and I had a number of discussions about the topic while he pursued an independent readings course on the frontier army as background to working on his doctoral dissertation. Throughout the subsequent years, Mickey has continued a marvelous publication record on various aspects of the military experience—especially on the African-American Buffalo Soldier regiments and on the symbiotic relationship between western forts and adjacent towns. Amid his own busy schedule, he has always been generous with his time and materials to help facilitate my own investigations.

Another friendship cultivated during my graduate school experience was one with William H. Leckie, who at that time served as Vice Chancellor of Academic Affairs at the University of Toledo. Not only did Bill graciously consent to serve on the committee for my dissertation on a Native American topic, he also loaned me material relevant to the Benjamin Grierson family. Ironically, those sources proved to be more important to me in the current book project than they did in my earlier dissertation pursuits. Likewise, Robert Utley provided me with information about printed guides and unpublished shelf lists to National Archives and other materials which I have treasured and made use of ever since. As a novice graduate student at that time, I was duly impressed with both men's generosity.

Another voice of support in the long climb to completion of this book was Ron Tyler, Director of the Texas State Historical Association. Ron saw merit in the concept and, whenever we met at conferences, he was always quick to ask, "Is it done yet?" I also wish to thank Ron Tyler and Edward Hake Phillips for their attention to me while they were professors at Austin College. They not only strengthened my interest in the academic field, but they also directed me along the path of becoming a better researcher and writer even as an undergraduate student. In a totally different regard, I owe a debt of gratitude to Don Rickey who not only gave the profession a wonderful book in the form of *Forty Miles a Day on Beans and Hay: The Enlisted Soldier Fighting the Indian Wars*, but he also long ago made me aware of the great value of soldier accounts in the obscure publication *Winners of the West.*

Aid in searching archival collections came from a variety of competent and helpful individuals over a long number of years: La Vera Rose, Manuscript Curator at the South Dakota State Historical Society; Bob Knecht, Manuscripts Curator at Kansas State Historical Society; and Reference Librarian Katherine Wyatt and Reference Assistant Ane McBride at the Nebraska State Historical Society. Much welcomed was the help of Clayton D. Laurie of the U.S. Army Center of Military History, who has recently published excellent case studies on the multipurpose army roles. Likewise, Rick Ewig, Editor of *Annals of Wyoming*, graciously granted permission to reproduce a revised form of my article from the winter 1997 issue of his journal as chapter two in this book.

Although the procurement of rights and permissions for this book proved to be a laborious task, a host of individuals deserve credit for locating archival photographs, reproducing them, and inquiring about any legal restrictions on those items. Especially noteworthy in this regard is Kevin Morrow, Photo Archivist at the National Archives, College Park, Maryland; Archivist John Dahlheim at Yellowstone National Park; Museum Curator Kitty Belle Deernose at Little Bighorn Battlefield National Monument; Superintendent Larry D. Reed and Park Historian Dean M. Knudson at Scotts Bluff National Monument; Reference Historian La Vaughn Bresnahan at Wyoming State Archives; Photo Service Coordinator Susan Sheehan at Arizona Historical Society; Curator Michael J. Winey at U.S. Army Military History Institute, Carlisle Barracks; Reference Assistant Chad Wall at Nebraska State Historical Society; State Archivist Richard L. Popp at South Dakota State Historical Society; and Director Don Snoddy and Archivist William Kratville at the Union Pacific Railroad Archives. In addition to these valuable photographs, the University of New Mexico Press agreed to the reproduction of three maps from Robert Utley's *The Indian Frontier of the American West.* I am particularly grateful to Dianne Edward of the University of New Mexico Press for helping me secure these rights.

Closer to home, Catherine Walker and the Interlibrary Loan staff at the University of Nebraska at Omaha Library have proven essential to my search for published and unpublished sources. Without their help, a project of this magnitude in time and space would have proven impossible. Colleagues within my own department—especially Professors Bruce Garver, Harl Dalstrom, Richard Overfield, William Pratt, Jerold Simmons and Tommy Thompson—have heard parts of the story before and have contributed ideas and needed encouragement along the way. Equally important were two summer research grants which aided my efforts. One was provided by the Summer Research Council of the University of Nebraska at Omaha. The second was made available by the Center for Great Plains Studies at the University of Nebraska-Lincoln; I wish to acknowledge the moral support of Frederick Luebke and John Wunder in seeking this award. My own university also provided a periodic professional leave during the Fall 1996 semester which enabled me to do a great deal of actual writing on the manuscript.

After expending so many years of thought and research on this project, it is an exhilarating feeling to reach the concluding stages. In this final pursuit, my association with staff members of the University of Oklahoma Press has been a rich and rewarding one. I appreciate the confidence that John Drayton, director, and Randolph Lewis, acquisitions editor, showed toward the manuscript and their guidance through various production stages. Editorial secretary Ursula Daly answered my many questions and kept me apprised of the publication schedule. Associate Editor Jo Ann Reece took over crucial duties as the project editor for the manuscript. Her close attention to detail, as well as the meticulous copyediting done by Noel Parsons, prevented some embarrassing errors and improved the quality of the final draft.

Likewise, two scholars widely recognized in the field of frontier military history—Robert Wooster and Robert Utley—served as outside readers of the manuscript, and they too made some important corrections and called for clarification of some imprecise information. My wife, Carol, not only assembled the final draft on computer disks, but she also discovered a number of stylistic errors and organizational oversights which needed immediate attention. To all of these people I owe an immense debt of gratitude for they have ensured that this extended project reached its maturity.

Finally, beyond mentioning all the people who have helped with this book in one form or another, I wish to acknowledge the special assistance of W. Eugene Hollon, former Ohio Regents Professor at the University of Toledo and a recognized authority on American frontier history. His importance as mentor and friend go far beyond any praise that I can list here.

The Frontier Army
in the Settlement of the West

CHAPTER ONE

Discoverers

MILITARY SCIENTISTS, ETHNOLOGISTS, AND ARTISTS IN THE NEW EMPIRE

When Meriwether Lewis and William Clark began their ascent of the Missouri River in May of 1804, they carried with them a list of specific instructions from President Thomas Jefferson. In addition to searching for an all-water route to the Pacific coast, judging the extent of British and Spanish influence among the Indian tribes, and assessing future economic potential along the line of march, they were to assiduously collect and catalog scientific data. The breadth of their instructions indicated that the exploratory mission served twin goals: to strengthen American claims to the Louisiana Purchase and to address intellectual curiosities about this exotic landscape.

Among other things, Jefferson directed the two captains to record geological, zoological, and botanical information with as much precision as possible. This type of detail about mineral resources, soil fertility, comparative temperatures, vegetation patterns, and populations of fur-bearing animals would aid future economic development of the Great Plains, Rocky Mountains, and Pacific Northwest. Yet the precise instructions also spoke to the excitement of an educated American elite who had been inspired by the boundless inquiry of the Enlightenment. Furthermore, these people wished to know more about the habits and customs of the Native Americans who dwelled in these distant lands, not merely for commercial and diplomatic reasons, but also to observe lifeways different from their own.[1] From out of the towering accomplishments of this corps of discovery emerged a century-long tradition of military exploration, scientific observation, and diligent record keeping which served a broader array of American interests than were first conceived.

President Jefferson's commitment to the pursuit of knowledge, as well as to the fulfillment of short-term geopolitical goals, was evidenced in two other western expeditions. Although largely remembered today as "spy missions" aimed at exploiting Spanish weaknesses in the southwestern borderlands, they, too, served a scientific need. Lt. Zebulon Pike's 1806–1807 exploration of the Central Plains resulted in capture and brief imprisonment in Ciudad Chihuahua. Similarly, the 1806 journey of Thomas Freeman, Peter Custis, and Capt. Thomas Sparks to locate the headwaters of the Red River resulted in failure when Spanish troops turned back their party at the eastern border of present-day Oklahoma. Yet in both cases the expeditions carried similar scientific instructions from the president, and they produced extensive facts about the geology, flora, fauna, and Indian peoples along the southern edges of the Louisiana Purchase.[2]

Following a hiatus of more than a dozen years, military reconnaissances of the Great Plains resumed under the guidance of Secretary of War John C. Calhoun, who shared Jefferson's earlier dream of government subsidy for western exploration and record keeping. Calhoun entrusted the primary mission to Maj. Stephen H. Long, who left the vicinity of Fort Atkinson, Nebraska, just as its construction was undertaken during the spring of 1820. The carefully selected party consisted of only twenty-two men—ten soldiers and twelve civilians—but it included an august group of specialists. Dr. Edwin James, a highly trained physician and scientist, served as the company surgeon, botanist, and geologist. Thomas Say fulfilled the primary obligation of collecting zoological specimens and describing them in his journals, but he also assumed an additional role as ethnologist and thus recorded much information about Plains tribes encountered along the trail. Samuel Seymour was principal artist of the party, but young Titian Ramsay Peale also contributed many sketches as he conducted work as assistant naturalist for the expedition.[3]

Long's reconnaissance produced an important assemblage of empirical evidence despite the major's unfortunate categorization of the Plains as the Great American Desert, "almost totally unfit for cultivation, and of course uninhabitable by a people depending upon agriculture for subsistence."[4] At the conclusion of the trip, Congress retained the scientists and artists on a per diem basis so that they could write their reports for publication and mount their specimens for permanent preservation. James, Say, and Peale had collected the skins of sixty new or rare animals, several thousand insects, between four hundred and five hundred plant specimens previously unknown to scientists, plus a wide assortment of minerals and shells, and Seymour had drawn and painted 150 landscapes. Renowned botanist John Torrey prepared the plant collections and completed a series of studies that were published within three volumes of *Annuals of the Lyceum of Natural History*.[5] Long also added a further contribution to the list of accomplishments by producing the most accurate map of the Central and Southern Plains that was available at that time. Originally published in 1823, it became the standard base map for other cartographers and explorers during the next several decades.[6]

The work accomplished by Long's expedition gradually ushered in a forty-year cycle of scholarly achievement by the army's most elite unit, the Corps of Topographical Engineers. Its officers, most of them trained at West Point, possessed an advanced education steeped in scientific, engineering, and cartographic skills.[7] Together with the civilian specialists who often accompanied their western travels, these savants amassed a collective scientific record unmatched anywhere else in the nation. They published their findings in notable journals, held membership in prestigious professional organizations, and collected the raw data that allowed scientists elsewhere to advance their own studies and theories.[8]

As early as 1834, Maj. Gen. Edmund Gaines instructed all officers involved in frontier exploration or other western field duties to keep journals of scientific information. Each officer was to enter "concisely, the position and military character of the country over which they travel, the nature and quality of the surface, the courses and distances travelled . . . noting the actual or estimated width, depth, general courses and velocity of the principal rivers and creeks, the character of the soil, the mineral and fossil appearances, the timber and other productions,

particularly such as belong to the military resources of the country; . . .
with sketches such as are usually and most conveniently made with a pen
or pencil in active reconnoissance."[9]

Although primarily intended to enhance the gathering of field reports
for map making, the order promoted recording of all kinds of observations in the following two decades. For the elite Topographical Engineers,
as well as other officers of the line, these instructions gave precise
substance to a host of scientific endeavors that transcended mere
exploration of unknown lands.

Typical of the accomplishments of these "topogs" during the antebellum period were the efforts of John C. Frémont during his three
primary western reconnaissances of 1842, 1843–44, and 1845. His published reports, along with the accompanying Charles Preuss maps that
were widely reprinted in civilian trail guides, helped stimulate American
migration to Oregon and California during mid-century. Frémont's
descriptions of the flora, fauna, and geological formations also were
quoted frequently in other studies of the period, and his numerous plant
specimens were cataloged and reported on by John Torrey.[10]

During the same era, Lt. James W. Abert, son of the chief of the Corps
of Topographical Engineers, conducted operations along the Santa Fe
Trail and through sections of Indian Territory and New Mexico. With
the sharp eye of a well-trained naturalist, Abert especially filled his
journals with information about birds and mammals. He subsequently
published ornithological articles within the prestigious *Proceedings of the
Academy of Natural Sciences* and the *Cincinnati Society for Natural History
Journal*.[11] Capt. Howard Stansbury evidenced the same mastery of
scientific observation in his 1849 trip to the Great Salt Lake. After the
assigned civilian naturalist deserted the party, Stansbury kept detailed
observations about the flora and fauna and collected unique specimens.
Princeton University's John Torrey used many of these plant and animal
samples in his own writings, but it was Stansbury's subsequent survey of
the route later followed by the Union Pacific Railroad that assured his
major claim to fame.[12]

The Corps of Topographical Engineers reached its high-water mark
during the 1850s as military officers and civilian scientists combined their
efforts to survey the best possible routes for a future transcontinental

railroad. Even though sectional politics and the approach of the Civil War precluded Congress from selecting a preferred route, the hard work paid off in other immediate ways. Congress funded publication of the thirteen-volume series of Pacific railroad studies under the title *Reports of the Explorations and Surveys to Ascertain the Most Practicable and Economical Route for a Railroad from the Mississippi River to the Pacific Ocean.* These volumes constituted the most extensive set of scientific records about *terra incognita,* but volumes seven, nine, and ten especially attracted the attention of scientists. They were exclusively devoted to botanical and zoological data, and they represented the federal government's most significant scientific publications of the nineteenth century. Also of monumental importance was volume eleven, which contained Lt. Gouverneur K. Warren's *Memoir* and his various maps, including the "General Map" of the entire Trans-Mississippi West.[13]

The Topographical Engineers left an immensely valuable scientific record for the American people, but they were not the only military officers to make their mark in the pre–Civil War era. A class of highly trained and intellectually inquisitive army surgeons maintained close associations with eastern scholars as well as their European counterparts. John Torrey, soon to be the nation's preeminent botanist, served as an assistant surgeon from 1824 to 1828 and as a professor at the U.S. Military Academy before finally leaving the army for academic life. He provided a tangible bridge between the frontier military officers who lived in the West and the eastern intellectuals who hungered for their reports and specimens.[14]

Assistant Surgeon Zina Pitcher began his collection of zoological objects while stationed at Fort Brady in Michigan's Upper Peninsula. He later bestowed these upon the Lyceum of Natural History in New York, and he remained a corresponding member of the group for many years. His subsequent scientific work while stationed at Fort Gibson, Indian Territory, during the 1830s attracted the attention of Torrey, who shepherded many of Pitcher's plant specimens to the New York Botanical Garden. In 1835, Major Pitcher became president of the Army Medical Board, and following retirement from service, he helped create the medical department at the University of Michigan and later served as regent at that institution for many years.[15]

Surgeon George Suckley held the important position as medical officer and naturalist for the 1853 Forty-seventh Parallel Survey headed by Governor Isaac Ingalls Stevens of Washington Territory. Together with his civilian assistant, contract surgeon James Graham Cooper, Suckley assembled a massive amount of information that appeared in the twelfth volume of the Pacific railroad survey reports. The value of its contents on mammals, waterfowl, fish, and geology was deemed so important that the volume was commercially reprinted as *The Natural History of Washington Territory* (1859). In the interim, Suckley continued this regional study from his new post at Fort Steilacoom and published a shorter descriptive article on Pacific Northwest fauna in *Transactions of the American Medical Association* (1857).[16]

At about the same time that Suckley was conducting his investigation in the Pacific Northwest, Assistant Surgeon Thomas Charlton Henry followed similar pursuits in the Southwest. As a member of Philadelphia's Academy of Natural Sciences, he maintained a steady stream of correspondence with his associates, who published his brief articles in local newspapers. Henry's most significant work came in the field of ornithology, and his writings on that subject filled one of the volumes in the Pacific railroad survey reports. His close association with civilian ornithologists also led to publication of his correspondence and formal reports in nongovernment sources. Most significant was inclusion of his southwestern avifauna descriptions in John Cassin's *Illustrations of the Birds of California, Texas, Oregon, British and Russian America* (1856).[17]

Also recognized by the scholarly community was Edward Perry Vollum, who served as post surgeon at Fort Belknap, Texas, in 1856 and later at Fort Umpqua, Oregon, and Fort Crook, California. From these widely dispersed locations this naturalist shipped many boxes of plants, animal skins, birds' eggs, fish, and other specimens preserved in alcohol solutions to the prestigious Smithsonian Institution. Likewise, the Smithsonian profited immensely from the collecting work of Surgeon John Frazier Head while he was stationed at Fort Ripley, Minnesota, during the mid-1850s, and at least one of his articles appeared within the Smithsonian's *Annual Reports.*[18]

Although these men gained stature in the scientific community of antebellum America, lesser known army medical officers also added to the scholarly record by writing down their observations and submitting specimens to eastern institutions during the same period. Joseph K. Barnes, who later served as surgeon general of the United States from 1864 to 1882, filed reports from Kansas; Rodney Glisan contributed from Indian Territory; and John Fox Hammond compiled information in New Mexico and California.[19] At Fort McKavett, Texas, Dr. S. Wylie Crawford made extensive studies of local plants and soil samples so that the army could better understand the relationship between environmental conditions and patterns of illness. His statistics and conclusions appeared prominently as "Medical Topography and Diseases of Fort McKavett" in a larger government report published in 1856. One hundred miles to the north, Surgeon Alex B. Hasson prepared a similar study on medical topography and diseases in the vicinity of Fort Phantom Hill. This was subsequently reprinted for broader public consumption in the *Texas State Gazette*, published in Austin.[20]

Perhaps the most unique contribution by a field naturalist with a medical connection came from John (János) Xántus. Although only an enlisted man serving as a hospital steward at Fort Riley, Kansas, Xántus received excellent scientific instruction from his superior, Surgeon William A. Hammond. He accompanied one of the Pacific railroad survey parties in 1855 and subsequently assembled for shipment to the Smithsonian Institution his personal collection of approximately three hundred snakes, two hundred lizards, seven hundred fish, and forty boxes of plants. Unfortunately, his considerable collecting efforts and his numerous reports published in scholarly tomes were tarnished by his propensity to exaggerate his accomplishments and even to plagiarize from other people's works. Even with these blemishes on his unofficial scientific career, Xántus was elected a life member of the Academy of Natural Sciences of Philadelphia in 1856. Following return to his native Hungary in 1857, he became director of the Zoological Gardens of Budapest and later headed the ethnographic division of the National Museum of Hungary.[21]

Despite the demise of the Corps of Topographical Engineers during the Civil War, military interest in exploration and scientific research continued unabated. Legendary were the four great surveys conducted between 1867 and 1879. Two were accomplished under the auspices of the Interior Department: the U.S. Geological and Geographical Survey, led by Ferdinand V. Hayden, and the U.S. Geographical and Geological Survey of the Rocky Mountain Region, conducted by John Wesley Powell. The War Department organized its own equivalent expeditions: the U.S. Geological Exploration of the Fortieth Parallel, headed by civilian Clarence King, and the U.S. Geographical Surveys West of the One Hundredth Meridian, commanded by Lt. George M. Wheeler. Although all four expeditions drew upon army aid in one form or another, Wheeler's party was the most thoroughly military in its composition and intent.[22] At its conclusion, Wheeler's officers, men, and civilian scientists had drawn 164 detailed maps and filed forty-one reports which ultimately would be published by the Government Printing Office. One later text dispassionately summarized the accomplishments of that effort: "The director and his associates had located and examined some 219 mining districts, made observations and delineations of 143 mountain ranges and of the profiles of 202 mountain passes, and charted the course of 90 streams. They determined the elevation of 395 high peaks, explored 25 lakes, discovered 50 terminal springs, and collected a few new species of birds, reptiles, fishes, and insects. The total collection of specimens later placed in the Smithsonian Institution numbered 61,659."[23]

The railroad surveys of the 1850s and the four great surveys of 1867–79 garnered immense national praise because of their thoroughness and their appeal to Americans' love for adventure. Lesser explorations, however, remained comparatively overlooked by the public, but they were highly touted within the scientific community. In the Department of the Platte alone, post–Civil War scientific exploration was robust as commanders routinely provided military escorts for even the smallest of civilian scientific parties and sometimes outfitted them with food and other supplies. When Professor J. A. Allen of the Museum of Comparative Zoology in Cambridge, Massachusetts, began his ornithological work in Wyoming during 1880, he received aid from Fort Fetterman's ranking officer.[24] Ten years earlier, troops stationed at Fort D. A. Russell, Wyoming, escorted celebrated Yale professor Othniel C. Marsh and thirty of his paleontology students on a search of the Agate Fossil Beds in northwestern Nebraska.[25]

When Marsh returned to the site in 1874 to resume digging for dinosaur bones, he received the help and good company of officers and soldiers dispatched from Fort Laramie. This eastern gentleman, known to the local Sioux as "Big Bone Chief," even persuaded his military escort to cross into the Great Sioux Reservation so that they could explore the Badlands for additional fossil deposits. Despite Oglala chief Red Cloud's opposition to troops' being on Sioux land, the expedition accomplished its mission without incident.[26]

A more notable scientific reconnaissance took place just to the northwest of the Badlands during the following year and had a profound effect on government relations with the Lakota Sioux and the Northern Cheyennes. Lt. Col. George A. Custer's 1874 cavalry expedition into the Black Hills had substantiated earlier rumors of gold deposits within the mountain streams.[27] To gain a more comprehensive geological knowledge of the area, the War Department ordered Col. Richard Irving Dodge to lead a second military column into the area during the summer of 1875. Included within this large party were Professor Walter P. Jenney of the New York School of Mines and a corps of seventeen civilian geologists, topographers, astronomers, naturalists, photographers, head miners, and laborers. Although the group performed excellent scientific work, they also directly contributed to the gold mining rush that would soon envelop the Black Hills. This area, sacred to the Sioux, formed the western end of the Great Sioux Reservation that had been guaranteed to the Lakotas in the 1868 Fort Laramie Treaty. With its defilement by legions of miners came the inevitable Sioux War of 1876–77, at exactly the same time that the scientific reports from the expedition were being prepared for publication.[28]

While military escorts for scientific parties were a common occurrence in the post–Civil War West, individual officers continued their own pattern of discovery and collecting that had been initiated by their antebellum brothers. During his assignment at Fort Wallace, Kansas, army physician Capt. Theophilus H. Turner discovered the rare fossil skeleton of a dinosaur, later identified as *Elasmosaurus platyurus*. He immediately contacted Edward D. Cope, curator of the Academy of Natural Sciences of Philadelphia, and, following a series of detailed correspondence, Cope instructed the officer to prepare shipment of the massive remains. The specimen became a major feature of the institution's permanent collection, and Turner was rewarded with membership in the academy.[29]

Even Custer proved to be an avid collector of certain types of scientific data as he moved from station to station on the Great Plains. During the 1874 Black Hills expedition, he learned much from the accompanying scientists, and he combined the new knowledge with pursuit of two of his favorite hobbies: paleontology and taxidermy. Fellow officers noted that he and his orderlies often worked well into the night mounting and protecting their specimens. Custer intended that these private collectibles would go to the Audubon Club, the University of Michigan, and similar institutions that could make further study of them. The fate of the majority of these objects is unclear, but a few live animals were shipped to New York City's Central Park Zoo. During the fall, the New York City Department of Parks formally thanked Custer for his donation of rattlesnakes, a badger, a porcupine, two marsh hawks, and a jackrabbit.[30]

Other post–Civil War officers began their military careers in relative obscurity but wound up as recognized authorities in their scientific specializations. Lt. Samuel Tillman reported to Fort Riley, Kansas, in 1869 for a brief tour of duty before a reassignment forever changed his life. He assumed a position as instructor of chemistry, mineralogy, and geology at the U.S. Military Academy, from which he took the opportunity to broaden his association with civilian scientists. Tillman performed admirably in George M. Wheeler's One Hundredth Meridian Survey, and he was assigned in 1874–75 as American military astronomer to Tasmania to observe the transit of the planet Venus. He eventually wrote several of the scientific textbooks used at West Point and became head of his academic department.[31]

One of the most precipitous climbs from obscurity to acclaim was found in the accomplishments of Charles E. Bendire. This German-born enlisted man rose through the ranks to become a captain in the First Cavalry. His major claim to ornithological fame rested upon publication of the two-volume *Life Histories of North American Birds* (1892–96) and upon his many years as honorary curator of the Department of Oology at the Smithsonian Institution.[32] Another former enlisted man and Swedish-born immigrant, Ivar F. Tidestrom, completed two terms as a cavalryman. He then resigned from the army to pursue academic studies in botany. In 1925 he published *Flora of Utah and Nevada,* and he followed that sixteen years later with *Flora of Arizona and New Mexico.*[33]

George Miller Sternberg, best remembered for his role as surgeon general of the United States from 1893 to 1902, began his career as a medical officer in frontier service. Even in the early years of his long career he demonstrated a desire to advance his chosen field of bacteriology. Sternberg also elected to pursue his personal experiments with chemical disinfectants. In 1883, while stationed at Fort Mason, California, he made the first photographs of the tubercle bacillus, the causative agent for tuberculosis. His continued search for a cure for this feared disease, as well as for yellow fever, earned him a respected place among physicians and research scientists alike.[34]

Perhaps the most widely recognized name among military officers who pursued an interest in natural sciences was that of Elliott Coues, and many experts have hailed him as the greatest American ornithologist of his era. During nineteen years of active service he efficiently carried out regular duties as assistant surgeon, but his real love was in the collection and identification of animal specimens. In 1872 he published a seminal reference work, *Key to North American Birds,* soon followed by similarly conceived avian books on the Northwest and the Colorado Valley. Though most celebrated for his identification and classification of bird species, he devoted equal time to mammals. With coauthor Joel Allen, Coues published the massive *Monographs of North American Rodentia* (1877), whose enduring value is still found in the contents of appendix B, entitled "Material for a Bibliography of North American Mammals." During that same year his *Fur Bearing Animals: A Monograph of North American Mustelidae* also appeared as part of a series published for Ferdinand V. Hayden's survey. He even helped prepare parts of the final reports for John Wesley Powell's and George M. Wheeler's western surveys.[35]

Throughout this period of intensive labor, Coues supplied a steady stream of scholarly articles to the journals of the Academy of Natural Sciences of Philadelphia, the Boston Society of Natural History, and the Essex Institute. He finally ended his long military career in 1880, when the army ordered him to routine field duty in Arizona. Rather than relinquish his intensive scientific work on the Hayden survey materials, he resigned his commission. The last decade of his life witnessed a steady publication of books that combined his continued interest in natural history with his talent for editing papers important in the exploration of the American West. Coues published multivolume editions of the *History of the Expedition of Lewis and Clark* (1893), *Expeditions of Zebulon Montgomery Pike* (1895), *Journals of Alexander Henry and David Thompson* (1897), *Journals of Major Jacob Fowler* (1898), *Forty Year a Fur Trader on the Upper Missouri by Charles Larpenteur* (1898), and the *Diary of Francisco Garces* (1900).[36]

Apart from the "natural sciences," which were investigated by many military officers and a few enlisted men, newly emerging interest in the "social science" of ethnology also attracted the attention of soldiers who wrote about American Indians. The simplest level of attention was manifested in the monthly reports of army physicians about the health, diet, and physical descriptions of Native Americans with whom they came in direct contact. Typical were the observations of Dr. J. G. Cooper, who accompanied one of the Pacific railroad surveys during the 1850s. He especially described the frequency of smallpox outbreaks among the Plains tribes and conjectured about why vaccination had done little to solve the problem. Surgeon J. Frazier Head, while stationed at Fort Riley, Kansas, in 1852, made similar studies about the prevalence of pneumonia, pleurisy, bronchitis, smallpox, and measles among surrounding tribes.[37]

The same problems among the Comanches drew the attention of Dr. Ebenizer Swift while he was stationed at Fort Chadbourne, Texas, in 1852. Swift evidenced even greater interest in the absences of certain kinds of medical problems among members of this tribe and in the remedies that they employed.[38] Most of these unsolicited monthly and annual field reports never reached the scientific community during the nineteenth century, but researchers have learned to mine them for valuable data in more recent decades.

Meanwhile, other officers and enlisted men did pursue knowledge of Indian ways with the full intent of sharing the information with scholars or even publishing the findings themselves. Assistant Surgeon Zina Pitcher sought the assistance of Indian medicine men to teach him about the power of healing herbs and ceremonies associated with their use. He especially collected instructions and medicinal plants from the diverse tribes of Indian Territory, and the results of his inquiries appeared as an extended section entitled "Indian Medicines" in Henry Rowe School-craft's six-volume *Historical and Statistical Information Respecting the History, Condition, and Prospects of the Indian Tribes of the United States* (1851–57).[39]

Native American languages were especially intriguing, because ethnologists of the nineteenth century relied heavily upon linguistic studies to understand the ancient origins of modern tribes. Again, army doctors provided some of the earliest word lists and even detailed vocabularies from Indian people who had never been visited by professional linguists. Assistant Surgeon John Moore included in his official monthly sanitary reports information about customs and languages of Indians encountered on the line of march to Camp Floyd, Utah, in 1857 as well as hearsay information he picked up from frontiersmen about Indian languages spoken elsewhere.[40] Even a lowly drummer boy such as Augustus Meyers maintained an interest in Indian customs and vocabularies during his mid-1850s service at Fort Pierre, Dakota Territory. Decades later, he recalled much of this ethnological detail and included extensive discussion of it in his published autobiography.[41]

After the Civil War, military interest in Indian languages increased at about the same rate that it grew among civilian ethnologists. For some, such as Surgeons James P. Kimball and William H. Corbusier, the intellectual pursuit became more than a passing fancy. The latter's wife reported from Arizona's Rio Verde Agency in 1875 that her husband was "making the best of his time. Teaching English [to the Indians] and learning the Indian language became almost an obsession with him." Likewise, Col. Philippe Régis de Trobriand compiled an extensive Lakota Sioux vocabulary while stationed in Dakota Territory, though he never tried to publish it.[42] More profound was the contribution of Capt. William Philo Clark, whose posthumously published *The Indian Sign Language* (1885) remained the standard source in the field for many years and contributed to numerous future studies.[43]

As always, some enlisted men made direct contributions to the ethnological record during the late nineteenth century. While stationed at Fort Wingate, New Mexico, during the 1880s, Cpl. Christian Barthelmess spent considerable time among Navajo elders, learning their language and lifeways. He published two articles about oral traditions and healing ceremonies in Chicago's German-language newspaper *Der Westen*. Over time he gained the friendship of respected tribal leaders and apparently was among the first non-Indians whom they invited to witness and record the events. Especially noteworthy was his transcription of the text of the "Dove Song," complete with the musical notation that accompanied the lyrics. Because the young infantryman was a trained musician and was then serving as principal musician of the Thirteenth Infantry, he possessed the skills to accurately record the song cycle.[44]

Barthelmess's real claim to fame rested upon his close association with post surgeon Dr. Washington Matthews, who was already a recognized figure among American ethnologists. The two friends cooperated in their pioneering work on the Navajos, and much of it appeared in various annual reports of the Bureau of American Ethnology. Further studies were published in newly emerging anthropological journals such as *American Anthropologist* and *Journal of American Folklore.* The urgency of their task was mandated by the fact that reservation conditions had already forced profound economic changes on the Navajos, and these, in turn, were significantly altering their life-styles.[45]

Although Matthews became best known for his pathbreaking Navajo studies, his Indian interests actually had antedated his arrival at Fort Wingate. As early as 1865 he had taken station at Fort Union, Dakota Territory, and this assignment ushered in a solid decade of field work among Northern Plains tribes. This productive period witnessed publication of many seminal works, which included *Grammar and Dictionary of the Language of the Hidatsa (Minnetarees, Grosventres of the Missouri)* (1873), *Hidatsa (Minnetaree) English Dictionary* (1874), and *Ethnography and Philology of the Hidatsa Indians* (1877). In addition to his exploration of cultural anthropology and comparative linguistics, Surgeon Matthews used his medical training to help pioneer the emerging field of physical anthropology.[46] He also infected other officers with his enthusiasm for science, as when he visited Fort Stevenson, Dakota Territory, in 1867 and enlisted the aid of post surgeon Maj. Charles Carroll Gray. Together they worked on Arikara linguistics, and with Gray's help Matthews was able to gain the critical cooperation of Arikara headman White Shield.[47]

Close behind Washington Matthews in recognition as a soldier-ethnologist was Capt. John Gregory Bourke. The two men not only shared a scientific interest in Native American life, but also a tolerance for ways that were different from their own. While both certainly reflected prevailing American values of their day, they were less likely than many of their civilian colleagues to make moral judgments about Indian customs or to dismiss the Native Americans as primitives and barbaric savages. Adolphe Francis Alphonse Bandelier, although not particularly tolerant toward the aboriginal societies that he studied, paid homage to officers such as Matthews and Bourke for their scholarly integrity as well as their commitment to the rights of native people. Furthermore, Bandelier noted the origins of important ethnographic work by remarking that "much of the work now attributed to civilians is in fact due to Army officers who have disinterestedly loaned it away."[48]

Yet Bourke was more than an observant recorder of Indian life; he was a participant in some of the primary campaigns against Sioux, Northern Cheyenne, Ute, and Nez Percé peoples as well as in Gen. George Crook's operations against Geronimo and other Apache leaders. In addition to two remarkable books chronicling those historical events—*On the Border with Crook* (1891) and *An Apache Campaign in the Sierra Madre* (1886)—Bourke published widely in ethnological journals and produced a 126-volume diary filled with ethnological data. His two most important scientific publications resulted from his intimate association with southwestern Indian tribes during tours of duty in the 1870s and 1880s. His *The Snake Dance of the Moquis of Arizona* (1884) offered the best information available on the Hopi at that time and was collected directly from Indian elders at the kivas of Walpi. The book received wide praise in both the United States and Great Britain. The *Nation* lauded its scientific and literary accomplishments as far above the usual publication of this type and placed it in the same category as the pioneering anthropological works of Lewis Henry Morgan and Alice Fletcher. The book also attracted the attention of celebrated historian Francis Parkman, and beginning with a regular exchange of correspondence between the two men, Bourke became Parkman's star protégé.[49]

Bourke's second ethnological classic resulted from his even closer association with another Indian people. His 1892 detailed study, *The Medicine Men of the Apache*, was published as the Ninth Annual Report of the Bureau of American Ethnology. It impressed national luminaries ranging from Theodore Roosevelt to Director of the Bureau of American

Ethnology John Wesley Powell, and they worked behind the political scene to have Bourke transferred from routine field duty so that he could devote full attention to ethnological publications. Although the reassignment strategy proved unsuccessful, Bourke continued to provide articles for the major scientific publications of the day, and he was elected to membership in the leading societies that advanced ethnological research. Until his death in 1896 he also served as a tireless advocate for Indian causes, especially for the release of the Apache prisoners of war who had been captured at the time of Geronimo's final surrender in 1886.[50] Yet, like most other ethnologists and policy reformers of the era, Bourke believed that Indian people could survive only if they yielded most of their traditional ways and gradually entered mainstream American society. Thus, he condemned the very medicine men who had entrusted him with their special knowledge, and he wrote disparagingly in the book, "So long as the 'medicine men' exist, the Indians never can follow the white man's road."[51]

While Bourke's harsh assessment about the future of Native American traditions mirrored the prevailing sentiments of ethnologists everywhere, it did not speak to a harsher reality about the search for specific anthropological data. By an 1867 order of the surgeon general, army personnel were instructed to secure the crania of dead Indians for scientific study. Military surgeons proved especially attuned to this directive, as they sought not only skulls but also complete skeletons for shipment to eastern institutions such as the Smithsonian Army Medical Museum and university and private museums.[52] Some of the excavations involved "prehistoric burials" such as the mound builder sites near Fort Wadsworth, Dakota Territory. There, army surgeon A. I. Comfort engaged in a sophisticated archeological endeavor that mapped the mound areas, divided them into quadrants, and collected funerary items as well as bones.[53]

More frequently, however, these collectors of skeletons and burial objects dealt with modern tribes whose recently deceased relatives became a source of contention. Captain Bourke related a story from the mid-1860s about how a newly assigned hospital steward at Fort Laramie had stolen the body of Sioux chief Spotted Tail's daughter from its burial scaffold so that he could have a human skeleton for medical consultation. Only after the surgeon reported the grisly act to post commander Col.

Henry Maynadier was the body returned to its original location, and a possible confrontation was averted.[54] Even Dr. William H. Corbusier, a military surgeon who otherwise maintained cordial relations with individual Indians, saw nothing wrong in cutting off the heads of four slain Apaches and sending them to the Army Medical Museum in 1875.[55]

Perhaps the barbarity reached its apex in 1867 when the post surgeon at Fort Harker, Kansas, beheaded at least six recently deceased Pawnees and sent the skulls to the Army Medical Museum for its newly created crania collection. No mention was made that these men had served in Luther and Frank North's celebrated detachment of Pawnee Scouts during the Civil War. This unit had gained lasting fame for its role in keeping the Overland Trail open during the war and for its protective aid to track layers of the Union Pacific Railroad in the immediate postwar era. The final irony of their undignified decapitations was seen in the fact that their skulls were used in a larger cranial study that concluded, "American Indians must be assigned a lower position in the human scale than was believed heretofore."[56]

Only a tiny percentage of military men engaged in the gruesome amassing of Indian skeletal material, yet many attempted to secure Native American cultural objects. Legitimate trade and the exchange of friendship gifts account for some of these transfers of Indian property to white hands, but much of the collecting resulted from economic pressure and even warfare. Illustrative of the latter case was Lt. Gouverneur K. Warren's remarkable compilation of Sioux artifacts. As a man interested in both ethnology and the natural sciences, the lieutenant recognized a unique opportunity following Gen. William S. Harney's 1855 defeat of Brulé Sioux chief Little Thunder at Blue Water Creek, Nebraska. This battle, fought near the Oregon Trail landmark of Ash Hollow, resulted in the fleeing Indians' leaving behind most of their camp accouterments and private possessions. Noting that these were the "proper booty of war" and that they would be destroyed if not immediately claimed, Warren loaded into a wagon as much property as he could take to Fort Laramie. Within the following year he shipped the greater part of the immense collection to the Smithsonian Institution, and a smaller portion eventually wound up in the Warren Collection at the New York State Library.[57] These items remain in the two repositories today, vital testimonies to nineteenth-century Lakota life and ethnological artifacts of inestimable value. Yet they also represent part of the nineteenth-century looting of Indian America.

An equally avid officer-collector was Ogden Benedict Read, who served on the Northern Plains during the last quarter of the nineteenth century. Not content merely to assemble the large numbers of artifacts, Read recorded detailed notes about each item, its tribal identity and use, and the method of procurement. He purchased many of the objects directly from the craftsmen, but a large number were taken from a Hunkpapa Sioux camp that was attacked by soldiers on January 2, 1881. As an active member of the Smithsonian Institution, American Ethnological Society, and American Antiquarian Society, Read knew what types of Native American objects were considered ethnologically important at that time, and he focused his search in those directions. From the inception of his effort he also sensed the need for a permanent home for this collection of valuable artifacts. Beginning in the fall of 1881, he made the first shipments to his alma mater, the University of Vermont. Thus, far from the Great Plains where they were gathered over a century ago, is today exhibited a stunning assemblage of Sioux and Crow artifacts created during the last stages of the buffalo hunting era.[58]

Military interest in accumulating scientific and ethnological data about the West did not confine itself to collecting specimens and compiling narrative reports. It also included the commissioning of an artistic record of the landscapes and the Indian peoples found within those diverse environments. Beginning with Stephen Long's 1820 exploration of the Great Plains, some government officials and army officers alike recognized the need to employ noted artists who could make sketches and watercolors of *terra incognita*. By doing so, the expeditions could appeal to a variety of constituencies that would, in turn, lobby funds from Congress and help finance future military exploration of the unknown lands. Scientists interested in new empirical evidence, businessmen drawn to exploitable natural resources, politicians intent upon continental expansion, and ordinary Americans fired by the spirit of adventure in an exotic land all added to the desire for further exploration and an artistic rendering of the great discoveries that lay ahead.

British-born watercolorist Samuel Seymour held the primary illustrator's position for Long's expedition. As directed in his written orders, Seymour worked diligently to sketch the great variety of Indians encountered between the Missouri River and the front range of the Rocky Mountains. Regrettably, of the roughly 150 drawings that he produced, fewer than two dozen survive today. More lasting were the contributions of Titian Ramsay Peale, who shared the talents of his renowned artist-father Charles Willson Peale. Although the younger Peale signed onto the reconnaissance principally to collect geological, zoological, ornithological, and botanical specimens, he found considerable time to fill his sketchbook with drawings and paintings.[59]

Long's expedition set an important precedent for assigning professional artists to military exploration parties, but the trend would have to await the decade of the Pacific railroad surveys before it would produce major results. From the 1820s through 1840s, Congress demonstrated a consistent opposition to subsidizing the compilation of a visual record of the West. Repeatedly, legislators even turned down George Catlin's offers to sell to the government his massive Indian gallery, a rich collection that had toured European capitals and had received the lobbying support of prominent American artists and businessmen.[60]

The most notable example of this failure of government patronage appeared in the 1854 publication of John Russell Bartlett's two-volume *Personal Narrative of Explorations and Incidents in Texas, New Mexico, California, Sonora, and Chihuahua, Connected with the United States and Mexican Boundary Commission, during the Years 1850, '51, '52 and 1853.* This detailed account of the official Southwestern Boundary Survey that established the international border between the two republics represented a wealth of scientific, ethnological, and historical information. Lamentably, the final published version contained only sixteen full-page sepia-toned lithographs and ninety-four full- or partial-page woodcuts in black and white, out of a larger collection assembled by artists Bartlett and Henry C. Pratt. Totally excluded were Capt. Seth Eastman's thirteen watercolors, which Bartlett had commissioned from the celebrated military artist. Some were based upon Bartlett's own drawings, but a greater number showed scenes from Texas, where Eastman previously had been stationed with the First Infantry. Again, congressional reluctance to pay the costs for a more fully illustrated edition robbed the final product of some of its richness.[61]

Despite this outcome, Eastman remained the most celebrated artist within the army, and he engaged in a number of important projects. From 1833 to 1840 he had served as assistant drawing instructor at West Point, and in 1837 he had published *Treatise on Topographical Drawing.* While stationed at Fort Snelling, Minnesota, during the 1840s, he had painted and sketched some of his finest renditions of army and Indian life, including the illustrations used by his wife, Mary Henderson Eastman, to illustrate her well-received *Dahcotah; or, Life and Legends of the Sioux around Fort Snelling* (1849).[62]

During 1849, after some strong lobbying in his behalf, Seth Eastman managed to secure an extended army leave so that he could pursue what he felt would be his most prized commission—to illustrate Henry Rowe Schoolcraft's six-volume *History of the Indian Tribes of the United States.* Unfortunately the partnership proved something of a nightmare for both men after government officials withheld some of the subsidies promised for the ambitious project. Schoolcraft drove a further wedge in the friendship when he denied Eastman's rights to reproduce his own plates in another privately published book. Although later efforts to gain compensation from Congress failed, Eastman maintained his reputation as a skilled artist who painted western scenes with both accuracy and aesthetic flare.[63]

No other soldier-artist achieved the same level of fame as Seth Eastman during the nineteenth century, but the Pacific railroad surveys of the 1850s provided excellent opportunities for linkage between respected civilian artists and heightened military exploration. The final multi-volume reports contained 147 lithographs prepared by artists who accompanied the various reconnaissances. These eleven artists included nine civilians: Richard H. Kern, John Mix Stanley, F. W. von Egloffstein, Heinrich B. Möllhausen, Albert H. Campbell, Charles Koppel, W. P. Blake, John Young, and Dr. Thomas Cooper. According to historian William Goetzmann, collectively they made a magnificent contribution to the nation's infatuation with the West, but the accuracy of their work ranged widely. While Möllhausen tended toward "twisted and exaggerated views" of the diverse landscapes, Egloffstein and Stanley drew scenes with remarkable accuracy, while still preserving an aesthetic sense of form and balance in their pictures.[64]

Two soldier-artists were also represented among the eleven illustrators. Gustave Sohon was only an infantry private when he served with Governor Isaac Ingalls Stevens's railroad survey of the Pacific Northwest. Approximately a dozen of his illustrations appeared in the final reports, but additional works were included in Capt. John Mullan's *Report on the Construction of a Military Road from Fort Walla-Walla to Fort Benton* (1863). Many of Private Sohon's original Indian sketches as well as his notable painting of Fort Benton now reside in the U.S. National Museum. In 1948 historian and ethnologist John C. Ewers pronounced this collection to be "the most extensive and authoritative pictorial series on Indians of the Northwest Plateau in prereservation days."[65]

Equally talented was Lt. John C. Tidball, a West Point–trained officer in the Corps of Topographical Engineers, who accompanied Lt. Amiel Weeks Whipple's Thirty-fifth Parallel Survey from Fort Smith, Arkansas, to Los Angeles, California, during 1853–54. Although Möllhausen served as the official artist for the expedition, Tidball contributed four of the approximately sixty-five woodcuts that appeared in the final twelve-volume set of Pacific railroad survey reports. He likewise made a number of sketches during the trip, but adequate time was never available for him to increase his portfolio as extensively as he had hoped. Because he often was designated to scout ahead of the main column to locate suitable campsites and forage for the animals—often ten days at a stretch—he barely had time to rest before assuming his next arduous task. Beyond his retirement in 1889 and to his death in 1906, Tidball remained proud of his artistic ability and his contributions to Whipple's expedition.[66]

A different type of art appeared from the pen of Capt. Clarence E. Dutton, who specialized in drawing exact geological representations of some of the West's most impressive sites. Between 1875 and 1885 this captain of ordnance worked first for John Wesley Powell's Geographical and Geological Survey of the Rocky Mountain Region and subsequently with the U.S. Geological Survey to produce definitive studies of the expansive mountain and canyon country. His precise landscape diagrams became the cornerstones for his four seminal scientific works: *Report on the Geology of the High Plateaus of Utah* (1880), *The Physical Geology of the Grand Cañon District* (1882), *The Tertiary History of the Grand Cañon District* (1882), and *Mount Taylor and the Zuñi Plateau* (1885). Although the detail of his art was unsurpassed, Dutton also had the gift for presenting evocative prose that virtually turned the arid landscape into a living creature. Likewise, he possessed a scientific curiosity that led him to develop new theories about geological formations, vulcanology, and isostasy that were, in turn, discussed by other prominent members of the world's scientific community.[67]

Three other officers deserve modern attention as recorders of military and Indian scenes, even though their artistic pursuits were more avocational than vocational. The irascible Col. Alfred Sully is better known for his hot temper, vindictive treatment of fellow officers, and service in a number of important Indian campaigns. Yet, as the son of celebrated painter Thomas Sully, he was exposed to artistic delights and instruction early in life. At the time of his death in 1879, he had assembled over a hundred paintings and sketches as well as two crates of letters and personal papers about his army career that stretched over three decades. Historian Ray Allen Billington, writing in 1974, acknowledged that Sully's mercurial character had kept him from winning national plaudits, and his life represented many lost opportunities, but the controversial officer had made a sizable contribution toward preserving an accurate portrayal of frontier army life. In Billington's estimation, the surviving canvases and sketchbooks reflected the work of "a competent artist, less gifted than his father, and inclined toward primitivism, but conveying a sense of realism that adds conviction to western scenes."[68]

A man of different temperament left an equally valuable artistic rendering of military settings in Texas during the 1850s. Capt. Arthur T. Lee of the Eighth Infantry made 154 watercolor and pen-and-ink sketches, primarily of Fort Davis and surrounding Davis Mountains scenes. Often compared to Seth Eastman in his overall style, and particularly in his portraits of Indians, Lee was allegedly trained by Philadelphia artists Bass Otis and Thomas Sully. He certainly knew Eastman when both were stationed at Fort Snelling, Minnesota, during the summer of 1848, and a number of his works reflect the same kinds of Indian and military scenes from the Upper Mississippi River.[69]

Popular with officers and men alike, Lee hoped to make a long career of frontier soldiering, but slowness of promotion sidetracked his aspirations, and he remained a second lieutenant for seven years and a captain for thirteen years. Following Civil War service and an 1867–72 stint as administrator of the Soldier's Home in Washington, D.C., he retired. Apparently Lee never sought a publisher for his artwork, but he did successfully complete two popular prose works: *Army Ballads and Other Poems* and "Reminiscences of the Regiment" in *History of the Eighth U.S. Infantry*, both published in 1871. In each he articulated a profound sympathy for Indians and a witty approach to the shortcomings of military life. Lee's family eventually donated his entire art collection to the Rush Rhees Library at the University of Rochester, where it resides today.[70]

The third officer in this triumvirate also mixed art and prose to gain some degree of fame in his lifetime. Col. Philippe Régis de Trobriand is best known as the author of a detailed diary that covered his almost daily activities on the Northern Plains between 1867 and 1868. This French-born officer also found time to sketch army and Indian scenes, including portraits of Arikara headman White Shield and Gros Ventres leaders Crow's Breast and Eagle Who Pursues the Eagle. As with his descriptive prose, de Trobriand strove for accuracy in his sketches and oil paintings. Especially noteworthy were his likenesses of Forts Totten, Stevenson, Berthold, Shaw, Ellis, and Fred Steele, which, in many cases, represent the only surviving drawings of those military installations at their peak periods. Though never as prolific an artist as Colonel Sully or Captain Lee, he nonetheless adjusted his duty schedule so that he would have time to draw and paint landscape scenes and people who interested him. When his diary was finally edited and published by Lucile M. Kane in 1951, she wisely chose to include much of de Trobriand's original art to illustrate the book.[71]

At least two military surgeons joined their fellow officers in making notable contributions to the artistic record. Dr. Joseph B. Girard joined the army in 1867 at age twenty and served the next five years in Wyoming. But it was not until his regiment was rotated to Arizona in 1872 that he quickened his output of pencil sketches, many of which were drawn while he was on field campaigns. Girard ultimately redid many of his sketches and made watercolor copies of them. Today, the prestigious Huntington Library in San Marino, California, houses five hundred of his works.[72]

Less polished in his style, but almost as prolific in sketching scenes from field campaigns, was Dr. Albert J. Myer, who, during the mid-1850s, drew many scenes of West Texas military life. Though his artistic endeavors were not of sufficient quality to ensure him lasting fame, Dr. Myer later gained the coveted title of "Father of the United States Signal Corps." His surviving sketches remain today at the Library of Congress in Washington, D.C.[73]

Another category of western military art went virtually unrecognized until the twentieth century, when historians and archivists rediscovered some of it within frontier newspapers, private papers, and even a few galleries. These were the sketches made by enlisted men to wile away the time, entertain their friends, and send to family members back east. Although few of these men had any formal artistic training, and the quality of their work ranged widely, they did leave an interesting visual record of frontier army life.

Among the most promising and recognized of these men was Sgt. Edward K. Thomas, who was stationed at Fort Snelling during the early 1850s. Although self-taught, he had done some portraits as a youth before joining the army in 1831 and subsequently serving in the Mexican War. Editor James M. Goodhue of Saint Paul's *Minnesota Pioneer* paid tribute to Sergeant Thomas in 1850 and described a number of his paintings of scenes in and around Fort Snelling that preserved "astounding fidelity . . . as the reflections of a mirror." Some of Thomas's Fort Snelling scenes were later mistakenly attributed to Seth Eastman because of similarities in composition and subject matter. Today his four Fort Snelling oil paintings hang in four recognized art collections, including that of the Minnesota State Historical Society. Following retirement in 1865, Thomas settled in the Detroit area, where his ongoing artwork gained him some local renown.[74]

Most of the surviving sketches done by enlisted men were of the posts where they served. For example, Sgt. H. Steiffel of the Fifth Infantry made a pencil drawing of Fort Bliss, Texas, in 1868. Eleven years later, Steiffel painted two watercolors of Fort Keogh and Miles City, Montana.[75] In the interim, Pvt. Robert F. Roche of the Second Infantry drew a panoramic four-piece sketch of Fort Larned, Kansas, just as it was being constructed. The nicely detailed work showed several completed adobe structures, but mostly the landscape was dotted with tents and unfinished buildings.[76]

The Civil War era also brought a number of eastern militia units to service on the Great Plains, and some of their officers and enlisted men drew and painted scenes similar to those undertaken by enlisted men of the regular army. The most famous of these men was Prussian-born Capt. Charles Frederick Moellmann of the Eleventh Ohio Volunteer Cavalry, which protected the Platte River Trail across Nebraska and Wyoming. During 1863–64, Moellmann produced at least sixty pencil, crayon, and watercolor drawings, most notably scenes in and around Fort Laramie. Noted for their remarkable accuracy and attention to detail, the majority of these works now reside in the University of Wyoming archives.[77] In addition to Capt. Moellmann, several enlisted men provided their own visual records of the Plains. Pvt. John Gaddis of the Twelfth Wisconsin Volunteer Infantry produced fourteen pen-and-ink sketches of 1862 Kansas military scenes that now hang in the Grand Army of the Republic Memorial Hall Museum in Madison, Wisconsin. Pvt. George P. Belden contributed a couple dozen sketches of the Second Nebraska Regiment's campaign in the Dakotas. Similarly, Pvt. Murtaugh Ryan painted a watercolor of Fort Logan, Montana, as it appeared in 1863, and on the reverse side he wrote about homesickness and the tedium of duty.[78]

But perhaps the most curious of the enlisted men's contributions from both the Civil War and post–Civil War eras came in the form of a six-panel pencil sketch in the 1880 diary of Pvt. C. C. Chrisman. These crudely drawn vignettes showed soldiers marching in parade, peeling potatoes, cleaning up the post, repairing buildings, conducting guard duty, and cooling their heels in the guardhouse. Chrisman's pictorial representation of army life certainly was not heroic or spectacular, but it represented a sad reality that faced soldiers daily.[79]

The nineteenth century represented a prolonged period of discovery for American citizens as their national borders spread ever westward to encompass a vast domain of diverse landscapes and native peoples. At the forefront of much of that discovery was the American army, which served as the right arm of federal exploration and scientific inquiry. Sometimes, as in the case of the Lewis and Clark expedition, the exploring parties carried full government sanction as well as specific instructions for conducting their scientific work. More often, however, officers and enlisted men conducted scientific and ethnological research as a secondary assignment, or even on their off-duty time. They not only manifested a deep and abiding intellectual curiosity, but many of them also possessed the academic training to make notable contributions to the collective scientific record. Their reports conveyed the invitation of the land itself—its beauty, its resources, and its native people—in such a way that they even captured the imaginations of people worldwide. Likewise, the artistic records assembled by some of these servicemen blended the romantic and realistic styles of the day to popularize the western landscapes and to provide an honest documentation of places and events that are now only a memory. It was only fitting that the federal organization that knew the western landscape and its populations most intimately would become so integrally involved in every facet of its settlement for the full extent of the century.

CHAPTER TWO

Encountering the Elephant

Army Aid to Emigrants on the Platte River Road

By the end of the Mexican War in 1848, Americans stood ready to hasten the great migration into the Far West. During the following two decades they would turn what had been a relative trickle into a flood of farmers, businessmen, gold miners, and Mormon faithful. Although some of the overlanders consciously reveled in the national spirit of Manifest Destiny, most made the journey for intensely personal reasons. Along the way many of them "saw enough of the elephant," a popular phrase denoting that they had reached the limits of endurance and privation.[1] Many would give up and return by way of the eastbound routes of the overland trails, but along the way they passed thousands of additional hopefuls headed optimistically for new lives in California, Oregon, and the Great Basin. On both legs of the journey military personnel played a pivotal role in aiding the prairie argonauts. That assistance came in many guises, and much of it had little to do with stereotypical notions of soldiers protecting beleaguered wagon trains from incessant Indian attacks. Even though protective duties were stressed during the early stages, the emphasis soon shifted to more important roles.

As early as 1840 some federal officials began to recognize the need for greater federal attention to the largely unimproved trails that crossed the Great Plains. Secretary of War Joel R. Poinsett recommended the establishment of three posts along the Oregon Trail to help protect overlanders and promote their travels. During the following year, Poinsett's successor, John C. Spencer, reiterated the special need for a "chain of posts" along the route.[2] These and other advocates pointed out that in 1824 and 1829 the federal government had helped subsidize commercial traffic along the Santa Fe Trail to the tune of thirty thousand dollars for road improvements in eastern Kansas and an equal amount for employment of 170 infantry to escort the wagons through dangerous Comanche lands.[3] Despite these aberrational precedents, politicians and army administrators were not yet ready to invest significant portions of annual military budgets into trail improvements.

The Mexican War era of 1846–48 changed the nature of the debate, for now the government was increasingly determined to assure its authority over the newly won Oregon Country and the Mexican Cession. Expansionist president James K. Polk had already recommended in his inaugural address of December 2, 1845, that the government create a suitable number of stockades and blockhouses on the Oregon and Santa Fe Trails. He also called for a special force of mounted riflemen to patrol between these strongholds during the nonwinter months to help protect civilian travelers.[4]

Authorization finally came for construction of a blockhouse and soldiers' quarters at Table Creek where present-day Nebraska City, Nebraska, stands. Because it was located on the Missouri River and represented the easternmost point on the Oxbow Trail that stretched westward to meet the Platte River at the western end of Grand Island, it was deemed a suitable place for inexpensive resupply and a logical jumping-off spot for emigrants headed to Oregon. Construction of this original Fort Kearny began in May 1846, but the site was quickly deemed to be too far east of the main Oregon Trail to be of much help to anyone.[5]

During September 1847, Lt. Col. Ludwell E. Powell instructed Lt. Daniel P. Woodbury to conduct a reconnaissance further west on the Platte River to locate a more viable site. Woodbury found on the south bank of the river a good location that he contended was adequately equipped with wood for fuel, grass for haying, and water for future irrigation. He also remarked that it was at an ideal place for emigrants who were already departing from the modern-day Kansas City area to intersect the Platte River near that juncture.[6]

The site was well chosen, but a minor debate erupted over whether this was the best and least expensive method for improving the trail. Two years earlier, Col. Stephen Watts Kearny, who had traversed the route as far west as South Pass, Wyoming, had reported that the creation of fixed posts would be expensive and confining to the mobility of soldiers. Better that the idea of permanent posts be dispensed with for now, and instead, a regiment of mounted riflemen periodically be sent up and down the trail to overawe the Indian tribes and maintain the peace.[7] Perhaps Kearny's observation made some budgetary sense, but it was offered in 1845 before massive migration had begun to Oregon, California, and the Salt Lake valley. Kearny's narrow interpretation of "protecting the trail" also missed the obvious point that permanent forts could provide far more diverse services to overlanders than merely overawing Indians.

A compromise plan had already been legislated as early as May 19, 1846, but the exigencies of the Mexican War had interrupted implementation of the concept. It authorized $76,500 for raising and equipping one regiment of mounted riflemen, but it also provided $3,000 for the establishment of each military post on the Oregon Trail plus $2,000 to compensate tribes for transfer of lands as military reservations. The legislation did not specify how many permanent installations were to be constructed, their size, or how they were to be continuously funded, but the paucity of designated funds left some doubt about the level of federal commitment.[8]

Despite wartime delays, inadequate funds, and continued debates over mounted riflemen versus fixed posts, construction began on a new Fort Kearny on the Platte River, 197 miles west of the original namesake fort at Table Creek. Government agents paid the Pawnees two thousand dollars to relinquish a military reservation of ten square miles, and work commenced during the spring of 1848.[9]

More significant discussion emerged about whether the privately owned trading post of Fort Laramie (Fort William) should be purchased from the American Fur Company and be occupied by the army, or whether a brand new post should be built somewhat west of that site. Capt. John C. Frémont had previously written in one of his official reports that the vicinity of Fort Laramie was ideal for a military post because it was on the Platte River line of overland march, influential in the widely spread fur trade, and would not interfere with the buffalo ranges of the Plains tribes.[10] In 1846, celebrated historian Francis Parkman traversed the area and wrote that troops stationed permanently at Fort Laramie could easily protect overlanders from the western Sioux and could help facilitate easier passage of the high plains region.[11]

Edwin Bryant, who had passed through the fur trading post on his way to California in June 1846, described it in a matter-of-fact way: "'The fort,' as it is called, is a quadrangle, the walls of which are constructed of adobes, or sun-dried bricks. The area enclosed is, I should suppose, about half or three-fourths of an acre of ground. Its walls are surmounted by watch-towers, and the gate is defended by two brass swivels. On three sides of the court, next to the walls, are various offices, store-rooms, and mechanical shops. The other side is occupied by the main building of the Fort, two stories high."[12]

Most people who traversed the trail in the last few years of the fort's private ownership described it in more emotional terms than did Bryant. Dr. William Thomas recorded in his journal on June 3, 1849, a positive assessment not only of the condition of the facilities, but also the beauty of the river and the low range of green hills immediately to the northwest. He was especially moved by the inspiring sight of the American flag which flew from its walls.[13] Less generous was Annie Ruff, whose husband was a captain among the dragoons who had been sent to patrol the trail. She had been at the place only a short time during June 1849 when she wrote to her mother that it "is the gloomiest most desolate looking place I ever saw. It looks exactly like a Penitentiary except there are *no* windows on the outside." She happily reported that Maj. Winslow F. Sanderson and Lt. Daniel P. Woodbury were scouting for a better site about fifty miles west on the Platte River, where the army could build a more reliable fort.[14]

Annie Ruff's hopeful prediction did not come true, but the old post did gradually evolve into a configuration that partially conformed to her vision. At a cost of four thousand dollars, the U.S. Army took transfer of Fort Laramie from the American Fur Company during the summer of 1849, and within a few years the installation had undergone a thorough transformation.[15] The old fur trade buildings gradually fell into disuse as the military laid out a larger parade ground, with living quarters and administrative structures dotting its periphery. No protective wall was necessary, because the size of the garrison and ever-present civilian travelers made the threat of an Indian attack exceedingly unlikely. It is fitting that this transfer took place in exactly the same year that the California Gold Rush began. Henceforth, Fort Laramie's importance on the Overland Trail to California, Oregon, and Salt Lake City would increase dramatically as the vast throngs of people accelerated their mass movement each year.

Ironically, companies of the Regiment of Mounted Riflemen were already camped at the fur trade post just at the time of its transfer to federal ownership. Maj. Winslow F. Sanderson immediately assigned them to cut hay along the riverbanks, harvest timber two miles to the north of the Platte River, and begin construction of new buildings. Although the Mounted Riflemen would continue escort service as far as the Oregon Country into 1850, the government had now made its commitment to fixed posts rather than large mobile units.[16] Furthermore, some civilian travelers had leveled complaints against the Mounted Riflemen. Lucius Fairchild complained that the troops were "always in the way" and were "the most perfect nusance [sic] on the whole road.[17] Others such as B. R. Biddle strongly rebuked the soldiers for seizing the ferry boats at Mormon Ferry to move their supplies across the Platte River ahead of the civilians.[18] Expenses for the Mounted Riflemen also made them unpopular with congressmen who more readily identified the nation's expanding sovereignty with military posts and towns.

Whatever the shortcomings of military protection on the overland trails, it quickly became evident that Forts Kearny and Laramie could also provide other forms of aid to travelers. In May 1849, government representatives instructed the post commander at Fort Kearny to hold out surplus commissary supplies "for the relief of emigrants broken down and returning to the states."[19] Such aid was already becoming essential because so many people had purchased wagons, teams, and supplies from the outfitting towns of western Missouri without fully comprehending the unique problems of the trail. A reporter writing under the pseudonym of "California" for the *Missouri Republican* had published a warning in late April. He contended that most supplies were readily available in Independence, but many of them were of inferior quality. Especially noteworthy were the old and feeble oxen and mules that were priced respectively at twenty-two dollars per yoke and thirty dollars per head. "California" asked rhetorically, "What men are thinking about, or calculating upon, when they provide themselves with such teams for a journey of near two thousand miles is a mystery; yet hundreds are doing so, and then confining themselves to a team barely sufficient to move their wagon." He further warned that many of these would surely break down in some isolated spot where no spares or help could be found.[20]

Col. Benjamin Bonneville, commander of Fort Kearny during the first summer of mass exodus, echoed that sentiment and reported directly to Adjutant General Roger Jones that greater control needed to be established in the Missouri outfitting towns. He suggested that the government, perhaps even the military, should provide information to overland novices about the best kinds of wagons and teams to purchase, as well as the types and quantities of supplies to procure.[21]

Apparently the formal advice was not given or heeded during the next few years as overlanders competed with each other in bidding wars to secure even the most inappropriate supplies at the outfitting towns. The description given by Margaret Frink of the great variety of wheeled vehicles approaching Fort Kearny during May 1850 spoke eloquently about the comedy of errors: "There were all conceivable kinds of convey-ances. There was a cart drawn by two cows, a cart drawn by one ox, and a man on horseback drove along an ox packed with his provisions and blankets. There was a man with a hand cart, another with a wheel barrow loaded with supplies. And we were not yet two hundred miles from the Missouri River."[22]

Others, such as Dr. Americus Powers and his wife Mary, found that horses could not pull wagons on a daily basis even along the fairly flat terrain of the Platte River valley. They tried to trade for oxen at Fort Laramie but were unsuccessful. Only a loan of three oxen by another, sympathetic wagon train provided them with the means to continue the journey. Their horses were reduced to such pitiable skeletons that Powers was forced to shoot one of them.[23]

The most fortunate people were those who realized their mistake early in the trip and made adjustments before departing Fort Kearny. Harriet Sherrill Ward lamented the fact that her family had not brought along extra livestock to replace the dead and dying animals. Yet she and her

husband wisely threw away many nonessential items, including one of
their beds, about five days east of Fort Kearny.[24] Even more resourceful
was 49er Giles Isham, who exchanged an exhausted yoke of oxen at the
post for a healthy replacement team. The following summer at the fort,
James Bennett traded a decrepit wagon for a stronger and heavier one.[25]

The problem of broken-down wagons and teams that first appeared
as overlanders neared Fort Kearny was even more evident by the time
they reached Fort Laramie. Elisha Douglass Perkins reported in the
summer of 1849 that his caravan wished to sell its largest wagon because
it was too heavy for the sandy soil of the trail. When offered only five
dollars for the wagon, its angry owner vowed he would burn it before he
would sell it at that price. Two other men of the same party were more
fortunate when they were able to purchase a light French wagon for only
twenty dollars at the fort.[26]

The experiences of the Perkins wagon train epitomized the anomaly
in the system of supply and demand that developed at the two military
installations. Many overlanders naïvely assumed that they could barter
or sell their excess goods along the trail. Yet because so many people were
jettisoning cargo from their overloaded wagons, the amount of goods
made this a buyer's market for most items. Dr. Caleb Ormsby reported
in June 1849 that prices of goods at Fort Laramie were still reasonably
high on flour, at $1.50 per hundredweight, and coffee, at $3.00 per
pound. But horses and mules were in such short supply that none could
be had at any price. On the opposite end of the spectrum, tools, broken
wagons, harnesses, and clothing littered the ground in great quantities,
and new waves of emigrants worried that they might share the fate of
their unfortunate predecessors. One party abandoned an entire sawmill
and its attendant equipment after transporting it five hundred miles to
Fort Laramie. Ormsby stood in awe of the virtual mountain of bacon that
had been stacked and scattered along the road near the fort. Fellow
traveler John H. Benson estimated that as much as two thousand pounds
of bacon was there and guessed that he had seen only about half of what
had been discarded in the immediate area.[27]

Frustration produced all manner of behavior. One 1850 emigrant
party was faced with the reality of receiving no more than one cent per
pound for their surplus flour and bacon, so they burned all of it as fuel

for their campfire.[28] Another traveler recorded that tempers flared over the apparent lack of resale value of food, so the owners maliciously destroyed the food surplus rather than turn it over to other destitute families. In the same vein, C. W. Smith witnessed two men throw their rifles into the Platte River after they were unable to sell them. They were determined that no one would profit from their loss.[29]

Not all the stories had such dreadful endings, because in many cases overlanders willingly helped the less fortunate along the trail. Some parties, such as the Buckeye Rovers, were virtually contracted together by longstanding friendships to look out for each other from the beginning of their 1849 excursion from Ohio to California. When one member of the group lost eight oxen to a single bolt of lightning, his compatriots replaced the animals from their own livestock and without complaint. During the same summer, other wagon trains willingly helped two forlorn young men make their way eastward across the Plains. The two had given up their California trek, and now, with worn-out mules and virtually no supplies, they lived off the charity of wagon trains that they encountered on the outbound leg of the trip. Despite no possibility of regaining later compensation from the young men, generous strangers helped facilitate their return to Indianapolis.[30]

Private charity, however, was not enough to rescue many of the migrants from their worst folly. Commanding officers at military posts always had some discretion to help civilians whose safety and welfare were threatened by disastrous circumstances. But with the advent of the 1849 California Gold Rush, army orders broadened these discretionary powers along all the western trails. During that year Congress authorized the War Department to sell at cost pistols, rifles, and ammunition to overlanders so that they could provide for their own protection. Unfortunately, this proved to be something of an empty gesture, since the army rarely had enough modern arms to supply its own soldiers.[31]

More significantly, the commanders at Forts Kearny and Laramie kept meticulous records on their food supplies so that they could release whatever was considered excess to truly desperate civilians. Often the ranking officer had to evoke the wisdom of Solomon to distinguish between the numerous pleadings presented to him. A three-tiered system of aid gradually developed on the frontier, completely separate from any official policy generated in Washington, D.C. At the highest level, the commander gave food to the most needy of all travelers—those whose very lives rested on this courtesy. No return payment was expected from these people, who often were headed east in dejection and without any attachment to a wagon train. A second level of help was granted to people who had to sign promissory notes of repayment, even though the majority probably never repaid any portion of the loan. The third and most frequently used level went to persons who were deemed needy but not desperate. The senior officer authorized them to purchase discounted food items from the post commissary as long as they paid cash for their share of the deal.[32] These subsidized amounts had to be absorbed by existing military budgets and could often work great hardship on a post if the commander was too generous. At the West Texas crossroads of Fort Davis, which served one of the primary southern trails to California, this liberality resulted in censure for the commander during an official inspection in 1856. Inspector General Joseph K. F. Mansfield strongly questioned the $42,099 spent that year to feed destitute overlanders and to repair their wagons.[33]

At the far western end of the trail a potential tragedy unfolded during the summer of 1849 along the supposed shortcut known as Lassen Cutoff into northern California. Graphic reports reached the gold camps by August that thousands of people were backed up along the route with winter fast approaching in the Sierra Nevada. Gen. Persifor F. Smith, military governor of California, authorized an immediate government relief fund of a hundred thousand dollars, and this was supplemented by several thousand dollars provided by Californians' private donations. Maj. Daniel H. Rucker oversaw the relief operations, which may have prevented a repeat of the experience of the ill-fated Donner party three years earlier.[34]

Although most travelers reached Forts Kearny and Laramie with some deficiencies in their supplies and livestock, they were not truly destitute or facing a life-and-death situation. Since they did not fit within the three emergency categories, they had to rely on the post sutler for additional items. The contents of these stores occupied considerable attention within their diaries, and most of their assessments were harsh. Many resented the monopolistic position of the post sutler because he held a government contract to be the only commercial establishment on the military reservation.[35]

The most persistent complaint was that the sutlers charged emigrants exorbitant amounts for even the most common of items. Overlanders such as Elisha Douglass Perkins found it especially galling that sutlers would buy only a few goods from the desperate civilians while marking up the prices of goods they sold back to the wagon trains. He doubted that any eastern merchants could profit as much as these noncompetitive sutlers.[36] In the following year of 1850, Eleazar Ingalls declared that the Fort Laramie sutler doubled his prices on just about every item, compared to the cost of goods in the Missouri outfitting towns. Another unidentified traveler estimated that the sutler's markup was four times the normal price, and yet when he bought items from overlanders, his payment was only about ten percent of the real value of the item.[37]

Some people recorded well-stocked shelves of canned foods, cigars, sardines, sugar, flour, tea, coffee, liquor, salt, medicines, and notions and even a selection of watch crystals.[38] But the ready supply of goods changed quickly during each trail season, and those people who passed through the forts later in the summer often found depleted stocks and higher prices. Some also received unpleasant surprises with the items that they purchased. Helen Carpenter recalled buying a block of cheese at Fort Kearny only to find out that it "should have been 'mustered' out long ago, it is too old to be in the service. One mere taste took the skin off the end of my tongue."[39] A worse fate befell Italian nobleman Count Leonetto Cipriani, whose eleven-wagon party purchased a thousand pounds of flour at the same place in 1853. By the time they reached Ash Hollow and began to break into this food stock, they found it crawling with worms.[40]

Even though many army sutlers made sizable fortunes in their monopolistic enterprises, and even Capt. Charles Ruff worked behind the scenes to create a sutler partnership between himself and famed Missouri traders Robert Campbell and John Dougherty, not everyone felt so oppressed by them.[41] One member of the "Wolverine Rangers" from Marshall, Michigan, concluded that the assertions of high sutler prices were greatly exaggerated in 1849, and he found most items to be fairly priced. Several Mormons who were headed east to escort more Saints to Salt Lake City commented in the same summer how helpful the Fort

Kearny officers were, especially in their sale of goods at considerably cheaper prices than those the American Fur Company agent had charged two years earlier.[42] Estimates of fairness and unfairness were measured in the eyes of the beholder, but army sutlers were united in their efforts to show why their goods cost more than those in eastern stores. Their high freight rates, spoilage rate, storage problems, and relatively brief trading season to overlanders drove up their costs of doing business. Likewise, they would not have survived financially had they purchased every broken-down wagon, ox, trunk, or supply of bacon that each traveler was trying to unload. The sutler, no matter how much maligned in some journals, served as an important agent in facilitating people's passage across the Great Plains.

Beyond the issuance of commissary supplies and sale of sutler goods to overlanders, the second biggest military contribution to trail development was in medical care. As with supplies, the extension of army hospital facilities was at the discretion of the fort commander and his surgeon. Cholera was a recurring problem that was especially virulent between 1849 and 1854, and it killed more civilians than any other single cause. Because most people contracted the disease in the Missouri River towns, they began to show the first symptoms just as their wagons were stretched out east of Fort Kearny, and the epidemic's ferocity was usually spent before they reached South Pass, Wyoming.[43] Thus, Forts Kearny and Laramie stood at the apex of the highest mortality rate on the trail.

Fort Laramie sutlers John S. Tutt and Lewis B. Dougherty ran an advertisement in an 1849 Saint Joseph, Missouri, newspaper indicating a large supply of medicines and an army surgeon committed to helping ill civilians at all times. Englishman Henry J. Coke found exactly this kind of humane treatment at Fort Laramie during the following year when he received paregoric, opium pills, and powders to ward off dysentery and cholera.[44] Sometimes the number of ill civilians exceeded the facilities available in the small post hospitals. During one especially difficult period in the summer of 1852, the hospitals at both forts were overwhelmed by cholera patients, and some of the civilians were placed in the regular barracks while soldiers camped beyond the parade ground in tents. Those who did not survive the epidemics were buried in the post cemetery—civilian and soldier alike.[45]

Medical help also was extended for other kinds of injuries. The surgeon at Fort Kearny treated a man's badly injured eye and charged him only two dollars for the treatment. Another unfortunate, severely wounded by the accidental discharge of a gun, was successfully treated after his friends brought him back from a point several days' travel to the west.[46] A member of the "Wolverine Rangers" was left at Fort Kearny by his compatriots because his knee was so shattered by an errant shot that he had no chance of continuing the trip to California. In another case, the Fort Kearny surgeon amputated the badly infected arm of an overlander who had been bitten by a rattlesnake. Two other men run over by wagons also found care in the hospital during the same month.[47]

Sometimes medicines and bandages were not enough to treat the ailments of certain overlanders. Maj. Osborne Cross discovered a man abandoned by his wagon train near Chimney Rock. The unfortunate soul seemed deranged and would surely have perished had the soldiers not escorted him to Fort Laramie for care by the post physician. During that same summer of 1849, the Boston-Newton party came across a naked and badly sunburned man just west of Fort Laramie. Despite his seeming insanity and dehydration from diarrhea, he foiled their elaborate attempts to capture him and take him to the fort.[48]

Two months later, Capt. John S. Perry escorted the military supply train from Fort Laramie to Missouri. Within the wagons he carried a number of sick and disabled emigrants who had been treated at the fort. He also carried the personal effects of some who had died. Despite frequent medical and relief aid for embattled migrants, officers could sometimes become victims of their own kindness. Annie Ruff witnessed soldiers rescuing a widow and her four children near Courthouse Rock. The woman had lost her husband and two children to cholera, and three of the survivors were ill with the disease. The officers provided her with every assistance—food, medicines, and drivers—but she proved her ingratitude by bribing two civilian teamsters to desert the military column and pilot her wagon.[49]

Because wagons and their teams were among the most crucial elements in making a western trek, blacksmithing and carpentry services provided at the isolated forts proved of inestimable value to many people. From their inceptions both posts employed a blacksmith to perform military tasks, but by the time of the California Gold Rush these craftsmen found their labors overwhelmed. During the summer of 1850, Assistant Quartermaster Stewart Van Vliet requested that the War Department authorize five thousand dollars to expand Fort Laramie blacksmithing services to meet the increased civilian demands. He recommended construction of a blacksmith shop with two forges plus a wagon maker's shop employing a carpenter. Van Vliet doubted that there would be any ongoing cost for this, because overlanders would gladly pay for these essential services. The plan was not approved, and when Lucena Parsons reached there two months later, she found the blacksmith too busy to accept any more jobs.[50]

To get around the labor problem, Forts Kearny and Laramie began to rent their forges and blacksmithing equipment so that overlanders could make some of their own repairs. This do-it-yourself approach seemed to work well for people who had the necessary skills, but even this flexible system did not guarantee speedy attention for the perpetually long line of wagons. Civilians could shoe livestock, repair and cut down wagons, replace wheels, manufacture simple tools, and overhaul other equipment.[51] Some overland companies avoided the alleged high cost and delays of fort blacksmiths and carpenters by relying on skilled craftsmen within their own ranks. Sarah Royce's wagon train contained its own blacksmith and had seen fit to carry tools and a supply of hardwood and metal to address its own needs. Likewise, Margaret Frink's party contained an experienced man who was able to salvage a good axle from a wagon that had broken down near Ash Hollow. He removed the axle and used it to replace the one that had bent on his own wagon. The demand for skilled artisans at the forts never seemed to decline during the peak years of the overland trails, and by 1860 a passerby could report "several blacksmith shops" at or very near Fort Laramie. Those reported as "nearby" were privately owned shops located outside of the official military reservation.[52]

Because the Great Plains appeared to stretch out forever for emigrants progressing at a rate of only twelve to fifteen miles per day, Forts Kearny and Laramie seemed like oases in the middle of nowhere. Isolated though these communities were, they provided the argonauts with another important tie to the East—communication facilities. During the summer of 1849, Fort Kearny commander Benjamin Bonneville requested that the postmaster general establish regular mail delivery at his post. He remarked that sending army mail by irregular supply trains had resulted in considerable problems with lost and delayed letters. If Fort Kearny could be established as an official post office under the charge of sutler Lewis B. Dougherty, Bonneville expected that military and civilian needs alike could be handled more expeditiously.[53]

By the following year, the Post Office Department had established a contract with Samuel A. Woodson to deliver and receive monthly mail between Independence, Missouri, and Salt Lake City, via Fort Kearny. In 1858 the service became weekly, thus virtually eliminating the need for special army couriers for the first time. During the short life of the Pony Express, from April 1860 to October 1861, Forts Kearny and Laramie served as important division stations for the unique express mail operation. Throughout the 1850s, overlanders not only deposited outgoing letters at both posts, but they also picked up mail that was sent to the two general military addresses by eastern friends and relatives.[54] No other official post offices existed along that immense section of the Platte River, though travelers sometimes still entrusted letters to freight trains headed east or deposited them with the private traders at Scotts Bluff or west of Fort Laramie. There was no guarantee of delivery by these haphazard methods, and unlike the official post offices in the two forts, there was no way to receive mail at these private trading establishments.[55] By mid-1861, telegraph services also had been established at the forts to carry military and civilian messages. These post and telegraph offices, which often shared the same facilities, became popular gathering points for migrants eager to maintain their connections with families and friends just at the time when they felt most isolated from the East.[56]

Attendant to these advances in communications, the army frequently made improvements to the trails themselves. Special units of the Army Corps of Topographical Engineers were particularly active during the 1850s as they laid out new trails to supplement the primary transcontinental routes. The Central Route along the Platte River received more than its share of attention, including a fifty-thousand-dollar appropriation for improvements along the Mormon Trail from Omaha to Fort Kearny. This 1856 survey by Lt. John H. Dickerson shortened the route by twenty-six miles. Other units made similar improvements on the western end of the Oregon Trail when, in 1857, soldiers graded the road, laid down wood planking, and built timber braces to prevent rock slides in the mountainous stretch between Forts Dalles and Vancouver. In 1857, Congress appropriated three hundred thousand dollars in an ambitious effort to modernize the Fort Kearny, South Pass, and Honey Lake wagon road to California. Although primarily built by civilian contract labor, this shorter route was clearly based on a military plan and partial military labor.[57]

Because all of the western trails served a military mission, enlisted men worked as the primary labor force for clearing large boulders, reducing steep grades, and damming up necessary water holes along the roads. They sometimes received additional compensation for special jobs, but for the most part this type of manual labor was considered part of their soldierly duties. Even after the roadway had been completed, army personnel still had to maintain it, and this necessitated continuous field work for virtually all infantry companies, even to the end of the frontier era. Busy army construction crews of the 1850s might well have understood Col. Zachary Taylor's 1820 observation that "the ax, pick, saw and trowel, has become more the implement of the American soldier than the cannon, musket, or sword."[58]

Along with physical improvements on the roads, military labor crews built bridges and operated ferries at key river crossings. A crude ferry consisting of several canoes lashed together did exist at Fort Laramie during the final years of ownership by the American Fur Company. But the army needed a larger and more reliable means of transporting heavy loads from one side of the Platte River to the other. By the summer of 1850 soldiers had established a substantial ferry at that point, but it sank within two months as a result of an overload of horses.[59] A replacement was soon open for brisk business, and its profits were directed into a fund for creation of a post library and other social improvements. Within two years a toll bridge was fully operational. Charges were two dollars per wagon with four yoke of oxen and twenty-five cents for each additional yoke. By 1864 a replacement bridge commanded a toll of three dollars per wagon.[60]

Because the Platte River crossing at Fort Kearny was relatively shallow, and its meandering channels made it too wide for bridge construction, the War Department did not authorize a bridge or ferry there. Yet many people crossed from the north bank on horseback to deliver or pick up mail at the post and to purchase goods in the sutler's store. As early as 1849, George Gibbs, a civilian naturalist traveling with the Mounted Riflemen, observed that the government should build a number of bridges across rivers and streams between Forts Leavenworth and Kearny to help facilitate movement of wagon trains.[61] Although soldiers did erect a few small bridges over the smaller creeks of Kansas and Nebraska, the major bridges and ferries across more substantial rivers such as the Big Blue, Little Blue, Wood, and Elkhorn were built by private interests, which charged regular tolls. Beyond Fort Laramie, important river crossings such as Mormon Ferry, Reshaw's (Richard's) Bridge, and Mountain Men's Ferry were also managed by other independent businessmen, who frequently made handsome profits.[62]

The army's physical improvements to the overland trails were subjects of considerable attention in journals and diaries, but less frequent were accounts of cooperation between civilians and soldiers in the maintenance of law and order. This unique spirit of cooperation was necessitated by the absence of regular courts and lawmen to administer justice in this remote country. To fill the void, officers occasionally used their own discretion to arrest, hold, and transport to eastern authorities those persons who had committed major crimes along the trail. Unfortunately, these military officers had no legal jurisdiction to confine civilians without a special court order, and they risked a possible lawsuit every time they did so.[63] Maj. Osborne Cross worried about this potentiality when he arrested several larcenous teamsters and turned them over to the commander at Fort Laramie. The latter, lacking clear authority to hold the men, released them after several days of confinement, and they continued their pattern of stealing from overland parties. A more effective use of discretion occurred at Fort Kearny in 1864 when four travelers killed a man from Indiana, threatened his wife if she told anyone, and took control of his livestock as if nothing had happened. Another member of the wagon train informed the post commander of the heinous crime, and he sent soldiers to arrest the culprits. After unearthing the remains of the victim and taking testimony from bystanders, they returned the prisoners to the fort for transfer to a civil court.[64]

One of the most bizarre cases of military cooperation with members of a wagon train came in 1850 when two couples quarreled and one man shot the other. Witnesses pursued the shooter for several miles across the Plains before apprehending him. Following a trial and guilty verdict among members of the train, they turned the man over to authorities at Fort Laramie for transfer to a Missouri court. While under military escort he made his escape, and three years later the two adversaries who had met in deadly combat on the Plains were partners in a blacksmith shop in Hangtown, California. The two women had since married soldiers at Fort Leavenworth, Kansas.[65]

Frequently, army officers served as arbitrators to settle civil questions among members of wagon trains. In 1850 the commander of Fort Laramie arrested and fined the leader of a train because he had not lived up to terms of a contract signed with a member of the party. That same year, John Hale lodged a formal complaint with the commander at Fort Laramie against three of his partners, who had merged their meager funds to buy a mule team, wagon, and supplies. Since leaving Independence, Missouri, Hale had a falling out with his partners over the slowness of their daily progress. He asked that the army officer make a division of the communal property so that he could join a faster-moving caravan. The officer heard the case and agreed that Hale was entitled to his share of the resources after they were sold at auction. Although the decision pleased Hale in theory, he was not happy that he had to buy back the two poorest mules with his share of the auction proceeds.[66]

The mutual law enforcement activities of soldiers and civilians sometimes led to even closer cooperation in the actual apprehension of offenders. When in 1849 four deserters from the Mounted Riflemen robbed an emigrant of two hundred dollars and raped his wife, soldiers pursued the men. Because of assistance given by other overlanders, they captured the felons on Green River, and the offenders were subsequently tried at Fort Laramie under military law. Several weeks earlier, Maj. Osborne Cross had arrested an overlander for the alleged theft of two army mules. Military and civilian representatives alike held a "mock court-martial" for the suspect, found him guilty, and threatened to hang him. By prearranged plan, they allowed the convicted man to "escape" while they fired their guns to hasten his speedy departure. On other occasions, the army's offer of a bounty of two hundred dollars for the apprehension of military deserters helped spark further cooperation between officers and civilians. Whether motivated by civic duty or monetary reward, migrants were more likely to surrender deserters than to harbor them.[67]

Other acts of kindness and cooperation came not in official military orders, but in highly personalized and informal ways. When Dr. Caleb Ormsby was forced to sell one of his wagons at Fort Laramie before continuing his journey to California, he loaded four large trunks with clothing and personal effects to send back to his Michigan home. Capt. John S. Perry, who had befriended the doctor during the latter's brief stay at the post, agreed to send the trunks free of charge with the next army supply train.[68] Likewise, the junior surgeon at Fort Laramie arranged for Elisha Douglass Perkins to procure a badly needed canteen when none were available for purchase or issue. Because both men were brothers of the Independent Order of Odd Fellows and shared a number of common interests, the junior surgeon coaxed a canteen from a soldier and made it a gift to his new friend. These associations and acts of personal kindness went both ways, as when Forty-Niner Sterling Clark disposed of his book collection at Fort Kearny by giving it to Capt. George McLane and Capt. Charles Ruff.[69]

The army also provided part-time employment to some overlanders who lacked the resources or inclination to continue their westward journey. At Fort Kearny, Maj. Robert B. Reynolds, quartermaster to one of the army supply trains, hired James Mason Hutchings as carpenter-mechanic. In return for his skilled services, Hutchings received a wage, rations, and free transportation. Although pleased with the job and proud of his civilian contribution to the army, he declined a later offer to extend his tenure. At Fort Laramie, Capt. Charles Ruff and his wife Annie hired an emigrant family in 1849 to cook and wash for them. They found the woman to be "smart, managing and obliging," well worth the room and board and one dollar per week that she was paid. Her husband, in marked contrast, was deemed by Annie to be the "slowest moving, laziest man, I ever saw."[70] More lucrative were the monthly salaries of the following civilians at Fort Kearny in 1853: blacksmith (fifty dollars), carpenter (fifty dollars), wagonmaster (seventy-five dollars), interpreters (fifty dollars), and teamsters (thirty dollars). Some among these were recruited directly from the ranks of skilled men from the wagon trains.[71]

From their inceptions, Forts Kearny and Laramie were designed as long-term federal improvements on the Central Route. Not surprisingly then, commanders experimented with a twenty-year cycle of agriculture to raise food for soldiers and overlanders alike, as well as to promote eventual settlement of the Great Plains. As early as June 1849, Col. Benjamin Bonneville wrote to the adjutant general that the government should expand its commitment to the emigration process by creating several farms at the various Platte River crossings. He surmised that small squads of soldiers could protect the farms, overlanders could be hired to tend them, and they could quickly become self-supporting.[72] The day before Bonneville penned this report, naturalist George Gibbs observed that several overlanders had already ended their westward migration and were preparing to put in crops near Fort Kearny. Maj. Osborne Cross noted the same occurrence and concluded that, given enough time and experimentation, "not only vegetables may be raised in abundance, but grain of every description."[73]

Initial success with the post farm five miles west of Fort Kearny gave way to partial failure by August. The post farmer, a civilian named Booth, reported that the corn crop was progressing nicely, but efforts to raise barley, rye, oats, and potatoes had suffered because of the "thin soil."[74] Anecdotal comments in overlanders' journals throughout the 1850s and 1860s reveal that there was no consistent pattern of agricultural production at either of the forts. Months with sufficient rains produced bumper crops, but cycles of aridity could come just as quickly and leave only a parched landscape.[75] Military commanders quickly learned that food supplies shipped from the Missouri River towns were still essential to feeding soldiers and migrants. Army experimentation, especially with corn and wheat, pointed the way for a later agricultural revolution on the Plains, but that transformation would come several decades later with the availability of a new technology and a generous Homestead Act to lure expectant farmers by the tens of thousands.

Although military agricultural experimentation did not solve the food problems along the Central Route, forts often helped spur the creation of nearby towns, which aided the overland migration. This is especially true of Fort Kearny, which gave rise to two civilian centers by the early 1850s: Dogtown (Valley City) to the east and Dobytown (Kearney) to the west. Because federal law disallowed any commercial establishments on a military reservation, these communities sprang up just beyond the jurisdictional confines of the fort commander. The two towns probably would have developed anyway to serve the soldier economy, but the presence of so many overlanders assured rapid growth for one of the two. Dogtown, named for its large prairie dog village, never matured beyond approximately a dozen buildings. For awhile it housed a swing station on the stagecoach line, a post office, and a general store, but the main overland traffic arriving from the southeast generally passed it by and pushed on to Fort Kearny.[76]

Dobytown offered a better location two miles from the fort and a larger collection of buildings for the stage line. In 1859 it boasted a population of approximately three hundred, and within the following year it was designated as county seat of newly created Kearney County. Although the settlement had a reputation for attracting undesirable elements to its saloons and gambling establishments, emigrants found an impressive selection of merchandise, telegraph service, a doctor, several tradesmen, and three blacksmiths by the eve of the Civil War. This symbolized how much the Nebraska portions of the Central Route had improved between 1849 and 1859. Not surprisingly, Dobytown entrepreneurs focused their attention on supplying exactly the same kinds of services that overlanders had been demanding since 1846, and which the army had only partially been able to deliver.[77]

The experiences of emigrants who followed the Platte River Road to Oregon, California and Salt Lake City during the midnineteenth century closely paralleled the ordeals of travelers who traversed similar trails across the Southern Plains and the Southwest. Editorials calling for army improvements along the Santa Fe Trail had appeared in many newspapers beginning in the 1820s, and debates about funding had repeatedly echoed through the halls of Congress. As in the case of the Platte River Road, Missouri Senator Thomas Hart Benton had played the essential role in securing appropriations for construction of military posts and other physical advancements along this trail. But, unlike its more northerly counterpart, the Santa Fe Trail primarily filled a commercial need rather than serving as a migratory conduit for settlement. Even though fewer families followed this pathway than the Platte River route, its military posts performed similar functions of repairing wagons, extending medical aid, selling supplies, rescuing people in distress, and providing information on local conditions.[78]

Between 1847 and 1870, the War Department established a line of posts across Kansas, continuing diagonally through northeastern New Mexico and into the central plaza at Santa Fe. Anchoring the eastern leg of this protected route was Fort Riley, from which freight wagons departed for the heart of the Great Plains. The initial line of small forts, including Mann and Atkinson near present Dodge City, gave way to a more substantial string of fortifications by the time of the Civil War. This second generation of posts included Larned, Zarah, and Dodge, all of which continued service into the post–Civil War era. At the western end of the road in 1851 the War Department established Fort Union, New Mexico, an installation that continued service for four additional decades.[79] During the 1860s, newly constructed Forts Harker, Hays, and Wallace furnished help to overland travelers and freighting companies bound from the Kansas City area to Denver by way of the Smoky Hill Trail.[80]

An even larger migration occurred along the various arteries that fanned out across Texas and through the Southwest. These routes primarily served people headed for the California gold fields and were numerically dominated by men who hoped to gain quick wealth and then return to their families in the East. In contrast to the greater number of families headed to Oregon and Salt Lake City in search of a permanent residence, most sojourners of the southwestern trails planned a two-way trip. Yet even amid their supreme naïveté about gaining instant riches, these desert argonauts eagerly sought out military protection and sustenance wherever it was offered. Sometimes the aid was of the most direct sort. For example, in 1849, Capt. Randolph B. Marcy formed a military escort to lead some two thousand would-be miners from Fort Smith, Arkansas, to Santa Fe. The pioneering of this Canadian River route across Indian Territory and the heart of the Texas Panhandle served the needs of tens of thousands of California gold seekers during the subsequent two decades.[81] Furthermore, Marcy's return trip through

West Texas helped popularize another important trail to California that soon saw the construction of Forts Belknap, Phantom Hill, Chadbourne, Stockton, and Bliss along the line of travel. Between 1857 and 1861 a portion of this route also served the Butterfield Overland Stage Line, which placed its relay stations at or near the posts.[82]

Across the southern quadrant of Texas another series of trails and military supply roads radiated toward El Paso under the watchful eyes and helping hands of Forts Inge, Terrett, Clark, McKavett, Lancaster, Hudson, Davis, and Bliss. California-bound travelers of the 1850s and 1860s could then continue their excursions along the southern boundaries of New Mexico and Arizona by following the line of installations that included Forts Fillmore, Cumings, McLane, and Buchanan. In 1849 alone, approximately fifteen thousand emigrants undertook the south-western migration by a variety of trails that passed through Texas and Indian Territory. An additional eight thousand to ten thousand made their way along a number of Mexican routes before joining this so-called Gila River Trail along the international boundary line. The exodus increased its numbers during the 1850s, but slowed considerably by the Civil War era because of problems with Apache raids, the difficulty of a long desert crossing, and the diminishing lure of the California gold discoveries.[83]

During the same two decades, the War Department expanded its protective role over the northern trails beyond Fort Laramie. Two of the most important additions occurred in 1849 and 1863 when the federal government authorized construction of Fort Hall and Fort Boise, respectively, along the present-day Idaho segment of the Oregon Trail. Equally important was the army's 1857 purchase of Jim Bridger's trading post in the southwest corner of present-day Wyoming. While still in private hands, the post had served many emigrants bound for California and Oregon. But, like the American Fur Company's original Fort Laramie, it had a bad reputation for allegedly gouging travelers with its inflated prices for goods and services. After the army took control of the old fortification and expanded its size, the facility gained a more credible reputation among overlanders.[84]

Desirous of keeping the trails open to the Great Basin and the Pacific coast during the Civil War, the army established additional posts and subposts along the traditional Platte River Road. In September 1863, Fort McPherson was constructed at the confluence of the North and South Platte Rivers in western Nebraska, and eleven months later Fort Mitchell began service as a subpost of Fort Laramie.[85] Even more important to the protection and advancement of the Oregon–California–Salt Lake routes was the May 1862 establishment of Fort Caspar at the present site of Casper, Wyoming. Its original designation as Platte Bridge Station precisely indicated the importance of this small military installation that protected the vital bridge across the North Platte River.[86]

The gradual creation of towns along the various western trails did not end the era of wagon travel across the Great Plains, but a significant modification in frontier transportation was underway during the years immediately after the Civil War. Along the Platte River Road through Nebraska and Wyoming, no technological advance had more profound effect than did the 1869 completion of the nation's first transcontinental railroad. Henceforth, travelers and their cargoes could traverse the two thousand miles from the Mississippi Valley to the Pacific coast in a matter of days rather than an average of six months. With that ribbon of iron eventually came farmers, town builders, cattlemen, and a host of other entrepreneurs who would forever change the landscape of the Great Plains. Across the Southern Plains and the Southwest, the Southern Pacific; Texas and Pacific; and Atchison, Topeka and Santa Fe Railroads followed the old overland trails during the 1870s and the 1880s, also to hasten settlement of those regions. Fort Kearny was abandoned in 1871, and Fort Laramie followed suit in 1890, but both had served as "spearheads of the frontier," and their impact was best symbolized in the nation's legendary migration to Oregon, California, and the Salt Lake valley.

In its many guises, the multipurpose army had helped make the migration possible and had earned the gratitude of many who had made that epic journey to begin new lives. Even for those who had "seen the elephant" and were giving up their search for the western dream, the army stood as the most important government institution to aid their return to the East. The trails truly ran both directions and the soldiers stood ready to assist the dreamers and the skeptics alike.

CHAPTER THREE

Across and On the Wide Missouri

THE ARMY'S ROLE IN WESTERN TRANSPORTATION AND COMMUNICATION

Although most Americans have long recognized the U.S. Army's key participation in frontier exploration, relatively few comprehend its cumulative role in improving transportation and communication networks during the nineteenth century. As road builders, surveyors of canals and railroads, deliverers of federal mails, pioneers of telegraphic services, developers of commercial river traffic, and innovators of well drilling, soldiers helped open the West. Many of these missions were militarily justifiable because the War Department needed an efficient system to link its far-flung outposts. But from their inception these efforts also served an imperial function by facilitating stronger federal authority over the vast empire. Likewise, private enterprise benefited financially from these internal improvements, and, over time, even the lifestyle of average Americans improved as regional isolation gave way to a national economy.

Road building within the expansive trans-Appalachian wilderness had its origins in 1802 when infantry regiments began to improve the rough-hewn forest trail between Nashville and Natchez known as the Natchez Trace. Exigencies of the War of 1812 furthered the effort as the army lobbied for and received permission to build roads throughout the South to serve defensive needs against foreign threats and defiant Indians. During the late 1820s Secretary of War William H. Crawford and Gen. Andrew Jackson oversaw the construction of the system, which ran from the Tennessee River to Mobile and New Orleans, and from the Tennessee border to Lake Pontchartrain, Louisiana. Similar activity appeared in the Lower Great Lakes region, where military roads soon linked Detroit with Fort Meigs, Ohio, and Sackets Harbor with Plattsburg, New York. Although most of these roads were little more than rudimentary trails hacked out of thick forests, augmented with occasional grading of steep hills and erection of simple wooden bridges, they readily accelerated the movement of soldiers and a small population of traders and squatters.[1]

When questioned in 1819 about the practical value of devoting so much of troops' time to these endeavors, Secretary of War John C. Calhoun defended the policy on two levels. First, he affirmed that road building and other "works of public utility" improved the discipline and health of troops far beyond the deleterious effects of monotonous drill. Yet he simultaneously recommended that soldiers receive a daily bonus of fifteen to twenty-five cents for performing the labor. Second, he tied military and civilian needs under a common banner when he noted that "the road or canal can scarcely be designated, which is highly useful for military operations, that is not equally required for the industry and political prosperity of the community."[2]

Military roads proliferated in the area between the Appalachian Mountains and the Mississippi River during the 1820s and 1830s, but it was the Cumberland Road that allowed army engineers to prove their full worth. Construction of this first national turnpike began in 1811 under the auspices of the Treasury Department. Aimed initially at linking the populated counties of Maryland with the promising trade of the Ohio country, the civilian-built enterprise lasted barely a decade before its rapid deterioration led Congress to order repairs, especially in the Maryland sections of the route. Finally, after budgeting delays, Lt. Joseph K. F. Mansfield and his army engineers began reconstruction of the horribly dilapidated highway in the areas east of the Ohio River. Between 1832 and 1835 the government spent more than nine hundred thousand dollars on the restoration of the Maryland section, a princely sum in that age of small national government, miserly budgets, and congressional debates about how far federal authority should extend into internal improvements. Despite the substantial outlay of capital, political nationalists and commercial leaders joined hands with Secretary of War Lewis Cass to praise the high quality of work performed by the army engineers and to promote subsequent extension of this National Road all the way to the Mississippi River. The engineers found themselves engaged not only in road work but also in surveying the routes for canals and railroads that would soon push into the Old Northwest and open future commercial and agricultural possibilities.[3]

As the civilian population began to move beyond the Mississippi River and into the lands formerly constituting the Louisiana Purchase, the clarion call for military and commercial roads was heard on many fronts. Within the territory of Iowa between 1839 and 1845 the federal government allocated approximately sixty thousand dollars for this purpose. Here, as elsewhere in the future prairie states, the U.S. Army Corps of Topographical Engineers surveyed, designed, and supervised the construction of projects. Yet because of a shortage of military manpower to tackle this extensive work, the corps employed a civilian engineer to supervise each undertaking, and most of the physical labor was carried out by salaried civilians. These federal roads were among the best constructed and most widely used of all transportation facilities within Iowa, and they continued to maintain that status well into the period of statehood. Furthermore, each civilian engineer maintained his role as supervisor, inspector, and disbursing agent throughout several decades while simultaneously submitting monthly reports and annual summaries to the secretary of war.[4]

The creation of a rudimentary transportation system in Indian Territory followed a slightly different pattern because, during the 1820s and 1830s, its population increased dramatically as eastern Indians were forcibly removed to these lands. To meet its treaty obligations for protecting these removed peoples from the indigenous Plains tribes just to the west and north, the government quickly raised troop strengths in Indian Territory and began the construction of additional posts. With the 1824 establishment of Fort Gibson in the heart of the Cherokee Nation, government officials saw the need for a road to link Fort Smith, Arkansas, with the new post at the confluence of the Grand and Arkansas Rivers. During the following year, Congress met the War Department's request for ten thousand dollars to survey and construct just such a road. Steep hills and extensive forests slowed progress, but soldiers of the Seventh Infantry performed the manual labor and completed the project by September 1827. Unfortunately, the men could not add bridges across the rivers and streams because no funds had been legislated for that purpose.[5]

Subsequent improvements of the existing artery, plus the laying out of military roads between Fort Smith and Fort Towson, Fort Smith and Fort Washita, and Fort Arbuckle and Fort Belknap, rounded out the 1830s and 1840s. The army also provided improvements on the heavily used route between Fort Smith and Santa Fe, New Mexico, which became one of the primary means for reaching the California gold fields during the busy decade of the 1850s. Following the conclusion of the Civil War, newly constructed Fort Sill guarded the western end of Indian Territory, and it served as the hub of a wheel with five roads extending like spokes into western Kansas, northwestern Texas, and the Texas Panhandle. Throughout forty years of road building projects in Indian Territory, soldiers provided most of the surveys, much of the initial labor, and some of the ongoing repair crews.[6]

Even though most lines of transportation were built along a general east-west axis, the army also perceived the need to connect its interior line of forts with roads that stretched along a north-south axis. The most extensive of these consisted of three segments that linked Fort Snelling, Minnesota, to Fort Washita, Indian Territory, and continued on to Fort Jesup, Louisiana. President Andrew Jackson approved the enabling act on July 2, 1836, for the expenditure of one hundred thousand dollars on this project. The vast sum represented Secretary of War Lewis Cass's commitment to establish an efficient transportation network within the area dubbed the Permanent Indian Frontier. This route, fully within the prairie regions just to the east of the Great Plains, traversed the lands where the eastern removed tribes had been resettled, but these regions also became the focus of considerable civilian commerce during the following two decades. As early as 1844 the quartermaster general's report reflected this increased traffic along the stretch of road between Fort Scott and Fort Leavenworth. It also requested an appropriation to replace all the bridges along the road and to regrade many of the surfaces that had been eroded by extensive rains. The report concluded that the appropriation would not have to be large, because troops would be available to perform all of the manual labor.[7]

Eleven years later, Lt. Francis T. Bryan of the Corps of Topographical Engineers recommended that bridges be built in Kansas over the Solomon, Saline, and Smoky Hill Rivers, but this time under the direction of civilian mechanics. The project was carried out during the following year, totally paid for by government funds that had been sought by the War Department. The civilian engineer who headed the project happily reported that the bridges had helped move the line of settlement about forty miles further west, and by spring he expected the advance to reach eighty-five miles west of Fort Riley, Kansas.[8]

Lieutenant Bryan's vision represented only a small portion of an extensive road building program on the Central Plains during the 1850s. With passage of the Kansas-Nebraska Act in 1854, the two territories were formally organized, and efforts were soon underway to clear Indian land titles from the eastern areas. During that year Congress approved a fifty-thousand-dollar allocation to construct a military road along the north bank of the Platte River, linking Omaha with Fort Kearny. A year later, fifty-thousand dollars was authorized to improve the wagon road between Fort Riley and Bridger's Pass in Wyoming, and a similar allocation went to improve the trail between Fort Riley and Bent's Fort in Colorado. Although these expenditures were defended as necessary for military supply, they simultaneously aided larger civilian populations in reaching Oregon, California, Salt Lake City, and Santa Fe by these routes. Soldiers conducted the surveys and escorted the civilian construction parties but performed little of the physical labor in these cases.[9]

Secretary of War Jefferson Davis proved to be a tireless advocate of road improvements in the areas recently acquired after the Mexican War and through American negotiations with Great Britain for the Oregon Country. During his tenure, Congress approved three bills appropriating $550,000 for wagon roads to California. The first stretched from Fort Ridgely, Minnesota, to South Pass in Wyoming; the second extended from Fort Kearny to the eastern boundary of California; and the third traversed the Southwest between El Paso, Texas, and Fort Yuma, Arizona. After completing surveys for these routes, the Corps of Topographical Engineers turned over construction duties to the secretary of the interior, who placed all work under civilian contractors.[10]

The Pacific Northwest mirrored a similar pattern of army surveys followed by civilian construction of wagon roads, but these efforts involved far more dissension and delay. In 1853, Oregon Territory received an allocation of twenty thousand dollars to build a road between Fort Steilacoom and Fort Walla Walla, as well as a route between Camp Stuart in the Rogue River Valley and Myrtle Creek. Expenditures were justified as a military necessity in the wake of the Rogue River Indian War of 1853. Unfortunately, competing settlers demanded that the roads pass through their specific communities. Only after extensive litigation did work begin, but progress suffered a second reversal when the secretary of war intervened. Davis may have been projecting some of his pro-Southern sympathies into these actions, or they may simply have resulted from his personal distaste for Lt. George H. Derby, who was conducting most of the field surveys in Oregon and Washington. Not until Lt. George H. Mendell succeeded Derby, and some obstructionist Whig representatives were challenged in the House of Representatives, did work resume. Poor timing proved deleterious to the resumption of activities, however, because the Fort Colville and Frazier River mining strikes created labor and equipment shortages. These unforeseen delays were then followed by the advent of the Civil War, which virtually ended wagon road construction in the Pacific Northwest.[11]

The decade of the 1850s witnessed an especially close association between military officers and private entrepreneurs in improving the byways across West Texas. Unlike the tightly knit north-to-south system that was constructed between the Red River and the Rio Grande, with forts placed about every 125 miles, no permanent post existed in the Trans-Pecos country of Texas before 1854.[12] Yet the huge area extending from Fort Clark, Texas, to Fort Fillmore, New Mexico, needed increased army protection during this period because of Apache and Comanche raids on freight wagons, mail coaches, and overlanders headed for the California gold fields. Accordingly, in June 1850 a massive supply train, consisting of 340 teams pulling fully loaded wagons driven by 450 civilian teamsters and escorted by 175 soldiers, set out from Fort Inge, in south central Texas, for El Paso. Commanded by Maj. John T. Sprague, the expedition faced 585 miles of arid and rocky land as well as unfriendly Indians. Though the journey cost several lives and considerable property,

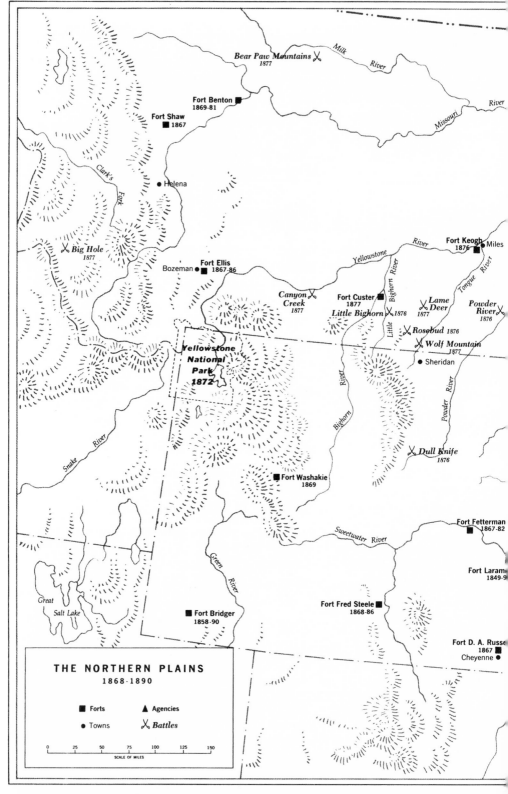

The Northern Plains, 1868–1890, from Robert M. Utley, *The Indian Frontier of the American W*

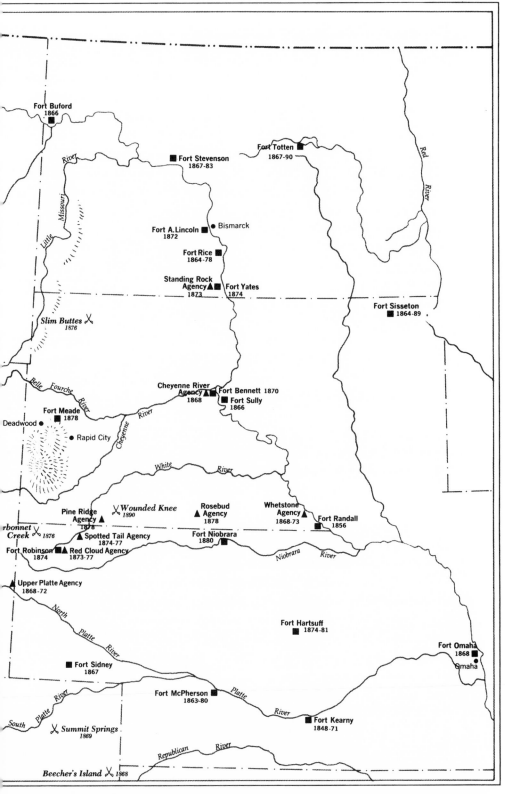

Fort Buford
1866

Fort Stevenson
1867-83

Fort Totten
1867-90

Fort A.Lincoln
1872

• Bismarck

Fort Rice
1864-78

Standing Rock
Agency ▲ Fort Yates
1873   1874

Fort Sisseton
■ 1864-89

Slim Buttes ⚔
1876

Cheyenne River
Agency ▲ Fort Bennett 1870
1868   ■ Fort Sully
1866

Fort Meade
1878

Deadwood •

• Rapid City

White   River

Wounded Knee ⚔
1890

Rosebud
▲ Agency
1878

Whetstone
▲ Agency
1868-73

Fort Randall
■ 1856

Pine Ridge
Agency ▲
1878

rbonnet ⚔ 1876
Creek

▲ Spotted Tail Agency
1874-77

Fort Robinson ■▲ Red Cloud Agency
1874   1873-77

Fort Niobrara
■ 1880

Niobrara   River

▲ Upper Platte Agency
1868-72

Fort Hartsuff
■ 1874-81

Fort Omaha
1868
■
• Omaha

■ Fort Sidney
1867

Fort McPherson ■
1863-80

Platte   River

Fort Kearny
■ 1848-71

⚔ Summit Springs
1869

Beecher's Island ⚔ 1868

46–1890. *Courtesy University of New Mexico Press.*

it proved the feasibility of modernizing this trail into the full-fledged Southern Military Road. During the following four decades this "army highway" served tens of thousands of civilians, ranging from merchants to cattlemen and homesteaders to gold seekers, thus becoming one of the most used of all southwestern travel arteries.[13]

From the inception of the Southern Military Road, civilians pleaded with political and military officials to improve conditions along the route. They especially wanted Uncle Sam to provide adequate sources of fresh water, because the alkali content of the Pecos River made it undrinkable, and only a few freshwater springs could be counted on year-round. On numerous occasions elsewhere on the frontier, soldiers had indeed erected temporary dams on creeks, dug shallow wells, and posted signs where the water was too fetid or poisonous for human or animal consumption. These improvements, plus the army's mapping of reliable water holes, had made western travel easier for many groups and undoubtedly had saved some of them from disaster. Partly to answer this call and partly to serve the future needs of a transcontinental railroad being planned along the thirty-second parallel, the War Department prepared a novel experiment that pioneered deep-water drilling in West Texas.[14]

Beginning in the summer of 1855, Capt. John Pope commenced drilling operations along the Pecos River near the Guadalupe Mountains, and within four months he had reached a depth of 360 feet, where a large underground pool of water was contacted. Unforeseen was the problem associated with the steam-powered pump, which could not draw the water to the surface. Further drilling at the site produced additional evidence of an even larger underground water supply, but the command moved its operations to the northwest near Fort Fillmore, New Mexico, where it hoped to reach the aquifer at a shallower level. Upon arriving at the camp in September 1855, Cpl. James A. Bennett reported that seventy-six soldiers of the Seventh Infantry and eighty civilians were working on the experiment. During three years of drilling at various locations, Pope struck several subterranean sources of water, yet the failure of his pump to draw up the precious resource, and the fact that he ran out of boring rods, forced the energetic commander finally to admit defeat.[15] Though arid sections of the Great Plains and the Southwest would have to await the development of the new technology of the 1870s and 1880s for successful deep-well pumping, Pope had at least proven the availability of water even for the driest parts of the nation.

Failure of the hundred-thousand-dollar well drilling experiment did not stop the army from seeking other cheaper solutions to the transportation problem in the Trans-Pecos country. During the 1870s and 1880s Col. Benjamin H. Grierson took the lead in building roads and providing better sources of water, first from his command post at Fort Concho and later at Fort Davis. In 1878 he laid out a shorter wagon road between Fort Concho and Fort Stockton, a route made usable by the recent army discovery of two reliable springs along the line of march. The following year he set up eight military subposts at various water holes in the District of the Pecos not only to limit Indian access to the valuable resources but also to improve the springs for use by soldiers and civilians alike. Sometimes that hospitality came back to haunt the colonel, as at his namesake Grierson's Spring, just west of Fort Concho. Once, in 1880, he permitted a freighter to water his expected ten head of livestock there, but the freighter watered at least fifty head and temporarily depleted the water supply. Nonetheless, using the various springs as essential guideposts, Grierson constructed new roads from Fort Stockton to Presidio, Fort Davis to Presidio, and Peña Blanca to Fort Stockton. Black soldiers of the Tenth Cavalry and Twenty-fourth and Twenty-fifth Infantries performed much of the labor by widening the rights-of-way, leveling the steepest grades, and cutting out the brush. Although powder was available for blasting the ledges, the bulk of the work had to be performed with pickaxes and shovels to make the roadbed even.[16]

Officers who had preceded Colonel Grierson into the area also had addressed the need for a bridge across the Pecos River, a cause long championed by people who had made the dangerous crossing. Army wife Lydia Spencer Lane recalled trying to make the difficult transit in 1869 at the most famous spot, known as Horsehead Crossing: "Then came the plunge into the treacherous, rapid stream, and the wagon trembled and careened as it struck the quicksands. The teamsters coaxed and scolded, urged and swore at the mules to prevent them stopping short of the opposite side of the river. I shut my eyes, and ears too. In the same team some of the mules were almost out of the water while others were nearly under it, caused by the quicksand shifting and changing position."[17]

Although the Pecos River was not very wide, it evidenced steep banks, quicksand, and a fast-flowing current during the spring. The 1870 construction of the Pontoon Bridge, about twenty miles downstream from Horsehead Crossing, offered travelers a safer means for traversing the dangerous waterway. Furthermore, soldiers from Fort Stockton maintained a small picket post called Camp Melvin at the crossing to protect the site and offer assistance to civilians. The bridge swung by iron chains stretched from both banks, and movable platforms standing on each side could be raised or lowered depending upon the elevation of the water. Unfortunately, the bridge was not strong enough to support the weight of a fully loaded freight wagon, and cursing teamsters could often be seen unloading and reloading some of their cargo.[18] When army wife Emily K. Andrews saw the structure in 1874, she warned that it was "not very safe" and noted that frightened mules balked at having to traverse its narrow width. Three years later, however, Dr. Ezra Woodruff, post surgeon at Fort Davis, pronounced it to be "a good pontoon bridge."[19]

The Pontoon Bridge across the Pecos River served another highly visible transportation facet in the West—the coaching of U.S. mail. Beginning with Article I, Section 8, of the U.S. Constitution, Congress was empowered to create a national postal system that could carry mail even to the most remote territories. When Fort Davis was founded in 1854, one of its primary duties was to protect the mail service along the San Antonio–El Paso route. Following the Civil War and the reactivation of the post in 1867, commander Col. Wesley Merritt authorized regular cavalry escorts of a dozen troopers between Barrilla Springs and Eagle Springs, places that had witnessed frequent Mescalero Apache attacks. The following year, Merritt switched to an alternate plan of stationing two or three soldiers at each of the civilian-owned stage stations located at intervals of about twenty-five miles throughout the exposed territory.[20]

Ironically, because most of the regiments rotated through Fort Davis during the 1870s were composed of black enlisted men, and because they were generally ordered to the stations without their white officers, racial problems sometimes arose. Virtually all of the stage stations and coaches were manned by white Southerners, many of them of the "unreconstructed" type who still viewed the Civil War as the defining moment in their lives. After a pattern of bad treatment by company employees and the failure of the station manager at Leon's Hole to even feed the soldiers, Fort Davis commander William Shafter issued an ultimatum in January 1872. He threatened to withdraw all protective units from the trail unless the issue was resolved immediately. To ameliorate the situation that now endangered their profitable operations, company executives agreed to a specific list of demands for the rights of soldiers guarding the mail stations and coaches. Even after the formal terms were agreed to, bad feelings still occasionally erupted. One particularly notorious driver who bullied white and black men alike met his end in November 1873 when Pvt. Frank Tall of the Twenty-fifth Infantry shot the abusive driver dead in his tracks.[21]

Francis C. Taylor, senior partner in the company that delivered mail along the San Antonio–El Paso route, soon found his enterprise facing a larger problem than merely maintaining good interpersonal relationships with the army. A political upheaval in Washington, D.C., forced the appointment of Marshall Jewell as the new postmaster general. Jewell began a reconsideration of many of the western mail contracts and cut Taylor's subsidy in half, pending the outcome of further reports. The company went into a financial tailspin as creditors called in their debts, and, by the fall of 1875, private mail service across far West Texas slowed to a trickle. For approximately six months the army transported virtually all of its own mail, as well as some of the federal mail that was piling up in San Antonio and El Paso. The crisis soon passed, but it had proven how vulnerable the federal mail service was in the most isolated regions of the nation.[22] Finally, in 1881 the army terminated its three decades of protective service to private mail companies operating in West Texas. The Apache threat to lone coaches had receded after the death of Victorio, and the road was now considered to be relatively safe for travel.[23]

Elsewhere, the need for army escorts had gradually subsided during earlier decades. Across the Central Plains, military patrols had been particularly active in protecting the overland mails between 1848 and the early 1870s. During the pre–Civil War era, Forts Kearny and Laramie had helped facilitate the movement of federal mails by freighting companies and later by the coaches owned by company giants such as Russell, Majors, and Waddell. Sometimes soldier escorts accompanied the freight trains and coaches, and less often, small squads were assigned to the stations. But, unlike the area traversed by the San Antonio–El Paso route, this trail along the Platte River was heavily used by civilian overlanders, and thus the need for special military protection was less critical.[24]

Amid the consequences of the Civil War, this reality changed as military manpower was withdrawn from the Plains and sent east, fewer civilians used the Platte River Road, and Indian pressures on the trail increased. During and immediately after the war, the army spent considerable portions of its resources in transporting and protecting the mails. In the most troubled times, four enlisted men were dispatched along with each coach, and four others were assigned on a permanent basis to each station.[25] On the Smoky Hill Trail across Kansas, other military units pursued a similar pattern, often relying upon Galvanized Yankees, former confederate soldiers recruited from Union prisoner-of-war camps, to fill their depleted ranks. As with the "galvanized" units stationed in Nebraska and Wyoming, these soldiers faced a steadily deteriorating situation. By the spring of 1866, Indian attacks and troop reductions forced the temporary abandonment of Fort Fletcher (forerunner of Fort Hays, Kansas) and the suspension of coaching operations by the Butterfield Overland Despatch.[26]

Even though reliable mail service was gradually reestablished in the years after the Civil War, not everyone was happy with the quality of delivery. In a letter mailed from Fort Dodge in April 1867, noted journalist Henry M. Stanley affirmed the truth of a rumor that was making the rounds on the Central Plains. It was alleged that stage drivers sometimes dumped mail when their loads became too heavy. Sure enough, in one of the creeks along the trail above Fort Larned, Stanley's party discovered five bags of mail, including one sack of books.[27] A year later, Julia Gilliss, wife of an officer stationed at Camp Warner, Oregon, noted a similar case of malfeasance. She joined other military and civilian families in charging the postmaster at Susanville with stealing about half of the packages addressed to the camp.[28]

Local postmasters could include virtually anyone willing to set up a small "office" and receive official designation from the U.S. Postal Department; such an informal arrangement was especially the case at far-flung military posts. At Fort Laramie, Sergeant Leodegar Schnyder received the job in 1859, and he held it for seventeen years during his active service and following retirement from the army. At Fort D. A. Russell, Lucinda Lester, wife of Sergeant Major Lester of the Seventeenth Infantry, secured appointment as postmistress in early 1887.[29] More often than not, however, the post sutler sought and won the designation, which allowed him to supplement his regular income without assuming a significant increase in workload.[30] When, in 1880, William S. Veck, former sutler at Fort Concho, got the postal assignment from the government, he moved his office from the fort across the Concho River to the fledgling town of Saint Angela. This created quite a controversy for Col. Benjamin H. Grierson, commander of the fort, because his men now had to cross the river to send and receive mail. In retaliation, Grierson had all military mail delivered to the station at Benficklin, about fifteen miles to the west, and he assigned the post chaplain as unofficial postmaster to make frequent trips there. Not until 1884 was the competition ended when the informal Fort Concho post office closed for good and all letters and packages were delivered at Saint Angela (by then renamed as San Angelo).[31]

The real test for the postal service, however, depended upon the perseverance and resourcefulness of the men who carried the mail in the West—including enlisted men of various regiments. Weather proved to be one of the most perplexing and dangerous realities encountered along the way, because without access to timely atmospheric reports, soldiers sometimes found themselves caught in rapidly developing storms. Pvt. Milton Spencer described how, in 1863, mail and supply wagons on their way to Fort Sully, Dakota Territory, became trapped in a blizzard. After losing four horses and twenty-five mules to the storm, the suffering men of the escort barely found their way into the post, but not until after temporarily abandoning the six wagons on the open prairie.[32] Eleven years later, three privates who were carrying mail to Camp Supply became disoriented in a blizzard and wandered for fifteen days on the Staked Plains of Texas. During that time for sustenance they had only meat from an antelope they killed and a dead horse they found on the prairie. Despite their horrible ordeal and subsequent confinement to a military hospital, the three dutifully brought in their bags of mail, and these were shipped on to their proper destinations.[33]

River crossings also created problems for mail riders, especially if they were traveling alone in the performance of their duties. During the winter of 1868, two troops of the Tenth Cavalry assumed the role of primary mail carriers between Forts Gibson and Arbuckle in Indian Territory. When one rider failed to report after his assigned thirty-mile ride, a detachment checked the trail, and upon not finding any trace, reported the man as a deserter. Some months later, the body of drowned nineteen-year-old Pvt. Filmore Roberts was found below the Canadian River crossing with the mail pouch still strapped around him. His status was changed from deserter to "having lost his life in the performance of his duty."[34]

The greatest fear of lone mail riders and escorted troops, however, involved attacks by Indians and bandits. In 1856, two soldiers carrying the mail from Fort Chadbourne, Texas, were captured, allegedly by Comanches; tied to a tree; and burned to death. During September 1867 two enlisted men escorting mails and building forts on the Bozeman Trail across the Powder River country of Wyoming and Montana were killed by Sioux intent upon closing down use of the trail by soldiers and miners. The troopers had no more than ten rounds of ammunition each, even though they were deployed in exceedingly dangerous territory.[35] A year later, six soldiers and two civilian scouts were ambushed at Palmer Spring while escorting a mail wagon to Fort Stevenson, Dakota Territory. Three soldiers were killed, but the survivors made their escape on foot and returned to Fort Totten safely. A relief column rode out the following morning to recover the wagon and its mail, which the attackers had left intact.[36] Less attentive to their duties were some of the men assigned to mail escort out of Fort Fetterman, Wyoming. In May 1874, seven of the twenty-three-man detail deserted while accompanying the mail wagon to Fort Laramie.[37]

Although timely delivery of military mail was necessary for the coordination of regimental and departmental business, it also served as a morale booster at the forts. Army wife Elizabeth Burt recollected the importance of mail call while she and her husband were stationed at Fort C. F. Smith, Montana, in 1868. Crow chief Iron Bull and one of his relatives brought the mail once a month from Fort Phil Kearny, and, on the appointed day, virtually the entire command would turn out for their arrival. Officers, men, and civilians alike gathered around as "each address was read out by a sergeant who then handed the letter or paper to a soldier to place in one of the various mail piles marked for company or for officer. How eagerly we watched the growth of our own pile and afterward devoured the month old letters and papers! To read the letter was a prolonged pleasure, shared with the officers and then passed on to the soldiers. To discuss the news with various friends helped pass many pleasant evenings."[38]

Thirteen years earlier, army clerk Charles E. Whilden had written to his sister in Charleston, South Carolina, indicating a similar feeling about the importance of the infrequent mail deliveries at his post in Santa Fe, New Mexico. Whilden movingly observed that "I never appreciated getting a letter where the mail was coming and going every day, but here, where it is only once a month that we can receive the slightest news, the arrival of the Mail is looked upon with the great eagerness."[39] To the west, at Fort Wingate, Lt. Frank Baldwin also lamented the slowness of a monthly mail call in the years immediately following the Civil War. Baldwin found reason to be jubilant at the arrival of eastern newspapers and periodicals, which, even though filled with "ancient history," were "begged and borrowed and read and passed down the line."[40]

If mail call provided a welcome respite for soldiers, it furnished an equally important boost to the lives of civilians who drew their mail at forts. Typical beneficiaries of this long-term practice were the residents of the eastern Texas Panhandle during the late 1870s and 1880s. Because no other official post offices existed across this vast Plains area, ranchers, sheep herders, railroad crews, and townspeople of Mobeetie relied almost exclusively upon officers at Fort Elliott to hold their mail. At first, freight wagons brought most of the civilian mail from Dodge City, Kansas, and the companies charged a hefty fifty cents for delivery of a single civilian letter to or from the post. By the summer of 1879, service had improved considerably at Fort Elliott, with delivery six times weekly from Fort Dodge, Fort Supply, and Fort Reno. Even though military necessity probably would have prompted this improved activity anyway, Panhandle civilians certainly played a major role in speeding and diversifying the delivery process. Because of citizens' early complaints about the initially poor service, Lee and Reynolds Company received a subcontract to transport the mail on a more frequent and cheaper basis. By the summer of 1879 the company likewise offered round-trip stage service from Dodge City to Fort Supply to Fort Reno for thirty-five dollars.[41]

Relaying messages over great distances in shorter amounts of time constituted an important dream for the nineteenth-century American army, but the amazingly simple method was not quickly adopted by the government. As early as 1844, Samuel F. B. Morse perfected the electromagnetic telegraph, with its ability to communicate almost instantaneously between distant points. Despite proven field tests and the relatively low cost of constructing extensive lines, Congress initially remained cool to the idea of subsidizing this new industry. It relied instead on private enterprise to develop and improve the concept. During the 1850s, California and Missouri led the way in creating their own statewide telegraph facilities, and military officers took their first look at the possible use of this system. Finally, in June 1860, Congress authorized forty thousand dollars a year for ten years to any firm that could establish transcontinental telegraphic services from western Missouri to San Francisco. By October 1861 a transcontinental line finally linked Omaha with San Francisco, and previously established eastern networks extended contact all the way to the Atlantic coast.[42]

Because the first transcontinental telegraph line generally followed the route of the Union Pacific and Central Pacific Railroads, it found itself in close association with the U.S. Army. Soldiers not only guarded telegraph construction and repair crews, but they also sometimes contributed physical labor to the building of what was otherwise a privately owned business. They dug holes, hauled poles, and repaired wire whenever civilian work crews were unavailable or frightened off by periodic Indian scares. The superintendent of the Western Union Telegraph Company made repeated requests to the Department of the Platte to provide protective and labor assistance, and many of them were answered affirmatively by departmental commanders.[43] The Civil War period proved especially difficult, because overtaxed soldiers were unable to meet the constant demand to repair broken lines. It was alleged that Indians cut the wires to lure small squads of soldiers into ambush, but more often than not, weather conditions interrupted the services.[44] One officer even suggested in 1867 that Plains Indians were cutting telegraphic lines to procure the stiff wire to make better arrows.[45]

As new telegraph companies established their own lines across the Central and Northern Plains during the 1870s and 1880s, they purposely linked themselves to military posts. Most were under contract to the government to handle military messages, and for this they received generous federal subsidies. Most often the association was a positive one, but sometimes companies neglected their end of the contractual bargain. In September 1883, Omaha newspaper correspondent William Annin reported from Fort Robinson, Nebraska, the general distress voiced by officers against the Cheyenne and Black Hills line, which operated a branch through their post and the nearby Sioux agency. Annin wrote: "It is owned by private parties who throw the labor of its maintenance on the government and remain sweetly oblivious whether it is up or down as long as they receive their monthly compensation for its use."[46]

Telegraph operators came from the ranks of both soldiers and civilians, but the purest form of a "military telegraph" extended across Texas and the Southwest. As early as 1868, Gen. Joseph J. Reynolds, commander of the District of Texas, requested a fully integrated telegraph system linking the tier of forts that stretched from the Red River to the Rio Grande. He observed that this was essential for the undermanned units that guarded such a vast area, for they would be better able to coordinate efforts against highly mobile Indians and outlaws. Reynolds, with the ardent support of the Texas legislature, repeated the call several times during the following years. One 1872 petition even provided quantitative evidence that between 1859 and 1872, Texans had sustained twenty-eight million dollars in property damage from Indian and bandit depredations. Finally, in the summer of 1874, Congress authorized one hundred thousand dollars to begin construction of the extensive system. Chief Signal Officer Albert J. Myer appointed Lt. Allyn Capron to begin the reconnaissance for possible routes and to start simultaneous construction at a number of different points. Lt. Adolphus W. Greely took Capron's place in the following spring and eventually completed 1,218 miles of military telegraph line in Texas.[47]

Fort Concho stood at the center of the integrated system and became a virtual clearinghouse for dispatches. The volume of monthly messages averaged between six hundred and seven hundred during the mid-1870s. Because this was officially a military system, soldier-telegraphers operated all the stations and substations. They also served as the repair crews for downed lines and sometimes received bonus pay for this "extra duty."

The special skills required of a telegraphic key operator allowed him to gain pay ranging anywhere from twenty-five to sixty-five dollars per month. Sometimes civilian helpers or young boys served as messengers at forty cents per day. Surviving records of telegraphic messages sent from Fort Concho and Fort Davis indicate the frivolous along with the important: Col. Benjamin Grierson trying to enhance his chances for promotion; Col. William Shafter ordering three bottles of the best claret, three quarts of the best champagne, and a dozen lemons; and a Captain Ward inquiring about the delivery of twenty pounds of malt to brew his own beer.[48]

As they did with army postal services, civilians made frequent use of the military telegraph. Ranchers, farmers, businessmen, and family consumers routinely placed orders for goods with firms as far away as San Francisco and New York. They likewise received emergency telegrams concerning their financial endeavors and private matters. Allegedly, one Atchison, Kansas, company transferring wagonloads of liquor across the Plains during the Civil War made a fortuitous use of the telegraph office at Fort Kearny. Learning that Congress had just imposed a new tax on their cargo, they raised their price and made an additional fifty thousand dollars' profit.[49] On a smaller scale, messenger boy Milo Burlingame assembled a sizable nest egg by delivering telegraph messages from Fort Elliott to civilians in and around the town of Mobeetie. Yet this all paled in comparison with the fifty dollars he received for taking an important message to Judge Frank Willis's distant ranch.[50]

Even though much of the West had been stereotyped as the Great American Desert by Maj. Stephen Long's 1821 pronouncement, river transportation actually played a prominent part in many regions. As a beneficiary of expanded frontier communication, and as a major player in the federal government's commitment to internal improvements, the army came to assume a significant role in developing the western river systems. As early as 1825, Col. Henry Atkinson envisioned improved transportation for the primary waterway of the West: the Missouri River. He loaded peace commissioners and a 450-soldier escort aboard a flotilla of nine side-wheeled keelboats. Despite frequent mechanical problems, the expedition proceeded against the strong current with greater speed and less effort than the usual flatboats and unpowered keelboats that were propelled by poling or cordelling techniques. The four-thousand-dollar cost of outfitting the flotilla seemed a bargain at first, but the side-wheelers never gained much popularity. Compared to conventional steamboats, which began to ply the Missouri River under civilian owner-ship during the following decade, the side-wheel keelboats were more expensive to operate, suffered more mechanical breakdowns, required more spare parts, and necessitated a crew twice as large as that of the stern-wheelers.[51]

Between 1842 and 1845, Congress funded more than $308,000 for improvements on the navigable western rivers. Work on the Missouri River consumed some of that amount as the Corps of Topographical Engineers worked steadily on a variety of projects.[52] Significantly larger funding came after the Civil War, based upon a comprehensive report filed by Maj. Charles W. Howell in December 1867. With great precision, Howell indicated which specific snags, boat wrecks, and boulders had to be removed; where deeper channels needed to be created by blasting and dredging; which landings should be improved; and where wood stations could be constructed to provide fuel for steamboats. He espe-cially highlighted the section of the river between Omaha and Sioux City, which carried considerable boat traffic but which was notorious for accumulating snags in its bends and for its unpredictable currents.[53]

The northern areas of the Missouri River gradually received a greater share of the annual funding as government officials tried to improve methods for supplying military posts and the mining towns of western Montana and southern Idaho. In comparison with the overland trails that crossed the Northern Plains during this era, river transportation offered a number of advantages. Freight could be moved by water more cheaply, in much greater quantities, and with fewer demands on main-tenance. Furthermore, passengers generally found that steamboats offered more creature comforts and less exertion than did stagecoaches, which bounced uncontrollably with each new rock or rut encountered along the roadway.[54]

Soldiers joined civilian crews in performing much of the labor along the rivers, all under the careful guidance of the Corps of Engineers, which planned and implemented the projects. One of the corps' key assignments was to determine how far west the Missouri River could be navigated by steamboats and which of its tributaries could also be used.

In 1875, Lt. Col. James W. Forsyth set out to answer these questions with the aid of scientists from the Smithsonian Institution and a 107-man escort of the Sixth Infantry. They confirmed Fort Benton, Montana, as the westernmost port on the Missouri River and concluded that the Yellowstone was navigable as far south as the Big Horn River. Finally, the Corps of Engineers created an exact map indicating where it would concentrate its activities so that no further money would be wasted in improving the Missouri River where the river's commercial use was not feasible.[55] Ironically, the largest expenditures on the "Mighty Mo" came in 1890, at the very time that river trade was decreasing because of the advent of railroads across the Central and Northern Plains.[56]

A second area offering possibilities for commercial and military use of rivers was Texas. As forts were constructed along the Rio Grande in the aftermath of the Mexican War, the army sought a way to supply them at the lowest possible cost. Likewise, Hispanic and Anglo businessmen recognized the economic potential of this traffic, and they turned increasingly to the steamboats that plied the river between Brownsville (Fort Brown) and Eagle Pass (Fort Duncan). Teresa Griffin Vielé, stationed with her officer husband at Ringgold Barracks (Rio Grande City), recalled how prolonged drought and the low level of water in the Rio Grande left the garrison virtually cut off from supplies in 1851. Steamboats could not make the transit because exposed sandbars threatened to ground and wreck them. Finally, the *Corvette* made its way up from Brownsville and reached a point some miles south of Rio Grande City before becoming stuck on a sandbar. Soldiers rode out and rescued food supplies, but not before the fort had been reduced to near starvation and Mrs. Vielé had even been compelled to eat her pet chicken.[57]

To test the broader commercial possibilities for the Rio Grande, the army conducted a number of reconnaissances upstream toward El Paso to determine if the river could be made navigable. As early as 1850, Capt. John Love led a twelve-man party on a keelboat to within 150 miles of El Paso before having to turn around. Subsequent military and private expeditions fared no better because the Big Bend area of the Rio Grande posed problems of negotiating narrow canyons. Thus, physical improvements were limited to the area along the southern reaches of the Rio Grande and a much smaller area near El Paso.[58]

Three other Texas rivers also occupied the attention of the Corps of Engineers: the Brazos, Colorado, and Red. The Brazos was potentially the most important, because it flowed across the cotton-rich counties of the east central part of the state. Private investors and county governments made the initial improvements during the 1850s, but these efforts were halted during the Civil War. Finally, in 1874 the corps was mandated to conduct the first systematic study of the waterway to determine if it warranted federal expenditures. The first formidable barrier of huge boulders was encountered at Rock Dam, barely thirteen miles below Waco, the starting point of the reconnaissance. Further difficulties with rocks, snags, and shoals, which required dragging the skiffs over bare stone, discouraged the party. Equally devastating was the final report of the corps, which concluded that clearing the Brazos and making it navigable year-round would be financially prohibitive. A second survey in 1895 was even more negative, and during the following year only five thousand dollars was appropriated to clear a small section near Richmond of snags, sandbars, and overhanging trees.[59]

The Colorado River fared even worse in attracting funds to develop its potential. In 1850, Lt. William F. Smith and two civilian surveyors followed the waterway from Austin northwestward to its source on the Staked Plains. They produced a detailed map showing the problem areas and estimated that it would cost about fifty-six thousand dollars to remove the main obstacles. Because so few white settlers had yet moved into the frontier areas above the capital city, the only money spent on the river's improvement was in those counties between Austin and the coast.[60] The Red River, marking the boundary between Texas and Indian Territory, also had a flurry of excitement at mid-century, but it never became a major shipping lane into the interior of the country. Especially notorious was the Red River Raft, a "great serpent" of trees and other debris that forced the river into frequent rechanneling. Even though the army cleared much of the barrier in 1835, new log jams quickly developed. Thus, despite the length of the Red River, only the area between New Orleans and Shreveport, Louisiana, remained commercially viable.[61]

The other Colorado River, marking the boundary between Arizona and California, also appeared to offer great potential for boat traffic. Following the 1850 establishment of Fort Yuma at that juncture, steamboat traffic began to develop, partly to help supply this and other forts in Arizona. During the winter of 1857–1858, Lt. Joseph C. Ives of the Topographical Engineers ascended the river by steamer. Despite the grueling nature of the trip because of numerous physical obstacles, Ives provided a detailed report favoring improvements along the river. For approximately three decades federal money was spent on the project, but the river was not destined to have a major function after railroads reached the area in the late 1870s.[62]

Along the California coast and in the Pacific Northwest the army took on an even bigger role, not only in river development but also in harbor work and reclamation. These innovations were hastened by the relatively quick settlement of Oregon by way of the Overland Trail and by the rush of miners into the California gold fields beginning in 1849. Among the earliest efforts was Lt. George H. Derby's 1853 rechanneling of the San Diego River by means of a levee that would prevent silting of San Diego harbor. This first federal harbor project west of the Mississippi River was partially washed away by a storm two years later, but it laid an important precedent for many other coastal modernizations soon to follow.[63]

After delays caused by the Civil War, Congress finally established, in 1866, a permanent San Francisco office for the Army Corps of Engineers, with the responsibility of surveying and refining important river and harbor sites all along the Pacific Coast. Within twelve years the corps had completed significant improvements of harbors at San Francisco and Los Angeles. Throughout the 1880s and 1890s it also dredged channels and built jetties at Humboldt Bay, approximately two hundred miles north of San Francisco. As a newly serviceable "deep water port," it handled much of the interior commerce into northern California and Oregon. Particularly reliant on this harbor facility was the burgeoning timber industry, which shipped logs and processed lumber worldwide.[64] To effect the safety of ships plying the harbors and inlets, the corps also constructed lighthouses along the full length of the coast. Even to the end of the century it continued to provide a team of lighthouse engineers and an engineer secretary to the Lighthouse Board of the Treasury Department. In 1910, with creation of the Bureau of Lighthouses, the Corps of Engineers ended its long association with these protective endeavors.[65]

Less heralded, but of vital importance to twentieth-century environmental policies, were the reclamation projects undertaken on California's
waterways. By the early 1880s more than five hundred mines, worth a
combined investment of one hundred million dollars, were destroying
the viability of many of the rivers flowing from the Sierra Nevada to the
coast. One estimate declared that between 1852 and 1909 at least one and
one-half billion cubic yards of dirt, rock, sand, and other debris had
washed down to the sea from the mines. Emerging agricultural and urban
interests, as well as shipping companies that feared future silting of the
major harbors, lobbied for environmental regulations. An 1884 court
decision finally forced Congress to act, and three years later it ordered
the Corps of Engineers to undertake a systematic reclamation study. From
this one-hundred-thousand-dollar scientific investigation came the first
efforts to save the Sacramento River, and this precedent led to work of even
larger scale on other California rivers throughout the twentieth century.[66]

Harbor and reclamation work would also occupy the attention of the
Corps of Engineers in the Pacific Northwest, but the earliest work was on
the Willamette and Columbia Rivers. Maj. R. S. Williamson initiated corps
activities in 1866 by dredging and removing snags from the Willamette.
He simultaneously prepared a report on the upper Columbia River
between Portland and the mouth of the Snake River. In close association
with the powerful Oregon Steam and Navigation Company, Williamson
proposed taming the three critical rapids at Umatilla, Homely, and John
Day, which had made riverboat traffic exceedingly difficult. Their blasting
experiment on John Day Rock marked the first permanent improvement
on the Columbia, and by 1873 the corps had eliminated all obstacles
associated with the rapids at that spot.[67] Even more complex was the
construction of a four-million-dollar canal around the huge physical barrier
on the Columbia known as the Cascades. Although work began as early
as 1878, the canal bypass was not finished until eighteen years later.
Despite huge expenditures on the Columbia, the would-be visionaries
were only mildly correct about the financial promise of long-term
shipping on the grand waterway.[68]

Of the army's numerous involvements with expanding transportation
and communication networks, no endeavor had more far-reaching
impact than its association with the western railroads. Because the rail

lines could build through the most imposing terrain, could economically serve areas with small populations, could carry heavy loads at reasonable rates, and could readily link frontier populations with eastern industry, they increasingly were viewed as the panacea for breaking patterns of frontier isolation. During the mid-1850s, Secretary of War Jefferson Davis oversaw the Pacific Railroad Surveys undertaken by the U.S. Army Corps of Topographical Engineers. Four main expeditions were launched: (1) between the forty-seventh and forty-ninth parallels from Saint Paul, Minnesota, to Puget Sound, Washington; (2) between the thirty-eighth and thirty-ninth parallels from Saint Louis to San Francisco; (3) along the thirty-fifth parallel from Fort Smith, Arkansas, to Los Angeles; and (4) along the thirty-second parallel from Vicksburg, Mississippi, to San Diego. The serious nature of this complex undertaking was seen in the congressional appropriation of $150,000 to make the explorations.[69]

Bitter sectional politics in the decade before the Civil War precluded initiation of construction as North and South argued over where the all-important eastern terminus would be located. During the war, however, secessionist Democrats led most of the South out of the Union and opened the door for a Republican-controlled Congress to fulfill its campaign promise for a transcontinental railroad. In the aftermath of the war, Union Pacific construction crews began work from Omaha westward across the Plains, and from California the Central Pacific began its slow advance eastward through the Sierra Nevada and into the vast Great Basin.[70]

Amid the building frenzy, Gen. William Tecumseh Sherman endorsed the transcontinentals and specifically the benefits that would accrue for the army. First, the rapid transport system would allow soldiers to move quickly to the scene of Indian threats and to readily supply expeditions that remained in the field for long periods. With this enhanced mobility some smaller forts and substations could be closed, and the regiments could be more efficiently consolidated at larger installations. Second, living conditions at the remaining posts would rapidly improve as new creature comforts were added. This would elevate soldier morale and increase the retention rate of experienced personnel. Third, and most important, the railroads would produce massive savings for the War Department by hauling supplies cheaply and offering half-fare rates to military passengers.[71]

Sherman's predictions proved correct on all three counts. Capt. Eugene F. Ware, a veteran of the Plains wars, would later describe events succinctly by saying, "Soon the Union Pacific Railroad was built, and the Indian problem was solved."[72] Even before completion of the line, one optimistic Chicago newspaper had already declared that the Union Pacific had done more to reduce Indian depredations than the entire army could have done with more direct punitive policies.[73] Likewise, conditions improved at some forts along the main construction paths within a matter of months. Army wife Elizabeth Burt noted how much Fort D. A. Russell and its adjoining town of Cheyenne had grown within the nine months of 1867–68 while her husband's command had been rotated to Montana. She declared that the frequent arrival of trains, regular deliveries of food from the Midwest and Pacific Coast, and friendly telegraph poles "made us feel we were again in 'God's Country.'"[74]

Yet, most important, financial figures showed the accuracy of Sherman's predictions about huge savings for the military budget. During the first seven years of Union Pacific freight service to military posts, the government saved an estimated $11,000,000. Throughout the late 1860s the average railroad freight rate for hauling army supplies was $.19 per hundred pounds per hundred miles. This compared favorably with the wagon rate of $1.45 to $1.99 for the same weight and distance. Furthermore, troops rode the rails for $.05 a mile, compared to $.125 by stagecoach, a total savings of $6,000,000 for the single year of 1873. For that same year, railroads transported seventy-three thousand military personnel, while wagons and stagecoaches handled a mere two thousand.[75]

In return for services rendered to the army, the War Department developed a close relationship with the western railroad companies during the 1870s and 1880s. Officers allowed civilian construction crews to secure timber and stone from military reservations without cost. They also permitted depots to be erected on post lands even though there was no clear legal authorization to do so. Patrols sometimes answered the call of executives to remove squatters from company-owned land grants, and officers infrequently loaned army rifles and ammunition to vulnerable work crews.[76] Despite the spirit of generosity engendered by General Sherman's 1867 directive to aid railroad construction in every possible way, some field officers found themselves mildly rebuked by their superiors.

Post commander Col. George L. Andrews routinely issued rations and tobacco to the engineers and survey teams of the Texas and Pacific Railroad as they worked through the mountainous areas around Fort Davis during late 1877 and early 1878. The practice ended in March, however, when departmental headquarters issued strict orders against the release of any more gifts.[77]

Protection against Indians constituted the most important reason for the army's relationship with railroad companies during the surveying and construction phases. Company M of the Sixth Infantry spent the entire spring of 1872 escorting representatives of the Atchison, Topeka, and Santa Fe as they surveyed right-of-way across Kansas. At about that same time, troops from Fort Abraham Lincoln, Dakota Territory, protected survey crews of the Northern Pacific Railroad across Dakota Territory. By prior plan, these soldiers released the civilian party to the responsibility of troops from Fort Ellis, who then provided escort for the Montana segment of the Plains. By the following year, some construction on the Northern Pacific had begun, and a company of soldiers from Fort Wadsworth, Dakota Territory, camped among the labor crews on the James River. In the Southwest, Company M of the Ninth Cavalry spent several winter months of 1881 protecting construction crews of the Southern Pacific Railroad from Apaches and bandits.[78]

The relative success of these missions contrasted sharply with the experiences of two earlier details that had helped guard Union Pacific crews and property. The unmerciful winter of 1866–67 had witnessed the stationing of a company of soldiers at North Platte, Nebraska. Obliged to live in tents that provided little protection against the bitterly cold winds, some of the soldiers plotted their escape. One night nine of them deserted, only to be apprehended quickly and confined to a makeshift guardhouse constructed of railroad ties piled twelve feet high.[79] Even more threatening to army credibility was the August 1867 Cheyenne attack upon a train at Plum Creek (today's Lexington, Nebraska). The Indians used workers' tools to remove the spikes and separate the rails so that a handcar and an engine pulling twenty-five boxcars crashed when they reached that point. Following this dramatic event, which left several railroad employees dead, the army increasingly relied upon Luther and Frank North's Pawnee Scouts to protect that section of the Union Pacific line.[80]

With completion of the arduous task of linking the Union Pacific and Central Pacific into the nation's first transcontinental railroad, the army found itself in the limelight of celebration. At the May 10, 1869, driving of the golden spike at Promontory Point, Utah, soldiers en route by train from Virginia to the Presidio of San Francisco joined in the festivities. Five companies of the Twenty-first Infantry, plus the regimental band, were appropriately outfitted for the occasion, and they performed with esprit, according to numerous spectators. Standing at attention in their dress blue uniforms and white gloves, shouldering their Springfield rifles with bayonets affixed, they made an impressive sight and added dignity to the grand event. Their officers participated in the main feature of the program by lightly striking their sabers against the famous golden spike after it had been placed in its predrilled hole. The regimental band then played for the assembled crowd of dignitaries, laborers, and prostitutes from the nearby town of Corrine. Their melodies continued well into the night, but "too much ardent spirit" finally broke up their extended soiree.[81]

The completion of the transcontinental railroads by the 1880s, and the expansion of "branch lines" and "short lines" during the same period, revolutionized life in the West. For the frontier army this was an especially exhilarating time, because the predictions of the late 1860s had proven accurate within two decades. The rapid decline of Indian wars, reduction and consolidation of military posts, substantial budgetary savings, and improved quality of life at posts all signaled the gradual end of a century of arduous and dangerous duty. Although the evolution of a frontier transportation and communication system had benefited tremendously from private investments and civilian use, the U.S. Army could take justifiable pride in its own contributions to the "westward movement." As surveyor, builder, and maintainer of roads, it had pointed the way into the wilderness. As innovator of well drilling techniques and pioneer of river, harbor, and reclamation projects, it had facilitated better use of the West's most precious resource, water. As deliverer of federal mails and telegraph messages, it had speeded communication beyond most people's wildest expectations. And as surveyor, protector, and frequent user of the railroads, the military had helped introduce the single most important piece of technology for closing the frontier era in the vast region from the Missouri River to the Pacific Ocean.

CHAPTER FOUR

Posse Comitatus *in Blue*

THE SOLDIER AS FRONTIER LAWMAN

One of the most daunting tasks to face the Founding Fathers was finding a way to establish federal policing powers without endangering the liberties of individual citizens. The generation that had fought for independence in the American Revolution steadfastly opposed the traditions of large standing armies and direct military authority over civilians. Thomas Jefferson's Declaration of Independence had specifically charged King George III with the "crimes" of illegally quartering troops in peacetime, hiring foreign mercenaries, inciting domestic insurrection, and resorting to martial law after suspending legally constituted colonial governments. Those refrains still echoed in the halls of the Constitutional Convention as the infant nation's leaders attempted to forge a new document for national guidance.

The most compelling evidence of their work toward a realistic compromise on policing powers appeared at two distinct places in the Constitution. Article I, Section 8, granted authority to Congress "to raise and support armies . . . [and] to provide for calling forth the militia to execute the law of the Union, to suppress insurrections, and repel invasions." Article IV, Section 4, went on to define the federal and state relationship by declaring the national government legally bound to protect each of the states against invasion and "on application of the legislature, or of the executive (when the legislature cannot be convened), against domestic violence."

The Judiciary Act of 1789 addressed the enforcement powers with greater specificity. Among other things, it established the federal courts, created a marshal system to execute the will of federal judges, and allowed each marshal to hire one or more part-time deputies. Section 27 of the Judiciary Act further instructed that when marshals and their deputies were unable to enforce the law by themselves, they could form a *posse comitatus*, translated as "the power of the county," of able-bodied, male, adult citizens.[1] This concept harkened back to a medieval English tradition whereby civil magistrates could enlist the direct aid of civilians in carrying out their enforcement duties. The practice had crossed the Atlantic Ocean and had been employed throughout the English colonies during the colonial period.[2]

Even though the *posse comitatus* model was well entrenched in America's Anglo tradition, it failed to address three problems. First, despite inferences from the Judiciary Act of 1789, no specific statute granted authority for marshals to assemble militiamen as a posse. Second, posses drawn from local militias or civilian groups often were more sympathetic to the lawbreakers, their neighbors, than they were to distant federal authority. Third, in remote frontier areas there often were not enough citizens to constitute either a civilian posse or a formal militia.[3]

These realities left only one other legally constituted body with enough manpower and proper mandate to fill the enforcement void—the U.S. Army. Predictably then, by the early nineteenth century, state, territorial, and local officials increasingly called upon regular military officers to augment civilian law enforcement, especially in cases of riots and civil disorder. To meet this demand and to answer the immediate emergency of the Aaron Burr conspiracy, Congress passed legislation on March 3, 1807, which provided "that in all cases of insurrection or obstruction to the laws, either of the United States or of any individual State or Territory, where it is lawful for the President of the United States to call forth the militia . . . it shall be lawful for him to employ, for the same purposes, such part of the land and naval force of the United States as shall be judged necessary."[4] While the phraseology echoed Article IV, Section 4, of the Constitution, it went further by bestowing ultimate authority on the president to call out federal troops for civil duty. The enabling legislation was finally in place, but a precise definition of "insurrection" had not been established. Over the coming decades the term often was interpreted in the most liberal of ways, and this led to many problems for the army, which could not escape the ambiguities of the law.

The only matter that appeared clear from the enabling legislation was that ultimate authority rested with the president, and thus no army officer could unilaterally order his men to serve as a *posse comitatus*. Nor could any officer turn over his troops to the command of civilian law officers unless specifically instructed by the chief executive.[5] Theoretically, the use of regular army forces for *posse comitatus* duty would be a rare occurrence, totally controlled from the executive office, and the soldiers would remain administratively separated from civilian law enforcement agencies. In short, the army would maintain its regular chain of command when called to *posse comitatus* status, and it would serve in that capacity only for a brief time. Unfortunately, as the nineteenth century wore on, beleaguered western territorial governors and marshals sometimes found themselves incapable of carrying out even the most basic tasks of law and order. Facing huge jurisdictions, inadequate manpower, lack of sufficient funding, political self-interest among territorial representatives, and sometimes an apathetic or even hostile local population, territorial governors and marshals came to rely increasingly on the regular army. Because they could somewhat deflect civilian resentment from themselves and could save money from their own budgets at the same time, some of these officials found it expedient to quickly call for military aid. Likewise, they could hide behind its shield if events went awry.[6]

By 1854, enforcement of the Fugitive Slave Act of 1850 brought a new burden to the army as Attorney General Caleb Cushing broadened the definition of *posse comitatus* and expanded the army's legal duties. Cushing declared all males above fifteen years old, including members of regular army, navy, and militia organizations, liable for this emergency service. This concept bypassed presidential approval by allowing civil officials to summon organized military units for suppressing major insurrections as well as arresting troublesome bandit gangs or individual felons. During the next twenty-three years the Cushing Doctrine was rarely invoked, but frustrated post–Civil War civil authorities returned to it as an important precedent.[7]

The first major western test of the Cushing Doctrine came two years after its inception, and ironically Attorney General Cushing himself ruled for the narrower interpretation of *posse comitatus* powers in this particular case. The conflict was limited to San Francisco, California, but it involved virtually all the residents of the city and created the potential for great bloodshed. A vigilance committee, composed of six thousand men and supported by perhaps seven-eighths of the city's population, took control of the local government and attempted to remove "undesirable elements" from the citizenry. Governor J. Neely Johnson and Maj. Gen. William Tecumseh Sherman, commander of the state militia, tried to wrest control of the city from the vigilantes and restore the legally elected political apparatus. Johnson and Sherman demanded that Maj. Gen. John E. Wool, federal commander of the Department of the Pacific, loan his stockpile of weapons and ammunition to the outgunned state militia. Wool refused on the grounds that only President Franklin Pierce could issue such an order. Cushing concurred by ruling that the vigilance committee had created a lawless situation and had usurped the power of the state government, but it had not violated the Constitution or federal law. Despite the narrowness of Cushing's legal definition, a single violent event almost triggered full-scale federal intervention anyway. A large group of vigilantes seized the city's armory and took several prisoners. U.S. Navy ships, already anchored in the harbor, prepared to do battle, but the vigilantes backed off and surrendered the stolen weapons.[8]

The San Francisco issue of 1856 did not constitute a direct challenge to the original Cushing Doctrine, since the matter involved the use of federal weapons instead of the use of federal troops by state authority. Events that transpired in eastern Kansas during 1855–60 did, however, create a crisis not so easily resolved. "Bleeding Kansas" evolved out of confrontations initiated by proslavery and antislavery factions who wanted to gain control of the territorial legislature. Territorial governor Wilson Shannon notified President Franklin Pierce in November, 1855, that law officers and courts were inadequate to handle the increasing wave of intimidation and violence. He cited cases of prisoners being forcibly taken from sheriffs, cattle being killed, property being burned, and illegal militia units being formed to terrorize the countryside. President Pierce responded that he would authorize federal troops to preserve order, but he took no action until January 1856.[9]

Prompted by rumors that a large force of Missourians, armed with artillery, was preparing to cross into Kansas to raid antislavery towns, the president sent instructions to his military commanders at Forts Leavenworth and Riley. Secretary of War Jefferson Davis carefully worded the directives to specify that "you will exercise much caution to avoid, if possible, collision with insurgent citizens, and will endeavor to suppress resistance to the laws and constituted authorities by that moral force which, happily, in our country is ordinarily sufficient to secure respect to the laws . . . [and] the government." Davis further advised the commanders to "use a sound discretion" and to look for the first opportunity to return to a purely defensive position.[10]

Such unrealistic double talk infuriated Fort Leavenworth commander Col. Edwin V. Sumner, who worried about whether the government would back him if the army had to resort to bloodshed against civilians. Even though the territorial governor made frequent calls for regular army help, Sumner did his utmost to avoid triggering further violence by not intruding too deeply into the civil unrest. His compatriots, Gen. William S. Harney and Col. Philip St. George Cooke, followed this cautious lead, but nonetheless they were quite active during the following four years. When the new territorial governor, Robert J. Walker, called for troops to protect the town of Lawrence during the fall of 1857, Cooke sent seven companies of dragoons to camp near this free-state community. This was only one among many cases in which the military commanders tried to anticipate trouble spots by sending troops to the area before events could get out of hand. Frequently they did so without even the presumption of having civil authorities request their aid. Their violations of the *posse comitatus* statutes were sometimes blatant, but success without much bloodshed silenced their critics.[11]

While the nation's attention was still riveted on Bleeding Kansas, another major conflict broke out in the heart of the Great Basin. A strong national anti-Mormon prejudice was further fanned by three newly appointed federal judges for Utah Territory. Two of these were rabidly apostate Mormons who had launched a personal vendetta against Brigham Young and the Quorum of Twelve Apostles. They propagandized about Mormon mistreatment of gentiles and disrespect for federal authority. Public demand for military action followed President James Buchanan's removal of Young from the position of territorial governor in 1858. Without much fanfare and without having first issued a "cease and desist" order to the Mormons, as apparently required by the 1807 law, Buchanan ordered Col. Albert Sidney Johnston to march twenty-five hundred federal troops to Salt Lake City.[12]

The entire Utah Expedition was mismanaged in the haste to assemble it, the inability to supply it in winter, and the underestimation of Mormon determination and ability to resist its advance. By using a scorched earth policy of destroying everything of use to the advancing army and guerrilla warfare tactics of destroying the supply column, the Mormons wrecked government plans for an easy victory.[13] Fortunately, a much larger war was averted by compromise, partly because of Colonel Johnston's realistic assessment of the no-win situation. The army withdrew the bulk of its troops in 1859, but as a symbol of federal authority it maintained a small garrison at Camp Floyd (renamed Fort Crittenden in 1861), approximately fifty miles southwest of Salt Lake City.[14]

While the concept of *posse comitatus* had been applied to regular army units in both the Kansas and Utah crises, several fundamental differences separated the two cases. In the former, the War Department had sanctioned the use of federal troops only under request by the territorial governor to the president. In the latter case, judges and marshals also had the authority to make the same request of the president through the War Department. Unlike the Kansas situation, in which governors and troop commanders coordinated their activities, Utah's new territorial governor Alfred Cummings repeatedly quarreled with Colonel Johnston. The issue of chain of command therefore remained confused throughout the duration of the Mormon War, and this caused military commanders to resent their policing duty even more. To Johnston's credit, however, he carried out his directives and helped restore order without significant bloodshed. Furthermore, throughout the duration of both the Kansas and Utah crises, no one invoked the Cushing Doctrine, bypassing presidential authority and allowing judges and marshals to expect the release of federal troops for law enforcement. In all cases, defenders of the *posse comitatus* concept acknowledged that the War Department (representing the president) retained all power over its soldiers and their deployment.[15]

While the three cases involving the San Francisco vigilantes, Bleeding Kansas, and the Mormon War attracted national attention to the *posse comitatus* issue, less visible frontier episodes spoke more eloquently of the need for military cooperation with civilian authorities. In 1853 the same Col. Edwin V. Sumner who would pursue such a cautious approach in the complex Kansas issue three years later stood as a strong advocate for decisive military action in New Mexico. Complaining about the territory's general state of lawlessness and the incompetence of civil administrators, he wrote to the secretary of war to request military intervention. Sumner alleged that local judges, federal justices, territorial officials, apathetic jurors, and skinflint taxpayers were preventing necessary expansion of the enforcement system.[16]

Six years later, an unidentified soldier reported from Fort Washita, Indian Territory, that "crime prevails to a great extent in this part of the country. Not a day passes but what we hear of somebody being killed. . . . Justice is slack and but rarely administered even if the rogues are caught."[17] The only hope for justice seemed to hinge on cooperation between civil and military officials. One such instance occurred in November, when a county sheriff from northern Texas enlisted the aid of twelve Fort Washita soldiers to arrest three murderers at Colbert's Ferry on the Red River. Unfortunately, the culprits escaped before the detachment could reach them. Thirteen months later, another patrol from the same post apprehended a murderer and held him in the guardhouse while awaiting transfer to federal court in Fort Smith, Arkansas.[18]

In locales where civilian law enforcement agencies were understaffed, constrained by local political conditions, or intimidated by public pressure, the army was well suited to temporary *posse comitatus* duty. In 1858 local officials at Doña Ana, New Mexico, refused to arrest some of their own citizens for brutally killing eight innocent Apaches. Armed with orders from a federal judge, soldiers made the arrests and ultimately delivered the prisoners to federal court at Socorro for a hearing.[19] Because of a shortage of jails in New Mexico during the 1850s, post guardhouses frequently held civilian prisoners, and army detachments helped escort prisoners when called upon. Whether in New Mexico during the 1850s or in one of the other territories later in the century, these types of *posse comitatus* services by the army only rarely caused a ripple of dissent. Likewise, they were carried out at the discretion of local commanders who apparently did not need to secure presidential or War Department authorization.[20]

Sometimes the cooperation between civilian and military officials went smoothly from the beginning of an operation. In 1852, Maj. James H. Carleton, commander at Fort Union, New Mexico, demanded that illegal saloons on and near the military reservation be closed immediately. Sympathetic to this predicament, territorial governor James Calhoun instructed the federal marshal's office to destroy the grog shops and their illegal contents. Deputy Marshal R. M. Stephens carried out the order with complete dedication, but the disgruntled owners launched lawsuits against him and Major Carleton. Fortunately, the court quickly dismissed the cases.[21]

Contrastingly, Maj. James Longstreet found himself on the receiving end of civil justice in 1856. Like many other officers stationed near the Mexican border, Longstreet purchased supplies from Ciudad Juárez, across the international boundary from El Paso, Texas. And like many other officers before him, he avoided paying customs duties on these goods. Deputy Marshal Samuel G. Bean traveled from Mesilla, New Mexico, into Texas, where he arrested the officer for customs violations. Longstreet ultimately had to pay a three-hundred-dollar fine and was none too happy with this particular case of civilian-military cooperation.[22]

Throughout the nineteenth century, all military officers who worked closely with local civilian law officials ran the risk of civil suits from aggrieved parties. This occurred because Congress never had passed legislation to establish specific arrest authority for the army. Doubtless, congressmen did not wish to create a national debate that had its philosophical roots in the American Revolution. Any discussion of expanded military power over civilians, even if statutorily limited to lightly inhabited frontier areas, would have caused an outburst of national indignation. Yet one generation of congressmen after another wanted the army to

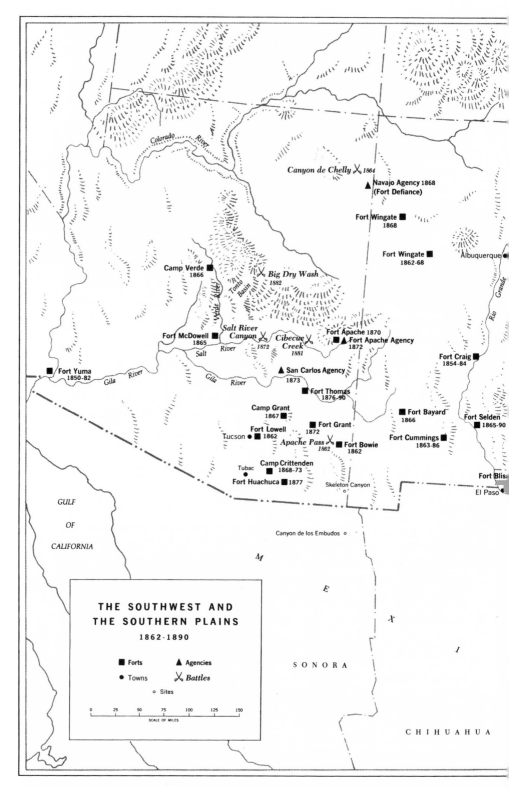

The Southwest and the Southern Plains, 1862–1890, from Robert M. Utley, *The Indian Fron*

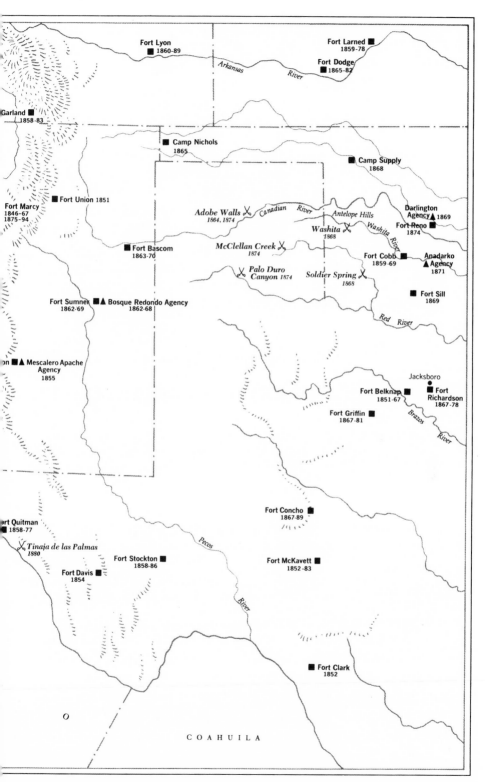

Fort Lyon
1860-89

Fort Larned
1859-78

Fort Dodge
1865-82

Arkansas *River*

Garland ■
1858-83

Camp Nichols
1865

Camp Supply
1868

Fort Marcy
1846-67
1875-94

Fort Union 1851

Darlington
Agency ▲ 1869
Fort Reno ■
1874

Adobe Walls
1864, 1874

Canadian *River*

Antelope Hills

Washita
1868

Washita River

Fort Bascom
1863-70

McClellan Creek
1874

Fort Cobb
1859-69

Anadarko
▲ Agency
1871

Palo Duro
Canyon 1874

Soldier Spring
1868

Fort Sumner ■ ▲ Bosque Redondo Agency
1862-69   1862-68

Fort Sill
1869

Red *River*

on ■ ▲ Mescalero Apache
Agency
1855

Jacksboro
●
■ Fort
Richardson
1867-78

Fort Belknap ■
1851-67

Fort Griffin
1867-81

Brazos River

Fort Concho ■
1867-89

rt Quitman
1858-77

Tinaja de las Palmas
1880

Pecos

Fort Stockton ■
1858-86

Fort McKavett ■
1852-83

Fort Davis ■
1854

River

Fort Clark ■
1852

O

COAHUILA

have a significant role in advancing law enforcement in the most remote regions. The complex issue could not be resolved to suit both viewpoints, and the matter was allowed to drift within a legal limbo. Predictably, military officers such as Maj. Gabriel René Paul turned out to be the victims of this dilemma. In 1857, Paul destroyed an illegal liquor supply in Young County on the frontier of northwest Texas. Invoking the federal law that banned alcohol in Indian country, this commander of Fort Belknap seemed to be well within his rights. However, one of the dealers, Hugh Harper, sued Paul for the astronomical sum of ten thousand dollars. Local citizens rallied to Harper's defense and helped pay his legal costs. The major, however, had to hire private legal counsel with the hope that the federal government would later reimburse him for those costs.[23]

The issue was not fully resolved eight months later when the new commander at Fort Belknap, Maj. George H. Thomas, found himself facing an even more complicated case. Thomas had discovered that the sheriff of Young County and an associate were illegally selling liquor to soldiers at sixty-five cents per gallon, and this was creating problems of rowdiness among the garrison. Thomas personally took an axe to the barrels of alcohol and soon found himself facing a ten-thousand-dollar damage suit, a hostile public, and even a disgruntled group of soldiers. His case went to civil court in the nearby town of Decatur, where he faced an even more hostile audience. The hearings dragged on for two years, never really being resolved but finally drifting into oblivion on the eve of Texas' secession from the Union in early 1861.[24] Similarly, when Lt. August V. Kautz arrested a man near Fort Orford, Oregon, in 1855, he could not possibly have anticipated the problem that it would cause. This particular crime of disturbing the peace on Indian land was a relatively minor one, and Kautz merely confined the man for six days in the post guardhouse. Yet the officer found himself facing a suit for false imprisonment of a civilian.[25]

Despite this obvious weakness in enforcement policy that left soldiers liable for litigation, most officers continued to exercise their own discretion in aiding civil authorities, and relatively few of them were targeted in lawsuits. They decided each issue on its own merit, declining some supplications for help while willingly accepting others. Ironically, the number of cases seemed to accelerate in the decade and a half after the Civil War, even though larger numbers of judges and marshals were gradually making their presence known in the western states and territories. Experiences at Fort Stockton, Texas, were fairly typical of those at many military posts during the era. Because the civilian town grew very slowly alongside the fort, and Pecos County was not officially organized until 1875, no jail or local courts existed to dispense justice. Hence, the post guardhouse held many civilian prisoners between 1869 and 1875, even though they technically were not supposed to be under military supervision. As soon as possible, various commanders at the post sent the prisoners under military guard to nearby Fort Davis, where a civil judge representing Jeff Davis County could try them. At the time of their transfer to civil authorities, these civilians ceased being an army problem.[26]

Although most arrests dealt with routine offenses such as theft, trespassing, and criminal mischief, capital crimes such as rape and murder frequently brought special cooperation between soldiers and civilian law officers. In one noteworthy incident near Fort Union, New Mexico, the army actually proved to be the only protection that several killers had, but that safeguard was only temporary. Following the arrests by soldiers and confinement in the post guardhouse, a local sheriff arrived to demand authority over the prisoners. Despite the men's pleadings that they be permitted to remain under the control of military personnel, the post commander released them to the law officer. Upon passing beyond the limits of the military reservation, the sheriff found himself confronted by a group of civilian vigilantes, who seized the prisoners and hanged them from telegraph poles. Mrs. Orsemus B. Boyd, wife of the officer who had made the initial arrests, recorded that the commanding officer had allowed this to happen knowing full well what the vigilantes would do. Since the offenders had set off the chain of events by murdering a soldier letter-carrier, he felt no compassion for them, and the work of the civilian vigilantes took care of the issue as far as he was concerned.[27]

Preventing trouble from spreading also occupied army attention when public officials were unable to handle the situation. On November 20, 1868, a riot broke out in the Union Pacific Railroad town of Bear River City, Wyoming. Track grading crews, angered at their poor treatment by some local business establishments and the town's newspaper, attacked the merchants and burned several buildings. Fearful of a second "invasion," citizens sent a messenger to Fort Bridger to seek immediate help. Capt. Henry R. Mizner arrived on the following day with fifty-five infantrymen, arrested the three alleged leaders of the riot, and removed them to the post guardhouse. Tensions remained high, but no further violence occurred, partly because Mizner went out of his way to placate both sides. The captain stabilized the situation and was able to withdraw his troops eleven days later. Quick action and a spirit of compromise had defused a potentially devastating crisis.[28]

A different kind of "state of riot and anarchy" drew soldiers to Colfax County, New Mexico, during 1875–76. A group of cowboys under the leadership of notorious gunslinger Clay Allison terrorized the opponents of their land baron patron Lucien B. Maxwell. When the county sheriff admitted that he could not preserve order, Governor Samuel B. Axtell sent his special agent, Ben Stevens, to Cimarron in the heart of outlaw country. Accompanying Stevens were regular troops who helped end the "Colfax County War" and persuaded Allison to surrender voluntarily.[29] Two years later, President Rutherford B. Hayes noted the growing state of lawlessness in several other New Mexico counties and ordered the cowboy factions to end their obstruction of justice. He further warned that since civil officials could no longer enforce the laws, regular army units would soon take the field unless the "unlawful assemblages" began to dissolve themselves.[30]

The relative ease of Captain Mizner's and Governor Axtell's successes contrasted sharply with the experiences of three companies of the Seventh Infantry that undertook a seemingly more mundane task during November 1871. Eighty-two men set out from Fort Shaw, Montana, and headed toward the Canadian border to arrest several whiskey traders. They never reached their destination because after having traveled only twenty-four miles from the post, they were overtaken by a blizzard. Of the total complement of troopers, fully seventy lost parts of their hands or feet to frostbite. One sergeant lost both hands and feet to amputation, and the suffering of all was made worse by the fact that no doctor or medical supplies accompanied the patrol.[31]

Although it was of little consolation to these maimed soldiers of the Seventh Infantry, Secretary of War William W. Belknap made special mention of the army's fine policing work in his annual report of 1871.

Belknap filled his summary with numerous examples of how soldiers had worked closely with civil magistrates and law officers to make arrests, deliver prisoners, evict illegal squatters, break up gangs of thieves, and prevent mob activities. Commanding General William Tecumseh Sherman echoed the sentiment and pronounced the cooperative effort to have been essential for maintaining law and order in the frontier regions.[32] Only two years earlier, Sherman had vented his own frustration at the state of lawlessness on the Northern Plains. In special instructions to commanders in the Department of Dakota, he had stressed the need to follow the letter of the law when working with civilian authorities. Yet he had also concluded the instructions with more unrestrained language: "When there are no courts or civil authorities to hold and punish such malefactors, we must of necessity use the musket pretty freely . . . ."[33]

Despite notable successes in the West for army policing roles, events in the South forced a change in national policy. Most Southern whites had long opposed federal military occupation of their region during the era of Reconstruction. Increasingly, in the early 1870s, as more Southern states gradually reentered the Union and the Democratic party reasserted its power, Congress began to consider new legislation that would severely limit the army's *posse comitatus* duties. Divided opinions were especially evident in Texas, where most white citizens resented federal military "occupation" to enforce Reconstruction policies but also liked having the troops stationed in frontier areas to protect them from Indians and outlaws. The Sixth Cavalry, assigned to Fort Richardson during the bitterest years of Reconstruction, found itself continuously assailed by public opinion for protecting freedmen and carpetbaggers from the former Confederate majority. Yet those same citizens were among the first to resist any effort to remove these soldiers further into the state's northwestern frontier. They were also among the most active groups to terrorize and kill blacks throughout all parts of Texas during Reconstruction.[34]

Beginning in the spring of 1878, Representative William Kimmel of Maryland offered an amendment to the year's army appropriation bill. His wording struck at the very heart of seven decades of loose interpretation of *posse comitatus* powers for the military. In its final approved version, the act ended all use of federal land and naval forces for policing duty except in specific cases expressly authorized by Congress or the president. Although some of the congressional speakers related the entire debate to the closing phases of military occupation of the South, others voiced more pragmatic concerns with the bill. Representative William Calkins of Indiana spoke against the sweeping language of the legislation. He correctly pointed out that in the western states and territories, where there were still inadequate militias and regular law enforcement authorities, military aid had performed a crucial task, and it would probably need to continue in that capacity for the foreseeable future. The outcome of the debate, however, was a victory for Kimmel's viewpoint.[35] Even more disturbing was an amendment by Representative J. Proctor Knott (Kentucky) to the bill which assessed a fine of up to ten thousand dollars and two years' imprisonment for anyone who violated the new provision. The amendment passed, and with its stinging promise of retribution the 1878 act seemed to have closed the door forever on military aid to civilian law enforcement.[36] The only routine exceptions allowed for the military were protection of Indians, public lands, and international neutrality laws, which were covered by other pieces of legislation.[37]

In compliance with the new law, War Department officials issued General Order No. 49 on July 7, 1878, to severely restrict military aid to civilian authorities. But as early as October 1, a second directive, General Order No. 71, again offered some discretionary power to local field commanders. It stated in less than precise language: "In cases of sudden and unexpected invasion, insurrection or riot, endangering the public property of the United States, or in cases of attempted or threatened robbery or interruption of the United States mails, or any other equal emergency, the officers of the Army may, if they think a necessity exists, take such action before the receipt of instructions from the seat of government, as the circumstances of the case and the law under which they are acting may justify."[38]

With the second directive, flexibility was restored to the system, but so was the ambiguity. The wording of General Order No. 71 sounded strangely similar to War Department instructions sent to Gen. George Gordon Meade in 1877, whereby each officer would make his own best judgment about every circumstance.[39] Unfortunately, the second directive offered no consolation to officers who were willing to take the initiative in handling emergency situations. They still could face the ten-thousand-dollar fine and two years in prison if they guessed wrong and exceeded their imprecisely defined authority.[40] Thus, military intervention into civilian law enforcement still remained a murky issue and everyone's guessing game. In late 1881, President Chester A. Arthur, under pressure from the wave of lawlessness in Arizona Territory, suggested broader latitude for army personnel to assist civil law enforcement, but his plan found little support in Congress.[41] Critics of expanded military powers pointed out that state and territorial governors should seize the moment to create and enlarge militias, which could take on the army's previous policing role. They also argued that in the wake of the 1878 law Congress had already created legislation to better coordinate activities among federal, county, and local law enforcement agencies.[42]

Within the first two years after passage of the 1878 law restricting army participation in *posse comitatus* duties, western governors, congressmen, and newspapers reported organized crime waves in some regions. During the late summer of 1878 alone, officials indicated that outlaws had robbed twelve stagecoaches between Cheyenne and Deadwood, had killed two law officers, and had intensified rustling activities. New Mexico officials lamented the upsurge in violence by a group who called themselves the Wrestlers. By the end of July, these desperadoes had already murdered six people, had raped a number of women, and had stolen considerable livestock from ranches. Arizona territorial governor John C. Frémont, a former soldier himself, also demanded an expanded role for the army in making arrests.[43] Joining him was John P. Clum, renowned former Apache agent and currently editor of the *Arizona Citizen*, who sarcastically remarked in August that five hundred troops were stationed in Arizona, and yet their hands were tied in dealing with the outlaw problem.[44] On the Northern Plains, Wyoming territorial governor John W. Hoyt called upon Congress to be more realistic, because the crimes were being "committed at places so remote from the main settled portions of the territory as well as by bands so large and desperate that the civil authorities are unequal to the work of breaking them up."[45] Even Secretary of War George W. McCrary worked toward relaxation of the restrictions, and Gen. William Tecumseh Sherman agreed that the relaxation would soon come.[46]

Among the most visible instances of legal instability were the large-scale rustling and robbery episodes in Arizona's southern counties. Here, the international border and lucrative black markets allowed a haven for brigands who could operate with virtual impunity on both sides of the boundary line. A complex tangle of outlaw groups, locally referred to as the Cowboys, posed special hazards for honest citizens in and around Cochise County. The 1881 Earp-Clanton feud, which reached legendary proportions in the infamous gunfight at the OK Corral and subsequent assassinations on both sides, revealed the deep political factionalism in the county and its law enforcement apparatus.[47]

Newly appointed Governor Frederick A. Tritle tried to restore order in the county seat of Tombstone by requesting military assistance from President Chester A. Arthur. Tritle indicated that Marshal Crawley P. Dake lacked the civilian manpower to conduct a roundup of violators and that Sheriff John H. Behan was so corrupt that he would have to be forcibly removed from office. When Gen. William Tecumseh Sherman visited the "besieged county" during the spring of 1882, he confirmed the governor's assessment and harshly criticized the restrictions of the 1878 *posse comitatus* act. President Arthur agreed, but Congress refused to create special legislation for this supposedly unique case.[48] Harkening back to the original 1807 law, which granted the president power to intervene in times of domestic insurrection, Arthur did call out troops to deal with this borderland unrest. Fortunately, no bloodshed occurred between federal troops and civilians in this case, so potential public outcry was minimized.[49]

Next door in New Mexico, an even bloodier event had already attracted national attention and had stirred passions on both sides about whether the army could maintain an impartial role when settling domestic disturbances. Within Lincoln County two factions vied for government contracts and economic domination through ranching and mercantile trade. Entrepreneur Lawrence G. Murphy and his associates, James J. Dolan and James H. Riley, held the upper hand because of their association with the powerful business-political clique known as the Santa Fe Ring. They were challenged by cattle baron John Chisum and his Lincoln County mercantile partners, Alexander McSween and John Tunstall. The February 1878 murder of Tunstall by a Dolan-controlled posse set off a chain of events later known as the Lincoln County War.[50]

During May, Tunstall supporters killed a herder who had been employed by Dolan and Riley. The latter parties requested help from Col. Nathan A. M. Dudley at nearby Fort Stanton. Dudley declined, pointing out that he could not commit troops merely on the request of individual citizens. The solicitation would have to come from the sheriff or some other public official. Two months later, a virtual war began in the town of Lincoln, where Billy the Kid and other members of the Tunstall-McSween faction came under a five-day siege by their rivals. In the midst of the bloody siege, the incumbent sheriff and a former sheriff urgently requested that Dudley send troops to halt the bloodshed. Both times the colonel refused, but when a soldier-messenger was fired upon, the colonel personally led officers and thirty-five enlisted men, armed with a Gatling gun and a mountain howitzer, into the town.[51]

Even though the McSween faction was under siege, Dudley indirectly sanctioned the assault on their stone fortress. McSween and four other men were killed, which prompted Mrs. McSween to prefer charges against Dudley. Although the court of inquiry exonerated the officer, his partisanship for the Murphy-Dolan faction had become widely apparent. So thoroughly poisoned was the atmosphere that in October, President Rutherford B. Hayes declared martial law in Lincoln County. Additional assassinations occurred, and the level of violence did not completely subside until Billy the Kid was killed in 1881 and John Chisum died of natural causes three years later. Army critics were quick to use this example to resist any congressional efforts to expand the military's *posse comitatus* powers.[52]

A different type of range war occurred on the Northern Plains fourteen years later when Wyoming's large cattle barons took the law into their own hands by driving out alleged rustlers from among the growing numbers of small ranchers and homesteaders. The Wyoming Stock Growers' Association, representing the cattle barons, hired twenty-two experienced gunmen and added them to their existing force of twenty-four men. Without any legal sanction, these so-called Invaders, or Regulators, began a sweep of the Powder River country above Casper in early April 1892. After killing several suspected rustlers, the vigilantes found themselves trapped at a ranch about thirteen miles south of Buffalo. Surrounded by over two hundred fully armed citizens, the Invaders faced annihilation unless they could be rescued by federal troops.[53] Acting Governor Amos Barber agreed, and he hurriedly wired Gen. John R. Brooke, commanding general of the Department of the Platte in Omaha, to authorize immediate deployment of soldiers from Fort McKinney, the nearest post to the site of the siege. He likewise beseeched President Benjamin Harrison to grant emergency *posse comitatus* status to federal troops, since, in his opinion, a full state of insurrection did exist. Barber also requested that Secretary of War Stephen B. Elkins release army guns and ammunition to the Wyoming National Guard so that it could aid the rescue if necessary.[54]

Following President Harrison's authorization of military action, elements of the Sixth Cavalry departed Fort McKinney and reached the besieged ranch on April 14. Their presence, and the threat that other soldiers would soon arrive to beef up the force, assured an end to the explosive crisis. The Invaders surrendered directly to Maj. Edmond G. Fechet, who provided an armed escort to Fort D. A. Russell near Cheyenne. At the behest of Acting Governor Barber, the prisoners were kept under guard in the post bowling alley because he feared turning them over to hostile civil authorities. The transfer to civilian jurisdiction did not occur until July 5, when they were placed in the custody of more sympathetic officials in Cheyenne.[55] Although questionable legal practices eventually gained the acquittal of the Invaders, bad feelings lingered for at least a decade. The army continued to be a target of some of the verbal abuse because, by performing its duty of preserving the peace, it seemingly had shown favoritism toward the wealthy cattle barons.[56]

Seven years earlier, Wyoming had been the scene of a different type of civil insurrection that could accurately be termed a race riot. At the Union Pacific Railroad town of Rock Springs in the southwestern corner of the state, Chinese laborers worked alongside whites in the coal mines that supplied the trains. Repeatedly, they had refused to join a strike called by the union, and other miners began to shower them with racial epithets and threats of reprisals. Of the 500 miners in the community, approximately 150 were white and the remainder were Chinese. There also were more than 100 additional unemployed white miners in Rock Springs who were convinced that the Chinese had taken their jobs during earlier labor disputes. A riot broke out on September 2, 1885, and by the end of the day 28 Chinese had been killed, 15 had been severely wounded, and the remainder had fled into the surrounding countryside. Virtually all the $147,000 in property damage was inflicted on Chinese stores and homes with the intent of driving them out forever.[57]

Because neither town nor county officials could restore order, and because more violence was expected against the defenseless Chinese, Governor Francis E. Warren telegraphed Department of the Platte commander Gen. Oliver Otis Howard to approve the deployment of troops as quickly as possible. Further messages to Secretary of War William C. Endicott and President Grover Cleveland resulted in the order to send elements of the Seventh Infantry from Fort Fred Steele and the Fourteenth Infantry from Fort D. A. Russell. Even before presidential approval had been granted, Endicott and Maj. Gen. John M. Schofield, commander of the Division of the Missouri, had already found a justification that would bypass the restrictive clauses of the 1878 *posse comitatus* act. They reasoned that since the Union Pacific Railroad had been established by an act of Congress, and since it transported federal troops and federal mails, then company property deserved special army protection. Thus, in the guise of safeguarding specific property, they dispatched soldiers whose real job was to protect Chinese families from further violence. They subsequently strengthened their legalistic maneuverings by citing an 1880 treaty signed between the United States and China guaranteeing that the federal government would protect all Chinese citizens who met ill treatment while in this country.[58]

Slowly, under military escort in many cases, most Chinese residents returned to Rock Springs. There they continued to face a hostile white population, especially after the sixteen arrested ringleaders of the riot were released by a grand jury. Yet the army maintained two new camps at Rock Springs and Evanston for several years to assure that no further violence would occur.[59]

Two months after the riot, however, white residents of Tacoma and Seattle, Washington, launched their own armed efforts to drive Chinese workers from their communities. Again, federal troops had to be summoned when local officials could not, or would not, meet the challenge. Unfortunately for Col. John Gibbon, commanding troops in the streets of Seattle, the experience turned out to be an embarrassing and frustrating one. Although he handled troop deployments well and restored peace, Gibbon illegally arrested and held civilian prisoners. This violated the 1878 *posse comitatus* act, since he had not been granted specific presidential authorization to make such arrests. Gibbon found himself officially reprimanded, even though he correctly pointed out the ambiguity of his orders, which had stated that he was supposed to support the civil authorities by any means possible.[60] Ironically, the federal government, whose passage of the 1882 Chinese Exclusion Act had fueled racist sympathies in the West and had helped precipitate these anti-Chinese outbreaks, actually came out of the crises looking like a benevolent guardian.

In far West Texas another episode involving race, economic rivalry, and political intrigue turned the border town of El Paso upside down. Tensions mounted throughout the late 1860s as Republican politicos Albert Fountain and W. W. Mills contested with Louis Cardis and his mostly Hispanic supporters for control of the valuable salt deposits near Guadalupe Peak, ninety miles to the east. In 1872 the Cardis faction joined with local Democratic leader Charles Howard to break the power of the Republican machine, but two years later Cardis and Howard separated into feuding factions. On October 10, 1877, Howard killed Cardis, and this precipitated a unified Hispanic call for Howard's arrest.[61]

While free on bail, Howard took a small group of his men to the nearby town of San Elizario, where they and some Texas Ranger allies became surrounded by the hostile Mexican American residents, who resented their acts of intimidation. Fourteen U.S. troops from Fort Bayard, New Mexico, under the command of Capt. Thomas Blair, arrived on December 12 to lift the siege but were unable to prevent the cold-blooded murders of Howard and two of his associates after they had surrendered. Several days later, Blair and his reinforced command attacked San Elizario, contending unfairly that this border town had become overrun by bandits from across the border. They killed four men, wounded several others, and drove many of the town's residents into the Mexican border town of Ciudad Juárez. No one from either side of the conflict was ever brought to trial, but Fort Bliss, which had been decommissioned a year earlier, was now reoccupied so that soldiers could watch over the tense situation. Hispanic residents of the region decried the army's seeming favoritism toward the Anglo faction that had supported Howard and his attempts to monopolize the salt deposits. At the same time, many Anglos harshly condemned the army for allowing the suspected murderers of Howard to escape unmolested.[62]

Whenever the army became embroiled in highly charged political, economic, and racial controversies, it usually suffered at the hands of public opinion—especially from groups that wound up the losers in these controversies. In contrast, military efforts against outlaw gangs generally won praise from the public, which saw these actions as the purest form of military cooperation with civilian law enforcement. Representative examples of this forceful and popular activity included soldiers working directly with sheriffs and other cases in which patrols performed on their own authority. In December 1875 a detachment of Ninth Cavalry operating from Fort Stanton, New Mexico, attacked the Mes brothers' gang at their hideout on the Rio Hondo. The soldiers killed or captured most of the band, including two of its leaders.[63] Eight years earlier, men of the Second Cavalry captured the notorious outlaw Sam Dugan near Cheyenne, Wyoming. They turned Dugan over to Colorado law authorities, and he was subsequently hanged in Denver.[64] Soldiers stationed at Fort Union, New Mexico, arrested William Coe and broke up his gang. While awaiting civil trial in Pueblo, Colorado, the prisoner was taken from jail by vigilantes and hanged.[65]

One of the most tragic episodes of military pursuit of deserters and horse thieves occurred in May 1881, when Lt. Samuel Cherry set out with a small patrol in the Sand Hills of northwestern Nebraska. One soldier within his command became drunk and unruly, and when Cherry tried to restrain him, the man fired a lethal volley. The remaining troopers not only captured the murderer but also arrested the horse thieves and returned all to Fort Niobrara for prosecution.[66]

Soldiers spent relatively little time chasing bank robbers, since banks had their own sophisticated detective systems. Such was not the case, however, with train robbers, especially if they tampered with the federal mails. One of the most celebrated and unique cases of military pursuit occurred following the September 18, 1877, robbery of a Union Pacific train at Big Springs, Nebraska. Led by Joel Collins and Sam Bass, the six gang members took thirteen hundred dollars in jewelry from the passengers and approximately sixty thousand dollars in gold coin from the express car. They then divided into two-man teams and headed south. The brazenness of the act, the notoriety surrounding "big time" outlaws such as Collins and Bass, and the amount of money lost compelled the railroad to offer a ten-thousand-dollar reward and a pro rata amount for any monies recovered.[67]

Along with various civilian posses, which began immediate searches, troops from Fort Robinson and Fort McPherson, Nebraska, as well as Fort Wallace, Kansas, also took the field under order of departmental commander Gen. George Crook. A force of eleven soldiers of the Sixteenth Infantry joined Sheriff George W. Bardsley of Hays City, Kansas, in hot pursuit and confronted Collins and Bill Heffridge near Buffalo Station, Kansas. The shootout resulted in the deaths of both outlaws, but it created a bitter legal controversy in its wake. Sheriff Bardsley took all the credit for this success and did not acknowledge the troopers' role at all. At stake were not simply the public accolades for a job well done, but also the impressive reward money. Not until May 1879 did the U.S. Circuit Court resolve the issue by awarding Bardsley $2,250, with the eleven soldiers receiving a total of $1,002, which they were to divide among themselves. The entitlement of soldiers to reward monies had never been decided previously by the legal system, probably because there had been so few cases of arrests that involved economic incentives. While senior commanders backed the right of their men to receive a share of the reward in this particular case, others worried about a conflict of interest that would again raise the specter of soldiers arresting civilians.[68] Although troopers apprehended felons throughout the nineteenth century, most did so in virtual anonymity and certainly without any financial rewards beyond their regular army pay. Those unknown numbers who were wounded or killed in the line of policing duty could likewise expect little more than treatment by a military surgeon or burial in a post cemetery.

General George Crook, commander of military departments on the Plains and in the Southwest throughout most of the 1870s and 1880s, generally favored a liberal interpretation of *posse comitatus* duties, and he frequently approved the use of troops to pursue outlaws. In one case, however, Crook's decisive action elicited a great deal of public attention and a severe reprimand from his superiors. The murder trial of Nebraska Sand Hills cattleman Isom Prentice "Print" Olive during the spring of 1879 represented the culmination of friction between large cattle operators who staked out the use of federal lands and smaller operators who wished to purchase and fence the land. Accused of killing two "homesteaders" and allegedly burning their bodies, Olive appeared smug at his trial, and this fueled rumors that his large assemblage of cowboys was on the way to raid Hastings and free their boss.[69]

The presiding judge wired Nebraska governor Albinus Nance to request the immediate deployment of federal troops from Fort Omaha to Hastings before the town was convulsed in gunfire. Upon receiving the urgent message, General Crook took it upon himself to send two companies of infantry and a Gatling gun to face down any possible street toughs. Although the potential for an armed rescue of Olive was probably overstated, the presence of these infantrymen dissuaded even the most loyal of Olive's lieutenants. Olive and several of his men were found guilty of the murders and sentenced to life in prison. They were released within two years because of the legal technicality that the trial had not been held in Custer County where the crime had been committed. A new trial was ordered, but it was never held because no witnesses could be found, and Olive soon moved his cattle herds into Kansas. Unfortunately, Commanding General Philip Sheridan rebuked Crook for violating the *posse comitatus* act of 1878. In this case Sheridan took the narrow view that the soldiers should not have been ordered into Hastings until after a violation of the law had occurred. The mere rumor of possible violence was not, in Sheridan's estimation, enough justification for military action.[70]

Crook's problems with the Olive trial paled in comparison with the potential troubles posed by labor strikes. Large and small, these confrontations constituted the most difficult duty that soldiers faced anywhere in the nation. Armed with virtually no training in how to handle these volatile situations, limited in their powers under the *posse comitatus* act, and despised by many Americans who saw them as armed strikebreakers, officers and men of the regular army hated this duty above all things. In these cases the enemies they faced were not stereotypical categories of Indians, outlaws, or conspirators against the government, but rather working men whose fare was not that different from their own.

Throughout the post–Civil War era, army personnel confronted a number of strike situations. Supposedly, presidential permission was necessary for the issuance of these orders, but as in the case of previously mentioned crises, senior officers often committed troops without clear orders. Most of the time their deployments were bloodless and of such short duration that the public supported the emergency action or at least did not protest strongly against it. For example, during the summer of 1868, troops from Fort Fred Steele moved into railroad construction camps at Green River, Wyoming, to contain anticipated labor violence. Three years later, General Christopher C. Augur sent two infantry companies to Carbon Station, Wyoming, where coal miners were striking against the Union Pacific Railroad and allegedly were threatening company property.[71]

Unlike these two cases, a full-scale riot broke out in Omaha, Nebraska, during March 1882 when the Burlington and Missouri River Railroad brought workers from nearby Plattsmouth to replace strikers who had been previously contracted for local construction. In addition to suffering numerous beatings, three Plattsmouth men were injured by gunshots. President Chester A. Arthur immediately answered the Nebraska governor's call by employing troops from Fort Omaha, two miles from the scene of the mob actions, and other troops from Fort Sidney in the western part of the state. Within nine days of military deployment, the threat of violence had subsided enough that the soldiers were withdrawn.[72] In each of the three examples, the controversies had remained localized and limited in duration, and the army never had to resort to any threatening gestures. Should all such labor difficulties have been resolved so easily, the military leadership would have rejoiced eternally.

This was not to be the case, however, and in the midst of growing union activities of the 1880s and 1890s, some officers tried to deal with the new reality by publishing educational articles within respected interservice magazines. The thematic intent of these articles could be divided into two categories. The first of these tried to win public sympathy for the army and especially for its individual soldiers, who were portrayed as simply doing their constitutional duty by preserving order. In an 1895 article for *United Service,* Theophilus Steward, black chaplain of the

Twenty-fifth Infantry, pointed out that servicemen and American wage laborers shared much in common. These same soldiers who had come under recent criticism for maintaining order in the streets had, in fact, spent far more time providing relief activities to destitute civilians. Chaplain Steward concluded his commentary by affirming that "the soldier may be relied upon to do his duty, even to bringing the bayonet against the breast of his own countrymen; but he will do it as a patriot, true to his oath and loyal to his flag, and not merely as a 'hired' instrument."[73] In somewhat the same vein, Capt. George F. Price, commenting on worsening relations between the army and elements of the civilian population, discussed precise ways in which the former could win over public sympathy. Price not only dealt with the policing duties of soldiers, but also other service practices that needed reform.[74]

The second type of article, of which many more examples appeared in print, offered precise how-to advice to officers who might face violent strikes or other forms of civil insurrection. Essays by Capt. James Regan, Lt. William Wallace, and John C. Gresham outlined the legal history of military policing duties and focused on laws regarding when troops could be used for maintaining domestic order and when they could not. Regan also remarked about practical matters such as equipping and feeding soldiers during riot duty and how commanders could avoid the use of force in most cases.[75] Gen. E. L. Molineux indicated how civilian police, National Guard, and regular army units could be coordinated in antiriot activities, and he offered special tactics that could be employed in facing down armed crowds. Col. Elwell S. Otis presented a detailed analysis of army successes and failures in handling the nationwide railroad labor disturbances of 1877 as a way of improving future strategies.[76] While Russell Thayer presented case studies on moving troops to trouble spots by rail, Capt. William N. Blow outlined hypothetical troop movements in a city besieged by armed mobs.[77] Because all of these articles were published within official military magazines that were routinely subscribed to by post libraries, they undoubtedly received a wide reading among military officers. How much influence they actually had on tactical policies is, however, more difficult to assess.

The 1877 Railroad Strike provided a wake-up call to military men that the rest of the nineteenth century would offer a different type of social disorder, one more difficult to contain because of its expansiveness, depth of public support, and propensity toward violence. During an eight-day interval of July 1877, nine governors called upon President Rutherford B. Hayes to suppress the violence associated with massive strikes against railroads that had implemented recent wage cuts for employees. Although primarily limited to states east of the Mississippi River, these events were anxiously viewed in the western states and territories, where other railroads were ripe for similar labor reprisal.

Within a matter of days the labor unrest had struck a dozen towns and cities between Philadelphia, Pennsylvania, and Jeffersonville, Indiana. The governor of West Virginia made the initial request for federal troops just at the time that coal miners joined the railroad workers in a common effort. Citing Section 5297 of the Revised Statutes (1875), which allows a state legislature or governor to request military aid from the president, Rutherford B. Hayes ordered troops into the troubled urban centers. He further alluded to the fact that federal mails and the trains that transported them were at risk, and thus they should be protected at all costs.[78]

The War Department found itself unprepared for this enormous task. No contingency plans existed, transportation for troops was inadequate, and no one had worked out coordination of the regular army with state militias, which had also been called into action. Within eleven days of mobilization, however, the army had twenty-seven hundred troops stationed in the trouble spots. These soldiers found themselves jeered, spat upon, and threatened with bodily harm wherever they went. Their officers also experienced a jurisdictional nightmare, because President Hayes had placed them at the disposal of the various governors. This allowed the state executives to decide tactical deployment of military personnel and to determine how long they would remain at the sites.[79] Maj. Winfield S. Hancock, commander of overall operations, bitterly complained about the vagary of his orders and the control exercised by the governors. He strongly asserted that the army "should not be made a police force" by state governments unwilling to perform the policing task themselves.[80]

By early August the most pronounced threats had passed, the strike had been broken, and the troops gradually returned to their regular stations. General Hancock praised his men's performance, especially citing the fact that they had restored order without bloodshed. Although no friend of the strikers, Hancock resented being used as a tool of corporate interests and politicians, and he knew that future labor disturbances of this magnitude would again bring the army into the imbroglio.[81] While General Hancock repeatedly alluded to the personal honor of the troops, the commander at Fort Dodge, Kansas, noted anything but a noble return for some of his men. During their strike duty in Saint Louis a large number of them contracted venereal diseases and had to spend the following winter in the post hospital. Their care from post surgeon William S. Tremaine was anything but sympathetic.[82]

The 1894 Pullman Strike, which posed even greater problems for the army, had its origins in policies similar to those of 1877. The Pullman Palace Car Company of Chicago had reduced workers' wages by 25 percent without making any pay cuts among corporate managers. In exacerbating the financial problems of workers, the company refused to reduce the housing rents that it charged employees. Defending the members' rights, the American Railway Union, under Eugene V. Debs, called a strike that quickly spread to railroad towns throughout the West. President Grover Cleveland sent regular soldiers to Chicago to enforce orders of federal courts, to protect railroad property, and to guarantee the continued flow of federal mails. This action came about despite Illinois governor John P. Altgeld's opposition to any use of regular troops and thus raised a question about possible violation of the 1878 *posse comitatus* act. Later, the Supreme Court upheld Cleveland's action and thereby set an important precedent for giving federal soldiers an enforcement role in states without the consent of state governments.[83]

By early July 1894, two thousand federal troops, four thousand militia, and five thousand deputy marshals patrolled Chicago streets. A crowd of well over five thousand people insulted the soldiers and pelted them with rocks on July 6, then overturned more than two dozen boxcars and blocked the tracks to prevent any train movements. On the following day, soldiers fired into a crowd of people who were wrecking a train and then dispersed them with a bayonet charge. Four demonstrators died, and seventeen were seriously wounded. On the July 8, another company of soldiers fired into a crowd at nearby Hammond, Indiana, and President Cleveland warned that anyone obstructing the trains would be forcibly dealt with.[84]

Although Chicago remained the centerpiece of strike activities, con-frontations spread quickly and taxed army resources to the maximum. The Seventeenth Infantry, which had been called from garrison at Fort D. A. Russell in May to protect railroad property at Green River, Wyoming, from a large group of unemployed laborers, was now dispatched to Pueblo, Colorado. There, several companies of the regiment protected property of the Santa Fe Railroad during the Pullman Strike. Other companies of the same regiment carried out similar functions at Rock Springs, Wyoming, and Pocatello, Idaho.[85] Likewise, troops from Fort Niobrara, Nebraska, protected railroad shops and yards at Laramie, Wyoming, and worked with federal marshals to safeguard Montana Union Railroad properties at Lima, Montana. Simultaneously, Lt. Col. William Shafter led almost three hundred soldiers from their post at Angel Island into downtown Los Angeles. The large force not only guarded the Southern Pacific and Santa Fe rail yards, but they also rode as armed escorts for outbound trains.[86]

These scattered military actions preserved the peace without employing counter-violence, but they also broke the back of the nationwide strike. While the Los Angeles Chamber of Commerce and other powerful businessmen held honoring banquets for Shafter and his troops, strikers and their supporters admonished the soldiers for acting as policemen for unscrupulous railroad magnates.[87] Friction also developed between Gen. Nelson A. Miles, who commanded the military occupation of Chicago, and his superior, Gen. John M. Schofield, commanding general of the army. Miles clearly became too cozy with the corporate interests against the workers, and when he tried to retain troops in the city after the crisis had passed, Schofield and Secretary of War Daniel Lamont roundly condemned his seeming conflict of interest.[88]

As the nineteenth century neared its end and the army celebrated its overwhelming victory in the Spanish-American War, another western labor dispute dragged reluctant officers and enlisted men into a no-win situation. The Coeur d'Alene, Idaho, mining district provided a perfect setting for labor violence as the unyielding philosophies of management conflicted with the militant tactics of the Western Federation of Miners. The first of three connected episodes occurred in July 1892 when union members dynamited one mine, killed several strikebreakers, and threatened other nonunion workers. Idaho governor Norman B. Willey requested federal help because the state's National Guard was inadequate to deal with the crisis. Following several days of delay, President Benjamin Harrison approved the dispatch of Col. William P. Carlin, who arrived with his troops at the Bunker Hill Mine on July 14. Detachments from various forts in Washington and Montana reinforced the regulars and helped make over three hundred arrests. Although nominally under the charge of federal marshals, the civilian prisoners actually remained under the watchful eye of the army. Gen. John Schofield and Secretary of War Stephen B. Elkins worked for the speedy withdrawal of troops, but the last infantry companies were not removed until mid-November. A renewed threat of violence during August 1894 brought a brief return of army personnel to protect mining property and the railroads, but the threat quickly subsided.[89]

The ultimate confrontation that had been brewing for almost a decade finally exploded in April 1899. Armed with thirty-five hundred pounds of stolen dynamite and aboard a commandeered Northern Pacific train, nearly one thousand union men descended upon the Bunker Hill Mine and blew up the $250,000 concentrator. President William McKinley responded immediately to Governor Frank Steunenberg's entreaties for military aid, because the entire Idaho National Guard was stationed in the Philippines at that time. Brig. Gen. Henry C. Merriam, commanding the Departments of the Colorado and Missouri, gathered over five hundred regular soldiers and headed for the trouble spot. Although Steunenberg had not yet called for a declaration of martial law, and President McKinley had not yet issued one, Merriam declared that he was proceeding as if one did exist. McKinley subsequently approved the officer's initiative, but labor organizations across the nation soon issued strong denunciations of Merriam's obvious favoritism toward the mine owners. All told, over a thousand people were arrested, and even though many were soon released, the others were forced to remain in wretched holding pens and boxcars.[90] One historian has recently labeled the 1899 handling of the Coeur d'Alene Strike as "one of the Army's most egregious failures." An earlier appraisal also condemned Merriam's zealousness and especially criticized President McKinley for "failure to give careful supervision" to the entire operation.[91] Thus, the nineteenth century ended not with images of universally respected cavalrymen dashing across the West in search of renegade Indians and outlaws, but with a growing public dissatisfaction with the army's continued service as a domestic constabulary.

Ever since passage of the 1807 act authorizing the president to use regular army and navy forces for the suppression of internal insurrections, military men had argued the pros and cons of their policing role. At times the majority preferred a loose interpretation of that power, thus allowing them to arrest and hold small numbers of outlaws and rioters for short periods of time. They well recognized that the more remote areas of the West lacked sufficient civilian law enforcement personnel to deal with some of these problems. Even under threat of possible legal reprisal for arresting civilians, most military officers carried out their duties with dedication. Yet in cases involving large numbers of people, in politically or economically charged atmospheres, and over protracted periods of time, the army met its severest tests and gained its greatest public enmity. In each of the major civil disorders, race riots, and violent strikes, officers inevitably favored one party over the other. The adversely affected side protested the one-sidedness of military action, and in many cases this damaged public confidence in an army that was supposed to remain above the controversies. As early as 1867, Gen. Christopher C. Augur acknowledged the ambiguities of military policing duties when he wrote: "It is a very delicate and unpleasant duty, and one from which we would gladly be relieved by the establishment and enforcement of civil laws."[92] His words proved prophetic for the rest of the century, and by the beginning of the twentieth century the army would face an even more difficult role as an "international constabulary" trying to maintain domestic order in its overseas empire.

CHAPTER FIVE

Dining at the Government Trough

ARMY CONTRACTS AND PAYROLLS AS COMMUNITY BUILDERS

During the summer of 1890, events were set in motion that would have a profound impact within Wheeler County and the larger Texas Panhandle. Acting on the recommendations of an earlier report, the War Department issued General Order No. 16 directing the permanent abandonment of Fort Elliott by October 1. This military post, which had guarded the eastern fringes of the Panhandle since its establishment in 1875, no longer had an identifiable function. The last Indian raid within the region had occurred in 1878, when a tiny Kiowa raiding party absconded from the Fort Sill Reservation and killed a lone white man to avenge an earlier Kiowa death. After that time only a few buffalo hunting parties of Comanches and Kiowas had entered the area under the watchful escort of soldiers. Yet by 1880, white hide hunters had exterminated the southern herds, and Indians no longer came into the territory under any circumstances. Furthermore, Fort Elliott's water supply had proven unhealthy for the soldiers and expensive for the army to maintain. With two railroads now crossing the area, and with both of them bypassing the fort, the installation's days seemed numbered.[1]

Yet, as in the case of so many western military establishments, the expected demise of Fort Elliott produced a unified outcry from the citizens of nearby Mobeetie. This tough frontier town owed its inception and its future to the post on Sweetwater Creek. Ten civilian residents were employed directly by the army, and the rest of the 250-person community consisted of ranchers, farmers, and merchants who were tied directly to the army payroll and contracting system. Every male adult inhabitant signed a petition to overturn General Order No. 16, and the petition was then forwarded to Texas governor Lawrence Sullivan "Sul" Ross. The state's chief executive, a celebrated Texas Ranger and Indian fighter during former days, agreed with the angry townspeople, and he sent the petition to President Benjamin Harrison. The document alleged that Fort Elliott was essential to the maintenance of peace throughout the Panhandle because this was the area of the state most exposed to Indian depredations. It falsely declared that Indian raids on area livestock had been "quite recent," and the removal of troops would certainly throw the entire tier of counties into panic. The petition further argued that the fort's water supply was healthy and adequate and that the existing railroads could only open the vast frontier area if they were protected by soldiers. In a final display of hypocrisy, Mobeetie residents implored: "We ask assistance in our behalf for the sole purpose of securing the needed protection of life and property to our citizens."[2]

Despite these impassioned pleas, the president, Congress, and the War Department remained convinced that money, not protection, was the real issue behind the petition. Fort Elliott was finally closed in October 1890. Its abandonment followed the same pattern that was seen in citizen petitions to retain Fort Griffin, Texas, in 1881 and Fort Stanton, New Mexico, in 1870. Only in the latter case did political leverage and recent Apache raids in the Sacramento Mountains help keep the post open another two and a half decades.[3] As in so many other incidents of fort closings, the town of Mobeetie limped along a few more years by serving the local cattle trade, but its population gradually diminished to 128 in 1900, and it lost its status as county seat seven years later.[4]

The experiences at Forts Elliott, Griffin, and Stanton were common throughout all decades of the nineteenth century. For wherever the army went, it carried with it a budget that, even in the leanest of years, was alluring to a sizable element of the diverse civilian population. Like camp followers all, they pursued military contracts and payrolls as major sources of income, and they did their best to protect the lucrative relationships whenever they were challenged by policy makers in Washington, D.C.

Historian Arthur Schlesinger, Sr., noted the symbiotic relationship between urban and rural development in a 1940 essay that stressed that more often than not, urban communities preceded farmers into the West, and they stimulated agricultural growth instead of becoming secondary by-products of the farmer's frontier.[5] Clearly, in many cases, such as Forts Abraham Lincoln, Dodge, Collins, Worth, Omaha, Scott, and Snelling, army towns helped shape the regional economies, but the communities were diversified enough to survive the loss of army revenues. In other cases, such as Forts Davis, Buford, Apache, Laramie, Bowie, and Union, the adjacent army towns were virtually the lone sources of economic growth for the surrounding areas. Once the soldiers left, these communities gradually faded into a state of somnambulance or they disappeared altogether.

The citizens of Mobeetie, in their desperate effort to preserve the Fort Elliott pork barrel, were at the chronological end of a process that had emerged widely in the West immediately after the Mexican War. For example, throughout the 1850s citizens of Minnesota repeatedly had trumpeted the call for increased military protection against Indians, even within the safest areas of the state. Individual frontier newspapers and local politicians incessantly competed with each other to attract the next established station. Secretary of War Jefferson Davis so worried about the proliferation of small camps and forts in 1853 that he demanded an end to the wholesale waste. He lamented that the public greed was bankrupting the army's yearly budget and leaving troops so dispersed that they could not receive adequate training or coordinate regimental affairs.[6]

At that very time, a new petition was circulated by the citizens of Pembina and Saint Joseph within the rich valley of the Red River of the North, which separated Minnesota from present-day North Dakota. The roughly twenty-five hundred residents of mostly French Canadian and Métis ancestry had long demanded protection against roaming tribes, but their relative remoteness and their "foreign racial composition" had gained them few supporters. The sympathetic editor of a Saint Paul newspaper blasted the simultaneous efforts of contractors and town site speculators who were trying to enlarge the facilities at Fort Abercrombie in the southeastern corner of Dakota Territory. The editor, dubbing himself "Veritas" (Truth), assailed the "cupidity of the mercenary bands of contractors and lobby agents" associated with Fort Abercrombie. He further demanded that the government station its troops where an Indian problem truly existed. Congress partially agreed with the editor, for in early 1855 it authorized five thousand dollars for the establishment of a post at or near Pembina.[7] Unfortunately, the appropriation was too small to erect a permanent facility, and the settlement had to wait another fifteen years before the plan came to fruition. Meanwhile, Fort Abercrombie received a larger sum of money, but the line of settlement quickly leaped beyond it during the immediate post–Civil War era, and it was deactivated in 1878.[8]

Fanning the fires of an "Indian Scare" became a common practice in the West when civilian contractors wished to expand their army business or save existing economic ties that were threatened by new policies. Pvt. Milton Spencer wrote disgustedly from Fort Randall, Dakota Territory, in February 1864 that "all the people in this territory and western Iowa, great and small, are doing their best to get another expedition set up the [Missouri] river (object to make money), and iff [sic] lying can effect anything they will gain their point."[9] The same anti-Indian hysteria was widely evident in the Sand Hills counties of western Nebraska during the 1880s as ranchers, farmers, and freighters pointed to nearby Pine Ridge Reservation as if it were a boiling cauldron of Sioux hostility. Rushville resident Jules Sandoz maintained good relations with Sioux families who frequently visited and dined with him, having left the starvation conditions of the reservation to hunt. Even during the controversial Ghost Dance period of 1889–90 and the resulting confusion of the Wounded Knee Massacre, Jules contended that white greed for army contracts had needlessly inflamed the volatile situation and had led to the disaster.[10]

Town site speculators proved especially adept at overdramatizing Indian threats in order to lure permanent garrisons. The growth of Wichita, Kansas, from a single trading house to an enterprising entrepôt in the years immediately after the Civil War was partly traceable to the creation of Camp Beecher. Promoted by Topeka businessmen who were incorporated as the Wichita Town Company, the small encampment hosted fewer than a hundred soldiers when it was established in 1868, but it fed vital revenues into the local dance halls and saloons. Despite community efforts to turn Camp Beecher into a permanent garrison, it was closed forever on June 3, 1869. By that time Wichita was beginning to attract Texas cattle along the Chisholm Trail, and the loss of military revenues was no longer crucial to the town's survival.[11] Further west, the editor of Denver's *Rocky Mountain News* stated financial realities more bluntly in an 1870 issue of the newspaper. In calling for the establishment of a large military depot within his city to supply all of Colorado's forts, he argued against economic naysayers by declaring, "Our people have a right to some of the patronage of the government."[12]

Even before a military encampment was officially established, dollars often dictated its location, size, and potential for permanence. If the post were located on federal land, the process was a relatively easy one, involving only the cost of construction and maintenance. But very often the choicest site was already in the hands of a private owner, who was in an excellent position to bargain with the government for a hefty selling or leasing fee. The problem was most acute in Texas, where, under the provisions of annexation in 1845, the state was allowed to retain possession of all of its public lands. Thus, when the army began its extensive fort building campaign in the state during the 1850s, it found the most favorable locations in the hands of either private developers or the state government.[13]

The sums of money involved in the purchase and leasing process were considered astronomical for the era. For example, Congress appropriated $100,000 for acquiring new sites throughout the West during the fiscal year 1854–55. When this proved to be inadequate for the task, legislators approved an additional $50,000 without ever undertaking serious debate. Five years later, as the nation faced a growing secession crisis and votes split more along sectional lines, the Senate refused to approve a more thrifty plan presented by the quartermaster general. The recommendation of $12,800 for rent and timber cutting privileges on the reservations of four Texas installations was considered excessive, but the official reason for rejection may have thinly masked Northern reluctance to aid a Southern state on the eve of the Civil War. The 1860 decision was in marked contrast to the events of 1854, when Congress routinely approved $43,000 to purchase a relatively small amount of land in the middle of San Antonio, Texas, for the creation of an arsenal and supply center.[14]

Not every private landowner tried to drive a hard bargain in his dealings with the army. Amid the arid terrain surrounding the remote West Texas post of Fort Stockton, land was valued at only about ten cents per acre in 1867, and civilian farmers and ranchers had not yet been drawn to the area in sufficient numbers to offer much opportunity for speculators. Deed holder Peter Gallagher therefore decided to make the army an excellent deal on the acreage necessary for the fort's expansion. For an annual fee of a mere $800, the army gained control of approximately 1,000 acres, including excellent cropland for a post garden and ample water from Comanche Springs. In addition to receiving the rent, Gallagher hoped to make a bigger sum of money in long-term army supply contracts and in sales of other parcels to settlers who would soon be attracted to the outpost.[15] A similar case presented itself approximately 150 miles to the east, where J. D. Robinson leased 2,373 acres for a mere $1,068 annually to assure construction of Fort McKavett. Like Gallagher, Robinson penned his hopes on a big payoff that would surely come after federal money had begun to roll into the local economy.[16]

More troublesome was the case of Fort Griffin, which was established in 1867 to protect the northwestern counties of Texas from Comanche and Kiowa raids. Not until 1873 did the government finally secure a lease with the multiple owners of the land on which the military reservation was located. Officers especially hated to negotiate with multiple claimants, because this tended to force up the asking prices. Even the army's threat to move the post elsewhere had little impact on the owners, who knew that they held the real bargaining power, since the buildings had already been constructed.[17] Similarly, the War Department wished to purchase lands outright for the establishment of Fort Concho because it was envisioned as a regimental headquarters with a promising future. But negotiations with various owners progressed so slowly that prices rose sharply on the stipulated 1,640-acre military reservation. Finally, the army settled for an annual leasing arrangement that wound up costing the government even more money in the long run.[18] On the Rio Grande, in the westernmost corner of Texas, the issues of ownership and lease contracts for Fort Quitman became so convoluted that only formal litigation through federal courts and the U.S. Court of Claims could settle the issue.[19]

Although purchase and lease arrangements for military reservation lands ran to large sums over protracted periods, only a few property owners profited from the negotiations. A far more lucrative source of civilian income resulted from the actual construction and constant repairs of the numerous posts throughout the West. While soldiers were the primary laborers in these construction projects, skilled carpenters and tradesmen frequently were hired to handle the more specialized tasks. In cases in which regiments could not spare men from drill, patrol, and other routine duties for long periods of time, the army contracted directly with private companies to do all of the construction work. In 1853 at Fort Ridgely, Minnesota, for example, master carpenters labored for $75 per month, masons earned up to $2.25 per day, and common laborers received $20 per month. By way of contrast, army privates made only 37 cents per day, often doing exactly the same work as the common laborers.[20]

Lower pay and lack of freedom led to considerable resentment by soldiers against their civilian counterparts. Sgt. H. H. McConnell was particularly acerbic in his description of the one hundred civilian workers who helped construct Fort Richardson, Texas, in 1867. He marveled at how "they did absolutely nothing; just put in their time and were in each other's way," while contrastingly, the soldiers were yelled at by their officers for even the slightest impropriety. McConnell especially poked fun at the foreman, assistant foreman, and eleven civilian carpenters who required several days to make a simple office table—a poor-quality one, at that.[21]

Other soldiers at Fort Fetterman, Wyoming, roundly condemned civilian workers who had neglected the maintenance of the post sawmill. Disinterested operator R. L. DeLay had reportedly responded to the criticism with the flippant remark, "Oh, if it kills anyone it will only be a soldier." On that same day in 1878, a private working on the woodcutting detail was killed when the poorly maintained blade snapped and hit him squarely in the face. Fellow soldiers threatened to kill DeLay, and on the following day they chased him from the military reservation. Inscribed on the soldier's tombstone were the words, "Killed through Criminal Negligence."[22]

At times, civilian workers were just as vociferous in their denunciation of army policies. During the summer of 1869, orders reached Fort Davis,

Texas, to discharge all laborers and mechanics who were involved in rebuilding the post. Henceforth, soldiers would perform virtually all of the physical labor under the guidance of twenty civilian foremen. One of the fired laborers, C. B. Owsley, wrote a contentious letter to the *San Antonio Herald.* Using the pen name "Argus" to protect his identity, Owsley blasted the quality of work performed by the troopers, contending that unfinished adobe walls were already beginning to collapse. He further charged the post quartermaster with malfeasance, but no formal action was ever taken.[23]

Much of the antipathy that existed between civilian and military laborers really masked a more important issue: the construction projects were so lucrative to contractors that they often represented the difference between whether or not a business could survive. The bidding process was highly competitive and sometimes involved illegal payoffs, cozy arrangements with key officers, and substandard inspections of the finished product. In frontier areas where people were optimistic about the future but strapped for cash in the present, these contracts were like manna from heaven. The Department of the Platte was authorized $130,000 for 1874–75 merely for the repair of existing buildings and the construction of a few new ones, a figure fairly consistent throughout the decade. At Fort Totten, Dakota Territory, replacement of temporary wooden buildings with permanent and more spacious brick facilities consumed over $106,000 to pay for materials, transportation, and labor costs. Even more astronomical was the estimated $800,000 expenditure on Fort Richardson, Texas, between 1868 and 1875. The high cost resulted because the site was moved twice and new buildings were quickly added to handle the unusually large number of troops who were originally housed in tents.[24] Even as late as 1887, at a time when many western posts were closing, Fort Robinson, Nebraska, underwent an expansion that lured numerous contractors and their workers into the upper Panhandle region. Work on the post accounted for 20 percent of Department of the Platte expenditures for the year, and its enlargement assured the immediate closing of the more isolated Fort Laramie, which was not on a rail line.[25]

Although most of these federal monies wound up in local economies, some of their impact was felt far away from the construction scene. When

Fort Quitman, Texas, was established in 1858 along the banks of the Rio Grande, all of its lumber was obtained from a privately owned sawmill two hundred miles away at Tularosa, New Mexico. Nineteen years later, as Fort Davis entered its own expansion phase, its commander also turned to Blazer's Mill at Tularosa to supply finished lumber. Previously, Fort Davis had hauled its lumber all the way from San Antonio at a high cost of $192 per thousand feet, but Blazer's Mill charged only $.03 per foot as long as the army carried the load in its own wagons. The New Mexico company sweetened the pot even more when it offered one free foot of lumber for each two feet purchased.[26]

During 1850 a more distant supplier had profited from construction of the Presidio at San Francisco, California. Because of a shortage of timber in the area and the high cost of local building materials in the inflated gold rush economy, Gen. Persifor Smith recommended that "iron houses" be sent for use as barracks. Six metal buildings, purchased from a company in Maine and assembled by soldiers in San Francisco, solved the post housing problem and demonstrated the long arm of the military contracting system.[27]

Aside from the huge construction budgets, the second most lucrative civilian contracts came from the delivery of beef, mutton, and other foods to military posts and to nearby Indian reservations, which were under a similar contracting system within the Interior Department. By the 1850s beef cattle generally were supplied from the local area, driven to the fort, and slaughtered when needed. Because beef was an army staple, extended contracts were among the most competitively bid of all civilian business arrangements. Advertisements appeared in local and regional newspapers outlining the delivery of specific quantities on exact dates. Even though the lowest bid was always given first consideration by the Commissary Department, low price alone did not assure a successful bid. Also taken into consideration were a contractor's past performance, local reputation, financial stability, and ability to pay a cash bond.[28]

Opportunities for profitable trade abounded in all areas served by a military installation. Even at a small outpost such as Camp Peña Colorado, near the rugged Big Bend country of West Texas, a single rancher supplied 4,715 pounds of edible beef during the short span of August through October 1884. At $.11 per pound, he received a payment of

$518, and he was only one among several contractors.[29] This contrasted sharply with the cost of monthly cattle deliveries at the larger Fort McKavett almost thirty years earlier. In that case, even though almost twice as much product was delivered each month, the total cost amounted to only $364 for the equivalent three months.[30] Supply and demand, plus the competitiveness of bidders, truly governed final sales prices more than any single factor.

Flour millers and other food producers also stood to make a good living with the military trade. In 1850, El Paso pioneer merchant Simeon Hart negotiated the first of many agreements to provide refined flour to Fort Bliss, Texas; to Fort Fillmore, New Mexico, a mere fifty miles further up the Rio Grande; and to Fort Davis, a hundred miles to the east. So lucrative and long-lasting were the contracts that all of the early merchant families of El Paso made their initial profits from the army. Hart and his competitors soon expanded into other food commodities such as beans and vegetables, many of which were transported from the Mexican state of Chihuahua.[31] Some of these trading houses were still in existence during the early 1870s and had expanded their food deliveries as far east as Fort Stockton. However, when Forts Davis and Stockton began to produce ample crops from their extensive post gardens, many of the contracts were scaled back or terminated altogether.[32]

Because many western posts were built in areas far removed from ample supplies of timber, contracting for wood for fuel to cook food and heat buildings was another means of expanding the civilian economy. Throughout the severe winter of 1866–67, Capt. Andrew Burt and his wife Elizabeth suffered mightily alongside the rest of Fort Bridger's garrison. The wood contract had been inadequate for this Wyoming post, which faced many weeks of sub-zero temperatures, and the inhabitants thought daily of this most basic necessity. Unfortunately, contracting for wood was a particularly inexact science, and many army posts were left unprepared for winter's capriciousness.[33]

Typical of these specialized contractors was Basil Clement, who doubled his income by providing firewood both to Fort Bennett, Dakota Territory, and to steamboats that moved seasonally along the Missouri River. Amid Clement's good fortune of 1869, however, his $700 profit for one cutting was lost when Indians from the nearby Cheyenne River

Agency ran off his herd of ninety horses and mules, which were used to haul the timber. Nineteen years of legal entanglement finally produced government compensation of $1,740 for his business. Like Clement, other entrepreneurs found that the golden goose of military supply could disappear almost as quickly as it had materialized. Denver business-men made steady incomes delivering wood at $105 per cord to Fort Sedgwick in the northeastern corner of Colorado during the mid-1860s. The lucrative contracts to the army and civilians in the nearby town of Julesburg lasted only a few years until the advance of rail service shattered the pricing system, and ultimately Wyoming coal put the wood cutting contractors out of the bidding competition.[34]

Wherever cavalry regiments were stationed, replacement horses also contributed to the growth of local economies. Likewise, mules pre-dominated at major supply posts, because they pulled most army freight wagons and occasionally served as temporary mounts for infantry regi-ments. Purchasing officers supposedly followed strict guidelines about the age, weight, and physical condition of each cavalry mount, but choices were sometimes limited. Before about 1870, reliable horses were scarce in some frontier areas, and they had to be purchased at premium prices from Midwestern states. After that date, however, local residents found ways to tap routinely into the thriving marketplace. A single sale could involve significant sums, as in 1861 when Alexander Warfield, former publisher of the *Santa Fe Republican*, sold eight hundred horses to New Mexico military authorities for a price of $90 to $150 apiece.[35]

At the end of the century, Fort Meade, South Dakota, served as a primary station for the purchasing of horses needed to outfit the newly organized Thirteenth Cavalry. With the animals commanding an average purchase price of $106 per head, four area businessmen stood to make significant profits from the sale of 683 equines. Furthermore, the entrepreneurs purchased most of these unbroken range animals from local ranchers for $85 each, and thus the money stayed within the immediate area. Unfortunately, the army sued two of the contractors on the grounds that they had delivered a number of mounts that did not meet specifications. The accused owners, Jack Hale and Abe Jones, lashed back that some of the army officers were biased in their favoritism for Kentucky-raised horses and that they had needlessly sabotaged the deal. A judge ruled in Hale's and Jones's favor, and a local newspaper praised the judicial decision for helping protect other military contracts within the area.[36]

Perhaps the nation's most unique plan for cashing in on the cavalry dollar appeared in an 1879 issue of *Army and Navy Journal.* This article described the six-thousand-acre New Mexico sheep ranch of J. Gordon Bryce, a former British Army officer who had served in the Cape Colony of South Africa. During his assignment there, Major Bryce had observed the use of ostriches for carrying men and supplies under extremely difficult field conditions. He now offered to sell enough ostriches from his ranch to allow the army a trial run with the strangely shaped animals. Bryce contended that the birds could move faster than horses, were more hardy in arid regions, and were far cheaper to maintain. Furthermore, they produced large eggs that could supplement a military diet, and allegedly they could retain their vigor for a longer period than the healthiest horse. Unlike the more famous camel freighting experiment of the mid-1850s, which had been undertaken with the blessings of Secretary of War Jefferson Davis, Bryce's plan never found any favor with the army or the government. Perhaps the $150 price per ostrich seemed excessive, but more important, no army officer could have seriously viewed himself leading men mounted atop the giant birds. To have promoted such a plan would have brought forth only derision from other officers and the public at large.[37]

Ostriches aside, horses and mules were destined to remain the preferred means of army transportation in the West. This reality afforded entrepreneurs with one other avenue for procuring a military contract: the delivery of hay and oats to feed the post livestock. Col. Philippe Régis de Trobriand recorded in an 1867 diary entry how he negotiated with two contractors at Fort Stevenson, Dakota Territory, to cut hay before the approaching winter arrived. With September almost half over, de Trobriand entered into an agreement whereby the men would provide a large supply of hay at thirty-three dollars per ton, which would be harvested from the open prairie about fifteen miles from the post. Work had to commence immediately on the project, and the colonel authorized it with the hope that the quartermaster general of the department would subsequently approve the deal.[38] During that same year a reverse situation of need arose when citizens of the Rio Abajo villages of New Mexico petitioned the quartermaster to direct part of the military hay contract to them. The mostly Hispanic residents of these Rio Grande villages were facing ruin because of massive flooding, and the haying business was about the only avenue of financial recovery that remained. Further downriver, the quartermaster at Fort Selden took the initiative, circumvented the usual bidding process, and bought a few tons of hay as a way of helping flooded residents of the Mesilla Valley.[39]

In its great variety of products and services, the army bidding system proved to be the Holy Grail for many western civilians. Acquisition of lucrative contracts supplemented incomes over the short run, and if successfully maintained for many years, those contracts could help insure financial independence for fortunate bidders. In her thorough study of this phenomenon in the Southwest between 1861 and 1885, historian Darlis Miller provided the definitive word on this government subsidy program. Her examination of financial records revealed a government expenditure of one and one-quarter to two million dollars annually flowing directly into the economies of New Mexico and Arizona alone.[40] Unlike the huge contracts that would feed the growth of the military-industrial complex during the Cold War of the 1950s to 1980s, the frontier bidding process apparently served a larger range of economic interests. Miller substantiated this point with statistics from which she concluded that "because large numbers of small entrepreneurs won government contracts, no clique of economic royalists emerged to greatly influence either military or civilian policies."[41] Thus, the government's indirect priming of the western economy produced significant benefits without unduly harnessing Uncle Sam to an eastern industrial establishment that many westerners came to hate by the end of the nineteenth century.

Even though the army contracting system for goods and services amounted to hundreds of millions of dollars during the late decades of the frontier era, smaller amounts paid to full-time civilian employees also found their way into local economies. At Fort Fred Steele, Wyoming, the post quartermaster employed as many as three civilian clerks throughout the 1870s. These accountants received excellent salaries averaging $100 to $150 monthly, much of which was then spent on other locally produced items. From time to time the same quartermaster hired sawmill engineers, carpenters, blacksmiths, wheelwrights, stonemasons, and other skilled tradesmen at monthly salaries ranging between $55 and $125, depending upon the proficiency and specialty of each man.[42] At Fort Richardson, Texas, the wagonmaster made $75 per month, his three assistants $45, and the forty teamsters $40 each.[43] During the same decade, Washington Hinman, interpreter at Fort McPherson, Nebraska, took home $50 monthly, plus a regular army issue of rations.[44] Added to the lists of civilian employees at many posts were scouts, telegraph operators, saddlers, tinners, ambulance drivers, herders, mail carriers, and even private cooks and servants.[45]

Monthly payrolls for civilians fluctuated widely over time, depending upon whether a post was merely employing its regular corps of civilian employees (usually less than thirty men) or was in the midst of a building boom that used short-term laborers. At the low end of the schedule, the expenditure of approximately $1,000–$1,500 monthly seemed about average for the total payment to permanent employees.[46] Yet when the temporary workers' wages were added to the sum, the totals reached astounding proportions. Fort Larned, Kansas, generated a monthly payroll of $15,830 for civilians during the construction boom of 1867. At nearby Fort Hays during the following year, the cumulative figure was $7,528. And at Fort Richardson for the same formative period, the amount reached approximately $8,100.[47]

With such vast sums of money at stake in the contracting system and in the civilian payrolls, it is little wonder that fraud and collusion sometimes occurred. Acting Assistant Surgeon Samuel Smith of Fort Concho, Texas, recorded in his diary that the entire Texas congressional delegation routinely inflated army contracts within the state. When other congressmen or military officers spoke against the wasteful process, the Texans allegedly employed threats and intimidation to get their way. In the entry dated July 4, 1879, Smith angrily wrote: "The whole state of Texas counts on expenditure of money for army supplies, and when a Congressman tackles the appropriation bill he joins issue with the whole state from Dan to Beersheba." In that same diary entry, the doctor recounted how post trader James L. Millspaugh continued to deliver inferior hay to the post, and yet the quartermaster still paid for the deliveries even though cavalry officers refused to feed the hay to their horses.[48]

Occasionally a post quartermaster was guilty of more than simply bad judgment. During the summer of 1871, Fort Davis quartermaster Capt. Thomas B. Hunt came under attack from post commander Col. William R. Shafter for malfeasance. Captain Hunt had sold thirty army horses to a civilian named Hiram Kelly on the grounds that these were condemned animals of no further use. Shafter contended, however, that these were serviceable mounts—the best thirty of the eighty-eight chosen for public sale—and that Kelly was covertly buying them for Hunt. Shafter further alleged that Hunt had contracted with a man named Tinkham and another civilian named Moses Kelly to provide an excessive amount of coal to the post at unusually high prices. Accusations of kickbacks filled the hearings, and the commanding officer even threatened to have Hunt charged in civil court.[49]

A more celebrated case occurred between senior officers when, in 1871, Department of Texas commander Gen. Joseph J. Reynolds began to prepare court-martial charges against Col. Ranald S. Mackenzie. Preparing for a major field campaign that spring, Mackenzie had invoiced new pack mules to his company commanders rather than through the regimental quartermaster. This technical violation of army regulations drew Reynolds's anger, but it really disguised his greater resentment that Mackenzie had just canceled a corn delivery at Fort Richardson from the firm of Adams and Wicks, whom Mackenzie suspected of fraud. Substantial rumors circulated that Reynolds was a protector and beneficiary of the company, and the potential for ruined military careers loomed. Fortunately for both officers, Mackenzie received only a mild reprimand from the judge advocate general, and Reynolds was soon transferred to a different military department.[50]

In addition to large contracts and civilian salaries, soldiers' pay also quickly found its way into the local economies. Within the five-year period of 1849–53, the Texas paymaster distributed a total of $519,000 to the garrisons at Forts Inge, Clark, and Duncan alone. Most of this served as a multiplier for the local businesses, because the troops had few avenues for spending their money elsewhere. Moreover, the payroll provided an important source of gold (and later silver) for a population that largely functioned on barter, promissory notes, private banknotes, and diverse credit arrangements.[51] Twenty years later, citizens of Yankton,

Dakota Territory, blessed the severe Easter blizzard that trapped elements of the Seventh Cavalry in their town. With the quartermaster paying four dollars a day to house and feed each soldier and each horse for almost two weeks, the town's businesses reaped an unforeseen financial bonanza.[52] Likewise, at the end of the century soldier pay at Fort Niobrara brought more than $12,000 monthly to the merchants of nearby Valentine, Nebraska.[53]

Sometimes enterprising civilians took their wares directly to the soldiers. Pvt. Hervey Johnson recalled that an itinerant peddler from Denver showed up at Fort Laramie in late 1865 and made himself quite popular by selling vegetables at fair prices. Three years later, soldiers at Fort Quitman, Texas, happily found that they could buy fruits and vegetables, as well as butter, eggs, and chickens, directly from Hispanic residents of the area. Another peddler marketed not only fresh vegetables, but also canned goods to men stationed at Fort Wingate, New Mexico.[54] At Fort Davis, Mrs. Phillip Halker Pruett amassed fifteen hundred dollars from milk and butter sales to soldiers and their families during a single year. Likewise, the widow of an army sergeant improved her financial lot by cooking meals for the twelve bachelor officers at Fort Riley, Kansas.[55]

Despite army efforts to somewhat regulate the businesses that could deal directly with servicemen, most of the monthly payroll clearly wound up in the hands of the "vice industries." No pressure or subterfuge was necessary on the part of these businessmen, because soldiers were always innovative and insatiable in their desire to find sources of alcohol, gambling, and prostitution. Sgt. H. H. McConnell, later mayor of Jacksboro, recalled how the town grew out of the Texas prairie almost overnight to serve the baser side of troopers' needs. He counted twenty-seven saloons at the peak of the community's growth and later wrote that "the sound of the fiddle and the crack of the six-shooter was heard the livelong night."[56] Another early resident similarly affirmed, "I am not exaggerating when I say I have seen the time when I could have walked on soldier[s] lying drunk along the road from the south side of the Square to the creek and not touched the ground."[57]

Contract surgeon Dr. Samuel Smith's 1878 description of the tiny settlement of Saint Angela (later San Angelo), Texas, virtually duplicated the eyewitness accounts of other people who visited forts throughout the West during the frontier period. Smith recorded in a letter to his sister: "There is a little town across the river, just outside the military reservation, that is full of human sharks, and as every inducement is held out there to soldiers to spend money, the nights succeeding pay day are hideous. There are so many gamblers, cut-throats, murderers, horse thieves living and finding harbor at San Angela, it is never considered safe to pass through there at night, and no officer even thinks of leaving the garrison after dark."[58]

Crudely built taverns and houses of prostitution, colloquially referred to as hog ranches, dotted the western landscape to serve all paying customers. Yet it was near military reservations that these illicit businesses reached their zenith and contributed to the greatest number of social problems. The area around Fort Laramie in 1867 supported a number of hog ranches with intriguing names such as Six Mile, Coon Dive, The Brewery, and Brown's Hotel. Fifteen years later, a black proprietor named Abe Hill operated a combination brothel and saloon known as the "Go As You Please House" in Sturgis, Dakota Territory, to serve the black soldiers at nearby Fort Meade.[59] Similarly, the nine drinking and whoring establishments at Winona, Dakota Territory, took the lion's share of soldiers' pay from nearby Fort Yates and created significant problems for Hunkpapa Sioux residents of the Standing Rock Reservation.[60]

In a successful effort to profit from the illicit trade, the municipal council of Crawford, Nebraska, charged a monthly "whore tax" as well as a sizable tavern fee. By 1906 town fathers collected nearly six thousand dollars yearly from these two taxes, accounting for over 60 percent of the annual revenues of this community, which so heavily depended on business from Fort Robinson. Unfortunately, the widespread vice industry created such a negative image for the town that the state of Nebraska refused to authorize the construction of a normal school at that location. Even conscious efforts to clean up this "stink pot of Northwest Nebraska" came too late and were too half-hearted to resurrect the school construction plan.[61]

Most army towns existed within the framework of boom and bust cycles, not unlike mining and cattle towns of the same era. As long as government contracts and payrolls flowed, these military communities could flourish, but most were not destined to survive much beyond the closing of their companion posts. In her visit of 1852, army wife Teresa Vielé described the remarkable growth of Brownsville, Texas, from a community of only two houses in 1848 to a bustling metropolis of four thousand inhabitants four years later. Because the town was on the northern bank of the Rio Grande, it provided a virtual doorway to international trade with Mexico, but it was the army payroll from Fort Brown that assured the earliest growth. Contrastingly, Lt. Rodney Glisan reported in 1850 that even though the little village of Rucklesville, Indian Territory, was trying its best to survive on the money of Fort Washita, it would never mature much beyond the primitive stage because no other economic ventures blessed the surrounding area.[62] An even sharper dissimilarity was seen in the small town that grew up alongside Fort Belknap on the northwestern frontier of Texas. Observers noted in 1856 that about two thousand acres were under cultivation, numerous cattle grazed on the open range, residents hired out as military suppliers, and local merchants thrived on the recycled money. Yet by 1878, within ten years after the closing of Fort Belknap, the town had virtually disappeared.[63]

Beyond the Southern Plains, the story of boom and bust was much the same elsewhere. When he arrived at Fort Hays, Kansas, in 1867, Capt. Albert Barnitz marveled at the rapid growth of Hays City. Within a matter of months after its founding, the community had grown to twenty frame houses, a host of wall tents, and a number of businesses under construction. So attractive were the military contracts and payrolls that the rival town of Rome had also started a building frenzy that brought the image of "civilization" to Barnitz's eyes and ears.[64] Less optimistic was Capt. Theophilus Turner, who described the growth of a town to serve newly established Fort Wallace, Kansas. Turner wrote in a letter home that "it is progressing favorably but its very existence is very uncertain. Cities as they are called in this country are exceedingly short lived."[65]

The rapid expansion of Pembina, Dakota Territory, was also directly attributable to army expenditures within the community. In 1870 only eight white men lived in this predominantly Métis settlement, six of whom were Bureau of Customs officials overseeing trade with Canada. Three years later, after the establishment of Fort Pembina to guard the area from roving Indians, the population had risen to over five hundred whites, along with forty new frame houses, eight saloons, several stores, and even a town marshal and a U.S. deputy marshal. The *Pembina Pioneer* proudly declared in 1879 that the town had grown to such affluence that it needed more women of marriageable age to pacify the huge male population. It instructed fathers with eligible daughters to quickly relocate there and promised that "speedy engagements are guaranteed" to civilians and soldiers alike.[66]

The economic stakes were even higher for the communities that served the Black Hills gold rush between 1875 and 1890. The military town of Sidney, Nebraska, became an important jumping off place to the gold fields because it was on the Union Pacific Railroad and because north-south freighting roads already existed between the two points. As a supply base for the miners, the town provided all the goods and services necessary for a successful venture. While these sources of income soon eclipsed the financial advantages that accrued from Fort Sidney, the army payroll and contracts still remained important to the expansion of the community.[67]

Even more in line to reap the benefits of the boom were the various towns that sprang up as rivals along the northern edge of the Black Hills. Although each of these settlements drew significant revenue from the gold deposits, three of them—Scooptown, Ruhlen City, and Dudley Town—made conscious efforts to grab a major share of the army dollar. Each experienced a brief flurry of growth, but ultimately they all lost out to the stronger Sturgis City, which was located nearest to what became the permanent military post of Fort Meade. Commander Col. Samuel Sturgis not only gave his name to the settlement, but he also became a financial investor and protector of the enterprise. Having a military insider in the speculative venture certainly aided the partnership and ultimately assured the growth and longevity of the town. Most of the other rivals quickly died out after the supremacy of Sturgis City was clearly established.[68]

While boom and bust cycles personified the early years of many western communities, one specific type of classification virtually assured the economic success of selected army towns: designation as a departmental quartermaster depot. Because these were created along the most extensive and reliable transportation networks of their time—military roads during the 1850s and mostly railroads after the Civil War—they were destined to last beyond the frontier era. Furthermore, they became the heart of the military contracting system as they handled the huge annual expenditures from within their offices and warehouses.

Among the chief beneficiaries of the expanded post–Civil War quartermaster system was Omaha, Nebraska. Although somewhat distant from the frontier counties on the Great Plains, and not totally reliant on government expenditures for its well-being, this Missouri River supply center was well situated as a depot. Ever since the 1850s, steamboats had brought military contract items upriver and unloaded them here for overland shipment to distant posts. This river freighting business actually increased during the late 1860s and early 1870s, but it was eventually surpassed by the amount of military cargo hauled by the newly constructed Union Pacific Railroad. As the nation's first transcontinental railroad, completed in 1869, this ribbon of iron remade the Omaha economy and helped open the doors to an accelerated settlement of the Plains and beyond.[69]

Three years before its maiden run, initial track had already been laid, and newly constructed Fort Omaha (then called Sherman Barracks) had been designated as headquarters for the vast Department of the Platte. An April 1866 issue of the *Omaha Weekly Herald* sensed the financial importance of this decision by declaring that Omaha would soon eclipse the role formerly played by Fort Leavenworth, Kansas, which had served as an eastern terminus for outfitting posts along the earlier Oregon and Santa Fe Trails.[70] Two years later, the city received even better news when the War Department announced that it would locate a huge depot in the downtown section near the Union Pacific rail yards. The *Omaha Weekly Herald* proudly crowed that the shipment of army supplies into town and their reshipment further west would produce a boom that could turn the village into a city:

> It will cause large and continuous disbursements of money, increasing local trade, and giving increased market facilities for the productions of the State at large. The fact will go far to stimulate the now rapid settlement of our unoccupied lands, and the direct and indirect benefits we are to derive from it can scarcely be overestimated.[71]

In addition to the military supplies that were brought into Omaha from eastern points and reshipped to western destinations, locally produced goods also found their way into the quartermaster commerce. The *Omaha Weekly Herald* contained frequent announcements about the army bidding process and the specific types and amounts of goods that were sought. Goods valued at $297,000 and $181,000 were disbursed among the forts of the Department of the Platte by the Omaha Depot quartermaster and the chief commissary officer, respectively, for the single year of 1874. How much of that total was paid directly to businessmen and farmers in and around Omaha is unclear, but they were certainly in a privileged position to bid competitively for the contracts.[72]

Five hundred and fifty miles to the west, the military depot established at Cheyenne, Wyoming, worked with the Omaha Depot to make purchases and disbursements of supplies. Like its eastern counterpart, Cheyenne Depot (also called Camp Carling) was opened within the protective embrace of a military post—Fort D. A. Russell in this case—and was located alongside the Union Pacific tracks for easy loading and unloading of freight. During 1868 alone, Cheyenne Depot contracted for and supplied forty-five thousand pounds of fresh vegetables to Forts D. A. Russell, Fetterman, and Laramie. Even though it was a quartermaster's operation, the depot relied heavily upon civilians for its day-to-day operations, employing a force averaging between five hundred and one thousand workers at various points within the western sectors of the Department of the Platte. Likewise, many of Cheyenne's most prominent citizens owed a substantial part of their livelihood to the depot and its government contracts.[73]

Remarks by N. A. Baker, editor of the *Cheyenne Daily Leader*, faithfully mirrored changing public opinion about the army's role during Cheyenne's formative years. In an October 17, 1867, article, Baker attacked the quality of regular soldiers sent to defend the region, and he promised that militia units enlisted from among the local frontiersmen would do a better job of fighting Indians. Nine months later he praised the quality of Fort D. A. Russell and its troops. In a convincing editorial he argued that the fort and Cheyenne Depot were the primary employers within the area and that they had already poured millions of dollars into the regional economy, including a considerable amount into Cheyenne's future.[74] Just how closely the town had tied itself to army expenditures was revealed in the wake of soldiers' complaints against local law officers during 1894. City Marshal T. Jeff Carr allegedly had arrested numerous soldiers for trivial matters and had harassed dozens of others, and now troops from Fort D. A. Russell and Cheyenne Depot were avoiding the town like a "pest house." The *Cheyenne Daily Leader* assumed the soldiers' side of the argument and reminded citizens that the army payroll brought six thousand dollars monthly to the town's economy, not to mention the Midas-like government contracts. Financial realities carried the day, and Marshal Carr soon found himself without a job.[75]

During their prime years the frontier military posts made their economic power evident, but even amid their death throes the forts offered economic opportunities to enterprising individuals. When it became evident that local citizens would not be able to delay the closing of their military facility, they circled like buzzards to acquire the surplus property. Commanding officers salvaged the most important transportable equipment, such as wagons, sawmills, engines, planing mills, lath mills, and shingle machines, routinely moving them with the regiment to their new assignment. In most cases then, the structures, rather than their contents, were declared as surplus. The auction of remaining buildings at Fort Fred Steele, Wyoming, in the summer of 1892 yielded only $1,316, a true bargain to purchasers, considering the original expense and ongoing maintenance costs of the structures.[76]

The earlier fate of Fort Ridgely, Minnesota, was perhaps even more typical of the trend. When abandoned in 1867, the post was left in charge of an ordnance sergeant, who was to oversee it in case the War Department cared to reestablish the post. In 1872, even the ordnance sergeant was withdrawn from the protective assignment, and local civilians immediately raided the entire complement of unsold structures. They removed the cut timbers, foundation stones, windows, doors, metal hardware, bricks, and interior fixtures to outfit their own homes.[77] At Fort Davis, abandoned in 1891, civilians simply appropriated the best houses on officers' row and turned them into private residences. The solid stone and adobe buildings provided excellent facilities that remained as occupied dwellings well into the twentieth century.[78]

Even the removal of bodies from post cemeteries offered financial opportunities to persons willing to undertake the unpleasant duty. Upon the closing of Fort Davis, the Chief Quartermaster's Office requested bids to remove the bodies of all soldiers, officers, and their families to the San Antonio National Military Cemetery. Exactly one hundred bodies were located and transferred, but presumably some burials were overlooked, because the post had used five different cemeteries since its establishment in 1854. Upon receiving the contract, local resident David Merrill exhumed the bodies, loaded them into boxes, and transported the entire load to San Antonio. Because of poorly maintained records, some of the earliest burials were identified merely as "unknown," but eighty-eight of the later ones still had complete or partial headstones, and these were transported along with the bodies.[79]

Purchasing land from abandoned military reservations provided the final opportunity for financially astute civilians, but the scenario varied widely from post to post. When Fort McKavett, Texas, was deactivated during the summer of 1883, a few local residents purchased small parcels of land. Former post sutler Sam Wallick paid three hundred dollars for a mere two and one-half acres, a princely sum indeed until it is revealed that he simultaneously gained ownership of the adobe buildings on the acreage. Two years later, James Callan purchased the land and buildings on "Captain's quarters row," and by the end of 1885, virtually all of the property in and around the former installation had been acquired by local families. The town of Fort McKavett, which had once served a flourishing army trade, found itself with only 138 inhabitants in 1965, but most of those residents could trace their roots to the era of military contracts and payrolls.[80]

Fort McKavett's transition to civilian ownership mirrored the fate of so many military reservations that were in relatively isolated spots and that were limited by monocausal economies. Yet lucrative financial deals accompanied the closings of other installations. After the army's abandonment of Fort Stevenson, Dakota Territory, in 1883, part of the facilities were used as a school for the Fort Berthold Indian Reservation. Following its transfer from the War Department to the Interior Department in 1895, the secretary of the interior authorized an appraisal of the land's value. Surprisingly, when the public auction finally occurred, an investment company organized by Lewis C. Black and other residents of Cincinnati, Ohio, paid a sum considerably higher than the appraised value. The investors were interested in employing the Missouri River port as a primary shipping depot for ranchers, farmers, and Indian reservations throughout the region.[81] Likewise, the demise of Fort Larned, Kansas, in 1878 resulted in the gradual disposal of the 10,240-acre military reservation. Within four years the General Land Office had surveyed, appraised, and begun selling 160-acre tracts to local civilians. The Atchison, Topeka, and Santa Fe Railroad also acquired title to a portion of the estate for a station house and storage area. The primary bidder, however, was the Pawnee Valley Stock Breeders' Association, which paid a total of $11,056 (or $17.27 per acre) to expand its ranching operations.[82]

By way of contrast, the speculative bubble burst soon after the 1891 army evacuation of Fort Davis. Ranchers and townspeople gradually bought much of the land from the former military reservation, but they did so at the lowest possible prices. Officers and soldiers who had heavily invested in lands adjacent to the reservation during more promising years watched as values fell precipitously. Former ordnance sergeant Charles Mulhern, a large land developer within the area, noted that at the time of the fort's closing, property assessed at sixty-five cents an acre could rarely fetch more than thirty-five cents on the open market. Two months later, Mulhern declared that "the Bottom is out of Fort Davis. There is no chance to sell property of any kind." Exactly three years later, the even more pessimistic former sergeant reported, "This place is going to the dogs fast."[83]

Unlike the case of Fort Davis, the founding fathers of some military towns developed innovative methods to meet the challenges, and they gradually weaned themselves from military dependency. Boosterism prevailed within the community of San Angelo at the time of Fort Concho's closing in 1889. Together with the town's two newspapers, the *Standard* and the *Enterprise*, the boosters waged a highly effective political and informational campaign against nearby Ballinger, which wanted to wrest the county seat from them. These men bonded themselves into a common effort not merely to maintain the status quo, but also to rapidly expand the business environment of the community. They immediately bought land and buildings from the former military reservation, and they advertised widely in newspapers and magazines to attract new settlers. Thirteen real estate and land firms flourished after the army's withdrawal, and they successfully drove prices up from one to five dollars per acre and prime town lots up to the value of thousands of dollars. Unlike so many army towns, San Angelo possessed a true vision for the future, and its leaders worked hard to accomplish their goals.[84] Ironically, the army later returned to this West Texas community by constructing Goodfellow Army Air Field during the exigencies of World War II. Although the air base was much welcomed by a new generation of residents and clearly was of great advantage to expanding the local economy, San Angelo had grown strong enough over the intervening fifty years that it no longer needed the government payroll or contracts to survive.[85]

Yet it was in another Texas military town at the conclusion of the frontier era that the symbiotic relationship between army money and local prosperity was best articulated. In an editorial article dated March 24, 1891, the *San Antonio Express* noted:

> Not only does this city feel the influence of the vicinity of the post [Fort Sam Houston] in a special way, but it profits from a financial standpoint. About $100,000 are expended here monthly by Uncle Sam. Of this sum, the quartermaster's department pays out something like $42,000; the commissary department about $30,000; and the pay department about $30,000. The greater portion of this money is spent in San Antonio, and in addition, the officers' families constitute quite a large amount of money every month to the coffers of local merchants. Hence the presence of the troops in our market adds over a million dollars annually to the local money market.[86]

In so many ways, the symbiotic relationship between military post and civilian community constituted a type of "company town" where "decisions regarding the nature and distribution of services emanated from a central authoritarian source."[87] Just as the fate of the community ebbed and flowed with each fundamental change in army finances, so too did the quality of military life improve alongside the expansion of business and social services within the towns. Amid this important context, it is little wonder that the entire citizenry of Mobeetie, Texas, had strived so mightily in 1890 to preserve Fort Elliott as their government trough. For them, there was no promising future, because they knew that their town would not rise phoenixlike out of the ashes of military abandonment.

Military officers at Fort Kearny, Nebraska, extended a host of services, including food, supplies, medical aid, and blacksmithing facilities, to emigrants on the Platte River Road during the 1840s and 1850s, as shown in William Henry Jackson's painting, *Old Fort Kearny*. *Courtesy Scotts Bluff National Monument, Gering, Nebraska.*

The Platte Bridge Station, which was located at present-day Casper, Wyoming, was one of the important pontoon bridges that the army maintained during the era of westward migration by wagon train. This particular crossing on the North Platte River was especially difficult for the army to maintain during the Civil War because of frequent Sioux and Cheyenne attacks within the region. *Courtesy Wyoming Division of Cultural Resources.*

The U.S. Army Corps of Engineers made numerous improvements to harbor facilities and on inland rivers during the second half of the nineteenth century. The U.S. *R. E. DeRussy* helped clear snags and other obstacles from the Missouri River to make it navigable for commerce and transportation of civilians. *Courtesy National Archives.*

U.S. Army troops prepared and distributed food to hungry civilians in the wake of San Francisco's 1906 earthquake. Despite its lack of clear authority to participate in these relief efforts, the army contributed relief in every possible way, including feeding citizens, offering medical help, fighting fires, and working directly with city fathers to restore order to the devastated city. *Courtesy National Archives.*

During the 1894 Pullman strike, Federal troops remained on guard to protect property of the Great Northern Railroad in Montana. Soldiers and officers especially hated strike duty, because they attracted the enmity of workers and were often simultaneously criticized by management for not being forceful enough in their handling of these delicate duties. Standing among the soldiers in this photo (*near center*) is Calamity Jane (Martha Canary). *Courtesy Montana Historical Society, Helena.*

Pvt. Henry Belike (left) and two other soldiers proudly display the bumper crop of vegetables that they raised in the post garden at Fort Assinniboine, Montana, during the mid-1880s. Agricultural efforts such as this not only improved the standard military diet and prevented dietary illnesses, but also instilled pride in soldiers who tended the crops. *Courtesy Little Bighorn Battlefield National Monument, National Park Service.*

Capt. John G. Bourke served as a field officer in the Apache wars and the Plains Indian wars, but he also left a greater legacy as a prolific author, ethnologist, and activist in the Indian reform movement of the late-nineteenth century. *Courtesy Nebraska State Historical Society.*

Dr. Washington Matthews combined his talents as an army assistant surgeon with his long-term ethnological interests in Native Americans. His published ethnological works ranged from Hidatsa linguistics to Navajo ceremonial studies. *Courtesy U.S. Army Military History Institute, Carlisle Barracks, Pennsylvania.*

Col. George Armstrong Custer's 1874 expedition to the Black Hills contained a contingent of geologists and other scientists who were to conduct scholarly investigations. But this violation of the 1868 Fort Laramie Treaty enraged the Lakota Sioux and the Northern Cheyennes, who viewed the Paha Sapa as sacred. The subsequent rush of gold miners into the mountains set off the Sioux War of 1876–77, which included the conflict at the Little Bighorn. In the foreground of this photograph is William H. Illingworth, the expedition's official photographer. *Courtesy South Dakota State Historical Society—State Archives.*

Between 1886 and 1916 the army protected and administered Yellowstone, Yosemite, Sequoia, and General Grant National Parks. Among the army's many important duties was the apprehension of illegal poachers within park boundaries. In this photograph, officers of the Sixth Cavalry pose with the confiscated heads of buffalo killed by a poacher in Yellowstone National Park during 1894. *Courtesy National Park Service, Yellowstone National Park.*

Elizabeth Custer, about 1900. "Libbie" Custer not only married one of the army's most controversial officers, but she also proved herself to be one of the most artful writers on the frontier army experience. Her trilogy of books provided several generations of readers with a glorious image of the Seventh Cavalry and, especially, of her "Dear Autie," Lt. Col. George Armstrong Custer. *Courtesy Little Bighorn Battlefield National Monument, National Park Service.*

The close association between the government, the army, and railroad executives assured that construction efforts would join government subsidy with private enterprise, and the army would be a major part of that government subsidy. Here, three companies of the Twenty-first Infantry and the regimental band help celebrate the "Wedding of the Rails," as the Union Pacific and Central Pacific railroads are joined at Promontory Point, Utah, May 10, 1869. *Courtesy Union Pacific Museum Collection, 1–53, Omaha, Nebraska.*

Soldiers made their true feelings known in newspaper articles, private letters, and drawings, such as this one made by Private C. C. Chrisman in Arizona Territory during the late 1880s. Private Chrisman dispelled the romantic image of army life when he drew this composite sketch of six realities facing soldiers on a daily basis. The drawings show (1) drill, (2) kitchen police, (3) post cleanup, (4) construction detail, (5) guard duty, and (6) guardhouse. *Courtesy Arizona Historical Society, Archives, MS152.*

Troops of the Seventh and Ninth Infantries were dispatched to Rock Springs, Wyoming, to protect Chinese residents during the aftermath of a race riot in 1885. Rioters had previously killed twenty-eight Chinese coal miners and laborers, wounded fifteen others, and driven several hundred others from town. Soldiers remained stationed at the hastily built Camp Pilot Butte as late as 1899. *Courtesy Wyoming Division of Cultural Resources.*

CHAPTER SIX

Uncle Sam's Farmers

SOLDIERS AS FRONTIER AGRICULTURALISTS AND METEOROLOGISTS

One of the most cherished notions in American history is the image of the proud and independent yeoman farmer pushing relentlessly westward, bringing civilization to the untamed frontier. Although disclaiming the oversimplified concept of a single wave of agricultural advance, historian Frederick Jackson Turner noted the symbiotic relationship between the frontier army post and farming. In his classic 1893 essay, first presented to an audience of the American Historical Association, Turner briefly remarked about how military installations provided the protective nucleus around which trans-Appalachian agriculture could flourish.[1] Over six decades later, historian Richard Wade took the point further by demonstrating how five towns—Pittsburgh, Cincinnati, Lexington, Louisville, and Saint Louis—partially owed their origins to military activities. Drawing upon lucrative army contracts for some of the their initial capital, the five entrepôts expanded their economies throughout the early nineteenth century. As commercial and industrial centers they grew quickly, but from their inceptions within a military setting they also helped spur agricultural development throughout the Ohio and Mississippi river valleys. They were, as Wade concluded, "spearheads of the frontier. . . . Planted far in advance of the line of settlement, they held the West for the approaching population."[2]

The ideas conveyed by Turner and Wade were indeed important correctives to the standard saga of frontier agriculture, but both articulated only part of the story. In their haste to establish the economic relationship between military and civilian societies on the frontier, they failed to demonstrate the more direct role assumed by officers and enlisted men during the nineteenth century and in a broader geographic expanse ranging from the Appalachian Mountains to the Pacific Ocean. Contrastingly, Francis Paul Prucha's magisterial *Broadax and Bayonet: The Role of the United States Army in the Development of the Northwest, 1815–1860* fully documented the history of the War Department's agricultural experimentation within the western Great Lakes region. In Prucha's context, soldiers were the primary farmers and beneficiaries of this grand endeavor. Like so many federal policies, this program grew out of budgetary and logistical necessity, transformed itself amid conflicting guidelines, achieved varying degrees of success and failure, and eventually gave way to improved transportation and technologies that revolutionized the feeding of the army. Ultimately, the entire nation benefited from the lessons learned by the army, especially in the more arid regions west of the ninety-eighth meridian. New crops, innovative planting and harvesting methods, sophisticated irrigation techniques, systematic meteorological records, and a proven record of success in many areas gradually encouraged civilian farmers of the post–Civil War era to attempt commercial agriculture on the Great Plains and beyond.

Because the U.S. Army was always underfunded and overcommitted in its duties, any method for saving money and improving the supply system was worth the scrutiny of senior officers. Yet not until 1818 did the War Department order virtually all posts to plant crops and begin raising livestock as food sources. Even though they were directed to become self-sufficient in these matters, the lofty goal was beyond the reach of many, because some fruits and vegetables required higher-quality soils and warmer climates for their growth. Also, many smaller posts would have to be exempted from the directive because their manpower was too limited for assignment to farm duties. For the successful cases, however, a significant savings could be attained by avoiding the high costs of contracting for civilian food items and transporting

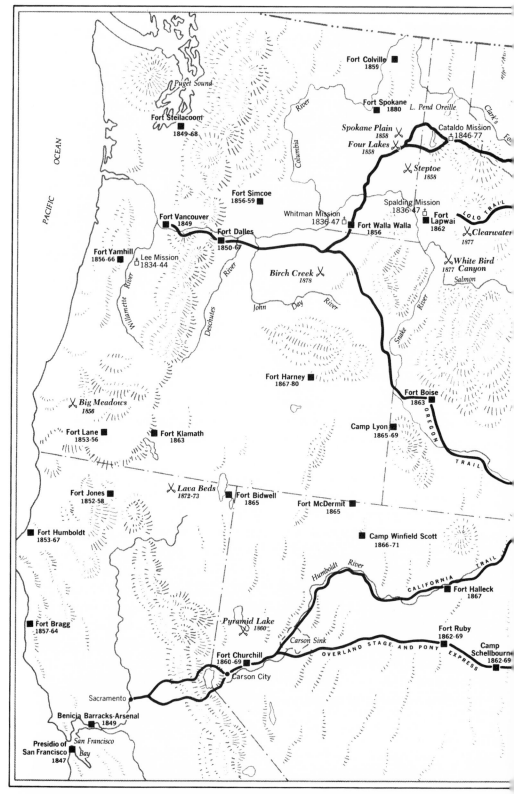

Fort Colville
1859

Fort Spokane
1880

L. Pend Oreille

Clark's

Puget Sound

Fort Steilacoom
1849-68

Columbia River

Fort Spokane
1880

Cataldo Mission
✝ 1846-77

Spokane Plain ⚔
1858

Four Lakes ⚔
1858

Steptoe ⚔
1858

OCEAN

PACIFIC

Fort Simcoe
1856-59

Fort Vancouver
1849

Fort Dalles
1850-67

Whitman Mission
1836-47 ✝

Fort Walla Walla
1856

Spalding Mission
1836-47 ✝

Fort
Lapwai
1862

LOLO TRAIL

⚔ Clearwater
1877

Fort Yamhill
1856-66

Lee Mission
✝ 1834-44

Birch Creek ⚔
1878

White Bird
1877 Canyon

Willamette River

Deschutes River

John Day River

Salmon

Snake River

Fort Harney
1867-80

Fort Boise
1863

Big Meadows ⚔
1856

Fort Lane
1853-56

Fort Klamath
1863

Camp Lyon
1865-69

OREGON TRAIL

Fort Jones
1852-58

Lava Beds ⚔
1872-73

Fort Bidwell
1865

Fort McDermit
1865

Fort Humboldt
1853-67

Camp Winfield Scott
1866-71

Humboldt River

CALIFORNIA TRAIL

Fort Halleck
1867

Fort Bragg
1857-64

Pyramid Lake ⚔
1860

Carson Sink

Fort Ruby
1862-69

Camp
Schellbourne
1862-69

Fort Churchill
1860-69

Carson City

OVERLAND STAGE AND PONY EXPRESS

Sacramento

Benicia Barracks-Arsenal
1849

Presidio of
San Francisco
1847

San Francisco

San Francisco
Bay

The Mountain Wars, 1850–1880, from Robert M. Utley, *The Indian Frontier of the American W*

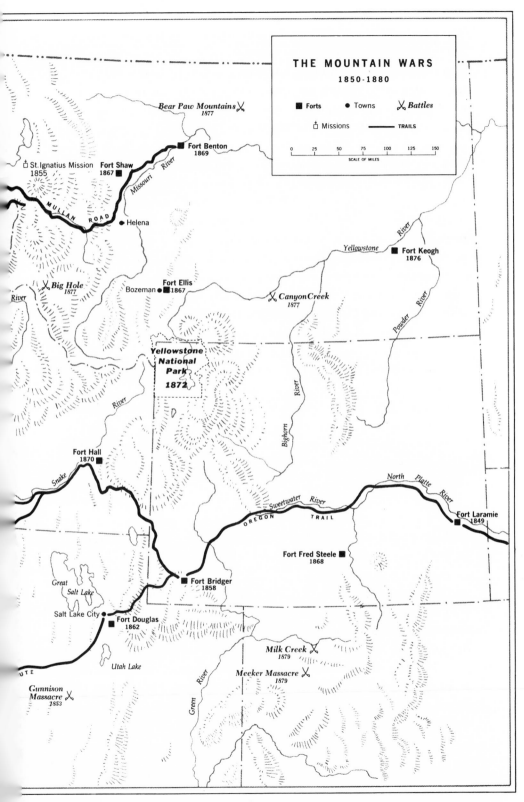

THE MOUNTAIN WARS

1850-1880

■ Forts   ● Towns   ✗ *Battles*

⛪ Missions   ▬▬ TRAILS

0   25   50   75   100   125   150

SCALE OF MILES

Bear Paw Mountains ✗
1877

Fort Benton
1869

⛪ St. Ignatius Mission   Fort Shaw
1855   1867 ■

Missouri River

MULLAN ROAD

● Helena

Yellowstone River

Fort Keogh
1876 ■

✗ *Big Hole*
1877

Fort Ellis
Bozeman ● ■ 1867

✗ *Canyon Creek*
1877

River

Powder River

**Yellowstone
National
Park
1872**

River

Bighorn River

Fort Hall
1870 ■

Snake

North Platte River

Sweetwater River

OREGON   TRAIL

Fort Laramie
1849 ■

Fort Fred Steele
1868 ■

*Great
Salt Lake*

Salt Lake City ●
Fort Bridger
1858 ■

Fort Douglas
1862 ■

UTE

Utah Lake

Milk Creek ✗
1879

Meeker Massacre ✗
1879

Green River

*Gunnison
Massacre* ✗
1853

46–1890. Courtesy University of New Mexico Press.

them great distances aboard lumbering wagon caravans. Moreover, a more balanced diet would certainly alleviate many of the health problems among soldiers and improve their morale. The 1818 directive also looked to the future of western agriculture by requiring that officers maintain records about their crops, weather, and soil content that could be used by scientists and government clerks in compiling systematic studies.[3]

Ironically, the most successful and widely debated of the earliest agricultural experiments occurred at the nation's westernmost garrison. Fort Atkinson, founded in 1819 on the west bank of the Missouri River in present-day Nebraska, housed over four hundred soldiers and was perhaps the most expensive post of its time to supply through a regular civilian contracting system. The first year of occupation proved disastrous, as the soldiers were forced to relocate their original campsite, were left with half-finished buildings when winter's fury set in, and were confronted with a scurvy outbreak that claimed 160 lives.[4] Spurred on by the ravages of the epidemic and the need for a better diet, Col. Henry Atkinson ordered troops to begin creating an extensive farm during the spring of 1820. Along the rich bottomland they cleared one hundred acres, which were planted mostly in corn, with smaller areas reserved for vegetable gardens. By the end of the season the men had added two hundred acres of corn, beans, and potatoes, with a plan to add thirty acres of turnips later. Unfortunately, some of the good work washed away in Missouri River floods.[5]

Despite an inauspicious beginning, the Fort Atkinson experiment proved to be a success, and the colonel predicted a harvest of ten thousand bushels of corn, eight thousand bushels of turnips, and six thousand to eight thousand bushels of potatoes during the first full year of operation. Several hundred more acres were cleared during the following two years, and under the guidance of Maj. Daniel Ketchum, director of agriculture for the post, watermelons, carrots, cabbages, beets, beans, and parsnips were added to the list of crops. Cases of scurvy and other dietary diseases dropped dramatically in the wake of these new vitamin-rich food sources.[6]

In keeping with the call for self-sufficiency, post commander Col. Henry Leavenworth rapidly expanded the livestock herd during 1823. By the end of the year, soldiers had cut and stacked 250 tons of hay for the 283 cattle and had harvested forty acres of oats for the horses and mules. They likewise tended six hundred hogs, some of which could be slaughtered at any time for fresh pork.[7] Even though soldiers could not be compensated with extra pay for the livestock tending and farm duties, most of them recognized the value of their work, and some openly expressed pride in the results of their labor. The work was certainly no more onerous than routine military drill, from which they were partly excused to attend these chores. Furthermore, the incentive of one additional daily cup of whiskey to each man on farm detail assured more than enough volunteers throughout the growing season.[8]

Despite short-term problems with flooding, insects, and weather, agricultural output increased with each passing year. This level of success not only made the post virtually self-sufficient in food production, but it also allowed the commander to sell surpluses to the Commissary Department headquartered in Saint Louis. In 1825 the surplus fetched $1,427, of which 15 percent went to the post officers and the remaining 85 percent was divided among the enlisted men.[9]

Beyond his submitting reports to Washington, D.C., about weather, soil content, insects, and other agricultural concerns, Colonel Atkinson demonstrated one more innovative talent. During 1820 he secured several barrels of corn from the neighboring Omaha Tribe, which had extended its friendship ever since the founding of the post. This strain of corn proved superior to the eastern varieties that had been sent out with the Sixth Infantry. Atkinson noted that it grew to maturity within ninety days, was more resistant to early frosts, was better attuned to the prairie environment, and produced substantially higher yields than anything he had seen elsewhere. He subsequently sent samples of the corn to Secretary of War John C. Calhoun and New York governor De Witt Clinton for further scientific analysis.[10]

Knowledge of the work at Fort Atkinson soon reached other civilian audiences as well. The Saint Louis County Agricultural Society honored the experiment by electing Colonel Atkinson to an honorary membership in 1823. Shortly before this, an Indiana newspaper editor praised the colonel and declared that he was "entitled to much credit for his zeal in promoting the interests of his agricultural countrymen."[11]

In the end, however, Fort Atkinson experienced too much of a good thing, for it came under the scrutiny of the Inspector General's Office.

When Col. George Croghan toured the remote post in 1826 as part of an official inspection, he paid homage to the soldiers' success when he declared, "You will see barn yards that would not disgrace a Pennsylvania farmer, [and] herds of cattle that would do credit to a Potomac grazier."[12] Yet Croghan went on to question the benefits of the entire operation for troops and the government. He had no quarrel with the maintenance of *small* gardens to improve the men's diet or with the provision for a *small* cattle herd to provide occasional fresh meat. Instead, he objected to the fact that on any given day sixty to eighty soldiers spent their time working in the fields. These were hours lost to the necessary drill and other military duties that supposedly produced a better-quality fighting man.[13]

As Croghan continued his tour of inspection, he leveled similar charges against Col. Josiah Snelling, commander of the Fifth Regiment at Fort Snelling, Minnesota. He fumed that forty-five days of military training had been sacrificed while soldiers processed five hundred tons of hay, and another ninety days would soon be lost to the collection of twelve hundred cords of firewood.[14] Croghan's point of view found support among other officers at far-flung installations. Capt. William Davenport remarked at Fort Smith, Arkansas, in 1823 that "raising and herding Cattle and Hogs is altogether foreign to the profession of the army and it has always been a matter of surprise to the thinking part of the army, what could have induced the Govt to undertake it. The same may be said of the cultivation of land by the soldiers." Davenport went on to complain that soldiers gained no advantage from these nonmilitary activities and that they were reaching such a state of lethargy that they could not adequately respond to an emergency.[15]

Croghan's impact on overall military policy was not immediate, but other realities helped tip the scales to his viewpoint. Fort Atkinson, the showcase of the agricultural experiment, harvested its last crop in the fall of 1826, and the post closed its gates forever during early 1827. Army retrenchment, not a failure of crops or deference to Croghan's philosophy, forced the recall of troops to Jefferson Barracks, Missouri. From there they could be readily supplied by civilian contractors at Saint Louis, and thus their expertise as farmers was no longer of value. Most garrison commanders continued to maintain small gardens for vegetable production, but gone were the days of massive farms and livestock management as had been seen at Fort Atkinson and a few other western installations. In 1833 the War Department officially relieved all commanders of the 1818 directive and left them with discretionary power to decide whether they would even cultivate small kitchen gardens.[16]

Following an interlude of almost twenty years in which agricultural experimentation remained a low priority among military men, a new perspective came out of the necessities produced by the Mexican War. American acquisition of Texas, California, and the Mexican Cession caused a rapid expansion of military presence into those areas. Likewise, the massive movement of overland pioneers along the trails that dotted the Great Plains necessitated construction of more forts in that region. Throughout the somewhat chaotic expansion period of the 1850s, then, the army built increased numbers of posts in relatively isolated areas of the frontier. As had been the case with Fort Atkinson for an earlier generation, these military settlements had to be supplied by slow and expensive methods, mostly by civilian contractors using wagon trains.

Again, the call went out for attaining some measure of self-sufficiency, especially at the more remote installations. Several orders spoke to the resumption of an agricultural experiment, but the key directives came from the War Department during January, 1851. This new plan eclipsed the vision of the 1820s and offered more encompassing provisions. It spelled out the need for detailed annual reports and agricultural balance sheets so that eastern experts could better assess the agrarian potential of the West. As further incentive for soldiers to work hard in the fields, it commanded that all crops and livestock raised on the military farms should be sold directly to post or regimental commissary officers at prevailing local market prices. The net proceeds would then be apportioned among the troops on an extra salary base and calibrated to the amount of farm work each man had performed during the season.[17] General Orders No. 1 of January 8, 1851, also declared that *all* posts had to maintain "kitchen gardens" to provide adequate vegetables for the entire garrison throughout the year. Larger forts, especially those built in the newly acquired areas, were directed to create and care for extensive farms that could support ample vegetables, corn, grains, hay, and livestock as food sources.[18] Without being specific, the War Department was now reversing the order of priorities laid down in Col. George

Croghan's 1826 inspection report. Farming was no longer a sidelight to be undertaken when all other duty was completed. It now was recognized as a vital military duty in its own right.[19]

Predictably, some posts proved more successful than others in this revival of an old experiment. Fort Leavenworth, Kansas, achieved phenomenal results largely because it had never terminated its farms during the interim years. Throughout the 1850s, acreage under production continued to expand, and by the end of the Civil War the post was cultivating 6,840 acres. Its soldiers even employed an arsenal of modern machinery, including plows, horse-powered reapers, mowing machines, cultivators, harrows, and threshers.[20] Fort Leavenworth's unparalleled accomplishments rested on the fact that it served as a jumping-off place for traffic on both the Santa Fe and Oregon Trails. Hence, part of its surplus production was sold to overland civilians, and the profits remained at the post. Likewise, some of its crops wound up on the open market in the Kansas City area, also encouraging greater output by soldiers who could share in the financial rewards. By contrast, the military farms at Forts Kearny and Laramie never achieved the size or productivity of Fort Leavenworth's during the 1850s. Despite their attempts to provide some food for travelers on the Oregon Trail, the respective Nebraska and Wyoming posts lacked the manpower for intensive agriculture, and they did not possess the water supply and fertile soil that Fort Leavenworth had.[21]

Near the western terminus of the Santa Fe Trail, Fort Union, New Mexico, experienced some of the same high level of success that Fort Leavenworth had achieved. Although the soil was not particularly rich, the soldiers created an ingenious irrigation system. They raised a wide assortment of vegetables, including corn, pumpkins, beets, peas, peppers, okra, onions, asparagus, carrots, cabbage, and turnips. Scarcely a farm of the rich Ohio River valley could have done better than this southwestern outpost. Soldiers also proved remarkably innovative in their new environment. When Irish potatoes failed to grow well, the men substituted small indigenous potatoes, which grew merely to the size of musket balls, but these flourished in the thinner soil. Other improvements included a fifty-foot by twenty-foot hothouse, with the entire southern wall encased in glass. This protected environment permitted vegetable production even during the coldest winter months, and a nearby ice house provided refrigeration for storage even during the hottest of summers.[22]

When Col. Joseph K. F. Mansfield conducted an 1853 inspection of the Department of New Mexico, he praised Fort Union's entire agricultural program. He likewise singled out the haying operations, the expanding herds of horses and cattle, and the irrigation system for special congratulations. Because the enterprise was so well established and because it truly saved money for the army, Mansfield recommended its full continuation at the fort.[23] In his subsequent inspection of posts throughout the rest of the department, however, the colonel was not so laudatory. One by one, he spelled out the agricultural difficulties at Forts Burgwin, Massachusetts, Marcy, Defiance, Conrad, Webster, and Fillmore and the camps at Albuquerque and Los Lunas. Although he pronounced some of them to be successful in food production, he recommended that all of them maintain no more than small vegetable gardens. He rationalized that food, hay, and beef could be purchased from civilian markets in the Rio Grande Valley and be delivered to the posts at relatively small freighting costs.[24] Mansfield further estimated that the Department of New Mexico was already $140,000 in debt as a result of overextension of its farming operations, though he did not explain how he derived that high figure.[25]

Just to the southeast, the Eighth Military Department, encompassing Texas, was undergoing similar analysis during the summer of 1853. Col. William G. Freeman reported that Texas hosted no large farms, as sanctioned in the 1851 General Orders No. 1, but his travels throughout the state discovered small kitchen gardens at all military installations. He noted the experiments at Forts Terrett and Worth to be successful not only in terms of money saved, but also in terms of improved health among the soldiers. At other locations, such as Fort Ewell and Ringgold Barracks, he found that heat and insufficient rainfall doomed all hopes for a meaningful crop.[26] Like Mansfield in New Mexico, Freeman concluded that large farms were a moot point for military endeavors in Texas, but the vegetable gardens were a proven commodity that should be preserved throughout the district.[27]

Army surgeon Alex B. Hasson, reporting from hard-luck Fort Phantom Hill in northwestern Texas during 1852, mirrored Freeman's glum assessment. Dr. Hasson remarked that most of the soil was too poor to raise any significant food crop and that sources of surface and sub-terranean water were inadequate for any form of irrigation. He further recorded that military livestock had barely survived on the dry range grasses, and most horses, mules, and cattle were in such poor condition that they were of little value. On a final ironic note, Hasson indicated that the summer drought had virtually finished off the vegetable garden, yet civilians to the east claimed this to be a rainy season.[28] When Col. Joseph K. F. Mansfield made an inspection of the Trans-Pecos area during 1856, he found Fort Davis to be at the beginning stages of a similar drought. Although normally well watered by the spring and summer showers that fell across the Davis Mountains, the post had received less than half its normal rainfall by midsummer.[29]

Across the Red River in Indian Territory, cases of success seemed more common than those in Texas, possibly because most of the forts had existed for a longer time and because surface water for irrigation was more widespread. Lt. Col. Dixon S. Miles reported from Fort Washita that he had divided the twenty-acre farm into plots and had assigned them to individual companies of the regiment. Each company began an intense competition with its fellows to produce the best crops, and Miles exclaimed his happiness that the experiment had raised troop enthusi-asm and esprit de corps.[30] At nearby Fort Arbuckle, however, Surgeon Rodney Glisan, superintendent of the post garden, doubted the need to keep expanding the operation. He recorded in his diary: "Small gardens are essential in a hygienic point of view—large ones are unnecessary, and exhaust too much of the soldiers' time."[31]

Experiences on the Northern Plains mirrored those in the southern regions, with the notable exception that commentators complained about special problems caused by shorter growing seasons. Augustus Meyers marveled at the astonishing size of potatoes, onions, and toma-toes grown at Fort Randall, Dakota Territory. He claimed them to be comparable to vegetables grown in the lush regions of the East, due more, he noted, to the careful attention shown by the soldiers than to the richness of the soil.[32] In the prairie region directly to the east, Fort Ridgely, Minnesota, attained local fame because of the success of its farm. The post council of administration approved fifteen dollars to pay freight charges on a new plow and seeds. During the following three meetings, it sanctioned the expenditure of over $140 for additional farming equipment and seeds. Among the subsequent purchases was a five-dollar subscription to *The Horticulturist* and an order for six agricultural pamphlets.[33]

Despite notable success with large farms and livestock herds at some well-established posts, the War Department program launched with such high hopes in 1851 collapsed in a mountain of debt and hostility. The expectations had been too high, the manpower too low, and the environmental conditions too harsh for the majority of large farms to thrive. At the same time, a change in administration had occurred in the nation's capital, and the new secretary of war, Jefferson Davis, demonstrated no support for the program that had been implemented by his predecessor, Charles Conrad. Perhaps more important to the demise of the experiment was the new adjutant general, Samuel Cooper, who made a preemptive strike against the army's farm budget. Quick to overstate the case of failure, Cooper orchestrated the discontinuation of the affair, and Jefferson Davis agreed wholeheartedly. By virtue of General Orders No. 3 in February 1854, the extensive agricultural program came to an end.[34] Unlike the 1818 directive, which had been overturned in 1833, this second attempt would see no subsequent revival. Thereafter, all gardening ventures were purely voluntary at the discretion of the fort commander, and the operating costs would have to come from existing post or regimental funds.[35]

The immediate post–Civil War era reflected many of the same problems that had been apparent during the early 1850s. As new forts had to be constructed and old ones had to be reoccupied after more than five years of neglect, army manpower was stretched to its limits on the frontier and in the Reconstruction South. Post gardens remained common throughout the late 1860s, but they were relatively small and primarily limited to vitamin-rich vegetable crops. Since their importance was principally of a dietary nature, post surgeons often managed the farms during this and subsequent decades. At the recently reoccupied Fort Davis, Texas, the doctor directed immediate tillage of three acres in the spring of 1868 so that a scurvy outbreak could be prevented.[36] Two months later at Fort Laramie, Wyoming, the surgeon reported two and one-half acres under production with more exotic plants such as straw-berries, raspberries, blackberries, rhubarb, and asparagus. Even after a decade the garden had expanded only to five acres and was still main-tained primarily to prevent medical problems.[37] In Dakota Territory, Forts Stevenson, Wadsworth, and Totten assiduously protected their gardens, because the nearest regular supply of fruits and vegetables had to be freighted more than two hundred miles from Minnesota. They also raised some cattle as sources of fresh beef to supplement protein in the diet and to serve as the main course at special holiday occasions.[38]

Throughout the 1870s, new technologies gradually made their appear-ance on the frontier, and these subtly changed the nature of military agriculture forever. The trend was already apparent at Fort D. A. Russell, Wyoming, as early as 1868. Because the post was located on the newly constructed Union Pacific Railroad, it could receive regular shipments from the Quartermaster's Office in Omaha within two days. Even though the post did maintain a vegetable garden throughout the 1870s, it never needed to strive for anything approaching self-sufficiency. Perhaps because of that reality, Fort D. A. Russell did not achieve much success with its agricultural endeavor, and its various commanders placed low priority on the enterprise.[39]

While the expansion of railroads was a relatively slow process during the 1870s and 1880s, regular roads developed quickly, even in the most remote frontier areas. With the growth of freighting, stagecoach lines, and other commercial transportation ventures, many army posts came more readily in contact with private means for supplying themselves. This gradually diminished the need for successful post farms and even small gardens. The Fort Fetterman, Wyoming, experiment encountered several successive years of bad weather and thus became increasingly reliant on crops purchased from civilians at Greeley and Fort Collins, Colorado. Likewise, when heavy rains and grasshopper infestations plagued the garden at Fort Pembina, Dakota Territory, officers redirected their efforts at contracting for readily available food grown by neighboring Red River valley settlers.[40] Fort Dodge, Kansas, also faced problems with several years of marginal rains and intense summer heat, but with the arrival of the Atchison, Topeka, and Santa Fe Railroad in late 1872, it, too, became less dependent on raising its own food. Some posts, however, did not benefit greatly from the comparatively rapid advancement in transportation. Along the Rio Grande in far West Texas, remote Fort Quitman represented a throwback example to the problems of the 1850s. Hot weather and an inadequate number of troops sabotaged its agricultural efforts so badly throughout the early 1870s that it remained dependent on food hauled in by wagon train from San Antonio, 595 miles to the southeast.[41]

Among the most important technological improvements during the 1870s and 1880s was the development of improved well drilling equipment and the refinement of irrigation techniques. Some posts were fortunate to have adequate surface water close at hand, and the soldiers merely channeled the water into their gardens. At Sidney Barracks, in the Nebraska Panhandle, Lodgepole Creek, a tributary of the Platte River, provided year-round sustenance for the three-and-one-half-acre plot. Years later, commanding officer Gen. Nathan A. M. Dudley proudly recalled how, for the first time anywhere, he had demonstrated how alkali soil could serve as a beneficial fertilizer. Even the agricultural society in Omaha sent delegates to inspect the irrigated crops at Sidney Barracks, and they came away much encouraged about the farming potential in western Nebraska.[42]

Other posts that lacked dependable water supplies began experimenting with deep well drilling equipment and windmills during the 1870s. Fort Wallace, Kansas, pioneered one of the earliest modern irrigation projects on the Great Plains in 1870 when it constructed a windmill and pump irrigation system. After several years of discouraging crop production at Camp Supply, in western Indian Territory, the commanding officer approved a windmill to provide enough subterranean water for irrigation. The experiment worked well, though problems with insects and unpredictable weather continued to plague the soldiers' efforts.[43] At Fort Niobrara, near the present-day border of Nebraska and South Dakota, officers erected a Halladay windmill over an existing well and pumped up to thirty-three thousand gallons of water into a holding tank at any given time. Eventually the water not only served the garden, but also was piped directly into the barracks and the officers' quarters.[44] Fort Stockton, in the Pecos River country of western Texas, grew an abundance of okra, melons, onions, and cucumbers, which were irrigated with the use of pumps. By the early 1870s, newly arrived civilians began duplicating this technology by also pumping water from nearby Comanche and Leon Creeks. Within a few years the town's population had grown to almost five hundred, with the majority of those working under military contracts or operating commercial farms.[45]

As in the case of the 1850s, many post commanders of the 1870s–80s allowed companies of enlisted men and even individual officers to reap the benefits of their own vegetable plots. This courtesy sometimes extended to private ownership of livestock as long as the animals did not create a health hazard or require time away from duty hours. At Fort Elliott, in the eastern Texas Panhandle, Mess Sgt. Mark Husselby started the post dairy of thirty cows from privately owned stock in 1880, and it provided fresh milk daily for the garrison. Officers and their families at Fort Fetterman bought milk cows and chickens to supplement their menu, and even army laundresses kept a few chickens and an occasional cow.[46]

Before the Civil War, civilian purchase of army produce was a common fact of life along the western trails and in remote areas, but by the 1870s military and civilian agricultural pursuits sometimes found themselves in direct competition. At Fort Concho, Texas, Chaplain Norman Badger directed soldiers' efforts on a ten-acre garden that was leased from the civilian owners of the widely heralded Bismarck Farm. Within two years the post vegetable crop had attained such a high level of productivity that the owners of the irrigated Bismarck Farm decried the unfair competition and their lost revenue from declining contracts to the fort. Following Badger's forfeiture of the lease, the post garden had to be moved closer to the post, and, without proper irrigation facilities, it never measured up to its predecessor.[47] At Fort Bennett, Dakota Territory, in 1871, Sioux leaders from the adjoining Cheyenne River Agency strongly objected to the soldiers' planting a garden outside the limits of the military reservation. Part of the opposition came from the fact that the land earmarked for this experiment belonged to the Indians. Other opposition arose because a successful post garden would diminish the supply of vegetables that the Indians raised under military contract.[48]

Just as army regulations about farming changed throughout the nineteenth century, so too did official regulations about distribution of rations. Congressional legislation of 1802 spelled out weekly rations per soldier of either one and one-half pounds of beef or three-fourths pound of pork, plus eighteen ounces of bread or flour and one gill of rum, whiskey, or brandy. In 1838 the alcohol allotment was abolished, and its replacement was set at six pounds of coffee and twelve pounds of sugar to be shared among every hundred rations issued.[49] The 1840s witnessed the addition of molasses to serve as a condiment and an antiscorbutic. The following decade led to new regulations for increased amounts of these items, but the only significant addition was eight quarts of peas or beans and ten pounds of rice for each one hundred rations issued.[50]

Curiously missing from all the official lists were the vegetables and fruits that were essential to a balanced diet. That is why the gardening experiments were so widely instituted, but even successful plots could not meet the demand for fruits and other varieties of food. Officers and enlisted men alike complained incessantly about the monotonous fare, but they were primarily left to their own devices for making improvements in the situation. Frederick C. Kurz, formerly a corporal of the Eighth Cavalry, later recalled that the men of his company were so afflicted with malnourishment and yellow jaundice that they voluntarily contributed two dollars from their pay every other month toward a mess fund. From this the company purchased fruits, vegetables, and a few canned goods. As bad as post food had been, Kurz remembered rations consumed on patrols and campaigns to have been even worse. The standard items were salt pork and hardtack, the latter being so filled with weevils as to be nauseating to the eye and palate. The men first dipped their hardtack into water "so as to let the little fellows creep out before eating." Kurz described the unappetizing grayish color of the hardtack and wondered if it had not been packaged fifteen years earlier during the Civil War.[51]

Shortages of many food items caused officers and their families to view them as luxuries and most enlisted men to view them as unattainable rare gems. Capt. Theophilus Turner wrote to his brother from Fort Wallace, Kansas, in 1867: "I nearly went wild over an apple today. The first I have had [*sic*] eaten in nearly two years. . . . If you ever see me in the East you will see me gluttonize, you bet—I am saving up an awful capacity for everything fresh as well as vile—I wonder how a fresh peach would look."[52] At nearby Fort Dodge during the same summer, Alice Baldwin, wife of Lt. Frank Baldwin, exclaimed over the dozen eggs the post surgeon had given to her. She likened them to "nuggets of gold . . . [that] could not have been more appreciated."[53]

Throughout the nineteenth century, officers and enlisted men found off-duty time to collect wild foods to supplement their monotonous diets. Hunting, of course, provided pleasant recreation as well as fresh meat from antelope, deer, rabbits, and even an occasional buffalo. Col. Philippe Régis de Trobriand recorded in his journal the special delicacies offered by a variety of wild birds, and Elizabeth Custer sprinkled her autobiographical trilogy with references to the hunts, her frequent participation, and the welcome supply of meat they provided.[54] Assistant Surgeon Rodney Glisan even recommended that since hunting was such a popular pastime with officers, enlisted men should be given more time to follow suit. He contended that this would improve their diet, morale, and marksmanship, which was sorely lacking throughout the ranks.[55]

Less spectacular, but nonetheless important, were the organized forays in search of wild fruits and vegetables. For officers and their families this often came in the guise of picnics, where recreation and camaraderie were greater goals than the actual collection of food. Yet the foraging aspect of this endeavor paid off handsomely for the dedicated person, whether from the officer corps or from among the common soldiers. At Fort Union, New Mexico, parties searched the nearby hills to readily find wild strawberries, raspberries, apricots, peaches, and plums that could be eaten in their fresh state or made into jams and jellies.[56] Some years earlier, enlisted men of the First Cavalry, while stationed in western Indian Territory, found an even more prized source near Antelope Hills. From a large beehive they extracted seventy-four pounds of pure honey, an additive that could make even the most bland of army food taste quite sweet.[57]

By the 1870s, as western transportation gradually improved, officers and soldiers alike found that they could buy more specialized foods, especially canned and packaged products, from distant markets. A partial list of items ordered during 1877–78 by individuals through Fort Union's unique supply system revealed an exotic array of choices. Among the tasty morsels and condiments shipped out from Missouri commercial establishments were Holland cheese, sardines, tapioca, nutmeg, mackerel, oysters, mustard, worcester sauce, syrup, lemon extract, olives, deviled ham, and canned lobster.[58] Locally produced foods also became more readily available wherever civilians and soldiers mixed. Unfortunately, some of the army families may have shared the earlier experience of Julia Gilliss at Fort Stevens, in northwestern Oregon. Although admitting that she was happy to have fresh beef available for purchase at the amazingly low price of six and a quarter cents per pound, she doubted the claims of the seller. The shape of the bones and cuts of meat hardly resembled a cow, and she wondered what animal they were actually eating.[59]

To facilitate greater diversity in soldiers' diets and a more flexible system of choice, Congress in 1866 authorized the Commissary Department to sell foodstuffs to army personnel at cost. Although individuals could make purchases, most transactions were conducted in bulk through each company's commissary sergeant. This system angered post traders and other civilians who sold food on the open market, because they could not easily match the subsidized commissary items. Commissary sergeants generally possessed the power to sell or trade excess food to civilians or even to local grocers, and the profits from these sales went into the company fund to facilitate later purchases. Thus, the bargaining skill of a commissary sergeant could make him a valuable asset within the company, or his abusive power could create hard feelings and a decline in morale.[60]

On his visit to Fort Robinson, Nebraska, in 1883, *Omaha Bee* reporter William E. Annin likened the commissary sergeants to "grocery store clerks" who had to account for every article's receipt and sale in special ledger books.[61] Annin agreed with an earlier assessment by Sgt. H. H. McConnell that real power rested with the post commissary officer, not with the company sergeants. Post commissary officers, in concert with fellow officers of the Board of Survey, had the authority to condemn army food supplies and then make use of those items for themselves. Chances for conspiracy and self-interest were rife in such a system if the commanding officer allowed such collusion to occur on a widespread basis.[62]

By the early 1890s the War Department began experimenting with a new system of food service as part of an efficiency drive. Because many western forts were being closed during that post–Indian War era and regiments were being consolidated at fewer places, more centralized food preparation was now possible. Instead of each company's providing its own cooks and menu, every fort would serve uniform meals prepared by a fully trained staff. Under the direction of a staff officer, a civilian cook and his trained army assistants could prepare healthier meals at cheaper costs and could end bickering among regimental companies about which ones seemed to be most favored at mealtime. Yet it was enlisted men who complained the most about this innovation, charging that companies would lose their freedom of choice and that the new system would not work well when troops were on campaigns away from the forts.[63]

Capt. Morris C. Foote of the Ninth Infantry published an article in an 1893 issue of the *Journal of the Military Service Institution of the United States* to dispute the charges. He pointed out that most company cooks lacked formal training in food preparation anyway, and they frequently were the targets of soldiers' derision. Trained cooks who devoted their full attention to this duty would certainly be superior to these part-time chefs. The relatively high costs of maintaining individual company messes and their equipment could be eliminated, and savings generated by bulk supply purchases would go into the post fund for the improvement of enlisted men's lives. Furthermore, when a regiment or companies from a regiment transferred to a new post, a meal service program would already exist there, and the various companies would not have to duplicate services for their men. Foote's arguments did not carry the debate for the moment, but his system for a centralized post mess eventually won out by the early twentieth century.[64] Individual company messes made little sense in the Spanish-American War of 1898 and even less sense at the sprawling stateside forts and training camps created during World War I. In its own small way, the gradual passing of the company mess system symbolized the passing of the Old Army that had grown up in frontier conditions that no longer existed.

Even though the army's nineteenth-century agricultural efforts were primarily directed at creating farms and vegetable gardens, experimenting with windmills and pump irrigation, and improving overall food preparation, another innovation began on the frontier and lasted into modern times. In 1814, Surgeon General James Tilton directed all military doctors to keep regular weather records at their stations. Four years later, his successor, Joseph Lovell, greatly expanded the program by requiring detailed records of weather patterns, climatic conditions, topography, and diseases prevalent at each fort. The purpose of Tilton's and Lovell's effort was to achieve a better scientific understanding of environmental conditions and their relationship to individual diseases. In 1825, only eighteen military posts were actively recording such information, but by 1853, ninety-seven reporting stations were active across the nation.[65]

While the program continued to retain its original medical component, it evolved by the 1870s into a meteorological service with both immediate and long-term goals. Surgeon General Lovell had pointed the way to this new line of inquiry by publishing *Meteorological Register for the Years 1822–'25 Inclusive, from Observations Made by the Surgeons of the Army at the Military Posts of the United States* in 1826. This represented the first attempt to coordinate four years of weather data from various regions to determine whether cultivation of soil or density of population had an effect on weather patterns. Fourteen years later, a second report under the auspices of Surgeon General Thomas Lawson examined similar information for the years 1826 through 1830. The results proved inconclusive, but proponents of this method of study continued to maintain their comparative work within smaller areas.[66]

While serving as Lawson's civilian assistant from 1843 to 1860, Professor James Pollard Espy turned the military record of weather observations toward the uncertain science of prediction. Espy was the foremost meteorologist of the day, and his close contacts with prominent scientists helped him gain support from military and government authorities for this practical use of weather knowledge. In addition to relying upon the daily records maintained at forts, he established a large group of voluntary observers from throughout the nation and sent them the same log books used by the army to enter its data. This allowed for more complete information and brought more national attention to the experiment. Using these readings of wind speeds, wind directions, barometric pressures, topographical characteristics, and comparative temperatures, Professor Espy worked out a theory of storms. The "Storm King" gained international fame for devising his convectional theory of precipitation and for creating a set of bulletins that showed the state of weather at all reporting stations for a given time. This became the foundation for future weather forecasting.[67]

The main feature that Espy lacked was a speedy method for transmitting updated information. Without this tool, predicting storms and relating warnings quickly to imperiled areas was virtually impossible. The military telegraph proved to be the answer, and Albert James Myer emerged as the founding father of this revolutionary process. Myer's army employment had begun at Fort Duncan, Texas, in 1854 when he received appointment as assistant surgeon at the post hospital. While stationed there, he began to experiment with a signaling system that received endorsement by the War Department in 1859. His line-of-sight method used flags during the daytime and kerosene torches at night; they were manipulated in a wig-wag motion to transmit representations of the alphabet. During the Civil War he introduced a dial type of magnetoelectric telegraph whose sending and receiving codes could be easily learned for distant transmission. Union armies made ample use of these communications during the war, and Colonel Myer became chief signal officer of the Army Signal Corps in 1867.[68]

With such a strong advocate of military telegraphy finally in a position of authority, the melding of meteorology and telegraphy could now open the door for predicting the weather. As separate entities the two services could not have survived the postwar budget cuts, but as a combined unit they were destined to expand their mission. Working with Congressman Halbert E. Paine of Wisconsin, Colonel Myer successfully promoted legislation in 1870 to establish a national weather service through the aegis of the Army Signal Corps. He likewise won the support of renowned civilian meteorologist Cleveland Abbe, who initially had opposed the idea of the collection and analysis of weather information by military men. Abbe resigned his position at the Cincinnati Astronomical Observatory to become chief forecaster and scientist, and the Myer-Abbe team worked well together. In 1872 they received increased federal money so that they could better predict weather patterns for the benefit of agricultural and commercial interests throughout the nation. The Signal Office in Washington, D.C., began to issue daily weather maps as well as publishing the *Daily Weather Bulletin*, the *Weekly Weather Chronicle*, and the *Monthly Weather Review* for sale to the public.[69]

To expand and professionalize the agency, Myer created a special school at Fort Whipple, Virginia, to educate officers and enlisted men in the special arts of signaling, telegraphy, and meteorology. With this highly trained group of observers he not only was able to man western military posts, but also to create fifty-six other weather stations across the nation. Among the most important assignments were the weather stations at Pike's Peak, Colorado, and Mount Washington, New Hampshire, which attracted the most promising observers. Eventually, stations opened in Alaska, Hawaii, and the West Indies.[70] To meet the mandate for supplying current information to shippers, farmers, commercial businesses, and the public at large, Myer worked out agreements with trade associations and newspapers to transmit them the latest predictions. Because of the close connections between army agriculture and the origins of the weather service, Myer paid special attention to communicating up-to-date information to civilian farmers. Special bulletins filled with meteorological data were sent daily to nineteen cities and to 6,042 rural subcenters, where local postmasters posted them for public inspection. Myer also created a "Weather Case," or "Farmer's Weather Indicator," complete with a barometer, wind disk, sunset disk, thermometer, and instructions, all of which could be purchased by farmers at cost. This would allow even the most isolated of farm families to predict violent shifts in weather and possibly prepare for disasters.[71] By 1879, Myer had also helped oversee the construction of more than forty-six hundred miles of military telegraph lines to help disseminate information and to provide what he termed "simultaneous observations."[72]

Several factors combined during the early 1880s to weaken the army's connection with the national weather service. First, Myer died in 1880, thus depriving the Signal Corps of its dynamic, long-term leader. Second, his successor, Col. William B. Hazen, tried to continue the full extent of the program, but several scandals, including embezzlement of over $100,000 by one of his assistants, undermined his administrative credibility at a crucial time.[73] Third, the Signal Corps annual budget had increased from a mere $15,000 in fiscal year 1871 to $375,000 in 1880. In the wake of political calls for drastic cuts in military spending, the Signal Corps found itself targeted even by General-in-Chief of the Army William Tecumseh Sherman. That sentiment would be echoed in 1885 by Gen. Philip Sheridan and Secretary of War William C. Endicott, both of whom advocated turning the expensive weather service over to civilian control.

As a result, Congress passed legislation on October 1, 1890, directing the Signal Corps to transfer all meteorological activities to a new weather bureau, which would be housed within the Department of Agriculture. When the transfer finally took place during the following July, an association that had stretched back to the War of 1812 was now officially concluded. With the exception of remote Alaska Territory, the army was now officially out of the weather reporting and predicting business.[74]

The U.S. Army had implemented a variety of agricultural experiments during the nineteenth century in order to save money and improve the health of its soldiers. These remained the primary goals throughout the century, but from the inception of the experiments, some army officers had recognized a second set of important accomplishments. By demonstrating the commercial prospects for agriculture in various areas of the West, they could hasten the advance of America's cities and farms. By trying different crops, growing techniques, irrigation networks, and pump technologies, they could help transform the image of the Great American Desert into the Great American Garden. By occasionally feeding destitute overlanders for free and selling surplus food at cost from commissary supplies, they could perform an important humanitarian service while simultaneously winning the accolades of a grateful public.[75] And with proper patience, they could witness the transfer of vital agricultural information to clerks in Washington, D.C., and to private scientific societies that would then disseminate the findings to the American people. Even local newspapers, as well as national publications, carried frequent articles about military farming accomplishments. For example, on the Northern Plains, Montana newspapers praised the dryland farming techniques used at Fort Assiniboine, and one editor pronounced them to "have a value to Montana equal to the discovery of the precious metals within her borders."[76] Another Montana newspaper highlighted the wheeled irrigation apparatus employed at Fort Custer in 1878 and wondered why its design was not used more by civilians in the region. Similarly, the *Minneapolis Tribune* ran a series about the productive gardens maintained at Fort Sisseton, Dakota Territory, and the unique planting methods used by soldiers there.[77]

In the attendant task of recording and predicting weather, the army also made a valuable contribution to advancing meteorological science and helping society at large. Beginning with the initial temperature and climate reports solicited by Surgeon General James Tilton in 1814, the effort grew into a nationwide weather service under the direction of the Army Signal Corps. By combining the talents of scientists and military men, the Signal Corps created a daily weather reporting system for the entire nation, and with the use of the extensive military telegraph network, they were able to collate the readings and make predictions. By the 1870s the weather office routinely issued frost advisories, hurricane alerts, flood warnings, and a variety of other information through an extensive dissemination program in cities and rural communities alike.[78]

A final fitting tribute to the military contribution came just two years after transfer of the weather bureau from the Army Signal Corps to the Department of Agriculture. In his speech to the 1893 International Meteorological Congress, Maj. Charles Smart confidently declared: "Meteorological science in the United States was conceived and brought forth by the Army Medical Department. It was nurtured in the then unknown West as in the East, and it gained strength year by year."[79] Few Americans heard the tribute, but none could deny the U.S. Army its proper credit.

CHAPTER SEVEN

Hippocrates in Blue

ARMY DOCTORS ON THE FRONTIER

The scarcity of doctors in the remote areas of the American frontier often spelled disaster for victims of accidents and disease. Home remedies were widely available, but without adequate treatment even the simplest of medical problems could quickly produce complications and possible death. In the sparsely settled Sand Hills of northwestern Nebraska during 1884, a prank among friends set the stage for an accident that almost ended the life of one of the region's most colorful and important characters.

Jules Ami Sandoz—experimental agriculturist, land developer, and entrepreneur—joined two recently arrived settlers in digging a well at his dugout. An afternoon of mischievousness escalated into stupidity when the two men began to raise Jules from the bottom of the sixty-five-foot hole. As they slowly pulled on the rope to draw him up in a large bucket, they began to jerk the rope violently to cause the bucket and its occupant to twist uncontrollably in the darkness. Just as Jules neared the top, the rope broke, and he fell the full length of the shaft onto a large rock. After eighteen days, with a crushed ankle, bloody pus dripping from the wound, and a spreading infection that discolored his entire leg, the badly injured man was beyond the level of help that his associates could provide at the homestead.

Finally, the two irresponsible "friends" loaded the delirious man into a wagon and had neighbors haul him to the nearest doctor—the post surgeon at Fort Robinson, sixty miles away. By the time Jules reached the office of Dr. Walter Reed, his normally robust body was emaciated and his face conveyed the look of death. So severe were the complications that Reed prepared to amputate the infected foot, but he was met by the full fury of Jules, who bellowed, "You cut my foot off, doctor and I shoot you so dead you stink before you hit the ground." The surgeon backed off and yielded to the man's rage but continued to care for him at the post hospital for over two months. Reed's flippant remark that any damn fool possessed with such meanness just might pull through proved providential. Jules not only survived the ordeal to become a major player in the settlement of the Niobrara River area, but he also established a lifetime friendship with the doctor he had once threatened to shoot.[1]

The experiences of Jules Sandoz and Dr. Walter Reed were unique only for the importance of the individuals involved. Cooperation between civilians and army doctors was a common occurrence in all regions of the nineteenth-century frontier, so much so that civilians routinely expected this care by the end of the century. Yet throughout the vast array of federal laws and policies, Congress never gave official authority for its military officers to treat any medical problems among civilians. Post commanders and their surgeons merely used their own discretion to meet the call of an expanding frontier population that had nowhere else to turn for aid. In today's litigious society, such nonsanctioned efforts at health care probably would lead to numerous lawsuits, but on the frontier common sense permitted the authorization of that assistance. Civilians generally could rely on ranking officers to approve treatment if medical supplies were readily available, if the surgeon had adequate time to handle the cases, and if the problem truly warranted immediate attention.

In the two decades following the Mexican War, extension of military medicine to civilians probably became most widespread among the million overlanders who traversed the various trails to Oregon, California, and Salt Lake City. With the founding of Fort Kearny in the spring of 1848 as the eastern pivot of the Platte River Road across Nebraska and Wyoming came the immediate call for a surgeon to staff the post.

Although no hospital had yet been constructed, Dr. Joseph Walker of the Mounted Riflemen carried out duties until his regiment was transferred west in October. During the following six months the fort had no official medical service despite repeated pleas from commanding officer Capt. Charles Ruff. When a replacement finally arrived in the spring of 1849, he became so ill that he was confined to bed and eventually withdrawn from service. By April, Captain Ruff reported that twenty-six soldiers were on sick call with scurvy. One soon died, and the fort cemetery was hastily prepared to accept the first of many victims. At that point no one in Fort Kearny could have predicted the ferocity of the cholera epidemics that would be brought by overlanders from the Missouri River outfitting towns during the 1849 and 1850 trailing seasons.[2] Soldiers suffered from the often fatal malady, but their rates of sickness never reached the proportions seen among civilian overlanders. Upon examining many of these patients, Fort Kearny's assistant surgeon, William Hammond, Jr., concluded that the emigrants were more prone to epidemics because of their "excessive imprudence in diet and exposure to many hardships on the plains, to which they were entirely unaccustomed at home."[3]

Military doctors ministered to overlanders plagued with every conceivable malady, but in addition to the threat of cholera, which ranked highest on the list of problems, they continuously faced accidental wounds. The most frequent and dangerous of the hazards involved falls from or being run over by wagons. In 1849, Dr. Caleb Ormsby noted that the Fort Laramie post surgeon was treating four civilians who had recently been run over by wagons and had been left behind by other members of their parties. One particularly unfortunate fellow had been severely lacerated across the groin, and in the delay of returning him to the post, his wound had become infected with maggots and the flesh had begun to rot. Before leaving Fort Laramie, Ormsby noted that three other emigrants had been brought in with gunshot wounds, and overlanders delivered a woman whose head had been partially crushed by a wagon.[4] More fortunate was four-year-old Walter Eakin, whose head was badly injured after he fell from his father's wagon. Not only was the boy's life saved by the Fort Laramie surgeon, but also the hospital steward furnished his own small room to the boy's ailing mother. Walter lived in

Oregon into his nineties, always reminded of that frightening plains experience by the deep wheel scar across his forehead.[5]

The frontier army that was called upon to extend its protective wings over ill and injured civilians was rarely in a position to stretch its largess very far. As of the summer of 1853, the national authorization was for 13,821 troops, but only 10,417 were actually in service. Of that number, only 6,918 were stationed on the frontier, while the remainder guarded coastal fortifications, were on detached service, or worked in eastern administrative offices. Once the men on sick call, on fatigue duty, and in training programs were subtracted from the understrength frontier regiments, it hardly seemed possible that soldiers could realistically supervise the vast area from the Mississippi River valley to the Pacific coast.[6]

Although Congress was slow to increase the size of the army before the Civil War, it did receive something of a wake-up call regarding medical service during the Mexican War of 1846–48. Approximately one hundred thousand regulars and volunteers were mustered for this confrontation, which was fought over a vast and inhospitable terrain extending from the bustling Mexican port of Vera Cruz to the sleepy port of San Francisco, California. In the diverse theaters of action, American casualties totaled approximately fifteen hundred killed in action and over ten thousand killed by disease and accidents. Journalists and a few congressmen inquired why soldiers had experienced a death rate from disease that was ten times higher than the rate encountered by their kinsmen back home. Among the assertions that consistently reappeared in the public debate was that ninety-four surgeons had been inadequate to meet the needs of such a large and dispersed army. Furthermore, critics condemned the poor quality of civilian volunteer and contract surgeons, who often seemed to lack fundamental medical knowledge. Worse were many of the enlisted men who served as medical attendants based upon their influence among officers instead of their educational backgrounds.[7]

In the wake of national acquisition of the Oregon Territory and the Mexican Cession in 1846 and 1848, respectively, the limited resources of the overextended army were stretched even further. Legislation in the latter year did add fourteen more surgeons to the army's total, but this minor increase hardly answered soldiers' needs, much less the demands of civilians who would begin a massive westward drive with the California Gold Rush.[8]

A great deal of the problem faced by military doctors was the general poor health record of men who sought military service. In 1852, 16,064 men volunteered, but only 2,726 (or 16.9 percent) were found acceptable for induction. Some were turned down because of height restrictions, age requirements, and inability to speak English, but the vast majority failed their army physicals.[9] Even if doctors did a reasonably good job of weeding out poor candidates, long years of frontier duty, inadequate diet, poor housing, and exposure to weather extremes could break the health and spirit of even the most robust soldier.

An 1853 survey of health conditions at all the Texas forts closely paralleled findings throughout the other western military districts during the same era. The summary from Fort Terrett, in the central part of the state, revealed that within the fiscal year of 1852–53, soldiers experienced 1,577 cases of disease among a command that averaged only 194 men, or a total of 800 percent. Most of these cases involved repeated intermittent fever, diarrhea, and dysentery. Approximately 170 miles to the north, Fort Belknap experienced a 374 percent incidence of disease for the same period—mostly intermittent fever, digestive disorders, and respiratory problems. Dr. Ebenizer Swift reported from Fort Chadbourne that unrealistic command decisions and a shortage of appropriate supplies were the root causes of suffering. Soldiers were forced to wear heavy woolen uniforms in summer temperatures that routinely ranged between 90 degrees and 105 degrees. They were required to wear forage caps and belts purely for military decorum and lived on a monotonous and non-nutritious diet of salt beef, pork, bacon, hardtack, bread, beans, sugar, and coffee.[10]

Because fevers and digestive disorders were the primary health problems in the nineteenth-century army, conscientious doctors updated their understanding of the causes of these maladies, and some sought their own local remedies. At midcentury the prevailing theory of disease causation was the miasmatic theory. This explanation stressed that poisonous vapors, or miasmas, were forced into the air in alarming amounts by decaying vegetable or animal matter. These were thought to be especially prevalent in areas of stagnant water and garbage dumps, where winds dispersed miasmas throughout the adjacent population. Standard treatment of an infected patient often involved bleeding and purgative doses of calomel or castor oil.[11] A few army surgeons, however, were already joining eastern colleagues in their questioning of the miasmatic theory. When Dr. W. W. Anderson at Fort Terrett found considerable intermittent fever at his garrison but no evidence of uncontrolled dumps or stagnant water, he began to doubt the concept and looked elsewhere for a cause.[12]

More successful were efforts to understand the persistent problem of scurvy within the ranks. By midcentury most army doctors agreed with their eastern counterparts that the disease resulted from inadequate consumption of fruits and vegetables. Some, such as Dr. S. P. Moore at Fort Laramie, however, believed that excessive physical labor on hot days followed by exposure to cool night air were the real culprits. Moore's thinking was focused on symptoms rather than causes, but most army doctors answered Surgeon General R. C. Wood's 1859 directive for a comparative study of all posts to isolate the causes of scurvy. The effort confirmed that dietary deficiency of vitamin C was the fundamental cause. Although diagnosis of cause was a significant step forward, most western posts continued to suffer from scurvy because shipments of antiscorbutics came rarely and in inadequate amounts.[13]

The Surgeon General's Office encouraged its army doctors to experiment with local sources of vitamin C that appeared in nature. Fort Laramie's assistant surgeon, Edward W. Johns, used watercress to supplement the soldiers' diet until the indigenous supply ran out. He next turned to cactus juice as a substitute, but the taste was so repugnant that troops refused to drink it unless it was mixed with a shot of whiskey. Other medical officers found that wild onions, wild artichokes, pokeweed, lamb's-quarter, and particular varieties of the aloe plant could serve the purpose when commissary departments were unable to supply antiscorbutics through lime juice, pickles, vegetables, dried fruits, and molasses. Although scurvy outbreaks were never entirely banished from the frontier army, the frequency of reported cases dropped significantly after the Civil War.[14]

Even though frontier military posts were far removed from the eastern settlements, they were never truly isolated from national health problems such as venereal diseases. A recent study of the Civil War era reveals that western garrisons had substantially higher rates of infection than did regiments that campaigned east of the Mississippi River. Statistics for the Department of the Pacific revealed that 1,587 soldiers sought treatment for sexually transmitted diseases between July 1, 1861, and June 30, 1862. These represented 461 men in every thousand, or over five times the rate of infection in the entire Union army. Within the Department of New Mexico, syphilis and gonorrhea cases were three times higher than the national military average. Historian Lawrence R. Murphy attributed the higher western rates to lax regulations among frontier militia units during the Civil War, their proximity to unregulated civilian communities, and the ready availability of prostitutes, who tied themselves to western army camps through fake marriages to soldiers and hiring on as laundresses. Despite the epidemic proportions that these diseases attained, most army doctors failed to see that these infections spread through the bloodstream. Accordingly, they treated visible sores with chemical salves or cauterized lesions with mercury, silver nitrate, or potassium iodide. Others prescribed rest, dietary restrictions, and saline or chemical solutions to purge the digestive system.[15]

At the conclusion of the Civil War, as the federal government began to reduce the million-man army to a more fiscally manageable size, the War Department wrestled with divergent plans to staff the medical service. It continued to designate three categories of military physicians: those in regular army service, volunteer physician-surgeons, and contract surgeons. Ever since the 1820s, doctors entering regular army medical service had begun as assistant surgeons with rank equal to that of a first lieutenant. After three to five years of praiseworthy duty they were elevated to rank and status equivalent to that of a captain. After a much longer term and passage of a difficult examination, they could be promoted to surgeon with rank equivalent to that of a major, with possibility of eventual promotion to equivalency of a colonel.[16]

Volunteer physician-surgeons were not a class who saw frontier duty, since they could be authorized only during periods of declared war. In contrast, contract physicians (acting assistant surgeons) became a significant feature of the frontier army from the 1850s to the end of the century. These were civilian doctors who were hired for fixed terms to treat military patients. Some were enlisted only for a few weeks or months, but others served for years through the annual renewal of their contracts. Although hiring contract physicians provided a budgetary advantage for the War Department and an ability to be more flexible with assignments, the relationship often was not a happy one. In addition to not possessing any job security, these "part-time doctors" were often poorly treated by officers at their posts. Since they held no official rank, they and their families had little choice about housing accommodations and other perquisites of fort life.[17]

The experiences of Acting Assistant Surgeon Samuel L. S. Smith at the West Texas post of Fort Concho were somewhat typical of these realities. Having graduated from the prestigious medical school at the University of Michigan in 1873, and having served his internship at the U.S. Marine Hospital in Louisville, Kentucky, Smith was a promising candidate for regular army medical service, but no slots were available when he applied. Upon transfer to Fort Concho in 1878, he found immediate problems with some officers. They resented his interference when they worked ill enlisted men to exhaustion and seemed to show no concern for any of the soldiers' welfare. Because he was junior to the regular army physician at Fort Concho, Smith found himself constantly rotated among the small outlying camps, one as far as two hundred miles away in the remote Guadalupe Mountains. Without amenities, he and the soldiers lived a life of isolation and hardship. Although anxious to obtain a regular army appointment, Smith quit his contract position in 1881 and entered private practice at the civilian community of San Angelo, which was adjacent to Fort Concho. He became a prominent school board member, civic organizer, postmaster, druggist, and county health officer over the following decades.[18]

Although the issue of contract physicians was a controversial one, their numbers grew throughout the remainder of the century. The surgeon general reported in 1869 that there were only 161 commissioned medical officers to serve almost thirty-three thousand men of the regular army in all the states and territories. At roughly the same time, 282 contract surgeons were filling the gaps in a badly overextended system.[19] Historian Percy Ashburn likened the contract physicians to army mules as he paid them homage: "Neither commissioned nor enlisted, without regiment or corps, having no hope of promotion and dubious rank, they survived because they were needed, were respected for their personalities, were as necessary as the mules, harder worked and quite as much an ever present help in trouble. They have never been accorded their just dues. Many were splendid men."[20]

No matter what the official status or background training of an army doctor, he was effective only if the quality of his hospital was high and his source of supplies was reliable. Unfortunately, before the 1880s most doctors faced grim realities on both counts. The experiences of Dr. William M. Notson at Fort Concho were fairly typical of the decade following the Civil War. This represented the rebuilding era during which old posts had to be repaired and new ones had to be constructed in even more remote areas of the west. Soldiers provided most of the physical labor because War Department budgets were inadequate for large numbers of civilian contractors. Not surprisingly, much of the construction that was performed during the late 1860s had to be redone during the early 1870s because of poor-quality building materials, improper design, and constant exposure to harsh weather.

When Dr. Notson arrived at the post in January 1868, tents still housed all medical facilities, and the foundation had been laid for only one structure. By November the hospital tents were in such poor condition that patients had to be moved into the unfinished hospital building, while surgery was still performed within a tent. Medical supplies had to be drawn from San Antonio, 230 miles away, and they were delivered only twice a year.[21]

At about the same time, the post surgeon at Fort Hays, Kansas, had to work in a small prefabricated pine structure shipped out from Saint Louis. The hospital actually consisted of two buildings joined by a passageway. Within the cramped quarters of one was the ward for patients, and the other side served as the surgeon's office, a dispensary, and a smaller ward.[22] Upon their arrival in 1868, Dr. R. H. McKay and his wife found deplorable working and living conditions at newly constructed Fort Sill, Indian Territory. They lived in a tent attached to a frame that was anchored into a dirt floor. In at least one storm they had to brace themselves against the frame to prevent the whole contraption from blowing away.[23]

By way of contrast, the Fort Richardson, Texas, hospital emerged as a modern, spacious, and elegant edifice upon its completion in 1870. Built of native stone by civilian architects and roofed by carefully cut cottonwood lumber, the two-story structure accommodated two wards, dispensary, main office, hospital steward's room, kitchen, and dining hall. Because Fort Richardson was designated a long-term military post, extra efforts were taken in its construction, and it was viewed as a good assignment by many soldiers. H. H. McConnell, who was stationed at the post with the Sixth Cavalry, observed, "No one institution of camp life is of more importance (or scarcely as much) to the well being of the soldier as is the hospital. . . . At many posts, if not at the majority of them, the hospital is so inhospitable as to present few attractions, and all keep away from it as long as possible, the prospect promising less comfort than the barracks."[24] The hospital at Fort Richardson turned out to be the one exception to his experiences, and he offered praise not only for the building, but also for the excellent medical staff.

Over a decade later and eight hundred miles to the north, Fort Robinson, Nebraska, guarded the southern edge of the Great Sioux Reservation and served as a primary supply center for the numerous campaigns during the late 1870s. When *Omaha Bee* newspaper correspondent William E. Annin visited the locale in 1883, he praised most aspects of military life, but he was especially complimentary toward the hospital. The two-story frame structure comprised an office, library, apothecary shop, storerooms, staff sleeping rooms, and a spacious ward. The beds seemed comfortable and were covered with clean linens. Furthermore, Dr. Henry McElderry had just received a windfall of eighteen hundred dollars from an unspent appropriation that he could now use to enlarge the hospital.[25]

Although military doctors had little control over the general quality of forts to which they were assigned, they could make specific health improvements. Virtually all of the post–Civil War surgeons tried to enhance the quality of water supplies and personal hygiene among troopers. They were not always sure of the exact connections between the spread of diseases and water supplies and their use, but they could see the dramatic effects of cleanup campaigns. Surgeon Daniel Weisel of Fort Davis, Texas, repeatedly tested the fresh springs of Limpia Creek and sent samples to Washington, D.C., for chemical analysis. Likewise, he chided soldiers for their aversion to bathing and called for a new regulation that required all soldiers to bathe at least twice a week.[26]

A similar appeal to superiors in Washington, D.C., came from the surgeon at Fort Dodge, Kansas, who could not even get soldiers to stop dumping the contents of their "slop wagon" into the Arkansas River from which they took their drinking water. More successful was Maj. George W. Schofield, commander at Fort Stockton, Texas, who directed all soldiers to bathe twice a week in nearby Comanche Springs during the warm months. Under his direction the officers took up a collection among themselves and built a small bathhouse that could be used most of the year because of the spring's almost constant temperature of 76 degrees. By 1889, soldiers at Fort Elliott, Texas, had even installed an ice machine whose daily capacity of thirty-nine hundred pounds provided ample means to preserve foods and cool their drinking water.[27]

No matter how well versed a late-nineteenth-century doctor was in modern surgery techniques, theory of disease origins, or treatment programs for epidemics, he needed a special flexibility for handling unexpected problems on the frontier. Fort Dodge's physician watched sixteen soldiers die during 1872 from bites inflicted by rabid skunks. At nearby Fort Larned, a rabid wolf killed several people, including Cpl. Mike McGuillicuddy, who refused to allow his lacerated finger to be amputated.[28] A blowfly epidemic at Fort Concho in 1878 pushed the limits on hospital admissions, which included one soldier who merely awoke from a night's sleep to find sundry screwworms deposited in his nostrils. Frequent tarantula bites at Fort McKavett, Texas, compelled Post Surgeon Andrew K. Smith to do his own research and to refute a treatment program outlined in a scientific article printed in *Harper's Magazine.*[29]

Army doctors clearly were better prepared to handle physical problems than mental ones. Fort Dodge surgeon William S. Tremaine performed several hundred successful amputations on frostbitten fingers, toes, and ears during his ten years in Kansas. When a Private Kensington partially severed his finger while working on a shingle machine at Fort Rice, Dakota Territory, Dr. Washington Matthews sewed it back on with a minimum of concern.[30] Less fortunate was Pvt. W. H. Henderson, who began experiencing hallucinations while on station guard at Eagle Spring, Texas, in 1878. No amount of restraint could calm down the terrified man, and he had to be confined at Fort Davis as if he were a common criminal. Another private named Deets, while serving at Camp Goodwin, Arizona, went berserk and threatened to shoot his Sixth Cavalry compatriots. After almost killing a sergeant, he was thrown into the guardhouse without any special treatment. At least in the last case the soldier ultimately was sent to the Government Hospital for the Insane in Washington, D.C.—the only institution in the entire army devoted to handling mental health problems.[31]

In addition to attending patients, post physicians performed a number of diverse tasks that often stretched their schedules to the limits. They had to check on living conditions, monitor water supplies, oversee cooking procedures, inspect all buildings, conduct daily sick calls, supervise hospital staff, and maintain the pharmacy. Like other officers, regular army doctors had to participate in various boards and courts-martial as well as serve at subposts and in extended field campaigns. As highly educated men, they were also expected to maintain detailed records of scientific value to eastern scholars and government clerks. They assembled daily meteorological reports, investigated local flora and fauna, studied Native American cultures, and collected scientific specimens to send to institutions in Washington, D.C. Much of this information was printed in the voluminous Congressional serial set of government publications and provided a valuable source of data to later generations of scholars.[32]

Army physicians generally had good reputations among the frontier population, but sinners certainly existed among the saints. There were the usual number of alcoholics, such as Contract Surgeon E. G. Umbstaetter, who eventually lost his position because of habitual drunkenness and "using for his private drinking most of the hospital brandy and whiskey."[33] Equally significant was the surgeon at Fort Bascom, New Mexico, who panicked in the midst of delivering a baby and left the whole task to a soldier's wife. The mother survived, but the baby died a few months later.[34] At least a few of the contract surgeons had ulterior motives when they accepted assignments in the western territories with the hopes of staking mining claims or making personal fortunes through land speculation. Contract Surgeon Samuel Brown McPheeters, serving at

Fort Robinson at the end of the frontier era, even outlined a plan to his family to serve only two years in that capacity, gain prestige and a grub-stake from the experience, and have Uncle Sam pay for his exotic travels.[35]

For every inept or opportunistic army doctor, however, there were scores of capable and committed men who risked their lives in the performance of duty. Dr. George Sternberg continued to treat cholera patients at Fort Harker, Kansas, even after his wife died in the epidemic and his own life was threatened by the disease. Likewise, Acting Assistant Surgeon Samuel Phillips volunteered to attend cholera cases at Fort Riley, Kansas, after the assigned surgeon fled the area with his family.[36] When the same 1867 epidemic struck Fort Lyon, Colorado, the surgeon also lost his wife, but he continued to treat soldiers of the Thirty-Eighth Infantry until his own health collapsed.[37]

The experiences of Dr. Redford Sharpe in San Antonio, Texas, during 1869 may have been even more reflective of how physicians' heroic performances could be overlooked in the official records. Sharpe argued with his commanding officer about how best to treat cholera cases among the Fourth Cavalry. His viewpoint finally prevailed, and the entire regiment moved to healthier surroundings thirteen miles out of town. The cholera threat quickly subsided after the relocation, but the obstructionist officer, rather than the physician, received a commendation from the War Department for having made the bold decision.[38]

Like other soldiers, army physicians spent most of their time in routine garrison duties, but when major campaigns were launched, they joined the men in the field. Small patrols rarely had a medical officer available, and when they did, he sometimes was not a surgeon. When troopers of the Second Cavalry pursued a Blackfeet raiding party in Montana during 1870, they remained on the trail for nine days in temperatures that plummeted to forty-two degrees below zero. Only a veterinary doctor accompanied the patrol, and he dispensed quinine and salts for the numerous frozen feet and other disabilities, because those were the only medical supplies available.[39]

Yet when the great Yellowstone expedition of 1876 was organized to force the Lakota Sioux and Northern Cheyennes into a series of decisive battles, the War Department outfitted its converging columns with seemingly ample physicians and medical supplies to handle any problem.

They did not, however, anticipate the magnitude of the Seventh Cavalry's defeat on the Little Big Horn on June 25. Assistant Surgeon George E. Lord and Acting Assistant Surgeon James Madison De Wolf were killed in the battle, while Acting Assistant Surgeon Henry R. Porter survived the desperate defense of Reno Hill. Fortunately, the other converging columns still had physicians and medicines available to treat the wounded. Drs. Holmes O. Paulding, Curtis E. Munn, John Ridgely, and Charles R. Stephens ministered to the survivors and helped evacuate them to Forts Abraham Lincoln, Reno, and Fetterman. Some of these men and their hospital stewards likewise remained in the field throughout the rigorous winter campaign of 1876–77 that forced many of the Indians onto the Great Sioux Reservation.[40]

Unfortunately for the wounded taken from General George Crook's column following the June 17 Battle of the Rosebud, conditions proved deplorable at Fort Fetterman. The hospital became so overcrowded that patients were placed on the floor, where at least one died. When the post surgeon returned from a visit to Fort Laramie, he ordered that the men be moved off the floor immediately. He also instructed that two hospital matrons clean up the filthy ward. When they refused to do so, he fired them and paid two laundresses to perform the task.[41]

Despite their usual role as noncombatants, four army surgeons received Medals of Honor for valor in the field. Assistant Surgeon Bernard J. D. Irwin of Fort Buchanan, Arizona, received the commendation for voluntarily taking command of a fourteen-man detachment and rushing to the aid of Lt. George N. Bascom's besieged unit at Apache Pass in 1861. Contract Surgeon Henry Tilton won the award for repeatedly risking his life in the rescue and treatment of wounded soldiers in the 1877 Battle of Bear Paw Mountain against Chief Joseph's Nez Percés. Contract Surgeon John O. Skinner received his honor for aiding the rescue and treating wounded men during the 1872 Modoc War. Most celebrated of the four honorees was Assistant Surgeon Leonard Wood, whose field service during the Geronimo campaign of 1886 demonstrated remarkable bravery and stamina. As a regular army officer, Wood continued his military medical service into the 1890s, commanded a Rough Rider unit in the Spanish-American War, was named military governor of Cuba, and served as army chief of staff from 1910 to 1914.[42]

As the numbers and quality of military hospitals gradually increased after the Civil War, post commanders found themselves under additional pressure to handle civilian medical needs. They operated under the same provisions as did prewar officers, who were allowed to use their own discretion in each specific case. When a life-or-death situation existed, permission for the physician to provide treatment was almost always forthcoming. The case of a sixty-year-old female settler at Fort Ridgely, Minnesota, provided just such a model for immediate authorization. The woman's feet had become frozen after she was exposed for three days and nights in a relentless snowstorm. Both legs had to be amputated. When several civilian woodcutters were brought into Fort Buford, Dakota Territory, in 1869, the surgeon operated on them for arrow and bullet wounds suffered in an Indian attack.[43] The same service was rendered for a citizen badly wounded in 1877 by Indians near Fort Keogh, Montana. He received not only treatment, but also generous rations from the commander. Surgeon Charles K. Winne, assigned to Sidney Barracks, Nebraska, in 1877, operated on a drunken civilian who had just been run over by a Union Pacific train. He removed both mangled legs, but the patient did not survive the trauma of the accident.[44]

Even with the absence of an official military regulation to extend medical service to civilians, no one would have questioned the actions taken in the above-mentioned cases. More debatable, however, were the humanitarian gestures of army physicians who traveled into the remote countryside to minister to ill civilians. Throughout the 1870s the various doctors who served at Fort Riley, Kansas, maintained a systematic rural health care program for residents within fifty miles of the post. They used a specially prepared saddlebag to carry medicines and instruments, and they occasionally employed a mule-drawn ambulance to transport a larger stock of supplies in a medical chest. During the diphtheria epidemic that struck northern New Mexico during the late 1880s, Fort Union surgeon Henry Lippincott drove a buckboard throughout the immediate area to tend patients who were too ill to come in to his office.[45]

Preventive techniques also seemed to be a regular part of army medical treatment after the Civil War and included immunization programs for soldiers and civilians alike. Smallpox was still a dreaded killer, but unlike cholera, its spread could be limited if a widespread immunization effort was undertaken quickly enough. When an outbreak occurred among the Fort Rice, Dakota Territory, garrison in 1869, the surgeon did not have enough vaccine to inoculate all the troops, and he was therefore unable to offer any to civilians, even those employed at the fort.[46] By way of contrast, the Department of Texas military commander had sufficient reserves available in 1873 to provide free vaccine to all civilian doctors who were willing to cooperate with a massive immunization effort. Likewise, Dr. Charles K. Winne at Sidney Barracks began an immediate vaccination drive among civilians in the railroad town of Sidney, Nebraska, after only a single smallpox case was discovered.[47]

When Fort Union authorities directed a forceful immunization drive during 1879 among all military and civilian residents of the post, they headed off an especially virulent smallpox epidemic. Unfortunately, the nearby New Mexico towns of Las Vegas, La Junta (Watrous), and Mora did not receive this aid and were devastated by the outbreak. The three communities suffered a combined total of 684 deaths.[48] Even a small group of transients could benefit from a larger immunization program when ample supplies of serum were readily available. The Fort Fetterman doctor offered to vaccinate anyone who requested the service during the spring 1877 outbreak. He especially instructed the post sutler and civilian scouts to pass the word to teamsters and other overlanders who might be especially prone to transferring the disease. Two years later, Fort Concho physician Samuel Smith and his orderly visited a ranch, approximately eighteen miles from the post, where they attempted to buy milk and eggs. The rancher reported that one of his sons was still ill from a recent smallpox vaccination and needed tending. Smith not only revaccinated the boy, but also the other five children—all at no cost to the family.[49]

Not since the days of the formation of the army had the issue of civilians' paying for military medical service been officially resolved. As for all other forms of aid, the decision was left entirely to the discretion of fort commanders, who had to balance public needs with the realities of meager army budgets, periodic shortages of supplies, and the work schedules of post surgeons. Most commanders tended to operate on a pay-as-you-can basis. At Fort Union, which treated 428 civilian cases in 1878, the going rate was fifteen cents to a dollar a day for treatment, depending on the person's financial status. At Fort Elliott, in the Texas

Panhandle, civilian patients were normally charged one dollar per day, with twenty-five cents of that sum divided among the hospital attendants and the remainder deposited in a hospital fund to be spent on improvements.[50] More lucrative was the practice of surgeon Charles K. Winne at Sidney Barracks. During his first five weeks of service there in 1875, he accumulated $163 from civilian patients, a handsome sum that went into post's coffers. During that time he lost only one client, and even then the man's brother paid the $40 hospital bill for the deceased.[51]

Even though civilians were to be charged informally for army medical aid, enforcement of those levies against civilian patients was virtually impossible. Payment depended upon the good will of the patient, especially if he or she was a local resident and wished to receive similar care in the future. Yet many of these clients were merely passing through the region when they sought out help at the fort, and once they had received it, they quickly moved along.

Most army doctors dispensed the aid anyway without pressing the issue, but some probably agreed with Dr. Albert James Myer's earlier assessment of the situation. Myer resented the use of scarce army supplies for treating civilians, and especially the free medical examinations that he was instructed to give. He also feared legal liability for damages in caring for nonmilitary patients. But his greatest philosophical reluctance stemmed from his view that his medical knowledge was his private property, and he should profit from it when treating civilians. Perhaps the Fort Fetterman commander of 1875 would have agreed substantially with Myer after the post hospital accumulated a large debt as a result of civilian care. One patient required fifty days of hospitalization but refused to pay for any of his treatment or rations during the extended stay.[52]

Oddly enough, army surgeons who fulfilled the Hippocratic oath sometimes gained the animosity of local residents. When a drunken cowboy began shooting up the civilian community near Fort Griffin, Texas, a posse followed and shot him repeatedly. Post surgeon J. L. Powell rescued the man, treated his wounds, and nursed him back to health. Powell earned the wrath of some citizens for the act of kindness, as did another doctor, at Fort Griffin, who presided over a similar case in 1874. A feud between rival factions in the community known disparagingly as "the Flats" resulted in several gunshot wounds that were treated at the post. Assistant Surgeon Rufus Choate identified nine of the worst offenders in this feud and refused to treat them for any more injuries. The tense situation subsided only after the commanding officer cleaned up the Flats and forced the worst hard cases out of town.[53]

Civilian demands on army medical care increased with each new decade of the nineteenth century, but changes in technology, transportation, and administration allowed the army to answer that challenge. By 1885 a consolidation of military posts lowered the numbers of soldiers necessary to staff them. Just as the Indian wars were winding down, budgets for scores of subposts and expensive campaigns were reduced. Forts that survived into the 1890s and beyond used the overall savings of these closings to improve their own infrastructures. Better-quality buildings, modernized water supplies, and more varied diets bettered health conditions throughout the army. Furthermore, expanded road and railroad service brought supplies and other advancements to even the most remote posts on a more timely basis.

On the national level, a new regulation in 1885 made it mandatory for each commanding officer to forward the medical officer's monthly sanitation report to Washington, D.C. This helped produce a more cohesive reporting system that could address hygienic conditions on the local level. Two years later, the Hospital Corps began to train staff to work in wards, operating rooms, and laboratories and in the field. The 1893 appointment of George M. Sternberg as surgeon general also brought a new professionalism and scientific advancement to the Army Medical Corps that presaged the era of modern medicine.[54]

Perhaps the public tribute to Dr. William S. Tremaine, post surgeon at Fort Dodge for a decade, best articulated the feelings that civilians everywhere in the West had for the most beloved army physicians. When Tremaine resigned in 1878, the citizens, as well as the soldiers, held a formal occasion to express their gratitude to the man who had delivered almost every baby born in the immediate area during the decade and who had handled thousands of cases ranging from cholera and gunshot wounds to minor burns and lacerations. To the members of the audience, Dr. Tremaine personified the best that the army had to offer, and he would be sorely missed by them.[55]

By 1893 the frontier army was an institution in search of a mission that would carry it beyond the era of the Indian wars. A congressional budgetary directive that year eliminated funds for all contract surgeons and reduced the number of assistant surgeons from 125 to 95. Even though the number of assistant surgeons was later raised to 110, this marked a substantial downturn in the size of the Medical Department, a downturn that would not be reversed in a significant way until American entry into World War I.[56] Ironically, the declining size of the agency also marked how far the army medical service had come since the first army surgeon pushed beyond the Mississippi River to assume his station at Fort Osage, Missouri, in 1808. Among the many vestiges of the army on the frontier, no feature rated higher among civilians than did the medical service.

CHAPTER EIGHT

Reform the Man

POST CHAPELS, SCHOOLS, AND LIBRARIES

Among the vast throngs of officers and men who joined the nineteenth-century frontier army, very few could be classified as loners who had turned their backs on the rest of the world. Indeed, the majority were motivated by quite the opposite goal. Even the most troubled of men who were escaping debts, failed marriages, dictatorial fathers, and past crimes saw the army not as the ultimate dead end to a fruitless life, but instead as an opportunity to begin a new life. Likewise, instead of turning their backs on the "civilized community," many soldiers relished the institutions of that society and participated in their renewal at even the most isolated of military posts.

Three institutions that promoted the army's civilizing process were apparent at many frontier stations by the 1850s: chapels, schools, and libraries. These closely entwined entities evolved slowly as the size of the army and the number of forts increased. They multiplied not because of new administrative edicts from Washington, D.C., but because the demand for their services were enthusiastically voiced among soldiers and civilians in the West. Their support and influence was always greatest at the local level, and some commanding officers demonstrated resource-fulness in funding these programs without having to draw from regular budgets. The long-term success of these agencies can be measured not only by the numbers of patrons who used them, but also by the less precise calculation of how they improved the quality of life at remote garrisons. Virtually every military diary, journal, or reminiscence published from the era devoted at least some attention to the joys associated with these three institutions. For some officers, their wives, and enlisted men, these associations merely provided a constructive way to while away their free time. For others, the churches, schools, and libraries ultimately gave them the knowledge to improve their personal lives.

As with so many aspects of soldiering, Congress and the War Department did not create a formal program for the spiritual well-being of federal troops. Special legislation in 1791 and 1812 gave Congress the power to appoint army and navy chaplains, but with the exception of brief service during the War of 1812, few were called.[1] Secretary of War Lewis Cass observed in his annual report of 1831 that soldiers were being placed far beyond the line of settlements, where they were asked to serve for years under conditions of personal sacrifice and great demoralization. He therefore hoped that lawmakers would appoint chaplains to attend to their spiritual, emotional, and material needs, but no legislation was immediately forthcoming.[2]

Junior and senior officers began to make similar appeals from the field at about the same time. Lt. Joseph S. Gallagher observed that the navy was spending over ten thousand dollars annually for chaplains to serve aboard its ships, while the army was doing virtually nothing. He also conjectured that ministers could be secured at many of the posts for annual salaries of only two hundred dollars to four hundred dollars each, because they could make the greater share of their compensation among civilian congregations within the general regions of the posts.[3] Lt. Col. Josiah Vose wrote from Fort Towson, Indian Territory, that his long military experience confirmed the absolute need for church services at military posts. He strongly believed that the presence of competent chaplains would produce "fewer desertions, less intoxication, and a more healthy command."[4]

Arguments for the necessary moral uplift of soldiers finally convinced Congress to authorize on July 5, 1838, that post councils of administration could employ up to twenty chaplains nationally. By subsequent War Department Order 29, these appointees would not only minister to the spiritual and educational needs of soldiers, but also serve as teachers for the children on assigned posts. They were to receive forty dollars per month, four daily ration allowances, and quarters equal to those of a captain.[5]

Despite this legislative breakthrough, the full extent of the chaplaincy service still remained unrealized during the 1850s. Early in the decade, the number of official slots was raised to thirty, but many went unclaimed. As of 1857, ten chaplains were sanctioned for the Department of the West, yet only half of the spaces were staffed. The Department of Texas received four positions for its fifteen widely scattered posts, but only three of these were manned. Likewise, in the Department of New Mexico only two of the three mandated positions were filled to serve the fifteen forts.[6]

As with so many other lukewarm attempts to improve army morale, the success of this program rested upon the degree of support from local commanding officers and the quality of the chaplains themselves. When chaplain David White wanted his superiors to close the Camp Verde, Arizona, trading post on the Sabbath and to suspend drinking and gambling, he was met with a total rebuff. Not only did his commander censure the young man, but he also recommended his transfer out of the territory.[7] Likewise, Capt. Nathaniel Lyon opposed the appointment of a chaplain to Fort Randall, Dakota Territory, in 1859 because each clergyman would allegedly indoctrinate the men with his particular brand of religion. Lyon also disliked the doctrine of penance and forgiveness that so many ministers preached because it conflicted with the military philosophy that all crimes and offenses should be swiftly punished.[8] Even as late as 1882, Gen. William Tecumseh Sherman, commanding general of the army, showed his disdain for the system that allegedly put too much emphasis on religious speculation and not enough on soldiering. He mused that any commanding officer who truly wanted the influence of a minister within his garrison should hire a part-time civilian out of post funds. But maintaining thirty chaplains in the service, allegedly half of whom were sick or refused service in isolated locations, made no budgetary sense, according to Sherman.[9]

Detractors of the overall system were short on specific charges against individual clerics but long on the imprecise list of generic complaints. They charged that chaplains collected reasonably good pay and allowances for light work, while simultaneously regarding the position as a temporary avocation until they found a regular church to serve. Critics also alleged that some of the appointments came as political plums, whereby chaplains held paid positions while dodging transfer to the frontier by assuming the status of "waiting orders" or "on leave" for an indefinite period. Allegedly, some retired clerks and aged sergeants were given the job by friendly officers as a sinecure. Once they secured the position, they did little or nothing toward attending the spiritual needs of fellow soldiers.[10]

Some officers resented chaplains because they seemed to have rights that exceeded normal military decorum. They especially complained that these civilian clerics had no military training, were not forced to abide by strict discipline, and could retire with a pension after only a few years of service. They also resented the fact that chaplains automatically held the rank of captain, while lieutenants among the line and staff officers often had to remain in rank for fifteen or more years before being promoted.[11]

These allegations seemed to offer evidence of widespread abuse, but few cases were ever brought against individual chaplains. Moreover, the charges offered no explanation about the ambiguous status facing these men. Even though they held officer rank and were qualified for pensions, they did not wear a regulation uniform or give orders. They were entitled to a salute from enlisted men but could rarely enforce regulations or rigid discipline. Furthermore, in the post–Civil War era they received only a first lieutenant's pay, and they could not be promoted beyond their entry status as a captain.[12]

Despite critics' suggestions that many chaplains received their appointments by chicanery and lived a privileged life, reality offered a different perspective. To receive an appointment, each cleric had to be a regularly ordained minister and be recommended by a recognized ecclesiastical denomination or by five accredited ministers from his own denomination. Letters from military officers, civic leaders, and other influential persons could also be used in his favor.[13] Far from being a man of leisure, the chaplain faced a busy round of official and unofficial duties. In addition to providing regular Sunday church services, he was expected to counsel individual soldiers, promote religious study groups, visit the sick, distribute "wholesome" literature to the men, and perform marriages, baptisms, and funeral services. Some chaplains, such as Norman Badger, demonstrated remarkable energy by moving beyond their assigned duties. At Fort Concho, Texas, during the early 1870s, Badger started a post garden, initiated a day and night school for children and enlisted men, taught telegraphic skills to soldiers, and served as post treasurer, bakery manager, and postmaster.[14]

Charges of denominational favoritism also plagued some people's perceptions of the chaplaincy service. Although all major Protestant denominations were included, and Episcopalians, Methodists, and Baptists dominated the ranks, Catholics were clearly underrepresented. This double standard existed because of the underlying anti-Catholic pre-judice that permeated American society. In spite of the high ratio of Catholic soldiers within the frontier army, especially among foreign-born enlistees, relatively few of their priests gained admission to the chaplain corps. Of the eighty men who held official army chaplain positions between 1813 and 1856, only three were Roman Catholic. That tiny percentage increased in the post–Civil War era, but never to the levels that would have provided fair representation.[15]

Some Catholics found ways to circumvent the biased system. During the 1850s soldiers at Fort Lincoln, Texas, traveled to the nearby town of D'Hanis, where they could receive communion from French priests who served the town on a part-time basis.[16] Even more fortunate were the troops at Fort Union, New Mexico, which was in the heart of a devout Catholic population. Throughout the late 1850s, Father Joseph Projectus Machebeuf made infrequent trips to the post and, with permission of the commander, conducted mass in the chapel. During the 1880s priests from the nearby community of Watrous continued the pattern of Catholic services on the fort premises, even though a Protestant held the official chaplain's position there.[17]

The most advanced case of accommodation between denominations came at Fort Leavenworth, Kansas. Because the like-named civilian community had grown up alongside the post, and because both grew to relatively large size, soldiers were able to attend Catholic services off the military reservation during the 1850s and 1860s. By 1870, money from the post building fund and private contributions allowed construction of a Catholic chapel at the military installation. Soldiers donated a thousand dollars toward the project, and civilians contributed the rest. Nineteen years later, an even larger Catholic church was constructed on the post following an agreement among the War Department, church authorities, and the local civilian population. At no cost to the government, the privately financed edifice became a landmark at Fort Leavenworth and a testament to gradual erosion of religious sectarianism that had so bitterly divided Catholics and Protestants in previous decades.[18]

Because military posts often lacked sufficient quarters and offices to meet their basic needs, it is little wonder that chaplains found themselves scrambling for facilities in which to hold services. This was especially true in the decade following the Civil War, when many new forts were established and many old ones were expanded. The changing situation at Fort Concho, Texas, mirrored experiences throughout the West. When chaplain Norman Badger arrived at the post in 1871, it was still under construction, and he constantly had to shift Sunday services among tents, the hospital ward, the enlisted men's mess hall, and his own quarters. Five years later, some soldiers of the Tenth Cavalry took the initiative and built a crude church of "upright mud plastered poles lined with flour bags." In 1879, a chapel measuring forty feet by twenty feet was finally constructed and was dubbed "by far the best finished room in the Post."[19]

At Fort Dodge, Kansas, the lack of space forced a moral dilemma on Chaplain A. G. White in 1867. He repeatedly protested to departmental headquarters that a suitable structure existed for church and school activities, but it had been turned into a recreational hall. In the spirit of compromise, White received use of the building during daylight hours of the week for school and on Sunday morning for religious services. Yet he was not satisfied, since he had to perform his duty in a notorious gambling hall and deliver sermons from a billiard table.[20] Facilities were equally deplorable at the Fort Leavenworth Military Prison, which had a chaplain assigned ever since its establishment in 1875. Six years later, however, Chaplain J. B. McCleery could happily report that approximately 30 percent of the Protestant inmates regularly attended weekly services, and an additional 15 percent of Roman Catholics held monthly religious meetings.[21]

Because too few chaplains existed to man all the military posts across the nation, ingenious ways were devised to meet the rising demands. The

most immediate innovations came from officers' wives, who organized
their own services. Some conducted Bible lessons and the singing of
sacred music, and others administered the Eucharist to themselves and
their families. Often their efforts spread beyond the confines of the
officer corps to include soldiers and civilian employees of the army as
well as their families. Elizabeth Burt recalled the diverse group that
attended her makeshift church at Fort Bridger, Wyoming, just after the
Civil War. Because no regular chaplain was assigned to the small post,
and enlisted men initially showed reluctance to join what was deemed to
be an officer's domain, she had to limit most of her energies to teaching
catechism to the children.[22]

Over 275 miles to the northeast, Margaret Irvin Carrington created
an even more active group of worshippers at Fort Phil Kearny. She
gleefully declared, "Few are the sanctuaries in civilized states where the
'Magnificat,' 'Gloria in Excelsis,' 'There is a light in the window,' 'Old
Hundred,' and 'Coronation' were supported by a better orchestra or
sung with more spirit."[23] At Fort Shaw, Montana, officer's wife Frances
Roe acted as music director for the chapel, and following each service
she sent a large cake and dozens of eggs to the bandsmen for their weekly
participation.[24]

Civilian clergymen often filled the void when no army chaplain was
available. Sometimes this was handled on an infrequent basis when a
cleric was passing through an area and was invited to hold services. While
stationed with her husband at Fort Bidwell, California, during the mid-
1880s, Elizabeth Burt handled events for the annual visit of the bishop of
the Episcopal diocese.[25] At Fort Bennett, Dakota Territory, soldiers and
their families were ministered to on a weekly basis by Rev. Henry Swift,
who was an Episcopal missionary at the nearby Cheyenne River Indian
Agency. Occasionally Father Rushman would tend to Catholics at the
post, though he had to journey from Fort Pierre to get there.[26]

In cases where army chapels and civilian churches existed in close
proximity to each other, the spirit of cooperation seemed to define their
associations. Rev. Endicott Peabody, founder of Saint Paul's Episcopal
Church of Tombstone and later of Groton School for Boys in Massachusetts, frequently shared services with the chaplain at Fort Huachuca,
Arizona. Likewise, Fort Whipple chaplain Alexander Gilmore worked

with civilians to establish three Protestant churches in Prescott, Arizona, in addition to helping to reorganize the Prescott Sunday School Society. Known as the "Marrying Parson" for officiating at so many military and civilian weddings, Gilmore became a familiar religious leader throughout the territory, and his tent meetings often led to the establishment of other churches.[27] Equally cooperative were Fort D. A. Russell chaplain E. B. Tuttle and his personal friend Rev. Joseph Cook at the adjoining railroad town of Cheyenne, Wyoming. Cook had many friends among the officers at the post, and he filled in for some of Tuttle's religious duties when the latter suffered from a prolonged illness in 1868.[28]

Even when no sizable community existed near a military post, some army chaplains took the initiative to serve civilians who were living on isolated farms and ranches throughout a large region. Eastern Texas Panhandle settlers met with Fort Elliott chaplains James Lavensky and a Reverend Watty during the late 1870s when the successive appointees visited their homesteads, and the families sometimes reciprocated by attending services at the post.[29] Exemplifying the best qualities of this profession was Father Eli Lindesmith, a Catholic chaplain stationed at Fort Keogh, Montana, from 1880 to 1891. He traveled widely to visit isolated civilian families, and some of them within the immediate vicinity of the post became regular members of his congregation. In one case, a Dakota Territory rancher and his wife rode horseback for twenty-one days to have Father Lindesmith baptize their child at the Fort Keogh chapel.[30]

Although the total of authorized army chaplains never exceeded thirty-four at any time in the nineteenth century, the second civilizing effort—the post schools—eventually involved larger numbers of people. Yet, as in the former case, Congress and the War Department were slow to address educational needs within the army. Some officers complained that formal schooling took time away from drill and other duties. Also, it allegedly drained post budgets to provide buildings, teachers, and instructional materials. Most important, however, many of those same officers harbored a deeply elitist view that enlisted men were their inferiors and that their education should be limited to the "school of hard knocks."[31]

The first congressional act for post schools, in 1821, authorized instruction for soldiers' children, creation of fort libraries, and ongoing use of military funds for their upkeep. The regulation went into effect at Fort Atkinson, Nebraska, late that year when Sgt. Thompson Mumford taught the students. In addition to army pay, he received two gallons of whiskey a month, which made him the envy of the garrison.[32] Not until seventeen years later did a second act provide that army chaplains would take charge of the schools where possible and offer courses of study to children and soldiers alike.[33] The real breakthrough to expanding this system came in Congressman James A. Garfield's 1866 proposal requiring the creation of schools and a uniform curriculum at all sizable posts. Because funds were inadequate and the army was in the midst of Reconstruction in the South and the rebuilding of forts in the West immediately after the Civil War, little was done to enforce Garfield's effort. Though delayed in widespread implementation, Garfield's concept found a true champion in George G. Mullins, chaplain of the Twenty-Fifth Infantry. Mullins's hard work paid off when in 1878, General Order No. 24 reaffirmed the 1866 act and ordered that educated enlisted men could be detailed to teaching duties and receive thirty-five cents a day as extra-duty pay. Post children were required to attend school, but enlisted men had the option of enrolling or not. In 1881, Mullins was appointed as officer in charge of education in the army, and under his direction the program quickly expanded.[34]

Although some officers groused about the use of military facilities to educate enlisted men, few opposed that part of the plan that guaranteed free education for their own children. Ranking officers generally enrolled their sons and daughters in post schools for a primary education of reading, writing, and arithmetic. When the children reached their early teenage years, they often traveled east to live with relatives or to attend private boarding schools. Junior-grade officers also aspired to send their children to eastern schools, but the meager pay of a lieutenant or even a captain made this difficult if more than one child in a family was sent away.[35]

The experiences of Martha Gray Wales, daughter of Maj. Charles C. Gray, somewhat mirrored the experiences of other military children during the post–Civil War era. When her father had been stationed at Fort Stevenson and Fort Sully, Dakota Territory, during the late 1860s, no teachers were assigned to the duty, so she received schooling from her mother and the wife of the commanding general, respectively. But when the family was transferred to the sprawling Fort Clark, Texas, during the mid-1870s, she was able to enroll in a civilian school in the adjoining community of Brackettville. Having reached the highest level of school locally available, teenaged Martha accompanied her Aunt Lilly back home to Burlington, Vermont, where she enrolled in a finishing school.[36]

Even as the system matured and more enlisted men were delegated to teach the classes, progress often had to be measured only over the short term. At Fort Fetterman, Wyoming, a school was in session by early 1871, and three years later, records showed fourteen children attending on a regular basis. By the summer of 1874, however, the school closed for unspecified reasons. Efforts to reopen it were repeatedly rebuffed because of budgetary and staffing problems. The entire project ended in 1880, when the commanding officer reported no money in the post coffers to purchase books for the school. Efforts to revive the experiment apparently died at that point.[37]

Rather than rely on a volunteer teacher from among the enlisted men, some civilian and army parents hired contract teachers. Most of these were men and were paid out of a small tuition fund assembled by the parents of the students. During the early 1880s Maria Corlett Riter took the Fort Laramie position at a higher salary than the one offered by Cheyenne schools. She lived and boarded with the officer of the Commissary Department, though the accommodations were only makeshift. During warm months she slept in a small tent-covered dwelling next to the officer's house. The free-standing structure offered some measure of privacy, but it was also a haven for rattlesnakes. Every child at the fort attended her school, and she thoroughly enjoyed the experience. Because of the cold winter and shortage of amenities, however, she did not renew her contract for the following year.[38]

Whether school was taught by an army chaplain, contracted civilian, or women of the garrison, rules usually followed a military regimen. At Fort Union, New Mexico, during the 1880s the daily school call was played on a cavalry trumpet or an infantry bugle. Times for classes were rigidly maintained, absences were reported to the post adjutant, children were required to dress neatly, and teachers were instructed to show no favoritism toward the children of officers over those of enlisted men.

Teachers could also reward and punish the students, but never whip them.[39] For children, the curriculum was generally limited to reading, writing, arithmetic, history, English, spelling, and elementary science. Books purchased from post funds for student use in the 1880s and 1890s included *McGuffie's Revised Reader, Eclectic or Spencerian System of Writing, Ray's New Elementary Arithmetic, McGuffie's Revised Speller,* and *Harvey's Elementary Grammar and Composition.*[40]

A specific regulation at each post segregated children's classes from those offered to enlisted men. Routinely, the former were held during daylight hours, and the latter were offered at night when men would be off duty. Although some of the subject matter was identical for children and adults, soldiers did not want to be embarrassed by sitting alongside youngsters, and parents did not want their sons and daughters mixed together with uncouth troopers.[41] Soldiers also had the opportunity to take higher-level instruction to enhance their chances for promotion and to master skills that could be used in civilian society. Accordingly, Chaplain Theophilus G. Steward offered classes on Spanish, American history, and civil government to black enlisted men of the Twenty-Fifth Infantry at Fort Niobrara, Nebraska. On posts where members of the four black regiments served, such as Fort Concho, Texas, not only were children and adults separated, but also the strict military policy of racial segregation was maintained. Thus, black soldiers had to hold their classes in a separate building from the one used by white children.[42]

Commanding officers possessed discretionary power to enroll civilians' children in post schools. They could accept these students without charging their parents, or they could demand some form of tuition. When this right was extended, civilian employees of the post—scouts, teamsters, woodcutters, mechanics, traders, and so on—always received priority for the limited positions. After them came the nearby farm and ranch families as well as occupants of any towns in the immediate vicinity of the post. Chaplain Allen Allensworth wrote in 1891 that the system should be expanded to include the children of all interested civilians in the area. To do otherwise, he argued, would be tantamount to sentencing thousands of innocent children to a life of illiteracy. Sometimes when a teacher permitted too many civilians' children to enroll, he could run into strong opposition from his commanding officer. In 1889, Lt. Col.

Elmer Otis, commander at Fort Meade, Dakota Territory, ordered the instructor to quit the practice. His reasoning, however, had less to do with budget than with preserving the elitism within the army. Otis finally approved allowing the civilians' sons and daughters to attend the post school if they attended classes only with enlisted men's children and never with those of the officers.[43]

A reversal of this relationship sometimes occurred when a neighboring town already had its own school. David White, chaplain at Fort Hays, Kansas, reported in 1878 that no post school was open at that time because army children were able to attend the public institutions in Hays City free of charge. He made no mention of the educational aspirations of enlisted men, but apparently their needs were not being addressed at that time.[44] Throughout the 1890s army families at Fort Robinson, Nebraska, sent all their sons and daughters to public schools in Crawford, three miles away. The more populous town of Leavenworth, Kansas, hosted several public and private schools in the post–Civil War years. One of those, Saint Mary's Academy, was started in 1868 by Jesuits and was run by the Sisters of Charity. It enrolled a number of army children from Fort Leavenworth, and within nine years a larger school had to be constructed to handle the increased number of civilian and military students.[45]

Although the post education program never seemed to generate the same level of controversy as the chaplains' corps issue did, efforts to expand it late in the century received stiff opposition. Chaplain George G. Mullins, officer in charge of education in the army during the early 1880s, called for creation of a regular corps of professional teachers, an integrated curriculum similar to that offered in eastern college preparatory schools, and increased expenditures for textbooks and supplies. His plan created contention within the powerful Adjutant General's Office and from its director, Adjutant General R. C. Drum, who was totally opposed to the suggestions. Drum especially disliked the proposal of mandatory schooling for all enlisted men, since this would have exempted the rank and file from supervision of line officers for several hours each day.[46] Mullins did win one battle in 1881 when the Quartermaster Department received funds to expand the number of post schools. Hypothetically, at least, after that date commanding officers no longer had to draw resources from other portions of their budgets to keep the schools operational. Three years later, Mullins lost much of his influence when his administrative post was discontinued.[47]

Another persistent voice in the call for expanded schools was Allen Allensworth, black chaplain of the Twenty-Fourth Infantry. Like Mullins, he focused on the welfare of the enlisted men and the procedures by which their lives could be enriched and their value to society increased. In an 1891 essay Allensworth contended that the army could no longer merely train enlistees for war because "it is now a recognized fact that to be a good soldier a man must be a good citizen, therefore the United States Government aims at giving its soldiers a fair English education. It does this not only with a view of utilizing their increased knowledge in its defence [sic], but with the object of returning him to civil life a more intelligent person."[48]

General Order No. 9, created in 1889, seemed to partially answer the pleas of Mullins and Allensworth by requiring all enlisted men who could not pass a literacy test to enroll in some form of classroom instruction during duty hours. But in truth little changed, because many commanding officers chose not to implement the order, and others made only token efforts at enforcing it. Two years later the order was rescinded by a half-hearted "reform measure" that forbade future enlistment of men who could not read, write, or speak English. Even that regulation was widely violated.[49]

The total number of people who enrolled in army schools during the entire nineteenth century can never be known, but partial figures suggest an average for the latter decades of the century. The official annual report of 1879 revealed 866 enlisted men, 834 children of enlisted men, 215 children of officers, and 218 children of civilians enrolled that year. A more generalized estimate for the 1880s and 1890s suggested 1,000 to 2,000 enlisted men actively involved in the educational program at any one time. Matching this against the overall number of about 20,000 enlisted men in that era, makes the 5 to 10 percent of participants seem relatively small, but it should not obscure a more important reality.[50] For most of those who did participate—children and adults, soldiers and civilians—this was their only chance at a formal education on the frontier. How they made specific use of their knowledge is impossible to document, but one can only surmise that most gained some maturity and confidence from the experience.

Closely allied with the concept of the army school was a third "civilizing" institution: the post library. Discussion of this idea began in the early decades of the army's formation, but not until 1821 did a specific directive address the issue. The same act that authorized instruction of soldiers' children and War Department expenditures for the upkeep of schools provided for creation of post libraries and special funds to purchase books and other reading materials. Gen. Winfield Scott, a strong supporter of the reform, wrote the wording into *General Regulations of the Army, 1821*, directing that proceeds for book purchases would be derived from a tax on each fort sutler. Secretary of War Jefferson Davis suspended this regulation in 1857, but it was restored four years later, only to again fall victim to Civil War exigencies. During the post–Civil War era the old, inefficient system was revived, but as some forts became larger and mail service improved, officers found ingenious ways to expand library facilities for the use of all people.[51]

Duties of post librarians remained much the same during both halves of the century. They ordered materials, cataloged them, judged suitability of publications, recorded names of patrons, assessed fines for damaged and late materials, made repairs on necessary items, enforced segregation of officers' hours of use from those of enlisted men, and sometimes conducted discussions of books and ideas. Since no regulation established the credentials of librarians, each commanding officer could make the assignment. Frequently it was the post treasurer, the chaplain, or an enlisted man who simultaneously served as teacher. In rarer cases the surgeon or an officer's wife might fill the position. No automatic financial remuneration came with the job, but any military personnel assigned to that duty could be compensated by relinquishment of some other assigned duties.[52]

As with the problems faced by chaplains and teachers, librarians found themselves to be a low priority when it came to assigning the limited space on a military post. The first library at Fort Richardson, Texas, was in a tent alongside a muddy creek. In 1872 it was moved into the commissary, and two years later into a nicely constructed picket building near the adjutant's office, where it remained throughout the life of the fort. Similarly, the Fort Concho library began in the hallway of the chaplain's quarters, but by 1876 it had found more spacious accommodations in the headquarters building.[53] By the time newspaper correspondent William E. Annin visited Fort Robinson, Nebraska, in 1883, he found a comfortable library that occupied half of the downstairs of the administration building. Sometimes the quality of the structure was not the problem, but rather that the facilities inside were inadequate. At Fort Wadsworth, Dakota Territory, the library was housed in a nice brick building that had been built for a different purpose. Yet because it was outfitted with only a single-burner oil lamp to illuminate the forty-foot by twenty-foot space, reading of the materials was almost impossible.[54]

Although the contents of a post collection were generally determined by the librarian and ultimately approved by the commanding officer, purchases had to reflect the reading habits of a diverse audience. Classical literature, incorporating the works of authors such as Charles Dickens, Sir Walter Scott, Shakespeare, Nathaniel Hawthorne, and James Fenimore Cooper, appeared in all collections. Religious studies were also standard fare, and many of them were donated to forts by missionary societies and the Young Men's Christian Association. Beyond improving the spiritual life of soldiers, other books were intended to improve their patriotism and sense of citizenship. Histories and biographies seemed to be popular choices among officers and enlisted men alike, although they leaned heavily toward military topics and presidential memoria. The Fort Laramie library of the 1870s was typical of the categories of distribution. Of its total book holdings, approximately 40 percent were literature, 30 percent history, and 20 percent biography. Religious studies were not reported by percentage, but apparently they were not a sizable component of the holdings.[55]

Two other small collections served specialized reading interests at some posts. Fort Ridgely, Minnesota, contained an impressive set of law books, including *Blackstone's Commentaries*, *Wheaton's International Law*, and *The Story of the Constitution of the United States*. In deference to the romantic reading tastes of officers and their wives, the Fort Laramie library contained numerous books by celebrated women authors of the era. Louisa May Alcott, Zadel (Barnes) Buddington, Maria Elizabeth (Jourdan) Westmoreland, Mary Louisa (Stewart) Molesworth, Katherine Sarah (Gadsden) McQuoid, and Lilian (Headland) Spender well articulated the ideals of the cult of true womanhood with their stress on the values of purity, piety, and domesticity. European female writers of greater acclaim, and three disguised by pseudonyms—George Eliot, George Sand, and Ouida—were also represented in the holdings.[56]

Periodicals were likewise an important part of each library collection, and they received continuous attention from patrons because new issues arrived weekly, monthly, and quarterly. Among the most popular were standard literary and current events magazines such as *Harper's Weekly*, *Scribner's*, *Atlantic*, *Harper's Monthly Magazine*, *North American Review*, *Century*, *Cosmopolitan*, and *Southern Literary Messenger*. More specialized were the service publications such as *Cavalry Journal*, *Infantry Journal*, *Journal of the Military Service Institution of the United States*, and especially the *Army and Navy Journal*. These contained useful information about military life and included articles written by officers whom the soldiers knew firsthand. The *Army and Navy Journal* also featured letters and brief articles from enlisted men, ranging from their experiences on patrols to recommendations for improving garrison life.[57]

Among the most popular of all library items were the various city newspapers, which were handled on a subscription basis. By 1880, Fort Concho received daily newspapers such as the *New York Herald*, *New York Tribune*, *Saint Louis Globe*, *Saint Louis Democrat*, *Cincinnati Commercial*, and *Louisville Courier-Journal*. Even though these sometimes reached the post a month after their publication, military patrons considered them to be filled with the most current information available on many topics. European and foreign-language publications printed in the United States also had broad appeal in a frontier army that contained so many ethnic enlistees. Issues of *Illustrated Zeitung*, *Chevron l'Illustration*, and various British publications such as *Blackwood's Magazine*, *Edinburgh Review*, *New London Monthly*, and *London Punch* dotted the shelves of most larger libraries. Perhaps the most ubiquitous of all was *Irish World*, which was published in New York City and bridged the news gap between Irish Americans and the motherland. For lowbrow tastes, the *Police Gazette* provided a flirtation with violence and unsubstantiated innuendo, but it was barred at some military posts.[58]

Over time, some post libraries grew to significant size. By 1873 the Fort Davis collection consisted of approximately twelve hundred books, plus numerous journals and newspapers. At the same time, the Fort

Richardson library boasted over eighteen hundred volumes. In the case of the large Fort Concho holdings, the post librarian made sure that even the soldiers stationed at outlying camps were able to take some of the books with them while they were on prolonged assignment. Military installations that contained medical officers also had access to more specialized medical publications. The surgeon at Fort Davis, Texas, loaned the fifty books in his collection to interested individuals, although it is doubtful that he had many patrons, considering the highly technical nature of the items.[59]

Among the forts that hosted one or more of the four black regiments during the post–Civil War era, libraries reflected an interest in African-American life. This was evidenced in the number of sustained subscriptions to eastern newspapers edited by blacks for blacks. By the end of the century, when Fort Robinson, Nebraska, housed the Ninth and Tenth cavalries consecutively, it received five African American periodicals— *The Colored American Magazine, Voice of the Negro, A.M.E. Church Review, A.M.E.Z. Church Review,* and *Howard's American*—plus three daily newspapers, eleven school papers, and dozens of weekly newspapers. The latter group included the *New York Age, Richmond Planet, Cleveland Gazette,* and *Indianapolis Freeman.*[60] Because black regiments were socially isolated from their eastern brothers and sisters, these publications played a major role in tying the military and civilian communities together. National issues, as well as local events, were adequately covered in the city newspapers, but each of the black regiments also produced its own newspapers and information sheets. In 1892, black chaplain Henry V. Plummer initiated the *Fort Robinson Weekly Bulletin* and managed the *Omaha Progress.* Both covered stories of interest to the larger African American population as well as specific concerns raised by black soldiers. The performances of these four regiments proved a source of great pride among their eastern kinsmen, and the stories of racial injustice were eye-opening.[61]

Regardless of the regiment involved, libraries seemed to be popular places on military reservations, even for illiterate soldiers who could at least peruse the pictures. Incomplete reports for 1881 revealed weekly attendance of 250 patrons at the Fort Concho library. Col. Philippe Régis de Trobriand observed an even more frequent use of the collection at Fort Stevenson, Dakota Territory, during the winter months of 1868 when other social and recreational outlets were limited by bad weather. Surprisingly, the number of books available at that time did not even surpass 60 volumes, but their number grew to 850 during the following year.[62] One former member of the Eighth Cavalry stationed at Fort Stanton, New Mexico, later recalled how no books were available during the formative years of that station. Desperate for reading material, enlisted men shared hometown newspapers that were occasionally sent through the mails by friends back east. According to his recollection, every man in the troop reread the valued newspapers until they were entirely worn out. As in the case with post schools and chapels, libraries could also be opened to civilian use if the commanding officer gave his consent.[63]

Some observers credited the libraries with elevating the character of soldiers and reducing the amount of antisocial behavior. Sgt. H. H. McConnell credited the joint effort of the chaplains and librarians with bringing a more civilized tone to Fort Richardson and producing better-quality citizens. Surgeon D. G. Caldwell, at nearby Fort Griffin, praised the library for introducing the troopers to "good readable novels" and turning them away from alcoholic excesses.[64] Pvt. Hervey Johnson found the Fort Laramie reading room to be a protected haven amid the rigorous demands of daily duty, and other soldiers joined him in what they considered to be a rare sanctuary. Members of the Twenty-fifth Infantry demonstrated their devotion to the Fort Davis library when, in 1873, they rescued all twelve hundred volumes from a raging fire.[65]

Although libraries supplied most of the reading materials on military posts, other means were used to supplement the collections. Authorities at Fort Union, New Mexico, established an exchange program with other forts in the territory to circulate magazines and newspapers more widely. When a sizable town existed within the fort's vicinity, soldiers could often use the civilian library. Surgeon J. H. Frantz reported in 1870 that Fort Sanders did not need to form a post library because the town of Laramie had a well-established Literary and Library Association, which made its facilities available to soldiers.[66] The most basic method of sharing resources occurred when officers and their families loaned favorite books to each other, often with the idea of sharing a discussion about the material. Elizabeth Custer recalled that her husband shared his small personal library with enlisted men while stationed at Fort Riley, Kansas, in the late

1860s. She stated that even the fashion pages of *Harper's Bazaar* "were not scorned in that dearth of reading, by the men about our fireside."[67]

The most important means of supplementing library holdings came when individual regiments and even individual companies purchased their own books, magazines, and newspapers. In 1875, Fort McPherson, Nebraska, possessed no official library, but two companies of Fifth Infantry owned a total of 387 books. When a newspaper reporter visited Fort Elliott, Texas, in 1879, he found that each cavalry company had its own case of books in the enlisted men's barracks. Furthermore, on that cold day, many of the men were gathered around a large stove reading from the selections.[68] Because these books belonged to army units that were periodically relocated to new assignments, they went with the units instead of remaining as part of a post library. The original library established at Fort D. A. Russell, Wyoming, in 1867 ceased to exist six years later when the Fifth Cavalry departed for Arizona and took the entire collection. When the Twenty-fifth Infantry replaced the recently transferred Ninth Cavalry at Fort Davis, it found a bill for $56.45 to cover books ordered by the latter for its regimental holdings.[69]

Even though the frontier army was never considered to be fertile ground for social experimentation, it was not entirely devoid of a desire to improve the lives of its soldiers. For every officer who opposed the reforms there were equal numbers who supported the expansion of the three primary "civilizing institutions." Chapels, schools, and libraries provided the means to "reform the man"—to teach him valuable skills, strengthen his self-esteem, and make him a better citizen. Well served were the immigrant soldiers who gained a better command of the English language, farm-boy recruits who mastered enough skills to land good jobs outside the army, and children who secured a basic moral and academic training that otherwise would not have been available to them. On a more practical level, the three institutions helped produce better soldiers. George G. Mullins's 1880 claim may have been overly generous, but it was not without some foundation: "The school-men were never found in the guard-house or arraigned before a court-martial, and they formed a large per cent of the garrison. The men were happier, cleaner, healthier, because of the school, for it was a grand sanitary measure in purifying the moral atmosphere."[70]

Military men who had campaigned for these reforms throughout the nineteenth century could not have summarized the results in more promising fashion. Whatever else they had gained from the three institutions, the participants had certainly become better soldiers, and in the final analysis, that is what the army demanded most.

CHAPTER NINE

Sharpening the Eagle's Talons for Domestic Duties

THE ARMY IN PUBLIC RELIEF WORK AND IN PROTECTING THE NATIONAL PARKS

At the beginning of the nineteenth century, most Americans perceived the army's primary role to be the maintenance of defense along the coastlines and on the frontier, but with a minimum of expense. Most citizens therefore remained content with the concept of an auxiliary militia composed of citizen-soldiers who could muster at any time to supplement the small regular army and deal with the nation's external or domestic threats. Accordingly, they supported congressional efforts to restrict the size of the full-time military, its budget, and its list of duties. Yet by midcentury, the army had well established its role in many domestic concerns. This gradual evolution of a "peacetime role" for the army came not from a sustained legislative drive, but from small, precedent-setting cases that found favor with the American public. Two activities—relief work during natural disasters and protection of federal resources—became among the most visible and popular areas for expansion of military authority. Not only were these "humanitarian efforts" generally approved by civilians, but they also provided officers and their men with a sense of self-satisfaction that they rarely could receive from more mundane duties.

In addition to early-nineteenth-century budgetary concerns and national apprehension about the involvement of large standing armies in the civilian sphere, several other intangible factors initially limited government relief work, and they would not be overcome until after the Civil War. Many Americans held a religiously based view that God created natural disasters to punish iniquity and to jolt transgressors into repentance of their sins. In that view of divine justice there was little intrinsic sympathy for the afflicted, and certainly no mandate for massive government aid to end the suffering. Another vantage point stressed that in times of major disaster that left large numbers homeless, diseased, or financially spent, private charity alone should meet the emergency. By this line of reasoning the charity should be briefly applied and then quickly withdrawn before it created a cycle of expectation and dependency among the recipients. A third perspective affirmed the apparent dangers of elected officials' becoming too compassionate and thus risking long-term social damage to the republic. Adherents of this philosophy contended that if various components of local, state, and federal government assumed official relief roles, all would drastically expand their budgets by rationalizing that they were preparing for potential calamities. These budgets allegedly would become bloated and inevitably would be drained off into other governmental expenditures over which taxpayers had no control. Furthermore, politicians at all levels could potentially misuse this largesse for the sake of their own reelection.

Given the depth of philosophical opposition to expanded federal powers, it is readily apparent that only crisis situations could force a gradual experimentation with the government's relief role. The original exemplars were indeed confined to helping small populations, within limited areas, for brief periods of time and with relatively small expenditures of federal money. The initial precedent was set in 1803, when a devastating fire leveled much of Portsmouth, New Hampshire, an important docking and supply center for the U.S. Navy. Although Congress did not authorize moneys for rebuilding the town, it granted a one-year extension on the repayment of federal bonds. It followed suit with similar arrangements for Norfolk, Virginia, in 1804, Portsmouth again in 1807, and New York City in 1836. All seemed to have been favored with this special consideration because their naval facilities were deemed important to national defense.[1]

When the great series of earthquakes struck the Mississippi River valley between December 16, 1811, and February 7, 1812, Missouri communities such as Cathersville were completely leveled, and New Madrid, second largest town in the territory, was severely damaged. After several months' delay, Congress approved a bill authorizing landowners to exchange flooded and silted property for 160 to 640 acres of federal land, depending upon the size of their original holdings.[2] Yet it was not until 1827 that a more direct financial connection was established between national authorities and a community devastated by a natural disaster. During February of that year a fire consumed a large section of Alexandria, Virginia, leaving most citizens homeless and the business establishments in shambles. Following acrimonious debate, Congress finally approved a direct appropriation of twenty thousand dollars to aid in feeding, clothing, and sheltering "the indigent sufferers." Congressional supporters defended the special grant by reasoning that the town of Alexandria was then a part of the federal district of Washington, D.C., and hence eligible for special aid, since it could not likely seek help from any state government. But among the several dozen communities that sought federal disaster relief in the pre–Civil War era, only these few received any consideration.[3]

Expansion of the size and power of the national government during the Civil War helped usher in a different public view of federal responsibilities to citizens. Large numbers of Union veterans who had served their country faithfully during its darkest hour eventually found themselves rewarded with cash bonuses, military bounty lands, and service pensions.[4] Creation of the Freedmen's Bureau during the last month of the war also provided the nation with an unparalleled example of government relief work on a grand scale. Employed throughout the Southern states during the era of Reconstruction, the Freedmen's Bureau provided schools, health care, and flood and famine relief to tens of thousands of poor people without regard to their race.[5]

The new era of expanded federal relief projects that was initiated in the aftermath of the Civil War also contrasted sharply with the prewar era on another important point. The army had played virtually no role in relief work during the first half of the century except for occasional distribution of emergency rations on the overland trails and emergency medical care to ill and injured civilians in remote sections of the frontier. The change that now came would be immediate, continuous, and dramatic in its impact on the rest of the century. Despite its relatively small size, inadequate budgets, and dispersal throughout all sections of the country, the army represented the one federal agency capable of responding to natural disasters with some degree of organization and alacrity. By necessity, not by grand plan, it rose to meet those challenges and left its mark of social activism for twentieth-century generations who would greatly expand the relief responsibilities of not only the regular army but also the state national guards.

Representative of this new activist role were the following examples of direct army intervention: the Chicago fire in 1871, the yellow fever epidemics in Memphis and Shreveport in 1873, the Mississippi River floods in 1874, a yellow fever outbreak in the South in 1878, the Missouri River floods in 1881, the Mississippi River floods in 1882, Mississippi and Ohio River floods in 1884, the Johnstown flood in 1889, the Seattle fire in 1889, the Indian Territory drought of 1890, Minnesota forest fires in 1894, Saint Louis tornadoes in 1896, Mississippi River and Rio Grande floods in 1897, and the Galveston hurricane of 1900.[6] The pattern of military involvement in each of these was fairly similar. Officers assessed the immediate relief needs, secured the supplies, delivered them to the scene, and maintained order if civil officials could not do so. For the most part, these officers turned the supplies over to local authorities and allowed them to make the actual distributions. Because this system preserved the concept of local civilian control and maintained the spirit of civilian voluntarism, few serious complaints were lodged against the various army missions.[7]

Not until the mid-1870s did the western frontier army face a major relief crisis that attracted national attention. The setting was the Central and Northern Plains, a vast area that had witnessed previous calls for government relief efforts in manmade disasters. Typical of these earlier pleas was the March 1869 inspection report of Col. N. H. Davis, who recommended distribution of army food and supplies to settlers within the Solomon, Saline, and Republican Valleys of Kansas. These homesteaders had suffered acutely from Indian attacks, and in Colonel Davis's estimation their ability to remain in the region rested upon the immediate delivery of supplies. But like most other requests for emergency relief expressed by officers stationed on the Plains between 1865 and 1900, this one never went beyond the lower departmental levels and was never sent to legislative delegations in Washington, D.C.[8] Senior commanders knew that Congress already had a system in place for handling private claims for Indian depredations, and though the process for compensation was slow, the government was not anxious to tie expensive relief payments to the course of Indian wars.[9]

Army officers demonstrated greater determination in dealing with short-term weather disasters that struck limited areas and affected relatively small numbers of people. During the winter of 1872, when snows interrupted the flow of Union Pacific freight and passenger trains through western Nebraska and Wyoming, local military commanders exercised good judgment in aiding weather victims with food supplies. They drew army rations from their stores and delivered them to snow-blocked trains and maintenance crews at isolated camps along the track. At the same time, the senior officer at Fort Stambaugh made a daring delivery to starving miners at South Pass City, Wyoming, and evacuated some of the worst medical cases to his post for proper care. When coal could not be delivered to the desperate civilian population at Cheyenne, the troops at nearby Fort D. A. Russell hauled their own surplus coal into town to be used by citizens at no cost. Although important in setting further precedents for direct army relief roles, these events went virtually unnoticed in the national press.[10]

More comprehensive and sustained was the army and government response to a natural disaster that devastated the Plains counties of Kansas, Nebraska, Colorado, and the Dakotas during 1874–75. The culprit was the Rocky Mountain locust, barely two inches long and, when confronted individually, hardly a threat to man or commercial crops. But the infestation that began to appear during the summer of 1874 numbered in the tens—perhaps hundreds—of millions, and no science or technology could slow its destructive progress. Farmers located in the prairie areas just to the east of the ninety-eighth meridian had encountered this menace on several occasions during the 1850s and 1860s, but the situation was now dramatically different.[11] The locusts came in far greater numbers than they ever had at any previous time. Furthermore, the spring and summer had been especially promising to the region's agriculturalists, who anticipated bumper crops of corn, wheat, and oats. Recently arrived families were especially vulnerable to the crisis because they had invested virtually all their assets in land and equipment and had nothing on which to fall back.[12]

Despite the fury of the summer onslaught, denial of the problem dominated newspaper editorials and speeches by state and territorial officials. Because community newspapers assumed a booster spirit for their regions, their editors were loath to print negative stories that would be circulated in the East and that might dissuade settlers and business-men from relocating there. Political leaders echoed a kindred sentiment and cautioned settlers not to overdramatize the events. The *Beatrice (Nebraska) Express* emphatically denied any significant problem and in an August 1874 editorial asserted that no people had left western Nebraska except a few who routinely wintered with relatives in eastern parts of the state. Even after the crisis had reached epic proportions, the *Nebraska Farmer* reprinted an article from the *Kansas Farmer* instructing settlers not to become discouraged or hysterical and, above all, not to request outside help that might send a defeatist message to the rest of the nation.[13]

By September 1874 conditions had deteriorated so severely in some counties of western Nebraska and Kansas that relief efforts could no longer be delayed. Drought had joined hands with the locust invasion to deliver a virtual knockout punch to the settlers. During that month, Nebraska's Governor Robert Furnas helped organize a private agency known as the Nebraska Relief and Aid Society. Governor Thomas A. Osborn of Kansas supported a similarly conceived Kansas Central Relief Committee in October, and each of the other afflicted states and territories followed suit within that month.[14] Furnas, like other political leaders, initially worried that he had no authority to use state funds for the sake of selected counties, and he therefore hoped that voluntary contributions from concerned citizens would meet the need. Public sympathy did translate into immediate action, for throughout the autumn private donations to the Nebraska effort totaled some thirty-seven thousand dollars in cash and thirty thousand dollars in supplies.[15]

Unfortunately, the private charity drive could not approximate anything near the level of aid that was needed. Furnas finally turned to the state legislature in early 1875 and requested the issuance of fifty thousand dollars in state bonds for the purchase of supplies for the endangered counties. The legislature approved his plan and set an important precedent for state action in disaster relief. Despite a promising beginning for private charity and state subsidy, the delivery process bogged down in poorly coordinated efforts. Furthermore, the collection of seed grain to help the farmers plant a new spring crop fell woefully short of projected needs. Even if the families could be sufficiently fed and clothed to survive the winter, they would have had no economic future on their homesteads and would certainly have had to abandon them in large numbers come the following spring.[16]

The catalyst for requesting federal help began with Maj. James S. Brisbin's inspection of the southwestern sections of Nebraska during September 1874. His reports, filed with the Adjutant General's Office during the following month, painted a bleak picture of overall conditions and an even more heart-rending portrayal of individual cases. At a dugout near the town of Arapahoe he found a desperate family who had just consumed a dinner of only two small pieces of bread and a watermelon. They were now reduced to a pint of milk and no other food staples. The elder daughter indicated that they had survived on a mere twenty dollars in cash since the previous April. With the exception of a few squash and melons, they had not been able to harvest any crops. At most other dwellings, the major found parents and children dressed in ragged, filthy clothing and already showing the effects of malnutrition. A majority of these poor farmers even lacked ammunition to hunt rabbits, and Brisbin recommended that two companies of cavalry be dispatched to kill fresh game for the starving people.[17]

Major Brisbin's firsthand observation of the problems gave credence to the extensiveness of the crisis and prompted Great Plains political leaders finally to seek help from federal authorities. An important key to the coordination of state and national relief efforts was the role assumed by Gen. Edward O. C. Ord, commander of the Department of the Platte, headquartered in Omaha. Ord joined the Nebraska Relief and Aid Society at its inception and, as vice-chairman, supervised all of its field operations. Because of his precise knowledge of the daily activities of the organization, he was also among the first to recognize that private charity and state aid were inadequate for the task. He was well aware that even when goods were delivered to the destitute, they often constituted low grades of flour and bacon, cast-off clothing, old blankets, and the cheapest types of groceries and dry goods.[18]

On October 24, Ord wrote to the adjutant general requesting authorization to send military personnel into the four worst stricken counties of Nebraska to distribute army stocks of flour and pork. Additionally seeking permission to use army transportation to deliver the supplies, he pointed out that narrow debates about the efficacy of this expanded military power should be tabled, lest hundreds of people die.[19] At first the commissary general of subsistence opposed the recommendation on the grounds that the army had already expended its subsistence authorization for the fiscal year, and in deference to the lack of a special relief budget, Secretary of War William W. Belknap upheld that decision. In the interim, however, appeals were pouring into Washington, D.C., at such an alarming rate that budgetary realities could no longer serve as the guiding hand behind relief policies.[20]

Secretary of War Belknap felt the public pressure, and on November 11, 1874, he presented part of Ord's plan to President Ulysses S. Grant. It called for the Army Quartermaster Department at Jeffersonville, Indiana, to ship several thousand "forage caps, lined and unlined, sack coats, jackets, boots and booties, and about one thousand unserviceable great coats which could be issued without much loss to the United States."[21] Belknap further remarked that even though no obvious precedent existed for dispersing such a large quantity of army clothing to civilians, this was a dire emergency that warranted immediate action. President Grant approved the operation on the following day, and the surplus clothing was sent directly to the hardest hit areas of the Central and Northern Plains. All told, during the winter of 1874–75 the army distributed 10,004 infantry coats, 6,285 other coats, 20,664 pairs of shoes and boots, 8,454 woolen blankets, and similar numbers of socks, hats, and trousers.[22]

The matter of food rations was handled in much the same manner after General Ord reported imminent starvation in the stricken areas. To establish the urgency of the crisis, the general relied heavily upon a report submitted early in November by Maj. Nathan A. M. Dudley, commander at Fort McPherson, Nebraska. Dudley had toured many of the same Nebraska counties visited by Major Brisbin over a month earlier and had found even worse conditions. He estimated that in Furnas

County alone, one-fifth of the thirteen hundred residents needed immediate food deliveries, and perhaps three-fourths would require some form of help by the following spring. In a most dire prediction, Dudley contended that hundreds would die during the winter if food was not sent immediately.[23]

The preponderance of evidence and Dudley's magnanimous offer to pay for relief supplies out of his own pocket struck a responsive chord in Washington. Congress passed a bill on February 10, 1875, appropriating $150,000 to guarantee immediate food shipments to all areas in question.[24] Ord would coordinate the logistics of the massive operation, and he would rely on junior officers to make sure that the food reached truly needy families. Already, younger officers such as Lt. Theodore E. True were in the field transporting army clothing to the settlers, and now they would add food distribution to their duties. True and his fellow officers worked closely with civilian officials to compile lists of eligible recipients and to prevent fraud in the process. Unfortunately, complaints poured in that some destitute families were bypassed while less needy ones successfully lied their way into getting free food. Other detractors pointed out that food shipments were delayed beyond their promised delivery dates, and some local businessmen worried that a long-term relief program might prevent customers from buying their goods.[25]

Despite these complaints, which arose during the confusing early stages of the operation, the army appeared to be much the hero of the story within a few months. Somewhat surprisingly, the most important and lingering opposition to Ord's herculean endeavor came from a fellow departmental commander and from Ord's superior, Gen. Philip Sheridan, commander of the Military Division of the Missouri. From his office in Chicago, Sheridan bellowed, "There may be a good deal of suffering in portions of Nebraska, but if the Government takes any advanced steps to relieve it, the suffering will be magnified a hundred times more than it really is." Although he approved Major Dudley's original outlay of supplies, he questioned any future generosity, which could lead to a continuous drain on the military budget and combat training time.[26] Unfortunately for many settlers in the Dakotas and western Minnesota, departmental commander Gen. Alfred Terry mirrored Sheridan's caution, and he only reluctantly implemented the army relief program. Despite public outcries against his seeming insensitivity, Terry expended only 72 percent of the rations and clothing allowance made available to him by Congress.[27] Clearly, the determined action of General Ord was unique in this crisis, and it set the tone for future large-scale army relief efforts in the twentieth century. Before his operations officially ended in western Nebraska on September 1, 1875, Ord had presided over the issuance of tons of surplus clothing as well as 1,081,122 ration units to over twenty-nine thousand hungry settlers.[28]

In his study of these events almost a hundred years later, historian Gilbert Fite concluded that the army was the best equipped federal agency to handle this crisis. Because it had the organization, transportation facilities, experience, and supplies to accomplish the mission, it likewise superseded the performance of all state and local aid programs. Furthermore, the officers stood above the bitterly partisan politics and local pressures that came to dominate most of the private relief efforts.[29]

Despite its basking in the light of public praise, the War Department was not anxious to take on this kind of duty every time someone pronounced a crisis. When the locusts returned during the summer of 1875, settlers again petitioned for army aid only to be met with stern resistance in Congress and among senior military officers. Because the infestation did not reach the same destructive levels as in the previous year, and because state governments were able to handle most of the problems, the issue was not pressed nationally. Furthermore, General Ord had been transferred to the Department of Texas during March, and the settlers had lost their foremost advocate.[30]

When a second great calamity—drought—struck western Nebraska and surrounding areas between 1890 and 1895, the probability of federal aid again seemed to be on everyone's mind. Farmers' lives and livelihoods were threatened not only by the new cycle of extreme aridity but also by the depression of 1893–97, which produced a high rate of farm foreclosures. Populist politics excited agriculturalists throughout the region and led to many victories in state houses and local governments alike. In Nebraska, Populists initially elected a sympathetic governor and legislature and helped organize the Nebraska State Relief Commission to deal with the drought problems. Even when more conservative Republicans returned to power in the elections of 1894, they continued to support some state economic aid and cooperated with the Nebraska State Relief Commission in dispensing privately donated goods.[31] Unlike the situation during the locust plague of the mid-1870s, no sustained public outcry for federal assistance through the army accompanied the second calamity. This time the regional and national debate centered more on economic policies than on food distribution, and the army was in no position to deal with the former.

Another type of natural disaster that sometimes elicited a military response was the numerous prairie fires that easily broke out among the dry grasses of the Great Plains. Soldiers were quick to respond to these emergencies whenever they threatened army property or lives. During a summer 1855 march from Fort Leavenworth, Kansas, to a new station near Santa Fe, elements of the Third Infantry found themselves in the midst of a huge fire accidentally started by one of their own number. The conflagration quickly spread through the dry grasses and consumed most of the camp equipment and weapons of five hundred soldiers. Four or five soldiers received wounds from exploding cartridges, and several others were treated for burns before they could extinguish the huge blaze.[32] Twenty-one years later the entire garrison at Fort Richardson, Texas, fought a large prairie fire that had been ignited by a lightning strike. Because they had no hoses, transportable water barrels, or other equipment, the men could only construct a fire break by clearing a path of all combustible materials. Unfortunately, gusty winds carried the flames beyond the cleared area, and the fire burned through fort property before extinguishing itself along the banks of Lost Creek.[33]

These kinds of cases were repeated perhaps hundreds of times in the Trans-Mississippi West during the latter half of the nineteenth century, but they remained only of localized interest. In many of these cases soldiers rode out to warn settlers of approaching fires and then helped them fight the menace with shovels and burlap bags.[34] No red tape or precise interpretations of army authority blocked these emergency actions, nor did they incur any opposition from War Department superiors in the capital. Instead, local public praise followed in the wake of these benevolent activities.[35]

The major exception to these spontaneous reactions to localized fire threats was an organized firefighting endeavor sanctioned by the War

Department in the postfrontier era. During the summer of 1910, northern Idaho was plagued by a series of interconnected forest fires sparked by electrical storms that ignited dry tinder. By early July, over three thousand separate fires were reported across the state, and the legislature approved appropriations to hire several thousand civilians for temporary fire-fighting duty. Just when the two-month effort seemed to bring the problem under some measure of control, fierce windstorms hit the region on August 20 and made conditions far worse. In the Coeur d'Alene National Forest district alone, one-third of the timber was burned, and seventy people were killed. The district forest ranger not only called for more civilian help, but he also requested that the War Department authorize the use of several companies of soldiers. Approval came quickly, though it was limited to only troops who were already stationed in the area.[36]

Among the military personnel dispatched into the crisis was Company G of the Twenty-fifth Infantry, whose black soldiers took up positions around the endangered town of Avery. In addition to serving on the fire lines, they presided over evacuation of women, children, and some men to safer areas. They loaded the frightened passengers aboard two special trains and guarded the doors of each car to prevent a panicked rush. Some of the soldiers stayed aboard the trains to preserve order and to put out fires that would surely flare up along the way because the track would carry them through the center of one approaching fire. The trains reached safety without losing anyone, but not before the passengers had suffered terribly from the heat and mental strain. Those who remained in town soon found themselves at the focal point of two converging fires that came roaring down the canyons. Soldiers and civilians alike desperately organized bucket brigades, dug pools for water storage, and created backfires as they grimly faced the approaching menace. Just as the converging walls of flame struck the path of the backfires at about 3:00 P.M. on August 21, the wind suddenly subsided and deprived the inferno of its energy. Exhaustion, not celebration, seemed to greet the defining movement. Even though the army relief role had been relatively small, considering that thousands of civilians had helped fight the fires and that the federal government had expended almost eight hundred thousand dollars in the crisis, the effort gained praise for the officers and men who had gallantly risked their lives.[37]

Another larger urban relief effort that had occurred only four years before the Idaho fires had generated some negative feelings toward the army. Precisely because the 1906 San Francisco earthquake and fire involved so many people, was so widespread in its devastation, and left the normal chain of civic command in such shambles, it had to be dealt with by instinct instead of being left to some plodding, prearranged disaster plan. The precise extent of the devastation would not be confirmed for two months, but even on the first day of the crisis citizens could already appreciate the fury of nature. By the final estimate, over 500 people were killed, over 5,000 were injured, 200,000 of the city's 450,000 residents were rendered homeless, and no fewer than 28,188 buildings were destroyed. Final computations placed real estate and personal property losses at five hundred million dollars, and the infrastructure of the city would have to be completely rebuilt.[38]

The sprawling city by the bay had not been built to withstand earthquakes, nor did it possess any contingency plan to handle such widespread destruction. Striking at 5:13 A.M. on April 18, 1906, the tremors brought walls down on sleeping residents, broke gas mains that fueled fires, made the streets instantly impassable with debris, and turned the entire population into a panicked and seemingly leaderless community. From his residence on fashionable Nob Hill, Brig. Gen. Frederick Funston, temporary commander of the Department of the Pacific, immediately called out the garrisons at the Presidio and smaller Fort Mason. Numbering less than two thousand men, the soldiers were certainly not equal to the task before them, but they were the first organized body of the government to react under unified direction.[39]

Funston, without any approval from his superiors in Washington, D.C., and without any prior communication from San Francisco political leaders, set up his headquarters at Fort Mason, near the center of the city. In the first hours of confused response, some soldiers failed to receive the order, and a few delayed the call to arms as they stopped to help injured civilians. Potential trouble also developed with Col. Charles Morris, commanding officer at the Presidio, who was no friend of Funston. Upon receiving the order to muster the troops and make them available for civilian relief efforts, Morris allegedly retorted, "Go back and tell that newspaperman [Funston] that he had better look up his army regulations, and there he will find that nobody but the President of the United States in person can order regular troops into any city."[40] Fortunately for everyone concerned, a Lieutenant Long, who had delivered the order to Morris, now exceeded his authority by directing that the bugler sound the call to arms, and then he personally led the assembled troops into the downtown district.[41]

Soon after establishing his headquarters and ordering troops into various rescue and firefighting operations, Funston went to the Hall of Justice, where he met with Mayor Eugene Schmitz. Their consultation was cordial, as both men sensed the need to work together closely and decisively; neither wanted to debate fine points of legal precedents, exact jurisdictions, or who would have ultimate authority over each thorny matter that was sure to arise. In fact, Funston clearly acknowledged at the first meeting that his troops would be placed under the "guidance" of Police Chief Jeremiah Dinan, even though they would retain their own officers in official command.[42]

The army's role was widely praised during the initial days of the crisis, and deservedly so. Squads prepared large amounts of food from army stores, often cooking and serving the fare in primitive, open-air environments because those were the only facilities available amid the vast throngs of homeless people. Soldiers also maintained a regular transport service from the outskirts of the city, bringing food and other supplies from businesses that were still intact, such as the city's largest bakery. They dug public latrines, rescued injured people from collapsed buildings, and helped fight the raging fires, which posed a greater threat to life and property than did the original earthquake.[43] Within several days they had established forty-two telegraph offices and seventy telephone stations, not for private use but to facilitate rapid communication between military officers, civilian officials, railroad freight offices, relief stations, and other key points.[44] Maj. C. R. Krauthoff of the Subsistence Department assumed charge of all food supplies and managed their delivery into the city, including goods brought by ships into the badly damaged port facilities. Col. G. H. Torney of the Medical Department oversaw all sanitary work within the temporary camps and within the broader city limits. Col. W. H. Heuer of the Corps of Engineers received orders to begin the immediate restoration of water supplies to help halt the fires and to provide a purified drinking source.[45]

Funston divided the city into various districts and assigned senior officers to coordinate efforts in each of them. They served as Funston's "eyes" in this campaign and constantly updated him on changing conditions from the field. His senior officers also received frequent eyewitness reports from their subordinates, first through military runners and later through the partially restored telegraph and telephone services. Army surgeon Wilson T. Davidson later recalled that to his amazement army personnel were able to respond quickly to medical crises because of the integrated communication system and because the doctors were not afraid to exercise their own discretion. Davidson described how he procured tents, bedding, and food from army stores and from the Red Cross and how he helped establish camps for injured and displaced persons. He likewise established a dispensary, complete with an adequate supply of medicines and dressings, and oversaw the efforts of seven civilian physicians and three trained nurses at his aid station.[46]

One of the boldest actions taken by Funston and his officers concerned the protection of the U.S. Mint, which was located in the center of the greatest destruction. Although the huge brick edifice had withstood the shocks of the earthquake, it supposedly was endangered by an armed gang intent upon robbing its two hundred million dollars in coin and bullion. Reports of this plot were probably never more than exaggerations, but Funston sent a company of Sixth Infantry to guard the building at all costs. The armed gang never showed up, but the soldiers soon found themselves in the middle of a firestorm, which was consuming all neighboring buildings on three sides. Although the mint possessed its own water supply, the water proved inaccessible because the quake had broken the pump that raised the water from a well below the building. For seven hours the soldiers and some civilian firefighters beat back the flames with wet mail sacks. Despite their desperate situation, and the fact that the exterior walls were blackened by the intense heat, they saved the interior of the building and its precious contents.[47]

Ironically, Funston's administrative task became increasingly difficult as more organizations joined the fight to save the city. By the second day, five separate agencies were performing relief work, but with no clear-cut jurisdictional lines drawn among each other. Although the municipal police, U.S. Army, U.S. Navy, citizen's committees, and California National

Guard sometimes coordinated activities, they more often acted independently of each other. On April 21, Funston met with Governor George Pardee, Mayor Schmitz, and Police Chief Dinan to redivide the city into three zones—one patrolled by the police, another by the regular army, and a third by the California National Guard.[48] Although more fragmented in command structure than units of the regular army, guardsmen performed the same types of duties. They fought the ever-present fires, escorted people from danger areas, transported food supplies, set up camps for homeless civilians, and transferred prisoners from damaged jails. The *San Francisco Chronicle* proudly claimed that the National Guard was feeding twenty-five thousand to thirty thousand people daily and that its improvised bakery was producing over a thousand loaves of bread per day.[49]

Most citizens praised the regulars and guardsmen for their countless heroic acts, but two controversial orders gradually eroded some of that public support and brought significant complaints against General Funston. The first of these decisive acts was Funston's order that soldiers could shoot on sight any person caught looting or committing a serious deed against the life or property of another resident. Mayor Schmitz played no role in establishing the policy, but he went along with it for the time being.[50] Unfortunately, rumors soon began to circulate that soldiers had killed several innocent bystanders with indiscriminate gunfire, had executed prisoners in cold blood, had conscripted hundreds of residents into burial details, and were now engaging in widespread looting. Unconfirmed stories from Green Street told how a woman found a soldier stealing goods from her parlor, and when she confronted him, he threatened to kill her. Other sources alleged that soldiers had driven a flour mill owner and his employees from their "fireproof building" at the point of bayonets and then allowed the $220,000 building to burn to the ground. Most frightening were the tales from the Southern Pacific rail yards, several of them substantiated by evidence and reliable witnesses. Each of these separate episodes affirmed that troops looted boxcars of liquor stocks, and in at least two of these cases soldiers were arrested by their superiors. The reports did not distinguish whether the culprits were from the regular army or the California National Guard.[51]

An ever greater controversy was stirred by Funston's early decision to dynamite large numbers of buildings in an effort to deprive the advancing fires of combustible materials. The plan had received initial support from the mayor and his staff, and under the direction of Capt. La Vert Coleman the dynamiting strategy seemed to pay huge dividends during the first two days of its implementation. When the fires regained momentum on the third day, Coleman began to expand his dynamiting operations in an effort to enlarge the downtown firebreak.[52] Alarmed that the army was becoming intemperate in its use of explosives, and fearful of many private lawsuits, Mayor Schmitz requested that no more buildings be purposely blasted until they clearly were on the verge of being overtaken by flames. Funston gave only token acknowledgment to this concern while simultaneously ordering his officers to destroy some of the city's most fashionable homes on Van Ness Avenue with dynamite and artillery shells. This episode left Funston and the city leaders polarized, but they had little time to harangue each other, because the fires leapt the firebreak and continued to burn in the center of the city.[53]

On April 23, Maj. Gen. Adolphus Greely, commander of the Department of the Pacific, returned to San Francisco and took control of relief operations. Although he in no way publicly criticized General Funston's controversial actions, he quickly changed the two policies that had created the tensions. Shoot-on-sight orders for looters were suspended, and the directive for dynamiting buildings ended even more abruptly. Greely's decision on these two matters came not because of public pressure, but because all the major fires had been contained or extinguished by the time he arrived in the city. The worst part of the crisis had now passed, and Greely was already busy trying to transfer some of the duties to civilian relief organizations. He soon stopped dispensing army clothing and persuaded Dr. Edward Devine of the Red Cross to assume the job. He also worked closely with the Citizen's Committee of Fifty, composed of prominent businessmen and civic leaders, to share part of the burden of food distribution. Despite the transfer of some tasks, the army still continued to play a prominent role in clothing and food distribution, as well as in the maintenance of refugee camps and health care facilities.[54]

Greely also defused another potential problem with Governor Pardee, who desired a larger role for the California National Guard. Pardee had already blocked the general's request for twenty-five hundred additional regular troops by appealing directly to President Theodore Roosevelt. In the meantime, Greely expressed his own determination not to federalize the state's National Guard because he felt that he would have little control over its use. The two men soon reached a workable compromise whereby regulars would continue to manage relief operations while state militia would supervise policing activities.[55] Ironically, not until April 27, four days after Greely's arrival and nine days after the earthquake, did the War Department finally authorize the use of regular army troops in the fight to save San Francisco. Only at that point did the military become an official participant in the massive firefighting and relief effort.[56]

Greely hoped to end all military operations in the city by June 1, but Mayor Schmitz's repeated appeals that the army remain pushed the separation date back by a month. Slowly, the army scaled down its work and proudly marched back to its assigned military stations on July 2 after seventy-five days of continuous duty. To most everyone's satisfaction, the less effective California National Guard had left the city on May 31. Most San Franciscans seemed to be genuinely supportive of the strong role that the army had played, and national newspapers and Washington politicians followed suit with trumpeted praise.[57] On June 12, 1906, the California state legislature passed Senate Concurrent Resolution No. 4, profusely thanking the regular army and the National Guard for their tireless and courageous work in the defense of a city convulsed by one of nature's greatest calamities.[58]

The army learned much from its San Francisco experiences, and the precedents prepared the way for expansion of its relief duties during the rest of the twentieth century. Officers of all ranks proved their innovativeness and flexibility in reacting quickly to a massive crisis despite the absence of clear-cut orders or jurisdiction. They gradually worked out guidelines for cooperation with civilian agencies as well as with city and state governments. The experience also conclusively proved that soldiers could be highly motivated and that they could take personal pride in answering the call of a beleaguered public. Although the army had performed well and was pleased with its newfound popularity, the War Department and its senior officers still preferred training for combat over training for natural disasters.[59]

While responding to natural disasters occupied only sporadic attention from the army, another role not foreseen by the Founding Fathers filled thirty-two years of continuous military attention. The numbers of soldiers committed to this new activity were relatively few, but the stakes were immense as the army assumed the guardianship role over the fledgling National Park System between 1886 and 1918. As with its other relief efforts and policing roles, the army was officially assigned this important mandate, but only slowly did Congress grant it sufficient authority to meet these obligations effectively. The officers and men who were committed to these duties achieved remarkable success, captured the support of distinguished environmentalists, and established a proper model for the civilian force of park rangers who would follow in their footsteps.[60]

Among the diverse group of public men who contributed to the creation of Yellowstone as America's first national park, none surpassed Gen. Philip Sheridan in their long-term vision for the vast wilderness area. As commander of the Division of the Missouri since 1869, Sheridan presided over the various military exploration parties that traversed the remote section of northwestern Wyoming. His appetite for new discovery in this area of unsurpassed physical beauty was whetted during the subsequent decade by the official reports of Lt. Gustavus C. Doane, Capt. John W. Barlow, and especially Capt. William Ludlow.[61] The general rejoiced when Congress legislated Yellowstone National Park into existence in 1872, but he lamented its despoliation by well-organized game poachers during the following years.

Sheridan realized that time was running out for the park when, in 1882, Secretary of the Interior Henry M. Teller gave the Yellowstone Park Improvement Company—an affiliate of the powerful Northern Pacific Railroad—control of forty-four hundred prime acres surrounding tourist meccas such as Old Faithful, Mammoth Hot Springs, Lake Yellowstone, and the Grand Canyon of the Yellowstone River. The general struck back against the immensely profitable leasing arrangement and condemned any effort to divert national resources into privately managed property. He further warned that he would use military patrols from Fort Washakie, Wyoming, and Forts Custer and Ellis, Montana, against poachers and other defilers of nature's wonders. With the aid of powerful allies such as William "Buffalo Bill" Cody and George Bird Grinnell, editor-in-chief of *Forest and Stream* magazine, he approached Senator George Graham Vest, chairman of the Senate Committee on Territories, to promote protective legislation. Despite stiff opposition, a March 1883 law provided some enforcement powers and authorized soldiers to patrol the park on a continuous basis. During that summer, Sheridan completed his plan by personally heading an excursion into Yellowstone for President Chester A. Arthur and other notables. This impressive party, properly accompanied by a seventy-five-man military escort, enjoyed the recreational aspects of the excursion, but it also saw first-hand the dramatic effects of environmental plundering. Two years later, Sheridan and his supporters finally achieved their goal by securing legislation authorizing transfer of the park from the ineffective Interior Department to the more energetic War Department.[62]

On August 20, 1886, Capt. Moses Harris led a company of First Cavalry into the park and assumed control of a situation that had badly deteriorated during the previous decade. Immediately his men extinguished several forest fires that had been started by careless campers and illegal hunters, who drove wild game out of the park boundaries with the use of raging flames. Although specific legislation for enforcement of park rules was not passed until 1894, the procession of military commanders followed Harris's common-sense strategy in posting and enforcing their own regulations. They ordered soldiers always to be courteous to tourists, inform them about safety requirements, and explain the philosophies of environmental protection. Most often warnings seemed to be sufficient, but should any tourists persist in endangering the wildlife, geysers, or rock formations, they could be placed in the guardhouse at Fort Yellowstone, which was constructed in the northwest corner of the park at Mammoth Hot Springs.[63]

Within the first few years of taking on this new task, the army increased the number of soldiers, and they were able to establish camps at all the major points within the park. During tourist season the men spent considerable time watching over the major sites and hiking the back trails. But most of their effort remained fixed year-round on the ubiquitous poachers, who always represented the greatest threat to the park's environmental integrity. Because these men were heavily armed and prone to the larcenous side of life, they also posed a threat to the soldiers' very lives. Other violators included prospectors looking for mineral wealth, illegal timber cutters, neighboring ranchers who drove cattle into the lush river valleys for free grazing, and fishermen who used more than a single hook and line. Four privates under the command of a noncommissioned officer wintered at each of the log-house substations, and despite temperatures that sometimes dipped to forty degrees below zero, they maintained patrols throughout their assigned districts. Several died from exposure during the performance of their duties, and others came away from the experience with frostbitten and amputated fingers and toes. With the 1891 addition of 2,000 square miles of forest reserve land to the east of the park, the army now assumed guardianship of over 5,350 square miles of rugged territory, constituting a region larger than the state of Connecticut. Underfunded throughout the era and limited to less than three companies of cavalry at any one time, the army must have thought that the task seemed impossible.[64]

Not until passage of the Lacey Act in May 1894 did the army have a prescribed set of federal rules to enforce and an established list of punishments for various offenses. The Lacey Act, signed immediately into law by President Grover Cleveland, dictated that henceforth Yellowstone National Park was within the U.S. judicial district of Wyoming. Military officers could now transport offenders to the existing court for prosecution instead of having to rely on brief guardhouse lockups or military escort beyond the boundaries of the park, where the culprits were merely turned loose. These weak actions had proven ineffective in the past, but now convicted violators could face fines of up to two thousand dollars or imprisonment of up to two years. To assure that the enforcement powers would work more smoothly, the legislation provided for a U.S. commissioner and one or more deputy marshals to reside permanently within the park and to work closely with the military authorities in making arrests.[65] Although not without its flaws, the Lacey Act helped to reduce poaching, trespassing, and vandalism significantly within the park.[66]

Four years before passage of this more effective legislation for Yellowstone, the federal government created three new national parks in California: Yosemite, Sequoia, and General Grant. Because of their proximity to the metropolis of San Francisco, which brought a flourishing tourist trade, and their attractiveness to illegal timber cutters and grazing interests, these parks faced an environmental assault from the moment of their inception. Organized poaching was certainly less of a problem than it had been in Yellowstone because Yosemite and Sequoia Parks lacked a sizable population of game animals, but the sheepherders more than made up the difference in their destruction of the grasses that protected the landscape from erosion. John Muir, famed resident of Yosemite, architect of its creation as a national park, and first president of the environmental advocacy group known as the Sierra Club, derisively labeled the sheep as "hooved locusts," and he plotted the strategy for their removal from the protected federal land.[67]

Despite the War Department's initial reluctance to take on the new task, a plan evolved whereby two troops of the Fourth Cavalry moved from their station at the Presidio of San Francisco into the three adjoining parks during the spring of 1891. From that time until 1912 the cavalry squadrons followed a routine pattern whereby they remained in the park throughout the "active months" but always returned to the Presidio during the winter. Because no adequate facilities existed within the parks to quarter the soldiers throughout the harsh winters, and because the threats to park property were minimized during the prolonged cold spells, patrols were maintained for only eight months of the year. Encompassing a total of 2,024 square miles, and containing land as rugged as any found in Yellowstone, the California parks presented an administrative nightmare. Yet from their camp near the town of Wawona on the southern boundary of Yosemite, the officers and men performed the herculean task with vigor and achieved even more notable results than their brothers stationed in Yellowstone.[68]

John Muir, a man exceedingly difficult to please in the safeguarding of what he considered to be "God's Temple in the Wilderness," was lavish in his praise of the army's protective performance over Yosemite. In an 1895 speech before the Sierra Club in San Francisco, this bearded sage of nature's loveliness proclaimed, "Blessings on UNCLE SAM's bluecoats! In what we may call homeopathic doses, the quiet, orderly soldiers have done this fine job, without any apparent friction or weak noise, in the still, calm way that the United States troops do their duty."[69] Muir was especially impressed with the persistence and dedication to duty that Capt. A. E. Wood, first acting superintendent of Yosemite National Park, evidenced during the formative years. Wood shared Muir's almost pathological hatred of the sheepmen, and he made their removal his number one priority. By the time of the captain's death in 1894, the sheep menace had all but been eliminated, and Muir portrayed this as the lasting legacy of his military compatriot.[70] In writing a feature article for the *Journal of the United States Cavalry Association* less than three years after Wood's death, Lt. N. F. McClure of the Fifth Cavalry also extolled the virtues of this commander and his successor, Capt. G. H. G. Gale, who had continued the noble fight. Furthermore, Lieutenant McClure took the occasion to blast Congress for withholding funds that could have improved the army's administration of the parks while simultaneously alleviating some of the soldiers' privation.[71]

Despite its nearly impossible mandate, the army had indeed made amazing progress toward protection of the California parks. In addition to driving out the worst human threats to the environment, soldiers had created elaborate projects for restocking lakes and rivers with fish from the state hatchery. They also had extensively mapped the parks; had constructed roads, bridges, and trails; and had aided scientific parties interested in the geology and diverse flora and fauna of the area. They had even attended to special delegations sent from Germany and Japan to study how Americans administered their parks and game refuges. Most importantly, when the soldiers finally completed their last patrol within Yosemite in 1914 and turned their responsibilities over to a force of civilian rangers, they delivered a proven system that necessitated no major changes or breaks within the continuity of activities. The National Park Service Act, signed by President Woodrow Wilson on August 26, 1916, signaled the final chapter of military duty within the parks and ushered in a system of Interior Department management that continues to the present.[72]

In spite of their close association with and admiration for John Muir, Captains Wood and Gale possessed an environmental philosophy that ran counter to his and that was common to fellow officers throughout the army. Unlike Muir and his "preservationists," who stressed aesthetic and ecological values in maintaining nature's near pristine state, the officers who had been sent to guard the national parks represented the more pragmatic group of "conservationists" within the broader environmental movement. These practical men promoted the *wise management* and *measured use* of natural resources for the greater good of contemporary society and for future generations of Americans. They represented the dominant wing of the turn-of-the-century environmental movement whom historian Samuel P. Hayes has identified with the "gospel of efficiency." The crux of their philosophy "lay in a rational and scientific method of making basic technological decisions through a single, central authority."[73] That central authority was the federal government, including its new legions of technocrats who presumably could make important decisions about natural resource management without being blinded by corporate greed or the misplaced sentimentality of Muir's romanticists.

In keeping with their pragmatic approach to environmental issues, army officers stationed throughout the West during the late nineteenth century embraced a philosophy of common sense when dealing with the larger human tragedies. Just as they had extended earlier aid to starving travelers on the overland trails and medical care to ill and injured frontier families, they gradually expanded their protective role as the century wore on. They had already learned the risks and legal pitfalls associated with enforcing laws against civilians, especially in controversial labor strikes and civil insurrections. But in the less risky atmosphere of directly aiding people with coordinated relief efforts, saving lives in natural disasters, and protecting the country's natural resources, they scored an impressive array of victories. In sharpening the eagle's talons for domestic duties, the army thus proved its resourcefulness, and from these ventures it gained public respect and a nation's gratitude.

CHAPTER TEN

In Defense of "Poor Lo"

MILITARY ADVOCACY FOR NATIVE AMERICAN RIGHTS

To avoid creation of thirteen separate Indian policies by thirteen different states, the Founding Fathers established Article I, Section 8, in the United States Constitution. This provision instituted exclusive federal jurisdiction over Indian affairs, and Article I, Section 10, specifically mandated that state governments had no authority over Indian people, who were not citizens of the United States. Throughout the 1790s, federal authorities refined the exact duties of the Great White Father toward Native American peoples by assigning day-to-day administration to the U.S. Army. Because soldiers were immediately dispatched into trans-Appalachia, where many tribes resided, War Department authority over this vast region and its peoples seemed a wise choice. Yet with the passage of the next five decades, military officers found themselves embroiled in one major controversy after another over their enforcement of federal law in the ill-defined "Indian country."

Some Americans claimed that soldiers spent too much time protecting "savages" and preventing whites from acquiring more of the "unoccupied" western lands. Other critics argued from an opposite viewpoint that the army was a merciless killer of innocent Native Americans who were perpetual victims of a nation steeped in the hypocrisy of Manifest Destiny. During the second half of the nineteenth century the acrimonious debate between War Department and Interior Department over administrative control of Indians symbolized a larger national conflict over defining the army's mission in the West. Trapped between the continuous onslaughts of "Indian haters" and "liberal reformers," officers and enlisted men found themselves in an impossible situation.[1] The laws were clear on what their general responsibilities toward Indians were, but the physical means and legal backing to carry out that mission were sadly lacking in Congress and among the citizenry.

Beginning in 1790, under the prodding of President George Washington and Secretary of War Henry Knox, Congress passed the first in a series of laws collectively known as the Trade and Intercourse Acts.[2] Although ostensibly aimed at regulating the fur trade in the vast area between the Appalachian Mountains and the Mississippi River, the various acts also tried to preserve harmony between whites and Indians. At the heart of this strategy was the absolute necessity of keeping most whites out of Indian country and properly licensing the relative few who could legally live and trade among the tribes. Critical to the enforcement of these regulations was the U.S. Army, the only government agency that had some official policing power there.[3]

Trade and Intercourse Acts passed in 1796 and 1799 authorized the President of the United States to use military personnel to remove unlicensed squatters, hunters, timber cutters, liquor dealers, and traders from Indian lands. Army officers were instructed to escort the accused parties to the nearest civil courts for trial. They were also ordered to show the utmost restraint in making these arrests and were to treat these prisoners with great respect while they were being transported to the settlements.[4] An 1802 act further integrated the three previous pieces of legislation, better defined some of the crimes and punishments, and remained in effect until 1834, when a new codification of Indian policy relaxed some of the standards of enforcement.[5]

From their inceptions the various Trade and Intercourse Acts had placed the army in an untenable position. With only 9,991 officers and men authorized in 1808, the War Department was mandated to protect Indian lands all the way to the Rocky Mountains by virtue of the added domain of the Louisiana Purchase. The numerous access points from the line of white settlements to the "protected" frontier areas leaked like a sieve, and soldiers could arrest only a tiny percentage of violators.

Furthermore, when the army escorted the accused to distant civil courts, it had to detach additional troops to serve as guard details. More often than not, sympathetic local judges and juries composed of frontiersmen immediately freed the arrested parties, who sometimes returned to their illegal activities even before the guard detail could reach its assigned station.[6]

The most significant barrier to proper enforcement of these laws rested upon some of the restrictive language within their texts. The letter of the law required that military officers could arrest civilians only after the President of the United States had given specific instructions for a specific case. The alternative was for civil magistrates to prepare proper warrants by which soldiers were temporarily empowered to apprehend a designated offender. With such great distances involved between Washington, D.C., and the frontier, and considering the anti-Indian prejudices of many magistrates, it is a wonder that effective warrants were issued against any trespassers in Indian country.[7]

Yet when officers took it upon themselves to enforce the intent of the laws, they found themselves penalized by the legalistic loopholes. For example, in 1829, when Maj. David E. Twiggs, commander at Fort Winnebago, removed illegal timber cutters from Wisconsin Indian lands, he found himself the victim of tangled litigation. The leader of the trespassers had Twiggs arrested by the sheriff, and the major was required to post sixteen hundred dollars' bail as he awaited trial at Green Bay. The case dragged on for two years, and although Twiggs escaped conviction on the charges of illegally arresting a civilian, he incurred legal costs of more than a thousand dollars. The federal government later reimbursed him for the full amount, but not without a long delay.[8]

A similar fate befell Maj. Stephen Watts Kearny, commander of Fort Crawford, Wisconsin, in the same year. Kearny joined with Indian Agent Joseph M. Street at Prairie du Chien to arrest Jean Brunett and his crew of unlicensed timber harvesters. Brunett filed charges in civil court on the grounds that no specific document from the president had authorized his removal from Indian lands. Despite Kearny's argument that he was merely protecting tribal resources as provided for by the Trade and Intercourse Acts, he and Agent Street were found guilty and assessed total damages of $1,375.[9] Even though Congress subsequently covered the two men's costs, these and similar events persuaded many officers that it was not worth their time, personal finances, and career aspirations to enforce the unpopular regulations. Simply turning a blind eye to all but the most flagrant violations became a growing trend that lasted until the end of the century. Ultimate culpability for the failure of these regulatory policies rested more with an irresolute Congress and a boisterous frontier population than it did with the officers and enlisted men who were entrusted to carry out the halfhearted regulations.

Without a doubt the federal government failed miserably in its treaty obligations to the tribes residing east of the Mississippi River. The theoretically protective Trade and Intercourse Acts never stemmed the tide of white advance into Indian lands, and the new philosophy of removal began to dominate national policy by the 1820s. One by one, most of the eastern tribes found themselves under intense pressure to relocate in the prairie regions just to the east of the Great Plains. It was during the thirty-year cycle of these removals that the army came to occupy another untenable role as it oversaw some of the most inhumane of the mass exoduses and as it offered protection and services to those same tribes in their new western homelands. Nowhere was this dual pattern more evident than in the settlement of Indian Territory by the Five Civilized Tribes: Cherokees, Choctaws, Chickasaws, Creeks, and Seminoles.

Even while the forced removals from the Southeast were underway, some officers already had voiced their opposition to the cruel actions and especially the fact that they had to administer the injustice. Gen. Winfield Scott, who oversaw one of the major Cherokee removals, praised the Indians for their cooperation, and he condemned the large number of whites who rushed in to steal their property and attack their defenseless families. Scott's aide, Erasmus D. Keyes, voiced his personal shame in the whole sordid affair and remarked that he felt like "a trespasser, one of a gang of robbers." Col. John E. Wool repeatedly interceded to drive Alabama and Georgia land pirates off of Indian property and to adjudicate disputes, only to find himself under attack from prominent citizens of the states.[10]

As the various tribes completed their unique Trails of Tears from the Southeast during the 1820s and 1830s, they found their new homes in Indian Territory already threatened. Raids by powerful Plains tribes such

as Comanches and Kiowas to the west and prairie tribes such as the
Osages to the north endangered not only their farms and towns, but also
their very lives. To protect the removed tribes from their neighbors, the
army constructed nine forts and camps across the present-day state of
Oklahoma before the Civil War. Among these were Fort Washita, situated
above the confluence of the Washita and Red Rivers, which protected
the Chickasaw and Choctaw lands from Plains tribes and from expansion-
minded Texans, and the original Fort Arbuckle on the Arkansas River,
which guarded the Kansas gateway. Some of these posts were guaranteed
by the removal treaties, and others were added at the behest of the
removed tribes. Despite chronic understaffing and shortage of supplies,
soldiers successfully reduced the level of intertribal conflict and by the
fall of 1858 had even established Camp Radziminski in the heart of
Comanche country near the Wichita Mountains.[11]

Of all the posts built in Indian Territory between the 1820s and the
1850s, none played a more important role in protecting Indians than did
Fort Gibson. Located in the heart of the Cherokee Nation, this post stood
at the apex of early commercial and military roads within Indian
Territory. Its government contracts spread badly needed capital among
the Five Civilized Tribes, and its palisades offered protection to Native
American leaders who wished to negotiate among themselves. Fort
Gibson's surviving records documented how attentive to duty commanders
such as Col. Matthew Arbuckle were in driving unlicensed traders, liquor
dealers, and squatters from the protected lands. Ironically, it was officers
such as Arbuckle who warned the government against settling the eastern
removed tribes so close to the Plains tribes. But their realistic appraisals
of the situation lost out to the assumptions of humanitarian reformers
such as Reverend Isaac McCoy, who downplayed the possibilities of
intertribal friction.[12]

While Arbuckle and other officers carried out their assigned duties in
Indian Territory, they also frequently served as advocates for Indian rights
and helped directly convey Native American viewpoints to policy makers
in Washington, D.C. In the most thoroughly researched history of Fort
Gibson, author Brad Agnew rescued the army from its critics and offered
dozens of examples to demonstrate how soldiers made a "sincere effort
to protect the well-being of the immigrant Indians within the limits of

their capabilities." Furthermore, he argued, at no time did the removed tribes demand the closing of Fort Gibson or its sister posts. On the contrary, they frequently requested that the government send more troops and establish additional installations.[13]

The precedents of military advocacy, material aid, and protection for Native Americans carried beyond the pre–Mexican War era in Indian Territory and multiplied in the broader western setting during the second half of the century. The most basic expression of humanitarian aid came in the form of rations and equipment that were often extended to Indian people in emergency situations. Because Washington bureaucracy moved slowly, and because the shipment of annuities over vast distances produced many delays, officers periodically released food stocks to starving Indians.

During the winter of 1868, Mandans traveled to Fort Stevenson, Dakota Territory, to protest the nondelivery of their guaranteed annuities and to request immediate food stocks from the quartermaster's supply. Col. Philippe Régis de Trobriand observed that Fort Stevenson itself was short of winter provisions, and it was only able to authorize the transfer of a few boxes of crackers and several barrels of salt port. De Trobriand sarcastically remarked that the crackers were "quite moldy" and the barrels of pork were "somewhat damaged." Both previously had been condemned by a board of survey as unfit for soldiers' consumption, but the Indians were in such a state of famine that they willingly accepted the stocks. On a happier note, at Fort Wingate, New Mexico, during the same year, Lt. Frank Baldwin routinely helped distribute all the food authorized for the Navajos. He also worked closely with elders to collect from the nearby hills grama grass that could be sold to the quartermaster for one cent per pound. By the end of the season, they had harvested more than six hundred thousand pounds of grama grass and had received all of their rations on schedule.[14]

No western tribes seemed immune from failures within the bureaucratic system, and officers realized that hunger and frustration caused Indians to remain away from the reservations. Between 1870 and 1874, several commanders at Fort Fetterman, Wyoming, made repeated efforts to deliver supplies to destitute Cheyenne and Arapaho families. They also favored creation of a new agency near the post so that they could better protect and control members of the two tribes.[15] At nearby Fort Laramie during 1870 the commander was authorized to distribute up to ten thousand rations to the Sioux and Cheyennes, "provided such amount can be spared from the supplies of the post."[16] At a crucial juncture in Northern Plains Indian affairs during the winter of 1867–68, Gen. William Tecumseh Sherman approved issuance of army rations from Forts Totten, Rice, Sully, and Randall to maintain the peace. As the number of reservation Indians increased, so did demands on army supplies. In 1870 alone the Dakota posts issued $1.6 million worth of subsistence from the commissary department, though they were supposedly reimbursed from Interior Department funds.[17]

At other times, officers gave or loaned equipment to Indians who were trying to make a living on the reservations. Most often these items came out of condemned or surplus stock, but senior commanders could take the initiative in transferring newer goods if they felt secure that the items would be subsequently replaced by the government. Items included wagons, horses, cattle, clothing, seed, tools, and milling equipment.[18] Among the many officers who championed liberal transfers of property was Gen. John Pope, commander of the Department of the Missouri during the late 1870s. Repeatedly he petitioned Washington, D.C., to release food supplies to starving Comanches, Kiowas, Southern Cheyennes, and Arapahos who had settled at the western Indian Territory agencies following the Red River War of 1874–75. He likewise chided civilian reformers for not providing the Indians with the proper means to adjust to the sedentary reservation life. Rather than hastily forcing these former buffalo-hunting peoples into small agricultural allotments, as most "Friends of the Indians" advocated, he proposed turning them into stock raisers. These Southern Plains tribes already owned large horse herds, possessed some familiarity with cattle, and greatly preferred a ranching lifestyle over yeoman farming. Pope devoted nine years of his military career to writing letters and filing reports, but to no avail. Most civilian policy makers were little interested in animal husbandry as a way of life for Indians, and they were even less committed to spending large sums of money to expand livestock programs on reservations.[19]

Army attention to Indian medical problems also increased with the establishment of additional western reservations during the second half of the century. Assistant Surgeon Rodney Glisan recalled that during the mid-1850s he treated many Indians while stationed at Fort Yamhill, Oregon. In addition to dispensing medicines and dressing small abrasions, he conducted surgical procedures when situations warranted. In one case he amputated the thigh of an Indian headman named Santiam Sampson. Yet despite Glisan's seemingly humanitarian gestures, he remained a complete racist who spoke often of Indians as superstitious savages. He especially singled out for criticism the medicine men, who opposed his methods, and he belittled the concept of spiritual healing.[20] At Fort Larned, Kansas, during the late 1860s Surgeon William H. Forwood found that Indians would routinely accept medication from the army dispensary but were reluctant to undergo any form of surgery. Only once did he find a young Cheyenne willing to take chloroform while undergoing amputation of a finger. In a different case, he operated on a Cheyenne man who had suffered a broken thigh bone from a gunshot. The second patient refused chloroform, but Dr. Forwood did not indicate what kind of anesthesia, if any, was used.[21]

On the Northern Plains, too, army medical officers regularly extended care to Indian patients, although without any official mandate or systematic plan. Colonel de Trobriand worked closely with army surgeon Charles E. Goddard to relieve the suffering of Arikara families at Fort Berthold, Dakota Territory, during an 1869 scurvy outbreak. Neither man had to seek higher approval for this act, since some of these Arikaras were employed as army scouts at that time. De Trobriand sent out ten kegs of sauerkraut and pickles to enrich the vitamin C intake of the afflicted individuals, and he blasted whites who had stolen the food and personal property of these same people.[22] At Fort Totten, Dakota Territory, Dr. Henry H. Ruger earned the gratitude of Indians as "Big Medicine Man."[23] While at Camp Sheridan, Dr. William H. Corbusier treated Oglala headman Red Cloud for tapeworm, and he treated many other Sioux patients as well. Dr. Valentine McGillycuddy, before he became agent at Pine Ridge Reservation, worked as contract surgeon at Fort Robinson, Nebraska, and cared for Sioux patients at the nearby Red Cloud Agency. During the summer of 1877, at the strong insistence of Crazy Horse, McGillycuddy tended the man's wife after she failed to respond to traditional Indian healing procedures. Because McGillycuddy's own wife, Fanny, bravely accompanied him on this and other sick calls, she became a favorite in the Sioux camps.[24]

Even in three of the most tragic episodes involving soldier and Indian conflict, medical aid was extended to victims of the violence. When Northern Cheyennes under Dull Knife and Little Wolf broke out of the horrible confinement conditions at Fort Robinson during the winter of 1879, full-scale carnage erupted. Although the exact number of Indian casualties has been debated, records indicate that at least twenty-three wounded Indians were taken to the post hospital. Assistant Surgeon Edward R. Moseley and Acting Assistant Surgeon Charles V. Petteys treated soldier and Indian casualties with apparent impartiality. Even though six of the wounded Cheyennes subsequently died, the others probably survived as a result of the medical care. Among those was a significant percentage of noncombatants who had offered no resistance during the indiscriminate killing.[25] Similarly, in the aftermath of the December 1890 massacre at Wounded Knee, which claimed at least two hundred Sioux lives, the small number of Indian wounded who could be found were transported to the hospital at Pine Ridge, where Sioux medical doctor Charles Eastman treated their wounds with army supplies.[26]

At the opposite end of the continent, Geronimo and other Apache prisoners-of-war who had been unjustly imprisoned at Forts Pickens and Marion, Florida, and Mount Vernon Barracks, Alabama, found themselves facing a 15 percent death rate. The hot, humid, malaria-infested environments contrasted sharply with the salubrious mountain climate of their Arizona homeland, and the entire population of prisoners and their families seemed doomed. Humanitarian efforts by Lt. William W. Wotherspoon and Dr. Curtis E. Munn finally reversed the trend by improving diet and living conditions as well as by moving them in 1894 to healthier conditions at Fort Sill, Indian Territory.[27]

Because alcohol was associated with many health and social problems, liberal reformers and military officers found a common ground in trying to stop its spread among the western tribes. Yet ever since the original Trade and Intercourse Acts of the 1790s had outlawed or severely limited its use in the fur trade, illegal liquor had been a prime commodity of exchange between whites and Indians. Conditions facing the army in western Indian Territory during the early 1870s demonstrated the rate of enforcement problems faced by other commanders throughout the West. The nefarious trade came from dealers who operated with virtual impunity just north of the border between Kansas and Indian Territory. Army patrols stationed along the Dodge City–Fort Supply road checked as many freighters as possible but had little impact on the flow of demon rum. In fact, until June 1871, officers had orders not even to pursue or arrest Indians with the contraband, and most Indians refused to identify the culprits or reveal their locations. When Arapaho chief Little Raven did request army help in arresting illegal dealers, Col. John Davidson had to await clarification from his superiors because the enforcement laws were so ambiguous. Finally, in January 1872 he received permission to move against the Kansas whiskey cabins, and three months later, Capt. Charles Viele captured three fully loaded liquor wagons.[28]

The heralded efforts of Davidson and Viele produced no more than a minor slowdown in delivery, because new dealers quickly set up shop along the Kansas border. Agent John D. Miles reported in January 1873 that wagons had delivered forty gallons of whiskey to the Cheyenne and Arapaho reservation and had created an uncontrollable bout of drunkenness. Colonel Davidson, using a liberal interpretation of the law, invaded the five liquor ranches, dumped more than four hundred gallons of whiskey, and arrested eight men, who were sent to Topeka for civil trial. The effort was impressive, but by July illegal traders from New Mexico had delivered two hundred kegs of whiskey into the Cheyenne and Arapaho camps for the exchange of horses. As long as the demand was high, the profits so dear, and the arrest rate so low, the illegal liquor trade would continue throughout Indian country into the twentieth century.[29]

During the post–Civil War era, the Interior Department retained administrative control over most reservations and the army dealt with off-reservation Indians, but a blurring of roles inevitably occurred. Army chaplains occasionally held religious services on reservations, and some of them became advocates for the Indians. Army surgeon Charles Carroll Gray drew upon his knowledge of French to become an unofficial interpreter for several Northern Plains tribes during the late 1860s.[30] Assistant Surgeon James Reagles, Jr., spent part of his duty time learning native languages wherever he was stationed, and he recorded considerable ethnographic data as well. At least one former soldier, C. H. Cook, who had fought against Indians in the Southwest, became a missionary to the Pimas and Maricopas.[31] In the same spirit of humanitarianism, the former hospital steward at Fort Davis, Texas, and his wife "adopted" two Apache children who had been captured in a skirmish along the Texas–New Mexico border. Likewise, Capt. James Burns "adopted" a seven-year-old Apache boy who lost his father in an 1872 skirmish in the Sierra Anchas of Arizona. The boy, renamed Mike Burns, received a rudimentary education from his new father and gained higher education through the financial efforts of Gen. George Crook, Gen. Wesley Merritt, and the Indian Rights Association. Unfortunately, their one-sided view of "civilizing" the boy left no consideration for allowing him to return to his own people and his own culture.[32]

Most military men clearly preferred to see Indians living on reservations where they could be more easily controlled. They also knew that the buffalo was the prime element in perpetuating the independence of the Plains tribes because it provided the essence of their spiritual and material life. This has led some scholars to allege that commanders such as Gen. Philip Sheridan fomented a plot during the 1870s to have hunters wipe out the buffalo so that the army could more easily perform its duty. Yet the evidence of this grand conspiracy is lacking, attributable more to anecdotal quotations and an overemphasis on army unity than to provable cases. While some officers certainly supported the buffalo slaughter, others, such as Col. William B. Hazen, Col. Albert Brackett, and Capt. Robert G. Carter, pronounced against it for a myriad of reasons.[33] More to the point, soldiers often escorted reservation Indians on buffalo hunts to protect them from whites. They also occasionally arrested buffalo hunters who stole Indian property or threatened their lives.[34] From time to time officers were also dispatched as translators and chaperones to Indian delegations that traveled to the nation's capital for negotiations.[35]

The most visible symbol of army authority on reservations occurred when officers served as official agents for designated tribes. The case of Capt. Frank Bennett of the Ninth Cavalry, who served as agent for the Navajos from 1869 to 1871, mirrored the problems faced by other officers in similar positions. This era marked a time of crisis in Navajo country, an era in which the Indians were trying to reestablish themselves in their traditional homeland following their forced confinement on the Bosque Redondo Reservation of eastern New Mexico during the Civil War. There, many had died, and many others took their sorrow and their motive of revenge with them when they returned to the Four Corners. Bennett worked tirelessly to help tribal members reestablish crops, fruit orchards, and sheep herds to rebuild their economy and social patterns. He dueled endlessly with bureaucrats and contractors within the Indian Bureau to assure the timely delivery of annuities to the malnourished Indians. He also demonstrated diplomatic skills in initially charming the white missionaries who were assigned to the reservation and in securing release of many Navajo women and children captives who previously had been forced into servitude.

Yet Bennett was at his best in dealing with the anger of local white settlers, who tended to blame all Navajos for the raids of a few. When in 1869 newly installed territorial governor William Pile called upon New Mexico residents to form posses and punish all "renegade" Indians, Bennett, reinforced by troops from nearby Fort Wingate, steadfastly refused to allow the armed force to enter the reservation and forcibly seize what its leaders claimed to be stolen livestock. He gave the armed men a few sheep as a good-will gesture and promised to punish any Navajos who participated in future livestock raids. Bennett's commitment to the welfare of his charges continued even in the face of other volatile situations and changing politics in Washington, D.C. When in 1871 government authorities notified the agent that he would soon be replaced by a civilian appointee as part of the reorganization brought on by the peace policy of President Ulysses S. Grant, Bennett offered to sacrifice his own military career. He indicated that he would resign his commission so that he could continue his position as agent for the Navajos. Such was not to be the case, however, because selection power rested with the Board of Foreign Missions, which already had other candidates under consideration.[36]

Placed in an equally difficult position was Capt. DeWitt Clinton Poole, who served as agent at Dakota Territory's Whetstone Agency for eighteen months during 1869–70. Despite intense pressure exerted on the Oglala and Brulé bands of western Sioux during that period and the growing factional struggles among band leaders, Poole maintained generally good relations with headmen such as Red Cloud and Spotted Tail. He worked tirelessly to secure their treaty annuities and accompanied them on the important trip to Washington, D.C., following the signing of the 1868 Fort Laramie Treaty.[37] More controversial was West Point graduate Thomas S. Twiss, who served as a lieutenant of engineers during the 1820s. Having resigned his commission in 1829, he held numerous jobs before being appointed as Indian agent for the Upper Platte in 1855, a position he held for six years. Even though Twiss was never above using nepotism to reward friends and family members, and was even suspected of some corruption, he ingratiated himself to many important Oglalas. He married an Oglala woman, fathered four sons by her, and maintained strong kinship ties until his death about 1871.[38]

Elsewhere, other officers on active duty found themselves serving as ex-officio agents. Among the Apaches of Arizona during the early 1880s, Capt. Emmett Crawford and his assistant, Lt. Britton Davis, supervised the San Carlos Reservation, while Lt. Charles Gatewood and his assistant, Lt. Hamilton Roach, oversaw events at Fort Apache. The situation they faced was somewhat unique, since the civilian agent at San Carlos still retained administrative control over the agencies. Precisely because so many small Apache groups kept leaving the reservations without permission, and thus fell under the army's purview, the dual system of administration continued into the following decade. The four men had good reputations among many Apache leaders because they spent so much time with the Indian families. As commanders of the army's Apache scouts, they often participated in tribal ceremonies, ranging from girls' puberty ceremonies to funerals for their friends. Often, Apache leaders who chose to remain on the reservations acknowledged that they trusted the military agents more than their civilian counterparts. The former seemed to speak more forthrightly, and they more often followed through on their promises.[39]

Even after the Indian wars had subsided, a few military men continued as agents on reservations. When Capt. Frank Baldwin took control of the Anadarko Agency in 1894, administrative chaos reigned, with Indians badly factionalized, white trespassers stealing reservation resources, and illegal traders operating freely. Baldwin not only removed the trespassers and destroyed barrels of liquor, but he also attempted to improve services on the reservation for the Comanches, Kiowas, and Kiowa-Apaches. Unfortunately, powerful trader Dudley P. Brown provoked an investigation of Baldwin's alleged "dictatorial" methods and initiated a lawsuit against him. From then on, the captain's efforts at reform were largely ineffective.[40]

In addition to military advocacy and material aid, calls for military protection of reservations and hunting lands emanated from diverse tribes throughout the West. During the 1850s, as Ojibwa, Winnebago, and Santee Sioux groups increasingly settled on Minnesota reservations, they found themselves subject to intertribal raids and invasions by white settlers. In the case of the Upper Sioux Agency at Yellow Medicine, civilian agent Joseph R. Brown listened to their demands and worked closely with Capt. A. A. Gibson at Fort Ridgely to provide extra protection for the reservation. He reported his charges to be making steady progress toward "civilization," but their resources, and even their lives, were being assaulted almost weekly by white farmers who had settled along the Minnesota River. Despite public outcries voiced in Minnesota newspapers, the transfer of troops nearer the agency was carried out in 1860. Progress was sacrificed two years later, however, when many starving Santees rose up on the Lower Sioux Agency under the nominal leadership of Little Crow.[41]

In 1854 the peaceful Omaha Tribe signed a new treaty with the government. Under duress from the advancing flood of white settlers into the Missouri River valley, the Omahas reluctantly agreed to return to their traditional homes in northeastern Nebraska. Although they still revered this land of their ancestors, they strongly opposed the removal northward because it would place them well within striking distance of their Yankton and Brulé Sioux enemies. To expedite the move, government representatives promised to meet their demands for continued military protection, possibly even the construction of a large post along the present Nebraska–South Dakota border that could blunt the horrific Sioux raids. Once the Omahas were situated on their exposed reservation, the promise was quickly forgotten in Washington, D.C., and they suffered devastating livestock and human losses during the following twenty years.[42]

On a more ironic note, forty years later the Choctaws of Indian Territory successfully requested federal troops to protect their coal mines during an 1894 labor strike. The Indians relied heavily upon royalties from these mineral deposits to provide essential tribal services, and thus they joined with white managers to crush the strike. Soldiers sent from Fort Reno and Fort Sill, including a cavalry troop armed with Gatling guns and an artillery piece, found the policing duty to be onerous and unpopular. They also disliked their portrayal in local newspapers that had sided with the strikers, including accusations that soldiers had beaten pregnant women with their rifle butts and had loaded the women onto flatcars like cattle. Following the army's removal of several hundred blacklisted miners from the Choctaw Nation, the strike ended. The Choctaws had their royalties restored; the mine owners reopened their lucrative enterprises; and the army, simply by following federal directives, came away with enemies on both sides of the conflict.[43]

As the government undertook rapid construction of western forts during the decade and a half following the Civil War, its experts made sure that many of these posts would be built near Indian agencies. Sometimes this was done to overawe the Indians with military power and to keep a better eye on them. But at other times it was undertaken to better protect the compliant reservation dwellers from enemy tribes, white interlopers, and even so-called "bronco" groups from among their own people. Fort Stevenson, located ninety miles above Bismarck, Dakota Territory, guarded the Three Affiliated Tribes—Mandans, Arikaras, and Gros Ventres—from Sioux attacks. During 1869, while many of the Indian men were away on a hunt, Sioux warriors threatened their families, but Maj. S. A. Wainwright sent soldiers and an artillery piece to the agency and drove off the attackers.[44] Further down the Missouri River, members of the First Infantry at Fort Randall gained the respect of Poncas, whom they protected against Sioux attacks during the mid-1870s.[45] Far to the west in Nevada, Sarah Winnemucca praised the soldiers for protecting her Paiute people from red and white raiders alike.[46]

Because white trespassers posed a greater threat to most reservations than did enemy tribes, post–Civil War military reports were filled with references to frequent dispersals and less frequent arrests. When a group of settlers left Cheyenne, Wyoming, for the Sweetwater mining district in 1870, they promised to bypass the Shoshone Reservation in order to receive government approval for their venture. Once beyond the arm of civil officials, they broke their covenant and found themselves pursued by a cavalry troop ordered out by Gen. Christopher C. Augur. By the time the pursuing column caught up with the illegal party, its members were so demoralized that they offered no resistance. Some moved on to the mining districts of western Montana, and the remainder headed for the Sweetwater mining district.[47] At about the same time, soldiers from Fort Stevenson, Dakota Territory, drove illegal timber cutters away from the Fort Berthold Agency, where the land and its resources were reserved for the Three Affiliated Tribes.[48]

While most searches for trespassers seemed to have ended in a fashion similar to the above-mentioned cases, some evidenced a more dangerous dimension. Creation of two small agencies in northwestern Texas during 1855 for two bands of Comanches and a smaller number of Caddo refugees precipitated a war of words between federal and state officials. Attacks against the agencies during 1858 and 1859 by Texas Rangers and vigilante frontiersmen killed some Indian noncombatants and almost triggered a confrontation with soldiers at nearby Fort Belknap. In the second encounter, federal troops pursued the vigilante raiders, whose anti-Indian banner declared, "Necessity Knows No Law." In the end, however, Washington policy makers, not protective army officers, decided the fate of these nonthreatening Indians. They were forcibly removed to western Indian Territory, and much of their property was forfeited to the Texans.[49]

Fifteen years later, Lt. Col. John M. Davidson, commanding at Fort Elliott on the eastern fringes of the Texas Panhandle, confronted George W. Arrington and his "Frontier Battalion" of Texas Rangers. Davidson charged that the Rangers were spoiling for a fight and wanted to attack one of the Comanche and Kiowa buffalo hunting parties from the Fort Sill Reservation. These reservation Indians, escorted by Fort Sill soldiers, had every right to enter the Texas Panhandle, and Davidson warned that he would protect them at all costs. Cooler heads finally prevailed, and the expected showdown never came.[50]

No western state or territory escaped the rancor produced by intruders invading Indian lands, but probably the most celebrated case occurred in the Black Hills of western Dakota Territory. Guaranteed as part of the Great Sioux Reservation by the Fort Laramie Treaty of 1868, these mountains, known in Lakota language as the Paha Sapa, were not only of material importance to the Sioux, but also sacred. The 1874 exploratory expedition led by Lt. Col. George Armstrong Custer to the mountains found enough gold in the streambeds to set off a major mining rush by the summer of 1875. To preserve the peace until a new treaty could be negotiated over transfer of the Black Hills, Washington authorities naïvely ordered the army to evict illegal miners for the time being. Units from Fort D. A. Russell, near Cheyenne, Wyoming, fanned out across a line through the Red Cloud and Spotted Tail Agencies of the Nebraska Panhandle and across the southern boundaries of the huge reservation. Officers carried clear orders to turn back all whites from the reservation and, more specifically, from the Black Hills. Yet in the meantime, the *Cheyenne Daily Leader* advertised the quickest routes to the mining areas and the best means to elude army patrols.[51]

The army was, in fact, receiving and sending mixed messages during the summer of 1875. Col. Richard Dodge had just led four hundred soldiers into the heart of the disputed Paha Sapa as he escorted geologists Newton Warren and Walter P. Jenney to discern the locations and extent of the first strikes. To gather information as quickly as possible, he worked with the illegal miners and inadvertently gave them the impression that they would not be bothered by authorities.[52] At that very moment, General Military Order No. 2 governed policy in the area, and it mandated the immediate removal of all miners. Realizing the magnitude of their task, officers were not content merely to request that trespassers leave the region, as had been done in countless cases elsewhere on the frontier. When Capt. Fergus Walker intercepted the first filibustering party on May 6, he arrested all and escorted them under strong guard to confinement at Fort Randall, on the Missouri River. Six days later, the same soldiers captured the John Gordon party of approximately 150 miners and forcibly disarmed them.[53]

Just as in the chaotic days of enforcing the original Trade and Intercourse Acts, officers found themselves pilloried in newspapers throughout the western territories. As they arrested additional trespassers, they also found themselves facing civil charges for illegally detaining civilians. Bowing to pressure, Secretary of War William W. Belknap ordered the unconditional release of prisoners and an investigation whether the arrests had been legal. A military tribunal presided over the hearings at

Fort Randall, but because of so much conflicting testimony, it declared that civilian charges of abuse were unfounded. U.S. District Judge Elmer S. Dundy, in Omaha, subsequently ruled that the military did have a legal right to repel trespassers in the Black Hills, but that it had no right to detain John Gordon for more than five days, not the three months that it did hold him.[54]

The court ruling turned out to be a hollow victory for the army and for the Sioux. Even though very few aggrieved miners chose to sue officers in court, they and thousands like them continued to pour into the contested area. One prospector, unimpressed with the army's staying power and the government's long-term commitment to preserving Indian lands, defiantly claimed that he had been captured four times within three months but could easily outlast the authorities.[55] Sgt. Charles Windolph later recalled the futility of it all when he said: "All the soldiers in the United States couldn't hold back the tide then. You could sign all the Indian treaties you could pack on a mule, but they wouldn't do any good. Men would get through. They'd go after gold in spite of hell and high water."[56]

And so it was, for the government quickly tired of the public outcry against its exclusionary policy. Instead of preserving the 1868 treaty rights, it ordered the army to drive all the Sioux from their Powder River hunting lands onto the reservation, where they were to be pressured into surrendering the Paha Sapa. This precipitated the massive military campaign of the summer of 1876 that resulted in army debacles at Rosebud Creek and Little Big Horn. Ironically, those disasters placed the army squarely on the side of the miners, and the relentless winter campaign of 1876–77 all but broke the back of the Sioux and Northern Cheyennes. Despite the punitive nature of those concluding events, the army's role had initially been a protective one. In his systematic study of the failed policies, historian Watson Parker gave high marks to the military officers for their sincere efforts to protect the Black Hills. He affirmed that it was "a credit to both the diligence and the ability of the soldiers, but the task was an impossible one and foredoomed to eventual failure."[57]

Even though the Black Hills provided the most celebrated case of failed army protection of Native American lands, Indian Territory supplied the most sustained examples of the post–Civil War era. In the eastern

half of present-day Oklahoma, where the removed tribes resided, trespassers appeared mainly in the guise of hunters, timber cutters, and
whiskey dealers. Tribal governments employed their own Indian police
to disperse these men, but they also repeatedly called for military help.[58]
Just as the frequency of these incidents increased during the 1870s and
1880s, two additional threats entered the area, especially in the massive
Cherokee Outlet, which stretched along the northern tier of Indian
Territory. The first of these were Texas and Kansas cattlemen, such as the
Cherokee Strip Live Stock Association, who grazed their animals on the
nutritious grasses without paying the customary tax or gaining permission
from the tribal government.[59]

The bigger threat came from "boomers," who illegally crossed the
Kansas border and tried to set up homesteads in the Outlet.[60] As early as
1879, President Rutherford B. Hayes issued a proclamation for soldiers
to stop the illicit migration and drive out the 300–350 families who were
already settled in the district. Some of the roundup operations were
conducted by black soldiers of the Ninth and Tenth Cavalries, and this
fact stirred up race-conscious newspapers even more. The unresolved
issue dragged on into the 1890s, when the government incrementally
opened the region to white settlement.[61] Years later, John H. Brandt,
formerly a private in the Fifth Cavalry, recalled his frustrating participation in the sweeps: "It was a job none like to do, yet it had to be done and
I think we were the best hated men in the United States, at least those
people who had to leave thought so."[62]

Further to the west, Plains tribes residing at the Fort Sill and Fort Reno
agencies found their lands overrun with Texas cattle on the way to Kansas
railheads. Most Texans paid the Comanches, Kiowas, Southern Cheyennes,
and Arapahos for passage of their herds, but some, such as George W.
Littlefield, refused. During one near-confrontation in 1879, a military
officer intervened, turned over some beeves to the Comanches, and
promised that Littlefield would be reimbursed by the government. The
Texas rancher never received his federal compensation, but violence was
averted.[63]

In addition to policing the trail herds, soldiers spent considerable time
pursuing white thieves who stole Indian horses from the two agencies.
Their 1875 arrest of "Red" McLaughlin and his gang helped stem some

of the thefts around Fort Sill, but only for a short time.[64] Ten years later, President Grover Cleveland responded to Indian petitions by requesting tougher laws for protecting reservations from cattlemen. Congress subsequently passed the law declaring a fine of up to five hundred dollars and one year's imprisonment for a first violation and double that for any subsequent violation. Although some cattlemen began withdrawing their herds from these two reservations in present-day western Oklahoma, other Texas cattle barons learned to bypass the protective system by working out grazing agreements with the agents and some compliant Indian leaders such as the Comanche Quanah Parker.[65]

Events in the Black Hills and in Indian Territory readily demonstrated the limits of power that military men faced in protecting reservation lands. Yet a less visible case in Montana proved that cooperation between Indians and soldiers could yield legal victories of major proportions. The Northern Cheyennes, defeated on the battlefield in 1877, decimated by disease on their reservation in western Indian Territory, and shocked by the bloody 1879 breakout from Fort Robinson, longed for a reservation in their original Tongue River homeland. As in so many cases involving other tribes, they found their enclave under relentless pressure from cattlemen, farmers, land speculators, and territorial politicians. In spite of great odds, the Northern Cheyenne people remained adamant and united in their efforts to preserve this part of their ancestral domain. Their twenty-year struggle, in concert with some politicians and eastern reform groups, surprisingly produced an enlargement of their reservation boundaries. Key to the Indians' legal victories were the sustained efforts of military officers such as Gen. Nelson A. Miles, Maj. Henry Carroll, and Capt. George W. H. Stouch. Not only did these officers physically keep trespassers off the reservation, but they also filed the sympathetic reports that ultimately won the day for the Northern Cheyennes. One lowly private, George Yoakam, shared in the ultimate victory of his Indian friends. As agency farmer since the early years of the reservation experience, Yoakam documented their rights to the land, and he helped teach white agricultural and ranching methods to bridge the gap between the old and new economies.[66]

Although the army's greatest impact on Indians, both for good and ill, was felt in the West, military officers also influenced national policies by working with civilian reform groups in the East. Sometimes they found themselves in heated debates with these reformers, but very often they discovered common ground in their advocacy for Native American rights. Historian Richard N. Ellis surveyed the contributions of a number of these officers, whom he dubbed the "humanitarian generals." Ellis did not contend that everything these men did was beneficial to Indians— after all, they also participated in some brutal campaigns against the western tribes—but their efforts at reforming federal Indian policy did go beyond mere words. Among the senior officers who fell into this category were Generals Benjamin Grierson, Oliver Otis Howard, Nelson Miles, and John Pope. At various times these men worked with groups such as the Boston Indian Citizenship Committee, the Indian Rights Association, and the Lake Mohonk Conferences toward the correcting of injustices. At other times, such as General Miles's duplicitous manipulation of the Apache prisoner-of-war issue and General Howard's mishandling of the 1877 Nez Percé flight to Canada, they found themselves rightfully blasted by the "Friends of the Indian."[67]

Perhaps the most consistent expression of the humanitarian concept came from Gen. George Crook. Even though he was a relentless campaigner and believed that tribes should be forced onto reservations, Crook championed their rights on many occasions.[68] The most important legalistic expression of his concern came in 1879 when Ponca chief Standing Bear guided about thirty of his people from their unhealthy Indian Territory reservation toward their former Niobrara River homeland in northern Nebraska. Orders to arrest the fleeing party reached Crook at Fort Omaha, and he carried out the directive. While holding the chief and his people, the general gained personal knowledge of their plight. His sympathy for the aggrieved Poncas prompted him not only to file reports about their conditions, but also to undertake a risky legal maneuver in their behalf. Acting in concert with Thomas Tibbles of the *Omaha Herald*, young lawyer John L. Webster, and Andrew J. Poppleton, chief attorney for the Union Pacific Railroad, he helped initiate the innovative plan. Poppleton filed a writ of *habeas corpus* in the court of Federal Judge Elmer S. Dundy. The writ challenged Crook's authority to hold the chief, and it demanded the immediate release of all the Poncas. Crook willingly allowed himself to become the defendant in this case so that Standing Bear could publicly relate the sufferings and injustices experienced by his people. The brief trial produced the desired results and helped establish an important legal principle for Indians throughout the United States. Judge Dundy ruled that not only was Standing Bear a "person" within the meaning of the law, but also the army had no authority to confine these people, who were at peace with the government. Crook was among the first to congratulate Standing Bear for his eloquence and his courtroom victory. Without Crook's cooperation in this case, its outcome would have been less certain.[69]

Army perceptions about Indians reflected a diversity of opinion similar to the myriad of views within broader society. Historian Sherry Smith's exhaustive study of the subject affirmed the conclusions of earlier scholars such as Thomas Leonard and William Skelton. All three found that military men from the lowest to the highest ranks evidenced an ambiguity about the character and cultural integrity of Native Americans. Many soldiers made major distinctions between different tribes by offering portrayals that ranged in extreme from "noble red men" to "unredeemable savages." Others judged individual Native Americans in categories that encompassed everything from tragic victims to inhuman villains.[70]

Still other officers and enlisted men changed their views over time after they became more closely associated with Indians. For example, Gen. Irvin McDowell, while commanding the Department of California during the late 1860s, became a firm friend of Pima chief Juan Chivaria, who headed a company of scouts. That close personal association helped modify some of McDowell's harsh feelings about Indians in general and about southwestern Indians in particular.[71] Capt. Frederick W. Benteen took the trouble to get to know a number of prominent Kiowas while he was stationed in western Indian Territory during 1868. On various occasions he invited Satank, Satanta, Lone Wolf, and Stumbling Bear to dine with him. He listened to their tales, extended gifts in the proper reciprocal manner, and praised the Kiowas for their manners, sagacity, and spirituality. He also became an outspoken critic of people who were cheating his friends, and when he returned to Fort Sill in 1884, he renewed relationships with those who had survived the Southern Plains wars.[72] Likewise, Lt. Elliott Coues, destined to become a celebrated ornithologist and ethnologist, underwent a major transformation in his association with Apaches during the late 1860s. He came not only to perceive their victimization in recent history, but also to understand the beauty of their culture and lifeways. Armed with that newfound sensitivity, he tried to educate the broader public about the dangers of stereotyping a group of people without first getting to know them.[73]

It is indeed true that even the most sympathetic of officers and enlisted men viewed Indian people through a prism of ethnocentrism and paternalism. Furthermore, they all shared a common sentiment that traditional native life would soon give way to the acculturative processes of making red men into white men. Yet to simply dismiss these soldiers as bigots, cultural chauvinists, or racists would unfairly take them out of their own milieu and hold them to a different standard than existed in their era. Such a typecasting would also homogenize all of their diverse feelings and experiences into one grand generalization. In truth, their views and actions were much too diverse for that easy analysis. For all their faults, military men certainly were not the inveterate "Indian haters" that Helen Hunt Jackson portrayed in her 1881 seminal book, *A Century of Dishonor.* Nor were they eternally unpopular with Indian people as *Council Fire* editor Thomas Bland alleged in an 1879 article entitled "Abolish the Army."[74]

By the same token, soldiers were not the frightened and incompetent martinets that many frontier newspapers claimed them to be.[75] In truth, the army was caught between two divergent philosophies of federal Indian policy. It could never entirely please either one, and the enforcement tools for carrying out its stated mission were never forthcoming from Washington officials or the public at large. Gen. William Tecumseh Sherman articulated the dilemma best when he stated: "There are two classes of people, one demanding the utter extinction of the Indians, and the other full of love for their conversion to civilization and Christianity. Unfortunately, the army stands between and gets the cuffs from both sides."[76]

CHAPTER ELEVEN

Documenting the Experience

SOLDIER JOURNALISTS, AUTOBIOGRAPHERS, AND NOVELISTS

From its inception, the American army was a prolific generator of private and public documents. The nineteenth-century volumes within the U.S. Congressional Serial Set abound with lengthy printings of military explorations, accounts of protracted Indian campaigns, discussions about experimental ordnance, descriptions of new fortifications, and diplomatic exchanges about problems along the international borders. Far more extensive than the printed documents were the records that made their way up the chain of command from far-flung military posts to divisional headquarters and eventually to the War Department in Washington, D.C. These massive files included fitness, daily, quartermaster, and meteorological reports as well as military correspondence on virtually every topic imaginable. Today, most of this data is housed in the National Archives, and it offers mountainous evidence of an army bureaucracy that documented its daily existence in incredible detail.

At the conclusion of the Mexican War in 1848, the United States enlarged its domain by more than a million square miles and, for the first time, truly became a continental nation. Mandated to the officers who would occupy the vast Trans-Mississippi West for the next half-century was the well-established record-keeping role. Yet amid the expanding production of official army reports and correspondence came another type of documenting endeavor—the labors of individual officers and enlisted men who wrote about their experiences for larger audiences. Greater numbers of nineteenth-century Americans read the memoirs of military officers and their wives than ever examined the published and unpublished records of the War Department. Although many of the memoirs were written to enhance careers and gain a moment of immortality in the public record, they also contained valuable information about frontier life. Moreover, some of them were written with enough introspection and literary grace to become minor classics among the reading public.

Other officers, such as Charles King, dominated a corner of the literary market with fictionalized accounts of army life that drew upon personal experiences to convey a sense of authenticity. The works of enlisted men rarely attracted the same level of national attention, but their words were not stilled by their lower status in the army hierarchy. As journalists and diarists they often conveyed a different perspective on military life than did their commanders, and their descriptions frequently were harsh. Although different in their styles and intentions, these men and women made valuable assessments of a significant time in American history, and their efforts remain important to today's scholars.

At no time did military policy ever require individual forts or regiments to sponsor their own newspapers. Yet experiments with journalism periodically appeared at some of the larger posts on the eastern frontier during the first half of the nineteenth century. None of them bore much resemblance to modern newspapers, but they were fairly typical of small community weeklies of that era. They generally were single-sheet publications, mostly filled with local news of the soldiering life in addition to a smattering of national news borrowed from other publications. If a printing press was available, the commanding officer approved the project, and someone was willing to take on the work, an army newspaper could spring up almost overnight.

The question of exactly which western fort used the first printing press cannot be answered conclusively, but among the present-day Plains states, Nebraska may have been home to the initial army newspaper. As early as 1822 the garrison at Fort Atkinson published a weekly tabloid to which the *Missouri Intelligencer* paid tribute as "on a royal sheet, elegantly and correctly executed in point of chirography; and in point of original matter not exceeded by the first eastern publications."[1] How long this newspaper continued to appear is unknown, but it was not mentioned in other Fort Atkinson correspondence much beyond the date of its founding. The very nature of this issue also assured that only a small number of copies ever were circulated. Because of the small printings and the great passage of time, none have survived into the modern era to allow a study of the contents.

Within the vast area between the Great Plains and the Pacific Ocean, post newspapers were rare until the 1860s. Typical of the new experiments during the Civil War era were the efforts of civilians who were closely associated with military garrisons. Unlike earlier newspapers produced completely by soldiers, these were the products of men interested in earning a profit by appealing simultaneously to civilian and military communities. In June 1863, Hiram Brundage, military telegraph operator at Fort Bridger, initiated the *Daily Telegraph*. This crude little news sheet, the first item ever printed in Wyoming, carried Brundage's title *The Fourth Infantry Press*, named for the unit stationed at the fort. After only a few issues, the editor suspended publication when he found that it could not pay its own way.[2]

Like other editors catering to both a military and civilian market, Brundage hoped to win contracts from the army as its local printer of government forms. He did print some items under military contract and for individual civilians, but these were inadequate to keep the enterprise going. Not until 1868 did a second newspaper appear at Fort Bridger, and this semiweekly moved to the mining boom town of South Pass City within three months after its founding. Yet as late as 1875, Brundage's *Fourth Infantry Press* was still doing work for Fort Bridger and other Wyoming posts. At that time it printed an artful New Year's Eve musical program for the garrison.[3]

Better known in the pantheon of Great Plains journalism was *The Frontier Index*, which was born at Fort Kearny, Nebraska, in December 1865. Editor Legh Freeman later contended that he and his brother Frederick had created the first newspaper at Fort Kearny more than a decade earlier, but in fact they built their enterprise on the efforts of three predecessors. Local businessman Moses H. Sydenham had created the *Kearney Herald* at the post in 1862 and had soon sold it to Seth P. Mobley, a soldier in the Seventh Iowa Cavalry, and Hiram Brundage, who was then serving as telegraph operator at the fort. In turn, the two partners sold out to the Freeman brothers at the end of 1865, and Brundage moved back to Fort Bridger to resume his *Fourth Infantry Press.*[4]

The Frontier Index was unique because of its frequent relocations. Aptly dubbed "the press on wheels," it followed the building line of the Union Pacific Railroad, and, in fact, the Freeman brothers remained one step ahead of construction, always moving into a railhead before it actually developed into a town. Sustained by their easily transportable press equipment, they often operated out of tents to provide a witty, opinionated, no-holds-barred brand of journalism that suited the frontier environment. Above all, they were perpetual economic boosters for the community in which they were temporarily located and bitter opponents of any rival community.[5]

Although acutely interested in selling advertisement space and serving as local printers for private jobs, the Freemans presented strong editorial opinions even if these cost them business. In the spirit of their masthead motto, "Independence in All Things, Neutrality in Nothing," they published endless tirades against the "Useless Slaughter" Grant administration, Black Republicanism, Credit Mobilier fraud, and Mormonism. With their easy access to telegraphic services, they were able to print national news soon after it was available in the East, and they maintained an exchange program with other newspapers. Unfortunately, their slanted presentation of national political stories and their firm stands on local issues alienated many people. At Bear River City, Wyoming, where the brothers briefly set up operations, an armed mob burned their offices and drove them from town in 1870.[6]

Controversy was also a part of their coverage of western military matters. They repeatedly editorialized about army failures to corral troublesome Indians and open the lands to white settlement. Even when they were located in military communities and seeking contracts from the army, they did not withhold their ire. While residing at Fort Sanders, Wyoming, Legh Freeman picked a fight with the post commander and wound up being thrown off the military reservation. He bitterly alleged in the next issue that the general had turned the newspaper office into a saloon, would eventually expand it into a billiard hall for illicit gambling, and would soon graze his flock of sheep on government land. Freeman, who had previously run into an unspecified problem with the Fort Kearny commander, now blasted both men for muzzling the free press and ruling by fiat.[7]

The Frontier Index was never strictly a military newspaper in the usual sense of the term. While headquartered at Fort Kearny and North Platte, Nebraska, and Fort Sanders and Laramie, Wyoming, it printed many stories about soldiers and larger military policy, but it primarily served civilian subscribers. Under a variety of names, *The Frontier Index* was published at approximately twenty different locations, and only a handful of them were on or near military reservations. Legh Freeman eventually wound up in the state of Washington, where he edited the *Northwest Farm and Home*, a dramatically revised publication that traced its roots to a Fort Kearney of twenty years earlier.[8]

Even before the days of the *Kearney Herald* and *The Frontier Index*, a newspaper written and distributed purely by military men had already made its appearance on the Plains. Fort Laramie's *Chugg Water Journal* was the creation of five officers who amused themselves with clever literary tricks and conundrums. Unable to mass produce the sheets, because no printing press was available, the men hand-copied a few issues for distribution around the post. Editors William Scott Ketchum, Benjamin Stone Roberts, Stewart Van Vliet, Thomas Grimke Rhett, and Dr. Samuel Preston Moore limited their small audience to other officers and civilians who worked at the fort. Their intent was not to deliver local or national news, but rather to provide humor through mock correspondence, features, editorials, quotations, and poetry. They mostly targeted the presumptions of military life, the foibles of individuals, and their own literary excesses. Hand-printed during 1849 and 1850, the *Chugg Water Journal* also contained intricately drawn sketches of scenes from fort life. These, too, were mostly on the humorous side rather than factual reporting of real events.[9]

More encompassing in its approach was the *Frontier Scout*, which made its debut at Fort Union, Dakota Territory, during the summer of 1864. When the Thirtieth Wisconsin Volunteers moved to Fort Rice, Dakota Territory, a few months later, the officers carried their printing press along, but it ultimately had to be left behind because the soldiers were transferred. Upon assuming replacement assignment at Fort Rice, members of the First U.S. Volunteer Infantry found the press and all of its supplies ready for use. Recognizing their good fortune, Capt. Enoch G. Adams, Lt. Charles H. Champney, and Cpl. William Johnson published the first of fifteen issues that would appear between June and October 1865. Unlike previously mentioned newspapers, the *Frontier Scout* truly delivered news to the regiment. It offered less in the way of satire and literary experimentation than did the *Chugg Water Journal* and more closely resembled community newspapers of the day.[10]

The most unusual factor governing the content of this newspaper was the composition of the enlisted men's ranks of the First U.S. Volunteer Infantry. This was largely a regiment of Galvanized Yankees, Confederate prisoners-of-war who were willing to accept frontier military service in return for release from federal stockades. Captain Adams set a positive tone in the first issue when he editorialized about the honesty and loyalty of these men who had once fought against the Union but now embraced it in order to protect exposed settlements from Indian attacks.[11]

Despite its generally upbeat approach, the *Frontier Scout* covered a wide range of pleasant and unpleasant topics. The premier issue contained a full list of all regimental members who had died between October 1864 and April 1865. Subsequent issues carried detailed and poignant accounts of deaths among the women and children as well as the soldiers. Showing no favoritism toward officers over enlisted men, the editors emphasized that all persons were linked in common station upon their passing from the temporal world. Equally egalitarian in their content were the biographical features that appeared in virtually all fifteen issues. Some of the articles profiled particular officers, but others summarized the accomplishments of individual companies within the regiment.[12]

Given the rigidly controlled nature of a frontier post, it is somewhat surprising how candid the *Frontier Scout* could be in dealing with controversial social issues. At least one column roundly chastised certain civilian "hangers-on" at the post for being brigands and for gouging the government by improperly fulfilling their supply contracts. Editor Adams also spoke in favor of women's employment rights at pay equal to the rate for men. Although no friend of the Indian, the newspaper did point out that corruption within the Indian Bureau was a major cause of uprisings and that the system of traders and agents should be cleaned out wholesale. Despite its direct approach toward some controversial matters, the newspaper never turned into a bitter sounding board for personal vendettas. While editor Adams had a running feud with his commanding officer throughout the year, neither man ever vented his rage within the publication. Thus, the *Frontier Scout* remained true to its humble beginnings by addressing real-life concerns at the post and allowing an open forum for enlisted men to voice their opinions.[13]

One month after the Fort Rice newspaper ended its publication, a similarly conceived newspaper was launched at Fort Larned, Kansas. Unlike its predecessor, however, *The Plains* did not continue beyond its premier issue. It consisted of three pages of news, personal commentary, and advertisements and a fourth blank page for soldiers to use in writing their relatives. This first newspaper ever printed in western Kansas had its origins among a group of officers who were socializing one day in the sutler's store. To raise money for the first issue, they collected three hundred dollars in advance subscriptions, and from that sum they purchased a job press and supplies from Saint Louis. Rather than make elaborate claims for their endeavor, the officers editorialized: "We are running a paper for our own amusement—for the fun of the thing— That's all—and why not, pray tell?"[14]

The short-lived effort mixed the comedic element with its more serious stories. One whimsical ad called for a half-dozen young ladies to learn the printing business under the constant instruction of the foreman of the office. But the matter-of-fact tone ended with the admonition that only "good looking ones need apply." Another front-page commentary strongly criticized a recommendation in Hall's *Journal of Health* that married people should not sleep with each other.[15]

The quick demise of *The Plains* was fairly typical of most soldier-produced newspapers. Writing columns, soliciting contributions, editing copy, and overseeing the printing process were time-consuming tasks. Yet the officers and enlisted men who worked on these projects did so on their private time. They were not routinely excused from military duties to perform this work, nor did their efforts appear as a priority to their commanders. Likewise, costs were high for purchasing a press, maintaining it, and acquiring ink and paper for printing. Thus, the men who performed the editorial work frequently had to solicit advertising and subscriptions to launch the enterprise and even more often had to use their personal finances to keep it going. The only salvation for some of the longer-running newspapers was to gain revenue by printing documents and forms that the commanding officer wanted. Only then would capital and release time from normal duties be sufficient for the editors to turn out a consistent product.[16]

The Texas frontier produced a number of army newspapers, but none was more famous than Fort Richardson's *The Flea*, which appeared between February 1 and June 15, 1869. This four-page newspaper drew its inspiration from two other "scandal sheets" published nearby at Fort Belknap and Camp Buffalo Springs, with the respective titles of *Big Injun* and *Grasshopper*. Evidencing considerable wit and charm, Sgt. H. H. McConnell wrote most of the features for *The Flea*, and it became a labor of love for him. In his later memoirs, McConnell explained how the newspaper was created entirely by Fort Richardson soldiers but was printed by a private firm in nearby Weatherford. Local businessmen in Jacksboro, who depended heavily on military trade, supported the newspaper with their advertisements, which enabled it actually to turn a profit. McConnell especially pointed with pride that a major Chicago newspaper reprinted the inaugural issue of *The Flea* for its Illinois audience, and it congratulated the Sixth Cavalry editor for producing the little gem. Although the post newspaper was a success by every definition, it ceased operation after releasing only six issues. Unlike other cases, this was not a result of lack of money or dedication by the staff, but instead because of the transfer of the regiment away from Fort Richardson.[17]

All army newspapers contained humorous articles to entertain and serious discussions to elicit reactions from their audiences, but some newspapers possessed special mandates for social commentary. Chaplain Henry V. Plummer edited the *Fort Robinson Weekly Bulletin* and served as the resident manager of the Fort Robinson department of the *Omaha Progress* during the early 1890s. As the black editor of a black regimental publication, Plummer forthrightly challenged the racism that existed in some corners of Crawford, Nebraska. He urged a general boycott of specific saloonkeepers and questioned the double standards employed by other businessmen in their dealings with black soldiers of the Ninth Cavalry. He also painfully recounted how an enlisted man named Charles Diggs had barely escaped a Crawford lynch mob and was only saved by the quick thinking of his comrades. In an unsigned series of articles, Plummer further warned that if the actions continued, "we will protect ourselves regardless of the consequences," and the white citizens might "arise some morning only to find that the town of Crawford WAS." Lt. Col. Reuben F. Bernard and other white officers at the post charged that the chaplain was inciting insurrection, but they could not prove the case. They then leveled other trumped-up charges against him, and this time he was found guilty and removed from military service.[18]

Because only a minority of forts had their own printing presses, many soldiers found outlets for journalist expression within civilian newspapers. Some served briefly as paid correspondents, but most simply created noms de plume and submitted articles wherever time allowed. Somewhat unique was Alfred Lee Runyon, who had briefly worked for two Manhattan, Kansas, newspapers before joining the Nineteenth Kansas Regiment in late 1868. The editor of one of those newspapers, the *Manhattan Standard*, promised that Private Runyon would send letters from the field campaign against Southern Plains Indians, and these would be duly published. The serialized letters continued to appear throughout the six months of regimental service until Runyon mustered out and headed back to the Manhattan printing trade. In 1874 he joined the *Junction City (Kansas) Tribune*, only to return and establish the *Manhattan Enterprise* two years later. He subsequently purchased the *Clay Center Times* and several other Kansas newspapers before getting out of the business altogether and moving to Pueblo, Colorado, to treat his wife's health problems. Their son, Damon Runyon, became a remarkable journalist in his own right.[19]

Soldiers who were primarily writing for civilian audiences included frequent discussions about the foibles of army life. One enlisted man writing from Fort Supply, Indian Territory, to the *Ford County (Kansas) Globe* in 1878 summarized how badly understrength most infantry companies were. At a recent parade, only six privates out of a company of thirty-seven were available to march. Others were on sick call, extra duty, and excused duty. The letter writer further affirmed that this was not an uncommon situation, and such understaffing grossly interfered with normal life. Another enlisted man writing from the same fort and to the same newspaper a few months later explained how excessive were the demands on soldiers for manual labor and how this contributed to a high desertion rate.[20]

Fort Supply produced an ample corps of journalists for both the *Dodge City Times* and the *Ford County Globe.* The former newspaper printed columns by unidentified soldiers with by-lines such as "Old Cactus" and "Young Cactus." The *Globe* published articles by "Jerry," "Reville [*sic*]," and "Domingo." Clearly, the most clever of this coterie was "Jerry," a satirist and social critic who targeted a wide range of issues.[21] Humor at the expense of other soldiers also appeared frequently in the columns and probably regaled military men and civilians alike. "Old Cactus" reported how a patrol from Fort Supply had encountered the bodies of several civilians who had been hanged from trees on the open prairie. Without making a close inspection, they rode to a nearby ranch and reported the incident. The owner went out to the site expecting to find the worst, but instead he discovered several pairs of pants that his cowboys had left in the limbs to dry.[22] One can only imagine the teasing that members of the patrol must have received when the story became widely disseminated.

Fort Union, New Mexico, produced a collection of soldier-correspondents who rivaled the output of Fort Supply journalists. Writing for the *Las Vegas (New Mexico) Daily Optic* and the *Las Vegas Daily Gazette* during the mid-1880s were "Two Stripes," "philo," and "Gus." Like so many other soldier-journalists elsewhere, they wrote seriously about needs for changes within the army and humorously about the types of people who occupied military posts. Unique among these reporters was Charles J. Scullin, who contributed articles to the *Las Vegas Daily Optic* under the pen name "Mars." A real champion of the rights of enlisted men, Scullin spent part of his writing career in the guardhouse. His repeated confrontations with the commanding officer, his frequent desertions, and his constant complaints about seemingly everything led to his incarceration but never his silence in the civilian newspaper. With the help of sympathetic enlisted men, Scullin smuggled his writings out of the guardhouse, and they soon appeared in print, only to create new controversies with his superiors. Col. Henry Douglas finally requested that the offender be

transferred to Fort Leavenworth Military Prison because he was unre-
pentant and because he was undermining morale among the troops.
Scullin's ultimate fate is not apparent from military files or newspapers,
but his journalistic flair must have remained a topic of conversation for
some time thereafter.[23]

Officers writing for civilian newspapers also used sobriquets, but unlike
Scullin, their identities generally remained protected. Under the nom
de plume of "Sabre," one ranking officer submitted numerous articles
to the *Los Angeles Star* during 1872. These were highly descriptive accounts
of a tour of Arizona and included information on towns, ranches, land-
marks, economic life, forts, and especially the Apache people. Avoiding
virtually all controversy, the columns offered a down-to-earth assessment
of the new land and its potential growth. Why the author even chose to
publish under a pseudonym is intriguing, for he was none other than
Gen. John M. Schofield, commander of the Division of the Pacific. The
informative and noncontroversial report might as well have been
published as a sanctioned government document rather than appearing
anonymously in a newspaper that catered to civilian reading tastes.[24]

Clearly the most interesting and sought-after articles emanated from
large-scale army campaigns against Indians. As with European armies,
which spread colonies around the world during the nineteenth century
and sent their civilian war correspondents to cover battles in these remote
and exotic areas, American newspapers sought to have their own staff
members report back from the field. Some officers relished having these
men cover their campaigns, because it brought them attention in Washington, D.C., and with the public at large. Despite specific orders to the
contrary, Lt. Col. George A. Custer made sure that the *Bismarck Tribune*
sent its assistant editor, Mark Kellogg, to cover the impending victory
against the Sioux and Cheyenne in the Yellowstone country. Unfortunately, the June 25, 1876, Battle of the Little Big Horn took Kellogg's life
along with the lives of more than 250 men of the Seventh Cavalry. In the
interest of selling newspapers, however, "Custer's Last Stand" proved to
be a wonderful saga during the weeks that followed.[25]

More representative of the war correspondents were Charles F.
Lummis, John Finerty, Henry M. Stanley, and DeBenneville Randolph
Keim, men with established journalistic reputations covering three of the

most celebrated Indian campaigns of the century. Lummis eventually gained minor literary fame as a regionalist author who articulated the flavor of Southwestern life. Yet it was his mid-1880s field reports on the Apache Wars that first captured the nation's attention. As field correspondent for the *Los Angeles Times*, he penned numerous articles from Gen. George Crook's headquarters at Fort Bowie, Arizona, and while accompanying army patrols. These reports, written at the time of Geronimo's final breakout from the reservation, made wonderful copy among a public eager for this exciting information.[26]

Finerty, an equally good storyteller in the right place at the right time, rode with General Crook's massive southern column during the 1876 Yellowstone expedition against the Sioux and Cheyennes. As correspondent for the *Chicago Times*, Finerty proved to be one of the best recorders of military life in the field, and his account of the "starvation march" made compelling reading. As a favorite among the soldiers, who dubbed him the "Fighting Irish Pencil Pusher," Finerty showed himself to be courageous under fire, a risk taker in seeking a good story, and attentive to the suffering of enlisted men. He also was exceptionally accurate in reporting these events, even when hyperbole and invented drama might have sold more newspapers. Stanley, later to immortalize himself in the search for Dr. David Livingston in Africa, received the coveted assignment of covering Gen. Winfield Scott Hancock's 1867 expedition through Kansas and western Indian Territory. As reporter for the *Saint Louis Missouri-Democrat*, he objectively recorded the ill-fated operation that subsequently produced rancor among some of the officers. Keim, correspondent for the *New York Herald*, covered Gen. Philip Sheridan's 1868 winter campaign against the Southern Cheyennes and allied tribes with equal skill and published a book-length account two years later.[27]

While civilian correspondents could be assets to enhancing the careers of military officers, they could also be a detriment during a campaign. In addition to Finerty, three other war correspondents—Joe Wasson, Robert E. Strahorn, and Reuben B. Davenport—accompanied Crook's 1876 campaign, all representing different newspapers. Davenport earned the enmity of almost every soldier from Crook down through the greenest of privates with his constant complaints about their performance. By publishing those accounts he could poison public sentiment about the regiment and possibly create pressure to investigate Crook for incompetence.[28]

More troubling were the exaggerated and inflammatory articles submitted from western Nebraska and South Dakota during the height of the 1890 Ghost Dance. Correspondents for regional newspapers clearly helped create an anti-Indian hysteria, and this in turn brought more troops to the area, causing further alarm among the Sioux. Selling more newspapers to an apprehensive public may have helped motivate this jingoism, but another financial consideration may even have outweighed that factor. Citizens in the Black Hills and Pine Ridge areas clearly desired the transfer of more soldiers not simply for protection, but also for the lucrative and immediate contracts that the army would bring to the area. Civilians could sell food and horses, hire out as freighters, and barter directly with the soldiers. The prospect of shifting tens of thousands of dollars of government money into the regional economy helped contribute to the poisoned atmosphere that produced the December 29, 1890, massacre at Wounded Knee.[29]

Although the civilian correspondents who were employed by major national newspapers reached the largest audiences, some officers also filed simultaneous stories from the field in national and regional newspapers. During early 1868, Lt. George Henry Palmer sent communiqués from Fort C. F. Smith, Wyoming, to the *Chicago Tribune* and his Illinois hometown newspaper, *The Monmouth Atlas*. These amazingly candid exposés explained the desperate situation that the army faced in securing the Bozeman Trail against repeated Sioux and Cheyenne attacks. Palmer blamed land speculators and contractors for prolonging the hopeless occupation, and he castigated agents for cheating the Indians and provoking their further resistance. The lieutenant clearly intended that his acerbic letters should produce public pressure and hasten the army's withdrawal from the indefensible Powder River country. Yet as an officer in the Twenty-seventh Infantry, he knew that discovery of his true identity could lead to court-martial. Hence, his published articles carried the byline of his name spelled backwards. Despite his antagonism toward government policy on the Bozeman Trail, Palmer remained in the army, rose to the rank of major, participated in the Spanish-American War, and received a belated Medal of Honor for heroic action in the Civil War battle at Lexington, Missouri.[30]

A number of enlisted men also filed reports from the field, but mostly with civilian newspapers located near their assigned posts. The targeted audiences, therefore, remained relatively small, but the public enthusiasm for their descriptions was large enough to sustain continued publication of their series. Throughout much of 1859 into early 1861 three members of the First Cavalry served as "special correspondents" to the *Leavenworth (Kansas) Daily Times*. With intriguing pen names of "Know Nothing," "Cato," and "Rover," they recorded notable events involving punishment of Comanche raiders in western Indian Territory.[31] Fourteen years later, Pvt. S. S. Peters provided articles for the *Junction City (Kansas) Weekly Union* from the midst of the Red River War against Comanches, Kiowas, and Southern Cheyennes in and near the Texas Panhandle. Civilian scout J. T. Marshall, accompanying Col. Nelson A. Miles's cavalry column in the same campaign, provided similar dispatches for the *Kansas Daily Commonwealth* in Topeka.[32] Throughout the 1876 Yellowstone expedition, "yellow-leg" journalists Sgt. John Powers, Pvt. Daniel Brown, and Pvt. Alfred McMackin, all of the Fifth Cavalry, filed dispatches with the *Ellis County Star* at Hays, Kansas.[33]

Newspapers provided the main outlet for army journalists and civilian war correspondents, but large-circulation magazines also offered a medium for expression. Lt. Col. George Custer published a lengthy series of articles about his service in Kansas and Indian Territory during the late 1860s. Written for the popular *Galaxy Magazine*, these twenty installments provided considerable detail about military life in the field, but they also were aimed at enhancing Custer's public image. Some members of the military, government, and press had severely criticized the "boy general's" performance in the 1868 Battle of the Washita when eighteen of his men had been cut off and killed by Southern Cheyenne warriors. The *Galaxy Magazine* articles, later republished in book form as *My Life on the Plains* (1874), argued Custer's side of the story in precise detail and produced broad public support for him.[34]

When Col. William B. Hazen challenged the veracity of major points in these autobiographical accounts, he felt the full fury of response from Custer and Gen. Philip Sheridan. Hazen's pamphlet, *Some Corrections on*

"My Life on the Plains" (1875), offered important revisions of the printed record but wound up in a no-win public debate that hurt Hazen in the long run.[35] Another detractor, Col. Samuel D. Sturgis, who lost a son at Little Big Horn, identified Custer as "a very selfish man . . . insanely ambitious for glory," whose heroic reputation was "to a great extent formed from his [own] writings and newspaper reports.[36]

Many senior officers followed Custer's lead in publishing their autobiographies, though most books were written near the end of military careers or following retirements. Yet even these after-the-fact memoirs often triggered a debate that became highly personalized and acrimonious. For example, Gen. Nelson A. Miles attempted throughout the 1890s to find a publisher for his life's story, hoping that this would further his anticipated political career. Deals to publish extracts in *Harper's Weekly* and the *Army and Navy Journal* fell through, but his book, *Personal Recollections and Observations of General Nelson A. Miles*, finally appeared in 1896. Unfortunately for him, it resembled less an incisive memoir than a rambling hodgepodge of disconnected thoughts and mundane descriptions.[37]

Among the several controversies that the book raised was the reopening of old wounds with supporters of Gen. George Crook. Although Crook had died six years earlier, many people resented the shabby treatment that he had received from the ambitious glory-seeker Miles at the end of the Apache Wars. Miles had taken undue credit for Geronimo's final surrender and had unfairly imprisoned the Apache scouts who had loyally served Crook for the better part of a decade. Critics blasted Miles and his book on these and other points, further reducing his credibility in the eyes of some Americans. His second book, *Serving the Republic* (1911), fared poorly in the hands of reviewers, not only for its dull and unimaginative prose but also for its flagrant propaganda. The experiences of General Miles proved that writing military memoirs could be a double-edged sword. When handled adeptly, it could provide a measure of fame and fortune, but when done purely for egotistical and self-serving reasons, it could have devastating consequences.[38]

Although subject to the same human frailties and desire for promotion as their superiors, junior officers frequently published the more valuable magazine articles. Among the many who did provide occasional stories, none was more polished or prolific than Capt. John G. Bourke. As aide-de-camp for General Crook throughout the 1870s and 1880s, he participated in the early phases of the Apache wars, the concluding phases of Geronimo's surrender, and the 1876–77 operations against the Sioux and Cheyennes. He published serially in *Outing Magazine* an important account of the 1883 pursuit of Apaches on both sides of the international boundary. Although accurate in its details, the publication went out of its way to rebut some criticisms of General Crook and to demonstrate the valor of officers and men who had undertaken such hazardous duty. Republished in book form by Charles Scribner's Sons in 1886, the work reached a large and appreciative audience. Five years later, the same publisher printed Bourke's more ambitious work, *On the Border with Crook*, which covered the Plains campaigns as well as the Southwestern years.[39]

The Apache Wars of the 1880s provided good copy for magazines and private printing houses throughout the rest of the century. Somewhat surprisingly, a few of the best eyewitness accounts did not see publication until after the frontier era had passed, even though the market was saturated with fictionalized tales from people who had never been to the Southwest. Lt. Britton Davis, commander of Crook's Apache scouts during the mid-1880s and participant in the next-to-final Geronimo surrender, later prepared a wonderful insider's account of events, but it was not published until 1929. Like Bourke, Lieutenant Davis used *The Truth about Geronimo* to pay homage to General Crook, the soldiers, loyal Apache scouts, and even to the "hostiles" whom they were pursuing.[40]

Amid all the people who wrote for newspapers and magazines, however, probably no one had more immediate impact than did civilian correspondent Frederic Remington. Although better known as a painter and sculptor, Remington achieved part of his claim to fame from his magazine articles, which appeared throughout the mid-1880s and 1890s. *Harper's Weekly* sent the twenty-five-year-old artist to Arizona during the summer of 1886 to draw sketches from the Geronimo campaign. Remington thrilled the reading public not only with his numerous sketches of soldiers and Indians, but also with his lively prose. The frontier army became one of the most prized subjects of his art, and he collected military equipment for his eastern studio so that he could accurately paint and sculpt the details. Many of the pen-and-ink drawings accompanied his first-hand stories for *Century Magazine, Outing Magazine, Harper's Weekly,* and *Harper's Monthly* as well as a host of important books authored by men such as Theodore Roosevelt and Richard Harding Davis. Frontier soldiers found a worthy advocate in Frederic Remington, whose art and journalism always paid tribute to their strength and courage.[41]

While officers frequently found outlets for publication in national magazines and with private publishing houses, enlisted men rarely did. Lower rates of literacy, less opportunity for writing, and apparent lack of public interest in the views of "common soldiers" combined to virtually shut them out of the marketplace. Yet even without much hope for literary fame or financial gain, some enlisted men did maintain journals, drafted detailed letters home, and even wrote full-length memoirs in their retirement years. Only slowly during the twentieth century did these primary sources of frontier military life emerge from dusty attics and archival collections to provide a wealth of information for researchers. Precisely because most of these writings were not originally intended for publication, they pulled no punches and were honest in their appraisals about people and situations.

Among those manuscripts that were later published, the format, quality and size ranged widely. Pvt. William Earl Smith, who later served prison time for desertion, praised his commanding officer, Col. Ranald Slidell Mackenzie, while simultaneously lambasting army policies and the brutality of Sgt. Maj. Stephen Walsh.[42] Likewise, Pvt. Theodore Ewert of the Seventh Cavalry kept a journal of Lt. Col. George Custer's 1874 expedition into the Black Hills. Although no great defender of Indians, Ewert criticized the government for violating the 1868 Fort Laramie Treaty and invading these lands that were sacred to the Sioux and Cheyennes. He correctly predicted the outcome of this invasion two years before his regiment met the same Indians at Little Big Horn.[43] Pvt. Josiah M. Rice produced a similar journal of his daily experiences and thoughts during Col. Edwin V. Sumner's 1851 expedition into the heart of Navajo country. As with Ewert's later experience on the Northern Plains, this march did not intimidate the Indians as expected; it only infuriated them more against military authorities.[44] Finally, among the records kept by enlisted men was the fine effort of Pvt. Hervey Johnson, who served along the dangerous stretch of military road between Fort Laramie and Platte River Station between 1863 and 1866. His letters home provided one of the most valuable collections of enlisted men's viewpoints from any theater of combat at any time.[45] Although these men and other common soldiers had to wait until after their deaths to be seen in print, their assessments of frontier military life now serve as important additions to a genre that traditionally was dominated by officers.

While officers and enlisted men wrote primarily about military duties and field campaigns, another type of literature appeared in magazines and books. This was the product of officers' wives such as Francis Anne Mullin Boyd, Teresa Vielé, Francis M. A. Roe, Martha Summerhayes, Alice Blackwood Baldwin, Margaret Irvin Carrington, Lydia Spencer Lane, Emily McCorkle FitzGerald, and Ellen McGowan Biddle.[46] They, too, were interested in promoting their husbands' careers and establishing a place in history through the written word, but they emphasized very different matters than did their male counterparts. Inculcated with the nineteenth-century virtues of "true womanhood"—piety, purity, submissiveness, and domesticity—most of these women accepted a lifestyle that placed their husbands and children at the center of their identity. Their autobiographies are filled with detailed information about living quarters; home furnishings; prized bric-a-brac; problems with servants; difficulty in obtaining adequate supplies; concerns about their children growing up in a restricted environment; pleasant days of parties, picnics, horseback riding and other recreations; and the long periods of loneliness when their husbands were away. Most officers' wives who wrote memoirs presented an overall happy portrayal of military life and expressed a fierce loyalty to the regiment and its exalted reputation. They often were not as kind in their judgments about the rough-and-tumble civilians with whom they came in contact. Just as they endorsed the military pecking order that separated officers' from enlisted men's worlds, they associated only with the civilians whom they considered equal to their station in life.[47]

The most unique and prolific writer among the officers' wives was Elizabeth Custer. Although very much a proponent of "feminine virtues" and always willing to live within her husband's shadow, Libbie Custer was a dynamic woman who became the dominant female figure at every post where she lived. She was the strong force who comforted the other Seventh Cavalry widows in the wake of the Little Big Horn debacle. Despite her own financial concerns, she spent the rest of her life waging a war for better army pensions and in preserving the glory of the frontier army. She wrote three books that helped gain income and, more importantly, that helped perpetuate the heroic image of her departed husband.[48] All three books sold well, and they became a virtual model for other officers' wives who wished to publish their own memoirs. Despite their propagandistic side, these books remain minor classics within this genre of military literature.[49]

Most army officers, their wives, and even enlisted men found their expressive medium in newspapers, magazines, and books, but a very specialized form of publication offered another option. The *Army and Navy Journal* became the unofficial but widely recognized mouthpiece for all levels of military life during the late nineteenth century. Although privately published by William Conant Church, it was warmly supportive of military policies and the men who served within the ranks. Articles covered wide ranges of topics, including the latest technologies, impending legislation, new War Department policies, and even military developments in Europe. But it also included many articles from officers and enlisted men stationed throughout the country. Most of their accounts were highly personalized and rarely contentious, although recommendations for change of policies were routinely included, even when the authors employed pseudonyms. The *Army and Navy Journal* served as a clearing-house for great varieties of experiences and viewpoints, and it heralded itself as part of the reform movement to improve soldiers' educations and their lives. Unlike the more elitist *Cavalry Journal, Infantry Journal,* and *Journal of the Military Service Institution of the United States,* which were dominated by officers' writings, it appealed to all the ranks.[50]

An even more egalitarian publication appeared in the post-frontier era to recapture the spirit of the old army and to work for passage of more liberal pension laws. *Winners of the West,* published by George and Lorena Jane Webb in Saint Joseph, Missouri, from 1922 to 1944, offered a unique forum for veterans to speak of past memories and current concerns. This newspaper represented the official publication of the National Indian War Veterans organization, which had been chartered in Denver, Colorado, in 1911. Dedicated to "The Men Who Protected the Frontier," it attracted donations and mounted a congressional lobbying effort to raise the level of benefits and to eliminate bureaucratic impasses within the Bureau of Pensions. Furthermore, it encouraged veterans to publish letters and reminiscences within the newspaper in order to reestablish contacts with comrades who would see the correspondence. Hundreds of former regulars, mostly enlisted men, not only provided information to *Winners of the West* but also created a highly personalized record of frontier army life.[51]

Amid all of the newspaper, magazine, and book publications by officers, their wives, and enlisted men, only one practitioner gained true fame and fortune from his writings. Captain Charles King served for over a decade in the Fifth Cavalry, fought Apaches during the early 1870s, participated in the 1876 Yellowstone expedition, and trailed Chief Joseph's Nez Percés across Montana during the following years. King loved military life and left it in 1879 only because of a disability from a wound suffered in the Battle of Sunset Pass in Arizona. He participated in the Spanish-American War as brigadier general of volunteers, fought in the Philippine Insurrection, became brigadier general of the Wisconsin National Guard in 1904, and trained troops for World War I. By the time of his retirement in 1932, he had served seventy years of active duty that stretched from the end of the Civil War to the beginning of the New Deal.[52]

King's factual *Campaigning with Crook* (1880) represented a worthy companion to journalist John F. Finerty's *Warpath and Bivouac* in their dual coverage of operations against the Sioux and Cheyennes during 1876. Three years after the appearance of this successful work, King published *The Colonel's Daughter*, the first of sixty-one books that would carry his name. The great majority of these were novels, and they were received with great enthusiasm by a receptive public. Almost all of the novels dealt with his favorite subject—the frontier army—and, despite their formulistic structure, they preserved impeccable accuracy in all details. *The Colonel's Daughter* went through sixteen reprintings, was translated into German, and found a receptive European market. In addition to the novels, biographies, and collections of short stories, King contributed 250 articles to *Cosmopolitan, Lippincott's Monthly Magazine, Saturday Evening Post,* the various *Harper's* magazines, numerous military publications, and a variety of newspapers.[53]

Within that busy publishing life, Charles King also worked with Buffalo Bill in making some of the nation's first movies about the West. Undoubtedly, in the decades that preceded director John Ford's retelling of the frontier army saga, he probably did more than any single person to elevate the old army to a heroic position among the American people. Only Frederic Remington might have been considered a close rival for the attention of the public, but his death in 1909 left King virtually alone in perpetuating the romantic image.[54]

Although American military journalism never had any formal structure or even official sanction during the nineteenth century, it existed because of a grassroots demand for it. Soldiers reveled in the humor of the scandal sheets that circulated from fort presses, and they spoke their minds in their columns and letters to the editor, even if they frequently penned their contributions anonymously. None of the soldier-editors became famous or left lasting literary legacies, but their newspapers entertained and informed their targeted audiences, and they left behind a primary record that is crucial to today's scholars who wish to reconstruct a social history of the frontier army.

On a national level, civilian war correspondents joined with soldier-reporters to document the grand campaigns of the western Indian wars. Most of them reported events as they saw them, and they were content to write about the mundane events of field operations rather than dwell only on rare moments of excitement. These civilian and military correspondents shared hardships with all other campaign personnel, and they found themselves experiencing the same frustrations of guerrilla warfare that provided few decisive battles. Most of the civilian correspondents remained journalists after their brief associations with the army, and a few, such as Henry Morton Stanley, James J. O'Kelly, Robert E. Strahorn, and John F. Finerty, gained a measure of fame.[55]

Ironically, the military and civilian journalists who wrote so much in newspapers and magazines about the West had less influence on the American public than did the smaller number of officers who wrote autobiographies and novels. The end of the nineteenth century produced a wave of nostalgia about the alleged passing of the frontier, and this newly awakened interest continued into the next century. Because officers and their wives effectively provided fond remembrances of the old army, with its code of personal honor, esprit, and regimental loyalty, post-frontier generations came to admire a lifestyle that had otherwise disappeared in the bloody excesses of World War I. The further Americans moved away in time and place from the frontier experience, the more they came to admire and venerate the old "blue coat" veterans. Just about the time that the last of these veterans were passing on, their writings were rediscovered by a post–World War II generation.

Yet it was not historians alone who made use of these rich resources, but also Hollywood moguls, who fed the public appetite for more movies about the frontier army. The cinematic portrayals released during the late 1940s through 1960s owed a debt of gratitude to the earlier soldiers who had recorded events as journalists, autobiographers, and novelists. Unfortunately, the new version of bygone days placed more emphasis on artistic license than it did on accuracy. Only in that manufactured guise did the public reach a comfort level with the legacy of the frontier army.

CHAPTER TWELVE

Life After Soldiering

Entrepreneurs, Investors, and Retirees

Many nineteenth-century Americans perceived the frontier army as an institution filled with drifters, men who served Uncle Sam for a brief time and then moved into oblivion as hired hands and laborers in civilian society. Except for a handful of senior commanders and a smaller number of junior officers who had gained fame in combat, the leadership corps seemed to follow a similar pattern as far as the public was concerned. With rare exceptions, neither the officers nor the enlisted men appeared to be heroes upon which the nation could affix its admiration. Instead, the public took them for granted and ignored their accomplishments. Sgt. H. H. McConnell of the Sixth Cavalry would later assail this spirit of benign neglect when he sarcastically observed that "the loss of one soldier, however, more or less, is not of much importance to anybody, as a general thing, and is hardly worth recording." On a more direct note, Teresa Griffin Vielé, while stationed with her officer husband in Texas, wrote that the unappreciative nation owed a debt of gratitude to this "chain of sentinels" who had sacrificed their lives and comforts to open the West to civilian occupation.[1]

Society's myopia about army life and its importance in frontier settlement also failed to grasp the nonmilitary contributions of these men and their families while on active duty and in the years beyond government service. Especially overlooked were the great number of former soldiers who remained in the West after their separation from the army. They continued to participate in the frontier story, and some of them left adequate records to establish at least a partial restoration of their diverse roles. As land speculators, investors, bankers, railroad executives, businessmen, homesteaders, ranchers, freighters, peace officers, and doctors and in other capacities they remained a vital part of the communities they once had protected as soldiers of the line. Even though many officers engaged in these economic pursuits while they were still in service, most enlisted men lacked the resources, time, and freedom to address these issues until after leaving the army. A few made fortunes, more discovered affluence, many made comfortable lives, and a large percentage undoubtedly failed in their ventures, only to redirect themselves and try again.

To understand why they undertook these enterprises, and how political and business influence was wielded, one must comprehend the nature of the officer corps. Officers always considered themselves to be badly underpaid, with second lieutenants earning only fourteen hundred dollars annually and colonels only thirty-five hundred dollars in 1880. Yet they were forced to live in frontier conditions where the cost of scarce goods was notoriously high. Furthermore, the burden of visiting relatives in the East and sending their children to distant boarding schools drained their resources in the prime years of their earning power. Likewise, government pensions were inadequate to maintain a comfortable standard of living in their declining years. For enlisted men, the situation was even more unpromising, because by 1880 monthly pay had only risen to seventeen dollars for sergeants and thirteen dollars for privates. Payday often came late for soldiers, sometimes several months behind schedule.[2]

The most graphic example of failure in the bureaucratic system came in 1877 when Congress neglected to approve the military appropriation bill, including monthly pay allotments. Locked in a bitterly partisan political battle at the conclusion of Reconstruction, the two parties fought to a budgetary impasse. While some eastern banks extended credit to officers, enlisted men had to rely on smaller credit extensions from post sutlers and local merchants. The Quartermaster Department ran up a deficit of $1.2 million on transportation alone. Even though the impasse was resolved during the following session of Congress, soldiers of all ranks had witnessed the vulnerability of their economic present and future.[3]

To attain financial security in retirement and to better protect against congressional whims, officers found ways to connect themselves with prominent businessmen and politicians. Sometimes, as in the case of Capt. Charles Ruff, this came through marriage. Repeatedly during 1849, Ruff beseeched his powerful father-in-law, John Dougherty, to use his considerable influence with Robert Campbell to create a partnership for him. As two powerful magnates in the fur trade and the Indian Department, Dougherty and Campbell supposedly could secure him a percentage of the government supplies that flowed to the recently constructed Fort Kearny, Nebraska. He proposed himself for a full share in the company, whereby he would be responsible for one-third of the profits and losses of the enterprise. He anticipated the annual sale of at least ten thousand bushels of grain and a huge beef contract for the post and the civilian wagon trains that stopped off there.[4]

In addition to providing capital for his share, Captain Ruff promised to remain at Fort Kearny for at least three years to oversee the operation. Ironically, he made this commitment at the same time he was serving in the Regiment of Mounted Riflemen, a special unit assigned to duty along the Oregon Trail. Dougherty and Campbell undoubtedly understood the hollowness of this pledge to remain at the post for three years, because this highly mobile regiment would surely be transferred within that time. Ruff's attempt to win part of the lucrative supply contract failed, and he was soon ordered to Oregon Territory. His persistence, however, did pay off seven years later when he was promoted to major and received a pay raise. In the meantime, Ruff entered into other Dougherty family investments, including Missouri land speculation, and his brother-in-law, Lewis Bissell Dougherty, received the coveted sutlership at Fort Kearny.[5]

Another ambitious officer who tied himself to the Dougherty political and commercial machine was Lt. Philip St. George Cooke. The young officer married Rachel Hertzog in 1830 after being introduced by Dougherty's wife, Mary, who was Rachel's sister. Like the Ruff marriage, this appeared to be a happy one, but it also provided Cooke with considerable military and government contacts. These enhanced his chances at attaining economic security and promotion, which carried him to the rank of brigadier general of volunteers by the beginning of the Civil War.[6] Likewise, the 1860 marriage of George B. McClellan and Mary Ellen Marcy enhanced the former's military career as well as providing him with an inside avenue toward several lucrative investments. While still a lieutenant, McClellan had served under the command of Capt. Randolph B. Marcy during the 1852 expedition to trace the course of the North Fork of the Red River through present-day western Oklahoma. The two men became close friends, and as Marcy's military career rose during the 1850s, so, too, did his son-in-law's. Through powerful political and private connections McClellan later acted as chief engineer of the Illinois Central Railroad, became president of the Ohio and Mississippi Railroad, and represented the U.S. Military Board in Europe. The situation somewhat reversed itself during the early stages of the Civil War, when General McClellan received command of the Army of the Potomac and Marcy served as his chief-of-staff during the Peninsular and Antietam campaigns.[7]

A relatively recent statistical study by historian John M. Gates has dramatized these types of connections between army officers and powerful civilians. Some relationships were cemented through marriage, but most arose from friendships or a shared investment idea that required cooperation in both spheres. Gates challenged the earlier views of historians Samuel P. Huntington and Allan Millett, who had stressed the "semi-cloistered" and "socially and intellectually isolated" lives of late-nineteenth-century officers. Drawing upon a large sample, Gates demonstrated that "at no time between the Civil War and 1898 does the Adjutant General's report show more than 50 percent of the Army's officers on duty in circumstances that physically isolated them from civilian society." Furthermore, even among those temporarily assigned to isolated posts, they continued to maintain their "eastern connections" as well as to broaden their associations with prominent western civilians. Many of the relationships were primarily social, but others were based on pocketbook issues.[8]

By the time of the Mexican War, the eastern frontier had already provided numerous precedents for high-stakes speculation by officers, especially in the acquisition of land. During the 1830s, Lt. Martin Scott bought four parcels amounting to more than eight hundred acres near Fort Howard, Wisconsin. When offered five thousand dollars for these plots, he declined, saying that he could double that price within six months. Dr. William Beaumont, who had already gained fame for his unique medical work on human digestion, also purchased land near Fort Crawford, Wisconsin, as a financial hedge against retirement. Likewise, Lieutenants Simon Bolivar Buckner and Winfield Scott Hancock invested heavily in strategic lands near Fort Snelling, Minnesota—lands that ultimately became part of the Minneapolis and Saint Paul communities.[9]

Senior officers often had the ability to use their personal knowledge and human contacts to produce private fortunes that were beyond the reach of junior officers. For example, Col. William Lindsay, commander of the Second Artillery, owned a Georgia plantation that was worked by slaves. By 1834 his profits from this enterprise had amounted to 80 percent of his annual military income. His influence must also have been strong within the War Department, because during that year his superiors agreed to establish his regimental headquarters at Athens, Alabama. This allowed him to be near his family and to take a more direct role in managing his plantation. Likewise, Gen. Zachary Taylor spent forty years in military service, all the time acquiring larger landholdings. The centerpiece of his efforts was a 1,923-acre Louisiana plantation worked by eighty-one slaves. By the time he became president in 1849, the value of his estate had risen to at least $135,000. Taylor's success well testified to the fact that he had followed his own maxim: always have a financial escape route from military life.[10]

Among the legion of active senior officers who became involved in wildly speculative schemes during the late nineteenth century, probably none surpassed Col. Benjamin H. Grierson in diversity of business interests. This hero of the Civil War and postwar commander of the celebrated Tenth Cavalry's Buffalo Soldiers made West Texas his financial bailiwick, because he spent much of the 1870s and early 1880s at Forts Concho and Davis. During those years he participated in numerous field assignments, and each patrol or inspection improved his intimate knowledge of the land, its people, and its economic potential. Benjamin and Alice Grierson were especially haunted by the fact that two of their sons, Charles and Robert, suffered from severe psychological problems that required periodic medical treatment, and they worried about the possibility that the sons would not be able to care for themselves in the future. Hoping to rescue all of his children from the "mental strains" that seemed to trigger the bouts of depression, Grierson purchased 5,843 acres near Fort Concho, intending that it would provide a ranch for Robert and two younger sons. Charles, who was a lieutenant in the Tenth Cavalry, also bought 1,417 acres in the vicinity of the post and intended to secure a sizable herd of cattle. Neither venture produced the anticipated windfall, because during that same spring of 1882 all units of the Tenth Cavalry were consolidated at the new regimental headquarters of Fort Davis. It was at this picturesque spot in the Davis Mountains that the Grierson family began their real diversification of investment.[11]

The Fort Davis area seemed to be a dream assignment for the military speculator of the early 1880s. The Indian wars were all but over, ranches were springing up amid the rich grazing lands, two railroads were pushing into the area, and the adjoining civilian town was already established as a commercial center. Grierson quickly secured 3,840 acres and an additional acreage on Limpia Creek even nearer the fort. This became the nucleus for the Grierson Brothers Spring Valley Ranch, which underwent improvements each year. Estimates made in 1906 showed that the family had at one time claimed approximately 45,000 acres in Jeff Davis, Brewster, and Presidio counties. They also owned 126 town lots in the unincorporated town of Valentine and 2,573 acres near old Fort Concho.[12]

Colonel Grierson was not above overtly using his considerable influence to cash in on a real estate deal. Throughout the early 1880s he tried to persuade the War Department to enlarge Fort Davis by purchasing more land around its perimeters. What he did not say in his communiqués was that some of this land was owned by his friends and relatives, who were riding his investment coattails. Likewise, he sent a troop of cavalry to Viejo Pass, forty miles west of Fort Davis, to establish a subpost there. Grierson owned twenty-five hundred acres of flat land at that location and hoped to sell it to the government for a handsome profit. Unfortunately for him, the army turned down the plan.[13]

But this was seemingly a minor setback, since the possibilities for making a small fortune appeared inexhaustible. In early 1884, while Grierson was in Washington, D.C., to strengthen his promotion chances, he made a side trip to New York City to seek advice from railroad moguls Collis P. Huntington and Thomas Pierce. He asked for their advice on building a shortline railroad from Fort Davis to Marfa, where it would intersect the mainline Southern Pacific Railroad. Having secured capital from the banking firm of M. P. Myers and Co. in his hometown of Jacksonville, Illinois, he prepared to start construction of the twenty-mile linkage track. Again, bad luck undermined his innovative plan, which might have paid off over the long run. On February 14, 1885, orders came for Grierson's Tenth Cavalry to transfer to Arizona, and the railroad deal fell through before construction could begin.[14]

Because Benjamin Grierson was loyal to his friends and extended family, some of his fellow officers were able to profit from his Fort Davis investment schemes. Lt. Mason Marion Maxon, who was married to Grierson's niece, Grace Fuller, became the chief beneficiary of this close association. Grierson appointed Maxon regimental quartermaster in 1882, and in that capacity the lieutenant sometimes detailed soldiers to undertake repair projects on Grierson's ranch. In addition to a sizable ranch near the post, Maxon also owned Fort Davis town lots, some of which he deeded to Grierson. By 1884, Maxon had introduced 869 goats to the ranch, including 300 valuable Angoras, as well as unspecified numbers of cattle.[15] Although the two ranches did not cause much controversy, civilian residents of the community resented the growing monopoly of town lots by the Grierson clique. Capt. William Wedemeyer later recorded in his memoirs that some of these residents worked to secure Grierson's transfer out of the region because of his tight grip on the town and its future.[16] Besides Colonel Grierson and Lieutenant Maxon, at least five other members of the Tenth Cavalry purchased significant numbers of town lots during that era: Lt. Charles Grierson, Lt. Samuel Woodward, Lt. Charles Nordstrom, Bandmaster George M. Brenner, and Ordnance Sergeant Charles Mulhern.[17]

Following his retirement from military service in 1890, Benjamin Grierson returned to his Spring Valley Ranch at Fort Davis. From there he also operated a telegraph service and employed family friend John L. Jones to handle the business. Even after his death in 1911, Grierson's sons continued to manage the cattle operation, and the youngest two, Harry and George, remained in the area as ranchers for over forty years. Ironically, despite all his efforts to provide a comfortable life for his family, Benjamin Grierson left a tangled web of debts and financial confusion because he had overextended himself and had taken on too many high-interest loans. His dream of creating a family dynasty thus remained but a fleeting memory for the second generation.[18]

The Trans–Pecos River area of Texas attracted three other officers to its potential riches during the same era that Grierson was seeking his fortune. Lt. John R. Bullis, commander of the Seminole-Negro Scout detachment, knew the area from his frequent patrols and from guarding Southern Pacific Railroad surveying crews. Between 1882 and 1884 he claimed over 53,000 acres in Pecos County alone, although much of it was desert land with little commercial value.[19] More lucrative was the partnership he formed in 1880 with Col. William R. Shafter, Lt. Louis Wilhelmi, and rancher John W. Spencer. Following Spencer's discovery of silver ore, the men filed on nine sections of state school lands in the rugged Chinati Mountains. Shortage of funds and a reconsideration of the area's geology caused them to purchase only four of the sections, but these proved to contain the silver deposits that they had been seeking. Wealthy San Francisco mining speculator Daniel Cook joined the partnership, which became known as the Presidio Mining Company.[20]

Despite contentiousness among the partners and Bullis's loss of a key property case in the Texas Supreme Court, the company prospered, even showing a profit in its first full year of operation. The adjoining town of Shafter housed several hundred miners and supported a thriving economy. It developed into a "company town," where the Presidio Mining Company provided everything, including the stores, the residences, and even the doctor. Between 1883 and 1942, the mine produced 32.6 million ounces of silver, valued at well over $120 million, and helped stimulate the previously dormant economy of the larger region. Unfortunately, as so often happened in hard-rock mining, which required considerable technology and capital and a trained work force, most of the profits flowed to California investors.[21]

Because of its promise of quick wealth, mining was an important lure to other army officers during the second half of the nineteenth century. In the midst of the California Gold Rush of the 1850s, officers stationed in that frontier region watched their pay devalued by rising inflationary prices of a boom economy. Capt. William Tecumseh Sherman felt the reality of the seventy dollars he received each month compared to the three hundred dollars that allegedly could be demanded by a common servant. Likewise, Capt. Ulysses S. Grant pointed out that a civilian cook routinely made more money than an army captain. Realizing that morale was fast declining among his staff, department commander Gen. Persifor F. Smith encouraged them to make money on the side. Responding to the open-ended invitation, his aide, Sherman, made six thousand dollars during a two-month leave. Lieutenants John Bell Hood and George Crook teamed up to net one thousand dollars from a bumper wheat crop. Other West Point–trained engineers bartered their services to survey mining districts, lay out townsites, and oversee construction projects. By far the most successful of these visionaries was Capt. Joseph L. Folsom, who eventually amassed over a million dollars, temporarily making him the richest man in California.[22]

Especially noteworthy were the mining operations of Samuel Peter Heintzelman, who had begun service in the Second Infantry in 1826 and had performed meritoriously during the Mexican War. While stationed in California during the early phases of the Gold Rush, he demonstrated his acumen by buying valuable town lots in the bustling port of San Diego. After being transferred to Fort Yuma, Arizona, in 1850, he created a partnership with important local residents such as Charles Poston and became president of the Sonora Exploring and Mining Company, capitalized at over two million dollars. Although he never cashed in on a big bonanza, Heintzelman maintained a sizable income and a comfortable lifestyle that exceeded the one provided by his army pay. Always one to maintain a policy of diversity in his investments, he owned or held stock in a ferry company, grocery business, ranch, and railroad. Despite his numerous business associations, Heintzelman was never accused of slighting his military duties.[23]

Another senior officer satisfied his mining and land speculation ambitions in the newly opened Black Hills of Dakota Territory. Col. Samuel D. Sturgis served during the late 1870s as commander of the military post that would eventually become known as Fort Meade. Established on the northeastern edge of the Black Hills, the fort was in close proximity to the numerous gold-field camps that were opening around Deadwood. Each of the small townsites competed with the others for dominance, and one of these, Sturgis City, received not only the commander's blessing but also his investments. In association with Jeremiah C. Wilcox, a cousin of his wife, Sturgis purchased several blocks of town lots. Sensing greater potential wealth beneath the ground, he joined a group of expectant capitalists to form the Fort Meade Hydraulic Gold Mining Company and became the president. Associated with the enterprise were Capt. Henry Jackson of the Seventh Cavalry and territorial delegate Granville Bennett. Together they built a mammoth tunnel along Rapid Creek to "obtain access and drainage of that extremely rich auriferous stream." The company was valued at a half million dollars, sold stock for five dollars a share, and marketed milled timber as a supplementary business.[24]

Because tremendous capitalization was necessary in hard-rock mining operations, and since most officers were not assigned to mining districts for extended periods, they generally speculated in a more proven venture: town lots. When French traveler Louis L. Simonin visited the emerging metropolis of Cheyenne, Wyoming, in 1867, he was awed by the powerful influence of Col. John Dunlap Stevenson, commander at nearby Fort D. A. Russell. Not only had Stevenson acquired choice corner lots, but he had also erected a sizable stone warehouse to handle the shipments of goods arriving daily by the Union Pacific Railroad. In describing the colonel's routine, Simonin might well have been describing a land baron or industrialist instead of a military officer: "Every day the General [by brevet, for Civil War service], in his 'buggy' drawn by two smart horses, visits his growing estates and calculates like Perette how much they will bring him."[25] A few months later, the *Cheyenne Daily Leader* noted that Stevenson had built a substantial plank sidewalk along the block of Seventeenth Street that he owned. He also had donated four lots to Catholic residents to build a church in the middle of the town.[26]

While most senior officers specialized in a certain type of investment and often in a region where they served for an extended period, some spread their holdings throughout the entire country. Gen. Nelson A. Miles, husband to the niece of powerful Ohio senator John Sherman and of Gen. William Tecumseh Sherman, blatantly used his familial relationships to enhance his military career and to engage in lucrative financial activities. When he finally reached the exalted position as Commander-in-Chief of the Army in 1895, he had accumulated a long list of influential friends and business associates. As early as 1867, he found opportunities under Southern Reconstruction to speculate in timber. Two years later, upon being transferred to the Great Plains, he used his savings and his wife's dowry to purchase land in Kansas and Colorado, partly in association with Senator Sherman. Powerful political friends also brought him into the Columbia Heights Association in 1883 to develop exclusive rental properties in that section of Washington, D.C. By the time of his death in 1925, Miles's financial empire included extensive western lands, western timber holdings, properties in Washington, D.C., mineral interest on Puget Sound, Texas oil interests, and an insider stock trading position through his brother-in-law, Colgate Hoyt, who was a Wall Street broker. Miles had wisely constructed a financial hedge against any decline in one part of his empire by backing it up with the profits of his other investments.[27]

Although on a much smaller scale, some junior officers and even some enlisted men also took ample advantage of the speculative market. Crawford, Nebraska, provided a natural lure for investments from nearby Fort Robinson by the 1880s. Capt. Augustus Corliss and Lts. Philip Betters, Edgar Hubert, and William McAnany, as well as Surgeon Walter Reed, offered rental properties there to soldiers and civilians alike. Several sergeants also offered similar kinds of housing. Post commander Col. James Biddle actually promoted this profitable system, because the fort could not adequately house all of its troops at that time.[28] During the same era, the *Billings (Montana) Post* reported that Pvt. John Stanley, stationed with the Fifth Infantry at Fort Custer, had recently invested fifteen hundred dollars in town lots. Yet the incredible story may have been apocryphal, intended to whip up the investment spirit in Billings. Certainly a private with a personal portfolio of fifteen hundred dollars would have been a significant story, and explaining how he came by that small fortune should have been a natural component of the article.[29]

Not everyone who turned to the lure of investments possessed the Midas touch. Some played the game for such big stakes that their financial empires perpetually tottered on the brink of disaster. No example of ego, ambition, greed, and bad luck better personified the problem than did that of John C. Frémont. Because of his various explorations in the West during the 1840s and his highly visible role in the conquest of California, Frémont became something of a household name by the following decade. His political and business associations came through his powerful father-in-law, Missouri Senator Thomas Hart Benton, who had long been active in expanding America's borders to the Pacific Ocean. During the California Gold Rush, and following the resignation of his commission, Frémont purchased extensive land and mining interests in the Mariposa District. Unfortunately for him, the large estate required constant infusions of developmental capital, and he spent considerable time in the East and in Europe seeking wealthy investors. Adding to the problem was the fact that he did not have clear title to the land, and in the end, the lengthy court battles all but ruined him. His own lack of business skill hastened the demise of his seventy-square-mile holdings, which passed out of his hands in 1864, just as his military and political dreams were on the wane.[30]

Trying to regain his lost fortune, Frémont became involved in a flurry of railroad investments, on which he staked the remainder of his money. He briefly held the Kansas Pacific franchise, acquired part interest in the Memphis and Little Rock Railroad, and became president of the Memphis and El Paso Railway. By 1871, however, he was virtually bankrupt, and his name had been sullied by the Memphis and El Paso's fraudulent business practices. Only the writings of his wife, Jessie, and help from friends kept the family solvent until Frémont received appointment as Arizona's territorial governor in 1878 from the Rutherford B. Hayes administration. Although it attained some small measure of social prestige in this political office, the family continued to face financial problems. Discovery of Frémont's secretive mining deals and charges of frequent absences from territorial duties forced his resignation in late 1881. By 1890, friends finally were successful in getting him restored to the army as a major general so that he could receive a pension and partially pay his creditors. His death that same year marked the end of a long history of personal triumphs and failures for this wildly ambitious American soldier, politician, and businessman.[31]

Less traumatic to a long-term career, but no less important at the moment, was William Tecumseh Sherman's experience with California banking during the height of the Gold Rush. Having graduated from West Point in 1840, having gained little fame in the Mexican War, and now facing a dismally slow promotion schedule, Sherman resigned his commission in 1853. He had already experienced the Gold Rush firsthand and had been present when James Marshall brought the first nuggets to Monterey to be assayed. He had also helped draft the official 1848 report to President James K. Polk that was ultimately published and became a clarion call for the great westward migration. Wisely recognizing that San Francisco would become the center of this boom, he entered into a partnership to create a branch of a prominent Saint Louis bank.[32]

Using personal savings and his numerous properties in San Francisco as collateral, Sherman became senior resident partner of the enterprise, and he stood to profit handsomely. The bank, however, soon became overextended and was unable to collect delinquent accounts from some of its biggest borrowers. A bank run in 1857, partly triggered by a nationwide financial panic, pushed Sherman's operation to bankruptcy. Despite his personal honesty in trying to meet corporate and personal responsibilities, his name became associated with ineptness and even corruption. With pocketbook empty and reputation sullied, he moved to Leavenworth, Kansas, where he tried to practice law. This endeavor also ended in failure, and he hesitatingly assumed the presidency of a small Louisiana college in 1859. Only the emergence of the Civil War saved Sherman from oblivion and provided him the forum to become Commander-in-Chief of the Army in 1869.[33]

While William Tecumseh Sherman demonstrated personal integrity in trying to save a tottering business, other officers held questionable ethical standards in their investments. Beginning with his 1857 entry into West Point, George Armstrong Custer seemed more motivated by the monthly payments of twenty-eight dollars and the free education than by a desire to serve the country. Even at that early date he wrote to his sister about how other West Point graduates had gone on to make fortunes through their associations with powerful men, and he hoped to do the same. Following his graduation and his gaining fame in the Civil War, young Custer eagerly sought a means to attain financial security. When representatives of Benito Juárez's Mexican government-in-exile offered him sixteen thousand dollars a year to serve as adjutant general in its war against Emperor Maximilian, he happily agreed. Yet when he applied for a year's leave of absence from the U.S. Army to accomplish this task, Secretary of State William Seward dashed his hopes by blocking the request on the grounds that it would upset American and French diplomatic relations.[34]

What Custer sought in his relationship with the Juárez government was not illegal but clearly was self-serving. It was during his subsequent fifteen years of duty on the frontier that his financial chicanery became more evident. In 1873, Lt. George D. Wallace accused Custer of taking kickbacks from the captain of the steamboat that was accompanying the Seventh Cavalry up the Missouri River. Wallace surmised that the column was marching only short distances each day before making camp because the captain received an extra twenty dollars of government money per hour while the boat was tied to the riverbank. Allegedly, Custer was taking a portion of this profit. Within two years Custer also seemed to be working with transportation king Ben Holladay in a secretive effort to establish coaching and freighting operations into the recently opened gold fields of the Black Hills. Custer's need for quick money was readily apparent in 1875 because he had become involved in a wild stock market scheme that cost him eighty-five hundred dollars. Later litigation in the District of Columbia Supreme Court revealed to the justices that he had indeed been involved in an "illicit business."[35]

Even before the Black Hills scheme unfolded, Custer had already shown a compulsion to invest in risky mining ventures. In 1871 he received a leave of absence while the Seventh Cavalry was stationed on Reconstruction duty in the South. He used the time to promote the Stevens silver mine near Georgetown, Colorado, and he wrote to wife Libbie: "If I succeed in this operation as now seems certain, it is to be but the stepping stone to large and more profitable undertakings."[36] He made the rounds of New York City, enlisting the aid of powerful financiers such as John Jacob Astor, Jim Fisk, August Belmont, Levi Morton, Leonard Jerome, and Jay Gould. Belmont subscribed fifteen thousand dollars to the mine, Astor provided ten thousand dollars, and Custer put in thirty-five thousand dollars, although most of his total represented contributions of small investors. The highly speculative and "watered" stock proved to be weak from the beginning and resulted in economic disaster for everyone concerned.[37]

Even when Custer seemed to assume the moral high ground on an issue, baser motivations often spurred his actions. He played a key role in the 1875–76 congressional hearings on corruption among traders who monopolized the flow of annuities to Indian reservations. Sounding like a defender of victimized Native Americans against a heartless machine of greed, he not only recounted specific instances of illegality, but he also named names. His allegations against Secretary of War William W. Belknap and President Ulysses S. Grant's younger brother as co-conspirators in the alleged Indian Ring temporarily cost him command of the Seventh Cavalry. Yet his seeming act of bravery also made him a hero in many people's eyes. His detractors, however, contended that Custer was trying to enhance his career while simultaneously creating a smoke screen around his own improprieties. Indeed, he previously had shaken down some of the traders who had refused to pay him kickbacks or perform other favors. He blackmailed some post sutlers and went into partnerships with others. Although these actions did not seem to reap great economic rewards for him, they clearly pointed out that he had crossed the accepted line of behavior.[38]

Ironically, Custer's greatest display of a conflict of interest came in the Black Hills just after his 1874 exploring party helped open the area to miners. Although guaranteed to the western Sioux by the Fort Laramie Treaty of 1868, these sacred lands became mere exploitable resources in his and many other white men's eyes. Custer's key role in this partnership with Ben Holladay and Col. Rufus Ingalls was to popularize the Black Hills and play upon his friendship with Gen. Philip Sheridan so that he could personally locate sites for all future military posts in the region. Advance knowledge of War Department construction plans would assure them a head start into the freighting and coaching operations, allow them to purchase the best lands for speculation, and perhaps entice the Northern Pacific Railroad to lay track into their dominion.[39] Ingalls, wartime friend of Custer and serving as acting quartermaster of the army in 1875, also discussed with Custer a plan to entice the army to purchase a large order of the controversial Goodenough horseshoes for its cavalry regiments. The private correspondence among these men raises questions about influence peddling and possible fraud, but it is insufficient to convict them of any crime. Potential charges of malfeasance were clearly negated by Custer's death at the Little Big Horn on June 25, 1876, because he quickly was raised to virtual sainthood in the eyes of most Americans.[40]

Not so lucky was Col. George Forsyth, who had also experienced a moment of glory when his civilian scouts held off a larger Cheyenne force in the 1868 defense of Beecher's Island. Twenty years later he faced a general court-martial at Fort Huachuca, Arizona, based largely on the claim that he had signed two months of his pay vouchers over to a local merchant. Then he allegedly drafted similar vouchers for the same two months and signed them over to Capt. William Tisdall. Added to this serious offense were separate charges that he had borrowed money from enlisted men and had appropriated a buggy from a sergeant without paying just compensation.[41]

Forsyth's financial problems stemmed from years of losses on the stock market. He fell into a cycle of increasing debt that he tried to shore up with even more speculative ventures in manufacturing and mining. Even after his transfer to the relatively isolated border post of Fort Huachuca, he continued to borrow money from individuals to cover previous loans. The charges brought by Capt. Abram E. Wood were compelling, although the motivation may have rested more on revenge. Drawing upon his earlier legal training, Forsyth ably defended himself before the thirteen members of the court-martial board but was found guilty on the main charge. The final sentence came directly from President Grover Cleveland, who labeled the offenses as "reprehensible" and "subversive of the honor and integrity of the service." He ordered that the guilty officer be suspended from the army for three years at half pay and that he be reprimanded in general orders.[42] Colonel Forsyth's fall from grace elicited a stern warning to other military personnel from Gen. John Schofield, who was serving as acting secretary of war. In executing the president's orders, Schofield especially directed young officers "to live modestly on the sufficient means provided for their support" and thereby avoid "the disasters which so often follow a greedy pursuit of money."[43]

Despite his personal tragedy, Forsyth maintained his dignity and received support from powerful military friends. Within a year after his punishment was issued, they successfully requested a hearing based upon new information about his health. Private doctors who had examined Forsyth had concluded that a head wound suffered in the Battle of Beecher's Island had created a condition known as hypomania. This malady supposedly worsened over time and produced behavioral problems that resulted in his indebtedness. This medical evidence led in January 1890 to his restoration to active duty, but also a simultaneous retirement because of disability. With pension and reputation restored, Forsyth had weathered the worst of the storm, but his financial problems remained.[44]

While Colonel Forsyth's personal problems attracted relatively little public attention, a more visible booster of frontier development was eliciting considerable notice. Col. James S. Brisbin published *The Beef Bonanza, or How to Get Rich on the Plains* in 1881, and this helped create a ranching boom on the Northern Plains. Although generally associated with cattle raising, Brisbin gave equal attention to Great Plains agriculture and was dubbed, "Grasshopper Jim" by his soldiers because of his homestead promotiveness. Despite already evident problems with the Homestead Act, he wrote in 1881: "The mighty West! . . . where the poor professional young man, flying from the over-crowded east and Tyranny of a monied aristocracy, finds honor and wealth . . . where there are lands for the landless, money for the moneyless . . . and above all, labor and its reward for every poor man who is willing to work. . . . No industries man can make a mistake in moving West, and if I had a son to advise, I should by all means say to him, 'Go West as soon as you can!'"[45]

Because military men were in the forefront of frontier investing, it is little wonder that many of them, like Brisbin, became powerful boosters for settling the West and exploiting its resources. A few, however, addressed the issue from a more realistic vantage point. Col. William B. Hazen served on the entire length of the Plains during the late 1860s and 1870s, and he strongly believed that the area was not suited for intensive agriculture. In an 1874 letter to the *New York Tribune,* he charged that financier Jay Cooke and the Northern Pacific Railroad were intentionally misrepresenting the climatic and soil conditions of the Dakotas and Montana to sell lands to gullible farmers and town builders. Lt. Col. George A. Custer, in service to this railroad, blasted Hazen's claims in a *Minneapolis Tribune* article, setting off a debate through other articles and speeches.[46]

Hazen's most authoritative word on the subject came in an 1875 pamphlet, *Our Barren Lands: The Interior of the United States West of the 100th Meridian, and East of the Sierra Nevadas.* Although the publication was overly pessimistic and failed to take into account the impact of new agricultural technology, it was more honest than the boomer literature coming from railroads and land speculators. Hazen's remarks presaged the even more damning 1878 report of Maj. John Wesley Powell, *Report on the Lands of the Arid Region of the United States*, which lambasted American land policies in the drier regions of the West. Given the high number of Homestead Act allotments undertaken on the Plains by 1910, it is evident that boosterism won out over the warnings of Hazen and Powell. Yet the high ratio of failed farmsteads also testified to the correctness of those warnings.[47]

Although the frontier army was filled with officers who sought big-stakes investments that would provide them with financial independence, most probably were content to supplement their military pay and seek a comfortable retirement. Fort Belknap, Texas, provided a haven for just such small-stakes land purchases during the 1850s. Col. Albert Sidney Johnston, Maj. George H. Thomas, Maj. Henry Hastings Sibley, Maj. James Duff, Col. Middleton Tate Johnson, and Capt. Newton G. Givens all bought land in the vicinity of the post. Lt. Edward F. Abbott later deeded fifty acres of his holdings for the county seat of Young County. Likewise, a number of enlisted men bought land and retired there to raise crops on contract to the army. Several of the former soldiers, as well as Major Duff, even remained in the area long enough to help organize the county government.[48]

Another officer destined to gain fame in the Civil War also considered early exit from the army and possible plantation life in Antebellum Texas. While stationed at Fort Mason, Lt. James Longstreet purchased 50 acres of choice land for future sale or possibly on which to settle. Exactly two decades later, Col. Ranald S. Mackenzie acquired 960 acres near San Antonio, Texas, in the hopes of marrying Florida Tunstall and ultimately retiring to the estate. With an even more determined eye fixed on retirement, Maj. Frank Baldwin purchased a farm near Denver, Colorado. He hoped to enjoy a leisurely life with his grandchildren, but his uncontrollable temper drove away his hired help and endangered the entire enterprise. Even a speculative gambler such as Gen. William Shafter was content to seek a farm in Kern County, California, as he neared retirement.[49]

Surprisingly resourceful were several enlisted men at Fort Dodge, Kansas, who looked forward to early discharge from the army. While still on active duty, each claimed a quarter-section of land and recorded it in the U.S. Land Office at nearby Larned. In doing so, they posed as civilians, and during their leaves they made the necessary improvements to meet the letter of the law. By the time they left the service, they had a sizable estate awaiting their full-time occupation or their sale to another party.[50]

The record of enlisted men and their lives after military service is of course an incomplete one. Yet the anecdotal evidence that survives indicates that a significant number of veterans found productive careers as civilians. Sgt. James A. Richardson retired after thirty-five years in the army to become a successful contractor for the New England Telephone Company. Pvt. Walter C. Harrington resigned from service in the mid-1890s, acquired a business education, and eventually established his own building supply company. At about the same time, Pvt. George Whitaker and Pvt. James G. Morrison became guides and rangers in Yellowstone National Park. Jacob Horner mustered out of the Seventh Cavalry and took employment as a butcher in Bismarck, North Dakota. Jacob Sobel, also of the Seventh Cavalry, experimented with even more diverse jobs after leaving the army in 1882. He first homesteaded near Billings, Montana, then opened a business college in the town and eventually became a major contractor who built roads and bridges throughout Montana, and especially in Yellowstone National Park. While Pvt. John Duke found success as a cattleman, dairyman, and hotel owner in Arizona, Pvt. Frank Heidelberger made a new life as a skilled blacksmith in the Black Hills mines. Sergeant Major W. H. Pickens, who had been a journeyman carpenter in Chicago before his 1873 enlistment, excelled in military life but mustered out within five years. He moved to Plattsmouth, Nebraska, where he became a highly sought after contractor.[51]

While many of these former servicemen found some measure of economic success in their new careers, a smaller number also discovered social and political prominence. George Eaton left the military in 1883, was elected to the first and second constitutional conventions of Montana Territory, and served five years as surveyor general. Former surgeon Henry H. Ruger and enlisted man Henry Hale both served in the North Dakota state legislature.[52] Danish-born Christian Madsen, of the Fifth Cavalry, gained fame as a U.S. deputy marshal in Indian Territory and as Oklahoma City's chief of police. The same regiment also produced

Medal of Honor awardee Sgt. Clay Beauford, who commanded the Apache police force at San Carlos Agency and who later was elected to Arizona's territorial legislature. William F. Morris, veteran of the 1876 Battle of the Little Bighorn, rose to prominence as justice of the New York City Municipal Court. Following his military service, Chaplain Winfield Scott became chairman of the Scottsdale, Arizona, school board and Maricopa County representative to the territorial legislature. The town itself carried his name, in deference to his popularity and importance as a pioneer of the region.[53]

While other veterans did not attain fame, they did preserve their military ties by settling near the forts to cater to soldiers and to compete for government contracts. Former soldier Ephraim Polly and his wife operated the stage station known as the Polly Hotel between Fort Elliott and Camp Supply from 1874 to 1884. Travelers considered their food and accommodations to be far superior to those of other establishments along the military road through present-day western Oklahoma. When Sgt. Charles Mulhern retired at Fort Davis in 1885, he owned thirty sections of grazing land and was a major supplier of local beef to the post.[54] Likewise, when Francis Rooney retired, he settled at Fort Stockton, Texas, where he developed an expansive irrigation project on Comanche Creek. He raised corn, barley, and oats, which were contracted to the fort, sometimes as many as twenty to forty wagons full at a time. Sgt. Frederick William Young also remained at Fort Stockton to become post trader and ultimately to establish the prosperous Diamond Y Ranch. He was elected the first county surveyor of Pecos County, was an early postmaster, and held the position of county judge.[55]

Perhaps the most successful of the former soldiers to operate as a military supplier on the Southern Plains was former quartermaster William McDole Lee. As early as 1869, he and civilian partner Albert E. Reynolds had begun to provide food to Camp Supply and the nearby Cheyenne and Arapaho Agency. They also expanded into trade with cowboys on the Western Trail from Texas to Dodge City. Profits from these ventures then went toward purchase of half-interest in the huge LS Ranch of the Texas Panhandle. Lee and Reynolds were notorious for using their money and influence to undermine competitors as they established the largest freighting operations out of Dodge City. Ultimately known as "the boss traders of the Southwest," they diversified their investments wisely. Just as the buffalo hide trade began its decline on the Southern Plains by 1878, Lee shifted much of his assets into ranching, and later into oil and ships.[56]

Some military posts provided better long-term opportunities for former servicemen than did others. Certainly Fort Robinson, Nebraska, made a likely magnet for continued interest among veterans who had served there during its glory days of the late 1870s. Because it continued as an active post well into the twentieth century, and because it helped create a lively economy for Crawford and the surrounding area, many retirees stayed beyond their term of duty. A relatively recent microcosmic social study indicates how white soldiers took up farms, started ranches, opened feed stores, started barbershops, organized a traveling orchestra, worked as clerks, created a restaurant, hired out as teamsters, and worked for the railroad. Some of them also served on the Crawford school board, city council, and fire department as well as holding county offices.[57]

Black veterans also found the area suitable for life beyond military service. Some maintained civilian jobs at the fort as cooks, bartenders, and attendants in the post exchange. The tasks and pay were menial, but for many black veterans the lack of an advanced education and the presence of a strongly racist society precluded opportunities elsewhere. Preston Brooks, formerly of the Ninth Cavalry, held a skilled and responsible civilian position as post engineer for eleven years. He managed the sawmill and waterworks, earning sixty dollars a month, until he lost his job after striking a white employee.[58]

Other black veterans worked on neighboring ranches. The most celebrated of these was Sgt. John Butler, a bronco buster for the famed 04 Ranch. He became a favorite employee of the Cook family and stayed on long after he had reached an advanced age. Butler lived the remainder of his life in poverty in Crawford after he was robbed of his life's savings. Also employed by the 04 Ranch was Alex Stepney, who worked as a bunkhouse cook for many years after his 1891 discharge from the military. Following his ranch years, he moved to Crawford with his wife, Fannie, and worked as a mail carrier between the fort and the railroad depot.[59]

Information on other black veterans who remained in the area is incomplete, but, as with white soldiers, their experiences varied. Henry

McClain and Rufus Slaughter established homesteads, while William Howard and his wife hired out as farm laborers. James Williams opened a restaurant but had to close its doors about a year later. George Wilson trained horses for Dawes County residents until he died at age sixty-seven. Sandy Tournage worked for a livery stable until he was killed in 1897 by an unknown assailant. Among all the black soldiers who remained near Fort Robinson, Charles Price emerged as the most financially successful. In 1916 he had personal property valued at one thousand dollars, much of it earned through gambling and bootlegging.[60]

Although blacks found limited job opportunities in northwestern Nebraska, and none ever held public office during the frontier era, they did create a viable community within the broader community. The black families helped each other through tough times, intermarried with each other, and formed their own social organizations to promote their unique identity. In 1895 they established a chapter of the Regular Army and Navy Union. They held their own masquerade balls and in 1913 opened their own church. The latter not only served as a religious institution, but also provided numerous socials, dinners, and fundraisers. White residents of Chadron sometimes attended these interracial functions, but the organizations primarily addressed black needs.[61]

The varied experiences of black and white soldiers at Fort Robinson and throughout the West help dispel the popular image of frontier army veterans as being unimportant elements in civilian society. On the contrary, large numbers found suitable employment and made comfortable lives for themselves and their families. Many of the officers invested in western lands, mines, railroads, and commercial enterprises, and a significant number of them remained in the frontier states and territories following their retirement. Enlisted men also seem to have speculated as far as their financial resources would allow, and an even higher percentage of them than of the officers apparently remained in the West. As farmers, ranchers, skilled tradesmen, clerks, freighters, and small businessmen, and in a host of other vocations, they continued to seek their futures in the lands they once had sworn to protect. They truly proved that there was a life beyond soldiering.

Conclusion

In a 1921 address at a dinner for the Order of the Indian Wars, Gen. Charles King summarized his experiences during the Sioux Campaign of 1876. Amid the rich detail about personalities, logistical planning, and the final clash at Little Big Horn, King offered a paean to the forgotten soldiers of America's long frontier era. He concluded with the honorific and yet melancholy words:

> A more thankless task, a more perilous service, a more exacting test of leadership, soldiership, morale and discipline no army in Christendom has ever been called upon to undertake than that which for eighty years was the lot of the little fighting force of regulars who cleared the way across the continent for the emigrant and settler, who summer and winter stood guard over the wide frontier, whose lives were spent in almost utter isolation, whose lonely death was marked and mourned only by sorrowing comrade. . . . There never was a warfare which, like this, had absolutely nothing to hold the soldier stern and steadfast to the bitter end, but the solemn sense of Soldier Duty.[1]

Although these words were intended to elicit the image of an Indian-fighting army engaged in well-matched combat with the masters of guerrilla warfare, King's description better suited the entire range of military experiences in the West. His further evocation of this "cherished memory" marked a sharp contrast in public viewpoint that had arisen from the passing of the frontier era. Americans of the first half of the twentieth century seemed to discover and romanticize the very institution that many nineteenth-century Americans had taken for granted and even neglected.

In truth, however, the real significance of the army was not measured in either romanticism or neglect, but instead in a wide range of tangible accomplishments. The military establishment was a federal agency in search of a mission throughout much of the nineteenth century. Except for the Civil War period, when budgets soared and regimental ranks swelled with hundreds of thousands of new recruits, the army constantly searched for novel methods to maintain and even expand its importance.[2] In casting the net widely in search of duties that would justify their existence, officers had to face the realities of limited budgets, inadequate manpower, and a public that perpetually feared creation of a large standing army. The fear of a martial threat to the nation's democratic traditions ensured that total strength never surpassed twenty-five thousand troops.[3]

The nature of the federal government also opened the door to a greater range of army duties even amid deficiencies in manpower and finances. Historian Wallace D. Farnham noted this "weakened spring of government" in a 1963 article for the *American Historical Review*. Drawing upon a phrase first coined in 1902 by M. I. Ostrogorski, Farnham argued that the national government was a hostage to prevailing public sentiment throughout the nineteenth century. Citizens and policy makers alike required the impossible of their government. They demanded that it "transfer the nation's resources into their hands without ensuring justice and order, [and] they made it certain that the 'spring of government' would be weakened and warped."[4] In his detailed discussion of the building of the Union Pacific Railroad, Farnham demonstrated that most Americans favored private enterprise over government ownership of this greatest of western transportation ventures. The federal government would have only a limited voice in the planning and management of the Union Pacific, but it would be expected to subsidize the operation from its inception.

This philosophy of "subsidies without interference" inadvertently increased federal reliance on the army, especially in the comparatively remote frontier regions. Farnham correctly noted that "the army was virtually loaned to the Union Pacific, and Grenville Dodge [a civilian employee of the railroad] became almost *de facto* commander of the Department of the Platte."[5] New forts were erected primarily to serve railroad interests, soldiers quelled workers strikes, patrols accompanied company surveyors, and officers frequently employed heavy-handed methods to remove illegal squatters from corporate property. Within the larger context of governing duties, Farnham concluded that the War Department came to be the most visible federal presence in the West. During a century when the government "subsidized but did not rule," a blurring of imperial and laissez-faire goals coalesced into a sometimes harmonious and sometimes disharmonious whole. A vacillating Indian policy, ravaged by numerous self-serving private interests, represented the latter category, with catastrophic results for all Native Americans. Yet the majority of Americans championed, and even came to routinely expect, the other diverse roles performed by the army. For them, the multipurpose concept of military action seemed not only wise but even essential to the improvement of western lives, whether they offered praise to it or not.[6]

Ironically, common soldiers were among the first to articulate the consequences of this expanded role for the frontier army. One unidentified enlistee poured out his disillusionment in a letter to the *Army and Navy Chronicle* during May 1838. Like other young men of his age, he had joined Uncle Sam's service to escape the monotony of home life and to find adventure and improved social station through gallant action against the nation's enemies. Instead, he summarized the brutal reality of a hard military life in which soldiers were expected to carry out augmented duties with comparatively fewer resources than the previous military generation:

> I am deceived; I enlisted for a soldier; I enlisted because I preferred military life to hard work; I never was given to understand that implements of agriculture and the mechanic's tools were to be placed in my hands before I had received a musket or drawn a

uniform coat. I never was told that I would be called on to make roads, build bridges, quarry stone, burn brick and lime, carry the hod, cut wood, hew timber, construct it into rafts and float it to the garrisons, make shingles, saw plank, build mills, maul rails, drive teams, make hay, herd cattle, build stables, construct barracks, hospitals, etc., etc., etc., which takes more time for their completion than the period of my enlistment. I never was given to understand that such duties were customary in the army, much less that I would be called on to perform them, or I never would have enlisted.[7]

The discontent voiced by this early recruit was echoed by officers and men alike throughout the rest of the century. Sgt. H. H. McConnell, a frequent critic and sometimes defender of army life, referred to himself and his men as "armed laborers, nothing less, nothing more." He further advised that youths who yearned for glory or sought the easy life should resist the melodious entreaties of recruitment officers. To the misinformed, McConnell sarcastically warned, "If he can find some soft and easy job working on a railroad for ten hours a day with a pick and shovel, driving a scraper, or pushing a wheelbarrow, he had better embrace that opening."[8] A decade earlier, during the 1850s, enlisted personnel at Fort Ridgely, Minnesota, complained about their servile labor assignments and similarly labeled themselves "brevet architects" instead of real soldiers.[9]

Officers frequently joined the debate by voicing their own sentiments against having the enlisted men serve in so many different capacities. Col. Joseph J. Reynolds, commander of the Department of Texas in 1870, lamented that troopers spent the great majority of their duty hours in construction work, road building, escort protection, and other nonmartial pursuits. Yet despite his fear that their soldierly abilities were declining as a result of so little time for drill, Reynolds acknowledged their vast list of accomplishments in opening the region to civilian settlement.[10] Fourteen years later, Capt. George Frederic Price of the Fifth Cavalry published an article in the *Las Vegas (New Mexico) Daily Optic* contending that no more than half the troops at nearby Fort Union were properly trained for extensive campaigning. In addition to endangering their future fighting ability, he argued, excessive manual labor had already sapped their morale. During the same year, an unidentified enlisted man at Fort Yates, Dakota Territory, pointed out that these endless demands on the soldier-laborer were the primary cause of desertion not only among his immediate compatriots, but also within the frontier army as a whole.[11]

The military establishment was thus locked in a century-long dilemma that it could not completely solve. The public, politicians, and special interest groups demanded that the army assume these multifaceted roles, and yet they remained unwilling to support adequate appropriations and troop strengths to accomplish the endless obligations. Ironically, the army's simultaneous search for a mission to justify its existence during relatively long periods of official peace compelled it to take on this multitude of diverse assignments. Most soldiers complained about their daily duties and rigid discipline, but officers knew that the future of a "peacetime army" rested upon its ability to perform the nonmartial tasks.

When the multipurpose duties are evaluated in their entirety, the record is indeed an impressive one. Probably most nineteenth-century western residents viewed the army not only as a "guardian of civilization," but also as a primary medium through which American culture and institutions were transferred from the Appalachian frontier to the Pacific coast. Within their collective perception of a beneficent Manifest Destiny relentlessly pushing back the rough and untamed wilderness, they saw the army as a prime player in the story. While the view was shamefully ethnocentric and ultranationalistic, few Americans of that time would have perceived it that way. Accordingly, as the century wore on, citizens demanded even more of the federal government and its "right arm in the wilderness."

A final assessment of the army's multipurpose role clearly indicates that most of the contributions were viewed in a favorable light by the public. During four and a half decades of exploration and mapping of the Trans-Mississippi expanse, the Corps of Topographical Engineers had popularized some of the earliest trails and provided some of the first government maps of terra incognita. Although ostensibly sent to protect the trails from Indian attacks during the 1840s and 1850s, the army made even more important nonmartial contributions to the overland wagon trains. Primary aid came in the form of food rations, medical services, timely information about trail conditions, blacksmithing and carpentry services for wagon repairs, and even infrequent attempts to dispense justice for mobile parties that had no means of incarcerating guilty offenders. Soldiers also helped beleaguered groups and individuals who had "seen the elephant" and were headed back east, often without adequate supplies, wagons, or livestock. Military posts stood like small oases in the midst of a hostile landscape, and the officers and men received frequent praise in the diaries and letters of overlanders for their humanitarian aid. Fortunately, the War Department broadened the discretionary powers of commanders during the increasing migration years of the California Gold Rush and helped alleviate some of the suffering.

What started out in the 1840s on the overland trails to Oregon, California, and Salt Lake City continued in more extensive ways as other trails branched out across the West throughout the rest of the century. In this close union of private enterprise and government subsidy, soldiers built roads and bridges, guarded railroad survey parties, dammed water sources along the trails, delivered federal mails, established telegraph networks, improved rivers for commercial traffic, and pioneered well-drilling experiments. Even though many of these efforts were justified by the War Department's desire to create an efficient transportation and communication system for its far-flung posts, individual civilians also profited immensely from the projects. Commercial enterprises also capitalized on the internal improvements by transporting their goods along the roads, using telegraph services at forts, shipping passengers and freight on safer rivers, and constructing the ribbons of iron that by the 1880s crisscrossed the states and territories. Only in the case of the railroads did significant criticism occur. Rising farmer discontent, reflected in the Farmers Alliance and Populist movements of the 1880s and 1890s, noted the close personal relationships between some senior officers and railroad executives. Doubting that they could get a fair hearing from these officers, some Populist spokesmen rhetorically branded the army as a mere minion of the corrupt railroads and their monopolistic practices.

Paradoxically, those same late-nineteenth-century farmers had profited from the army's ongoing agricultural experiments. Since 1819 the War Department and the officer corps had debated the efficacy of allowing garrisons to take time away from drill to raise crops and livestock for food.

This effort to achieve partial self-sufficiency rested upon a desire to reduce transportation costs and to improve the health of soldiers through a more balanced diet. Along the way to attaining these goals, the army produced some important ancillary benefits. It collected new seeds from Indian tribes and observed Native American agricultural methods in the more arid regions of the nation. Furthermore, officers and surgeons recorded soil chemistry throughout the various landscapes, introduced different planting and harvesting techniques, established mechanical irrigation systems, and experimented with livestock production in plains and desert environments.

Daily meteorological record keeping, standardized since 1814, blossomed by the 1870s into a national weather service under the auspices of the Army Signal Corps. This sophisticated reporting system tracked storms across the continent and alerted civilian and military agencies through its extensive telegraphic service. Groups as diverse as farmers, shipping enterprises, and municipal governments benefited from these early warning systems. Scientists profited additionally from the empirical data that figured into weather predictions and from the historical data that could reveal long-term weather cycles from the past.

In areas remote from formal medical care, army doctors also became an essential part of civilians' lives. Even though no statutory requirement existed to compel or even allow military care for civilians, discretionary powers for commanding officers again came into play. Most of this aid was extended on an emergency basis and frequently with no cost incurred by the patient. This necessitated not only the dispensing of medicines and physical treatments, but also sometimes long-term convalescent care in the post hospital. Because army doctors had to undertake formal medical training, possess certified medical degrees, and pass rigid examinations for service positions, their quality matched or surpassed that of civilian doctors in private practice. Criticism of army medical care stemmed more from the unreliable supply system, the poor quality of hospital structures, and the overwhelming demands caused by sudden epidemics or dietary deficiencies among large numbers of people. The small corps of regimental doctors was never adequate to meet army and civilian needs in the West, but their presence was highly applauded. A few of the elite physicians elected to remain in the West after their stints in the army, and they continued to contribute to the civilian population through their private practices.

Although not as critical as the life-saving services provided by army doctors, frontier posts offered additional conveniences to civilians and military personnel alike. The forts stood as "harbingers of civilization" that could help duplicate some of the cultural aspects of the urbane East in the unpolished West. Officers especially demanded the amenities of civilization that would befit their social station and that would enrich the lives of their families, who lived with them on the frontier. Post chapels, schools, and libraries multiplied not because of federal directives, but because of the grassroots demands for them among service personnel of all ranks and even among adjacent civilian communities.

While chaplains could improve the quality of life at forts, they also could create endless controversy by launching purity campaigns against gambling, swearing, prostitution, and other vices. Soldiers expected to hear sermons on these subjects, but they did not tolerate rigid enforcement of restrictions. In addition to serving the garrisons, many chaplains cooperated with clergymen in nearby communities. Some even filled the need for circuit riders as they carried religion to outlying farms and ranches by performing baptisms, funerals, and a host of other welcome services. Likewise, the post schools offered a basic curriculum to children of officers, interested enlisted men, and civilian families if approved by the commanding officer. For many children and soldiers, this was the only formal education available. The chapels and schools also anchored part of each fort's social life as they provided a range of recreational and educational activities. Additionally, post libraries offered a wide variety of reading materials to all ranks and provided a quiet place away from the confines of barracks life. In its efforts to "reform the man," the army could take justifiable pride in conveying valuable educational skills, strengthening self-esteem, and preparing the soldiers and civilians for lives as more informed citizens.

In its search for peacetime roles, the army found two of its most celebrated activities: relief work following natural disasters and protection of the fledgling national parks. The move toward these expanded duties was initially slowed by public fears of bloated national budgets and dangerous shifts toward private dependency on government aid. Although a few isolated precedents were set on the East Coast and in the Mississippi River valley before 1820, real expansion of the federal role came in the post–Civil War era with Reconstruction duties in the South and a host of public relief projects in the West. Floods, hurricanes, fires, and epidemics all attracted some government help through military aegis. Yet it was the drought and locust relief to the Great Plains during the mid-1870s that best demonstrated the army's innovativeness, as well as its limitations, in overcoming the resultant problems of starvation, illness, and public demoralization. Less heralded were the numerous rescues of lost travelers, snowbound miners, fever-ridden ranchers, and wildfire-threatened home-steaders that were recorded only in officers' day reports or sometimes in local newspapers.

Army firefighting activities during the 1910 inferno in Idaho's Coeur d'Alene Forest were one of the rare exceptional examples of sustained effort that saved possibly hundreds of lives and garnered national press attention. Equally dramatic was the military's decisive participation in confronting the huge blaze produced by the 1906 San Francisco earth-quake and in managing the subsequent relief efforts. Less visible, but of equal importance, was the army's thirty-two-year guardianship of the infant national park system. The premier parks of Yellowstone and Yosemite were havens for exploitation by illegal timber cutters, ranchers, miners, and poachers, but small squads of soldiers provided a measure of protection and even earned praise from uncompromising preserva-tionist John Muir. By the time soldiers finally turned these tasks over to civilian rangers in 1914, they had created important precedents for resource management that would survive into later generations sensitized to the new wave of scientific environmentalism.

Clearly, the most important contribution of the frontier army con-cerned its payroll and contracting system. For a full century and beyond, these two examples of federal largesse provided badly needed specie to remote areas, prompted the growth of many financial enterprises, and helped produce the towns that served as nuclei for further settlement. Yet these important infusions of capital also initiated cycles of dependency from which some frontier populations were unable to wean themselves. Communities fought hard to maintain their military connections and to prevent inevitable closings of posts as the century neared its conclusion.

Some ended up as virtual ghost towns, while others found ways to diversify and restore their financial health in agriculture, ranching, mining, and a host of other endeavors. An even smaller number capitalized upon advantageous locations near major transportation networks, and they barely even missed the passing of the military phase.

Townsite promoters, local land speculators, construction contractors, wood suppliers, farmers interested in marketing their crops, and livestock operators intent upon selling their horses and cattle all saw Uncle Sam as a logical source of lucrative revenue. Legitimate dry goods merchants and itinerant peddlers joined vice lords of the saloons and gambling and prostitution establishments to draw the last possible dollar from soldiers' pay. Equally alert to the economic possibilities were the civilian mechanics, teamsters, telegraph operators, sawmill engineers, clerks, wheelwrights, blacksmiths, saddlers, and scouts who found long-term employment at the posts that provided their families with a decent living. Estimates of annual government subsidies of $1,250,000 to $2,000,000 in New Mexico and Arizona between 1861 and 1885 testified eloquently to the magnitude of the contracting and payroll bonanzas. Without those incentives, fewer civilians would have been drawn into the area, and fewer yet would have been able to remain there. Because the money was recycled through many hands within the broader region, the multiplier effect seems to have been almost endless. Even a deactivated fort offered a final round of economic opportunity. Some farsighted individuals purchased the lands and buildings of the former military reservations. Others simply absconded with everything not sold or nailed down and used it to improve their own domiciles.

While military budgets brought smiles to the faces of most westerners, the army found itself steeped in controversy amid its efforts to serve as an unofficial frontier lawman. Military pursuits of outlaws and other criminals who had no public support rarely stirred passions, especially in areas where a shortage of sheriffs, marshals, and judges precluded routine enforcement of laws. However, when soldiers found themselves carrying out unpopular policies—as during the Mormon War, Bleeding Kansas, and Reconstruction in the South—they became targets of public indignation. Since the constitutional concept of insurrection had never been defined in a precise way, and because military authorities had no clear legal authority to act as policemen without a presidential directive, officers sometimes appeared both powerless and dictatorial at the same time.

Lack of clear instructions and an inability to avoid favoring one side over another in disputes continually plagued officers, and these cases demanded the wisdom of Solomon. Quick military actions during New Mexico's Lincoln County War, Wyoming's Rock Springs Massacre, and Wyoming's Johnson County War probably saved lives, but they also prompted bitter invective from disgruntled citizens who wound up on the losing sides. This became even more apparent when troops were ordered into action against industrial strikes. In their efforts to preserve order, well-meaning officers generally found themselves favoring the side of the industrialists and attracting the animosity of pro-labor forces. Military personnel predictably came to hate these "political assignments," which could only spoil their public image and perhaps even invite civil suits against them.

As in the case of the military's imprecise law enforcement powers, civilians remained bitterly divided about the army's relationship with Native Americans. While many citizens condemned the soldiers as shameless tormentors of Indians and instigators of inhumane slaughters, others criticized the same troops for mollycoddling Indian raiders and living in utter fear of them. Caught between the relentless onslaught of the "liberal reformers" and the "Indian haters," officers and enlisted men found themselves in another untenable situation.

From the inception of the United States, Congress entrusted the army with a mandate to keep illegal trespassers out of Indian country, but it never provided a mechanism for enforcement. Halfhearted regulations left officers vulnerable to civil suits and made a mockery of treaties that supposedly guaranteed federal protection of tribal lands. Yet in the face of impossible odds, some officers demonstrated great courage in protecting Indians and their property from abuse. Gen. George Crook best epitomized the concept of the "humanitarian generals" by his advocacy for the Apache prisoners-of-war and for the civil rights of Standing Bear and his Ponca kinsmen. In truth, military opinions about Indians were never monolithic, and failure to protect the sacred Black Hills and the Cherokee Outlet rested more on government duplicity than on army incompetence or inhumanity.

Even though the frontier military was much praised for its multi-purpose contributions to settlement and, to a lesser extent, maligned for its policing and Indian advocacy roles, two other of its functions were more benign and overlooked. As a generator of government records—both published and archival—the army stood almost unmatched in the nineteenth century. The Government Printing Office and its privately owned predecessors published annual reports from the War Department as well as the more specific records of explorations, field campaigns, engineers' projects, transportation of supplies, and a host of other topics. Records not deemed worthy of immediate publication were dutifully turned over to the National Archives, where they remain today.

More important to that age, however, were the publications that were intended for sale to a larger audience. Senior officers, intent upon promoting their professional careers or securing themselves a favorable place in history, assembled memoirs of their experiences. On a similar level of literacy and insightfulness, a number of officers' wives also published their reminiscences, often with a different sensitivity and from a different vantage point. But it was the historical novels of Capt. Charles King, veteran of the Fifth Cavalry and participant in the celebrated 1876 Yellowstone Expedition against the Sioux and Cheyenne, that excited Americans with their romanticized images of the frontier army.

Although less financially lucrative to their authors, publications by junior officers and enlisted men remain equally valuable records of military life. Their nineteenth-century post newspapers were often crude, but these tabloids provided a grassroots look at daily events and concerns. Some of the officers reached a broader audience by writing for the service magazines such as *Cavalry Journal, Infantry Journal,* and *Journal of the Military Service Institution of the United States.* At the same time, enlisted men served as correspondents for civilian newspapers and later wrote about their experiences in *Winners of the West.* The full importance of much of this early material, as well as unpublished diaries, journals, and letters that only recently have been edited and printed by scholars, still remains to be realized. Only after modern scholars have systematically examined and synthesized broader themes from these rich primary sources can the full story of frontier soldiers' lives be related to a new generation of readers. The old veterans thus continue to speak to us in a way that they probably never envisioned.

Also overlooked by nineteenth-century civilians and modern generations of Americans is the fact that soldiers of all ranks continued to participate in the western story even after their retirement from active service. As land speculators, investors, bankers, railroad executives, businessmen, homesteaders, ranchers, freighters, peace officers, doctors, and day laborers, and in other capacities, they remained a vital part of the communities they once had protected as soldiers of the line. These new careers were necessitated by the relatively small pay earned by military personnel and the even more minuscule pension plans that awaited them upon retirement. Some well-connected officers found financial security through marriage into prominent families, but most actively had to seek out sound investments and job opportunities to suffice in their golden years. Enlisted men had fewer "inside relationships" to exploit, but it did not keep them from trying.

For example, Col. Benjamin Grierson's inner circle of friends who joined him in speculative schemes at Fort Davis, Texas, included four lieutenants, a bandmaster, and an ordnance sergeant. Similarly, Col. William R. Shafter's mining partnership in the rugged Chinati Mountains of West Texas included two lieutenants and the civilian rancher who had first made the silver discovery. A relatively few former officers, such as Joseph Folsom and Peter Heintzelman, made comfortable lives from their investments, but others, such as flamboyant John C. Frémont, made and lost a fortune. More representative of the Gilded Age ethic was Lt. Col. George Armstrong Custer, who clearly evidenced a conflict of interest when he helped open the Black Hills to a mining rush and then tried to profit from a transportation company that would serve the mining camps. Influence peddling and outright fraud seemed evident in numerous cases, but few were ever brought to public accountability in the milieu of laissez-faire economics.

In evaluating the importance of the frontier army a full century after it passed from the scene, one is struck by how little we really understand about its many roles. It truly was a multipurpose army that made far greater contributions to the western landscape than as a mere campaigner against hostile Indians. Perhaps when the persistently romanticized cinematic images of John Ford finally give way to the more accurate appraisals first voiced by historian Francis Paul Prucha, the truth can be known. Then, and only then, can Americans clearly understand the wisdom of Col. Zachary Taylor's 1820 observation that "the ax, pick, saw and trowel, has become more the implement of the American soldier than the cannon, musket, or sword."[12] Until that understanding is ultimately achieved, the frontier army will remain a one-dimensional entity within the collective public consciousness, and its true historical significance will be misperceived on a grand scale.

Notes

PREFACE

1. Francis Paul Prucha, *Broadax and Bayonet: The Role of the United States Army in the Development of the Northwest, 1815–1860*, viii.

2. Francis Paul Prucha, *The Sword of the Republic: The United States Army on the Frontier, 1783–1846*, xvii.

3. Robert M. Utley, *Frontiersmen in Blue: The United States Army and the Indian, 1848–1865*, 5; Robert M. Utley, *Frontier Regulars: The United States Army and the Indian, 1866–1891*, xiii–xiv.

4. "Letter" of Albert Van Zant, in *Winners of the West*, September 1924, 2.

5. Roger L. Nichols, "The Army and the Indians, 1800–1830—A Reappraisal: The Missouri Valley Example," *Pacific Historical Review* 41 (May 1972): 168.

6. Leo E. Oliva, "Frontier Forts and the Settlement of Western Kansas," in *Kansas and the West: Bicentennial Essays in Honor of Nyle H. Miller*, ed. Forrest R. Blackburn et al., 62–73.

7. Leo E. Oliva, "The Army and Continental Expansion," in *The United States Army in Peacetime*, ed. Robin Higham and Carol Brandt, 21.

8. Ibid., 37.

9. Robert W. Frazer, *Forts and Supplies: The Role of the Army in the Economy of the Southwest, 1846–1861*, ix.

10. Darlis A. Miller, *Soldiers and Settlers: Military Supply in the Southwest, 1861–1885*, xiii–xv.

11. Frank N. Schubert, *Buffalo Soldiers, Braves, and the Brass: The Story of Fort Robinson, Nebraska*, v–vi.

12. Patricia Nelson Limerick, *The Legacy of Conquest: The Unbroken Past of the American West;* Richard White, *"It's Your Misfortune and None of My Own": A New History of the American West.*

13. The pros and cons of the New Western History, as well as evidence of omission of the multipurpose army story, is demonstrated in Patricia Nelson Limerick, Clyde A. Milner II, and Charles E. Rankin, eds., *Trails: Toward a New Western History;* Gene M. Gressley, ed., *Old West/New West: Quo Vadis?;* Clyde A. Milner II, ed., *A New Significance: Re-Envisioning the History of the American West;* and Larry McMurtry, "How the West Was Won or Lost," *New Republic,* October 22, 1990, 32–38.

14. A good historiographical article that shows the richness of research in this field and offers limited commentary on what still needs to be done is Paul A. Hutton, "The Frontier Army," in *American Frontier and Western Issues: An Historiographical Review,* ed. Roger L. Nichols, 253–74.

15. Michael L. Tate, "The Multi-Purpose Army on the Frontier: A Call for Further Research," in *The American West: Essays in Honor of W. Eugene Hollon,* ed. Ronald Lora, 171–208.

16. Three excellent studies of twentieth-century military roles in modernizing western societies and economies are Gerald D. Nash, *The American West Transformed: The Impact of the Second World War;* Gerald D. Nash, *The American West in the Twentieth Century: A Short History of an Urban Oasis;* and Michael P. Malone and Richard W. Etulain, *The American West: A Twentieth-Century History.*

17. Quoted in Prucha, *Broadax and Bayonet,* 104.

CHAPTER 1. DISCOVERERS

1. Jefferson's instructions are quoted at length in David Freeman Hawke, *Those Tremendous Mountains: The Story of the Lewis and Clark Expedition,* 26–32.

2. Elliott Coues, ed., *The Expeditions of Zebulon Montgomery Pike, to Headwaters of the Mississippi River, through Louisiana Territory, and in New Spain, during the Years 1805–6–7,* vol. 2; Dan L. Flores, ed., *Jefferson and Southwestern Exploration: The Freeman and Custis Accounts of the Red River Expedition of 1806.*

3. Phillip Drennen Thomas, "The United States Army as the Early Patron of Naturalists in the Trans-Mississippi West, 1803–1820," *Chronicles of Oklahoma* 56 (Summer 1978): 187–90. For a more complete record of the scientific work of the expedition, see George J. Goodman and Cheryl A. Lawson, *Retracing Major Stephen Long's 1820 Expedition: The Itinerary and Botany.*

4. Quoted in Richard G. Wood, *Stephen Harriman Long, 1784–1864: Army Engineer, Explorer, Inventor,* 116.

5. Thomas, "United States Army as Early Patron," 192.

6. Roger L. Nichols, "Stephen Long and Scientific Exploration on the Plains," *Nebraska History* 52 (Spring 1971): 61.

7. James L. Morrison, Jr., *"The Best School in the World": West Point, the Pre–Civil War Years, 1833–1866*, 91–94.

8. William H. Goetzmann, *Army Exploration in the American West, 1803–1863*, 4–6.

9. John B. Garver, Jr., "Practical Military Geographers and Mappers of the Trans-Mississippi West, 1820–1860," in *Mapping the North American Plains: Essays in the History of Cartography*, ed. by Frederick C. Luebke, Frances W. Kaye, and Gary E. Moulton, 116.

10. Typical of Frémont's reports and Torrey's botanical work is the following publication based on the 1842 reconnaissance: John C. Frémont, *A Report on an Exploration of the Country Lying between the Missouri River and the Rocky Mountains, on the Line of the Kansas and Great Platte Rivers*, 27th Cong., 3d sess., 1843, S. Doc. 243, esp. 79–94.

11. "Notes of Lieutenant J. W. Abert," in William H. Emory, *Notes of a Military Reconnaissance*.

12. Brigham D. Madsen, "Stansbury's Expedition to the Great Salt Lake, 1849–50," *Utah Historical Quarterly* 56 (1988): 148–59. The full report is found in Howard Stansbury, *Exploration and Survey of the Great Salt Lake of Utah, Including a Reconnoissance of a New Route through the Rocky Mountains*.

13. Goetzmann, *Army Exploration in the American West*, 262–304, 446–47; Leo E. Oliva, "The Army and Continental Expansion," in *The United States Army in Peacetime*, ed. Robin Higham and Carol Brandt, 34–35. Warren's meticulous attention to scientific detail is evidenced in Gouverneur K. Warren, *Preliminary Report of Explorations in Nebraska and Dakota, in the Years 1855–'56–'57*.

14. Michael J. Brodhead, "Contributions of Medical Officers of the Regular Army to Natural History in the Pre–Civil War Era," in *History and Humanities: Essays in Honor of Wilbur S. Shepperson*, ed. Francis X. Hartigan, 4.

15. Susan Delano McKelvey, *Botanical Exploration of the Trans-Mississippi West, 1790–1850*, 443–47.

16. Brodhead, "Contributions of Medical Officers," 6–7; Michael J. Brodhead, "The Military Naturalist: A Lewis and Clark Heritage," *We Proceeded On* 9 (November 1983): 8.

17. Brodhead, "Contributions of Medical Officers," 8–9; Edgar Erskine Hume, *Ornithologists of the United States Army Medical Corps*, 207–20.

18. Brodhead, "Contributions of Medical Officers," 9–10. Civilian contract surgeons also frequently accompanied military expeditions to record scientific observations. One of the best examples of this kind of work is found in John S. Tomer and Michael J. Brodhead, eds., *A Naturalist in Indian Territory: The Journals of S. W. Woodhouse, 1849–1850*.

19. Brodhead, "Contributions of Medical Officers," 10.

20. Margaret Bierschwale, *Fort McKavett, Texas: Post on the San Saba*, 35; Alex B. Hasson, "Report of the Post Surgeon at Fort Phantom Hill, for 1852," *West Texas Historical Association Year Book* 1 (June 1925): 73–77.

21. Henry Miller Madden, *Xántus: Hungarian Naturalist in the Pioneer West*, 41–49, 203–207, 211–50.

22. Richard A. Bartlett, *Great Surveys of the American West*, xiv–xv.

23. LeRoy R. Hafen, W. Eugene Hollon, and Carl Coke Rister, *Western America: The Exploration, Settlement, and Development of the Region Beyond the Mississippi*, 391.

24. David P. Robrock, "A History of Fort Fetterman, Wyoming, 1867–1882," *Annals of Wyoming* 48 (Spring 1976): 70–71.

25. Richard Guentzel, "The Department of the Platte and Western Settlement, 1866–1877," *Nebraska History* 56 (Fall 1975): 403–404; Gerald M. Adams, *The Post Near Cheyenne: A History of Fort D. A. Russell, 1867–1930*, 44.

26. Merrill J. Mattes, *Indians, Infants, and Infantry: Andrew and Elizabeth Burt on the Frontier*, 193–97.

27. The "scientific corps" of Custer's 1874 expedition is detailed in Donald Jackson, *Custer's Gold: The United States Cavalry Expedition of 1874*, 46–72.

28. Mattes, *Indians, Infants, and Infantry*, 200–204; Wayne R. Kime, *The Black Hills Journals of Colonel Richard Irving Dodge*, 3–26.

29. Kenneth J. Almy, ed., "Thof's Dragon and the Letters of Capt. Theophilus H. Turner, M.D., U.S. Army," *Kansas History* 10 (Fall 1987): 184–89.

30. Robert M. Utley, *Cavalier in Buckskin: George Armstrong Custer and the Western Military Frontier*, 118, 137–38.

31. Dwight L. Smith, ed., "The Kansas Frontier, 1869–1870: Lt. Samuel Tillman's First Tour of Duty," *Kansas History* 12 (Winter 1989–90), 202.

32. Hume, *Ornithologists of the United States Army*, 22–31.

33. Brodhead, "The Military Naturalist," 9–10; Hume, *Ornithologists of the United States Army*, 413–17.

34. Peter D. Olch, "Medicine in the Indian-Fighting Army, 1866–1890," *Journal of the West* 21 (July 1982): 36.

35. Michael Brodhead, "Of Mice and Mastodons: Contributions to the Literature of Mammalogy by Officers and Men of the United States Army in the Nineteenth Century," *Archives of Natural History* 18, no. 3 (1991): 366–67.

36. Michael J. Brodhead, "A Dedication to the Memory of Elliott Coues, 1842–1899," *Arizona and the West* 13 (Spring 1971): 2–4; Michael J. Brodhead, *A Soldier-Scientist in the American Southwest: Being a Narrative of the Travels of Elliott Coues*, 62–67.

37. Wilfred W. Black, "The Army Doctor in the Trans-Mississippi West, 1775–1860," *Southwestern Social Science Quarterly* 24, no. 2 (1943): 126–27.

38. B. J. Fisher, "Medical Conditions at West Texas Military Posts in the 1850s," *West Texas Historical Association Year Book* 62 (1986): 112–13.

39. McKelvey, *Botanical Exploration of the Trans-Mississippi West*, 447.

40. Marie H. Erwin, comp., "Statistical Reports on the Sickness and Mortality of the Army of the United States, 1819–1860," *Annals of Wyoming* 15 (1943): 358–61.

41. Augustus Meyers, *Ten Years in the Ranks, U.S. Army*, 77–90, 96–100.

42. James A. Wier, "19th Century Army Doctors on the Frontier and in Nebraska," *Nebraska History* 61 (Summer 1980): 207; Philippe Régis de Trobriand, *Military Life in Dakota: The Journal of Philippe Régis de Trobriand*, ed. Lucile M. Kane, 183–84.

43. William P. Clark, *The Indian Sign Language*.

44. Maurice Frink and Casey Barthelmess, *Photographer on an Army Mule*, 33–51.

45. Ibid., 28–29; Washington Matthews, *Navaho Legends Collected and Translated by Washington Matthews, M.D., LL.D., Major U.S. Army, ex-President of the American Folk-Lore Society*, vol. 5, *Memoirs of the American Folk-lore Society*.

46. Ray H. Mattison, ed., "The Diary of Surgeon Washington Matthews, Fort Rice, D.T.," *North Dakota History* 21 (January 1954): 5–6. The most complete interpretation of Dr. Matthews and his ethnographic work is found in Katheryn Spencer Halpern and Susan Brown McGreevy, eds., *Washington Matthews: Studies of Navajo Culture, 1880–1894*.

47. Martha Gray Wales, "When I Was a Little Girl: Things I Remember from Living at Frontier Military Posts," ed. Willard B. Pope, *North Dakota History* 50 (Spring 1983): 13–14.

48. John A. Turcheneske, Jr., "Historical Manuscripts as Sources for the Anthropological Study: The Ethnological Correspondence of John Gregory Bourke," *New Mexico Historical Review* 59 (July 1984): 271.

49. Ibid., 266–72; Joseph C. Porter, *Paper Medicine Man: John Gregory Bourke and His American West*, 203–205.

50. Porter, *Paper Medicine Man*, 302–304; John A. Turcheneske, Jr., "John G. Bourke—Troubled Scientist," *Journal of Arizona History* 20 (Fall 1979): 328–42.

51. John G. Bourke, *The Medicine Men of the Apache: Ninth Annual Report of the Bureau of Ethnology, 1887–1888*, 75.

52. Walter R. Echo-Hawk and Roger Echo-Hawk, "Repatriation, Reburial, and Religious Rights," in *Handbook of American Indian Religious Freedom*, ed. Christopher Vecsey, 67.

53. Larry J. Zimmerman, *Peoples of Prehistoric South Dakota*, 19.

54. John G. Bourke, *On the Border with Crook*, 399–400.

55. William T. Corbusier, *Verde to San Carlos: Recollections of a Famous Army Surgeon and His Observant Family on the Western Frontier, 1869–1886*, 278.

56. Echo-Hawk and Echo-Hawk, "Repatriation, Reburial, and Religious Rights," 72.

57. James A. Hanson, *Little Chief's Gatherings: The Smithsonian Institution's G. K. Warren 1855–1856 Plains Indian Collection and the New York State Library's 1855–1857 Warren Expeditions Journal*, 11–18.

58. Glenn E. Markoe, Raymond J. DeMallie, and Royal B. Hassrick, *Vestiges of a Proud Nation: The Ogden B. Read Northern Plains Indian Collection*, 13–16.

59. Kenneth Haltman, "Between Science and Art: Titian Ramsay Peale's Long Expedition Sketches, Newly Recovered at the State Historical Society of Iowa," *Palimpsest* 74 (Summer 1993): 63–81.

60. Brian W. Dippie, "Government Patronage: Catlin, Stanley, and Eastman," *Montana, Magazine of Western History* 44 (Fall 1994): 46–47.

61. Lucretia Hoover Giese, "Artist Collaborators: A Surrogate Hand—Seth Eastman's for Bartlett's," in *Drawing the Borderline: Artist-Explorers of the U.S.–Mexico Boundary Survey*, 81–90; Robert Hine, *Bartlett's West: Drawing the Mexican Boundary*, 85–90.

62. John Francis McDermott, *Seth Eastman: Pictorial Historian of the Indian*, 22–23, 50–62. See also John Francis McDermott, *Seth Eastman's Mississippi: A Lost Portfolio Recovered*. A helpful analysis of the art training that was provided to cadets at West Point is found in Marilyn Anne Kindred, "The Army Officer Corps and the Arts: Artistic Patronage and Practice in America, 1820–85," Ph.D. diss., University of Kansas, 1980, 86–124.

63. McDermott, *Seth Eastman*, 80–96; Sarah E. Boehme, Christian Feest, and Patricia Condon Johnston, *Seth Eastman: A Portfolio of North American Indians*, 19–27. Further evidence of Eastman's artistic renderings of specific military fortifications is found in Willard B. Robinson, *American Forts: Architectural Form and Function*.

64. Goetzmann, *Army Exploration in the American West*, 331–36.

65. Robert Taft, *Artists and Illustrators of the Old West, 1850–1900*, 276.

66. Eugene C. Tidball, "John C. Tidball: Soldier-Artist of the Great Reconnaissance," *Journal of Arizona History* 37 (Summer 1996): 108–25. For a more complete account of the expedition, see Grant Foreman, ed., *A Pathfinder in the Southwest: The Itinerary of Lieutenant A. W. Whipple during His Explorations for a Railway Route from Fort Smith to Los Angeles in the Years 1853–1854*.

67. Wallace Stegner, "The Scientist as Artist: Clarence E. Dutton and the Tertiary History of the Grand Cañon District," *American West* 15 (May–June 1978): 18–19, 61. William H. Goetzmann, *Exploration and Empire: The Explorer and the Scientist in the Winning of the American West*, 567–68.

68. Langdon Sully, *No Tears for the General: The Life of Alfred Sully, 1821–1879*, 9–12.

69. W. Stephen Thomas, *Fort Davis and the Texas Frontier: Paintings by Captain Arthur T. Lee, Eighth U.S. Infantry*, ix, 34–35.

70. Ibid., 5–6, 32.

71. De Trobriand, *Military Life in Dakota*, xi, 308, 330, 380–81.

72. Jim Schreier, "Joseph B. Girard: Army Doctor and Artist of the Frontier," *Arizona Highways* 67 (March 1989): 43–45.

73. David A. Clary, ed., "'I Am Already Quite a Texan': Albert J. Myer's Letters from Texas, 1854–1856," *Southwestern Historical Quarterly* 82 (July 1978): 25–76.

74. Rena Neumann Coen, "Edward K. Thomas: Fort Snelling Artist," *Minnesota History* 41 (Fall 1969): 317–26.

75. Richard K. McMaster, "Records and Reminiscences of Old Fort Bliss," *Password* 8 (Spring 1963): 28; Louis L. Pfaller, "Eli Washington John Lindesmith, Fort Keogh's Chaplain in Buckskin," *Montana, Magazine of Western History* 27 (January 1977): 17.

76. Leo E. Oliva, *Fort Larned on the Santa Fe Trail*, 10–11.

77. Hervey Johnson, *Tending the Talking Wire: A Buck Soldier's View of Indian Country, 1863–1866*, ed. William E. Unrau, 17; James H. Nottage, "A Centennial History of Artist Activities in Wyoming, 1837–1937," *Annals of Wyoming* 48 (Spring 1976): 86.

78. Dennis K. McDaniel, "Kansas in 1862 as Seen by the 12th Wisconsin Infantry: The Sketches of Pvt. John Gaddis," *Kansas Historical Quarterly* 40 (Winter 1974): 465, 473–74; Richard D. Rowen, ed., "The Second Nebraska's Campaign against the Sioux," *Nebraska History* 44 (March 1963): 3–53; Thomas Twichel, "Fort Logan and the Urban Frontier," *Montana, Magazine of Western History* 17 (Fall 1967): 46–47.

79. David Nevin, *The Soldiers*, 56.

CHAPTER 2. ENCOUNTERING THE ELEPHANT

1. Merrill J. Mattes, *The Great Platte River Road: The Covered Wagon Mainline via Fort Kearny to Fort Laramie*, 62.

2. Report of Secretary of War Joel R. Poinsett, in *Annual Report of the Secretary of War, 1840*, 1–3; Report of Secretary of War John C. Spencer, in *Annual Report of the Secretary of War, 1841*, 61–62.

3. *Register of Debates*, 18th Cong., 2d sess., 1825, 1–5; Otis E. Young, *The First Military Escort on the Santa Fe Trail, 1829, from the Journal and Reports of Major Bennet Riley and Lieutenant Philip St. George Cooke*, 15–29.

4. James K. Polk, First Annual Message, December 2, 1845, in James D. Richardson, comp., *A Compilation of the Messages and Papers of the Presidents*, 4:396.

5. Lillian M. Willman, "The History of Fort Kearny," in *Publications of the Nebraska State Historical Society*, 21:215–23.

6. Lt. Daniel P. Woodbury to Col. Joseph G. Totten, November 10, 1847, Adjutant General's Office [hereafter cited as AGO], Letters Sent, Records of the Army Continental Commands, RG 393, National Archives, and reel 6, Nebraska State Historical Society [hereafter cited as NSHS].

7. Stephen Watts Kearny, "Report of a Summer Campaign to the Rocky Mountains, etc., in 1845," in *Annual Report of the Secretary of War, 1845*, 212.

8. *U.S. Statutes at Large* 9 (1851): 13–14.

9. Report of Secretary of War William L. Marcy, in *Annual Report of the Secretary of War, 1848,* 79–80; John D. Unruh, Jr., *The Plains Across: The Overland Emigrants and the Trans-Mississippi West, 1840–60,* 207.

10. John C. Frémont, *Report of the Exploring Expedition to the Rocky Mountains in the Year 1842, and to Oregon and North California in the Years 1843–1844,* 47.

11. Francis Parkman, *The Oregon Trail,* 90.

12. Edwin Bryant, *What I Saw in California: Being the Journal of a Tour, by the Emigrant Route and South Pass of the Rocky Mountains, across the Continent of North America, the Great Desert Basin, and through California, in the Years 1846, 1847,* 109.

13. Dr. William L. Thomas, "Diary," 9–10, unpublished manuscript in the Bancroft Library, University of California, Berkeley.

14. Annie Ruff to Mary Dougherty, June 24, 1849, in Charles and Annie Ruff Papers, NSHS.

15. Maj. Winslow F. Sanderson to Adjutant General Roger Jones, June 27, 1849, AGO, Letters Sent, RG 393, NA.

16. Report of Secretary of War George C. Crawford, in *Annual Report of the Secretary of War, 1849,* 95.

17. Joseph Schafer, ed., *California Letters of Lucius Fairchild,* Wisconsin Historical Society Publications *Collections,* 31:31.

18. Dale L. Morgan, "The Ferries of the Forty-Niners," *Annals of Wyoming* 31 (April 1959): 22–23.

19. Raymond W. Settle, ed., *The March of the Mounted Riflemen: First United States Military Expedition to Travel the Full Length of the Oregon Trail from Fort Leavenworth to Fort Vancouver May to October 1849, as Recorded in the Journals of Major Osborne Cross and George Gibbs and the Official Report of Colonel Loring,* 301.

20. *Missouri Republican,* April 29, 1849. Complete listings of prices of various types and conditions of livestock available at Independence, Weston, and Westport, Missouri, are given in *Missouri Republican,* April 7, 1849.

21. Col. Benjamin L. E. Bonneville to Adj. Gen. R. Jones, July 2, 1849, AGO, Letters Sent, RG 393, NA.

22. Margaret A. Frink, "Adventures of a Party of Gold-Seekers," in *Covered Wagon Women: Diaries and Letters from the Western Trails, 1840–1890,* ed. Kenneth L. Holmes, 2:87. S. H. Taylor wrote home to Watertown, Wisconsin, to publish in the local newspaper his specific recommendations on types of livestock, wagons, and food to buy for the trip. Residents intending to make the journey depended upon this kind of newspaper information, as well as the guidebooks, to help make better decisions during the 1850s, but the problems of ignorance persisted throughout the era; see S. H. Taylor, "Oregon Bound, 1853: Letters of S. H. Taylor to the Watertown [Wisconsin] Chronicles," *Oregon Historical Quarterly* 22 (1921): 133–34, 139–43.

23. Mary Rockwood Powers, *A Woman's Overland Journal to California,* ed. W. B. Thorsen, 25–33.

24. Ward G. DeWitt and Florence Stark DeWitt, *Prairie Schooner Lady: The Journal of Harriet Sherrill Ward, 1853*, 63.

25. Giles S. Isham, *Guide to California and the Mines*, 14; James Bennett, *Overland Journey to California: Journal of James Bennett, Whose Party Left New Harmony in 1850 and Crossed the Plains and Mountains until the Golden West Was Reached*, 29.

26. Elisha Douglass Perkins, *Gold Rush Diary: Perkins on the Overland Trail in the Spring and Summer of 1849*, ed. Thomas D. Clark, 52.

27. Russell E. Bidlack, *Letters Home: The Story of Ann Arbor's Forty-Niners*, intro. F. Clever Bald, 22; John H. Benson, "Journal," unpublished manuscript in NSHS.

28. Howard Stansbury, *An Expedition to the Valley of the Great Salt Lake of Utah*, 30.

29. Susan Badger Doyle and Donald E. Buck, eds., *The 1849 California Trail Diaries of Elijah Preston Howell*, 34; C. W. Smith, *Journal of a Trip to California: Across the Continent from Weston, Missouri, to Weber Creek, California, in the Summer of 1850*, ed. R. W. G. Vail, 42.

30. Howard L. Scamehorn, ed., *The Buckeye Rovers in the Gold Rush*, 26–27; Alonzo Delano, *Life on the Plains and among the Diggings*, 67.

31. Unruh, *Plains Across*, 229.

32. Ibid.; D. Ray Wilson, *Fort Kearny on the Platte*, 33; Merrill J. Mattes, *Great Platte River Road*, 514–15.

33. Barry Scobee, *Fort Davis, Texas, 1583–1960*, 16–17.

34. Doyle and Buck, *California Trail Diaries*, xix–xx.

35. Lyle E. Mantor, "Fort Kearny and the Westward Movement," *Nebraska History* 29 (September 1948): 203; Lewis E. Atherton, "The Merchant Sutler in the Pre–Civil War Period," *Southwestern Social Science Quarterly* 19 (September 1938): 140–47.

36. Perkins, *Gold Rush Diary*, 29.

37. Eleazar Stillman Ingalls, *Journal of a Trip to California by the Overland Route across the Plains in 1850–51*, 36; John Phillip Reid, *Law for the Elephant: Property and Social Behavior on the Overland Trail*, 109n.

38. Owen Cochran Coy, *The Great Trek of Dr. E. A. Tompkins*, 140; Perkins, *Gold Rush Diary*, 29; William H. Woodhams, "1852–1853, New York to San Francisco by Ship," and "1854, St. Joseph to California Overland," in "Journals," unpublished manuscripts in NSHS, n.p. (entry of May 26, 1854).

39. Helen Carpenter, "A Trip across the Plains in an Ox Wagon, 1857," in *Ho for California! Women's Overland Diaries from the Huntington Library*, 105.

40. Mattes, *Great Platte River Road*, 204.

41. Charles Ruff to John Dougherty, June 24, 1849, and Charles Ruff to John Dougherty, February 7, 1850, in Charles and Annie Ruff Papers, NSHS.

42. *The Gold Rush: Letters from the Wolverine Rangers to the Marshall, Michigan Statesman, 1849–1851*, 46; LeRoy R. Hafen and Francis Marion Young, *Fort Laramie and the Pageant of the West, 1834–1890*, 155.

43. Richard L. Rieck, "A Geography of Death on the Oregon and California Trails, 1840–1860," *Overland Journal* 9, no. 1 (1991): 14–15.

44. Unruh, *Plains Across*, 229; Henry J. Coke, *A Ride over the Rocky Mountains to Oregon and California*, 158.

45. Unruh, *Plains Across*, 229–30; Mattes, *Great Platte River Road*, 513.

46. Reid, *Law for the Elephant*, 122; Bennett, *Overland Journey to California*, 29.

47. *The Gold Rush*, 45; Unruh, *Plains Across*, 229; Bidlack, *Letters Home*, 22.

48. Settle, *March of the Mounted Riflemen*, 75; Jessie Gould Hannon, *The Boston-Newton Company Venture: From Massachusetts to California in 1849*, 129.

49. Bidlack, *Letters Home*, 54; Annie Ruff to Mary Dougherty, June 24, 1849, in Charles and Annie Ruff Papers, NSHS.

50. Hafen and Young, *Fort Laramie*, 165–66; Lucena Parsons, "An Overland Honeymoon," in *Covered Wagon Women*, ed. Kenneth L. Holmes, 2:255.

51. Mattes, *Great Platte River Road*, 205.

52. Sarah Royce, *A Frontier Lady: Recollections of the Gold Rush and Early California*, ed. Ralph Henry Gabriel, 21; Frink, "Adventures of a Party," 94; Mary Jane Guill, "The Overland Diary of a Journey from Livingston County, Missouri, to Butte County, California (1860)," unpublished manuscript in California State Library, Sacramento, 5.

53. Col. Benjamin Bonneville to Postmaster General, June 4, 1849, AGO, Letters Sent, RG 393, NA.

54. Mantor, "Fort Kearny," 191–95; Hafen and Young, *Fort Laramie*, 171–73, 265–71.

55. Ingalls, "Journal of a Trip," 27; William Richard Brown, *An Authentic Wagon Train Journal of 1853 from Indiana to California*, 36.

56. Mantor, "Fort Kearny," 195–200; Hafen and Young, *Fort Laramie*, 305–306; Doyle and Buck, California Trail Diaries, 16.

57. Unruh, *Plains Across*, 235–36; W. Turrentine Jackson, *Wagon Roads West: A Study of Federal Road Surveys and Construction in the Trans-Mississippi West, 1846–1869*, 167–72.

58. Quoted in Francis Paul Prucha, *Broadax and Bayonet: The Role of the United States Army in the Development of the Northwest*, 1815–1860, 104.

59. William J. Pleasants, *Twice across the Plains, 1849 and 1856*, 27; Hafen and Young, *Fort Laramie*, 159–60.

60. Ingalls, *Journal of a Trip*, 36; Origen Thomson, *Crossing the Plains: Narrative of the Scenes, Incidents, and Adventures Attending the Overland Journey of the Decatur and Rush County Emigrants to the "Far Off" Oregon, in 1852*, 37; Elizabeth Lee Porter, "Iowa to Oregon, 1864," in *Covered Wagon Women*, ed. Kenneth L. Holmes, 9:22.

61. Settle, *March of the Mounted Riflemen*, 289.

62. Sarah Sutton, "A Travel Diary in 1854," in *Covered Wagon Women*, ed. Kenneth L. Holmes, 7:46; William K. Sloan, "Autobiography of William K. Sloan,"

Annals of Wyoming 4 (July 1926): 245–46; Mary Burrell, "Council Bluffs to California, 1854," in *Covered Wagon Women*, ed. Kenneth L. Holmes, 6:233.

63. Henry P. Walker, "When the Law Wore Army Blue," *Military Collector and Historian* 29 (Spring 1977): 7.

64. Settle, *March of the Mounted Riflemen*, 100; Lucretia Lawson Epperson, "A Journal of Our Trip, 1864," in *Covered Wagon Women*, ed. Kenneth L. Holmes, 8:169.

65. D. A. Shaw, *Eldorado, or California As Seen by a Pioneer, 1850–1900*, 32–33.

66. S. L. Grow, "Journal," unpublished manuscript in the Beinecke Library, Yale University; John Hale, *California As It Is: Description of a Tour by the Overland Route and South Pass of the Rocky Mountains*, 5–14.

67. Unruh, *Plains Across*, 231, 463; Settle, *March of the Mounted Riflemen*, 325–26.

68. Bidlack, *Letters Home*, 21–22.

69. Perkins, *Gold Rush Diary*, 53; Sterling B. F. Clark, *How Many Miles from St Jo? The Log of Sterling B. F. Clark, a Forty-Niner*, 12.

70. Shirley Sargent, ed., *Seeking the Elephant, 1849: James Mason Hutchings' Journal of His Overland Trek to California, Including His Voyage to America, 1848, and Letters from the Mother Lode*, 109–10; Annie Ruff to Mary Dougherty, June 24, 1849, in Charles and Annie Ruff Papers, NSHS.

71. Fort Kearny, Post Returns for November 1853, in Office of Adjutant General, reel 2, NSHS.

72. Benjamin Bonneville to Adj. Gen. Roger Jones, June 2, 1849, AGO, Letters Sent, RG 393, NA.

73. Settle, *March of the Mounted Riflemen*, 58 and 304.

74. Robert H. Chilton to Adj. Gen. R. Jones, August 23, 1849, in Office of Adjutant General, Letters Sent, RG 393, NA.

75. Parsons, "Overland Honeymoon," 246; Stansbury, *Expedition to Great Salt Lake*, 53; Louis C. Butscher, ed., "An Account of Adventures in the Great American Desert by His Royal Highness, Duke Paul Wilhelm Von Wurttemberg," *New Mexico Historical Review* 17 (1942): 199–201; Epperson, "Journal of Our Trip," 168–69.

76. Mattes, *Great Platte River Road*, 33; Harriet Hitchcock, "Thoughts by the Way, 1864–1865," in *Covered Wagon Women*, ed. Kenneth L. Holmes, 8:238; Wilson, *Fort Kearny*, 80.

77. Wilson, *Fort Kearny*, 80–86; Eugene F. Ware, *The Indian War of 1864*, 32–35; Violet A. Saltzgaber, "Doby Town," unpublished manuscript, NSHS.

78. Ray Allen Billington, *The Far Western Frontier, 1830–1860*, 26–40.

79. Leo E. Oliva, *Soldiers on the Santa Fe Trail*, 93–130; Chris Emmett, *Fort Union and the Winning of the Southwest*, 14–20. For a more detailed account of the various forts' protective roles, see William Y. Chalfant, *Dangerous Passages: The Santa Fe Trail and the Mexican War*.

80. Leo E. Oliva, *Fort Hays, Frontier Army Post, 1865–1889*, 1–12.

81. Grant Foreman, *Marcy and the Gold Seekers: The Journal of Captain R. B. Marcy, with an Account of the Gold Rush over the Southern Route*, 3–38.

82. A. C. Greene, *900 Miles on the Butterfield Trail*: 45–107.

83. Patricia A. Etter, "To California on the Southern Route—1849," *Overland Journal* 13 (Fall 1995): 2–10.

84. Robert L. Munkres, "Fort Bridger," *Overland Journal* 8, no. 2 (1990): 26–33.

85. Louis A. Holmes, *Fort McPherson, Nebraska, Fort Cottonwood, N.T.: Guardian of the Tracks and Trails*, 1–22; Merrill J. Mattes, "Old Fort Mitchell, Nebraska, Revisited," *Overland Journal* 7, no. 2 (1989): 2–9.

86. J. W. Vaughn, *The Battle of Platte Bridge*, 14–21.

CHAPTER 3. ACROSS AND ON THE WIDE MISSOURI

1. Francis Paul Prucha, *The Sword of the Republic: The United States Army on the Frontier, 1787–1846*, 186–88.

2. Richard K. Crallé, ed., *The Works of John C. Calhoun*, 5:40–54.

3. Harold Kanarek, "The U.S. Army Corps of Engineers and Early Internal Improvements in Maryland," *Maryland Historical Magazine* 72 (Spring 1977): 99–109; George Rogers Taylor, *The Transportation Revolution, 1815–1860*, 17–31.

4. W. Turrentine Jackson, "The Army Engineers as Road Builders in Territorial Iowa," *Iowa Journal of History and Politics* 47 (January 1949): 24–33.

5. William P. Corbett, "Rifles and Ruts: Army Road Builders in Indian Territory," *Chronicles of Oklahoma* 60 (Fall 1982): 294–300.

6. Corbett, "Rifles and Ruts," 301–304; Louise Barry, ed., "With the First U.S. Cavalry in Indian Country, 1859–1861," *Kansas Historical Quarterly* 24 (Fall 1958): 275; Frederick W. Rathjen, "The Federal Role in Opening the Panhandle," *Panhandle-Plains Historical Review* 49 (1976): 11.

7. Louise Barry, "The Fort Leavenworth–Fort Gibson Military Road and the Founding of Fort Scott, "*Kansas Historical Quarterly* 11 (May 1942): 117–27.

8. Leo E. Oliva, "Frontier Forts and the Settlement of Western Kansas," *Kansas and the West: Bicentennial Essays in Honor of Nyle H. Miller*, ed. Forrest R. Blackburn et al., 66. For post–Civil War developments in Kansas, see David K. Clapsaddle, "The Fort Hays–Fort Dodge Road," *Kansas History* 14 (Summer 1991): 101–12"; and David K. Clapsaddle, "Conflict and Commerce on the Santa Fe Trail: The Fort Riley–Fort Larned Road, 1860–1867," *Kansas History* 16 (Summer 1993): 124–37.

9. W. Turrentine Jackson, "The Army Engineers as Road Surveyors and Builders in Kansas and Nebraska, 1854–1858," *Kansas Historical Quarterly* 17 (February 1949): 39–40; John B. Garver, Jr., "The Role of the United States Army

in the Colonization of the Trans-Missouri West: Kansas, 1804–1861," Ph.D. diss., Syracuse University, 1981, 611–41.

10. Jackson, "Army Engineers as Road Surveyors and Builders," 58–59. A good overview of the impact of military roads across the Northern Plains is found in Gary S. Freedom, "Moving Men and Supplies: Military Transportation on the Northern Great Plains, 1866–1891," *South Dakota History* 14 (Summer 1984): 114–33.

11. William H. Goetzmann, *Army Exploration in the American West, 1803–1863,* 353–60; Thomas W. Prosch, "The Military Roads of Washington Territory," *Washington Historical Quarterly* 2 (January 1908): 118–126; Merrill Burlingame, "The Influence of the Military in the Building of Montana," *Pacific Northwest Quarterly* 29 (April 1938): 137–40. The most complete account of the entire wagon roads program is found in W. Turrentine Jackson, *Wagon Roads West: A Study of Federal Road Surveys and Construction in the Trans-Mississippi West, 1846–1869.*

12. J. W. Williams, "Military Roads of the 1850s in Central West Texas," *West Texas Historical Association Year Book* 18 (1942): 77–91.

13. Ben E. Pingenot, "The Great Wagon Train Expedition of 1850," *Southwestern Historical Quarterly* 98 (October 1994): 183–225; John T. Sprague, "Journal of a Wagon Train Expedition from Fort Inge to El Paso del Norte in 1850," ed. Ben E. Pingenot, *Military History of the West* 25 (Spring 1995): 69–105.

14. Homer T. Fort, "John Pope, the First Great Wildcatter," *Greater Llano Estacado and Southwest Heritage* 7 (Fall 1977): 13.

15. Lee Myers, "Pope's Wells," *New Mexico Historical Review* 38 (October 1963): 273–99; Clinton E. Brooks and Frank D. Reeve, eds., *Forts and Forays: James A. Bennett, a Dragoon in New Mexico, 1850–1856,* 76–77.

16. Frank M. Temple, "Colonel B. H. Grierson's Administration of the District of the Pecos," *West Texas Historical Association Year Book* 38 (1962): 88–93; Mary Sutton, "Glimpses of Fort Concho through the Military Telegraph," *West Texas Historical Association Year Book* 32 (1956): 129.

17. Lydia Spencer Lane, *I Married a Soldier, or Old Days in the Army,* 165.

18. Patrick Dearen, *Crossing Rio Pecos,* 71–86; Clayton Williams, *Texas' Last Frontier: Fort Stockton and the Trans-Pecos, 1861–1895,* 126–27, 159.

19. Sandra L. Myres, ed., "A Woman's View of the Texas Frontier, 1874: The Diary of Emily K. Andrews," *Southwestern Historical Quarterly* 86 (July 1982): 49–50, 72; Elvis Joe Ballew, "Supply Problems at Fort Davis, Texas, 1867–1880," master's thesis, Sul Ross State University, 1971, 19.

20. Douglas C. McChristian, "Apaches and Soldiers: Mail Protection in West Texas," *Periodical: Journal of the Council on America's Military Past* 13, no. 3 (1985): 6–9.

21. Ibid., 10–11.

22. Wayne R. Austerman, *Sharps Rifles and Spanish Mules: The San Antonio–El Paso Mail, 1851–1881,* 279–82.

23. McChristian, "Apaches and Soldiers," 14.

24. Merrill J. Mattes, *The Great Platte River Road: The Covered Wagon Mainline via Fort Kearny to Fort Laramie*, Publications of the Nebraska State Historical Society, 25:174, 206, 515; Lyle E. Mantor, "Stage Coach and Freighter Days at Fort Kearny," *Nebraska History* 29 (December 1948): 324–26.

25. Richard Guentzel, "The Department of the Platte and Western Settlement, 1866–1877," *Nebraska History* 56 (Fall 1975): 397.

26. Leo E. Oliva, *Fort Hays, Frontier Army Post, 1865–1889*, 1–7; Dee Brown, *The Galvanized Yankees*, 199–204.

27. Henry M. Stanley, *My Early Travels and Adventures in America and Asia*, 1:49.

28. Julia Gilliss, *So Far From Home: An Army Bride on the Western Frontier, 1865–1869*, ed. Priscilla Knuth, 180.

29. Merrill J. Mattes, "The Sutler's Store at Fort Laramie," *Annals of Wyoming* 18 (July 1946): 103; Gerald M. Adams, *The Post Near Cheyenne: A History of Fort D. A. Russell, 1867–1930*, 97.

30. Paul L. Hedren, "On Duty at Fort Ridgely, Minnesota: 1853–1867," *South Dakota History* 7 (Spring 1977): 187.

31. Bill Green, *The Dancing Was Lively: Fort Concho Texas: A Social History, 1867 to 1882*, 69–70; Susan Miles, "The Post Office War," *Fort Concho Report* 12 (Spring 1980): 5–13.

32. Carol G. Goodwin, "The Letters of Private Milton Spencer, 1862–1865: A Soldier's View of Military Life on the Northern Plains," *North Dakota History* 37 (Fall 1970): 253–54.

33. S. S. Peters, "Letters of a Sixth Cavalryman Stationed at 'Cantonment' in the Texas Panhandle, 1875," ed. Lonnie J. White, *Texas Military History* 7 (Summer 1968): 81.

34. "Letter of Sgt. George W. Ford," *Winners of the West*, April 1924, 1.

35. Martin L. Crimmins, "Experiences of an Army Surgeon at Fort Chadbourne," *West Texas Historical Association Year Book* 15 (1939): 32; Merrill J. Mattes, *Indians, Infants, and Infantry: Andrew and Elizabeth Burt on the Frontier*, 127.

36. Dana Wright, "The Fort Totten–Fort Stevenson Trail, 1867–1872," *North Dakota History* 20 (April 1953): 82–83. For additional accounts of mail delivery problems on this trail, see Ray H. Mattison, "Old Fort Stevenson, a Typical Missouri River Military Post," *North Dakota History* 18 (April–June 1951), 61–64.

37. David P. Robrock, "A History of Fort Fetterman, Wyoming, 1867–1882," *Annals of Wyoming* 48 (Spring 1976): 39.

38. Quoted in Mattes, *Indians, Infants, and Infantry*, 146. Further evidence of the army's use of Indian scouts such as the famed Arikara Bloody Knife as mail couriers is seen in Philippe Régis de Trobriand, *Military Life in Dakota: The Journal of Philippe Régis de Trobriand*, ed. Lucile M. Kane, 162–63, 237n.

39. Charles E. Whilden, "Letters from a Santa Fe Army Clerk, 1855–1856," ed. John Hammond Moore, *New Mexico Historical Review* 40 (April 1965): 151.

40. Alice Blackwood Baldwin, *Memoirs of the Late Frank D. Baldwin, Major General, U.S.A.*, 162. Letters between Lt. Clinton W. Lear at Fort Towson, Indian Territory, and his wife in Louisiana capture the deep pains of their separation and the former's bout with depression that pushed him close to suicide. See George H. Shirk, "Mail Call at Fort Washita," *Chronicles of Oklahoma* 33 (Spring 1958): 14–20.

41. James M. Oswald, "History of Fort Elliott," *Panhandle-Plains Historical Review* 32 (1959): 25; Robert C. Carriker, *Fort Supply, Indian Territory: Frontier Outpost on the Plains*, 147–48.

42. Robert L. Thompson, *Wiring a Continent: The History of the Telegraph Industry in the United States, 1832–1866*, 345–71.

43. Guentzel, "Department of the Platte," 398.

44. Hervey Johnson, *Tending the Talking Wire: A Buck Soldier's View of Indian Country, 1863–1866*, ed. William E. Unruh, 268.

45. Kenneth J. Almy, ed., "Thof's Dragon and the Letters of Capt. Theophilus H. Turner, M.D., U.S. Army," *Kansas History* 10 (Fall 1987): 183.

46. Quoted in William E. Annin, "Fort Robinson during the 1880s: An Omaha Newspaperman Visits the Post," *Nebraska History* 55 (Summer 1974): 193.

47. L. Tuffly Ellis, ed., "Lieutenant A. W. Greely's Report on the Installation of Military Telegraph Lines in Texas, 1875–1876," *Southwestern Historical Quarterly* 69 (July 1965): 67–85; Adolphus W. Greely, *Reminiscences of Adventure and Service: A Record of Sixty-five Years*, 153–55.

48. Sutton, "Glimpses of Fort Concho through the Military Telegraph," 122–32; Williams, *Texas' Last Frontier*, 200.

49. Mantor, "Stage Coach and Freighter Days at Fort Kearny," 337.

50. Oswald, "History of Fort Elliott," 26.

51. Roger L. Nichols, "Army Contributions to River Transportation, 1818–1825," *Military Affairs* 33 (April 1969): 247–48. For a discussion of the important Platte River tributary and its failure as a navigable waterway, see Lawrence C. Allin, "'A Mile Wide and an Inch Deep': Attempts to Navigate the Platte River," *Nebraska History* 63 (Spring 1982): 1–15.

52. Averam B. Bender, "Military Transportation in the Southwest, 1848–1860," *New Mexico Historical Review* 32 (April 1957): 140.

53. Charles W. Howell, "An Army Engineer on the Missouri in 1867," ed. Leland R. Johnson, *Nebraska History* 53 (Summer 1972): 253–85.

54. Freedom, "Moving Men and Supplies," 125; *The Federal Engineer: Damsites to Missile Sites: A History of the Omaha District, U.S. Army Corps of Engineers*, 4–12.

55. Maurice Frink and Casey Barthelmess, *Photographer on an Army Mule*, 74–75; Joseph Mills Hanson, *The Conquest of the Missouri, Being the Story of the Life and Exploits of Captain Grant Marsh*, chap. 25; William Molchert, "Sergeant Molchert's Perils: Soldiering in Montana," ed. John G. James, *Montana, Magazine of Western History* 34 (Spring 1984): 63.

56. William E. Lass, *A History of Steamboating on the Upper Missouri River*, 176.

57. Teresa Griffin Vielé, *Following the Drum: A Glimpse of Frontier Life*, 137–40.

58. Pat Kelley, *River of Lost Dreams: Navigation on the Rio Grande*, 48–56; Ron C. Tyler, *The Big Bend: A History of the Last Texas Frontier*, 76–100.

59. Pamela Ashworth Puryear and Nath Winfield, Jr., *Sandbars and Stern-wheelers: Steam Navigation on the Brazos*, 29–33.

60. Robert Sidney Martin, "United States Army Mapping in Texas, 1848–50," in *The Mapping of the American Southwest*, ed. Dennis Reinhartz and Charles C. Colley, 52.

61. Bender, "Military Transportation in the Southwest," 142–43. Problems of making the Arkansas into a navigable river are discussed in Brad Agnew, *Fort Gibson: Terminal on the Trail of Tears*, 33–34; and H. Craig Miner, *Wichita: The Early Years, 1865–1880*, 149–50.

62. Bender, "Military Transportation in the Southwest," 144–45; Goetzmann, *Army Exploration in the American West*, 384–94; Edward S. Wallace, *The Great Reconnaissance: Soldiers, Artists, and Scientists on the Frontier, 1848–1861*, 175–203.

63. Susan Pritchard O'Hara and Gregory Graves, *Saving California's Coast: Army Engineers at Oceanside and Humboldt Bay*, 9–10.

64. Ibid., 9–18.

65. Joseph J. Hagood, Jr., *Engineers at the Golden Gate: A History of the San Francisco District, U.S. Army Corps of Engineers, 1866–1890*, 36–43.

66. Joseph J. Hagood, Jr., *Commitment to Excellence: A History of the Sacramento District, U.S. Army Corps of Engineers, 1929–1973*, 7–9.

67. Henry R. Richmond III, *The History of the Portland District, Corps of Engineers, 1871–1969*, 13–18.

68. William F. Willingham, *Army Engineers and the Development of Oregon: A History of the Portland District, U.S. Army Corps of Engineers, 1929–1973*, 28–36.

69. George L. Albright, *Official Explorations for Pacific Railroads*, 37–43; Goetzmann, *Army Exploration in the American West*, 275. Excellent coverage of army engineers' roles in the surveying and construction of eastern and western railroads alike is found in Forest G. Hill, *Roads, Rails, and Waterways: The Army Engineers and Early Transportation*, 96–152.

70. Taylor, *Transportation Revolution*, 86; John F. Stover, *The Life and Decline of the American Railroad*, 45–50.

71. Robert G. Athearn, *Union Pacific Country*, 199–210.

72. Eugene F. Ware, *The Indian War of 1864*, 405.

73. Athearn, *Union Pacific Country*, 201–202.

74. Mattes, *Indians, Infants, and Infantry*, 176.

75. Athearn, *Union Pacific Country*, 210.

76. Guentzel, "Department of the Platte," 395; Raymond L. Welty, "The Policing of the Frontier by the Army, 1860–1870," *Kansas Historical Quarterly* 7 (August 1938): 253–54.

77. Ballew, "Supply Problems of Fort Davis," 39. Examples of "cozy deals" between railroad executives and specific military officers are found in Frink and Barthelmess, *Photographer on an Army Mule,* 120–21; Robert M. Utley, *Cavalier in Buckskin: George Armstrong Custer and the Western Military Frontier,* 126; Mary Patience Magwire Carr, "Fort McPherson in 1870: A Note by an Army Wife," ed. James T. King, *Nebraska History* 45 (March 1964): 106.

78. "Letter of William Fetter," *Winners of the West,* May 1925, 5; Burlingame, "Influence of the Military," 146; Paul M. Edwards, "Fort Wadsworth and the Friendly Santee Sioux, 1864–1892," *South Dakota Department of History Report and Historical Collections* 31 (1962): 142; Monroe Billington, "Black Soldiers at Fort Selden, New Mexico, 1866–1891," *New Mexico Historical Review* 62 (January 1987): 75.

79. Athearn, *Union Pacific Country,* 61–62.

80. Ibid., 203.

81. Paul L. Hedren, "A Footnote to History: The U.S. Army at Promontory, Utah, May 10, 1869," *Utah Historical Quarterly* 49 (Fall 1981): 363–73.

CHAPTER 4. *POSSE COMITATUS* IN BLUE

1. *U.S. Statutes at Large* 1 (1789): 73; H. W. C. Furman, "Restrictions upon the Use of the Army Imposed by the Posse Comitatus Act," *Military Law Review* 7 (January 1960): 86–87.

2. Jerry M. Cooper, "Federal Military Intervention in Domestic Disorders," in *The United States Military under the Constitution of the United States, 1789–1989,* ed. Richard H. Kohn, 133.

3. Furman, "Restrictions upon the Use," 87; Clayton D. Laurie, "Filling the Breach: Military Aid to the Civil Power in the Trans-Mississippi West," *Western Historical Quarterly* 25 (Summer 1994): 151.

4. *U.S. Statutes at Large* 2 (1807): 443. Dumas Malone, *Jefferson the President, Second Term, 1805–1809,* 252–55; G. Norman Lieber, *The Use of the Army in Aid of the Civil Power,* 18.

5. James Regan, "Military Duties in Aid of the Civil Power," *Journal of the Military Service Institution of the United States* 18 (March 1896): 285.

6. Cooper, "Federal Military Intervention," 134; Laurie, "Filling the Breach," 149–50.

7. Robert W. Coakley, *The Role of Federal Military Forces in Domestic Disorders, 1789–1878,* 140–44; Larry D. Ball, *The United States Marshals of New Mexico and Arizona Territories, 1846–1912,* 16.

8. Frederick T. Wilson, *Federal Aid in Domestic Disturbances, 1787–1903,* 57th Cong., 2d sess., 1903, S. Doc. 209, 86–92; William Tecumseh Sherman, *Memoirs of General William T. Sherman,* 1:146–60.

9. Igor I. Kavass and Adolph Sprudzs, *Military Aid to the Civil Power*, 187–88.

10. Quoted in ibid., 189; Cooper, "Federal Military Intervention," 134.

11. Henry P. Walker, "When the Law Wore Army Blue," *Military Collector and Historian* 29 (Spring 1977): 7; Coakley, *Role of Federal Military Forces*, 154–63.

12. Norman F. Furniss, *The Mormon Conflict, 1850–1859*, 62–94.

13. Ibid., 105–18, 168–201.

14. Donald R. Moorman and Gene A. Sessions, *Camp Floyd and the Mormons: The Utah War*, 54–58.

15. Coakley, *Role of Federal Military Forces*, 225–26.

16. Ball, *United States Marshals*, 29–30.

17. Louise Barry, ed., "With the First U.S. Cavalry in Indian Country, 1859–1861," *Kansas Historical Quarterly* 24 (Fall 1958): 278.

18. Ibid., 278–79, and (Winter 1958): 419–20.

19. Walker, "When the Law Wore Army Blue," 7.

20. Ball, *United States Marshals*, 26; Walker, "When the Law Wore Army Blue," 7.

21. Ball, *United States Marshals*, 29.

22. Ibid., 27.

23. Barbara A. Neal Ledbetter, *Fort Belknap Frontier Saga: Indians, Negroes, and Anglo-Americans on the Texas Frontier*, 65–66.

24. Ibid., 80.

25. Rodney Glisan, *Journal of Army Life*, 231. Two other examples of soldiers facing fines and lawsuits from civilians are found in H. Craig Miner, *Wichita: The Early Years, 1865–1880*, 40–41; and James M. Oswald, "History of Fort Elliott," *Panhandle-Plains Historical Review* 32 (1959): 39–41.

26. Clayton Williams, *Texas' Last Frontier: Fort Stockton and the Trans-Pecos, 1861–1895*, ed. Ernest Wallace, 110, 195–96.

27. Ibid., 110; Mrs. Orsemus Bronson Boyd, *Cavalry Life in Tent and Field*, 201–203.

28. D. Claudia Thompson, "Driven from Point to Point: Fact and Legend of the Bear River Riot," *Montana, Magazine of Western History* 46 (Winter 1996): 24–34. A similar set of events during 1867–68 in Cheyenne, Wyoming, and other railroad towns was handled by troops from Fort D. A. Russell. See Gerald M. Adams, *The Post Near Cheyenne: A History of Fort D. A. Russell, 1867–1930*, 11–12.

29. Ball, *United States Marshals*, 59–60, 80–81; Howard R. Lamar, *The Far Southwest 1846–1912: A Territorial History*, 151–55.

30. Lieber, *The Use of the Army*, 24.

31. William Molchert, "Sergeant Molchert's Perils: Soldiering in Montana," ed. John G. James, *Montana, Magazine of Western History* 34 (Spring 1984): 61–62.

32. *Annual Report of the Secretary of War, 1871*, 16–33.

33. Quoted in Raymond L. Welty, "The Policing of the Frontier by the Army, 1860–1870," *Kansas Historical Quarterly* 7 (August 1938): 254.

34. Donald W. Whisenhunt, *Fort Richardson: Outpost on the Texas Frontier*, 9, 16; Wilson, *Federal Aid in Domestic Disturbances*, 127–29.

35. Furman, "Restrictions upon the Use," 94–97; Lieber, *Use of the Army*, 9–10. The entire debate is presented in the *Congressional Record*, 45th Cong., 2d sess., 1878, 3538, 3645, 3845, 3847–50, 3877–78.

36. Lieber, *Use of the Army*, 3–4.

37. Laurie, "Filling the Breach," 158.

38. Quoted in ibid., 160.

39. Walker, "When the Law Wore Army Blue," 8.

40. Laurie, "Filling the Breach," 160.

41. U.S. Congress, House, *Message from the President of the United States in Relation to Disorders and Lawlessness in Arizona*, 47th Cong., 1st sess., 1882, H. Exec. Doc. 188.

42. Laurie, "Filling the Breach," 161.

43. Ibid., 159.

44. Ball, *United States Marshals*, 113.

45. Laurie, "Filling the Breach," 159.

46. Ibid.

47. Lamar, *Far Southwest, 1846–1912*, 464–71; John Myers Myers, *The Last Chance: Tombstone's Early Years*, 136–69.

48. Ball, *United States Marshals*, 125–26.

49. Laurie, "Filling the Breach," 159–60.

50. Maurice G. Fulton, *History of the Lincoln County War*, ed. Robert N. Mullin, 70–120.

51. Walker, "When the Law Wore Army Blue," 10–11.

52. Robert M. Utley, *High Noon in Lincoln: Violence on the Western Frontier*, 66–78, 92–124, 125–36; Frederick Nolan, *The Lincoln County War: A Documentary History*, 395–96.

53. Helena Huntington Smith, *The War on Powder River: The History of an Insurrection*, 190–219.

54. Ibid., 220–25; Robert A. Murray, "The United States Army in the Aftermath of the Johnson County Invasion, April through November, 1892," in Robert A. Murray, *The Army on the Powder River*, 40–42.

55. Murray, "United States Army in Aftermath," 43–46; Adams, *Post Near Cheyenne*, 116.

56. An example of continued local resentment against the army that was directed in racial terms against black soldiers of the Ninth Cavalry is seen in Frank N. Schubert, "The Suggs Affray: The Black Cavalry in the Johnson County War," *Western Historical Quarterly* 4 (January 1973): 57–68.

57. Roger Daniels, *Asian America: Chinese and Japanese in the United States since 1850*, 61–62.

58. Murray L. Carroll, "Governor Francis E. Warren, the United States Army, and the Chinese Massacre at Rock Springs," *Annals of Wyoming* 59 (Fall 1987):

18–23; Clayton D. Laurie, "Civil Disorder and the Military in Rock Springs, Wyoming: The Army's Role in the 1885 Chinese Massacre," *Montana, Magazine of Western History* 40 (Summer 1990): 52–59.

59. Carroll, "Governor Francis E. Warren," 21–23.

60. Clayton D. Laurie, "'The Chinese Must Go': The United States Army and the Anti-Chinese Riots in Washington Territory, 1885–1886," *Pacific Northwest Quarterly* 81 (January 1990): 25–28. See also Jules A. Karlin, "The Anti-Chinese Outbreak in Tacoma, 1885," *Pacific Historical Review* 23 (August 1954): 271–83; and Jules A. Karlin, "The Anti-Chinese Outbreaks in Seattle, 1885–1886," *Pacific Northwest Quarterly* 39 (1948): 103–30.

61. C. L. Sonnichsen, *Ten Texas Feuds*, 108–35; Walter Prescott Webb, *The Texas Rangers: A Century of Frontier Defense*, 345–54.

62. Sonnichsen, *Ten Texas Feuds*, 135–54; George Ruhlen, "Quitman: 'The Worst Post at Which I Ever Served,'" *Password* 12 (Fall 1966): 120–21.

63. Walker, "When the Law Wore Army Blue," 10.

64. Adams, *Post Near Cheyenne*, 27.

65. J. Evetts Haley, *Charles Goodnight, Cowman and Plainsman*, 222–24.

66. Thomas R. Buecker, "Fort Niobrara,1880–1906: Guardian of the Rosebud Sioux," *Nebraska History* 65 (Fall 1984): 306. Details of other army pursuits on the Central Plains, including public outcries against alleged brutality, are found in James David Drees, "The Army and Horse Thieves," *Kansas History* 11 (Spring 1988): 35–53.

67. Larry D. Ball, "The United States Army and the Big Springs, Nebraska Train Robbery of 1877," *Journal of the West* 34 (January 1995): 34–35; Louis A. Holmes, *Fort McPherson, Nebraska, Fort Cottonwood, N.T.: Guardian of the Tracks and Trails*, 59–60.

68. Ball, "United States Army and Big Springs Train Robbery," 35–44. Other notable examples of army pursuits of train robbers who violated the federal mails are found in: Laurie, "Filling the Breach," 156, 161; and David K. Strate, *Sentinel to the Cimarron: The Frontier Experience of Fort Dodge, Kansas*, 62.

69. Merrill J. Mattes, *Indians, Infants, and Infantry: Andrew and Elizabeth Burt on the Frontier*, 239–40; Solomon D. Butcher, *Pioneer History of Custer County*, 43–62.

70. Mattes, *Indians, Infants, and Infantry*, 240–41; Martin Schmitt, ed., *General George Crook: His Autobiography*, 230–31.

71. Robert A. Murray, "Fort Fred Steele: Desert Outpost on the Union Pacific," *Annals of Wyoming* 44 (Fall 1972): 152; *Annual Report of the Secretary of War, 1871*, 32.

72. Walter C. Sharp, Jr., "Fort Omaha and the Winning of the West," master's thesis, University of Nebraska at Omaha, 1967, 96–98; Ronald M. Gephart, "Politicians, Soldiers, and Strikes: The Reorganization of the Nebraska Militia and the Omaha Strike of 1882," *Nebraska History* 46 (June 1965): 100–20.

73. Theophilus G. Steward, "Starving Laborers and the 'Hired' Soldier," *United Service* 15 (October 1895): 366.

74. George F. Price, "The Necessity for Closer Relations between the Army and the People, and the Best Method to Accomplish the Result," *Journal of the Military Service Institution of the United States* 6 (December 1885): 303–32.

75. James Regan, "Military Duties in Aid of the Civil Power," *Journal of the Military Service Institution of the United States* 18 (March 1896): 285–97; William Wallace, "The Army and the Civil Power," *Journal of the Military Service Institution of the United States* 17 (September 1895): 235–66; John C. Gresham, "Civil Employment of Troops," *United Service* 7 (May 1892): 476–82.

76. E. L. Molineux, "Riots in Cities and Their Suppression," *Journal of the Military Service Institution of the United States* 4 (1883): 335–70; Elwell S. Otis, "The Army in Connection with the Labor Riots of 1877," *Journal of the Military Service Institution of the United States* 5 (1884): 292–323.

77. Russell Thayer, "Movements of Troops in Cities in Cases of Riots or Insurrection," *United Service* 1 (January 1879): 92–99; William N. Blow, "Use of Troops in Riots," *Journal of the Military Service Institution of the United States* 25 (July 1899): 45–57.

78. Otis, "Army in Connection with Labor Riots of 1877," 292–96; Bennett M. Rich, *The Presidents and Civil Disorder*, 72–83.

79. Jerry M. Cooper, *The Army and Civil Disorder: Federal Military Intervention in Labor Disputes, 1877–1900*, 45–65.

80. Cooper, "Federal Military Intervention," 134.

81. Cooper, *Army and Civil Disorder*, 61.

82. Strate, *Sentinel to the Cimarron*, 62.

83. Louis Adamic, *Dynamite: The Story of Class Violence in America*, 115–22; Walker, "When the Law Wore Army Blue," 12.

84. Louise Carroll Wade, "Hell Hath No Fury Like a General Scorned: Nelson A. Miles, the Pullman Strike, and the Beef Scandal of 1898," *Illinois Historical Quarterly* 79, no. 3 (1986): 168–71; Robert Wooster, *Nelson A. Miles and the Twilight of the Frontier Army*, 198–201.

85. Adams, *Post Near Cheyenne*, 119; William H. Bisbee, *Through Four American Wars*, 232–33.

86. Buecker, "Fort Niobrara," 318; Paul H. Carlson, *"Pecos Bill": A Military Biography of William R. Shafter*, 156–57. Two larger studies of federal troop movements in the West are W. Thomas White, "Boycott: No Pullman Strike in Montana," *Montana, Magazine of Western History* 29 (October 1979): 2–13; and Clayton D. Laurie, "Extinguishing Frontier Brushfires: The U.S. Army's Role in Quelling the Pullman Strike in the West, 1894," *Journal of the West* 32 (April 1993): 54–63.

87. Carlson, *Pecos Bill*, 157–58.

88. Wooster, *Nelson A. Miles*, 200–201; Wade, "Hell Hath No Fury," 171–72; John M. Schofield, *Forty-Six Years in the Army*, 491–512.

89. Robert Wayne Smith, *The Coeur d'Alene Mining War of 1892: A Case Study of an Industrial Dispute*, 80–96; Clayton D. Laurie, "The United States Army and

the Labor Radicals of the Coeur d'Alenes: Federal Military Intervention in the Mining Wars of 1892–1899," *Idaho Yesterdays* 37 (Summer 1993): 12–21.

90. Laurie, "United States Army and Labor Radicals," 21–29; Cooper, *The Army and Civil Disorder*, 172–96.

91. Cooper, "Federal Military Intervention," 135; Rich, *The Presidents and Civil Disorder*, 119.

92. *Annual Report of the Secretary of War*, 1867, 60.

CHAPTER 5. DINING AT THE GOVERNMENT TROUGH

1. James M. Oswald, "History of Fort Elliott," *Panhandle-Plains Historical Review* 32 (1959): 50.

2. Oswald, "History of Fort Elliott," 51–52.

3. David E. Kyvig, "Policing the Panhandle: Fort Elliott, Texas, 1875–1890," *Red River Valley Historical Review* 1 (Fall 1974): 231–32; Oswald, "History of Fort Elliott," 53; Report of Gen. John Pope, in *Annual Report of the Secretary of War, 1870*, 15–16.

4. "Mobeetie, Texas," in Walter Prescott Webb and H. Bailey Carroll, *The Handbook of Texas*, 2:220.

5. Arthur M. Schlesinger, "The City in American History," *Mississippi Valley Historical Review* 27 (June 1940): 48–49.

6. Report of Secretary of War Jefferson Davis in *Annual Report of the Secretary of War, 1853*, 6.

7. Francis Paul Prucha, "The Settler and the Army in Frontier Minnesota," *Minnesota History* 29 (September 1948): 235–36.

8. Robert W. Frazer, *Forts of the West*, 109, 112–13.

9. Carol G. Goodwin, "The Letters of Private Milton Spencer, 1862–1865: A Soldier's View of Military Life on the Northern Plains," *North Dakota History* 37 (Fall 1970): 255.

10. Mari Sandoz, *Old Jules*, 128–32. Further examples of contrived efforts to attract army money through Indian scares are found in Merrill G. Burlingame, "The Influence of the Military in the Building of Montana," *Pacific Northwest Quarterly* 29 (April 1938): 148–49.

11. H. Craig Miner, *Wichita: The Early Years, 1865–1880*, 35–42.

12. Robert G. Athearn, "The Firewagon Road," *Montana, Magazine of Western History* 20 (April 1970): 10.

13. Sandra L. Myres, "Fort Graham: Listening Post on the Texas Frontier," *West Texas Historical Association Year Book* 59 (1983): 33. See Oswald, "History of Fort Elliott," 43–47, for a discussion of special problems created by Texas' "donation" of land to the federal government for creation of this Panhandle post.

14. Leonora Barrett, "Transportation, Supplies, and Quarters for the West Texas Frontier under the Federal Military System, 1848–1861," *West Texas Historical Association Year Book* 5 (1929): 97–98.

15. Clayton Williams, *Texas' Last Frontier: Fort Stockton and the Trans-Pecos, 1861–1895*, ed. Ernest Wallace, 173.

16. Margaret Bierschwale, *Fort McKavett, Texas: Post on the San Saba*, 42.

17. Eula Haskew, "Stribling and Kirkland of Fort Griffin," *West Texas Historical Association Year Book* 32 (October 1956): 61–69.

18. Bill Green, *The Dancing Was Lively: Fort Concho Texas, a Social History, 1867 to 1882*, 8. The situation of multiple owners also prevailed at Fort Davis and created major complications; see Barry Scobee, *Fort Davis, Texas, 1583–1960*, 20–21, 94–97.

19. George Ruhlen, "Quitman's Owners: A Sidelight on Frontier Reality," *Password* 5 (April 1960): 54–62; George Ruhlen, "Quitman: The Worst Post at Which I Ever Served," *Password* 12 (Fall 1966): 115–16.

20. Paul L. Hedren, "On Duty at Fort Ridgely, Minnesota: 1853–1867," *South Dakota History* 7 (Spring 1977): 179–80.

21. H. H. McConnell, *Five Years a Cavalryman, or Sketches of Regular Army Life on the Texas Frontier, 1866–1871*, 91.

22. David P. Robrock, "A History of Fort Fetterman, Wyoming, 1867–1882," *Annals of Wyoming* 48 (Spring 1976): 71.

23. Elvis Joe Ballew, "Supply Problems of Fort Davis, Texas, 1867–1880," master's thesis, Sul Ross State University, 1971, 88–89.

24. Richard Guentzel, "The Department of the Platte and Western Settlement, 1866–1877," *Nebraska History* 56 (Fall 1975): 410–11; Charles De Noyer, "The History of Fort Totten," *Collections of the State Historical Society of North Dakota* 3 (1910): 188; Donald W. Whisenhunt, *Fort Richardson: Outpost on the Texas Frontier*, 8–9.

25. Thomas R. Buecker, "The 1887 Expansion of Fort Robinson," *Nebraska History* 68 (Summer 1987): 89–91. This article gives precise information on the cost of each new building as well as the dispute between two senior officers over the method of releasing funds to civilian contractors.

26. Ruhlen, "Quitman: Worst Post," 108; Ballew, "Supply Problems of Fort Davis," 92–95.

27. Averam B. Bender, "Military Transportation in the Southwest, 1848–1860," *New Mexico Historical Review* 32 (April 1957): 127–28.

28. Richard D. Gamble, "Garrison Life at Frontier Military Posts, 1820–1860," Ph.D. diss., University of Oklahoma, 1956, 109.

29. Martin L. Crimmins, "Camp Pena Colorado, Texas," *West Texas Historical and Scientific Society Bulletin* 56, no. 6 (1935): 16.

30. Bierschwale, *Fort McKavett, Texas*, 33.

31. W. H. Timmons, "The Merchants and the Military, 1849–1854," *Password* 27 (Summer 1982): 55; Scobee, *Fort Davis*, 17.

32. Williams, *Texas' Last Frontier*, 212.

33. Merrill J. Mattes, *Indians, Infants, and Infantry: Andrew and Elizabeth Burt on the Frontier*, 91.

34. Harry H. Anderson, "A History of the Cheyenne River Agency and Its Military Post, Fort Bennett, 1868–1891," *South Dakota Report and Historical Collections* 28 (1956): 412; Athearn, "Firewagon Road," 4.

35. Ballew, "Supply Problems of Fort Davis," 101; Robert W. Frazer, *Forts and Supplies: The Role of the Army in the Economy of the Southwest, 1846–1861*, 180.

36. Robert Lee, *Fort Meade and the Black Hills*, 170–71.

37. "Ostriches for Our Cavalry," *Army and Navy Journal* 16 (August 2, 1879): 955. For a first-hand account of the army's camel experiment, see Lewis Burt Lesley, ed., *Uncle Sam's Camels: The Journal of May Humphreys Stacey, Supplemented by the Report of Edward Fitzgerald Beale (1857–1858)*.

38. Philippe Régis de Trobriand, *Military Life in Dakota: The Journal of Philippe Régis de Trobriand*, ed. Lucile M. Kane, 71–73.

39. Darlis A. Miller, *Soldiers and Settlers: Military Supply in the Southwest, 1861–1885*, 100.

40. Ibid., 354.

41. Ibid., xv.

42. Robert A. Murray, "Fort Fred Steele: Desert Outpost on the Union Pacific," *Annals of Wyoming* 44 (Fall 1972): 172–73.

43. Allen Lee Hamilton, *Sentinel of the Southern Plains: Fort Richardson and the Northwest Texas Frontier, 1866–1878*, 41.

44. Louis A. Holmes, *Fort McPherson, Nebraska, Fort Cottonwood, N.T.: Guardian of the Tracks and Trails*, 7.

45. Robrock, "History of Fort Fetterman," 30–32; Ballew, "Supply Problems of Fort Davis," 48; Robert A. Murray, "Prices and Wages at Fort Laramie, 1881–1885," *Annals of Wyoming* 36 (April 1964): 19–20.

46. These low-end averages for long-term civilian employees are taken from Guentzel, "The Department of the Platte," 410; Oswald, "History of Fort Elliott," 27–31; and Leo E. Oliva, "Frontier Forts and the Settlement of Western Kansas," in *Kansas and the West: Bicentennial Essays in Honor of Nyle H. Miller*, ed. Forrest R. Blackburn et al., 68–69.

47. The larger averages, reflective of both full- and part-time civilian employees, are taken from Leo E. Oliva, *Fort Larned on the Santa Fe Trail*, 62; Oliva, "Frontier Forts," 68; and Hamilton, *Sentinel of the Southern Plains*, 41.

48. John Neilson, ed., "'I Long to Return to Fort Concho': Acting Assistant Surgeon Samuel Smith's Letters from the Texas Military Frontier, 1878–1879," *Military History of the West* 24 (Fall 1994): 164–65.

49. Ballew, "Supply Problems of Fort Davis," 87, 103.

50. Michael D. Pierce, *The Most Promising Young Officer: A Life of Ranald Slidell Mackenzie*, 106–107, 176–77.

51. Thomas T. Smith, "Fort Inge and the Texas Frontier Economy, 1849–1869," *Military History of the Southwest* 21 (Fall 1991): 152.

52. Usher L. Burdick, *The Army Life of Charles "Chip" Creighton*, 7.

53. Thomas R. Buecker, "Prelude to Brownsville: The Twenty-Fifth Infantry at Fort Niobrara, Nebraska, 1902–06," *Great Plains Quarterly* 16 (Spring 1996): 97.

54. Hervey Johnson, *Tending the Talking Wire: A Buck Soldier's View of Indian Country, 1863–1866*, ed. William E. Unrau, 296; James C. Cage, comp., *Fort Quitman*, 11; Alice Blackwood Baldwin, *Memoirs of the Late Frank D. Baldwin, Major General, U.S.A.*, 162.

55. Scobee, *Fort Davis, Texas*, 141; Dwight L. Smith, ed., "The Kansas Frontier, 1869–1870: Lt. Samuel Tillman's First Tour of Duty," *Kansas History* 12 (Winter 1989–90): 203.

56. McConnell, *Five Years a Cavalryman*, 160.

57. Thomas F. Horton, *History of Jack County*, 120.

58. Quoted in Green, *The Dancing Was Lively*, 63.

59. Douglas McChristian, "The Bug Juice War," *Annals of Wyoming* 49 (Fall 1977): 256–57; Thomas R. Buecker, "Confrontation at Sturgis: An Episode in Civil-Military Race Relations, 1885," *South Dakota History* 14 (Fall 1984): 246.

60. Ray H. Mattison, "The Army Post on the Northern Plains, 1865–1885," *Nebraska History* 35 (March 1954): 34–35.

61. Frank N. Schubert, *Buffalo Soldiers, Braves, and the Brass: The Story of Fort Robinson, Nebraska*, 170, 173. This excellent book offers detailed discussion of how army payrolls and contracts impacted various sectors of Crawford's and the surrounding region's economies.

62. Teresa Griffin Vielé, *Following the Drum: A Glimpse of Frontier Life*, 108–109; Rodney Glisan, *Journal of Army Life*, 46.

63. Barbara A. Neal Ledbetter, *Fort Belknap Frontier Saga: Indians, Negroes, and Anglo-Americans on the Texas Frontier*, 51; Earl Burk Braly, "Fort Belknap of the Texas Frontier," *West Texas Historical Association Year Book* 30 (1954): 107–108.

64. Robert M. Utley, ed., *Life in Custer's Cavalry: Diaries and Letters of Albert and Jennie Barnitz, 1867–1868*, 102.

65. Kenneth J. Almy, ed., "Thof's Dragon and the Letters of Capt. Theophilus H. Turner, M.D., U.S. Army," *Kansas History* 10 (Fall 1987): 192.

66. William D. Thomson, "History of Fort Pembina: 1870–1895," *North Dakota History* 36 (Winter 1969): 30, 35.

67. Thomas R. Buecker, ed., "Letters of Caroline Frey Winne from Sidney Barracks and Fort McPherson, Nebraska, 1874–1878," *Nebraska History* 62 (Spring 1981): 3.

68. Lee, *Fort Meade and the Black Hills*, 28–35.

69. Lawrence H. Larsen and Barbara J. Cottrell, *The Gate City: A History of Omaha*, 15–31.

70. *Omaha Weekly Herald*, April 6, 1866, 1.

71. *Omaha Weekly Herald*, July 29, 1868, 2.

72. Guentzel, "The Department of the Platte," 412–13. Guentzel (p. 410) lists the specific occupations of the sixty-one civilians who were employed at the Omaha Military Depot in 1875.

73. Gerald M. Adams, *The Post near Cheyenne: A History of Fort D. A. Russell, 1867–1930*, 6–7, 81, 103–107.

74. Ibid., 10–11.

75. Ibid., 118–19.

76. Murray, "Fort Fred Steele," 175, 202.

77. Hedren, "On Duty at Fort Ridgely," 190.

78. Scobee, *Fort Davis*, 185.

79. Mary L. Williams, "Care of the Dead (and Lack of It) at 19th Century Posts," *Periodical: Journal of the Council on America's Military Past* 13, no. 1 (1984): 14–24.

80. Bierschwale, *Fort McKavett, Texas*, 85–86.

81. Ray H. Mattison, "Old Fort Stevenson, a Typical Missouri River Military Post," *North Dakota History* 18 (April–July 1951): 77.

82. Oliva, *Fort Larned on the Santa Fe Trail*, 77.

83. Bruce J. Dinges, "Colonel Grierson Invests on the West Texas Frontier," *Fort Concho Report* 16 (Fall 1984): 9–10.

84. James Holm Ware, "San Angelo and San Antonio: A Comparative Study of the Military City in Texas, 1865–1898," master's thesis, Southwest Texas State University, 1973, 59–60; JoAnne Caldwell, "Community at a Crossroads: San Angelo and the Closing of Fort Concho, 1889," *Fort Concho Report* 20 and 21 (Winter 1988–Spring 1989): 7–19.

85. Rupert N. Richardson, Ernest Wallace, and Adrian N. Anderson, *Texas: The Lone Star State*, 355–56.

86. Quoted in Mary Olivia Handy, *History of Fort Sam Houston*, 49.

87. Schubert, *Buffalo Soldiers, Braves, and the Brass*, vi. A helpful geographical study of three models of fort relationships with civilian populations is found in Gary S. Freedom, "The Role of the Military and the Spread of Settlement in the Northern Great Plains, 1866–1891," *Midwest Review* 9 (Spring 1987): 1–11.

CHAPTER 6. UNCLE SAM'S FARMERS

1. Frederick Jackson Turner, "The Significance of the Frontier in American History," *Annual Report of the American Historical Association for the Year 1893*, 211–12.

2. Richard C. Wade, *The Urban Frontier: The Rise of Western Cities, 1790–1830*, 1–26, 63.

3. *American State Papers: Military Affairs* 2:265.

4. Sally A. Johnson, "The Sixth's Elysian Fields: Fort Atkinson on the Council Bluffs," *Nebraska History* 40 (March 1959): 2–5; Roger L. Nichols, "Scurvy at Cantonment Missouri, 1819–1820," *Nebraska History* 49 (Winter 1968): 338–46.

5. Roger L. Nichols, "Soldiers as Farmers: Army Agriculture in the Missouri Valley, 1818–1827," *Nebraska History* 52 (Fall 1971): 242–43.

6. Ibid., 243; Edgar Bruce Wesley, "Life at Fort Atkinson," *Nebraska History* 30 (December 1949): 352.

7. Virgil Ney, *Fort on the Prairie: Fort Atkinson on the Council Bluff, 1819–1827*, 142; Edward M. Coffman, *The Old Army: A Portrait of the American Army in Peacetime, 1784–1898*, 169.

8. Miller J. Stewart, "To Plow, to Sow, to Reap, to Mow: The U.S. Army Agriculture Program," *Nebraska History* 63 (Summer 1982): 200.

9. Everett Dick, *Vanguards of the Frontier: A Social History of the Northern Plains and Rocky Mountains from the Earliest White Contacts to the Coming of the Homemaker*, 83.

10. Nichols, "Soldiers as Farmers," 249–50.

11. Ney, *Fort on the Prairie*, 146.

12. Francis Paul Prucha, ed., *Army Life on the Western Frontier: Selections from the Official Reports Made between 1826 and 1845 by Colonel George Croghan*, 7.

13. Ibid., 6–7; Stewart, "To Plow, to Sow," 200.

14. Prucha, *Army Life on the Western Frontier*, 7–8; Stewart, "To Plow, to Sow," 195.

15. Edwin C. Bearss and Arrell M. Gibson, *Fort Smith: Little Gibraltar on the Arkansas*, 58–59.

16. Stewart, "To Plow, to Sow," 202–203.

17. *Annual Report of the Secretary of War, 1851*, 164–165; Richard D. Gamble, "Garrison Life at Frontier Military Posts, 1820–1860," Ph.D. diss., University of Oklahoma, 1956, 127–28.

18. *Annual Report of the Secretary of War, 1851*, 164–65.

19. Robert W. Frazer, "Army Agriculture in New Mexico, 1852–1853," *New Mexico Historical Review* 50 (October 1975): 315.

20. Gamble, "Garrison Life," 126; Report of Colonel Ogden in *Annual Report of Secretary of War, 1851*, 292–93.

21. Merrill J. Mattes, *The Great Platte River Road: The Covered Wagon Mainline via Fort Kearny to Fort Laramie*, Publications of the Nebraska State Historical Society 25:184, 204, 512; Gamble, "Garrison Life," 125–26.

22. Dale F. Giese, "Soldiers at Play: A History of Social Life at Fort Union, New Mexico, 1851–1891," Ph.D. diss., University of New Mexico, 1969, 56–57.

23. Joseph K. F. Mansfield, *Mansfield on the Condition of the Western Forts*, ed. Robert W. Frazer, 34–35.

24. Ibid., 38–57.

25. Ibid., 34.

26. Martin L. Crimmins, ed., "W. G. Freeman's Report on the Eighth Military Department," *Southwestern Historical Quarterly* 51 (January, 1948): 252–53, 257–58; 52 (October 1948): 231–33; 53 (January 1950): 317–19; 53 (April 1950) 460–62.

27. Ibid., 54 (October 1950): 210.

28. Alex B. Hasson, "Report of the Post Surgeon at Fort Phantom Hill, for 1852," *West Texas Historical Association Year Book* 1 (June 1925): 74.

29. Gamble, "Garrison Life," 137.

30. Ibid., 128–29.

31. Quoted in Coffman, *The Old Army*, 170.

32. Augustus Meyers, *Ten Years in the Ranks, U.S. Army*, 128; Paul L. Hedren, "On Duty at Fort Ridgely, Minnesota: 1853–1867," *South Dakota History* 7 (Spring 1977): 178–79.

33. Gamble, "Garrison Life," 135–36.

34. Frazer, "Army Agriculture," 328; Prucha, *Broadax and Bayonet*, 127–28.

35. Gamble, "Garrison Life," 135.

36. Barry Scobee, *Fort Davis, Texas, 1583–1960*, 64.

37. Ray H. Mattison, "The Army Post on the Northern Plains, 1865–1885," *Nebraska History* 35 (March 1954): 27.

38. Philippe Régis de Trobriand, *Military Life in Dakota: The Journal of Philippe Régis de Trobriand*, ed. Lucile M. Kane, 314–16; Paul M. Edwards, "Fort Wadsworth and the Friendly Santee Sioux, 1864–1892," *South Dakota Department of History Report and Historical Collections* 31 (1962): 93; Mildred Wertenberger, comp., "Fort Totten, Dakota Territory, 1867," *North Dakota History* 34 (Spring 1967): 134; Gary S. Freedom, "Military Forts and Logistical Self-Sufficiency on the Northern Great Plains, 1866–1891," *North Dakota History* 50 (Spring 1983): 6.

39. Gerald M. Adams, *The Post Near Cheyenne: A History of Fort D. A. Russell, 1867–1930*, 42–43.

40. David P. Robrock, "A History of Fort Fetterman, Wyoming, 1867–1882," *Annals of Wyoming* 48 (Spring 1976): 36–37; William D. Thomson, "History of Fort Pembina, 1870–1895," *North Dakota History* 36 (Winter 1969): 33.

41. David K. Strate, *Sentinel to the Cimarron: The Frontier Experience of Fort Dodge, Kansas*, 52–53; George Ruhlen, "Quitman: The Worst Post at Which I Ever Served," *Password* 12 (Fall 1966): 119.

42. R. Eli Paul, ed., "Battle of Ash Hollow: The 1909–1910 Recollections of General N. A. M. Dudley," *Nebraska History* 62 (Fall 1981): 384.

43. A. Bower Sageser, "Windmill and Pump Irrigation on the Great Plains, 1890–1910," *Nebraska History* 48 (Summer 1967): 107; Robert C. Carriker, *Fort Supply, Indian Territory: Frontier Outpost on the Plains*, 140.

44. Thomas R. Buecker, "Fort Niobrara, 1880–1906: Guardian of the Rosebud Sioux," *Nebraska History* 65 (Fall 1984): 305.

45. Clayton Williams, *Texas' Last Frontier: Fort Stockton and the Trans-Pecos, 1861–1895*, ed. Ernest Wallace, 137.

46. Giese, "Soldiers at Play," 58–62; James M. Oswald, "History of Fort Elliott," *Panhandle-Plains Historical Review* 32 (1959): 20–21; Robert A. Murray, *Military Posts in the Powder River Country of Wyoming, 1865–1894*, 61–63.

47. Bill Green, *The Dancing Was Lively: Fort Concho, Texas, a Social History, 1867 to 1882*, 34–35.

48. Harry H. Anderson, "A History of the Cheyenne River Agency and Its Military Post, Fort Bennett, 1868–1891," *South Dakota Report and Historical Collections* 28 (1956): 420.

49. Philip A. Kalisch and Beatrice J. Kalisch, "Indian Territory Forts: Charnel Houses of the Frontier, 1839–1865," *Chronicles of Oklahoma* 50 (Spring 1972): 68; Gamble, "Garrison Life," 112.

50. *Regulations for the Army of the United States, 1857*, 206.

51. *Winners of the West*, March 30, 1931, 11.

52. Kenneth J. Almy, ed., "Thof's Dragon and the Letters of Capt. Theophilus H. Turner, M.D., U.S. Army," *Kansas History* 10 (Fall 1987): 183.

53. Alice Blackwood Baldwin, *Memoirs of the Late Frank D. Baldwin, Major General, U.S.A.*, 144.

54. Mattison, "Army Post on the Northern Plains," 29; De Trobriand, *Military Life in Dakota*, 175; Elizabeth Custer, *Tenting on the Plains, or General Custer in Kansas and Texas*, 121–24.

55. Rodney Glisan, *Journal of Army Life*, 54.

56. Giese, "Soldiers at Play," 57.

57. Louise Barry, ed., "With the First U.S. Cavalry in Indian Country, 1859–1861," *Kansas Historical Quarterly* 24 (Fall 1958): 269–70.

58. Giese, "Soldiers at Play," 59–61.

59. Julia Gilliss, *Far From Home: An Army Bride on the Western Frontier, 1865–1869*, ed. Priscilla Knuth, 100.

60. Thomas J. Caperton and LoRheda Fry, "U.S. Army Food and Its Preparation during the Indian Wars, 1865–1900, with Selected Recipes," *El Palacio* 80 (Winter 1974): 31; Douglas McChristian, "The Commissary Sergeant: His Life at Fort Davis," *Military History of Texas and the Southwest* 14, no. 1 (1978): 21–32.

61. William E. Annin, "Fort Robinson during the 1880s: An Omaha Newspaperman Visits the Post," ed. Vance E. Nelson, *Nebraska History* 55 (Summer 1974): 194.

62. H. H. McConnell, *Five Years a Cavalryman, or Sketches of Regular Army Life on the Texas Frontier, 1866–1871*, 206–208.

63. Caperton and Fry, "U.S. Army Food," 32–34; Morris C. Foote, "The Post Mess," *Journal of the Military Service Institution of the United States* 14 (1893): 519–21.

64. Foote, "The Post Mess," 521–24.

65. Kalisch and Kalisch, "Indian Territory Forts," 65; Donald R. Whitnah, *A History of the United States Weather Bureau*, 10–11; Charles C. Bates and John F. Fuller, *America's Weather Warriors, 1814–1985*, 4–5.

66. Edgar Erskine Hume, "The Foundation of American Meteorology by the United States Army Medical Department," *Bulletin of the History of Medicine* 8 (January–May 1940): 208–14.

67. Ibid., 214–19.

68. Rebecca Robbins Raines, *Getting the Message Through: A Branch History of the U.S. Army Signal Corps*, 5–31.

69. Paul J. Scheips, "'Old Probabilities': A. J. Myer and the Signal Corps Weather Service," *Arlington Historical Magazine* 5 (October 1974): 36–38; Raines, *Getting the Message Through*, 49.

70. Scheips, "'Old Probabilities,'" 37–38; Frederick J. Hughes, Jr., "Albert James Myer: Army Physician and Climatologist," *Transactions of the American Clinical and Climatological Association* 81 (1969): 126; Phyllis Smith, *Weather Pioneers: The Signal Corps Station at Pikes Peak*, 1–6; Michael J. Brodhead, "The United States Army Signal Service and Natural History in Alaska, 1874–1883," *Pacific Northwest Quarterly* 86 (Spring 1995): 72–81.

71. Scheips, "'Old Probabilities,'" 38–39.

72. Hughes, "Albert James Myer," 124–26.

73. Raines, *Getting the Message Through*, 54–61.

74. Scheips, "'Old Probabilities,'" 39; Bates and Fuller, *America's Weather Warriors*, 13–14; Joseph M. Hawes, "The Signal Corps and Its Weather Service, 1870–1890," *Military Affairs* 30 (Summer 1966): 74–76.

75. John D. Unruh, Jr., *The Plains Across: The Overland Emigrants and the Trans-Mississippi West, 1840–60*, 229; Oswald, "History of Fort Elliott," 22; Jerome A. Greene, "Army Bread and Army Mission on the Frontier, with Special Reference to Fort Laramie, Wyoming, 1865–1890," *Annals of Wyoming* 47 (Fall 1975): 214.

76. Freedom, "Military Forts and Logistical Self-Sufficiency," 7.

77. Ibid.

78. Bates and Fuller, *America's Weather Warriors*, 11–13; Whitnah, *History of United States Weather Bureau*, 25–36.

79. Quoted in Bates and Fuller, *America's Weather Warriors*, 3.

CHAPTER 7. HIPPOCRATES IN BLUE

1. Mari Sandoz, *Old Jules*, 41–46, 237–38.

2. Merrill J. Mattes, *The Great Platte River Road: The Covered Wagon Mainline via Fort Kearny to Fort Laramie*, 172; Raymond W. Settle, ed., *The March of the Mounted Riflemen: First United States Military Expedition to Travel the Full Length of the Oregon Trail from Fort Leavenworth to Fort Vancouver, May to October 1849, as Recorded in the Journals of Major Osborne Cross and George Gibbs and the Official Report of Colonel Loring*, 44–47, 74–75.

3. Marie H. Erwin, comp., "Statistical Reports on the Sickness and Mortality of the Army of the United States, 1819–1860," *Annals of Wyoming* 15 (1943): 317.

4. Russell E. Bidlack, *Letters Home: The Story of Ann Arbor's Forty-Niners*, intro. F. Clever Bald, 22–23.

5. Shirley Ewart, Jane Anderson, and John Anderson, eds., *A Long and Wearisome Journey: The Eakin Family Diaries 1866*, 92–95.

6. Report of Secretary of War Charles Conrad, in *Annual Report of the Secretary of War, 1853*, 116–23.

7. Mary C. Gillett, *The Army Medical Department, 1818–1865*, 124–25.

8. Ibid., 127–28.

9. Richard H. Coolidge, *Statistical Report on the Sickness and Mortality in the Army of the United States, Compiled from the Records of the Surgeon General's Office, Embracing a Period of Sixteen Years, from January, 1839, to January, 1855*, 625–26.

10. Surgeon General Thomas Lawson, *Report on Sickness and Mortality among the Troops in Texas*, 34th Cong., 1st sess., 1855–56, S. Exec. Doc. 96, 373–96.

11. Charles Caldwell, *Analysis of Fever*, 15; Lawson, *Report on Sickness and Mortality*, 399–410.

12. Lawson, *Report on Sickness and Mortality*, 395–96.

13. Erwin, "Statistical Reports," 322–31.

14. Edward W. Johns, "Sanitary Report from Fort Laramie," in *Statistical Report on the Sickness and Mortality in the Army of the United States, from January, 1855, to January, 1860*, 47; Peter D. Olch, "Medicine in the Indian-Fighting Army, 1866–1890," *Journal of the West* 21 (July 1982): 37.

15. Lawrence R. Murphy, "'The Enemy Among Us': Venereal Disease among Union Soldiers in the Far West, 1861–1865," *Civil War History* 31 (September 1985): 259–65.

16. James A. Wier, "19th Century Army Doctors on the Frontier and in Nebraska," *Nebraska History* 61 (Summer, 1980): 203–204.

17. Ibid., 204; H. H. McConnell, *Five Years a Cavalryman, or Sketches of Regular Army Life on the Texas Frontier, 1866–1871*, 165–66.

18. John Neilson, "'I Long to Return to Fort Concho': Acting Assistant Surgeon Samuel Smith's Letters from the Texas Military Frontier, 1878–1879," *Military History of the West* 24 (Fall 1994): 124–30, 186.

19. Olch, "Medicine in the Indian-Fighting Army," 32.

20. Percy M. Ashburn, *A History of the Medical Department of the United States Army*, 150–51.

21. William M. Notson, "Fort Concho, 1868–1872: The Medical Officer's Observations," ed. Stephen Schmidt, *Military History of Texas and the Southwest* 12 (Fall 1975): 128–33.

22. Leo E. Oliva, *Fort Hays, Frontier Army Post, 1865–1889*, 25, 49.

23. Allen Lee Hamilton, *Sentinel of the Southern Plains: Fort Richardson and the Northwest Texas Frontier, 1866–1878*, 33–36.

24. McConnell, *Five Years a Cavalryman*, 164–65.

25. William E. Annin, "Fort Robinson during the 1880's: An Omaha Newspaperman Visits the Post," ed. Vance E. Nelson, *Nebraska History* 55 (Summer 1974): 195.

26. Barry Scobee, *Fort Davis, Texas, 1583–1960*, 64–66; David A. Clary, "The Role of the Army Surgeon in the West: Daniel Weisel at Fort Davis, Texas, 1868–1872," *Western Historical Quarterly* 3 (January 1972): 57–59.

27. David K. Strate, *Sentinel to the Cimarron: The Frontier Experience of Fort Dodge, Kansas*, 51–53; Clayton Williams, *Texas' Last Frontier: Fort Stockton and the Trans-Pecos, 1861–1895*, ed. Ernest Wallace, 191; James M. Oswald, "History of Fort Elliott," *Panhandle-Plains Historical Review* 32 (1959): 14.

28. Strate, *Sentinel to the Cimarron*, 69; Leo E. Oliva, *Fort Larned on the Santa Fe Trail*, 70–71.

29. Neilson, "'I Long to Return to Fort Concho,'" 142; B. J. Fisher, "Medical Conditions at West Texas Military Posts in the 1850s," *West Texas Historical Association Year Book* 62 (1986): 113–14.

30. Strate, *Sentinel to the Cimarron*, 69; Ray H. Mattison, ed., "The Diary of Surgeon Washington Matthews, Fort Rice, D.T.," *North Dakota History* 21 (January 1954): 65.

31. Scobee, *Fort Davis*, 67–68; *Winners of the West*, March 30, 1926, 7; Olch, "Medicine in the Indian-Fighting Army," 39.

32. Olch, "Medicine in the Indian-Fighting Army," 36; Clary, "The Role of the Army Surgeon," 54–57; Erwin, "Statistical Reports," 315.

33. H. Craig Miner, *Wichita: The Early Years, 1865–1880*, 42.

34. Forrest R. Blackburn, "Army Families in Frontier Forts," *Military Review* 49 (October, 1969): 23.

35. Olch, "Medicine in the Indian-Fighting Army," 34; Samuel Brown McPheeters, "A Young Medical Officer's Letters from Fort Robinson and Fort Leavenworth, 1906–1907," ed. Willard E. Wight, *Nebraska History* 37 (June 1956): 137, 143.

36. Wier, "19th Century Army Doctors," 196; Alice Blackwood Baldwin, *Memoirs of the Late Frank D. Baldwin, Major General, U.S.A.*, 133–34.

37. Robert M. Utley, ed., *Life in Custer's Cavalry: Diaries and Letters of Albert and Jennie Barnitz, 1867–1868*, 85.

38. Eldon Cagle, Jr., *Quadrangle: The History of Fort Sam Houston*, 21.

39. *Winners of the West*, September 1924, 7.

40. Mary C. Gillett, "United States Army Surgeons and the Big Horn–Yellowstone Expedition of 1876," *Montana, Magazine of Western History* 39 (Winter 1989): 20–23; Thomas R. Buecker, ed., "A Surgeon at the Little Big Horn: The Letters of Dr. Holmes O. Paulding," *Montana, Magazine of Western History* 32 (Fall 1982): 34–49.

41. David P. Robrock, "A History of Fort Fetterman, Wyoming, 1867–1882," *Annals of Wyoming* 48 (Spring 1976): 58.

42. Wier, "19th Century Army Doctors," 193.

43. Paul L. Hedren, "On Duty at Fort Ridgely, Minnesota: 1853–1867," *South Dakota History* 7 (Spring 1977): 188; Philippe Régis de Trobriand, *Military Life in Dakota: The Journal of Philippe Régis de Trobriand*, ed. Lucile M. Kane, 337.

44. Maurice Frink and Casey E. Barthelmess, *Photographer on an Army Mule*, 96; Thomas R. Buecker, ed., "Letters of Caroline Frey Winne from Sidney Barracks and Fort McPherson, Nebraska, 1874–1878," *Nebraska History* 62 (Spring 1981): 28.

45. George E. Omer, Jr., "An Army Hospital: From Dragoons to Rough Riders—Fort Riley, 1853–1903," *Kansas Historical Quarterly* 23 (Winter 1957): 347; Dale F. Giese, "Soldiers at Play: A History of Social Life at Fort Union, New Mexico, 1851–1891," Ph.D. diss., University of New Mexico, 1969, 189.

46. Mattison, "Diary of Surgeon Washington Matthews," 57.

47. Donald W. Whisenhunt, *Fort Richardson: Outpost on the Texas Frontier*, 21; Buecker, "Letters of Caroline Frey Winne," 29–30.

48. Giese, "Soldiers at Play," 189.

49. Robrock, "History of Fort Fetterman," 67; Neilson, "'I Long to Return to Fort Concho,'" 154–55.

50. Giese, "Soldiers at Play," 188; Oswald, "History of Fort Elliott," 23–24.

51. Buecker, "Letters of Caroline Frey Winne," 8.

52. Frederic J. Hughes, Jr., "Albert James Myer: Army Physician and Climatologist," *Transactions of the American Clinical and Climatological Association* 81 (1969): 123; Robrock, "History of Fort Fetterman," 33.

53. Carl Coke Rister, *Fort Griffin on the Texas Frontier*, 126–32.

54. Olch, "Medicine in the Indian-Fighting Army," 40; Mary C. Gillett, *The Army Medical Department*, 1865–1917, 93–109.

55. Strate, *Sentinel to the Cimarron*, 71.

56. Gillett, *Army Medical Department, 1865–1917*, 96–97.

CHAPTER 8. REFORM THE MAN

1. Richard D. Gamble, "Army Chaplains at Frontier Posts, 1830–1860," *Historical Magazine of the Protestant Episcopal Church* 27, no. 4 (1958): 287.

2. *American State Papers: Military Affairs* 4:209.

3. Ibid., 6:119–30.

4. Ibid., 6:148.

5. *U.S. Statutes at Large* 5 (1838): 259.

6. Office of the Chief of Chaplains, *American Army Chaplaincy: A Brief History*, 17–21.

7. Richard K. Smith, "For God . . . for Country . . . for the Territory," *Arizona Highways* 49 (April 1973): 8.

8. Richard D. Gamble, "Garrison Life at Frontier Military Posts, 1820–1860," Ph.D. diss., University of Oklahoma, 1956, 267.

9. Orville J. Nave, "The Status of Army Chaplains," in Theophilus G. Steward, ed., *Active Service, or Religious Work among United States Soldiers*, 43.

10. Gamble, "Garrison Life," 264; Smith, "For God," 8.

11. John H. Macomber, "The Army Chaplaincy," in Theophilus G. Steward, ed., *Active Service, or Religious Work among United States Soldiers*, 22.

12. David H. Stratton, "The Army and the Gospel in the West," *Western Humanities Review* 8 (Spring 1954): 248–51.

13. Carol Schmidt, "The Chaplains of Fort Concho," *Fort Concho Report* 16 (Summer 1984): 33.

14. Stratton, "Army and the Gospel," 249; Schmidt, "Chaplains of Fort Concho," 31, 36.

15. Stratton, "Army and the Gospel," 250; Gamble, "Garrison Life," 262.

16. Cornelia Crook and Garland Crook, "Fort Lincoln, Texas," *Texas Military History* 4 (Fall 1964): 154.

17. Dale F. Giese, "Soldiers at Play: A History of Social Life at Fort Union, New Mexico, 1851–1891," Ph.D. diss., University of New Mexico, 1969, 10–11.

18. Henry Shindler, *Fort Leavenworth: Its Churches and Schools*, 92–94, 101–103.

19. Schmidt, "Chaplains of Fort Concho" *Fort Concho Report* 16 (Summer 1984): 30–37.

20. David K. Strate, *Sentinel to the Cimarron: The Frontier Experience of Fort Dodge, Kansas*, 53–54.

21. Shindler, *Fort Leavenworth*, 77–80.

22. Stratton, "Army and the Gospel," 261; Merrill J. Mattes, *Indians, Infants, and Infantry: Andrew and Elizabeth Burt on the Frontier*, 82.

23. Margaret Irvin Carrington, *Absaraka, Home of the Crows: Being the Experiences of an Officer's Wife on the Plains*, 178–79.

24. Frances M. A. Roe, *Army Letters from an Officer's Wife, 1871–1888*, 338–40.

25. Julia Gilliss, *So Far from Home: An Army Bride on the Western Frontier, 1865–1869*, ed. Priscilla Knuth, 134; Mattes, *Indians, Infants, and Infantry*, 248.

26. Harry H. Anderson, "A History of the Cheyenne River Agency and Its Military Post, Fort Bennett, 1868–1891," *South Dakota Report and Historical Collections* 68 (1956): 527–28.

27. Smith, "For God," 11.

28. Gerald M. Adams, *The Post Near Cheyenne: A History of Fort D. A. Russell, 1867–1930*, 16–17.

29. James M. Oswald, "History of Fort Elliott," *Panhandle-Plains Historical Review* 32 (1959): 35.

30. Louis L. Pfaller, "Eli Washington John Lindesmith: Fort Keogh's Chaplain in Buckskin," *Montana, Magazine of Western History* 27 (January 1977): 15–18.

31. Stratton, "Army and Gospel," 249; William Bruce White, "ABCs for the American Enlisted Man: The Army Post School System, 1866–1898," *History of Education Quarterly* 8 (Winter 1968): 479.

32. Miller J. Stewart, "A Touch of Civilization: Culture and Education in the Frontier Army," *Nebraska History* 65 (Summer 1984): 268; Edgar B. Wesley, "Life at Fort Atkinson," *Nebraska History* 30 (December 1949): 357.

33. *U.S. Statutes at Large* 2 (1838): 259.

34. White, "ABCs," 479–482; George G. Mullins, "Education in the Army," *United Service* 2 (April 1880): 478–85.

35. Forrest R. Blackburn, "Army Families in Frontier Forts," *Military Review* 49 (October 1969): 24; Rodney Glisan, *Journal of Army Life*, 462.

36. Martha Gray Wales, "'When I Was a Little Girl: Things I Remember from Living at Frontier Military Posts," ed. Willard B. Pope, *North Dakota History* 50 (Spring 1983): 12–22.

37. David P. Robrock, "A History of Fort Fetterman, Wyoming, 1867–1882," *Annals of Wyoming* 48 (Spring 1976): 34.

38. Maria Inez Corlett Riter, "Teaching School at Old Fort Laramie," *Annals of Wyoming* 51 (Fall 1979): 24–25.

39. Giese, *Soldiers at Play*, 17–18.

40. Stewart, "Touch of Civilization," 271; Anderson, "History of Cheyenne River Agency," 528.

41. Leo E. Oliva, *Fort Hays, Frontier Army Post, 1865–1889*, 58.

42. William Seraile, "Theophilus G. Steward, Intellectual Chaplain, 25th U.S. Colored Infantry," *Nebraska History* 66 (Fall 1985): 284–85; Bill Green, *The Dancing Was Lively: Fort Concho, Texas: A Social History, 1867 to 1882*, 80–84.

43. Allen Allensworth, "Military Education in the United States," *National Education Association Journal of Proceedings and Addresses*, 224; Robert Lee, *Fort Meade and the Black Hills*, 99.

44. Leo E. Oliva, "Frontier Forts and the Settlement of Western Kansas," *Kansas and the West: Bicentennial Essays in Honor of Nyle H. Miller*, ed. Forrest R. Blackburn et al., 70.

45. Betty Loudon, ed., "Pioneer Pharmacist J. Walter Moyer's Notes on Crawford and Fort Robinson in the 1890s," *Nebraska History* 58 (Spring 1977): 91; Shindler, *Fort Leavenworth*, 155–58.

46. Robert D. Miewald, "The Army Post Schools: A Report from the Bureaucratic Wars," *Military Affairs* 39 (February 1975): 9–10.

47. U.S. War Department, *Regulations of the Army of the United States and the General Orders in Force on the 17th of February 1881*, 57; Stanley S. Graham, "Duty, Life, and Law in the Old Army, 1865–1890," *Military History of Texas and the Southwest* 12, no. 4 (1970): 280; Miewald, "Army Post Schools," 10.

48. Allensworth, "Military Education," 221–22.

49. Miewald, "Army Post Schools," 10–11; Stewart, "Touch of Civilization," 274; Allensworth, "Military Education," 223.

50. Mullins, "Education in the Army," 483; White, "ABCs," 488–89.

51. Stewart, "Touch of Civilization," 258–59.

52. Ibid., 265.

53. Allen Lee Hamilton, *Sentinel of the Southern Plains: Fort Richardson and the Northwest Texas Frontier, 1866–1878*, 32; Green, *Dancing Was Lively*, 85.

54. William E. Annin, "Fort Robinson during the 1880s: An Omaha News-paperman Visits the Post," ed. Vance E. Nelson, *Nebraska History* 55 (Summer 1974): 185–86; Paul M. Edwards, "Fort Wadsworth and the Friendly Santee Sioux, 1864–1892," *South Dakota Department of History Report and Historical Collections* 31 (1962): 137–38.

55. Walter Edens, "Wyoming's Fort Libraries: The March of Intellect," *Annals of Wyoming* 51 (Fall 1979): 58.

56. Gamble, "Garrison Life," 201–202; Edens, "Wyoming's Fort Libraries," 58.

57. Elvis Joe Ballew, "Supply Problems of Fort Davis, Texas, 1867–1880," master's thesis, Sul Ross State University, 1971, 71; Mary Sutton, "Glimpses of Fort Concho through the Military Telegraph," *West Texas Historical Association Year Book* 32 (1956): 132.

58. Sutton, "Glimpses of Fort Concho," 132; Stewart, "Touch of Civilization," 260; Jack D. Foner, "The Socializing Role of the Military," in *The American Military on the Frontier: Proceedings of the Seventh Military History Symposium*, ed. James P. Tate, 98.

59. Ballew, "Supply Problems," 71–72; Hamilton, *Sentinel of the Southern Plains*, 32; Sutton, "Glimpses of Fort Concho," 132; Giese, "Soldiers at Play," 24.

60. Frank N. Schubert, "The Fort Robinson Y.M.C.A., 1902–1907: A Social Organization in a Black Regiment," *Nebraska History* 55 (Summer 1974): 177–79.

61. Earl F. Stover, *Up From Handymen: The United States Army Chaplains, 1865–1920*, 89–90.

62. Schmidt, "Chaplains at Fort Concho" *Fort Concho Report* 16 (Summer 1984): 39; Philippe Régis de Trobriand, *Military Life in Dakota: The Journal of Philippe Régis de Trobriand*, ed. Lucile M. Kane, 232–33.

63. *Winners of the West* (November 1925): 3.

64. H. H. McConnell, *Five Years a Cavalryman, or Sketches of Regular Army Life on the Texas Frontier, 1866–1871*, 119; Carl Coke Rister, *Fort Griffin on the Texas Frontier*, 126.

65. Hervey Johnson, *Tending the Talking Wire: A Buck Soldier's View of Indian Country, 1863–1866*, ed. William E. Unruh, 70; Barry Scobee, *Fort Davis, Texas, 1583–1960*, 68.

66. Giese, "Soldiers at Play," 23; Edens, "Wyoming's Fort Libraries," 57.

67. Elizabeth B. Custer, *Tenting on the Plains, or General Custer in Kansas and Texas*, 260.

68. Ray H. Mattison, "The Army Post on the Northern Plains, 1865–1885," *Nebraska History* 35 (March 1954): 36–37; James M. Oswald, "History of Fort Elliott," *Panhandle-Plains Historical Review* 32 (1959): 16.

69. Adams, *Post Near Cheyenne*, 49–50; Ballew, "Supply Problems," 72.

70. Mullins, "Education in the Army," 484.

CHAPTER 9. SHARPENING THE EAGLE'S TALONS FOR DOMESTIC DUTIES

1. Gaines M. Foster, *The Demands of Humanity: Army Medical Disaster Relief,* 12.

2. *U.S. Statutes at Large* 3 (1815): 211–12. Malcolm J. Rohrbough, *The Land Office Business: The Settlement and Administration of American Public Lands, 1789–1837,* 106–107, explores the "New Madrid land claims" and the widespread speculative mania created by them.

3. *U.S. Statutes at Large* 6 (1848): 356–57; Foster, *Demands of Humanity,* 12–13.

4. *U.S. Statutes at Large* 17 (1873): 566–77; Charles Barron McIntosh, *The Nebraska Sand Hills: The Human Landscape,* 202–205.

5. David H. Donald, *Liberty and Union,* 178–82.

6. Foster, *Demands of Humanity,* 16. For more details about army relief work amid these mostly "Eastern disasters," see B. Franklin Cooling, "The Army and Flood and Disaster Relief," in *The United States Army in Peacetime,* ed. Robin Higham and Carol Brandt, 62–67.

7. Foster, *Demands of Humanity,* 16–17; Cooling, "Army and Flood and Disaster Relief," 62.

8. James B. Rhoads, "The Taming of the West: Military Archives as a Source for the Social History of the Trans-Mississippi Region to 1900," in *People of the Plains and Mountains: Essays in the History of the West Dedicated to Everett Dick,* ed. Ray Allen Billington, 194.

9. Larry C. Skogen, *Indian Depredation Claims, 1796–1920,* 207–12.

10. Richard Guentzel, "The Department of the Platte and Western Settlement, 1866–1877," *Nebraska History* 56 (Fall 1975): 406.

11. Sam S. Kepfield, "Grasshoppers, Destitution, and Public Relief in Western Nebraska, 1874–1875," *Journal of the West* 34 (July 1995): 94–95; Everett Dick, *Conquering the Great American Desert,* 191–92.

12. Gary D. Olson, ed., "Relief for Nebraska Grasshopper Victims: The Official Journal of Lieutenant Theodore E. True," *Nebraska History* 48 (Summer 1967): 119–20.

13. Dick, *Conquering the Great American Desert,* 199–201.

14. Gilbert C. Fite, "The United States Army and Relief to Pioneer Settlers, 1874–1875," *Journal of the West* 6 (January 1967): 99; Olson, "Relief for Nebraska," 120.

15. Kepfield, "Grasshoppers, Destitution, and Public Relief," 96.

16. Ibid.

17. Fite, "United States Army and Relief," 99–100.

18. Everett Dick, *The Sod-House Frontier, 1854–1890: A Social History of the Northern Plains from the Creation of Kansas and Nebraska to the Admission of the Dakotas*, 207–208.

19. Fite, "United States Army and Relief," 100.

20. U.S. Congress, Senate, 43rd Cong., 2d sess., 1874, S. Exec. Doc. 5, 4.

21. Fite, "United States Army and Relief," 102.

22. U.S. Congress, House. "Relief of Grasshopper Sufferers," 44th Cong., 1st sess., 1875, H. Exec. Doc. 28, 2.

23. "Report of Maj. N. A. M. Dudley," November 6, 1874, in 43rd Cong., 2d sess., 1874, S. Exec. Doc. 5, 5–8.

24. *U.S. Statutes at Large* 18 (1875): 314.

25. Lt. Theodore E. True's Journal in Olson, "Relief for Nebraska," 124–39.

26. Annette Atkins, *Harvest of Grief: Grasshopper Plagues and Public Assistance in Minnesota, 1873–78*, 115. For General Sheridan's activist role in providing protection and relief supplies during the 1871 Chicago fire, see Paul A. Hutton, *Phil Sheridan and His Army*, 209–12.

27. Atkins, *Harvest of Grief*, 120.

28. Olson, "Relief for Nebraska," 140.

29. Fite, "United States Army and Relief," 106.

30. Robert N. Manley, "In the Wake of the Grasshoppers: Public Relief in Nebraska, 1874–1875," *Nebraska History* 44 (December 1963): 274–75; Atkins, *Harvest of Grief*, 121.

31. Sam S. Kepfield, "'A Great Deal Like Smallpox': 'Destitution Business' and State Drought Relief in Nebraska, 1890–1895," *Heritage of the Great Plains* 26 (Summer 1993): 39–44.

32. Charles E. Whilden, "Letters from a Santa Fe Army Clerk, 1855–1856," ed. John Hammond Moore, *New Mexico Historical Review* 40 (April 1965): 142–43.

33. Donald W. Whisenhunt, *Fort Richardson: Outpost on the Texas Frontier*, 16.

34. David K. Strate, *Sentinel to the Cimarron: The Frontier Experience of Fort Dodge, Kansas*, 62.

35. Eyewitness descriptions of army efforts to fight large fires appear in John Neilson, ed., "'I Long to Return to Fort Concho': Acting Assistant Surgeon Samuel Smith's Letters from the Texas Military Frontier, 1878–1869," *Military History of the West* 24 (Fall 1994): 151–52, and Philippe Régis de Trobriand, *Military Life in Dakota: The Journal of Philippe Régis de Trobriand*, ed. Lucile M. Kane, 343–47.

36. Marvin Fletcher, "Army Fire Fighters," *Idaho Yesterdays* 16 (Summer 1972): 12.

37. Ibid., 13–15.

38. Report of Gen. Adolphus Greely in *Annual Report of the Secretary of War, 1906*, 99–103; Gordon Thomas and Max Morgan Witts, *The San Francisco Earthquake*, 138.

39. Richard Patterson, "Funston and the Fire," *American History Illustrated* 10 (December 1975): 35–37.

40. Thomas and Witts, *San Francisco Earthquake*, 85.

41. Patterson, "Funston and the Fire," 36.

42. Thomas and Witts, *San Francisco Earthquake*, 95–96.

43. Ibid., 173–74.

44. William Strobridge, "Soldiers in the Streets, 1906," *Pacific Historian* 22 (Spring 1978): 6.

45. Carroll A. Devol, "The Army in the San Francisco Disaster," *Journal of the United States Infantry Association* 4 (July 1907): 70.

46. Wilson T. Davidson, *Years of an Army Doctor: An Autobiography*, 82; Devol, "Army in the San Francisco Disaster," 71–72.

47. Thomas and Witts, *San Francisco Earthquake*, 118–20, 138.

48. James J. Hudson, "The California National Guard in the San Francisco Earthquake and Fire of 1906," *California Historical Quarterly* 55 (Summer 1976): 142.

49. Ibid., 138–43.

50. Thomas and Witts, *San Francisco Earthquake*, 95.

51. Ibid., 192, 228–29. Allegations of widespread army impropriety appear in Henry A. Lafler, *How the Army Worked to Save San Francisco*, but many of the book's descriptions cannot be authenticated by other sources.

52. Thomas and Witts, *San Francisco Earthquake*, 172–73, 197–98.

53. Patterson, "Funston and the Fire," 38–40.

54. Strobridge, "Soldiers in the Streets," 3–5; Thomas and Witts, *San Francisco Earthquake*, 249.

55. Strobridge, "Soldiers in the Streets," 5.

56. Cooling, "Army and Flood and Disaster Relief," 65.

57. Strobridge, "Soldiers in the Streets," 6–7; Thomas and Witts, *San Francisco Earthquake*, 249; Patterson, "Funston and the Fire," 45. A more sympathetic view of the overall role of the National Guard is found in Hudson, "California National Guard," 145–47.

58. Hudson, "California National Guard," 147.

59. Strobridge, "Soldiers in the Streets," 7.

60. Richard A. Bartlett, *Yellowstone: A Wilderness Besieged*, 257.

61. For details of the army and civilian explorations, see Aubrey L. Haines, *Yellowstone National Park: Its Exploration and Establishment*, 56–106; Orrin H. and Lorraine Bonney, *Battle Drums and Geysers: The Life and Journals of Lt. Gustavus Cheyney Doane, Soldier and Explorer of the Yellowstone and Snake River Regions*; and William Ludlow, *Exploring Nature's Sanctuary: Captain William Ludlow's Report of a*

Reconnaissance from Carroll, Montana Territory, on the Upper Missouri to the Yellowstone National Park, and Return Made in the Summer of 1875, intro. Paul K. Walker, Engineer Historical Studies No. 3.

62. Paul A. Hutton, "Phil Sheridan's Crusade for Yellowstone," *American History Illustrated* 19 (February 1985): 7, 10–15.

63. H. Duane Hampton, "The Army and the National Parks," *Montana, Magazine of Western History* 22 (July 1972): 67–72. Army efforts to safeguard the park's declining buffalo herd are examined in Paul Schullery, "'Buffalo' Jones and the Bison Herd in Yellowstone: Another Look," *Montana, Magazine of Western History* 26 (July 1976): 40–51.

64. Hampton, "Army and the National Parks," 71–72; George S. Anderson, "Work of the Cavalry in Protecting the Yellowstone National Park," *Journal of the United States Cavalry Association* 10 (March 1897): 5–10. Two revealing essays written by Frederic Remington and Emerson Hough describe their adventures with Capt. George S. Anderson in pursuing notorious poachers and enforcing other park rules and are reprinted in Paul Schullery, ed., *Old Yellowstone Days,* 117–57.

65. *U.S. Statutes at Large* 28 (1895): 73.

66. H. Duane Hampton, *How the U.S. Cavalry Saved Our National Parks,* 128–29.

67. Ibid., 130–45, 156–57.

68. Ibid., 146–51; N. F. McClure, "The Fourth Cavalry in the Yosemite National Park," *Journal of the United States Cavalry Association* 10 (June 1897): 113.

69. Quoted in McClure, "Fourth Cavalry in Yosemite," 118.

70. Ibid., 118–19.

71. Ibid., 118.

72. Ibid., 117, 120; Hampton, "Army and the National Parks," 76–79; Richard A. Bartlett, "The Army, Conservation, and Ecology: The National Park Assignment," in *The United States Army in Peacetime,* ed. by Robin Higham and Carol Brandt, 56.

73. Samuel P. Hayes, *Conservation and the Gospel of Efficiency: The Progressive Conservation Movement, 1890–1920,* 271. The distinction between "preservationist" and "conservationist" is dramatized in the struggle over Yosemite's Hetch Hetchy Valley in Roderick Nash, *Wilderness and the American Mind,* 161–81.

CHAPTER 10. IN DEFENSE OF "POOR LO"

1. Donald J. D'Elia, "The Argument over Civilian or Military Indian Control, 1865–1880," *Historian* 24 (February 1962): 207–25.

2. *U.S. Statutes at Large* 1 (1790): 137–38.

3. Francis Paul Prucha, *American Indian Policy in the Formative Years: The Indian Trade and Intercourse Acts, 1790–1834,* 44–45.

4. *U.S. Statutes at Large* 1 (1796): 470–73; 1 (1799): 748.

5. Ibid., 2 (1802): 139–46; 4 (1832): 729–35.

6. Robert W. Frazer, *Forts of the West*, xviii; Prucha, *American Indian Policy*, 62–63, 73–75, 125–26.

7. Francis Paul Prucha, *Broadax and Bayonet: The Role of the United States Army in the Development of the Northwest, 1815–1860*, 62–63.

8. Francis Paul Prucha, *The Sword of the Republic: The United States Army on the Frontier, 1783–1846*, 202–203.

9. Ibid., 203; Prucha, *Broadax and Bayonet*, 65–66.

10. Edward M. Coffman, *The Old Army: A Portrait of the American Army in Peacetime, 1784–1898*, 74; Grant Foreman, *Indian Removal: The Emigration of the Five Civilized Tribes of Indians*, 8–9.

11. Vinson Lackey, *The Forts of Oklahoma*, 1–25; Frazer, *Forts of the West*, 116–26; William B. Morrison, "Fort Washita," *Chronicles of Oklahoma* 5 (June 1927): 251–56.

12. Brad Agnew, *Fort Gibson: Terminal on the Trail of Tears*, 208–11.

13. Ibid., 207–10 (quote is on 207).

14. Philippe Régis de Trobriand, *Military Life in Dakota: The Life of Philippe Régis de Trobriand*, ed. Lucile M. Kane, 235; Robert H. Steinbach, *A Long March: The Lives of Frank and Alice Baldwin*, 38.

15. David P. Robrock, "A History of Fort Fetterman, Wyoming, 1867–1882," *Annals of Wyoming* 48 (Spring 1976): 74.

16. Richard Guentzel, "The Department of the Platte and Western Settlement, 1866–1877," *Nebraska History* 56 (Fall 1975): 409.

17. Raymond L. Welty, "The Policing of the Frontier by the Army, 1860–1870," *Kansas Historical Quarterly* 7 (August 1938): 251–52.

18. Ibid., 252–53.

19. Richard N. Ellis, "General John Pope and the Southern Plains Indians, 1875–1883," *Southwestern Historical Quarterly* 72 (October 1968): 154–69.

20. Rodney Glisan, *Journal of Army Life*, 448–50.

21. Leo E. Oliva, *Fort Larned on the Santa Fe Trail*, 71.

22. De Trobriand, *Military Life in Dakota*, 360–61.

23. Mildred Wertenberger, comp., "Fort Totten, Dakota Territory, 1867," *North Dakota History* 34 (Spring 1967): 142.

24. James A. Wier, "19th Century Army Doctors on the Frontier and in Nebraska," *Nebraska History* 61 (Summer 1980): 207; Julia B. McGillycuddy, *McGillycuddy, Agent*, 75–76.

25. Roger T. Grange, Jr., "Treating the Wounded at Fort Robinson," *Nebraska History* 45 (September 1964): 274–94.

26. Robert M. Utley, *The Last Days of the Sioux Nation*, 227–28; Charles A. Eastman, *From the Deep Woods to Civilization: Chapters in the Autobiography of an Indian*, 107–14; Mary C. Gillett, *The Army Medical Department, 1865–1917*, 86–87.

27. Woodward B. Skinner, *The Apache Rock Crumbles: The Captivity of Geronimo's People*, 119–305.

28. Robert C. Carriker, *Fort Supply, Indian Territory: Frontier Outpost on the Plains,* 60–65.

29. Ibid., 73–82; William E. Unrau, *White Man's Wicked Water: The Alcohol Trade and Prohibition in Indian Country, 1802–1892,* 103–16.

30. David H. Stratton, "The Army and the Gospel in the West," *Western Humanities Review* 8 (April 1954): 252–53; Richard D. Gamble, "Garrison Life at Frontier Military Posts, 1820–1860," Ph.D. diss., University of Oklahoma, 1956, 258; Martha Gray Wales, "When I Was a Little Girl: Things I Remember from Living at Frontier Military Posts," ed. Willard B. Pope, *North Dakota History* 50 (Spring 1983): 14.

31. Jere W. Roberson, ed., "A View from Oklahoma, 1866–1868: The Diary and Letters of Dr. James Reagles, Jr., Assistant Surgeon, U.S. Army," *Red River Valley Historical Review* 3 (Fall 1978): 22–40; Oliver Otis Howard, *My Life and Experiences among Our Hostile Indians,* 137–42.

32. Barry Scobee, *Fort Davis, Texas, 1583–1960,* 91; Dan L. Thrapp, *The Conquest of Apacheria,* 125–26.

33. David D. Smits, "The Frontier Army and the Destruction of the Buffalo: 1865–1883," *Western Historical Quarterly* 25 (Fall 1994): 313–38; William A. Dobak, "The Army and the Buffalo: A Demur," *Western Historical Quarterly* 26 (Summer 1995): 197–202; David D. Smits, "More on the Army and the Buffalo: The Author's Reply," *Western Historical Quarterly* 26 (Summer 1995): 203–208.

34. Carriker, *Fort Supply,* 108–109, 135; David E. Kyvig, "Policing the Panhandle: Fort Elliott, Texas, 1875–1890," *Red River Valley Historical Review* 1 (Fall 1974): 225.

35. Herman J. Viola, *Diplomats in Buckskins: A History of Indian Delegations in Washington City.*

36. Norman J. Bender, *"New Hope for the Indians": The Grant Peace Policy and the Navajos in the 1870s,* 23–36.

37. D. C. Poole, *Among the Sioux of Dakota: Eighteen Months' Experience as an Indian Agent, 1869–70,* intro. Raymond J. DeMallie, xi–xxii, xxxvi–liii.

38. Burton S. Hill, "Thomas S. Twiss, Indian Agent," *Great Plains Journal* 6 (Spring 1967): 85–96.

39. Britton Davis, *The Truth about Geronimo,* viii–xi, 29–54; Jason Betzinez, and Wilbur S. Nye, *I Fought with Geronimo,* 126–33; Eve Ball, *In the Days of Victorio: Recollections of a Warm Springs Apache,* 159–61.

40. Steinbach, *A Long March,* 163–65.

41. Francis Paul Prucha, "The Settler and the Army in Frontier Minnesota," *Minnesota History* 29 (September 1948): 237–38, 243–44; Kenneth Carley, *The Sioux Uprising of 1862,* 1–24.

42. Judith A. Boughter, "Betraying Their Trust: The Dispossession of the Omaha Nation, 1790–1916," master's thesis, University of Nebraska at Omaha, 1995, 93–101.

43. Don F. Badinelli, "Struggle in the Choctaw Nation: The Coal Miners Strike of 1894," *Chronicles of Oklahoma* 72 (Fall 1994): 295–307.

44. Ray H. Mattison, "Old Fort Stevenson, a Typical Missouri River Military Post," *North Dakota History* 18 (April–June 1951): 53–65; Welty, "Policing of the Frontier," 250–51.

45. John E. Cox, "Soldiering in Dakota Territory in the Seventies: A Communication," *North Dakota Historical Quarterly* 6 (October 1931): 63–64.

46. Sarah Winnemucca Hopkins, *Life among the Piutes: Their Wrongs and Claims,* ed. Mrs. Horace Mann, 92–93.

47. Welty, "Policing of the Frontier," 248–49.

48. Mattison, "Old Fort Stevenson," 70.

49. Kenneth F. Neighbors, "Indian Exodus Out of Texas in 1859," *West Texas Historical Association Year Book* 36 (1960): 80–97.

50. John M. Oswald, "History of Fort Elliott," *Panhandle-Plains Historical Review* 32 (1959): 41–42.

51. Donald Jackson, *Custer's Gold: The United States Cavalry Expedition of 1874,* 104–18; Gerald M. Adams, *The Post Near Cheyenne: A History of Fort D. A. Russell, 1867–1930,* 53; Grant K. Anderson, "The Black Hills Exclusion Policy: Judicial Challenges," *Nebraska History* 58 (Spring 1977): 2–4.

52. Wayne R. Kime, ed., *The Black Hills Journals of Colonel Richard Irving Dodge,* 3–26.

53. Anderson, "Black Hills Exclusion Policy," 5–8; Cox, "Soldiering in Dakota Territory," 66–67.

54. Anderson, "Black Hills Exclusion Policy," 1–20; Erik Erikkson, "Sioux City and the Black Hills Gold Rush 1874–1877," *Iowa Journal of History and Politics* 20 (July 1922): 334.

55. Agnes Wright Spring, *The Cheyenne and Black Hills Stage and Express Routes,* 67.

56. Frazier Hunt and Robert Hunt, *I Fought with Custer: The Story of Sergeant Windolph, Last Survivor of the Battle of the Little Big Horn,* 42.

57. Watson Parker, "The Majors and the Miners: The Role of the U.S. Army in the Black Hills Gold Rush," *Journal of the West* 11 (January 1972): 103. Army efforts to protect Indian lands during the California Gold Rush also receive praise in William F. Strobridge, *Regulars in the Redwoods: The U.S. Army in Northern California, 1852–1861,* 183–210.

58. *Winners of the West,* June 24, 1926, 6; Louise Barry, ed., "With the First U.S. Cavalry in Indian Country, 1859–1861," *Kansas Historical Quarterly* 24 (Fall 1958): 281; (Winter 1958): 419–20; Roberson, "A View From Oklahoma," 21.

59. Carriker, *Fort Supply,* 182–203; Edward Everett Dale, *The Range Cattle Industry: Ranching on the Great Plains from 1865 to 1925,* 135–46.

60. Carriker, *Fort Supply,* 133–34, 181–220; *Winners of the West,* October 1925, 7.

61. W. Sherman Savage, "The Role of Negro Soldiers in Protecting the Indian Territory from Intruders," *Journal of Negro History* 36 (January 1951): 25–34.

62. *Winners of the West,* June 24, 1926, 6.

63. Jimmy M. Skaggs, "Military Operations on the Cattle Trails," *Texas Military History* 6 (Summer 1967): 143–47; Jean L. Zimmerman, "Colonel Ranald S. Mackenzie at Fort Sill," *Chronicles of Oklahoma* 44 (Spring 1966): 12–21; Carriker, *Fort Supply,* 161–81.

64. Henry P. Walker, "When the Law Wore Army Blue," *Military Collector and Historian* 29 (Spring 1977): 8–9; Carriker, *Fort Supply,* 111–19.

65. Kyvig, "Policing the Panhandle," 228; Skaggs, "Military Operations," 147; William T. Hagan, *Quanah Parker, Comanche Chief,* 28–39.

66. Orlan J. Svingen, *The Northern Cheyenne Indian Reservation, 1877–1900,* 29–44, 130–47.

67. Richard N. Ellis, "The Humanitarian Soldiers," *Journal of Arizona History* 10 (Summer 1969): 53–66; Richard N. Ellis, "The Humanitarian Generals," *Western Historical Quarterly* 3 (April 1972): 169–78.

68. James T. King, "George Crook: Indian Fighter and Humanitarian," *Arizona and the West* 9 (Winter 1967): 333–48.

69. Thomas Henry Tibbles, *The Ponca Chiefs: An Account of the Trial of Standing Bear,* ed. Kay Graber, vii–xiii; James T. King, "'A Better Way': General George Crook and the Ponca Indians," *Nebraska History* 50 (Fall 1969): 239–56.

70. Sherry L. Smith, *The View from Officers' Row: Army Perceptions of Western Indians,* 182–85; Thomas C. Leonard, "The Reluctant Conquerors: How the Generals Viewed the Indians," *American Heritage* 27 (August 1976): 34–41; William B. Skelton, "Army Officers' Attitudes Toward Indians, 1830–1860," *Pacific Northwest Quarterly* 67 (July 1976): 113–24.

71. Constance Wynn Altshuler, "Men and Brothers," *Journal of Arizona History* 19 (Fall 1978): 315–22.

72. Charles A. Bentley, "Captain Frederick W. Benteen and the Kiowas," *Chronicles of Oklahoma* 56 (Fall 1978): 344–47.

73. Michael J. Brodhead, "Elliott Coues and the Apaches," *Journal of Arizona History* 14 (Summer 1973): 87–94.

74. Helen Hunt Jackson, *A Century of Dishonor: A Sketch of the United States Government's Dealings with Some of the Indian Tribes;* Thomas A. Bland, "Abolish the Army," *Council Fire,* March 1879, 36.

75. Robert G. Athearn, "Frontier Critics of the Western Army," *Montana, Magazine of Western History* 5 (Spring 1955): 16–28; Adams, *Post Near Cheyenne,* 10–11.

76. Raymond L. Welty, "The Indian Policy of the Army 1860–1870," *Cavalry Journal* 36 (July 1927): 378.

CHAPTER 11. DOCUMENTING THE EXPERIENCE

1. Anne P. Diffendal, comp., *A Guide to the Newspaper Collection of the State Archives Nebraska State Historical Society,* 1.

2. Douglas C. McMurtrie, "The Fourth Infantry Press at Fort Bridger," *Annals of Wyoming* 13 (October 1941): 347.

3. Ibid., 347–51.

4. Thomas H. Heuterman, *Movable Type: Biography of Legh R. Freeman*, 18–19.

5. Robert F. Karolevitz, *Newspapering in the Old West: A Pictorial History of Journalism and Printing on the Frontier*, 169–71.

6. John A. Lent, "The Press on Wheels: A History of *The Frontier Index* of Nebraska, Colorado, Wyoming, Elsewhere?" *Annals of Wyoming* 43 (Fall 1971): 169–70, 191–96; Elizabeth Wright, *Independence in All Things, Neutrality in Nothing: The Story of a Pioneer Journalist of the American West*, 77, 109–14.

7. Lent, "Press on Wheels," 174–79.

8. Heuterman, *Movable Type*, 24–26, 133–37.

9. Thomas B. Brumbaugh, "Fort Laramie Hijinks: A New Manuscript Account," *Annals of Wyoming* 58 (Fall 1986): 6–9.

10. John D. McDermott, "The *Frontier Scout*: A View of Fort Rice in 1865," *North Dakota History* 61 (Fall 1994): 27–29.

11. McDermott, "*Frontier Scout*," 25–29; Dee Brown, *The Galvanized Yankees*, 94–110.

12. McDermott, "*Frontier Scout*," 30–31.

13. Ibid., 30–35.

14. Leo E. Oliva, *Fort Larned on the Santa Fe Trail*, 67–68.

15. Ibid., 69.

16. Gordon S. Chappell, "Surgeon at Fort Sidney: Captain Walter Reed's Experiences at a Nebraska Military Post, 1883–1884," *Nebraska History* 54 (Fall 1973): 423.

17. H. H. McConnell, *Five Years a Cavalryman, or Sketches of Regular Army Life on the Texas Frontier, 1866–1871*, 173–74; Donald W. Whisenhunt, *Fort Richardson: Outpost on the Texas Frontier*, 17.

18. Earl F. Stover, "Chaplain Henry V. Plummer, His Ministry and His Court-Martial," *Nebraska History* 56 (Spring 1975): 29–44 (quote is on 29).

19. A. L. Runyon, "A. L. Runyon's Letters from the Nineteenth Kansas Regiment," *Kansas Historical Quarterly* 9 (February 1940): 58–61; C. Robert Haywood, *Trails South: The Wagon-Road Economy in the Dodge City–Panhandle Region*, 24, 262.

20. Robert C. Carriker, *Fort Supply, Indian Territory: Frontier Outpost on the Plains*, 140–44.

21. Ibid., 143–44; David Strate, *Sentinel to the Cimarron: The Frontier Experience of Fort Dodge, Kansas*, 63.

22. Haywood, *Trails South*, 33.

23. Dale F. Giese, "Soldiers at Play: A History of Social Life at Fort Union, New Mexico, 1851–1891," Ph.D. diss., University of New Mexico, 1969, 166–67, 174–77.

24. Henry Winfred Splitter, ed., "Tour in Arizona: Footprints of an Army Officer," *Journal of the West* 1 (July 1962): 74–97; Henry Winfred Splitter, "The Adventures of an Editor in Search of an Author," *Journal of the West* 1 (October 1962): 201–14.

25. J. W. Vaughn, "The Mark H. Kellogg Story," *Westerners New York Posse Brand Book* 7 (1961): 73–75, 84–91.

26. Dan L. Thrapp, ed., *Dateline Fort Bowie: Charles Fletcher Lummis Reports on an Apache War.*

27. John F. Finerty, *War-Path and Bivouac, or the Conquest of the Sioux: A Narrative of Stirring Personal Experiences and Adventures in the Big Horn and Yellowstone Expedition of 1876, and in the Campaign on the British Border in 1879*, vii–xvi; Henry M. Stanley, *My Early Travels and Adventures in America and Asia*, vol. 1; De B. Randolph Keim, *Sheridan's Troopers on the Border: A Winter Campaign on the Plains.*

28. Oliver Knight, *Following the Indian Wars: The Story of the Newspaper Correspondents among the Indian Campaigns*, 234–44.

29. Elmo Scott Watson, "The Last Indian War, 1890–91: A Study of Newspaper Jingoism," *Journalism Quarterly* 20 (September 1943): 205–19; Philip S. Hall, *To Have This Land: The Nature of Indian/White Relations, South Dakota, 1888–1891*, 27–36, 71–82; William Fitch Kelley, *Pine Ridge 1890: An Eye Witness Account of the Events Surrounding the Fighting at Wounded Knee*, ed. Alexander Kelley and Pierre Bovis.

30. Herbert Krause and Gary D. Olson, *Prelude to Glory: A Newspaper Accounting of Custer's 1874 Expedition to the Black Hills*; George Henry Palmer, "'We Do Not Know What the Government Intends to Do . . .': Lt. Palmer Writes from the Bozeman Trail, 1867–68," ed. Jerome A. Greene, *Montana, Magazine of Western History* 28 (July 1978): 17–35.

31. Louise Barry, ed., "With the First U.S. Cavalry in Indian Country, 1859–1861," *Kansas Historical Quarterly* 24 (Fall 1958): 257–84; (Winter 1958): 399–425.

32. S. S. Peters, "Letters of a Sixth Cavalryman Stationed at 'Cantonment' in the Texas Panhandle, 1875," ed. Lonnie J. White, *Texas Military History* 7 (Summer 1968): 77–102; J. T. Marshall, *The Miles Expedition of 1874–1875: An Eyewitness Account of the Red River War*, ed. Lonnie J. White, v–xi.

33. William A. Dobak, "Yellow-Leg Journalists: Enlisted Men as Newspaper Reporters in the Sioux Campaign, 1876," *Journal of the West* 13 (January 1974): 86–94.

34. George A. Custer, *My Life on the Plains*, ed. Milo Milton Quaife, xxxvii–xli.

35. William B. Hazen, *Some Corrections on "My Life on the Plains."*

36. Brian W. Dippie, "George A. Custer," in *Soldiers West: Biographies from the Military Frontier*, ed. Paul A. Hutton, 101.

37. Robert Wooster, *Nelson A. Miles and the Twilight of the Frontier Army*, 202–203.

38. Ibid., 254.

39. John G. Bourke, *An Apache Campaign in the Sierra Madre: An Account of the Expedition in Pursuit of the Hostile Chiricahua Apaches in the Spring of 1883*; John G. Bourke, *On the Border with Crook.*

40. Britton Davis, *The Truth about Geronimo.*

41. Peggy Samuels and Harold Samuels, *Frederic Remington: A Biography*, 67–113.

42. Sherry L. Smith, ed., *Sagebrush Soldier: Private William Earl Smith's View of the Sioux War of 1876.*

43. John M. Carroll and Lawrence A. Frost, eds., *Private Theodore Ewert's Diary of the Black Hills Expedition of 1874.*

44. Richard H. Dillon, ed., *A Cannoneer in Navajo Country: Journal of Private Josiah M. Rice, 1851.*

45. Hervey Johnson, *Tending the Talking Wire: A Buck Soldier's View of Indian Country, 1863–1866*, ed. William E. Unrau.

46. Mrs. Orsemus Bronson Boyd, *Cavalry Life in Tent and Field*; Teresea Griffin Vielé, *Following the Drum: A Glimpse of Frontier Life*; Francis M. A. Roe, *Army Letters from an Officer's Wife, 1871–1888*; Martha Summerhayes, *Vanished Arizona: Recollections of the Army Life of a New England Woman*, 2d ed.; Alice Blackwood Baldwin, *Memoirs of the Late Frank D. Baldwin, Maj. General, U.S.A.*; Margaret Irvin Carrington, *Absaraka: Home of the Crows: Being the Experience of an Officer's Wife on the Plains*; Lydia Spencer Lane, *I Married a Soldier, or Old Days in the Army*; Emily McCorkle FitzGerald, *An Army Doctor's Wife on the Frontier: Letters from Alaska and the Far West, 1874–1878*, ed. Abe Laufe; Ellen McGowan Biddle, *Reminiscences of a Soldier's Wife.*

47. Sandra L. Myres, "Army Women's Narratives as Documents of Social History: Some Examples from the Western Frontier, 1840–1900," *New Mexico Historical Review* 65 (April 1990): 175–98; Sandra L. Myres, "The Ladies of the Army: Views of Western Life," in *The American Military on the Frontier: Proceedings of the Seventh Military History Symposium*, ed. James P. Tate, 135–50.

48. Elizabeth B. Custer, *Boots and Saddles, or Life in Dakota with General Custer*; Elizabeth B. Custer, *Tenting on the Plains, or General Custer in Kansas and Texas*; Elizabeth B. Custer, *Following the Guidon.*

49. Michael L. Tate, "The Girl He Left Behind: Elizabeth Custer and the Making of a Legend," *Red River Valley Historical Review* 5 (Winter 1980): 5–22.

50. Donald N. Bigelow, *William Conant Church and the Army and Navy Journal*, 192–208; William A. Dobak, "Licit Amusements of Enlisted Men in the Post–Civil War Army," *Montana, Magazine of Western History* 45 (Spring 1995): 36–38.

51. Lora Taylor Gray, "'Winners of the West': A Personal Reminiscence of Lauren Winfield Aldrich," *Journal of the West* 33 (January 1994): 96–98; Don Rickey, Jr., *Forty Miles a Day on Beans and Hay: The Enlisted Soldier Fighting the Indian Wars*, 369.

52. Oliver Knight, "A Dedication to the Memory of Charles King, 1844–1933," *Arizona and the West* 15 (Fall 1973): 209–12.

53. Charles King, *Campaigning with Crook: The Fifth Cavalry in the Sioux War of 1876*; Don Russell, *Campaigning with King: Charles King, Chronicler of the Old West*, ed. Paul L. Hedren, 69–83; Paul L. Hedren, "Charles King," in *Soldiers West: Biographies from the Military Frontier*, ed. Paul A. Hutton, 250–52.

54. Harry H. Anderson, "The Friendship of Buffalo Bill and Charles King," *Milwaukee History* 9 (Winter 1986): 119–32; Oliver Knight, *Life and Manners in the Frontier Army*, 3–38.

55. Knight, *Following the Indian Wars*, 320–25.

CHAPTER 12. LIFE AFTER SOLDIERING

1. H. H. McConnell, *Five Years a Cavalryman, or Sketches of Regular Army Life on the Texas Frontier, 1866–1871*, 101; Teresa Griffin Vielé, *Following the Drum: A Glimpse of Frontier Life*, 174–75.

2. Robert A. Murray, "Prices and Wages at Fort Laramie, 1881–1885," *Annals of Wyoming* 36 (April 1964): 19–21; Harry A. Anderson, "A History of the Cheyenne River Indian Agency and Its Military Post, Fort Bennett, 1868–1891," *South Dakota Historical Collections* 28 (1956): 525–26; Cornelia Crook and Garland Crook, "Fort Lincoln, Texas," *Texas Military History* 4 (Fall 1964): 153.

3. Henry P. Walker, "Bugler! No Pay Call Today! The Year the Army Went Payless," *Montana, Magazine of Western History* 21 (Summer 1971): 34–43.

4. Charles Ruff to John Dougherty, 1849, and Charles Ruff to John Dougherty, June 24, 1849, in Charles and Annie Ruff Papers, Nebraska State Historical Society.

5. Charles Ruff to John Dougherty, Dec. 8, 1849, and Charles Ruff to John Dougherty, Feb. 7, 1850, in Ruff Papers, NSHS.

6. Hamilton Gardner, "Romance at Old Cantonment Leavenworth: The Marriage of 2d Lt. Philip St. George Cooke in 1830," *Kansas Historical Quarterly* 22 (Summer 1956): 97–113; Daniel D. Holt and Marilyn Irvin Holt, "'The Pleasures of Female Society' at Cantonment Leavenworth," *Kansas History* 8 (Spring 1985): 21–35; William Garrett Piston, "Petticoats, Promotions, and Military Assignments: Favoritism and the Antebellum Career of James Longstreet," *Military History of the Southwest* 22 (Spring 1992): 15–30.

7. W. Eugene Hollon, *Beyond the Cross Timbers: The Travels of Randolph B. Marcy, 1812–1887*, 236–44; Michael L. Tate, "Randolph B. Marcy: First Explorer of the Wichitas," *Great Plains Journal* 15 (Spring 1976): 81–113.

8. John M. Gates, "The Alleged Isolation of U.S. Army Officers in the Late 19th Century," *Parameters: The Journal of the U.S. Army War College* 10 (September 1980): 32–44 (quote is on 34).

9. Edward M. Coffman, *The Old Army: A Portrait of the American Army in Peacetime, 1784–1898*, 84–85.

10. Ibid., 84–85.

11. Bruce J. Dinges, "Colonel Grierson Invests on the West Texas Frontier," *Fort Concho Report* 16 (Fall 1984): 6–7.

12. Ibid., 7–8.

13. Mary L. Williams, "Empire Building: Colonel Benjamin H. Grierson at Fort Davis, 1882–1885," *West Texas Historical Association Year Book* 61 (1985): 61–64.

14. Dinges, "Colonel Grierson Invests," 8.

15. Douglas C. McChristian, ed., *Garrison Tangles in the Friendless Tenth: The Journal of First Lieutenant John Bigelow, Jr., Fort Davis, Texas*, 8–14; Williams, "Empire Building," 67–68.

16. Williams, "Empire Building," 68–69.

17. Dinges, "Colonel Grierson Invests," 5, 12.

18. Barry Scobee, *Fort Davis, Texas, 1583–1960*, 90; Williams, "Empire Building," 70; William H. Leckie and Shirley A. Leckie, *Unlikely Warriors: General Benjamin H. Grierson and His Family*, 305–308.

19. Dinges, "Colonel Grierson Invests," 5.

20. Julia Cauble Smith, "The Shafter Mining District," *Permian Historical Annual* 28 (December 1988): 76–77.

21. Ibid., 77–82; Paul H. Carlson, "The Discovery of Silver in West Texas," *West Texas Historical Association Year Book* 54 (1978): 60–63.

22. Coffman, *Old Army*, 86.

23. Diane M. T. North, *Samuel Peter Heintzelman and the Sonora Exploring and Mining Company*, 8–45.

24. Robert Lee, *Fort Meade and the Black Hills*, 34, 48–49.

25. Louis L. Simonin, *The Rocky Mountain West in 1867*, trans. and ed. Wilson O. Clough, 71.

26. Gerald M. Adams, *The Post Near Cheyenne: A History of Fort D. A. Russell, 1867–1930*, 12–13.

27. Robert Wooster, *Nelson A. Miles and the Twilight of the Frontier Army*, 50, 59–60, 137–38, 249–50.

28. Frank N. Schubert, *Buffalo Soldiers, Braves, and the Brass: The Story of Fort Robinson, Nebraska*, 155.

29. William A. Dobak, "Yellow-Leg Journalists: Enlisted Men as Newspaper Reporters in the Sioux Campaign, 1876," *Journal of the West* 13 (January 1974): 94.

30. Mary Lee Spence, ed., *The Expeditions of John Charles Frémont*, vol. 3, *Travels from 1848 to 1854*, xli–lxxvii.

31. Allan Nevins, *Frémont: Pathmarker of the West*, 594–610.

32. Dwight L. Clarke, *William Tecumseh Sherman: Gold Rush Banker*, ix–x.

33. Ibid., 105–99; Robert G. Athearn, *William Tecumseh Sherman and the Settlement of the West*, xiii–xv.

34. Robert M. Utley, *Cavalier in Buckskin: George Armstrong Custer and the Western Military Frontier*, 14–15, 39.

368   NOTES TO PAGES 295–302

35. Ibid., 153–55.

36. Ibid., 109.

37. Ibid. See also Duane A. Smith, "'Where a Bird Could Hardly Obtain a Footing': George Armstrong Custer and the Stevens Mine," *Colorado Heritage,* Spring 1997, 25–37.

38. Richard Slotkin, ". . . and Then the Mare Will Go!: An 1875 Black Hills Scheme by Custer, Holladay, and Buford," *Journal of the West* 15 (July 1976): 73–74.

39. Ibid., 63–69.

40. Ibid., 70–71; Utley, *Cavalier in Buckskin,* 153–54.

41. David Dixon, *Hero of Beecher Island: The Life and Military Career of George A. Forsyth,* 168–69.

42. Ibid., 170–82.

43. Ibid., 182.

44. Ibid., 183–87.

45. James S. Brisbin, *The Beef Bonanza, or How to Get Rich on the Plains,* 13–14.

46. Edgar I. Stewart, ed., *Penny-an-Acre Empire in the West,* 35–42, 78–113.

47. Marvin E. Kroeker, *Great Plains Command: William B. Hazen in the Frontier West,* 120–42.

48. Barbara A. Neal Ledbetter, *Fort Belknap Frontier Saga: Indians, Negroes, and Anglo-Americans on the Texas Frontier,* 41, 47.

49. Piston, "Petticoats, Promotions, and Military Assignments," 27; Soren W. Nielsen, "Ranald S. Mackenzie: The Man and His Battle," *West Texas Historical Association Year Book* 64 (1988): 150; Robert H. Steinbach, *A Long March: The Lives of Frank and Alice Baldwin,* 186–87; Paul H. Carlson, *"Pecos Bill": A Military Biography of William R. Shafter,* 158.

50. David K. Strate, *Sentinel to the Cimarron: The Frontier Experience of Fort Dodge, Kansas,* 96.

51. Don Rickey, Jr., *Forty Miles a Day on Beans and Hay: The Enlisted Soldier Fighting the Indian Wars,* 344–48.

52. Don Russell, *Campaigning with King: Charles King, Chronicler of the Old Army,* ed. by Paul L. Hedren, 147; Mildred Wertenberger, comp., "Fort Totten, Dakota Territory, 1867," *North Dakota History* 34 (Spring 1967): 142.

53. William A. Dobak, "Yellow-Leg Journalists," 95; Richard K. Smith, "For God . . . for Country . . . for the Territory," *Arizona Highways* 49 (April 1973): 12; Homer Croy, *Trigger Marshal: The Story of Chris Madsen,* 44–215.

54. Scobee, *Fort Davis,* 102–103; C. Robert Haywood, *Trails South: The Wagon-Road Economy in the Dodge City–Panhandle Region,* 52.

55. Clayton Williams, *Texas' Last Frontier: Fort Stockton and the Trans-Pecos, 1861–1895,* ed. Ernest Wallace, 140–42, 193–94.

56. Donald F. Schofield, "The Making of a West Texas Ghost Town: Tascosa vs. W. M. D. Lee," *West Texas Historical Association Year Book* 61 (1985): 31–37;

Donald F. Schofield, "W. M. D. Lee, Indian Trader," *Panhandle-Plains Historical Review* 54 (1981): 3–39, 101–107.

57. Schubert, *Buffalo Soldiers*, 158–60.
58. Ibid., 149–53.
59. Ibid., 153.
60. Ibid., 153–54.
61. Ibid., 156–58.

CONCLUSION

1. "Address by General Charles King," in *The Papers of the Order of Indian Wars*, comp. and ed. John M. Carroll, 46.

2. Jerry M. Cooper, "The Army's Search for a Mission, 1865–1890," in *Against All Enemies: Interpretations of American Military History from Colonial Times to the Present*, ed. Kenneth J. Hagan and William R. Roberts, 173–95.

3. Lester D. Langley, "The Democratic Tradition and Military Reform, 1878–1885," *Southwestern Social Science Quarterly* 48 (September 1967): 192–98.

4. Wallace D. Farnham, "The Weakened Spring of Government: A Study in Nineteenth-Century American History," *American Historical Review* 68 (April 1963): 680.

5. Ibid., 669.

6. Ibid., 670–80.

7. Quoted from *Army and Navy Chronicle* 6 (May 17, 1838): 314–15, in Francis Paul Prucha, *Broadax and Bayonet: The Role of the United States Army in the Development of the Northwest, 1815–1860*, 105.

8. H. H. McConnell, *Five Years a Cavalryman, or Sketches of Regular Army Life on the Texas Frontier, 1866–1871*, 104–105.

9. Paul L. Hedren, "On Duty at Fort Ridgely, Minnesota: 1853–1867," *South Dakota History* 7 (Spring 1977): 185.

10. Raymond L. Welty, "The Daily Life of the Frontier Soldier," *Cavalry Journal* 36 (1927): 585–87.

11. Dale F. Giese, "Soldiers at Play: A History of Social Life at Fort Union, New Mexico, 1851–1891," Ph.D. diss., University of New Mexico, 1969, 167–68.

12. Quoted in Prucha, *Broadax and Bayonet*, 104.

Bibliography

MANUSCRIPT COLLECTIONS

Benson, John H. "Journal." Manuscript. Nebraska State Historical Society, Lincoln.

Bourke, John G. "Memorandum, Giving Certain Information in Connection with the Campaigns against the Apache Indians in Arizona and New Mexico from June 1871 to April 1885." Typescript in File 1066, Adjutant General's Office, 1883. National Archives and Records Service, Washington, D.C.

Day, Hannibal. "Papers." Unpublished diary and map. Nebraska State Historical Society, Lincoln.

Grierson, Robert K. "Journal Kept on the Victorio Campaign in 1880." Manuscript made available by Dr. William H. Leckie to the author.

Grow, S. L. "Journal." Manuscript. Beinecke Library, Yale University, New Haven, Connecticut.

Hamilton, George F. "History of the Ninth Regiment, U.S. Cavalry." Manuscript. U.S. Military Academy, West Point, New York.

Letters Sent, Records of the Army Continental Commands, Record Group 393, National Archives, reel 6. Nebraska State Historical Society, Lincoln.

McDonald, Charles. "Papers." Account ledgers and letters. Nebraska State Historical Society, Lincoln.

Nickerson, Azor. "Major General George Crook and the Indians." Manuscript. Walter S. Schuyler Papers, Henry Huntington Library, San Marino, California.

Ruff, Charles, and Annie Ruff. Papers. Nebraska State Historical Society, Lincoln.

Saltzgaber, Violet A. "Doby Town." Manuscript. Nebraska State Historical Society, Lincoln.

Thomas, Dr. William L. "Diary." Manuscript. Bancroft Library, University of California, Berkeley.

Woodhams, William H. "Journals." Manuscript. Nebraska State Historical Society, Lincoln.

GOVERNMENT DOCUMENTS

Abert, James W. "Notes of Lieutenant J. W. Abert." In William H. Emory, *Notes of a Military Reconnaissance.* New York: H. Long and Brother, 1848.

Annual Report of the Secretary of War, 1798–1895.

Baldwin, Kenneth H. *Enchanted Enclosure: The Army Engineers and the Yellowstone National Park, a Documentary History.* Washington, D.C.: Office of the Chief of Engineers, United States Army, 1976.

Bell, William Gardner. *Commanding Generals and Chiefs of Staff 1775–1991: Portraits and Biographical Sketches of the United States Army's Senior Officer.* Washington, D.C.: Center for Military History, United States Army, 1992.

Billings, John S. *A Report on Barracks and Hospitals, with Descriptions of Military Posts.* War Department Surgeon General's Office Circular 4. Washington, D.C.: Government Printing Office, 1870.

——. *Report on the Hygiene of the United States Army, with Descriptions of Military Posts.* War Department Surgeon General's Office Circular 8. Washington, D.C.: Government Printing Office, 1875.

Blauch, Lloyd E., and William L. Iverson. "Education of Children on Federal Reservations." In *Advisory Committee on Education.* Staff Study No. 17. Washington, D.C.: Government Printing Office, 1939.

Bourke, John G. *The Medicine Men of the Apache.* Ninth Annual Report of the Bureau of Ethnology, 1887–88. Washington, D.C.: Government Printing Office, 1892.

Brown, Harvey E., comp. *The Medical Department of the United States Army from 1775 to 1873.* Washington, D.C.: Surgeon General's Office, 1873.

Carey, Asa B. *A Sketch of the Organization of the Pay Department of the U.S. Army from 1775 to 1876.* Washington, D.C.: Paymaster General's Office, 1876.

Clary, David A., and Joseph W. A. Whitmore. *The Inspectors General of the United States Army, 1777–1903.* Washington, D.C.: Office of the Inspector General and Center for Military History, United States Army, 1987.

Coakley, Robert W. *The Role of Federal Military Forces in Domestic Disorders, 1789–1878.* Washington, D.C.: Center for Military History, United States Army, 1988.

Coolidge, Richard H. *Statistical Report on the Sickness and Mortality in the Army of the United States, Compiled from the Records of the Surgeon General's Office Embracing a Period of Sixteen Years from January, 1839, to January, 1855.* Washington, D.C.: AOP Nicholson, 1856.

Davis, George B., ed. *The Military Laws of the United States.* Washington, D.C.: Government Printing Office, 1897.

Ellis, Richard N. "The Political Role of the Military on the Frontier." In *The American Military on the Frontier: Proceedings of the Seventh Military History Symposium,* pp. 71–83. Ed. James P. Tate. Washington, D.C.: Office of Air Force History, 1978.

Exley, Thomas M. *A Compendium of the Pay of the Army from 1785 to 1888.* Washington, D.C.: Government Printing Office, 1888.

The Federal Engineer: Damsites to Missile Sites, A History of the Omaha District, U.S. Army Corps of Engineers. Omaha, Nebr.: U.S. Army Corps of Engineers, 1985.

Foner, Jack D. "The Socializing Role of the Military." In *The American Military on the Frontier: Proceedings of the Seventh Military History Symposium,* pp. 85–99. Ed. James P. Tate. Washington, D.C.: Office of Air Force History, 1978.

Foster, Gaines M. *The Demands of Humanity: Army Medical Disaster Relief.* Washington, D.C.: Center for Military History, United States Army, 1983.

Frémont, John C. *A Report on Exploration of the Country Lying between the Missouri River and the Rocky Mountains, on the Line of the Kansas and Great Platte Rivers.* 27th Cong., 3d sess., 1843, S. Doc. 243.

———. *Report of the Exploring Expedition to the Rocky Mountains in the Year 1842, and to Oregon and North California in the Years 1843–1844.* Washington, D.C.: Gales and Seaton, 1845.

Gillett, Mary C. *The Army Medical Department, 1775–1818.* Washington, D.C.: Center for Military History, United States Army, 1981.

———. *The Army Medical Department, 1818–1865.* Washington, D.C.: Center for Military History, United States Army, 1987.

———. *The Army Medical Department, 1865–1917.* Washington, D.C.: Center for Military History, United States Army, 1995.

Hagood, Joseph J., Jr. *Commitment to Excellence: A History of the Sacramento District, U.S. Army Corps of Engineers, 1929–1973.* Sacramento, Calif.: U.S. Army Corps of Engineers, 1976.

———. *Engineers at the Golden Gate: A History of the San Francisco District, U.S. Army Corps of Engineers, 1866–1980.* San Francisco: U.S. Army Corps of Engineers, 1982.

Haines, Aubrey L. *Yellowstone National Park: Its Exploration and Establishment.* Washington, D.C.: U.S. Department of the Interior, National Park Service, 1974.

Hershler, N. *The Soldier's Hand-Book: For the Use of the Enlisted Men of the Army.* Washington, D.C.: Government Printing Office, 1884.

Honeywell, Roy J. *Chaplains of the United States Army.* Washington, D.C.: Office of the Chief of Chaplains, 1958.

Huston, James A. *The Sinews of War: Army Logistics, 1775–1953.* Washington, D.C.: Government Printing Office, 1960.

Laurie, Clayton D., and Ronald H. Cole. *The Role of Federal Military Forces in Domestic Disorders, 1877–1945.* Washington, D.C.: Center for Military History, United States Army, 1997.

Lieber, G. Norman. *The Use of the Army in Aid of the Civil Power.* Washington, D.C.: Government Printing Office, 1898.

Ludlow, William. *Exploring Nature's Sanctuary: Captain William Ludlow's Report of a Reconnaissance from Carroll, Montana Territory, on the Upper Missouri to the Yellowstone National Park, and Return Made in the Summer of 1875.* Intro. Paul K. Walker. Engineer Historical Studies, No. 3. Washington, D.C., Historical Division, Office of Chief of Engineers, 1985.

Morton, Desmond. "Comparison of U.S./Canadian Military Experience on the Frontier." In *The American Military on the Frontier: Proceedings of the Seventh Military History Symposium,* pp. 17–35. Ed. James P. Tate. Washington, D.C.: Office of Air Force History, 1978.

Myres, Sandra L. "The Ladies of the Army: Views of Western Life." In *The American Military on the Frontier: Proceedings of the Seventh Military History Symposium,* pp. 135–50. Ed. James P. Tate. Washington, D.C.: Office of Air Force History, 1978.

Norton, Herman A. *Struggling for Recognition: The United States Army Chaplaincy, 1791–1865.* Washington, D.C.: Office of the Chief of Chaplains, Department of the Army, 1977.

Otis, George A. *A Report to the Surgeon General on the Transport of the Sick and Wounded by Pack Animals.* Circular No. 9, March 1, 1877. Washington, D.C.: Government Printing Office, 1877.

Outline Descriptions of the Posts in the Military Division of the Missouri. Chicago: Military Division of the Missouri, 1876.

Prucha, Francis Paul. "Commentary." In *The American Military on the Frontier: Proceedings of the Seventh Military History Symposium,* pp. 174–77. Ed. James P. Tate. Washington, D.C.: Government Printing Office, 1978.

Raines, Rebecca Robbins. *Getting the Message Through: A Branch History of the U.S. Army Signal Corps.* Washington, D.C.: Center of Military History, U.S. Army, 1996.

Richardson, James D., comp. *A Compilation of the Messages and Papers of the Presidents.* 10 vols. Washington, D.C.: Government Printing Office, 1897.

Richmond, Henry R., III. *The History of the Portland District, Corps of Engineers, 1871–1969.* Portland, Ore.: U.S. Army Corps of Engineers, 1970.

Risch, Erna. *Quartermaster Support of the Army: A History of the Corps, 1775–1939.* Washington, D.C.: Government Printing Office, 1962.

Roberts, Thomas P. *Report of a Reconnaissance of the Missouri River in 1872.* Washington, D.C.: Government Printing Office, 1875.

Scheufele, Roy W. *The History of the North Pacific Division, U.S. Army Corps of Engineers, 1888–1965.* Portland, Ore.: U.S. Army Corps of Engineers, 1969.

Schubert, Frank N., ed. *The Nation Builders: A Sesquicentennial History of the Corps of Topographical Engineers 1838–1863.* Fort Belvoir, Va.: Office of History, United States Army Corps of Engineers, 1988.

————. *Vanguard of Expansion: Army Engineers in the Trans-Mississippi West, 1819–1879.* Washington, D.C.: Office of the Chief of Engineers, n.d.

Seward, William H. *Speech of William H. Seward on the Army Bill: The Army of the United States Not to Be Employed as a Police to Enforce the Laws of the Conquerors of Kansas.* Washington, D.C.: Buell and Blanchard, 1856.

Smith, Cornelius C., Jr. *Fort Huachuca: The Story of a Frontier Post.* Washington, D.C.: Government Printing Office, 1976.

Stanley, D. S. *Report on the Yellowstone Expedition of 1873.* Washington, D.C.: Government Printing Office, 1874.

Stansbury, Howard. *Exploration and Survey of the Valley of the Great Salt Lake of Utah, Including a Reconnoissance of a New Route through the Rocky Mountains.* Philadelphia: Lippincott, Grambo and Co., 1852.

Stover, Earl F. *Up From Handymen: The United States Army Chaplains, 1865–1920.* Washington, D.C.: Office of the Chief of Chaplains, Department of the Army, 1977.

Traas, Adrian George. *From the Golden Gate to Mexico City: The U.S. Army Topographical Engineers in the Mexican War, 1846–1848.* Washington, D.C.: Office of History, Corp of Engineers and Center of Military History, 1993.

Tyler, Ron C. *The Big Bend: A History of the Last Texas Frontier.* Washington, D.C.: National Park Service, U.S. Department of the Interior, 1975.

U.S. Congress. *American State Papers: Military Affairs.* 7 vols. Washington, D.C.: Gales and Seaton, 1832–61.

————, House. *Message from the President of the United States in Relation to Disorders and Lawlessness in Arizona.* 47th Cong., 1st sess., 1882, H. Exec. Doc. 188.

————. *Providing Indemnity to Certain Chinese Subjects.* 49th Cong., 1st sess., 1886, H. Exec. Doc. 2044.

————. *The Purchase of Military Sites in Texas.* 43rd Cong., 1st sess., 1873, H. Exec. Doc. 282.

————. *Testimony Taken by Committee on Military Affairs in Relation to Texas Border Troubles.* 45th Cong., 2d sess., 1879, H. Misc. Doc. 64.

U.S. Congress, Senate. *Costs of the Late War with the Sioux Indians.* 45th Cong., 2d sess., 1877, S. Exec. Doc. 33.

————. *Report on Sickness and Mortality among the Troops in Texas.* 49th Cong., 1st sess., 1886, S. Exec. Doc. 96.

————. *Reports of Explorations and Surveys to Ascertain the Most Practicable and Economical Route for a Railroad from the Mississippi River to the Pacific Ocean.* 33rd Cong., 2d sess., S. Exec. Doc. 78. Washington, D.C.: Beverly Tucker Printer, 1856.

U.S. Statutes at Large, 1803–1885.

Utley, Robert M. "The Contribution of the Frontier to the American Military Tradition." In *The American Military on the Frontier: Proceedings of the Seventh Military History Symposium*, pp. 3–13. Ed. James P. Tate. Washington, D.C.: Office of Air Force History, 1978.

Walker, Henry P. "The Enlisted Soldier on the Frontier." In *The American Military on the Frontier: Proceedings of the Seventh Military History Symposium*, pp. 119–33. Ed. James P. Tate. Washington, D.C.: Office of Air Force History, 1978.

War Department. *Regulations of the Army of the United States, 1857*. Washington, D.C.: Government Printing Office, 1857.

———. *Regulations of the Army of the United States and the General Orders in Force on the 17th of February 1881*. Washington, D.C.: Government Printing Office, 1881.

Warren, Francis E. *Report of the Governor of Wyoming to the Secretary of the Interior, 1885*. Washington, D.C.: Government Printing Office, 1885.

Warren, Gouverneur K. *Preliminary Report of Explorations in Nebraska and Dakota, in the Years 1855, '56, '57*. Washington, D.C.: Government Printing Office, 1875.

Willingham, William F. *Army Engineers and the Development of Oregon: A History of the Portland District, U.S. Army Corps of Engineers*. Washington, D.C.: Government Printing Office, 1983.

Wilson, Frederick T. *Federal Aid in Domestic Disturbances, 1787–1903*. 57th Cong., 2d sess., 1903, S. Doc. 209, 1–394.

THESES AND DISSERTATIONS

Acker, G. Dudley, Jr. "Nantan Lupan: George Crook on America's Frontiers." Ph.D. diss., Northern Arizona University, 1995.

Ballew, Elvis Joe. "Supply Problems of Fort Davis, Texas, 1867–1880." M.A. thesis, Sul Ross State University, 1971.

Blackman, Patricia R. "The History of Disability Legislation for Regular Army Widows of the Indian Wars, 1790–1890." M.A. thesis, University of Nebraska at Omaha, 1982.

Boughter, Judith A. "Betraying Their Trust: The Dispossession of the Omaha Nation, 1790–1916." M.A. thesis, University of Nebraska at Omaha, 1995.

Bowie, Chester W. "Redfield Proctor: A Biography." Ph.D. diss., University of Wisconsin, 1980.

Brown, Wallace. "George L. Miller and the *Omaha Herald*, 1854–1869." M.A. thesis, University of Nebraska, 1959.

Buchanan, John S. "Functions of the Fort Davis Military Bands and Musical Proclivities of the Commanding Officer, Colonel Benjamin H. Grierson, Late Nineteenth Century." M.A. thesis, Sul Ross State University, 1968.

Buss, Stephen Ralph. "The Military Theatre: Soldier-Actor Theatricals on the Frontier Plains." Ph.D. diss., Washington State University, 1982.

Christian, Garna L. "Sword and Plowshare: The Symbiotic Development of Fort Bliss and El Paso, Texas, 1849–1918." Ph.D. diss., Texas Tech University, 1977.

Crouch, Thomas W. "The Making of a Soldier: The Career of Frederick Funston, 1865–1902." Ph.D. diss., University of Texas, 1969.

Falk, Stanley L. "Soldier-Technologist: Major Alfred Mordecai and the Beginnings of Science in the United States Army." Ph.D. diss., Georgetown University, 1958.

Fisher, Barbara E., ed. "Forrestine Cooper Hooker's Notes and Memoirs on Army Life in the West, 1871–1876." M.A. thesis, University of Arizona, 1963.

Fleming, William F. "San Antonio: The History of a Military City, 1865–1880." Ph.D. diss., University of Pennsylvania, 1963.

Freeman, William H., Jr. "An Analysis of Military Land Use Policy and Practice in the Pacific Northwest: 1849–1940." Ph.D. diss., University of Washington, 1974.

Gamble, Richard D. "Garrison Life at Frontier Military Posts, 1820–1860." Ph.D. diss., University of Oklahoma, 1956.

Garver, John B., Jr. "The Role of the United States Army in the Colonization of the Trans-Missouri West: Kansas, 1804–1861." Ph.D. diss., Syracuse University, 1981.

Giese, Dale F. "Soldiers at Play: A History of Social Life at Fort Union, New Mexico, 1851–1891." Ph.D. diss., University of New Mexico, 1969.

Hoge, William, Jr. "The Logistical System of the U.S. Army during the Indian Wars, 1866–1889." M.A. thesis, Washington State University, 1968.

Iverson, William L. "U.S. Military Post Schools, 1821–1921." Ph.D. diss., Stanford University, 1936.

Kindred, Marilyn Anne. "The Army Officer Corps and the Arts: Artistic Patronage and Practice in America, 1820–85." Ph.D. diss., University of Kansas, 1980.

Knecht, Robert Lee. "Ado Hunnius, Great Plains Cartographer." M.A. thesis, Emporia State University, 1987.

McBride, Donald B. "The Military Metropolis: The Unique Military-Civilian Relationship and Military Influences in San Antonio, Texas." M.A. thesis, Trinity University, 1959.

Marcum, Richard T. "Fort Brown Texas: The History of a Border Post." Ph.D. diss., Texas Tech University, 1964.

Nacy, Michele Joan. "Members of the Regiment: Army Officers' Wives on the Western Frontier, 1865–1890." Ph.D. diss., Kansas State University, 1995.

Pederson, Lyman C., Jr. "History of Fort Douglas, Utah." Ph.D. diss., Brigham Young University, 1967.

Poor, Robert. "Washington Matthews: An Intellectual Biography." M.A. thesis, University of Nevada-Reno, 1975.

Rue, Norman L. "Words by Wire: Construction of the Military Telegraph in Arizona Territory, 1873–1877." M.A. thesis, University of Arizona, 1967.

Shackett, Phyllis. "Brass Button Belle; or the Life of Cynthia J. Capron, Frontier Military Wife." M.A. thesis, Northeast Missouri State University, 1980.

Sharp, Walter C., Jr. "Fort Omaha and the Winning of the West." M.A. thesis, University of Nebraska at Omaha, 1967.

Stone, Jerome. "A History of Fort Grant." M.A. thesis, University of Arizona, 1941.

Sutherland, Edwin V. "The Diaries of John Gregory Bourke: Their Anthropological and Folklore Content." Ph.D. diss., University of Pennsylvania, 1965.

Uglow, Loyd Michael. "Standing in the Gap: Subposts, Minor Posts, and Picket Stations and the Pacification of the Texas Frontier, 1866–1886." Ph.D. diss., University of North Texas, 1995.

Walker, Gary Lee. "A History of Fort Duchesne, including Fort Thornburgh: The Military Presence in Frontier Uinta Basin, Utah." 2 vols. Ph.D. diss., Brigham Young University, 1992.

Ware, James Halm. "San Angelo and San Antonio: A Comparative Study of the Military City in Texas, 1865–1898." M.A. thesis, Southwest Texas State University, 1973.

White, William Bruce. "The Military and the Melting Pot: The American Army and Minority Groups, 1865–1924." Ph.D. diss., University of Wisconsin, 1968.

Wright, Peter M. "Fort Reno, Indian Territory, 1874–85." M.A. thesis, University of Oklahoma, 1965.

Zwink, Timothy A. "Fort Larned: Garrison on the Central Great Plains." Ph.D. diss., Oklahoma State University, 1980.

PRIMARY BOOKS AND PAMPHLETS

Alexander, Eveline. *Among the Pimas, or the Mission to the Pima and Maricopa Indians.* Albany, N.Y.: Ladies' Union Mission School Association, 1893.

Allensworth, Allen. "Military Education in the United States." In *National Education Association Journal of Proceedings and Addresses,* 224–34. New York: J. J. Little and Co., 1891.

Annual Report of the U.S. Military Post Library Association, 1871–72. New York: Headquarters of the Library Association, 1872.

Armes, George A. *Ups and Downs of an Army Officer.* Washington, D.C.: n.p., 1900.

Baldwin, Alice Blackwood. *Memoirs of the Late Frank D. Baldwin, Major General, U.S.A.* Los Angeles: Wetzel Publishing Co., 1929.

Ball, Eve. *In the Days of Victorio: Recollections of a Warm Springs Apache.* Tucson: University of Arizona Press, 1970.

Bandel, Eugene. *Frontier Life in the Army, 1854–1861.* Trans. Olga Bandel and Richard Jente. Ed. Ralph A. Bieber. Glendale, Calif.: Arthur H. Clark, 1932.

Beecher, George Allen. *A Bishop of the Great Plains*. Philadelphia: Church Historical Society, 1950.

Bennett, James. *Overland Journal to California: Journal of James Bennett Whose Party Left New Harmony in 1850 and Crossed the Plains and Mountains until the Golden West Was Reached*. Fairfield, Wash.: Ye Galleon Press, 1987.

Bergey, Ellwood. *Why Soldiers Desert from the United States Army*. Philadelphia: W. F. Fell & Co., 1903.

Betzinez, Jason, and Wilbur S. Nye. *I Fought with Geronimo*. Harrisburg, Pa.: Stackpole Co., 1959.

Biddle, Ellen McGowan. *Reminiscences of a Soldier's Wife*. Philadelphia: J. B. Lippincott and Co., 1907.

Bidlack, Russell E. *Letters Home: The Story of Ann Arbor's Forty-Niners*. Intro. F. Clever Bald. Ann Arbor, Mich.: Ann Arbor Publishers, 1960.

Bisbee, William H. *Through Four American Wars*. Boston: Meador Publishing Co., 1931.

Bourke, John G. *An Apache Campaign in the Sierra Madre: An Account of the Expedition in Pursuit of the Hostile Chiricahua Apaches in the Spring of 1883*. New York: Charles Scribner's Sons, 1886.

―――. *On the Border with Crook*. New York: Charles Scribner's Sons, 1891.

Boyd, Mrs. Orsemus Bronson. *Cavalry Life in Tent and Field*. New York: J. S. Tait, 1894.

Brisbin, James S. *The Beef Bonanza, or How to Get Rich on the Plains*. Philadelphia: J. B. Lippincott, 1881.

Brooks, Clinton E., and Frank D. Reeve, eds. *Forts and Forays: James A. Bennett, a Dragoon in New Mexico, 1850–1856*. Albuquerque: University of New Mexico Press, 1948.

Brown, William Richard. *An Authentic Wagon Train Journal of 1853 from Indiana to California*. Mokelumne Hill, Calif.: Horseshoe Printing, 1985.

Bryant, Edwin. *What I Saw in California: Being the Journal of a Tour, by the Emigrant Route and South Pass of the Rocky Mountains, across the Continent of North America, the Great Desert Basin, and through California, in the Years 1846, 1847*. New York: D. Appleton and Co., 1848.

Bunky [Irving Geffs]. *The First Eight Months of Oklahoma City*. Oklahoma City: McMaster Printing Co., 1890.

Byrne, Bernard. *A Frontier Army Surgeon*. Cranford, N.J.: Allen Printing Co., 1935.

Carriker, Robert C., and Eleanor R. Carriker, eds. *An Army Wife on the Frontier: The Memoirs of Alice Blackwood Baldwin, 1867–1877*. Salt Lake City: University of Utah, 1975.

Carrington, Frances C. *My Army Life and the Fort Phil Kearney [sic] Massacre*. Philadelphia: J. B. Lippincott Co., 1910.

Carrington, Margaret Irvin. *Absaraka, Home of the Crows: Being the Experience of an Officer's Wife on the Plains*. Philadelphia: J. B. Lippincott and Co., 1868.

Carroll, John M. *Camp Talk: The Very Private Letters of Frederick W. Benteen to His Wife, 1871 to 1888*. Mattituck, N.Y.: J. M. Carroll and Co., 1983.

————, ed. *Custer's Chief of Scouts: The Reminiscences of Charles A. Varnum*. Lincoln: University of Nebraska Press, 1987.

————, and Lawrence A. Frost, eds. *Private Theodore Ewert's Diary of the Black Hills Expedition of 1874*. Piscataway, N.J.: CRI Books, 1976.

Carter, Robert G., ed. *The Old Sergeant's Story: Winning the West from the Indians and Bad Men in 1870 to 1876*. New York: Frederick H. Hitchcock, 1926.

————. *On the Border with Mackenzie*. Washington, D.C.: Eynon Printing Co., 1935.

————. *On the Trail of Deserters*. Washington, D.C.: Gibson Brothers, Printers, 1920.

Carter, W. H. *From Yorktown to Santiago with the Sixth U.S. Cavalry*. Baltimore: Lord Baltimore Press, 1900.

Clark, Sterling B. F. *How Many Miles from St Jo? The Log of Sterling B. F. Clark, a Forty-Niner*. Fairfield, Wash.: Ye Galleon Press, 1988.

Clark, William P. *The Indian Sign Language*. Philadelphia: L. R. Hamersly and Co., 1885.

Coke, Henry J. *A Ride Over the Rocky Mountains to Oregon and California*. London: Richard Bentley, 1852.

Coker, Caleb, ed. *The News from Brownsville: Helen Chapman's Letters from the Texas Military Frontier, 1848–1852*. Austin: Texas State Historical Association, 1991.

Cooke, Philip St. George. *Scenes and Adventures in the Army, or Romance of Military Life*. Philadelphia: Lindsay and Blakiston, 1857.

Corbusier, William T. *Verde to San Carlos: Recollections of a Famous Army Surgeon and His Observant Family on the Western Frontier, 1869–1886*. Tucson: Dale Stuart King Publisher, 1968.

Coues, Elliott, ed. *The Expeditions of Zebulon Montgomery Pike, to Headwaters of the Mississippi River, through Louisiana Territory, and in New Spain, during the Years 1805–6–7*. 2 vols. Minneapolis: Ross and Haines, Inc., 1965.

Crallé, Richard K., ed. *The Works of John C. Calhoun*. 6 vols. New York: D. Appleton, 1854–57.

Crane, Charles J. *Experiences of a Colonel of Infantry*. New York: Knickerbocker, 1923.

Croffut, W. A., ed. *Fifty Years in Camp and Field: Diary of Major General Ethan Allen Hitchcock, U.S.A.* New York: G. P. Putnam's Sons, 1909.

Custer, Elizabeth B. *Boots and Saddles, or Life in Dakota with General Custer*. New York: Harper and Row, 1885.

————. *Following the Guidon*. New York: Harper and Brothers, 1890.

————. *Tenting on the Plains, or General Custer in Kansas and Texas*. New York: C. L. Webster, 1887.

Custer, George A. *My Life on the Plains*. Ed. Milo Milton Quaife. Chicago: Lakeside Press, 1952.

Davidson, Wilson T. *Years of an Army Doctor: An Autobiography*. San Antonio, Texas: Naylor Co., 1944.

Davis, Britton. *The Truth About Geronimo.* New Haven: Yale University Press, 1929.

Davis, George B. *A Treatise on Military Law.* New York: J. Wiley and Sons, 1898.

De Trobriand, Philippe Régis. *Military Life in Dakota: The Journal of Philippe Régis de Trobriand.* Ed. Lucile M. Kane. Saint Paul: Alvord Memorial Commission, 1951.

Delano, Alonzo. *Life on the Plains and Among the Diggings.* Auburn and Buffalo, New York: Miller, Orton and Mulligan, 1854.

DeWitt, Ward G., and Florence Stark DeWitt. *Prairie Schooner Lady: The Journal of Harriet Sherrill Ward, 1853.* Los Angeles: Westernlore Press, 1959.

Dickson, Arthur Jerome, ed. *Covered Wagon Days: From the Private Journals of Albert Jerome Dickson.* Cleveland: Arthur H. Clark, 1929.

Dillon, Richard H., ed. *A Cannoneer in Navajo Country: Journal of Private Josiah M. Rice, 1851.* Denver: Old West Publishing Co., 1970.

Doyle, Susan Badger, and Donald E. Buck, eds. *The 1849 California Trail Diaries of Elijah Preston Howell.* Independence, Mo.: Oregon-California Trails Association, 1995.

Dyer, Mrs. D. B. *"Fort Reno," or Picturesque "Cheyenne and Arrapahoe Army Life" before the Opening of "Oklahoma."* New York: G. W. Dillingham, 1896.

Eastman, Charles A. *From the Deep Woods to Civilization: Chapters in the Autobiography of an Indian.* Boston: Little, Brown and Co., 1936.

Eastman, Mary Henderson. *The American Aboriginal Portfolio.* Philadelphia: Lippincott, Grambo Co., 1853.

————. *Dahcotah, or Life and Legends of the Sioux around Fort Snelling.* New York: Wiley, 1849.

Elder, Jane Lenz, and David J. Weber, eds. *Trading in Santa Fe: John M. Kingsbury's Correspondence with James Josiah Webb, 1853–1861.* Dallas: Southern Methodist University/De Golyer Library, 1996.

Farmer, James E. *My Life with the Army in the West.* Ed. Dale F. Giese. Santa Fe, N.M.: Stagecoach Press, 1967.

Finerty, John F. *War-Path and Bivouac, or the Conquest of the Sioux: A Narrative of Stirring Personal Experiences and Adventures in the Big Horn and Yellowstone Expedition of 1876, and in the Campaign on the British Border in 1879.* Norman: University of Oklahoma Press, 1961.

FitzGerald, Emily McCorkle. *An Army Doctor's Wife on the Frontier: Letters from Alaska and the Far West, 1874–1878.* Ed. Abe Laufe. Pittsburgh: University of Pittsburgh Press, 1962.

Flores, Dan L., ed. *Jefferson and Southwestern Exploration: The Freeman and Custis Accounts of the Red River Expedition of 1806.* Norman: University of Oklahoma Press, 1984.

Foreman, Grant. *Marcy and the Gold Seekers: The Journal of Captain R. B. Marcy, with an Account of the Gold Rush Over the Southern Route.* Norman: University of Oklahoma Press, 1939.

————, ed. *A Pathfinder in the Southwest: The Itinerary of Lieutenant A. W. Whipple during His Explorations for a Railway Route from Fort Smith to Los Angeles in the Years 1853–1854.* Norman: University of Oklahoma Press, 1941.

Forsyth, George A. *The Story of the Soldier.* New York: D. Appleton and Co., 1900.

————. *Thrilling Days in Army Life.* New York: Harper and Brothers, 1902.

Fougera, Katherine Gibson. *With Custer's Cavalry.* Caldwell, Idaho: Caxton Printers, 1940.

Gilliss, Julia. *So Far from Home: An Army Bride on the Western Frontier, 1865–1869.* Ed. Priscilla Knuth. Portland: Oregon Historical Society, 1993.

Glisan, Rodney. *Journal of Army Life.* San Francisco: A. L. Bancroft and Co., 1874.

Gold Rush, The: Letters from the Wolverine Rangers to the Marshall, Michigan Statesman, 1849–1851. Mount Pleasant, Mich.: Cumming Press, 1974.

Gordon, Mary McDougall, ed. *Through Indian Country to California: John P. Sherburne's Diary of the Whipple Expedition, 1853–1854.* Stanford: Stanford University Press, 1988.

Greely, Adolphus W. *Reminiscences of Adventure and Service: A Record of Sixty-five Years.* New York: Charles Scribner's Sons, 1927.

Greene, Duane N. *Ladies and Officers of the United States Army, or American Aristocracy, A Sketch of the Social Life and Character of the Army.* Chicago: Central Publishing Co., 1880.

Hagemann, E. R., ed. *Fighting Rebels and Redskins: Experiences in the Army Life of Colonel George B. Sanford, 1861–1892.* Norman: University of Oklahoma Press, 1969.

Hale, John. *California As It Is: Description of a Tour by the Overland Route and South Pass of the Rocky Mountains.* Rochester, N.Y.: W. Heughes, 1851.

Harris, Theodore, ed. *Negro Frontiersman: The Western Memoirs of Henry O. Flipper.* El Paso: Texas Western College Press, 1963.

Hazen, William B. *Some Corrections on "My Life on the Plains."* Saint Paul, Minn.: n.p., 1875.

Hine, Robert V., and Savoie Lottinville, eds. *Soldier in the West: Letters of Theodore Talbot during His Services in California, Mexico, and Oregon, 1845–53.* Norman: University of Oklahoma Press, 1972.

Hopkins, Sarah Winnemucca. *Life among the Piutes: Their Wrongs and Claims.* Ed. Mrs. Horace Mann. New York: G. P. Putnam's Sons, 1883.

Howard, Oliver Otis. *My Life and Experiences among Our Hostile Indians.* Hartford, Conn.: Worthington, 1907.

Hunt, Frazier, and Robert Hunt. *I Fought with Custer: The Story of Sergeant Windolph, Last Survivor of the Battle of the Little Big Horn.* New York: Scribner, 1954.

Ingalls, Eleazar Stillman. *Journal of a Trip to California by the Overland Route Across the Plains in 1850–51.* Fairfield, Wash.: Ye Galleon Press, 1979.

Johnson, Hervey. *Tending the Talking Wire: A Buck Soldier's View of Indian Country, 1863–1866.* Ed. William E. Unrau. Salt Lake City: University of Utah Press, 1979.

Keim, De B. Randolph. *Sheridan's Troopers on the Border, a Winter Campaign on the Plains.* Philadelphia: Claxton, Remsen and Haffelfinger, 1870.

Kelley, William Fitch. *Pine Ridge 1890: An Eye Witness Account of the Events Surrounding the Fighting at Wounded Knee.* Ed. Alexander Kelley and Pierre Bovis. San Francisco: Pierre Bovis, 1971.

Kennedy, W. J. D. *On the Plains with Custer and Hancock: The Journal of Isaac Coates, Army Surgeon.* Boulder, Colo.: Johnson Books, 1996.

Kimball, Maria Brace. *A Soldier-Doctor of Our Army: James P. Kimball, Late Colonel and Assistant Surgeon-General, U.S. Army.* Boston: Houghton Mifflin Co., 1917.

Kime, Wayne R., ed. *The Black Hills Journals of Colonel Richard Irving Dodge.* Norman: University of Oklahoma Press, 1996.

King, Charles. *Campaigning with Crook: The Fifth Cavalry in the Sioux War of 1876.* Milwaukee, Wis.: Sentinel Co., 1880.

Krause, Herbert, and Gary D. Olson. *Prelude to Glory: A Newspaper Accounting of Custer's 1874 Expedition to the Black Hills.* Sioux Falls, S.Dak.: Brevet Press, 1974.

Lafler, Henry A. *How the Army Worked to Save San Francisco.* San Francisco: Calkins Newspaper Syndicate, 1906.

La Guardia, Fiorello H. *The Making of an Insurgent: An Autobiography, 1882–1919.* Philadelphia: J. B. Lippincott Co., 1948.

Lane, Lydia Spencer. *I Married a Soldier, or Old Days in the Army.* Philadelphia: J. B. Lippincott and Co., 1910.

Langley, Harold D., ed. *To Utah with the Dragoons and Glimpses of Life in Arizona and California, 1858–1859.* Salt Lake City: University of Utah Press, 1974.

Larson, James. *Sergeant Larson, 4th Cavalry.* San Antonio: Southern Literary Institute, 1925.

Leckie, Shirley A., ed. *The Colonel's Lady on the Western Frontier: The Correspondence of Alice Kirk Grierson.* Lincoln: University of Nebraska Press, 1989.

Leefe, Laurence. *Daughter of the Regiment: Memoirs of a Childhood in the Frontier Army, 1878–1898.* Ed. Thomas T. Smith. Lincoln: University of Nebraska Press, 1996.

Lesley, Lewis Burt, ed. *Uncle Sam's Camels: The Journal of May Humphreys Stacey, Supplemented by the Report of Edward Fitzgerald Beale (1857–1858).* Glorietta, N.M.: Rio Grande Press, Inc., 1929.

McCall, George A. *Letters from the Frontiers: Written during a Period of Thirty Years' Service in the Army of the United States.* Philadelphia: n.p., 1968.

———. *New Mexico in 1850: A Military View.* Ed. Robert W. Frazer. Norman: University of Oklahoma Press, 1968.

McChristian, Douglas C., ed. *Garrison Tangles in the Friendless Tenth: The Journal of First Lieutenant John Bigelow, Jr., Fort Davis, Texas.* Bryan, Texas: J. M. Carroll and Co., 1984.

McConnell, H. H. *Five Years a Cavalryman, or Sketches of Regular Army Life on the Texas Frontier, 1866–1871.* Jacksboro, Texas: J. N. Rogers and Co., 1889.

McGillicuddy, Julia B. *McGillycuddy, Agent.* Palo Alto, Calif.: Stanford University Press, 1941.

McKay, R. H. *Little Pills.* Pittsburgh, Kans.: Pittsburgh Headlight, 1918.

McNitt, Frank, ed. *Navaho Expedition: Journal of a Military Reconnaissance from Santa Fe, New Mexico, to the Navaho Country Made in 1849 by Lieutenant James H. Simpson.* Norman: University of Oklahoma Press, 1964.

Madsen, Brigham D., ed. *Exploring the Great Salt Lake: The Stansbury Expedition of 1849–50.* Salt Lake City: University of Utah Press, 1989.

Mansfield, Joseph K. F. *Mansfield on the Condition of the Western Forts, 1853–54.* Ed. Robert W. Frazer. Norman: University of Oklahoma Press, 1963.

Marcy, Randolph B. *Border Reminiscences.* New York: Harper and Brothers, 1872.

———. *Thirty Years of Army Life on the Border.* New York: Harper and Brothers, 1866.

Marshall, J. T. *The Miles Expedition of 1874–1875: An Eyewitness Account of the Red River War.* Ed. Lonnie J. White. Austin: Encino Press, 1971.

Mattes, Merrill J. *Indians, Infants and Infantry: Andrew and Elizabeth Burt on the Frontier.* Denver: Old West Publishing Co., 1960.

Matthews, Washington. *Navaho Legends Collected and Translated by Washington Matthews, M.D., LL.D., Major U.S. Army, Ex-President of the American Folk-Lore Society,* vol. 5, *Memoirs of the American Folk-Lore Society.* Boston: Houghton, Mifflin and Co., 1897.

Merington, Marguerite, ed. *The Custer Story: The Life and Intimate Letters of General George A. Custer and His Wife Elizabeth.* New York: Devin-Adair, 1950.

Meyers, Augustus. *Ten Years in the Ranks, U.S. Army.* New York: Stirling Press, 1914.

Miles, Nelson A. *Personal Recollections and Observations of General Nelson A. Miles.* Chicago: Werner Co., 1896.

———. *Serving the Republic: Memoirs of the Civil and Military Life of Nelson A. Miles.* New York: Harper and Brothers, 1911.

Mills, Anson. *My Story.* Ed. C. H. Claudy, 2d ed. Washington, D.C.: Press of Byron S. Adams, 1921.

Mollhausen, H. B. *Diary of a Journey from the Mississippi to the Coasts of the Pacific, with a United States Government Expedition.* 2 vols. London: n.p., 1858.

Mulford, Ami Frank. *Fighting Indians in the 7th United States Cavalry.* Corning, New York: Paul Lindsley Mulford, 1879.

Myres, Sandra L., ed. *Cavalry Wife: The Diary of Eveline M. Alexander, 1866–1867.* College Station: Texas A&M University Press, 1977.

Nelson, Oliver. *The Cowman's Southwest.* Ed. Angie Debo. Glendale, Calif.: Arthur H. Clark Co., 1953.

Nichols, Roger L., ed. *The Missouri Expedition, 1818–1820: The Journal of Surgeon John Gale.* Norman: University of Oklahoma Press, 1969.

Parker, James. *The Old Army: Memories, 1872–1918.* Philadelphia: Dorrance and Co., 1929.

Paulding, Holmes Offley. *Surgeon's Diary with the Custer Relief Column.* Ed. W. Boyes. Washington, D.C.: WJBM Associates, 1974.

Perkins, Elisha Douglass. *Gold Rush Diary: Perkins on the Overland Trail in the Spring and Summer of 1849.* Ed. Thomas D. Clark. Lexington: University of Kentucky Press, 1967.

Pingenot, Ben E., ed. *Paso del Aguila: A Chronicle of Frontier Days on the Texas Border as Recorded in the Memoirs of Jesse Sumpter.* Austin: Encino Press, 1969.

Poole, D. C. *Among the Sioux of Dakota: Eighteen Months' Experience as an Indian Agent, 1869–70.* Intro. by Raymond J. DeMallie. Saint Paul: Minnesota Historical Society Press, 1988.

Powers, Mary Rockwood. *A Woman's Overland Journal to California.* Ed. W. B. Thorsen. Fairfield, Wash.: Ye Galleon Press, 1985.

Pratt, Richard Henry. *Battlefield and Classroom: Four Decades with the American Indian, 1867–1904.* Ed. Robert M. Utley. New Haven: Yale University Press, 1964.

Price, George F. *Across the Continent with the Fifth Cavalry.* New York: Van Nostrand, 1883.

Prucha, Francis Paul, ed. *Army Life on the Western Frontier: Selections from the Official Reports Made between 1826 and 1845 by Colonel George Croghan.* Norman: University of Oklahoma Press, 1958.

Roe, Frances M. A. *Army Letters from an Officer's Wife, 1871–1888.* New York: D. Appleton, 1909.

Royce, Sarah. *A Frontier Lady: Recollections of the Gold Rush and Early California.* Ed. Ralph Henry Gabriel. New Haven: Yale University Press, 1932.

Sargent, Alice Applegate. *Following the Flag: Diary of a Soldier's Wife.* Kansas City: E. B. Barnett, 1919; 2d ed., 1928.

Scamehorn, Howard L., ed. *The Buckeye Rovers in the Gold Rush.* Athens: Ohio University Press, 1965.

Schmitt, Martin, ed. *General George Crook: His Autobiography.* Norman: University of Oklahoma Press, 1960.

Schofield, John M. *Forty-Six Years in the Army.* New York: Century Co., 1897.

Scott, Hugh L. *Some Memories of a Soldier.* New York: Century Co., 1928.

Settle, Raymond W., ed. *The March of the Mounted Riflemen: First United States Military Expedition to Travel the Full Length of the Oregon Trail from Fort Leavenworth to Fort Vancouver, May to October 1849, as Recorded in the Journals of Major Osborne Cross and George Gibbs and the Official Report of Colonel Loring.* Glendale, Calif.: Arthur H. Clark Co., 1940.

Shaw, D. A. *Eldorado, or California As Seen By a Pioneer, 1850–1900.* Los Angeles: B. R. Baumgardt and Co., 1900.

Sheridan, Philip H. *Personal Memoirs of P. H. Sheridan.* 2 vols. New York: Charles L. Webster, 1888.

Sherman, William Tecumseh. *Memoirs of General William T. Sherman.* 2 vols. 2d ed. revised. New York: D. Appleton and Co., 1904.

Simonin, Louis L. *The Rocky Mountain West in 1867.* Trans. and ed. Wilson O. Clough. Lincoln: University of Nebraska Press, 1966.

Slaughter, Linda W. *From Fortress to Farm, or Twenty-three Years on the Frontier.* Intro. by Hazel Eastman. New York: Exposition Press, 1972.

Smith, C. W. *Journal of a Trip to California: Across the Continent from Weston, Missouri, to Weber Creek, California, in the Summer of 1850.* Ed. R. W. G. Vail. Fairfield, Wash.: Ye Galleon Press, 1974.

Smith, Sherry L., ed. *Sagebrush Soldier: Private William Earl Smith's View of the Sioux War of 1876.* Norman: University of Oklahoma Press, 1989.

Smith, Thomas T., ed. *A Dose of Frontier Soldiering: The Memoirs of Corporal E. A. Bode, Frontier Regular Infantry, 1877–1882.* Lincoln: University of Nebraska Press, 1994.

Spence, Mary Lee, ed. *The Expeditions of John Charles Frémont,* vol. 3, *Travels from 1848 to 1854.* Urbana: University of Illinois Press, 1984.

Spotts, David L. *Campaigning with Custer and the Nineteenth Kansas Volunteer Cavalry on the Washita Campaign, 1868–69.* Ed. E. A. Brininstool. Los Angeles: Wetzel Publishing Co., 1928.

Springer, Charles H. *Soldiering in the Sioux Country, 1865.* Ed. Benjamin F. Cooling III. San Diego: Frontier Heritage Press, 1971.

Stanley, Henry M. *My Early Travels and Adventures in America and Asia.* Vol. 1. London: S. Low, Marston, 1895.

Stansbury, Howard. *An Expedition to the Valley of the Great Salt Lake of Utah.* Philadelphia: Lippincott, Grambo and Co., 1852.

Steele, James W. *Frontier Army Sketches.* Albuquerque: University of New Mexico Press, 1969.

Steward, Theophilus G., ed. *Active Service, or Religious Work among United States Soldiers.* New York: United States Army Aid Association, 189[?].

———, ed. *From 1864 to 1914: Fifty Years in the Gospel Ministry.* Philadelphia: A.M.E. Book Concern, 1921.

Stillman, J. D. B. *Wanderings in the Southwest in 1855.* Ed. Ron Tyler. Spokane: Arthur H. Clark, 1990.

Summerhayes, Martha. *Vanished Arizona: Recollections of the Army Life of a New England Woman.* 2d ed. Salem, Mass.: Salem Press, 1911.

Thomson, Origen. *Crossing the Plains: Narrative of the Scenes, Incidents and Adventures Attending the Overland Journey of the Decatur and Rush County Emigrants to the "Far Off" Oregon, in 1852.* Fairfield, Wash.: Ye Galleon Press, 1983.

Thrapp, Dan L., ed. *Dateline Fort Bowie: Charles Fletcher Lummis Reports on an Apache War.* Norman: University of Oklahoma Press, 1979.

Tibbles, Thomas Henry. *The Ponca Chiefs: An Account of the Trial of Standing Bear.* Ed. Kay Graber. Lincoln: University of Nebraska Press, 1972.

Tomer, John S., and Michael J. Brodhead, eds. *A Naturalist in Indian Territory: The Journals of S. W. Woodhouse, 1849–50.* Norman: University of Oklahoma Press, 1992.

Utley, Robert M. ed. *Life in Custer's Cavalry: Diaries and Letters of Albert and Jennie Barnitz, 1867–1868.* New Haven: Yale University Press, 1977.

Vielé, Teresa Griffin. *Following the Drum: A Glimpse of Frontier Life.* New York: Rudd and Carleton, 1858.

Ware, Eugene F. *The Indian War of 1864.* Topeka: Crane and Co., 1911.

Wheeler, Homer W. *Buffalo Days, Forty Years in the Old West: The Personal Narrative of a Cattleman, Indian Fighter, and Army Officer.* Indianapolis: Bobbs-Merrill Co., 1925.

Will, George Francis. *Army Life in Dakota.* Trans. Milo M. Quaife. Chicago: R. R. Donnelley and Sons., Inc., 1941.

Yost, Nellie Snyder, ed. *Boss Cowman: The Recollections of Ed Lemmon, 1857–1946.* Lincoln: University of Nebraska Press, 1969.

SECONDARY BOOKS AND PAMPHLETS

Abbe, Truman. *Professor Abbe and the Isobars: The Story of Cleveland Abbe, America's First Weatherman.* New York: Vantage Press, 1955.

Adamic, Louis. *Dynamite: The Story of Class Violence in America.* New York: Harper and Row, 1931.

Adams, Gerald M. *The Post Near Cheyenne: A History of Fort D. A. Russell, 1867–1930.* Boulder, Colo.: Pruett Publishing Co., 1989.

Agnew, Brad. *Fort Gibson: Terminal on the Trail of Tears.* Norman: University of Oklahoma Press, 1980.

Alberts, Don E. *Brandy Station to Manila Bay: A Biography of General Wesley Merritt.* Austin: Presidial Press, 1980.

Albright, George L. *Official Explorations for Pacific Railroads.* Berkeley: University of California Press, 1921.

Alexander, Charles. *Battles and Victories of Allen Allensworth.* Boston: Sherman French and Co., 1914.

Altshuler, Constance Wynn. *Cavalry Yellow and Infantry Blue: Army Officers in Arizona between 1851 and 1886.* Tucson: Arizona Historical Society, 1991.

Amchan, Arthur J. *The Most Famous Soldier in America: A Biography of Lt. Gen. Nelson A. Miles, 1839–1925.* Alexandria, Va.: Amchan Publications, 1989.

Ashburn, Percy M. *A History of the Medical Department of the United States Army.* Boston: Houghton Mifflin Co., 1929.

Athearn, Robert G. *Forts of the Upper Missouri.* Englewood Cliffs, N.J.: Prentice-Hall, 1967.

————. *Union Pacific Country*. Chicago: Rand McNally Co., 1971.

————. *William Tecumseh Sherman and the Settlement of the West*. Norman: University of Oklahoma Press, 1956.

Atkins, Annette. *Harvest of Grief: Grasshopper Plagues and Public Assistance in Minnesota, 1873–78*. Saint Paul: Minnesota Historical Society Press, 1984.

Austerman, Wayne R. *Sharps Rifles and Spanish Mules: The San Antonio–El Paso Mail, 1851–1881*. College Station: Texas A&M University Press, 1985.

Bailey, John W. *Pacifying the Plains: General Alfred Terry and the Decline of the Sioux, 1866–1890*. Westport, Conn.: Greenwood Press, 1979.

Baker, Robert Orr. *The Muster Roll: A Biography of Fort Ripley, Minnesota*. Saint Paul, Minn.: H. M. Smyth Co., 1972.

Ball, Larry D. *The United States Marshals of New Mexico and Arizona Territories, 1846–1912*. Albuquerque: University of New Mexico Press, 1978.

Barry, Louise. *The Beginning of the West: Annals of the Kansas Gateway to the American West, 1540–1854*. Topeka: Kansas State Historical Society, 1972.

Bartlett, Richard A. *Great Surveys of the American West*. Norman: University of Oklahoma Press, 1962.

————. *Nature's Yellowstone: The Story of an American Wilderness That Became Yellowstone National Park in 1872*. Albuquerque: University of New Mexico Press, 1974.

————. *Yellowstone: A Wilderness Besieged*. Tucson: University of Arizona Press, 1985.

Bates, Charles C., and John F. Fuller. *America's Weather Warriors, 1814–1985*. College Station: Texas A&M University Press, 1986.

Bearss, Edwin C., and Arrell M. Gibson, *Fort Smith: Little Gibraltar on the Arkansas*. Norman: University of Oklahoma Press, 1969.

Bender, Averam B. *The March of Empire: Frontier Defense in the Southwest, 1848–1860*. Lawrence: University Press of Kansas, 1952.

Bender, Norman J. *"New Hope for the Indians": The Grant Peace Policy and the Navajos in the 1870s*. Albuquerque: University of New Mexico Press, 1989.

Berman, Edward. *Labor Disputes and the President of the United States*. New York: Columbia University Press, 1924.

Berthrong, Donald J. *The Cheyenne and Arapaho Ordeal: Reservation and Agency Life in the Indian Territory, 1875–1907*. Norman: University of Oklahoma Press, 1976.

Bieber, Ralph P. *Southern Trails to California in 1849*. Glendale, Calif.: Arthur H. Clark Co., 1939.

Bieder, Robert E. *Science Encounters the Indian, 1820–1880: The Early Years of American Ethnology*. Norman: University of Oklahoma Press, 1986.

Bierschwale, Margaret. *Fort McKavett, Texas: Post on the San Saba*. Salado, Texas: Anson Jones Press, 1966.

Bigelow, Donald N. *William Conant Church and the Army and Navy Journal*. New York: Columbia University Press, 1952.

Billington, Monroe. *New Mexico's Buffalo Soldiers, 1866–1900.* Niwot, Colo.: University Press of Colorado, 1991.

Billington, Ray Allen. *The Far Western Frontier, 1830–1860.* New York: Harper and Row, 1956.

Birkhimer, William E. *Military Government and Martial Law.* Kansas City: Franklin Hudson Publishing Co., 1914.

Blackman, John L., Jr. *Presidential Seizures in Labor Disputes.* Cambridge: Harvard University Press, 1967.

Blocker, Jack S., Jr. *American Temperance Movements: Cycles of Reform.* Boston: Twayne Publishing, 1989.

Boehme, Sarah E.; Christian Feest; and Patricia Condon Johnston. *Seth Eastman: A Portfolio of North American Indians.* Afton, Minn.: Afton Historical Society Press, 1995.

Bonney, Orrin H., and Lorraine Bonney. *Battle Drums and Geysers: The Life and Journals of Lt. Gustavus Cheyney Doane, Soldier and Explorer of the Yellowstone and Snake River Regions.* Chicago: Swallow Press, 1970.

Brandes, Ray. *Frontier Military Posts of Arizona.* Globe, Ariz.: Dale Stuart King, Publishers, 1960.

Brecher, Jeremy. *Strike!* San Francisco: Straight Arrow Books, 1972.

Brimlow, George F. *Cavalryman Out of the West: Life of General William Carey Brown.* Caldwell, Idaho: Caxton Printers, 1944.

Brodhead, Michael L. *A Soldier-Scientist in the American Southwest: Being a Narrative of the Travels of Elliot Coues.* Tucson: Arizona Historical Society, 1973.

Brown, Dee. *The Galvanized Yankees.* Urbana: University of Illinois Press, 1963.

Bruce, Robert V. *1877: Year of Violence.* Indianapolis: Bobbs-Merrill, 1959.

Burdick, Usher L. *The Army Life of Charles "Chip" Creighton.* Paris, Md.: National Reform Associates Printers and Publishers, 1937.

Burton, William L. *Melting Pot Soldiers: The Union's Ethnic Regiments.* Ames: Iowa State University Press, 1988.

Butcher, Solomon D. *Pioneer History of Custer County.* Broken Bow, Nebr.: n.p., 1901.

Cage, James C., comp. *Fort Quitman.* McNary, Texas: n.p., 1972.

Cagle, Eldon, Jr. *Quadrangle: The History of Fort Sam Houston.* Austin: Eakin Press, 1985.

Calhoun, Frederick S. *The Lawmen: United States Marshals and Their Deputies, 1789–1989.* Washington, D.C.: Smithsonian Institution Press, 1990.

Carley, Kenneth. *The Sioux Uprising of 1862.* Saint Paul: Minnesota Historical Society, 1976.

Carlson, Paul H. *"Pecos Bill": A Military Biography of William R. Shafter.* College Station: Texas A&M University Press, 1989.

Carriker, Robert C. *Fort Supply, Indian Territory: Frontier Outpost on the Plains.* Norman: University of Oklahoma Press, 1970.

Carter, William Harding. *The Life of Lieutenant General Chaffee.* Chicago: University of Chicago Press, 1917.

Chalfant, William Y. *Dangerous Passage: The Santa Fe Trail and the Mexican War.* Norman: University of Oklahoma Press, 1994.

Chandler, Melbourne C. *Of Garry Owen in Glory: The History of the Seventh United States Cavalry Regiment.* Annandale, Va.: Turnpike Press, 1960.

Christian, Garna L. *Black Soldiers in Jim Crow Texas, 1899–1917.* College Station: Texas A&M University Press, 1995.

Clarke, Dwight L. *William Tecumseh Sherman: Gold Rush Banker.* San Francisco: California Historical Society, 1969.

Clendenen, Clarence C. *Blood on the Border: The United States Army and the Mexican Irregulars.* New York: MacMillan Co., 1969.

Coffman, Edward M. *The Old Army: A Portrait of the American Army in Peacetime, 1784–1898.* New York: Oxford University Press, 1986.

Colton, Ray C. *The Civil War in the Western Territories: Arizona, Colorado, New Mexico, and Utah.* Norman: University of Oklahoma Press, 1959.

Conkling, Roscoe P., and Margaret B. Conkling. *The Butterfield Overland Mail, 1857–1869.* 3 vols. Glendale, Calif.: Arthur H. Clark Co., 1947.

Conover, G. W. *Sixty Years in Southwest Oklahoma.* Anadarko, Okla.: N. T. Plummer, 1927.

Cooper, Jerry M. *The Army and Civil Disorder: Federal Military Intervention in Labor Disputes, 1877–1900.* Westport, Conn.: Greenwood Press, 1980.

Corning, Leavitt, Jr. *Baronial Forts of the Big Bend: Ben Leaton, Milton Faver and Their Private Forts in Presidio County.* San Antonio: Trinity University Press, 1969.

Cox-Paul, Lori A., and James W. Wengert, comps. *A Frontier Army Christmas.* Lincoln: Nebraska State Historical Society, 1996.

Coy, Owen Cochran. *The Great Trek of Dr. E. A. Tompkins.* Los Angeles: Powell Publishing Co., 1931.

Croy, Homer. *Trigger Marshal: The Story of Chris Madsen.* New York: Duell, Sloan and Pearce, 1958.

Cusack, Michael F. *Fort Clark: The Lonely Sentinel.* Austin: Eakin Press, 1985.

Cutright, Paul Russell. *Lewis and Clark: Pioneering Naturalists.* Urbana: University of Illinois Press, 1969.

Dale, Edward Everett. *The Range Cattle Industry: Ranching on the Great Plains from 1865 to 1925.* Norman: University of Oklahoma Press, 1960.

Daniels, Roger. *Asian America: Chinese and Japanese in the United States since 1850.* Seattle: University of Washington Press, 1988.

Davidson, Homer K. *Black Jack Davidson: A Cavalry Commander on the Western Frontier.* Glendale, Calif.: Arthur H. Clark Co., 1974.

Dearen, Patrick. *Crossing Rio Pecos.* Fort Worth: Texas Christian University Press, 1996.

Delo, David Michael. *Peddlers and Post Traders: The Army Sutler on the Frontier*. Salt Lake City: University of Utah Press, 1992.

Dick, Everett. *Conquering the Great American Desert*. Nebraska State Historical Society Publications, Vol. 27. Lincoln: Nebraska State Historical Society, 1975.

———. *The Sod-House Frontier, 1854–1890: A Social History of the Northern Plains from the Creation of Kansas and Nebraska to the Admission of the Dakotas*. New York: Appleton-Century Co., 1954.

———. *Vanguards of the Frontier: A Social History of the Northern Plains and Rocky Mountains from the Earliest White Contacts to the Coming of the Homemaker*. New York: D. Appleton-Century Co., 1941.

Diffendal, Anne P., comp. *A Guide to the Newspaper Collection of the State Archives Nebraska State Historical Society*. Lincoln: Nebraska State Historical Society, 1977.

Dixon, David. *Hero of Beecher Island: The Life and Military Career of George A. Forsyth*. Lincoln: University of Nebraska Press, 1994.

Dodds, Gordon B. *Hiram Martin Chittenden: His Public Career*. Lexington: University Press of Kentucky, 1973.

Donald, David H. *Liberty and Union*. Lexington, Mass.: D. C. Heath and Co., 1978.

Dowell, Cassius. *Military Aid to the Civil Power*. Fort Leavenworth, Kans.: General Service Schools, 1925.

Downey, Fairfax, and J. N. Jacobsen, Jr. *The Red-Bluecoats: The Indian Scouts*. Fort Collins, Colo.: Old Army Press, 1973.

Dunlay, Thomas W. *Wolves for the Blue Soldiers: Indian Scouts and Auxiliaries with the United States Army, 1860–1890*. Lincoln: University of Nebraska Press, 1982.

Dupree, A. Hunter. *Science in the Federal Government: A History of Policies and Activities to 1940*. New York: Harper and Row, 1964.

Eales, Anne Bruner. *Army Wives on the American Frontier: Living within the Sound of Bugles*. Boulder, Colo.: Johnson Books, 1996.

Eggert, Gerald G. *Railroad Labor Disputes: The Beginnings of Federal Strike Policy*. Ann Arbor: University of Michigan Press, 1967.

Ellison, R. S. *Fort Bridger: A Brief History*. Cheyenne: Wyoming State Archives, Museums and Historical Department, 1981.

Emmett, Chris. *Fort Union and the Winning of the Southwest*. Norman: University of Oklahoma Press, 1965.

Faulk, Odie B. *The U.S. Camel Corps: An Army Experiment*. New York: Oxford University Press, 1976.

Fletcher, Marvin E. *The Black Soldier and Officer in the United States Army, 1891–1917*. Columbia: University of Missouri Press, 1974.

Foner, Jack D. *Blacks and the Military in American History: A New Perspective*. New York: Praeger Publishers, 1974.

———. *The United States Soldier between Two Wars: Army Life and Reforms, 1865–1898*. New York: Humanities Press, 1970.

Foote, Cheryl J. *Women of the New Mexico Frontier, 1846–1912*. Niwot, Colo.: University Press of Colorado, 1990.

Foreman, Grant. *Indian Removal: The Emigration of the Five Civilized Tribes of Indians*. Norman: University of Oklahoma Press, 1932.

Fowler, Arlen L. *The Black Infantry in the West, 1869–1891*. Westport, Conn.: Greenwood Publishing Co., 1971.

Frazer, Robert W. *Forts and Supplies: The Role of the Army in the Economy of the Southwest, 1846–1861*. Albuquerque: University of New Mexico Press, 1983.

———. *Forts of the West*. Norman: University of Oklahoma Press, 1965.

Frink, Maurice, and Casey Barthelmess. *Photographer on an Army Mule*. Norman: University of Oklahoma Press, 1965.

Frost, Lawrence A. *General Custer's Libbie*. Seattle: Superior Publishing Co., 1976.

Fulton, Maurice G. *History of the Lincoln County War*. Ed. Robert N. Mullin. Tucson: University of Arizona Press, 1968.

Furniss, Norman F. *The Mormon Conflict, 1850–1859*. New Haven: Yale University Press, 1960.

Gard, Wayne. *Frontier Justice*. Norman: University of Oklahoma Press, 1949.

Georgi-Findlay, Brigitte. *The Frontiers of Women's Writing: Women's Narratives and the Rhetoric of Westward Expansion*. Tucson: University of Arizona Press, 1996.

Germain, Aidan Henry. *Catholic Military and Naval Chaplains, 1776–1917*. Washington, D.C.: Catholic University, 1929.

Getlein, Frank. *The Lure of the Great West*. Waukesha, Wis.: Country Beautiful Corporation, 1973.

Gibson, Arrell Morgan, and John S. Whitehead. *Yankees in Paradise: The Pacific Basin Frontier*. Albuquerque: University of New Mexico Press, 1993.

Gibson, John M. *Soldier in White: The Life of General George Miller Sternberg*. Durham: Duke University Press, 1958.

Glass, E. L. N., comp. *The History of the Tenth Cavalry, 1866–1921*. N.p.: n.p., 1921.

Glasson, William H. *Federal Military Pensions in the United States*. New York: Oxford University Press, 1918.

Glick, Edward Bernard. *Peaceful Conflict: The Non-Military Use of the Military*. Harrisburg, Pa.: Stackpole Books, 1967.

Goetzmann, William H. *Army Exploration in the American West, 1803–1863*. New Haven: Yale University Press, 1959.

———. *Exploration and Empire: The Explorer and the Scientist in the Winning of the American West*. New York: Alfred A. Knopf, 1971.

Goodman, George J., and Cheryl A. Lawson. *Retracing Major Stephen Long's 1820 Expedition: The Itinerary and Botany*. Norman: University of Oklahoma Press, 1995.

Green, Bill. *The Dancing Was Lively: Fort Concho Texas, a Social History, 1867 to 1882*. San Angelo, Texas: Fort Concho Sketches Publishing Co., 1974.

Greene, A. C. *900 Miles on the Butterfield Trail.* Denton: University of North Texas Press, 1994.

Greene, Jerome A. *Slim Buttes, 1876: An Episode of the Great Sioux War.* Norman: University of Oklahoma Press, 1982.

Gressley, Gene M., ed. *Old West/New West: Quo Vadis?* Worland, Wyo.: High Plains Publishing Co., 1994.

Grinnell, George B. *Two Great Scouts and Their Pawnee Battalion.* Cleveland: Arthur H. Clark Co., 1928.

Grinstead, Marion C. *The Life and Death of a Frontier Fort: Fort Craig, New Mexico, 1854–1885.* Socorro, N.Mex.: Socorro County Historical Society, 1973.

Hafen, LeRoy R. *The Overland Mail, 1849–1869: Promoter of Settlement, Precursor of Railroads.* Cleveland: Arthur H. Clark Co., 1926.

————, and Francis Marion Young. *Fort Laramie and the Pageant of the West, 1834–1890.* Glendale, Calif.: Arthur H. Clark Co., 1938.

————; W. Eugene Hollon; and Carl Coke Rister. *Western America: The Exploration, Settlement, and Development of the Region Beyond the Mississippi.* 3d ed. Englewood Cliffs, N.J.: Prentice-Hall, Inc., 1970.

Hagan, William T. *Quanah Parker, Comanche Chief.* Norman: University of Oklahoma Press, 1993.

————. *United States–Comanche Relations: The Reservation Years.* Norman: University of Oklahoma Press, 1976.

Hagedorn, Herman. *Leonard Wood: A Biography.* 2 vols. New York: Harper and Brothers, 1931.

Haines, Aubrey L. *The Yellowstone Story: A History of Our First National Park.* 2 vols. Yellowstone National Park, Wyo.: Yellowstone Library and Museum Association, 1977.

Haites, Erik F.; James Mak; and Gary Walton. *Western River Transportation: The Era of Early Internal Development, 1810–1860.* Baltimore: Johns Hopkins University Press, 1975.

Haley, J. Evetts. *Charles Goodnight, Cowman and Plainsman.* Boston: Houghton Mifflin Co., 1936.

————. *Fort Concho and the Texas Frontier.* San Angelo, Texas: *San Angelo Standard-Times,* 1952.

Hall, Philip S. *To Have This Land: The Nature of Indian/White Relations, South Dakota, 1888–1891.* Vermillion: University of South Dakota Press, 1991.

Halpern, Katheryn Spencer, and Susan Brown McGreevy, eds. *Washington Matthews: Studies of Navajo Culture, 1880–1894.* Albuquerque: University of New Mexico Press, 1996.

Hamilton, Allen Lee. *Sentinel of the Southern Plains: Fort Richardson and the Northwest Texas Frontier, 1866–1878.* Fort Worth: Texas Christian University Press, 1988.

Hampton, H. Duane. *How the U.S. Cavalry Saved Our National Parks.* Bloomington: Indiana University Press, 1971.

Handy, Mary Olivia. *History of Fort Sam Houston.* San Antonio: Naylor Company, 1951.

Hannon, Jessie Gould. *The Boston-Newton Company Venture: From Massachusetts to California in 1849.* Lincoln: University of Nebraska Press, 1969.

Hanson, James A. *Little Chief's Gatherings: The Smithsonian Institution's G. K. Warren 1855–1856 Plains Indian Collection and the New York State Library's 1855–1857 Warren Expeditions Journal.* Crawford, Nebr.: Fur Press, 1996.

Hanson, Joseph Mills. *The Conquest of the Missouri, Being the Story of the Life and Exploits of Captain Grant Marsh.* New York: Murray Hill, 1946.

Havins, Thomas R. *Camp Colorado: A Decade of Frontier Defense.* Brownwood, Texas: Brown Press, 1964.

Hawke, David Freeman. *Those Tremendous Mountains: The Story of the Lewis and Clark Expedition.* New York: W. W. Norton and Co., 1980.

Hayes, Samuel P. *Conservation and the Gospel of Efficiency: The Progressive Conservation Movement, 1890–1920.* New York: Atheneum, 1969.

Haywood, C. Robert. *Trails South: The Wagon-Road Economy in the Dodge City–Panhandle Region.* Norman: University of Oklahoma Press, 1986.

Hedren, Paul L. *Fort Laramie in 1876: Chronicle of a Frontier Post at War.* Lincoln: University of Nebraska Press, 1988.

———. *With Crook in the Black Hills: Stanley J. Morow's 1876 Photographic Legacy.* Boulder, Colo.: Pruett Publishing Co., 1985.

Heuterman, Thomas H. *Movable Type: Biography of Legh R. Freeman.* Ames: Iowa State University Press, 1979.

Hill, Forest G. *Roads, Rails, and Waterways: The Army Engineers and Early Transportation.* Norman: University of Oklahoma Press, 1957.

Hine, Robert V. *Bartlett's West: Drawing the Mexican Boundary.* New Haven: Yale University Press, 1968.

Hinsley, Curtis M., Jr. *Savages and Scientists: The Smithsonian Institution and the Development of American Anthropology, 1846–1910.* Washington, D.C.: Smithsonian Institution Press, 1981.

Hoig, Stan. *The Oklahoma Land Rush of 1889.* Oklahoma City: Oklahoma Historical Society, 1984.

Hollon, W. Eugene. *Beyond the Cross Timbers: The Travels of Randolph B. Marcy, 1812–1887.* Norman: University of Oklahoma Press, 1955.

Holmes, Louis A. *Fort McPherson, Nebraska, Fort Cottonwood, N.T.: Guardian of the Tracks and Trails.* Lincoln: Johnsen Publishing Co., 1963.

Holt, W. Stull. *The Office of the Chief of Engineers of the Army: Its Non-Military History, Activities, and Organization.* Baltimore: Johns Hopkins University Press, 1923.

Horan, James. *The Life and Art of Charles Schreyvogel: Painter-Historian of the Indian-Fighting Army of the American West.* New York: Crown Publishers, 1969.

Horton, Thomas F. *History of Jack County.* Jacksboro, Texas: Gazette Publishing Co., n.d.

Hume, Edgar Erskine. *Ornithologists of the United States Army Medical Corps.* Baltimore: Johns Hopkins University Press, 1942.

Hunt, Elvid. *History of Fort Leavenworth, 1827–1927.* Fort Leavenworth, Kans.: General Service Schools Press, 1926.

Hunter, Louis C. *Steamboats on Western Rivers.* Cambridge: Harvard University Press, 1949.

Huseman, Ben W. *Wild River, Timeless Canyons: Baldwin Möllhausen's Watercolors of the Colorado.* Tucson: University of Arizona Press for the Amon Carter Museum, 1995.

Hutton, Paul A. *Phil Sheridan and His Army.* Lincoln: University of Nebraska Press, 1985.

———, ed. *Soldiers West: Biographies from the Military Frontier.* Lincoln: University of Nebraska Press, 1987.

Jackson, Donald. *Custer's Gold: The United States Cavalry Expedition of 1874.* New Haven: Yale University Press, 1966.

Jackson, Helen Hunt. *A Century of Dishonor: A Sketch of the United States Government's Dealings with Some of the Indian Tribes.* New York: Harper and Brothers, 1881.

Jackson, W. Turrentine. *Wagon Roads West: A Study of Federal Road Surveys and Construction in the Trans-Mississippi West, 1846–1869.* Berkeley: University of California Press, 1952.

Jensen, Richard E.; R. Eli Paul; and John E. Carter. *Eyewitness at Wounded Knee.* Lincoln: University of Nebraska Press, 1991.

Johnson, Virginia W. *The Unregimented General: A Biography of Nelson Miles.* Boston: Houghton Mifflin Co., 1962.

Johnston, William Preston. *The Life of Gen. Albert Sidney Johnston.* New York: D. Appleton and Co., 1878.

Karolevitz, Robert F. *Newspapering in the Old West: A Pictorial History of Journalism and Printing on the Frontier.* New York: Bonanza Books, 1965.

Kavass, Igor I., and Adolph Sprudzs. *Military Aid to the Civil Power.* Fort Leavenworth, Kans.: General Service Schools Press, 1925.

Keleher, William A. *Violence in Lincoln County, 1869–1881.* Albuquerque: University of New Mexico Press, 1957.

Kelley, Pat. *River of Lost Dreams: Navigation on the Rio Grande.* Lincoln: University of Nebraska Press, 1986.

Kemble, C. Robert. *The Image of the Army Officer in America: Background for Current Views.* Westport, Conn.: Greenwood Press, 1983.

King, James T. *War Eagle: A Life of General Eugene A. Carr.* Lincoln: University of Nebraska Press, 1963.

Knight, Oliver. *Following the Indian Wars: The Story of the Newspaper Correspondents among the Indian Campaigns.* Norman: University of Oklahoma Press, 1960.

———. *Fort Worth: Outpost on the Trinity.* Norman: University of Oklahoma Press, 1953.

————. *Life and Manners in the Frontier Army.* Norman: University of Oklahoma Press, 1978.

Kroeker, Marvin E. *Great Plains Command: William B. Hazen and the Frontier West.* Norman: University of Oklahoma Press, 1976.

Lackey, Vinson. *The Forts of Oklahoma.* Tulsa, Okla.: Tulsa Printing Co., 1963.

Lamar, Howard R. *The Far Southwest 1846–1912: A Territorial History.* New York: W. W. Norton and Co., 1970.

Larsen, Lawrence H., and Barbara J. Cottrell. *The Gate City: A History of Omaha.* Boulder, Colo.: Pruett Publishing Co., 1982.

Larson, Robert W. *New Mexico's Quest for Statehood, 1846–1912.* Albuquerque: University of New Mexico Press, 1968.

Lass, William E. *From the Missouri to the Great Salt Lake: An Account of Overland Freighting.* Lincoln: Nebraska State Historical Society, 1972.

————. *A History of Steamboating on the Upper Missouri River.* Lincoln: University of Nebraska Press, 1962.

Lawson, Merlin P. *The Climate of the Great American Desert: Reconstruction of the Climate of Western Interior United States, 1800–1850.* University of Nebraska Studies, No. 46. Lincoln: University of Nebraska, 1974.

Leckie, William H. *The Buffalo Soldiers: A Narrative of the Negro Cavalry in the West.* Norman: University of Oklahoma Press, 1963.

————, and Shirley A. Leckie. *Unlikely Warriors: General Benjamin H. Grierson and His Family.* Norman: University of Oklahoma Press, 1984.

Ledbetter, Barbara A. Neal. *Fort Belknap Frontier Saga: Indians, Negroes and Anglo-Americans on the Texas Frontier.* Burnet, Texas: Eakin Press, 1982.

Lee, Robert. *Fort Meade and the Black Hills.* Lincoln: University of Nebraska Press, 1991.

————. *Fort Meade: The Peacekeeper Post on the Dakota Frontier, 1878–1944.* Fort Meade, S.Dak.: Old Fort Meade Museum and Historic Research Association, 1987.

Limerick, Patricia Nelson. *The Legacy of Conquest: The Unbroken Past of the American West.* New York: W. W. Norton and Co., 1987.

————; Clyde A. Milner II; and Charles E. Rankin, eds. *Trails: Toward a New Western History.* Lawrence: University Press of Kansas, 1991.

Lindsey, Almont. *The Pullman Strike: The Story of a Unique Experiment and a Great Labor Upheaval.* Chicago: University of Chicago Press, 1942.

McCaffrey, James M. *Army of Manifest Destiny: The American Soldier in the Mexican War, 1846–1848.* New York: New York University Press, 1992.

McDermott, John D. *Dangerous Duty: A History of Frontier Forts in Fremont County, Wyoming.* Lander, Wyo.: Fremont County Historic Preservation Commission, 1993.

McDermott, John Francis. *Seth Eastman: Pictorial Historian of the Indian.* Norman: University of Oklahoma Press, 1961.

————. *Seth Eastman's Mississippi: A Lost Portfolio Recovered.* Urbana: University of Illinois Press, 1973.

McGavin, E. Cecil. *U.S. Soldiers Invade Utah.* Boston: Meador Publishing Co., 1937.

McIntosh, Charles Barron. *The Nebraska Sand Hills: The Human Landscape.* Lincoln: University of Nebraska Press, 1996.

McKelvey, Susan Delano. *Botanical Exploration of the Trans-Mississippi West, 1790–1850.* Jamaica Plain, Mass.: Arnold Arboretum of Harvard University, 1955.

Madden, Henry Miller. *Xántus: Hungarian Naturalist in the Pioneer West.* Palo Alto, Calif.: Books of the West, 1949.

Madsen, Brigham D. *Glory Hunter: A Biography of Patrick Edward Connor.* Salt Lake City: University of Utah Press, 1990.

Malone, Dumas. *Jefferson the President: Second Term 1805–1809.* Boston: Little Brown and Co., 1974.

Malone, Michael, and Richard W. Etulain. *The American West: A Twentieth Century History.* Lincoln: University of Nebraska Press, 1989.

Malsch, Brownson. *Indianola, The Mother of Western Texas.* Austin: Shoal Creek Publishers, 1977.

Manning, Thomas J. *Government in Science: The U.S. Geological Survey, 1867–1894.* Lexington: University Press of Kentucky, 1967.

Markoe, Glenn E.; Raymond J. DeMallie; and Royal B. Hassrick. *Vestiges of a Proud Nation: The Ogden B. Read Northern Plains Indian Collection.* Lincoln: University of Nebraska Press, 1986.

Marshall, Max L., ed. *The Story of the U.S. Army Signal Corps.* New York: Franklin Watts, 1965.

Mattes, Merrill J. *The Great Platte River Road: The Covered Wagon Mainline via Fort Kearny to Fort Laramie.* Publications of the Nebraska State Historical Society, No. 25. Lincoln: Nebraska State Historical Society, 1969.

Miles, Susan. *Fort Concho in 1877.* San Angelo, Texas: Bradley Co., 1972.

Miller, Darlis A. *Captain Jack Crawford: Buckskin Poet, Scout and Showman.* Albuquerque: University of New Mexico Press, 1993.

————. *Soldiers and Settlers: Military Supply in the Southwest, 1861–1885.* Albuquerque: University of New Mexico Press, 1989.

Mills, Charles K. *Harvest of Barren Regrets: The Army Career of Frederick William Benteen, 1834–1898.* Glendale, Calif.: Arthur H. Clark Co., 1985.

Milner, Clyde A., II, ed. *A New Significance: Re-Envisioning the History of the American West.* New York: Oxford University Press, 1996.

Miner, H. Craig. *West of Wichita: Settling the High Plains of Kansas, 1865–1890.* Lawrence: University Press of Kansas, 1986.

————. *Wichita: The Early Years, 1865–1880.* Lincoln: University of Nebraska Press, 1982.

Moorman, Donald R., and Gene A. Sessions. *Camp Floyd and the Mormons: The Utah War.* Salt Lake City: University of Utah Press, 1992.

Morrison, James L., Jr. *"The Best School in the World": West Point, the Pre–Civil War Years, 1833–1866.* Kent, Ohio: Kent State University Press, 1986.

Morrison, William B. *Military Posts and Camps in Oklahoma.* Oklahoma City: Harlow Publishing Co., 1936.

Murray, Robert A. *Military Posts in the Powder River Country of Wyoming, 1865–1894.* Lincoln: University of Nebraska Press, 1968.

Myer, Jesse S. *Life and Letters of Dr. William Beaumont.* Saint Louis: C. V. Mosby Co., 1912.

Myers, John Myers. *The Last Chance: Tombstone's Early Years.* New York: E. P. Dutton and Co., 1950.

Nankivell, John H., comp. *The History of the Twenty-Fifth Regiment United States Infantry.* Denver: Smith-Brooks Printing Co., 1927.

Nash, Gerald D. *The American West in the Twentieth Century: A Short History of an Urban Oasis.* Englewood Cliffs, N.J.: Prentice-Hall, 1973.

———. *The American West Transformed: The Impact of the Second World War.* Bloomington: Indiana University Press, 1985.

Nash, Roderick. *Wilderness and the American Mind.* New Haven: Yale University Press, 1967.

Nenninger, Timothy K. *The Leavenworth Schools and the Old Army: Education, Professionalism, and the Officer Corps of the United States Army, 1881–1918.* Westport, Conn.: Greenwood Press, 1978.

Nevin, David. *The Soldiers.* New York: Time-Life Books, 1973.

Nevins, Allan. *Frémont: Pathmarker of the West.* New York: Longman's, Green and Co., 1955.

Ney, Colonel Virgil. *Fort on the Prairie: Fort Atkinson on the Council Bluff, 1819–1827.* Washington, D.C.: Command Publications, 1978.

Nolan, Frederick. *The Lincoln County War: A Documentary History.* Norman: University of Oklahoma Press, 1992.

North, Diane M. T. *Samuel Peter Heintzelman and the Sonora Exploring and Mining Company.* Tucson: University of Arizona Press, 1980.

Nye, Wilbur S. *Carbine and Lance: The Story of Old Fort Sill.* Norman: University of Oklahoma Press, 1942.

Office of the Chief of Chaplains. *American Army Chaplaincy: A Brief History.* Washington, D.C.: Chaplains Association, 1946.

O'Hara, Susan Pritchard and Gregory Graves, *Saving California's Coast: Army Engineers at Oceanside and Humboldt Bay.* Spokane: Arthur H. Clark Co., 1991.

Oliva, Leo E. *Fort Hays, Frontier Army Post, 1865–1889.* Topeka: Kansas State Historical Society, 1980.

———. *Fort Larned on the Santa Fe Trail.* Topeka: Kansas State Historical Society, 1982.

———. *Fort Scott on the Indian Frontier.* Topeka: Kansas State Historical Society, 1984.

————. *Soldiers on the Santa Fe Trail.* Norman: University of Oklahoma Press, 1967.

Olson, James C. *Red Cloud and the Sioux Problem.* Lincoln: University of Nebraska Press, 1965.

Parker, William Thornton. *Annals of Old Fort Cummings, New Mexico, 1867–8.* Northampton, Mass.: n.p., 1916.

Pirtle, Caleb, III, and Michael F. Cusack. *Fort Clark: The Lonely Sentinel on Texas's Western Frontier.* Austin: Eakin Press, 1985.

Pohanka, Brian C. *Nelson A. Miles: A Documentary Biography of His Military Career, 1861–1903.* Glendale, Calif.: Arthur H. Clark Co., 1985.

Porter, Joseph C. *Paper Medicine Man: John Gregory Bourke and His American West.* Norman: University of Oklahoma Press, 1986.

Pride, Woodbury F. *The History of Fort Riley.* Fort Riley, Kans.: Cavalry School, Book Department, 1926.

Prucha, Francis Paul. *American Indian Policy in the Formative Years: The Indian Trade and Intercourse Acts, 1790–1834.* Cambridge, Mass.: Harvard University Press, 1962.

————. *Broadax and Bayonet: The Role of the United States Army in the Development of the Northwest, 1815–1860.* Madison: State Historical Society of Wisconsin, 1953.

————. *The Sword of the Republic: The United States Army on the Frontier, 1783–1846.* New York: Macmillan Co., 1969.

Puryear, Pamela Ashworth, and Nath Winfield, Jr. *Sandbars and Sternwheelers: Steam Navigation on the Brazos.* College Station: Texas A&M University Press, 1976.

Railsback, Thomas C., and John P. Langellier. *The Drums Would Roll: A Pictorial History of U.S. Army Bands on the American Frontier, 1866–1900.* New York: Arms and Armour Press, 1987.

Reed, Bill. *The Last Bugle Call: A History of Fort McDowell Arizona Territory, 1865–1890.* Parsons, W.Va.: McClain Printing Co., 1977.

Reeves, Ira L. *Military Education in the United States.* Burlington, Vt.: Free Press Printing Co., 1914.

Reid, John Phillip. *Law for the Elephant: Property and Social Behavior on the Overland Trail.* San Marino, Calif.: Huntington Library, 1980.

Reinhartz, Dennis, and Charles C. Colley, *The Mapping of the American Southwest.* College Station: Texas A&M University Press, 1987.

Remele, Larry, ed. *Fort Totten: Military Post and Indian School, 1867–1959.* Bismarck: State Historical Society of North Dakota, 1986.

Reneau, Susan C. *The Adventures of Moccasin Joe: The True Life Story of Sgt. George S. Howard.* Missoula, Mont.: Blue Mountain Publishing, 1994.

Rich, Bennett M. *The Presidents and Civil Disorder.* Washington, D.C.: Brookings Institution, 1941.

Richter, William L. *The Army in Texas during Reconstruction, 1865–1870.* College Station: Texas A&M University Press, 1987.

Rickey, Don, Jr. *Forty Miles a Day on Beans and Hay: The Enlisted Soldier Fighting the Indian Wars.* Norman: University of Oklahoma Press, 1963.

Rister, Carl Coke. *Border Command: General Phil Sheridan in the West.* Norman: University of Oklahoma Press, 1944.

———. *Fort Griffin on the Texas Frontier.* Norman: University of Oklahoma Press, 1956.

———. *Land Hunger: David L. Payne and the Oklahoma Boomers.* Norman: University of Oklahoma Press, 1942.

———. *Robert E. Lee in Texas.* Norman: University of Oklahoma Press, 1946.

Robinson, Charles, III. *The Frontier World of Fort Griffin: The Life and Death of a Western Town.* Spokane: Arthur H. Clark Co., 1992.

Robinson, Willard B. *American Forts: Architectural Form and Function.* Urbana: University of Illinois Press, 1977.

Rohrbough, Malcolm J. *The Land Office Business: The Settlement and Administration of American Public Lands, 1789–1837.* New York: Oxford University Press, 1968.

Roland, Charles P. *Albert Sidney Johnston: Soldier of Three Republics.* Austin: University of Texas Press, 1964.

Rosenberg, Charles S. *The Cholera Years: The United States in 1832, 1849, and 1866.* Chicago: University of Chicago Press, 1962.

Russell, Don. *Campaigning with King: Charles King, Chronicler of the Old Army.* Ed. Paul L. Hedren. Lincoln: University of Nebraska Press, 1991.

———. *Custer's Last, or The Battle of the Little Big Horn in Picturesque Perspective.* Fort Worth: Amon Carter Museum of Western Art, 1968.

Samuels, Peggy, and Harold Samuels. *Frederic Remington: A Biography.* Austin: University of Texas Press, 1982.

Sandoz, Mari. *Old Jules.* New York: Hastings House, 1935.

Schlicke, Carl Paul. *General George Wright: Guardian of the Pacific Coast.* Norman: University of Oklahoma Press, 1988.

Schofield, Donald F. *Indians, Cattle, Ships, and Oil: The Story of W. M. D. Lee.* Austin: University of Texas Press, 1985.

Schubert, Frank N. *Buffalo Soldiers, Braves and the Brass: The Story of Fort Robinson, Nebraska.* Shippensburg, Pa.: White Mane Publishing Co., 1993.

Schuler, Harold H. *Fort Sully: Guns at Sunset.* Vermillion, S.Dak.: University of South Dakota Press, 1992.

Scobee, Barry. *Fort Davis, Texas, 1583–1960.* El Paso: Hill Printing Co., 1963.

Scott, Robert M. *An Analytical Digest of the Military Laws of the United States.* Philadelphia: J. B. Lippincott and Co., 1873.

Selcer, Richard F. *The Fort that Became a City: An Illustrated Reconstruction of Fort Worth, Texas, 1849–1853.* Fort Worth: Texas Christian University Press, 1995.

Seraile, William. *The Voice of Dissent: Theophilus Gould Steward (1843–1924) and Black America.* Brooklyn, N.Y.: Carlson Publishing, 1991.

Settle, Raymond W., and Mary Lund Settle. *War Drums and Wagon Wheels: The Story of Russell, Majors, and Waddell.* Lincoln: University of Nebraska Press, 1966.

Sharp, Paul F. *Whoop-Up Country: The Canadian-American West, 1865–1885.* Norman: University of Oklahoma Press, 1973.

Shindler, Henry. *Fort Leavenworth: Its Churches and Schools.* Fort Leavenworth, Kans.: Army Service Schools Press, 1912.

———. *History of the United States Military Prison.* Fort Leavenworth, Kans.: Army Service Schools Press, 1911.

Skelton, William B. *An American Profession of Arms: The Army Officer Corps, 1784–1861.* Lawrence: University Press of Kansas, 1992.

Skinner, Woodward B. *The Apache Rock Crumbles: The Captivity of Geronimo's People.* Pensacola, Fla.: Skinner Publications, 1987.

Skogen, Larry C. *Indian Depredation Claims, 1796–1920.* Norman: University of Oklahoma Press, 1996.

Smith, Cornelius C., Jr. *Don't Settle for Second: Life and Times of Cornelius Smith.* San Rafael, Calif.: Presidio Press, 1977.

Smith, Helena Huntington. *The War on Powder River: The History of an Insurrection.* New York: McGraw-Hill Book Co., 1966.

Smith, Phyllis. *Weather Pioneers: The Signal Corps Station at Pikes Peak.* Athens, Ohio: Swallow Press/Ohio University Press, 1993.

Smith, Robert W. *The Coeur D'Alene Mining War of 1892: A Case Study of an Industrial Dispute.* Corvallis: Oregon State University Press, 1961.

Smith, Sherry L. *The View from Officers' Row: Army Perceptions of Western Indians.* Tucson: University of Arizona Press, 1990.

Smith, Thomas T. *Fort Inge: Sharps, Spurs, and Saber on the Texas Frontier, 1849–1869.* Austin: Eakin Press, 1993.

Sonnichsen, C. L. *Ten Texas Feuds.* Albuquerque: University of New Mexico Press, 1957.

Spring, Agnes Wright. *The Cheyenne and Black Hills Stage and Express Routes.* Glendale, Calif.: Arthur H. Clark Co., 1949.

Stallard, Patricia Y. *Glittering Misery: Dependents of the Indian Fighting Army.* Fort Collins, Colo.: Old Army Press, 1978.

Stanley, F. [Stanley Francis Louis Crocchiola]. *Fort Stanton.* Pampa, Texas: Pampa Print Shop, 1964.

Stegner, Wallace E. *Beyond the Hundredth Meridian: John Wesley Powell and the Second Opening of the West.* Boston: Houghton Mifflin Co., 1953.

Steinbach, Robert H. *A Long March: The Lives of Frank and Alice Baldwin.* Austin: University of Texas Press, 1990.

Sternberg, Martha L. *George Miller Sternberg, a Biography.* Chicago: American Medical Association, 1920.

Stewart, Edgar I., ed. *Penny-an-Acre Empire in the West.* Norman: University of Oklahoma Press, 1968.

Stover, John F. *The Life and Decline of the American Railroad.* New York: Oxford
University Press, 1970.

Strate, David K. *Sentinel to the Cimarron: The Frontier Experience of Fort Dodge, Kansas.*
Dodge City, Kans.: Cultural Heritage and Arts Center, 1970.

Strobridge, William F. *Regulars in the Redwoods: The U.S. Army in Northern
California, 1852–1861.* Spokane: Arthur H. Clark Co., 1993.

Sully, Langdon. *No Tears for the General: The Life of Alfred Sully, 1821–1879.* Palo
Alto, Calif.: American West Publishing Co., 1974.

Svingen, Orlan J. *The Northern Cheyenne Indian Reservation, 1877–1900.* Niwot,
Colo.: University Press of Colorado, 1993.

Taft, Robert. *Artists and Illustrators of the Old West, 1850–1900.* New York: Charles
Scribner's Sons, 1953.

Taylor, George Rogers. *The Transportation Revolution, 1815–1860.* New York:
Harper and Row, 1951.

Thomas, Gordon, and Max Morgan Witts. *The San Francisco Earthquake.* New York:
Dell Publishing Co., 1971.

Thomas, W. Stephen. *Fort Davis and the Texas Frontier: Paintings by Captain Arthur
T. Lee, Eighth U.S. Infantry.* College Station: Texas A&M University Press, 1976.

Thompson, Gerald. *The Army and the Navajo: The Bosque Redondo Reservation
Experiment, 1863–1868.* Tucson: University of Arizona Press, 1976.

Thompson, Neil Baird. *Crazy Horse Called Them Walk-a-Heaps: The Story of the
Foot Soldier in the Prairie Indian Wars.* Saint Cloud, Minn.: North Star Press,
1979.

Thompson, Richard A. *Crossing the Border with the 4th Cavalry: Mackenzie's Raid
into Mexico, 1873.* Waco, Texas: Texian Press, 1986.

Thompson, Robert L. *Wiring a Continent: The History of the Telegraph Industry in
the United States, 1832–1866.* Princeton: Princeton University Press, 1947.

Unrau, William E. *White Man's Wicked Water: The Alcohol Trade and Prohibition in
Indian Country, 1802–1892.* Lawrence: University Press of Kansas, 1996.

Unruh, John D., Jr. *The Plains Across: The Overland Emigrants and the Trans-
Mississippi West, 1840–60.* Urbana: University of Illinois Press, 1979.

Upton, Richard, ed. *Fort Custer on the Big Horn, 1877–1898: Its History and
Personalities as Told and Pictured by Its Contemporaries.* Glendale, Calif.: Arthur
H. Clark Co., 1973.

Utley, Robert M. *Cavalier in Buckskin: George Armstrong Custer and the Western
Military Frontier.* Norman: University of Oklahoma Press, 1988.

———. *Custer and the Great Controversy: The Origin and Development of a Legend.* Los
Angeles: Westernlore Press, 1962.

———. *Four Fighters of Lincoln County.* Albuquerque: University of New Mexico
Press, 1986.

———. *Frontier Regulars: The United States Army and the Indian, 1866–1890.* New
York: Macmillan Co., 1973.

————. *Frontiersmen in Blue: The United States Army and the Indian, 1848–1865.* New York: Macmillan Co., 1967.

————. *High Noon in Lincoln: Violence on the Western Frontier.* Albuquerque: University of New Mexico Press, 1987.

————. *The Last Days of the Sioux Nation.* New Haven: Yale University Press, 1963.

Vaughn, J. W. *The Battle of Platte Bridge.* Norman: University of Oklahoma Press, 1963.

Vestal, Stanley. *Queen of Cowtowns: Dodge City, "The Wickedest Little City in America," 1872–1886.* New York: Harper and Brothers, 1952.

Viola, Herman J. *Diplomats in Buckskins: A History of Indian Delegations in Washington City.* Bluffton, S.C.: Rivilo Books, 1995.

Wade, Richard C. *The Urban Frontier: The Rise of Western Cities, 1790–1830.* Cambridge: Harvard University Press, 1959.

Wagner, Glendolin Damon. *Old Neutriment.* Boston: Ruth Hill, Publisher, 1934.

Walker, Henry P. *The Wagonmasters: High Plains Freighting from the Earliest Days of the Santa Fe Trail to 1880.* Norman: University of Oklahoma Press, 1966.

Wallace, Edward S. *The Great Reconnaissance: Soldiers, Artists and Scientists on the Frontier, 1848–1861.* Boston: Little, Brown and Co., 1955.

Webb, Walter Prescott, and H. Bailey Carroll, eds. *The Handbook of Texas.* 2 vols. Austin: Texas State Historical Association, 1952.

Weber, David J. *Richard Kern, Expeditionary Artist in the Far Southwest, 1848–1853.* Albuquerque: University of New Mexico Press, 1985.

West, Elliott. *Growing Up with the Country: Childhood on the Far Western Frontier.* Albuquerque: University of New Mexico Press, 1989.

Whisenhunt, Donald W. *Fort Richardson: Outpost on the Texas Frontier.* Southwestern Studies, Monograph No. 20. El Paso: Texas Western Press, 1968.

Whitnah, Donald R. *A History of the United States Weather Bureau.* Urbana: University of Illinois Press, 1961.

Williams, Clayton. *Texas' Last Frontier: Fort Stockton and the Trans-Pecos, 1861–1895.* Ed. Ernest Wallace. College Station: Texas A&M University Press, 1982.

Wilson, D. Ray. *Fort Kearny on the Platte.* Dundee, Ill.: Crossroads Communications, 1980.

Wilson, John P. *Merchants, Guns, and Money: The Story of Lincoln County and Its Wars.* Santa Fe: Museum of New Mexico Press, 1987.

Winther, Oscar O. *The Transportation Frontier: Trans-Mississippi West, 1865–1890.* New York: Holt, Rinehart and Winston, 1964.

Wood, Laura N. *Walter Reed: Doctor in Uniform.* New York: Julian Messner, 1943.

Wood, Richard G. *Stephen Harriman Long, 1784–1864: Army Engineer, Explorer, Inventor.* Glendale, Calif.: Arthur H. Clark Co., 1966.

Wood, Robert L. *Men, Mules and Mountains: Lieutenant O'Neil's Olympic Expeditions.* Seattle: The Mountaineers, 1976.

Wooster, Robert. *The Military and United States Indian Policy, 1865–1903.* New Haven: Yale University Press, 1988.

————. *Nelson A. Miles and the Twilight of the Frontier Army.* Lincoln: University of Nebraska Press, 1993.

————. *Soldiers, Sutlers and Settlers: Garrison Life on the Texas Frontier.* College Station: Texas A&M University Press, 1987.

Wright, Elizabeth. *Independence in All Things, Neutrality in Nothing: The Story of a Pioneer Journalist of the American West.* San Francisco: Miller Freeman Publications, 1973.

Young, Otis E. *The First Military Escort on the Santa Fe Trail 1829: From the Journal and Reports of Major Bennet Riley and Lieutenant Philip St. George Cooke.* Glendale, Calif.: Arthur H. Clark Co., 1952.

Zimmerman, Larry J. *Peoples of Prehistoric South Dakota.* Lincoln: University of Nebraska Press, 1985.

PRIMARY ARTICLES

Adams, Donald K., ed. "The Journal of Ada A. Vogdes, 1868–71." *Montana, Magazine of Western History* 13 (Summer 1963): 2–17.

Almy, Kenneth J., ed. "Thof's Dragon and the Letters of Capt. Theophilus H. Turner, M.D., U.S. Army." *Kansas History* 10 (Autumn 1987): 170–200.

Anderson, E. "The Pay of Our Soldiers Affecting Desertion and Re-Enlistment." *American Review of Reviews* 33 (1906): 330–40.

Anderson, George. "Work of the Cavalry in Protecting the Yellowstone National Park." *Journal of the United States Cavalry Association* 10 (March 1897): 3–10.

Annin, William E. "Fort Robinson during the 1880's: An Omaha Newspaperman Visits the Post." Ed. Vance E. Nelson. *Nebraska History* 55 (Summer 1974): 181–202.

Archambeau, Ernest R., ed. "Monthly Reports of the Fourth Cavalry 1872–1874." *Panhandle-Plains Historical Review* 38 (1965): 95–154.

Archibald, J. F. "A Cavalry March to the Yosemite." *Illustrated American* 7 (November 1896): 27–34.

Barry, Louise, ed. "With the First U.S. Cavalry in Indian Country, 1859–1861." *Kansas Historical Quarterly* 24 (Autumn 1958): 257–84; (Winter 1958): 399–425.

Bland, Thomas A. "Abolish the Army." *Council Fire* (March 1879): 36.

Blow, William N. "Use of Troops in Riots." *Journal of the Military Service Institution of the United States* 25 (July 1899): 45–57.

Brimlow, George F., ed. "Two Cavalrymen's Diaries of the Bannock War, 1878." *Oregon Historical Quarterly* 68, nos. 3 and 4 (1967): 221–58, 293–316.

Brust, James S. "John H. Fouch, First Post Photographer at Fort Keogh." *Montana, Magazine of Western History* 44 (Spring 1994): 2–17.

Buecker, Thomas R., ed. "Letters from a Post Surgeon's Wife: The Fort Washakie Correspondence of Caroline Winne, May 1879–May 1880." *Annals of Wyoming* 53 (Fall 1981): 44–63.

———, ed. "Letters of Caroline Frey Winne from Sidney Barracks and Fort McPherson, Nebraska, 1874–1878." *Nebraska History* 62 (Spring 1981): 1–46.

———, ed. "A Surgeon at the Little Big Horn: The Letters of Dr. Holmes O. Paulding." *Montana, Magazine of Western History* 32 (Autumn 1982): 34–49.

Campbell, C. E. "Down among the Red Men." *Kansas Historical Collections* 17 (1926–28): 623–91.

Carbaugh, H. C. "The Contract of Enlistment and Its Violation in the United States Army." *Army and Navy Life* 10 (February 1907): 176–95.

Carr, Mary Patience Magwire. "Fort McPherson in 1870: A Note by an Army Wife." Ed. James T. King. *Nebraska History* 45 (March 1964): 99–107.

Clary, David A., ed. "'I Am Already Quite a Texan': Albert J. Myer's Letters from Texas, 1854–1856." *Southwestern Historical Quarterly* 82 (July 1978): 25–76.

Conway, Walter C., ed. "Colonel Edmund Schriver's Inspector-General Report on Military Posts in Texas, November 1872–January 1873." *Southwestern Historical Quarterly* 67 (April 1964): 559–83.

Cox, John E. "Soldiering in Dakota Territory in the Seventies: A Communication." *North Dakota Historical Quarterly* 6 (October 1931): 62–81.

Crandall, Genia Rood. "Fort Hartsuff and the Local Pioneer Life: A School Teacher's Recollections of Fort Hartsuff." *Nebraska History* 12 (April–June 1929): 140–57.

Crimmins, Martin L. ed., "W. G. Freeman's Report on the Eighth Military Department." *Southwestern Historical Quarterly* 51 (July 1947): 54–58; (October 1947): 167–74; (January 1948): 252–58; (April 1948): 350–57; 52 (July 1948): 100–108; (October 1948): 227–33; (January 1949): 349–53; (April 1949): 444–47; 53 (July 1949): 71–77; (October 1949): 202–208; (January 1950): 308–19; 53 (April 1950): 443–73; 54 (October 1950): 204–18.

Danker, Donald F., ed. "The Journal of an Indian Fighter: The 1869 Diary of Major Frank J. North." *Nebraska History* 39 (June 1958): 87–177.

Devol, Carroll A. "The Army in the San Francisco Disaster." *Journal of the United States Infantry Association* 4 (July 1907): 59–87.

Dungan, Hugh E. "Still in Texas." Ed. Llerena Friend. *Southwestern Historical Quarterly* 72 (October 1968): 223–39.

Dupuy, Raoul. "A Study of the Cavalry of the United States." *Journal of the United States Cavalry Association* 12 (March 1899): 68–92.

Eldridge, W. Heath. "An Army Boy in Colorado." *Colorado Magazine* 32 (October 1955): 299–310.

Ellis, John M., and Robert E. Stowers, eds. "The Nevada Uprising of 1860 as Seen by Private Charles A. Scott." *Arizona and the West* 3, no. 4 (1961): 355–76.

Ellis, L. Tuffly, ed. "Lieutenant A. W. Greely's Report on the Installation of Military Telegraph Lines in Texas, 1875–1876." *Southwestern Historical Quarterly* 69 (July 1965): 66–87.

Erwin, Marie H., comp. "Statistical Reports on the Sickness and Mortality of the Army of the United States, 1819–1860." *Annals of Wyoming* 15 (1943): 315–75.

Foote, Morris C. "The Post Mess." *Journal of the Military Service Institution of the United States* 14 (1893): 519–24.

Goodwin, Carol G. "The Letters of Private Milton Spencer, 1862–1865: A Soldier's View of Military Life on the Northern Plains." *North Dakota History* 37 (Fall 1970): 233–69.

Gresham, John C. "Civil Employment of Troops." *United Service* 7 (May 1892): 476–82.

Gressley, Gene M., ed. "A Soldier with Crook: The Letters of Henry Porter," *Montana, Magazine of Western History* 8, no. 3 (1958): 33–47.

Heistand, Mary Ripply. "Scraps from an Army Woman's Diary: An Old Army Christmas." *Army and Navy Life* 9 (December 1907): 626–31.

Hill, Michael D., and Ben Innis, eds. "The Fort Buford Diary of Private Sanford, 1876–1877." *North Dakota History* 52 (Summer 1985): 2–40.

Holcomb, Freeborn P. "The Use of the Bicycle in the Army." *Journal of the United States Cavalry Association* 15 (January 1905): 598–604.

Howell, Charles W. "An Army Engineer on the Missouri in 1867." Ed. Leland R. Johnson. *Nebraska History* 53 (Summer 1972): 253–91.

Hull, Myra E., ed. "Soldiering on the High Plains: The Diary of Lewis Byram Hull, 1864–1866." *Kansas Historical Quarterly* 7 (February 1938): 3–53.

Jordan, Weymouth T., Jr., ed. "A Soldier's Life on the Indian Frontier, 1876–1878: Letters of 2Lt. C. D. Cowles." *Kansas Historical Quarterly* 38 (Summer 1972): 144–55.

Koch, F. J. "Protecting National Parks against Poachers." *Overland Monthly* 65 (February 1915): 117–22.

Kramer, Adam. "An Army Officer in Texas, 1866–1867." Ed. Brit Allan Storey. *Southwestern Historical Quarterly* 72 (October 1968): 242–52.

Landrum, Francis S., ed. "From the Sketchbook of 1st Sergeant Michael McCarthy, Troop H, 1st US Cavalry: Excerpts, 1873." *Journal of the Shaw Historical Library* 9 (1995): 1–18.

Larned, Charles W. "The Regeneration of the Enlisted Soldier." *International Quarterly* 12 (January 1906): 189–207.

"Lawlessness in the Army." *Frank Leslie's Illustrated Weekly* 85 (December 9, 1897): 370.

Lee, J. G. C. "Suggestions for Consideration, Relative to the Quartermaster's Department, U.S. Army." *Journal of the Military Service Institution* 15 (March 1894): 257–80.

Lindsay, Charles, ed. "The Diary of Dr. Thomas G. Maghee." *Nebraska History* 12 (July–September 1929): 247–304.

Lockwood, John A. "Uncle Sam's Troopers in the National Parks of California." *Overland Monthly* 33 (April 1899): 356–368.

Loudon, Betty ed., "Pioneer Pharmacist J. Walter Moyer's Notes on Crawford and Fort Robinson in the 1890s." *Nebraska History* 58 (Spring 1977): 89–117.

Luce, Edward S., ed. "The Diary and Letters of Dr. James D. DeWolf, Acting Assistant Surgeon, U.S. Army: His Record of the Sioux Expedition of 1876 As Kept until His Death." *North Dakota History* 25 (April–July 1958): 33–81.

McAnaney, William D. "Desertion in the United States Army." *Journal of the Military Service Institution of the United States* 10 (1889): 450–65.

McAndrews, Eugene V., ed. "An Army Engineer's Journal of Custer's Black Hills Expedition, July 2, 1874–August 23, 1874." *Journal of the West* 13 (January 1974): 78–85.

McClure, N. F. "The Fourth Cavalry in the Yosemite National Park." *Journal of the United States Cavalry Association* 10 (June 1897): 113–21.

McDaniel, Dennis K. "Kansas in 1862 as Seen by the 12th Wisconsin Infantry: The Sketches of Pvt. John Gaddis." *Kansas Historical Quarterly* 40 (Winter 1974): 465–74.

McPheeters, Samuel Brown "A Young Medical Officer's Letters from Fort Robinson and Fort Leavenworth, 1906–1907." Ed. Willard E. Wight. *Nebraska History* 37 (June 1956): 135–47.

Mattison, Ray H., ed. "An Army Wife on the Upper Missouri: The Diary of Sarah E. Canfield, 1866–1868." *North Dakota Historical Quarterly* 20 (October 1953): 191–220.

———, ed. "The Diary of Surgeon Washington Matthews, Fort Rice, D.T." *North Dakota History* 21 (January 1954): 5–74.

———, ed. "The Harney Expedition Against the Sioux: The Journal of Capt. John B. S. Todd." *Nebraska History* 43 (June 1962): 89–130.

Miles, Nelson A. "Our Indian Question." *Journal of the Military Service Institution* 2 (1881): 278–92.

Miles, Susan, ed. "Mrs. Buell's Journal, 1877." *Edwards Plateau Historian* 2 (1966): 33–43.

Molchert, William "Sergeant Molchert's Perils: Soldiering in Montana." Ed. John G. James. *Montana, Magazine of Western History* 34 (Spring 1984): 60–65.

Molineux, E. L. "Riots in Cities and Their Suppression." *Journal of the Military Service Institution of the United States* 4 (1883): 335–70.

Mullins, George G. "Education in the Army." *United Service* 2 (April 1880): 478–85.

Myres, Sandra L., ed. "A Woman's View of the Texas Frontier, 1874: The Diary of Emily K. Andrews." *Southwestern Historical Quarterly* 86 (July 1982): 49–80.

Neilson, John, ed. "'I Long to Return to Fort Concho': Acting Assistant Surgeon Samuel Smith's Letters from the Texas Military Frontier, 1878–1879." *Military History of the West* 24 (Fall 1994): 122–186.

Notson, William M. "Fort Concho, 1868–1872: The Medical Officer's Observations." Ed. Stephen Schmidt. *Military History of Texas and the Southwest* 12 (Fall 1975): 125–49.

Oliva, Leo E., ed. "'A Faithful Account of Everything': Letters from Katie Bowen on the Santa Fe Trail, 1851." *Kansas Historical Quarterly* 19 (Winter 1996–97): 262–81.

Olson, Gary D., ed. "Relief for Nebraska Grasshopper Victims: The Official Journal of Lieutenant Theodore E. True." *Nebraska History* 48 (Summer 1967): 119–40.

"Ostriches for Our Cavalry." *Army and Navy Journal* 16 (August 2, 1879): 955.

Otis, Elwell S. "The Army in Connection with the Labor Riots of 1877." *Journal of the Military Service Institution of the United States* 5 (1884): 292–23.

Palmer, George Henry. "'We Do Not Know What the Government Intends to Do . . . ,': Lt. Palmer Writes from the Bozeman, 1867–68." Ed. Jerome A. Greene. *Montana, Magazine of Western History* 28 (July 1978): 17–35.

Paul, R. Eli, ed. "Battle of Ash Hollow: The 1909–1910 Recollections of General N. A. M. Dudley." *Nebraska History* 62 (Fall 1981): 373–99.

Payne, John Scott. "Conflict in Dakota Territory: Episodes of the Great Sioux War." Ed. Jerome A. Greene. *South Dakota History* 23 (Spring 1993): 1–47.

Peters, S. S. "Letters of a Sixth Cavalryman Stationed at 'Cantonment' in the Texas Panhandle, 1875." Ed. Lonnie J. White. *Texas Military History* 7 (Summer 1968): 77–102.

"Poetry of an Army Private." *Frank Leslie's Illustrated Weekly* 78 (May 31, 1894): 372.

Pope, J. Worden. "Desertion and the Military Prison." *Cosmopolitan Magazine* 10 (November 1890): 111–20.

Powell, William H. "The Indian as a Soldier." *United Service* 3 (March 1890): 229–38.

Price, George F. "The Necessity for Closer Relations between the Army and the People, and the Best Method to Accomplish the Result." *Journal of the Military Service Institution of the United States* 6 (December 1885): 303–30.

Reeve, Frank D., ed. "Frederick E. Phelps: A Soldier's Memoirs." *New Mexico Historical Review* 25 (July 1950): 187–221; (October 1950): 305–27.

Regan, James "Military Duties in Aid of the Civil Power." *Journal of the Military Service Institution of the United States* 18 (March 1896): 285–97.

Remington, Frederic. "Policing the Yellowstone." *Harper's Weekly* 39 (January 12, 1895): 35–38.

———. "Stirrups or Pedals? The Colonel of the First Cycle Infantry." Ed. Ted C. Hinckley. *American West* 11 (September 1974): 10–13, 58–59.

Rhoda, Jean. "Uncle Sam in the Yosemite." *Overland Monthly* 61 (June 1913): 590–94.

Roberson, Jere W., ed. "A View from Oklahoma, 1866–1868: The Diary and Letters of Dr. James Reagles, Jr., Assistant Surgeon, U.S. Army." *Red River Valley Historical Review* 3 (Fall 1978): 19–46.

Robertson, C. S. "Our Indian Contingent." *Harper's Weekly* 30 (February 13, 1892): 156–60.

Roland, Charles P., and Richard C. Robbins, eds. "The Diary of Eliza (Mrs. Albert Sidney) Johnston: The Second Cavalry Comes to Texas." *Southwestern Historical Quarterly* 60 (April 1957): 463–500.

Rowen, Richard D., ed. "The Second Nebraska's Campaign against the Sioux." *Nebraska History* 44 (March 1963): 3–53.

Runyon, A. L. "A. L. Runyon's Letters from the Nineteenth Kansas Regiment." *Kansas Historical Quarterly* 9 (February 1940): 58–75.

Sanford, Wilmont P. "The Fort Buford Diary of Private Wilmont P. Sanford." Ed. Ben Innis. *North Dakota History* 33 (Fall 1966): 335–78.

Schreier, Jim, ed. "'For This I Had Left Civilization': Julia Davis at Camp McDowell, 1869–1870." *Journal of Arizona History* 29 (Summer 1988): 185–98.

Sehon, John L. "Post Schools in the Army." *Journal of the Military Service Institution of the United States* 14 (May 1892): 522–34.

Sharpe, Alfred C. "Post Schools." *Journal of the Military Service Institution of the United States* 12 (November 1891): 1177–88.

Smith, Dwight L., ed. "The Kansas Frontier, 1869–1870: Lt. Samuel Tillman's First Tour of Duty." *Kansas History* 12 (Winter 1989–90): 202–209.

Splitter, Henry Winfred, ed. "Tour in Arizona: Footprints of an Army Officer." *Journal of the West* 1 (July 1962): 74–97.

Sprague, John T. "Journal of a Wagon Train Expedition from Fort Inge to El Paso del Norte in 1850." Ed. Ben E. Pingenot. *Military History of the West* 25 (Spring 1995): 69–105.

Spring, Agnes Wright, ed. "An Army Wife Comes West: Letters of Catharine Wever Collins (1863–1864)." *Colorado Magazine* 31 (October 1954): 241–73.

———, ed. "Old Letter Book: Discloses Economic History of Fort Laramie, 1858–1871." *Annals of Wyoming* 13 (October 1941): 237–330.

Steward, Theophilus G. "Starving Laborers and the 'Hired' Soldier." *United Service* 15 (October 1895): 363–66.

Thayer, Russell. "Movements of Troops in Cities in Cases of Riots or Insurrection." *United Service* 1 (January 1879): 92–99.

Theisen, Lee Scott. "The Fight in Lincoln, N.M., 1878: The Testimony of Two Negro Participants." *Arizona and the West* 12 (Summer 1970): 173–98.

Thompson, Jerry D., ed. "With the Third Infantry in New Mexico, 1851–1853: The Lost Diary of Private Sylvester W. Matson." *Journal of Arizona History* 31 (Winter 1990): 349–404.

Twitchell, Phillip G., ed. "Camp Robinson Letters of Angeline Johnson, 1876–1879." *Nebraska History* 77 (Summer 1996): 89–95.

Vance, Zebulon V. "The Indian Soldier." *Journal of the Military Service Institution* 14 (November 1893): 1203–1207.

Wales, Martha Gray. "When I Was a Little Girl: Things I Remember from Living at Frontier Military Posts." Ed. Willard B. Pope. *North Dakota History* 50 (Spring 1983): 12–22.

Walker, Henry P., ed. "The Reluctant Corporal: The Autobiography of William Bladen Jett." *Journal of Arizona History* 12 (Spring 1971): 1–50.

Wallace, William. "The Army and the Civil Power." *Journal of the Military Service Institution of the United States* 17 (September 1895): 235–66.

Weaver, E. M. "The Military Schools of the United States." *United Service* 3 (May 1890): 457–69.

"What a Good Chaplain Can Do." *Army-Navy Journal* (September 9, 1876): 74.

Whilden, Charles E. "Letters from a Santa Fe Army Clerk, 1855–1856." Ed. John Hammond Moore. *New Mexico Historical Review* 40 (April 1965): 141–64.

Woodhull, Alfred A. "The Enlisted Soldier." *Journal of the Military Service Institution* 8 (March 1887): 18–70.

Woodward, George A. "The Difference Between Military and Martial Law." *United Service* 1 (October 1879): 635–43.

SECONDARY ARTICLES

Allin, Lawrence C. "'A Mile Wide and an Inch Deep': Attempts to Navigate the Platte River." *Nebraska History* 63 (Spring 1982): 1–15.

———. "'A Thousand and One Little Delays': Training the Missouri River at Omaha, 1877–1883." *Nebraska History* 66 (Winter 1985): 349–71.

Altshuler, Constance Wynn. "Men and Brothers." *Journal of Arizona History* 19 (Autumn 1978): 315–22.

Ambrose, David C. "The Major Reasons for Army Desertions at Fort Davis, Texas, 1882–1885." *Panhandle-Plains Historical Review* 45 (1972): 38–45.

Anderson, Grant K. "The Black Hills Exclusion Policy: Judicial Challenges," *Nebraska History* 58 (Spring 1977): 1–24.

Anderson, Harry H. "The Benteen Base Ball Club: Sports Enthusiasts of the Seventh Cavalry." *Montana, Magazine of Western History* 20 (July 1970): 82–87.

———. "The Friendship of Buffalo Bill and Charles King." *Milwaukee History* 9 (Winter 1986): 119–32.

———. "A History of the Cheyenne River Agency and Its Military Post, Fort Bennett, 1868–1891." *South Dakota Report and Historical Collections* 28 (1956): 390–551.

Athearn, Robert G. "The Firewagon Road." *Montana, Magazine of Western History* 20 (April 1970): 2–19.

————. "Frontier Critics of the Western Army," *Montana, Magazine of Western History* 5 (Spring 1955): 16–28.

Atherton, Lewis E. "The Merchant Sutler in the Pre–Civil War Period." *Southwestern Social Science Quarterly* 19 (September 1938): 140–51.

Ayres, Mary C. "History of Fort Lewis, Colorado." *Colorado Magazine* 8 (May 1931): 81–92.

Badinelli, Don F. "Struggle in the Choctaw Nation: The Coal Miners Strike of 1894." *Chronicles of Oklahoma* 72 (Fall 1994): 292–311.

Ball, Larry D. "The United States Army and the Big Springs, Nebraska, Train Robbery of 1877." *Journal of the West* 34 (January 1995): 34–45.

————. "The United States Army as a Constabulary on the Northern Plains." *Great Plains Quarterly* 13 (Winter 1993): 21–32.

Ball, Eve. "The Apache Scouts: A Chiricahua Appraisal." *Arizona and the West* 7 (Winter 1965): 315–28.

Barrett, Arrie. "Western Frontier Forts of Texas, 1845–1861." *West Texas Historical Association Year Book* 7 (1931): 115–39.

Barrett, Leonora. "Transportation, Supplies, and Quarters for the West Texas Frontier Under the Federal Military System 1848–1861." *West Texas Historical Association Year Book* 5 (1929): 87–99.

Barry, Louise. "The Fort Leavenworth–Fort Gibson Military Road and the Founding of Fort Scott." *Kansas Historical Quarterly* 11 (May 1942): 115–29.

Bartlett, Richard A. "The Army, Conservation, and Ecology: The National Park Assignment." In *The United States Army in Peacetime*, 41–59. Ed. Robin Higham and Carol Brandt. Manhattan, Kans.: Military Affairs–Aerospace Historian Publishing, 1975.

Beck, Paul N. "Military Officers' Views of Indian Scouts, 1865–1890." *Military History of the West* 23 (Spring 1993): 1–19.

Beers, Henry P. "Military Protection of the Santa Fe Trail to 1843." *New Mexico Historical Review* 12 (April 1937): 113–33.

Bell, William Gardner. "A Dedication to the Memory of John Gregory Bourke, 1846–1896." *Arizona and the West* 13 (Winter 1971): 319–22.

————. "John Gregory Bourke: A Soldier Scientist in the Southwest." In *Military History of the Spanish-American Southwest: A Seminar*, 121–42. Ed. Bruno J. Rolak. Fort Huachuca, Ariz.: Fort Huachuca Museum, 1976.

Bender, Averam B. "Military Transportation in the Southwest, 1848–1860." *New Mexico Historical Review* 32 (April 1957): 123–50.

————. "Opening Routes across West Texas, 1848–1850." *Southwestern Historical Quarterly* 37 (October 1933): 116–35.

————. "The Soldier in the Far West, 1848–1860." *Pacific Historical Review* 8 (June 1939): 159–78.

Bentley, Charles A. "Captain Frederick W. Benteen and the Kiowas." *Chronicles of Oklahoma* 56 (Fall 1978): 344–47.

Bierschwale, Margaret. "Mason County, Texas, 1845–1870." *Southwestern Historical Quarterly* 52 (April 1949): 379–97.

Billington, Monroe. "Black Soldiers at Fort Selden, New Mexico, 1866–1891." *New Mexico Historical Review* 62 (January 1987): 65–80.

Black, Wilfred W. "The Army Doctor in the Trans-Mississippi West, 1775–1860." *Southwestern Social Science Quarterly* 24, no. 2 (1943): 118–28.

Blackburn, Forrest R. "Army Families in Frontier Forts." *Military Review* 49 (October 1969): 17–28.

Bluthardt, Robert F. "Baseball on the Military Frontier." *Fort Concho Report* 19 (Spring 1987): 17–26.

———. "The Men of Company F." *Fort Concho Report* 15 (Summer 1983): 3–9.

Bluthardt, Valerie C., ed. "Town Building on the Texas Frontier." *Fort Concho Report* 18 (Winter 1986–87): 1–46.

Braly, Earl Burk. "Fort Belknap of the Texas Frontier." *West Texas Historical Association Year Book* 30 (1954): 83–114.

Bradley, L. E. "Government Ice Harbors on the Upper Missouri." *North Dakota History* 60 (Summer 1993): 28–37.

Breeden, James O. "The Army and Public Health." In *The United States Army in Peacetime*, 83-105. Ed. Robin Higham and Carol Brandt. Manhattan, Kans.: Military Affairs–Aerospace Historian Publishing, 1975.

———. "Health of Early Texas: The Military Frontier." *Southwestern Historical Quarterly* 80 (April 1977): 357–98.

Briggs, Harold E. "Early Freight and Stage Lines in Dakota." *North Dakota Historical Quarterly* 3 (July 1929): 229–61.

Brodhead, Michael J. "Contributions of Medical Officers of the Regular Army to Natural History in the Pre–Civil War Era." In *History and Humanities: Essays in Honor of Wilbur S. Shepperson*, 3–14. Ed. Francis X. Hartigan. Reno: University of Nevada Press, 1989.

———. "A Dedication to the Memory of Elliott Coues, 1842–1899." *Arizona and the West* 13 (Spring 1971): 1–4.

———. "Elliott Coues and the Apaches." *Journal of Arizona History* 14 (Summer 1973): 87–94.

———. "The Military Naturalist: A Lewis and Clark Heritage." *We Proceeded On* 9 (November 1983): 6–10.

———. "Of Mice and Mastodons: Contributions to the Literature of Mammalogy by Officers and Men of the United States Army in the Nineteenth Century." *Archives of Natural History* 18 (1991): 363–74.

———. "Notes on the Military Presence in Nevada, 1843–1988." *Nevada Historical Quarterly* 32, no. 4 (1989): 261–77.

Brown, A. W. "The Administration of Justice in the Army." *Cornell Law Quarterly* 3 (1917–18): 178–210.

Brown, Lisle G. "The Yellowstone Supply Depot." *North Dakota History* 40 (Winter 1973): 24–33.

Brumbaugh, Thomas B. "Fort Laramie Hijinks: A New Manuscript Account." *Annals of Wyoming* 58 (Fall 1986): 4–9.

Brust, James S., and Lee H. Whittlesey. "'Roughing It Up the Yellowstone to Wonderland': The Nelson Miles/Colgate Hoyt Party in Yellowstone National Park, September 1878." *Montana, Magazine of Western History* 46 (Spring 1996): 56–64.

Buecker, Thomas R. "Can You Send Us Immediate Relief'? Army Expeditions to the Northern Black Hills, 1876–1878." *South Dakota History* 25 (Summer 1995): 95–115.

———. "Confrontation at Sturgis: An Episode in Civil-Military Race Relations, 1885." *South Dakota History* 14 (Fall 1984): 238–61.

———. "The 1887 Expansion of Fort Robinson." *Nebraska History* 68 (Summer 1987): 83–93.

———. "Fort Niobrara, 1880–1906: Guardian of the Rosebud Sioux." *Nebraska History* 65 (Fall 1984): 300–25.

———. "Prelude to Brownsville: The Twenty-Fifth Infantry at Fort Niobrara, Nebraska, 1902–06." *Great Plains Quarterly* 16 (Spring 1996): 95–106.

Burlingame, Merrill G. "The Influence of the Military in the Building of Montana." *Pacific Northwest Quarterly* 29 (April 1938): 135–50.

Butler, Anne. "Military Myopia: Prostitution on the Frontier." *Prologue* 13 (Winter 1981): 233–50.

Caldwell, JoAnne. "Community at a Crossroads: San Angelo and the Closing of Fort Concho, 1889." *Fort Concho Report* 20 and 21 (Winter 1988–Spring 1989): 5–21.

Caperton, Thomas J., and LoRheda Fry. "U.S. Army Food and Its Preparation during the Indian Wars, 1865–1900, with Selected Recipes." *El Palacio* 80 (Winter 1974): 29–45.

Carlson, Paul H. "Baseball's Abner Doubleday on the Texas Frontier, 1871–1873." *Military History of Texas and the Southwest* 12, no. 4 (1974): 236–43.

———. "The Discovery of Silver in West Texas." *West Texas Historical Association Year Book* 54 (1978): 55–64.

———. "William R. Shafter, Black Troops, and the Finale to the Red River War." *Red River Valley Historical Review* 3 (Spring 1978): 247–58.

———. "William R. Shafter, Black Troops, and the Opening of the Llano Estacado, 1870–1875." *Panhandle-Plains Historical Review* 47 (1974): 1–18.

Carroll, John M. "The Doubleday Myth and Texas Baseball." *Southwestern Historical Quarterly* 92 (April 1989): 597–612.

Carroll, Murray L. "Governor Francis E. Warren, the United States Army, and the Chinese Massacre at Rock Springs." *Annals of Wyoming* 59 (Fall 1987): 16–27.

Cashion, Ty. "(Gun) Smoke Gets in Your Eyes: A Revisionist Look at 'Violent' Fort Griffin." *Southwestern Historical Quarterly* 99 (July 1995): 81–94.

————. "Life on Government Hill: Fort Griffin before the Boom." *West Texas Historical Association Year Book* 70 (1994): 113–25.

Cass, Edward C. "Flood Control and the Corps of Engineers in the Missouri Valley, 1902–1973." *Nebraska History* 63 (Spring 1983): 108–22.

Chappell, Gordon S. "Surgeon at Fort Sidney: Captain Walter Reed's Experiences at a Nebraska Military Post, 1883–1884." *Nebraska History* 4 (Fall 1973): 419–43.

Chaput, Donald. "The Early Missouri Graduates of West Point: Officers or Merchants?" *Missouri Historical Review* 72 (April 1978): 262–70.

Clapsaddle, David K. "Conflict and Commerce on the Santa Fe Trail: The Fort Riley–Fort Larned Road, 1860–1867." *Kansas History* 16 (Summer 1993): 124–37.

————. "The Fort Hays–Fort Dodge Road." *Kansas History* 14 (Summer 1991): 101–12.

Clark, Christopher G. "The Myth of Indian Aggression in Early Nebraska." *Platte Valley Review* 14 (Spring 1986): 26–34.

Clark, Michael J. "Improbable Ambassadors: Black Soldiers at Fort Douglas, 1896–1899." *Utah Historical Quarterly* 46 (Summer 1978): 282–301.

Clary, David A. "The Role of the Army Surgeon in the West: Daniel Weisel at Fort Davis, Texas, 1868–1872." *Western Historical Quarterly* 3 (January 1972): 53–66.

Coen, Rena Neumann, "Edward K. Thomas: Fort Snelling Artist." *Minnesota History* 41 (Fall 1969): 317–26.

Coffin, Edward M. "Army Life on the Frontier, 1865–1898." *Military Affairs* 20 (Fall 1956): 192–201.

Coker, Caleb, and Janet G. Humphrey. "The Texas Frontier in 1850: Dr. Ebenezer Swift and the View from Fort Martin Scott." *Southwestern Historical Quarterly* 96 (January 1993): 393–413.

Connelly, Thomas L. "The American Camel Experiment: A Reappraisal." *Southwestern Historical Quarterly* 69 (April 1966): 442–62.

Conrad, David E. "The Whipple Expedition in Arizona, 1853–1854." *Arizona and the West* 11 (Summer 1969): 147–78.

————. "Whipple's Pacific Railroad Survey in the Indian Territory." *Red River Valley Historical Review* 1 (Winter 1974): 391–415.

Cooling, B. Franklin. "The Army and Flood and Disaster Relief." In *The United States Army in Peacetime*, 61–81. Ed. Robin Higham and Carol Brandt. Manhattan, Kans.: Military Affairs–Aerospace Historian Publishing, 1975.

Cooper, Jerry M. "The Army as Strikebreaker–The Railroad Strikes of 1877 and 1894." *Labor History* 18 (Spring 1977): 179–96.

————. "The Army's Search for a Mission, 1865–1890." In *Against All Enemies: Interpretations of American Military History from Colonial Times to the Present*,

173–95. Ed. Kenneth J. Hagan and William R. Roberts. Westport, Conn.: Greenwood Press, 1986.

———. "Federal Military Intervention in Domestic Disorders." In *The United States Military under the Constitution of the United States, 1789–1989*, 120–50. Ed. Richard H. Kohn. New York: New York University Press, 1991.

Coppersmith, Clifford P. "Indians in the Army: Professional Advocacy and Regularization of Indian Military Service, 1889–1897." *Military History of the West* 26 (Fall 1996): 159–85.

Corbett, William P. "Rifles and Ruts: Army Road Builders in Indian Territory." *Chronicles of Oklahoma* 60 (Fall 1982): 294–309.

Corbusier, William T. "Camp Sheridan, Nebraska." *Nebraska History* 29 (March 1961): 29–53.

Crimmins, Martin L. "Camp Peña Colorado, Texas." *West Texas Historical and Scientific Society Bulletin* 56 (1935): 8–22.

———. "Experiences of an Army Surgeon at Fort Chadbourne." *West Texas Historical Association Year Book* 15 (1939): 31–39.

———. "Fort Fillmore." *New Mexico Historical Review* 6 (October 1931): 327–33.

———. "Fort McKavett, Texas." *Southwestern Historical Quarterly* 38 (July 1934): 28–39.

———. "Fort Massachusetts, First United States Military Post in Colorado." *Colorado Magazine* 14 (July 1937): 128–33.

———. "General Albert J. Myer: The Father of the Signal Corps." *West Texas Historical Association Year Book* 29 (1953): 47–66.

Crook, Cornelia, and Garland Crook. "Fort Lincoln, Texas." *Texas Military History* 4 (Fall 1964): 145–61.

Culpin, Alan. "A Brief History of Social and Domestic Life Among the Military in Wyoming, 1849–1890." *Annals of Wyoming* 45 (Spring 1973): 93–108.

Daniel, Wayne. "Fort Concho's Water Supply." *Fort Concho Report* 16 (Spring 1984): 22–26.

Davis, W. N. "The Sutler at Fort Bridger." *Western Historical Quarterly* 2 (January 1971): 37–54.

D'Elia, Donald J. "The Argument over Civilian or Military Indian Control, 1865–1880." *Historian* 24 (February 1962): 207–25.

De Lorme, Roland L. "The Long Arm of the Law: Crime and Federal Law Enforcement in the Northern Tier Territories." In *Centennial West: Essays on the Northern Tier States.* Ed. William L. Lang. Seattle: University of Washington Press, 1991.

De Noyer, Charles. "The History of Fort Totten." *Collections of the State Historical Society of North Dakota* 3 (1910): 178–236.

Dinges, Bruce J. "Colonel Grierson Invests on the West Texas Frontier." *Fort Concho Report* 16 (Fall 1984): 2–13.

———. "The Court-Martial of Lieutenant Henry O. Flipper: An Example of Black-White Relationships in the Army, 1881." *American West* 9 (January 1972): 12–17, 59–61.

———. "The Irrepressible Captain Armes: Politics and Justice in the Indian-Fighting Army." *Journal of the West* 32 (April 1993): 38–52.

———. "Leighton Finley: A Forgotten Soldier of the Apache Wars." *Journal of Arizona History* 29 (Summer 1988): 163–84.

———. "New Directions in Frontier Military History: A Review Essay." *New Mexico Historical Review* 66 (January 1991): 103–16.

———. "Scandal in the Tenth Cavalry: A Fort Sill Case History." *Arizona and the West* 28 (Summer 1986): 125–40.

———. "The Victorio Campaign of 1880: Cooperation and Conflict on the United States–Mexico Border." *New Mexico Historical Review* 62 (January 1987): 81–94.

Dippie, Brian W. "Government Patronage: Catlin, Stanley, and Eastman." *Montana, Magazine of Western History* 44 (Autumn 1994): 40–53.

———. "'What Valor Is': Artists and the Mythic Moment." *Montana, Magazine of Western History* 46 (Autumn 1996): 40–55.

Dobak, William A. "The Army and the Buffalo: A Demur." *Western Historical Quarterly* 26 (Summer 1995): 197–202.

———. "Black Regulars Speak." *Panhandle-Plains Historical Review* 47 (1974): 19–27.

———. "Licit Amusements of Enlisted Men in the Post–Civil War Army." *Montana, Magazine of Western History* 45 (Spring 1995): 34–45.

———. "Yellow-Leg Journalists: Enlisted Men as Newspaper Reporters in the Sioux Campaign, 1876." *Journal of the West* 13 (January 1974): 86–112.

Dollar, Charles M. "Putting the Army on Wheels: The Story of the Twenty-Fifth Infantry Bicycle Corps." *Prologue* 17 (Spring 1985): 7–23.

Drees, James David "The Army and Horse Thieves." *Kansas History* 11 (Spring 1988): 35–53.

Duke, Escal F. "O. M. Smith, Frontier Pay Clerk." *West Texas Historical Association Year Book* 45 (1969): 45–57.

Dunn, Adrian R. "A History of Old Fort Berthold." *North Dakota History* 30 (October 1963): 157–240.

Dykstra, Robert R. "Field Notes: Overdosing on Dodge City." *Western Historical Quarterly* 27 (Winter 1996): 505–14.

Echo-Hawk, Walter R., and Roger Echo-Hawk. "Repatriation, Reburial, and Religious Rights." In *Handbook of American Indian Religious Freedom*, 63–80. Ed. Christopher Vecsey. New York: Crossroad Publishing Co., 1991.

Edens, Walter. "Wyoming's Fort Libraries: The March of Intellect." *Annals of Wyoming* 51 (Fall 1979): 54–62.

Edrington, Thomas S. "Military Influence on the Texas–New Mexico Boundary Settlement." *New Mexico Historical Review* 59 (October 1984): 371–93.

Edwards, Paul M. "Fort Wadsworth and the Friendly Santee Sioux, 1864–1892." *South Dakota Department of History Report and Historical Collections* 31 (1962): 74–156.

Egan, Ferol. "The Building of Fort Churchill: Blueprint for a Military Fiasco, 1860." *American West* 9 (March 1972): 4–9.

Ellis, Catherine. "A Common Soldier at Camp Douglas, 1866–68." *Utah Historical Quarterly* 65 (Winter 1997): 49–63.

Ellis, Richard N. "General John Pope and the Southern Plains Indians, 1875–1883." *Southwestern Historical Quarterly* 72 (October 1968): 152–69.

———. "The Humanitarian Generals." *Western Historical Quarterly* 3 (April 1972): 169–78.

———. "The Humanitarian Soldiers." *Journal of Arizona History* 10 (Summer 1969), 53–66.

Eppinga, Jane. "Henry O. Flipper in the Court of Private Land Claims: The Arizona Career of West Point's First Black Graduate." *Journal of Arizona History* 36 (Spring 1995): 33–54.

Erikkson, Erik. "Sioux City and the Black Hills Gold Rush 1874–1877." *Iowa Journal of History and Politics* 20 (July 1922): 319–47.

Etter, Patricia A. "To California on the Southern Route—1849." *Overland Journal* 13 (Fall 1995): 2–12.

Ewy, Marvin. "The United States Army in the Kansas Border Troubles, 1855–1856." *Kansas Historical Quarterly* 32 (Winter 1966): 385–400.

Farnham, Wallace D. "The Weakened Spring of Government: A Study in Nineteenth Century American History." *American Historical Review* 68 (April 1963): 662–80.

Feaver, Eric. "Indian Soldiers, 1891–95: An Experiment on the Closing Frontier." *Prologue* 7 (Summer 1975): 109–18.

Field, William T. "Fort Duncan and Old Eagle Pass." *Texas Military History* 6 (Summer 1967): 160–71.

Fine, Harry L. "Fort Laramie: Post Office in the Old West." *Posta: Postal History Journal* 8 (November 1977): 2–5.

Fisher, B. J. "Medical Conditions at West Texas Military Posts in the 1850s." *West Texas Historical Association Year Book* 62 (1986): 108–18.

———. "Military Justice on the Texas Frontier." *West Texas Historical Association Year Book* 64 (1988): 123–39.

Fite, Gilbert C. "The United States Army and Relief to Pioneer Settlers, 1874–1875." *Journal of the West* 6 (January 1967): 99–107.

Flanagan, Vincent J. "Gouverneur Kemble Warren, Explorer of the Nebraska Territory." *Nebraska History* 51 (Summer 1970): 171–98.

Fletcher, Marvin E. "The Army and Minority Groups." In *The United States Army in Peacetime*, 107–27. Ed. Robin Higham and Carol Brandt. Manhattan, Kans.: Military Affairs–Aerospace Historian Publishing, 1975.

———. "Army Fire Fighters." *Idaho Yesterdays* 16 (Summer 1972): 12–15.

———. "The Black Bicycle Corps." *Arizona and the West* 16 (Autumn 1974): 219–32.

Foote, Cheryl J. "'My Husband Was a Madman and a Murderer': Josephine Clifford McCrackin, Army Wife, Writer, and Conservationist." *New Mexico Historical Review* 65 (April 1990): 199–224.

Foreman, Carolyn Thomas. "Military Discipline in Early Oklahoma." *Chronicles of Oklahoma* 6 (June 1928): 140–44.

Fort, Homer T. "John Pope, the First Great Wildcatter." *Greater Llano Estacado and Southwest Heritage* 7 (Fall 1977): 11–15.

Foster, James M., Jr. "Fort Bascom, New Mexico." *New Mexico Historical Review* 35 (January 1960): 30–62.

Frazer, Robert W. "Army Agriculture in New Mexico, 1852–1853." *New Mexico Historical Review* 50 (October 1975): 313–34.

———. "Purveyors of Flour to the Army: Department of New Mexico, 1849–1861." *New Mexico Historical Review* 47 (July 1972): 213–38.

Freedom, Gary S. "Military Forts and Logistical Self-Sufficiency on the Northern Great Plains, 1866–1891." *North Dakota History* 50 (Spring 1983): 4–11.

———. "Moving Men and Supplies: Military Transportation on the Northern Great Plains, 1866–1891." *South Dakota History* 14 (Summer 1984): 114–33.

———. "The Role of the Military and the Spread of Settlement in the Northern Great Plains, 1866–1891." *Midwest Review* 9 (Spring 1987): 1–11.

Friis, Herman R. "The Image of the American West at Mid-Century (1840–60): A Product of the Scientific Geographical Exploration by the United States Government." In *The Frontier Re-examined*, 49–63. Ed. John Francis McDermott. Urbana, Ill.: University of Illinois Press, 1967.

———. "The Role of the United States Topographical Engineers in Compiling a Cartographic Image of the Plains Region." In *Images of the Plains: The Role of Human Nature in Settlement*, 59–74. Ed. Brian W. Blouet and Merlin P. Lawson. Lincoln: University of Nebraska Press, 1975.

Furman, H. W. C. "Restrictions upon the Use of the Army Imposed by the Posse Comitatus Act." *Military Law Review* 7 (January 1960): 85–129.

Gamble, Richard D. "Army Chaplains at Frontier Posts, 1830–1860." *Historical Magazine of the Protestant Episcopal Church* 27, no. 4 (1958): 287–304.

Gardner, Hamilton. "Romance at Old Cantonment Leavenworth: The Marriage of 2d Lt. Philip St. George Cooke in 1830." *Kansas Historical Quarterly* 22 (Summer 1956): 97–113.

Garver, John B., Jr. "Practical Military Geographers and Mappers of the Trans-Mississippi West, 1820–1860." In *Mapping the North American Plains: Essays in the History of Cartography*, 111–26. Ed. Frederick C. Luebke, Frances W. Kaye, and Gary E. Moulton. Norman: University of Oklahoma Press, 1987.

Gates, John M. "The Alleged Isolation of U.S. Army Officers in the Late 19th Century." *Parameters: The Journal of the U.S. Army War College* 10 (September 1980): 32–45.

―――. "Indians and Insurrectos: The U.S. Army's Experience with Insurgency." *Parameters: The Journal of the U.S. Army War College* 13 (March 1983): 59–68.

Gates, Paul Wallace. "Major Powell's 'Arid' Lands in Kansas." In *Kansas and the West: Bicentennial Essays in Honor of Nyle H. Miller.* Ed. Forrest R. Blackburn. Topeka: Kansas State Historical Society, 1976.

Gephart, Ronald M. "Politicians, Soldiers and Strikes: The Reorganization of the Nebraska Militia and the Omaha Strike of 1882." *Nebraska History* 46 (June 1965): 89–120.

Giese, Lucretia Hoover. "Artist Collaborators: A Surrogate Hand—Seth Eastman's for Bartlett's." In *Drawing the Borderline: Artist-Explorers of the U.S.-Mexico Boundary Survey,* 79–94. Albuquerque, N.Mex.: Albuquerque Museum, 1996.

Gillett, Mary C. "United States Army Surgeons and the Big Horn–Yellowstone Expedition of 1876." *Montana, Magazine of Western History* 39 (Winter 1989): 16–27.

Goplen, Arnold O. "Fort Abraham Lincoln, A Typical Frontier Military Post." *North Dakota History* 13 (October 1946): 176–221.

Graham, Roy Eugene. "Federal Fort Architecture in Texas during the Nineteenth Century." *Southwestern Historical Quarterly* 74 (October 1970): 165–88.

Graham, Stanley S. "Duty, Life and Law in the Old Army, 1865–1890." *Military History of Texas and the Southwest* 12, no. 4 (1970): 273–81.

―――. "Routine at Western Cavalry Posts, 1833–1861." *Journal of the West* 15 (July 1976): 49–59.

Grange, Roger T., Jr. "Fort Robinson, Outpost on the Plains." *Nebraska History* 39 (September 1958): 191–240.

―――. "Treating the Wounded at Fort Robinson." *Nebraska History* 45 (September 1964): 273–94.

Gray, John S. "Sutler on Custer's Last Campaign." *North Dakota History* 43 (Summer 1976): 14–21.

―――. "Veterinary Service on Custer's Last Campaign." *Kansas Historical Quarterly* 43 (Autumn 1977): 249–63.

Gray, Lora Taylor. "'Winners of the West': A Personal Reminiscence of Lauren Winfield Aldrich." *Journal of the West* 33 (January 1994): 96–100.

Green, Curtis E. "Captain Charles King: Popular Military Novelist." *Arizoniana* 2 (Summer 1961): 23–26.

Green, Donald E. "The Oklahoma Land Run of 1889: A Centennial Re-Interpretation." *Chronicles of Oklahoma* 67 (Summer 1989): 116–49.

Greene, Jerome A. "Army Bread and Army Mission on the Frontier, with Special Reference to Fort Laramie, Wyoming, 1865–1890." *Annals of Wyoming* 47 (Fall 1975): 191–219.

Greenleaf, J. Cameron. "Captain Jack" Crawford: The Poet Scout." *Arizoniana* 2 (Summer 1961): 18–21.

Guentzel, Richard. "The Department of the Platte and Western Settlement, 1866–1877." *Nebraska History* 56 (Fall 1975): 389–417.

Hacker, Barton C. "The United States Army as a National Police Force: The Federal Policing of Labor Disputes, 1877–1898." *Military Affairs* 33 (April 1969): 255–64.

Hale, Henry. "The Soldier, the Advance Guard of Civilization." *Mississippi Valley Historical Association Proceedings* 7 (1913–1914): 93–98.

Haltman, Kenneth. "Between Science and Art: Titian Ramsay Peale's Long Expedition Sketches, Newly Recovered at the State Historical Society of Iowa." *Palimpsest* 74 (Summer 1993): 62–81.

Hammer, Kenneth M. "Railroads and the Frontier Garrisons of Dakota Territory." *North Dakota History* 46 (Summer 1979): 24–34.

Hampton, H. Duane. "The Army and the National Parks." *Montana, Magazine of Western History* 22 (July 1972): 64–79.

Hardeman, Nicholas P. "Brick Stronghold of the Border: Fort Assinniboine, 1879–1911." *Montana, Magazine of Western History* 29 (April 1979): 54–67.

Hargreaves, Reginald. "The Idle Hours." *Military Review* 46 (December 1966): 29–35.

Harte, John Bret. "Conflict at San Carlos: The Military-Civilian Struggle for Control, 1882–1885." *Arizona and the West* 15 (Spring 1973): 27–44.

Haskew, Eula. "Stribling and Kirkland of Fort Griffin." *West Texas Historical Association Year Book* 32 (October 1956): 55–69.

Hasson, Alex B. "Report of the Post Surgeon at Fort Phantom Hill, for 1852." *West Texas Historical Association Year Book* 1 (June 1925): 73–77.

Hatcher, John H. "Fort Phantom Hill." *Texas Military History* 3 (Fall 1963): 154–64.

Hatfield, Shelley Bowen. "The Death of Emmet Crawford: Who Was to Blame?" *Journal of Arizona History* 29 (Summer 1988): 131–48.

Hawes, Joseph M. "The Signal Corps and Its Weather Service, 1870–1890." *Military Affairs* 30 (Summer 1966): 68–76.

Hedren, Paul L. "Captain King's Centennial Year Look at Fort Laramie, Wyoming." *Annals of Wyoming* 48 (Spring 1976): 100–108.

―――. "A Footnote to History: The U.S. Army at Promontory, Utah, May 10, 1869." *Utah Historical Quarterly* 49 (Fall 1981): 363–73.

―――. "Fort Laramie and the Sioux War of 1876." *South Dakota History* 17 (Fall–Winter 1987): 223–40.

―――. "On Duty at Fort Ridgely, Minnesota: 1853–1867." *South Dakota History* 7 (Spring 1977): 168–92.

―――. "The Sioux War Adventures of Dr. Charles V. Petteys, Acting Assistant Surgeon." *Journal of the West* 32 (April 1993): 29–37.

Herbert, Paul. "Fort Concho: A State Asset." *Texas Military History* 7 (Summer 1968): 128–45.

Hill, Burton S. "Thomas S. Twiss, Indian Agent." *Great Plains Journal* 6 (Spring 1967): 85–96.

Hinds, James R. "The Army and Las Vegas: A Century of Association." *Periodical: Journal of the Council on America's Military Past* 17, no. 2 (1990): 35–46.

Hinton, Harwood P. "Life and Death on the Goodnight-Loving Trail." *West Texas Historical Association Year Book* 70 (1994): 102–12.

Hoeckman, Steven. "The History of Fort Sully." *South Dakota Historical Collections* 26 (1952): 222–77.

Holt, Daniel D., and Marilyn Irvin Holt. "'The Pleasures of Female Society' at Cantonment Leavenworth." *Kansas History* 8 (Spring 1985): 21–35.

Hoop, Oscar W. "History of Fort Hoskins, 1856–65." *Oregon Historical Quarterly* 30 (December 1929): 346–61.

Hudson, James J. "The California National Guard in the San Francisco Earthquake and Fire of 1906." *California Historical Quarterly* 55 (Summer 1976): 137–49.

Huey, William G. "Making Music: Brass Bands on the Northern Plains, 1860–1930." *North Dakota History* 54 (Winter 1987): 3–13.

Hughes, Frederic J., Jr. "Albert James Myer: Army Physician and Climatologist." *Transactions of the American Clinical and Climatological Association* 81 (1969): 119–29.

Hughes, Willis B. "The First Dragoons on the Western Frontier, 1834–1846." *Arizona and the West* 12 (Summer 1970): 115–38.

Hume, Edgar Erskine. "The Foundation of American Meteorology by the United States Army Medical Department." *Bulletin of the History of Medicine* 8 (January–May 1940): 202–38.

Hummell, Edward A. "The Story of Fort Sisseton." *South Dakota Historical Review* 2 (April 1937): 126–44.

Hurt, R. Douglas. "The Construction and Development of Fort Wallace, Kansas, 1865–1882." *Kansas Historical Quarterly* 43 (Spring 1977): 44–55.

———. "Fort Wallace, Kansas, 1865–1882: A Frontier Post during the Indian Wars." *Red River Valley Historical Review* 1 (Spring 1974): 132–45.

Huseas, Marion M. "Touched Nothing to Drink . . .: Frontier Army Leisure." *Periodical: Journal of the Council on America's Military Past* 12 (January 1981): 11–23.

Hutton, Paul A. "'Fort Desolation': The Military Establishment, the Railroad, and Settlement on the Northern Plains." *North Dakota History* 56 (Spring 1989): 21–30.

———. "The Frontier Army." In *American Frontier and Western Issues: A Historiographical Review*, 253–74. Ed. Roger L. Nichols. New York: Greenwood Press, 1986.

————. "Phil Sheridan's Crusade for Yellowstone." *American History Illustrated* 19 (February 1985): 7, 10–15.

Innis, Ben. "Bottoms Up! The Smith and Leighton Yellowstone Store Ledger of 1876." *North Dakota History* 51 (Summer 1984): 24–38.

Isern, Thomas D. "The Controversial Career of Edward W. Wynkoop." *Colorado Magazine* 56 (Winter–Spring 1979): 1–18.

Ivey, James. "'The Best Sutler's Store in America': James E. Barrow and the Formation of Trader's Row at Fort Union, New Mexico, 1867–1891." *New Mexico Historical Review* 70 (July 1995): 299–327.

Jackson, W. Turrentine. "The Army Engineers as Road Builders in Territorial Iowa." *Iowa Journal of History and Politics* 47 (January 1949): 15–33.

————. "The Army Engineers as Road Surveyors and Builders in Kansas and Nebraska, 1854–1858." *Kansas Historical Quarterly* 17 (February 1949): 37–59.

Jennings, Jan. "Frank J. Grodavent: Western Army Architect." *Essays and Monographs in Colorado History* 11 (1990): 2–23.

Johnson, Sally A. "The Sixth's Elysian Fields: Fort Atkinson on the Council Bluffs." *Nebraska History* 40 (March 1959): 1–38.

Kalisch, Philip A., and Beatrice J. Kalisch. "Indian Territory Forts: Charnel Houses of the Frontier, 1839–1865." *Chronicles of Oklahoma* 50 (Spring 1972): 65–81.

Kanarek, Harold. "The U.S. Army Corps of Engineers and Early Internal Improvements in Maryland." *Maryland Historical Magazine* 72 (Spring 1977): 99–109.

Kane, Randy. "'An Honorable and Upright Man': Sidney R. DeLong as Post Trader at Fort Bowie." *Journal of Arizona History* 19 (Autumn 1978): 297–314.

Karlin, Jules A. "The Anti-Chinese Outbreak in Tacoma, 1885." *Pacific Historical Review* 23 (August 1954): 271–83.

————. "The Anti-Chinese Outbreaks in Seattle, 1885–1886." *Pacific Northwest Quarterly* 39 (1948): 103–30.

Kenner, Charles. "Guardians in Blue: The United States Cavalry and the Growth of the Texas Range Cattle Industry." *Journal of the West* 34 (January 1995): 46–54.

Kepfield, Sam S. "Grasshoppers, Destitution, and Public Relief in Western Nebraska, 1874–1875." *Journal of the West* 34 (July 1995): 93–100.

————. "'A Great Deal Like Smallpox': 'Destitution Business' and State Drought Relief in Nebraska, 1890–1895." *Heritage of the Great Plains* 26 (Summer 1993): 37–46.

King, James T. "'A Better Way': General George Crook and the Ponca Indians." *Nebraska History* 50 (Fall 1969): 239–56.

————. "George Crook: Indian Fighter and Humanitarian." *Arizona and the West* 9 (Winter 1967): 333–48.

————. "The Sword and the Pen: The Poetry of the Military Frontier." *Nebraska History* 47 (September 1966): 229–45.

Kirkus, Peggy D. "Fort David A. Russell: A Study of Its History from 1867 to 1890, with a Brief Summary of Events from 1890 to the Present." *Annals of Wyoming* 40 (October 1968): 161–92; 41 (April 1969): 83–111.

Knight, Oliver. "A Dedication to the Memory of Charles King, 1844–1933." *Arizona and the West* 15 (Autumn 1973): 209–12.

———. "Toward an Understanding of the Western Town." *Western Historical Quarterly* 4 (January 1973): 27–42.

Kyvig, David E. "Policing the Panhandle: Fort Elliott, Texas, 1875–1890." *Red River Valley Historical Review* 1 (Autumn 1974): 222–32.

Lamkin, Patricia E. "Blacks in San Angelo: Relations between Fort Concho and the City, 1875–1889." *West Texas Historical Association Year Book* 66 (1990): 26–37.

———. "Fort Concho: The Lost Years, 1889–1930." *Fort Concho Report* 20, no. 4 (1988); and 21, no. 1 (1989): 22–35.

Lang, William L. "Charles A. Broadwater and the Main Chance in Montana." *Montana, Magazine of Western History* 39 (Summer 1989): 30–36.

Langellier, James P. "Desert Documentary: The William Lee Diary Account of the James H. Simpson Expedition, 1858–1859." *Annals of Wyoming* 59 (Fall 1987): 36–47.

Langley, Lester D. "The Democratic Tradition and Military Reform, 1878–1885." *Southwestern Social Science Quarterly* 48 (September 1967): 192–200.

Langum, David J. "Pioneer Justice on the Overland Trails." *Western Historical Quarterly* 5 (October 1974): 421–39.

Larew, Karl G. "Frederick Phisterer and the Indian Wars." *Journal of the West* 30 (October 1991): 22–28.

Laurie, Clayton D. "'The Chinese Must Go': The United States Army and the Anti-Chinese Riots in Washington Territory, 1885–1886." *Pacific Northwest Quarterly* 81 (January 1990): 22–29.

———. "Civil Disorder and the Military in Rock Springs, Wyoming: The Army's Role in the 1885 Chinese Massacre." *Montana, Magazine of Western History* 40 (Summer 1990): 44–59.

———. "Extinguishing Frontier Brushfires: The U.S. Army's Role in Quelling the Pullman Strike in the West, 1894." *Journal of the West* 32 (April 1993): 54–63.

———. "Filling the Breach: Military Aid to the Civil Power in the Trans-Mississippi West." *Western Historical Quarterly* 25 (Summer 1994): 149–62.

———. "The United States Army and the Labor Radicals of the Coeur d'Alenes: Federal Military Intervention in the Mining Wars of 1892–1899." *Idaho Yesterdays* 37 (Summer 1993): 12–29.

Layton, Stanford J. "Fort Rawlins, Utah: A Question of Mission and Means." *Utah Historical Quarterly* 42 (Winter 1974): 68–83.

Leckie, Shirley A. "Fort Concho: Paradise for Children." *Fort Concho Report* 19 (Spring 1987): 1–15.

————. "Reading between the Lines: Another Look at Officers' Wives in the Post–Civil War Frontier Army." *Military History of the Southwest* 19 (Fall 1989): 137–60.

Leckie, William H. "Black Regulars on the Texas Frontier, 1866–85." In *The Texas Military Experience: From the Texas Revolution through World War II*, 86–96. Ed. Joseph G. Dawson III. College Station: Texas A&M University Press, 1995.

Lee, Robert. "Warriors in Ranks: American Indian Units in the Regular Army, 1891–1897." *South Dakota History* 21 (Fall 1991): 263–316.

Leiker, James N. "Black Soldiers at Fort Hays, Kansas, 1867–1869: A Study in Civilian and Military Violence." *Great Plains Quarterly* 17 (Winter 1997): 3–17.

Lent, John A. "The Press on Wheels: A History of *The Frontier Index*." *Journal of the West* 10 (October 1971): 662–99.

————. "The Press on Wheels: A History of *The Frontier Index* of Nebraska, Colorado, Wyoming, Elsewhere." *Annals of Wyoming* 43 (Fall 1971): 165–204.

Leonard, Thomas C. "Red, White and the Army Blue: Empathy and Anger in the American West." *American Quarterly* 26 (May 1974): 176–90.

————. "The Reluctant Conquerors: How the Generals Viewed the Indians." *American Heritage* 27 (August 1976): 34–41.

Levine, Richard R. "Indian Fighters and Indian Reformers: Grant's Indian Peace Policy and the Conservative Consensus." *Civil War History* 31 (December 1985): 329–50.

Libby, Orin G. "Fort Abercrombie, 1857–1877." *Collections of the State Historical Society of North Dakota* 2 (1908): 1–163.

Lindberg, Christer, ed. "Foreigners in Action at Wounded Knee." *Nebraska History* 71 (Winter 1990): 171–81.

Lubick, George M. "Soldiers and Scientists in the Petrified Forest." *Journal of Arizona History* 29 (Winter 1988): 391–412.

McChristian, Douglas C. "Apaches and Soldiers: Mail Protection in West Texas." *Periodical: Journal of the Council on America's Military Past* 13, no. 3 (1985): 3–17.

————. "The Bug Juice War." *Annals of Wyoming* 49 (Fall 1977): 253–61.

————. "The Commissary Sergeant: His Life at Fort Davis." *Military History of Texas and the Southwest* 14, no. 1 (1978): 21–32.

————. "'Dress On the Colors, Boys!' Black Noncommissioned Officers in the Regular Army, 1866–1898." *Colorado Heritage* (Spring 1996): 38–44.

McClernard, Edward J. "Service in Montana, 1870 and 1871." *Military Affairs* 15 (Winter 1951): 192–98.

McDermott, John D. "Crime and Punishment in the United States Army: A Phase of Fort Laramie History." *Journal of the West* 7 (April 1968): 246–55.

————. "The *Frontier Scout*: A View of Fort Rice in 1865." *North Dakota History* 61 (Fall 1994): 25–35.

McElroy, Harold L. "Mercurial Military: A Study of the Central Montana Frontier Army Policy." *Montana, Magazine of Western History* 4 (Fall 1954): 9–23

McKale, William. "Military Photography." *Journal of the West* 28 (January 1989): 83–88.

McMaster, Richard K. "Records and Reminiscences of Old Fort Bliss." *Password* 8 (Spring 1963): 18–32.

McMurtrie, Douglas C. "The Fourth Infantry Press at Fort Bridger." *Annals of Wyoming* 13 (October 1941): 347–51.

McMurtry, Larry. "How the West Was Won or Lost." *New Republic* (October 22, 1990): 32–38.

Madsen, Brigham D. "Stansbury's Expedition to the Great Salt Lake, 1849–50." *Utah Historical Quarterly* 56 (1988): 148–59.

Manley, Robert N. "In the Wake of the Grasshoppers: Public Relief in Nebraska, 1874–1875." *Nebraska History* 44 (December 1963): 255–75.

Mantor, Lyle E. "Fort Kearny and the Westward Movement." *Nebraska History* 29 (September 1948): 175–207.

———. "Stage Coach and Freighter Days at Fort Kearny." *Nebraska History* 29 (December 1948): 324–38.

Mardock, Robert W. "The Plains Frontier and the Indian Peace Policy, 1865–1880." *Nebraska History* 49 (Summer 1968): 187–201.

Martin, Michael. "Dr. Beaumont's Miracle." *American History Illustrated* 23 (September 1988): 14, 28–29.

Martin, Robert Sidney. "United States Army Mapping in Texas, 1848–50." In *The Mapping of the American Southwest*, 37–56. Ed. Dennis Reinhartz and Charles C. Colley. College Station: Texas A&M University Press, 1987.

Mattes, Merrill J. "Fort Mitchell, Scotts Bluff, Nebraska Territory." *Nebraska History* 33 (March 1952): 1–34.

———. "The Old Fort Mitchell, Nebraska, Revisited." *Overland Journal* 7, no. 2 (1989): 2–11.

———. "The Sutler's Store at Fort Laramie." *Annals of Wyoming* 18 (July 1946): 93–137.

———, and Paul Henderson. "The Pony Express: Across Nebraska from St. Joseph to Fort Laramie." *Nebraska History* 41 (June 1960): 83–122.

Matthews, James T. "Using the Deity's Name in Reverence: The Chaplains at Fort Concho." *Panhandle-Plains Historical Review* 68 (1995): 37–44.

Mattison, Ray H. "The Army Post on the Northern Plains, 1865–1885." *Nebraska History* 35 (March 1954): 17–43.

———. "Fort Rice, North Dakota's First Missouri River Military Post." *North Dakota History* 20 (April 1953): 87–108.

———. "Old Fort Stevenson, a Typical Missouri River Military Post." *North Dakota History* 18 (April–June 1951): 53–91.

May, Robert E. "Invisible Men: Blacks and the U.S. Army in the Mexican War." *Historian* 49, no. 4 (1987): 463–77.

Mayes, William G., Jr. "Did Murphy Blunder? The Closing of Fort Hays, Kansas."
  Journal of the West 15 (July 1976): 38–48.
Meketa, Jacqueline Dorgan. "A Soldier in New Mexico, 1847–1848." *New Mexico
  Historical Review* 66 (January 1991): 15–32.
Miewald, Robert D. "The Army Post Schools: A Report from the Bureaucratic
  Wars." *Military Affairs* 39 (February 1975): 8–11.
Miles, Susan. "The Post Office War." *Fort Concho Report* 12 (Spring 1980): 5–13.
———. "The Soldiers Riot." *Fort Concho Report* 13 (Spring 1981): 1–20.
Miller, Darlis A. "Captain Jack Crawford: A Western Military Scout on the
  Chautauqua Circuit." *South Dakota History* 21 (Fall 1991): 230–46.
———. "Civilians and Military Supply in the Southwest." *Journal of Arizona History*
  23 (Summer 1982): 115–38.
———. "Foragers, Army Women and Prostitutes." In *New Mexico Women: Inter-
  cultural Perspectives*, 141–68. Ed. Joan M. Jensen and Darlis A. Miller.
  Albuquerque: University of New Mexico Press, 1986.
———. "The Perils of a Post Sutler: William H. Moore at Fort Union, New
  Mexico, 1859–1870." *Journal of the West* 32 (April 1993): 7–18.
———. "The Role of the Army Inspector in the Southwest: Nelson H. Davis in
  New Mexico and Arizona, 1863–1873." *New Mexico Historical Review* 59 (April
  1984): 137–64.
Montgomery, Mrs. Frank C. "Fort Wallace and Its Relation to the Frontier."
  Collections of the Kansas State Historical Society 17 (1928): 189–282.
Morrison, William B. "Fort Washita." *Chronicles of Oklahoma* 5 (June 1927):
  251–58.
Morton, Desmond. "Cavalry or Police: Keeping the Peace on Two Adjacent
  Frontiers, 1870–1900." *Journal of Canadian Studies* 12 (Spring 1977): 27–37.
Munkres, Robert L. "Fort Bridger." *Overland Journal* 8, no. 2 (1990): 25–34.
Murphy, Lawrence R. "'The Enemy Among Us': Venereal Disease among Union
  Soldiers in the Far West, 1861–1865." *Civil War History* 31 (September 1985):
  257–69.
Murray, Robert A. "Fort Fred Steele: Desert Outpost on the Union Pacific."
  Annals of Wyoming 44 (Fall 1972): 139–206.
———. "Prices and Wages at Fort Laramie, 1881–1885." *Annals of Wyoming* 36
  (April 1964): 19–21.
———. "The United States Army in the Aftermath of the Johnson County
  Invasion, April through November, 1892." In Robert A. Murray, *The Army on
  the Powder River*, 37–53. Bellevue, Nebr.: Old Army Press, 1969.
Myers, Lee. "Military Establishments in Southwestern New Mexico: Stepping
  Stones to Settlement." *New Mexico Historical Review* 43 (January 1968): 5–48.
———. "Mutiny at Fort Cummings." *New Mexico Historical Review* 38 (October
  1971): 337–50.
———. "Pope's Wells." *New Mexico Historical Review* 38 (October 1963): 273–99.

Myhra, Thomas J. "The Economic Influence of Steamboats on Early Bismarck." *North Dakota History* 28 (April–July 1961): 54–78.

Myres, Sandra L. "Army Women's Narratives as Documents of Social History: Some Examples from the Western Frontier, 1840–1900." *New Mexico Historical Review* 65 (April 1990): 175–98.

———. "Evy Alexander: The Colonel's Lady at McDowell in Arizona." *Montana, Magazine of Western History* 24 (July 1974): 26–38.

———. "Fort Graham: Listening Post on the Texas Frontier." *West Texas Historical Association Year Book* 59 (1983): 33–51.

———. "Frontier Historians, Women, and the 'New' Military History." *Military History of the Southwest* 19 (Spring 1989): 27–37.

———. "Romance and Reality on the American Frontier: Views of Army Wives." *Western Historical Quarterly* 13 (October 1982): 409–27.

Nalty, Bernard C., and Truman R. Strobridge. "Captain Emmet Crawford: Commander of Apache Scouts, 1882–1886." *Arizona and the West* 6 (Spring 1964): 30–40.

Nankivell, John H. "Fort Garland, Colorado." *Colorado Magazine* 16 (January 1939): 13–28.

———. "Fort Crawford, Colorado, 1880–1890." *Colorado Magazine* 11 (March 1934): 54–64.

Neighbors, Kenneth F. "Indian Exodus Out of Texas in 1859." *West Texas Historical Association Year Book* 36 (1960): 80–97.

Neilson, John. "Military Medicine on the Frontier: Charles M. Gandy in Texas, 1886–1890." *Fort Concho Report* 21, no. 2 (1989): 22–36.

———. "Soldiers and Surgeons: Army Medical Practice at Fort Concho, Texas, 1867–1889." *West Texas Historical Association Year Book* 69 (1993): 45–58.

Newman, Doris Nelson. "Nothing But His Country." *Daughters of the American Revolution Magazine* 120, no. 9 (1986): 756–60, 770, 791.

Nichols, Roger L. "Army Contributions to River Transportation, 1818–1825." *Military Affairs* 33 (April 1969): 242–49.

———. "The Army and Early Perceptions of the Plains." *Nebraska History* 56 (Spring 1975): 121–35.

———. "The Army and the Indians, 1800–1830—A Reappraisal: The Missouri Valley Example." *Pacific Historical Review* 41 (May 1972): 151–68.

———. "Scurvy at Cantonment Missouri, 1819–1820." *Nebraska History* 49 (Winter 1968): 333–48.

———. "Soldiers as Farmers: Army Agriculture in the Missouri Valley, 1818–1827." *Nebraska History* 52 (Fall 1971): 239–54.

———. "Stephen Long and Scientific Exploration of the Plains." *Nebraska History* 52 (Spring 1971): 51–64.

Nielsen, Soren W. "Ranald S. Mackenzie: The Man and His Battle." *West Texas Historical Association Year Book* 64 (1988): 140–52.

"None So Beautiful." *Fort Concho Report* 16 (Winter 1984–85): 36–37.

Nottage, James H. "A Centennial History of Artist Activities in Wyoming, 1837–1937." *Annals of Wyoming* 48 (Spring 1976): 77–100.

Obst, Janis. "Abigail Snelling, Military Wife, Military Widow." *Minnesota History* 54 (Fall 1994): 98–111.

Olch, Peter D. "Medicine in the Indian-Fighting Army, 1866–1890." *Journal of the West* 21 (July 1982): 32–41.

Oliva, Leo E. "The Army and Continental Expansion." In *The United States Army in Peacetime*, 21–39. Ed. Robin Higham and Carol Brandt. Manhattan, Kans.: Military Affairs–Aerospace Historian Publishing, 1975.

———. "The Army and the Fur Trade." *Journal of the West* 26 (October 1987): 21–26.

———. "Frontier Forts and the Settlement of Western Kansas." In *Kansas and the West: Bicentennial Essays in Honor of Nyle H. Miller*, 59–73. Ed. Forrest R. Blackburn et al. Topeka: Kansas State Historical Society, 1976.

Omer, George E., Jr. "An Army Hospital: From Dragoons to Rough Riders—Fort Riley, 1853–1903." *Kansas Historical Quarterly* 23 (Winter 1957): 337–67.

Oswald, John M. "History of Fort Elliott." *Panhandle-Plains Historical Review* 32 (1959): 1–59.

Palmieri, Anthony, and Chris Humberson. "Medical Incidents in the Life of Dr. John H. Finfrock." *Annals of Wyoming* 53 (Fall 1981): 64–69.

Parker, Watson. "The Majors and the Miners: The Role of the U.S. Army in the Black Hills Gold Rush." *Journal of the West* 11 (January 1972): 79–113.

Pate, J'Nell. "The Red River War of 1874: An Enlisted Man's Contribution." *Chronicles of Oklahoma* 54 (Summer 1976): 263–75.

Patterson, Richard. "Funston and the Fire." *American History Illustrated* 10 (December 1975): 34–45.

Pennanen, Gary. "Sitting Bull, Indian Without a Country." *Canadian Historical Review* 51 (June 1970): 123–40.

Pfaller, Louis L. "Eli Washington John Lindesmith: Fort Keogh's Chaplain in Buckskin." *Montana, Magazine of Western History* 27 (January 1977): 14–25.

Pingenot, Ben E. "The Great Wagon Train Expedition of 1850." *Southwestern Historical Quarterly* 98 (October 1994): 183–225.

Piston, Garrett. "Petticoats, Promotions, and Military Assignments: Favoritism and the Antebellum Career of James Longstreet." *Military History of the Southwest* 22 (Spring 1992): 15–30.

Porter, Joseph C. "'The American Congo': Captain John G. Bourke and the Texas Military Experience." In *The Texas Military Experience: From the Texas Revolution through World War II*, 113–27. Ed. Joseph G. Dawson III. College Station: Texas A&M University Press, 1995.

Powers, Ramon S., and Gene Younger. "Cholera and the Army in the West: Treatment and Control in 1866–1867." *Military Affairs* 39 (April 1975): 49–54.

————. "Cholera on the Overland Trails, 1832–1869." *Kansas Quarterly* 5 (Spring 1973): 32–49.

Prosch, Thomas W. "The Military Roads of Washington Territory." *Washington Historical Quarterly* 2 (January 1908): 118–26.

Prucha, Francis Paul. "The Settler and the Army in Frontier Minnesota." *Minnesota History* 29 (September 1948): 231–46.

Railsback, Thomas C. "Military Bands and Music at Old Fort Hays, 1867–1889." *Journal of the West* 22 (July 1983): 28–35.

Raines, Edgar F., Jr. "Major General J. Franklin Bell, U.S.A.: The Education of a Soldier, 1856–1899." *Register of the Kentucky Historical Society* 83 (Autumn 1985): 315–46.

Rathjen, Frederick W. "The Federal Role in Opening the Panhandle." *Panhandle-Plains Historical Review* 49 (1976): 1–24.

Reedy, Michael J. "Army Doctors—Pioneers and Peacemakers." *Military Medicine* 126 (December 1961): 891–94.

Rhoads, James B. "The Taming of the West: Military Archives as a Source for the Social History of the Trans-Mississippi Region to 1900." In *People of the Plains and Mountains: Essays in the History of the West Dedicated to Everett Dick*, 175–203. Ed. Ray Allen Billington. Westport, Conn.: Greenwood Press, 1973.

Rickards, Colin. "'The Christian General Investigates the Camp Grant Massacre." *The English Westerners' 10th Anniversary Publication*, 37–45. London: English Westerners' Society, 1964.

Riley, Paul. "Dr. David Franklin Powell and Fort McPherson." *Nebraska History* 51 (Summer 1970): 153–71.

Rister, Carl Coke. "The Border Post of Phantom Hill." *West Texas Historical Association Year Book* 14 (October 1938): 3–13.

Riter, Maria Inez Corlett. "Teaching School at Old Fort Laramie." *Annals of Wyoming* 51 (Fall 1979): 24–25.

Robrock, David P. "A History of Fort Fetterman, Wyoming, 1867–1882." *Annals of Wyoming* 48 (Spring 1976): 5–76.

Roome, Richard T. "A Cavalry Company on the Indian Frontier: A Short History of Troop L, 10th U.S. Cavalry." *Permian Historical Annual* 34 (December 1994): 25–43.

Ruhlen, George. "Fort Hancock—Last of the Frontier Forts." *Password* 4 (January 1959): 19–30.

————. "Quitman: The Worst Post at Which I Ever Served." *Password* 12 (Fall 1966): 107–26.

————. "Quitman's Owners: A Sidelight on Frontier Reality." *Password* 5 (April 1960): 54–64.

Russell, Don. "How Many Indians Were Killed?" *American West* 10 (July 1973): 42–47, 61–63.

Sageser, A. Bower. "Windmill and Pump Irrigation on the Great Plains 1890–1910." *Nebraska History* 48 (Summer 1967): 107–18.

Savage, W. Sherman. "The Role of Negro Soldiers in Protecting the Indian Territory from Intruders." *Journal of Negro History* 36 (January 1951): 25–34.

Scheips, Paul J. "Albert James Myer, an Army Doctor in Texas, 1854–1857." *Southwestern Historical Quarterly* 82 (July 1978): 1–24.

———. "'Old Probabilities': A. J. Myer and the Signal Corps Weather Service." *Arlington Historical Magazine* 5 (October 1974): 29–43.

———. "Will Croft Barnes, Soldier and Citizen of Arizona." *Arizona and the West* 2 (Autumn 1960): 205–12.

Schlesinger, Arthur M. "The City in American History." *Mississippi Valley Historical Review*, 27 (June 1940): 43–66.

Schmidt, Carol. "The Chaplains of Fort Concho." *Fort Concho Report* 16 (Spring 1984): 27–32; (Summer 1984): 31–40.

Schnell, J. Christopher, and Patrick E. McLear. "Why the Cities Grew: A Historiographical Essay on Western Urban Growth, 1850–1880." *Bulletin of the Missouri Historical Society* 28 (Spring 1972): 162–77.

Schofield, Donald F. "The Making of a West Texas Ghost Town: Tascosa vs. W. M. D. Lee." *West Texas Historical Association Year Book* 61 (1985): 30–41.

———. "W. M. D. Lee, Indian Trader." *Panhandle-Plains Historical Review* 54 (1981): 1–113.

Schreier, Jim. "Joseph B. Girard: Army Doctor and Artist of the Frontier." *Arizona Highways* 67 (March 1989): 43–45.

Schubert, Frank N. "Black Soldiers on the White Frontier: Some Factors Influencing Race Relations." *Phylon* 32 (Winter 1971): 410–15.

———. "The Fort Robinson Y.M.C.A., 1902–1907: A Social Organization in a Black Regiment." *Nebraska History* 55 (Summer 1974): 165–79.

———. "The Suggs Affray: The Black Cavalry in the Johnson County War." *Western Historical Quarterly* 4 (January 1973): 57–68.

———. "The Violent World of Emanuel Stance, Fort Robinson, 1887." *Nebraska History* 55 (Summer 1974): 203–19.

Schullery, Paul. "'Buffalo' Jones and the Bison Herd in Yellowstone: Another Look." *Montana, Magazine of Western History* 26 (July 1976): 40–51.

Scott, Douglas D. "An Officeres' Latrine at Fort Larned and Inferences on Status." *Plains Anthropologist* 34 (February 1989): 23–34.

Seraile, William. "Saving Souls on the Frontier: A Chaplain's Labor." *Montana, Magazine of Western History* 42 (Winter 1992): 29–41.

———. "Theophilus G. Steward, Intellectual Chaplain, 25th U.S. Colored Infantry." *Nebraska History* 66 (Fall 1985): 272–93.

Shideler, Frank J. "Custer Country: One Hundred Years of Change." *American West* 10 (July 1973): 25–31.

Shields, Alice Mathews. "Army Life on the Wyoming Frontier." *Annals of Wyoming* 13 (October 1941): 331–43.

Shirk, George H. "Mail Call at Fort Washita." *Chronicles of Oklahoma* 33 (Spring 1958): 14–35.

Sibbald, John R. "Camp Followers All." *American West* 3 (Spring 1966): 56–67.

———. "Frontier Inebriates with Epaulets." *Montana, Magazine of Western History* 19 (Summer 1969): 50–57.

Skaggs, Jimmy M. "Military Operations on the Cattle Trails." *Texas Military History* 6 (Summer 1967): 137–48.

Skelton, William B. "Army Officers' Attitudes toward Indians, 1830–1860." *Pacific Northwest Quarterly* 67 (July 1976): 113–24.

Slotkin, Richard ". . . and Then the Mare Will Go!: An 1875 Black Hills Scheme by Custer, Holladay, and Buford." *Journal of the West* 15 (July 1976): 60–77.

Smith, Duane A. "'Where a Bird Could Hardly Obtain a Footing': George Armstrong Custer and the Stevens Mine." *Colorado Heritage* (Spring 1997): 25–37.

Smith, Julia Cauble "The Shafter Mining District." *Permian Historical Annual* 28 (December 1988): 75–84.

Smith, Richard K. "For God . . . For Country . . . For the Territory." *Arizona Highways* 49 (April 1973): 8–12.

Smith, Sherry L. "Beyond Princess and Squaw: Army Officers' Perceptions of Indian Women." In *The Women's West*, 63–75. Ed. Susan Armitage and Elizabeth Jameson. Norman: University of Oklahoma Press, 1987.

———. "Officers' Wives, Indians and Indian Wars." *Journal of the Order of Indian Wars* 1 (Winter 1980): 35–46.

———. "Reimagining the Indian: Charles Erskine Scott Wood and Frank Linderman." *Pacific Northwest Quarterly* 87 (Summer 1996): 149–58.

———. "A Window on Themselves: Perceptions of Indians by Military Officers and Their Wives." *New Mexico Historical Review* 64 (October 1989): 447–61.

Smith, Thomas T. "Fort Inge and the Texas Frontier Economy, 1849–1869." *Military History of the Southwest* 21 (Fall 1991): 135–56.

———. "U.S. Army Combat Operations in the Indian Wars of Texas, 1849–1881." *Southwestern Historical Quarterly* 99 (April 1996): 501–31.

Smits, David D. "The Frontier Army and the Destruction of the Buffalo: 1865–1883." *Western Historical Quarterly* 25 (Autumn 1994): 313–38.

———. "More on the Army and the Buffalo: The Author's Reply." *Western Historical Quarterly* 26 (Summer 1995): 203–208.

Splitter, Henry Winfred. "The Adventures of an Editor in Search of an Author." *Journal of the West* 1 (October 1962): 201–14.

Stegner, Wallace. "The Scientist as Artist: Clarence E. Dutton and the Tertiary History of the Grand Cañon District." *American West* 15 (May–June 1978): 17–29.

Stewart, Miller J. "Army Laundresses: Ladies of the 'Soap Suds Row.'" *Nebraska History* 61 (Winter 1980): 421–36.

———. "To Plow, to Sow, to Reap, to Mow: The U.S. Army Agriculture Program." *Nebraska History* 63 (Summer 1982): 194–215.

———. "A Touch of Civilization: Culture and Education in the Frontier Army." *Nebraska History* 65 (Summer 1984): 257–82.

Stover, Earl F. "Chaplain Henry V. Plummer, His Ministry and His Court-Martial." *Nebraska History* 56 (Spring 1975): 21–50.

Stratton, David H. "The Army and the Gospel in the West." *Western Humanities Review* 8 (Spring 1954): 247–62.

Strobridge, William. "Soldiers in the Streets, 1906." *Pacific Historian* 22 (Spring 1978): 3–8.

Sutton, Mary "Glimpses of Fort Concho through the Military Telegraph." *West Texas Historical Association Year Book* 32 (1956): 122–34.

Tanner, George C. "History of Fort Ripley, 1849–1859, Based on the Diary of Rev. Solon W. Manney, D.D., Chaplain of the Post 1851–1859." *Collections of the State Historical Society of Minnesota* 10 (February 1905): 179–202.

Tapson, Alfred J. "The Sutler and the Soldier." *Military Affairs* 21 (Winter 1957): 175–81.

Tate, Michael L. "The Girl He Left Behind: Elizabeth Custer and the Making of a Legend." *Red River Valley Historical Review* 5 (Winter 1980): 5–22.

———. "The Multi-Purpose Army on the Frontier: A Call for Further Research." In *The American West: Essays in Honor of W. Eugene Hollon*, 171–208. Ed. Ronald Lora. Toledo, Ohio: University of Toledo Press, 1980.

———. "Randolph B. Marcy: First Explorer of the Wichitas." *Great Plains Journal* 15 (Spring 1976): 81–113.

———. "Soldiers of the Line: Apache Companies in the U.S. Army, 1891–1897." *Arizona and the West* 16 (Winter 1974): 343–64.

Taylor, Morris F. "The Mail Station and Military Camp on Pawnee Fork, 1859–1860." *Kansas Historical Quarterly* 36 (Spring 1970): 27–39.

Taylor, Quintard. "Comrades of Color: Buffalo Soldiers in the West: 1866–1917." *Colorado Heritage* (Spring 1996): 3–27.

Temple, Frank M. "Colonel B. H. Grierson's Administration of the District of the Pecos." *West Texas Historical Association Year Book* 38 (1962): 85–96.

———. "Discipline and Turmoil in the Tenth U.S. Cavalry." *West Texas Historical Association Year Book* 59 (1982): 103–18.

Thomas, Philip D. "The United States Army as the Early Patron of Naturalists in the Trans-Mississippi West, 1803–1820." *Chronicles of Oklahoma* 56 (Summer 1978): 171–93.

Thompson, D. Claudia. "Driven from Point to Point: Fact and Legend of the Bear River Riot." *Montana, Magazine of Western History* 46 (Winter 1996): 24–37.

Thompson, Erwin N. "The Negro Soldiers on the Frontier: A Fort Davis Case Study." *Journal of the West* 7 (April 1968): 217–35.

Thompson, Richard A. "Rainbow Cliffs: Camp Pena Colorado, Texas." *Fort Concho and the South Plains Journal* 22, no. 2 (1990): 6–26.

Thomson, William D. "History of Fort Pembina: 1870–1895." *North Dakota History* 36 (Winter 1969): 5–39.

Tidball, Eugene C. "John C. Tidball: Soldier-Artist of the Great Reconnaissance." *Journal of Arizona History* 37 (Summer 1996): 107–30.

Timmons, W. H. "The Merchants and the Military, 1849–1854." *Password* 27 (Summer 1982): 51–61.

Tudor, W. G. "Ghost Writers of the Palo Duro." *Southwestern Historical Quarterly* 99 (April 1996): 533–41.

Turcheneske, John A., Jr. "Historical Manuscripts as Sources for Anthropological Study: The Ethnological Correspondence of John Gregory Bourke." *New Mexico Historical Review* 59 (July 1984): 267–87.

———. "John G. Bourke—Troubled Scientist." *Journal of Arizona History* 20 (Autumn 1979): 323–44.

———. "The United States Congress and the Release of the Apache Prisoners of War at Fort Sill." *Chronicles of Oklahoma* 54 (Summer 1976): 199–226.

Turner, Alvin O. "Order and Disorder: The Opening of the Cherokee Outlet." *Chronicles of Oklahoma* 71 (Summer 1993): 154–73.

Turner, Frederick Jackson. "The Significance of the Frontier in American History." *Annual Report of the American Historical Association for the Year 1893.* Washington, D.C.: American Historical Association, 1894.

Twichel, Thomas. "Fort Logan and the Urban Frontier." *Montana, Magazine of Western History* 17 (Autumn 1967): 44–49.

Unrau, William E. "Indian Agent vs. the Army: Some Background Notes on the Kiowa-Comanche Treaty of 1865." *Kansas Historical Quarterly* 30 (Summer 1964): 129–52.

———. "Justice at Fort Laramie: The Trial and Tribulations of a Galvanized Yankee." *Arizona and the West* 15 (Summer 1973): 107–32.

———. "The Story of Fort Larned." *Kansas Historical Quarterly* 23 (Autumn 1957): 257–80.

Utley, Robert M. "Arizona Vanquished: Impressions and Reflections Concerning the Quality of Life on a Military Frontier." *American West* 6 (November 1969): 16–20.

———. "A Chained Dog: The Indian-Fighting Army." *American West* 10 (July 1973): 18–24, 61.

———. "The Frontier Army: John Ford or Arthur Penn?" In *Indian-White Relations: A Persistent Paradox*, 133–45. Ed. Jane F. Smith and Robert Kvasnicka. Washington, D.C.: Howard University Press, 1976.

Vaughn, J. W. "The Mark H. Kellogg Story." *Westerners New York Posse Brand Book* 7 (1961): 73–75, 84–91.

Wade, Arthur P. "The Military Command Structure: The Great Plains, 1853–1891." *Journal of the West* 15 (July 1976): 5–22.

———. "A Military Offspring of the American Philosophical Society." *Military Affairs* 38 (September 1974): 103–107.

Wade, Louise Carroll. "Hell Hath No Fury Like a General Scorned: Nelson A. Miles, the Pullman Strike, and the Beef Scandal of 1898." *Illinois Historical Quarterly* 79, no. 3 (1986): 162–84.

Walker, Henry P. "Bugler! No Pay Call Today! The Year the Army Went Payless." *Montana, Magazine of Western History* 21 (Summer 1971): 34–43.

———. "George Crook, 'The Gray Fox': Prudent, Compassionate Indian Fighter." *Montana, Magazine of Western History* 17 (April 1967): 2–13.

———. "When the Law Wore Army Blue." *Military Collector and Historian* 29 (Spring 1977): 4–14.

Watson, Elmo Scott. "The Last Indian War, 1890–91: A Study of Newspaper Jingoism." *Journalism Quarterly* 20 (September 1943): 205–19.

Weist, Katherine M. "Ned Casey and His Cheyenne Scouts: A Noble Experiment in An Atmosphere of Tension." *Montana, Magazine of Western History* 27 (January 1977): 26–39.

Welty, Raymond L. "The Army Fort of the Frontier." *North Dakota Historical Quarterly* 2 (January 1928): 85–99; (April 1928): 155–67.

———. "The Daily Life of the Frontier Soldier." *Cavalry Journal* 36 (1927): 584–94.

———. "The Indian Policy of the Army 1860–1870." *Cavalry Journal* 36 (July 1927): 367–81.

———. "The Policing of the Frontier by the Army, 1860–1870." *Kansas Historical Quarterly* 7 (August 1938): 246–57.

———. "Supplying the Frontier Military Posts." *Kansas Historical Quarterly* 7 (May 1938): 154–69.

Wengert, James W. "The Contract Surgeon." *Journal of the West* 36 (January 1997): 67–76.

Werne, Joseph Richard. "Surveying the Rio Grande, 1850–1853." *Southwestern Historical Quarterly* 94 (April 1991): 535–54.

Wertenberger, Mildred, comp. "Fort Totten, Dakota Territory, 1867." *North Dakota History* 34 (Spring 1967): 125–46.

Wesley, Edgar B. "Life at Fort Atkinson." *Nebraska History* 30 (December 1949): 348–58.

White, William Bruce. "ABCs for the American Enlisted Man: The Army Post School System, 1866–1898." *History of Education Quarterly* 8 (Winter 1968): 479–96.

———. "The American Indian as Soldier, 1890–1919." *Canadian Review of American Studies* 7 (Spring 1976): 15–25.

White, W. Thomas. "Boycott: The Pullman Strike in Montana." *Montana, Magazine of Western History* 29 (October 1979): 2–13.

Wier, James A. "19th Century Army Doctors on the Frontier and in Nebraska." *Nebraska History* 61 (Summer 1980): 192–214.

Will, Drake W. "Lewis and Clark: Westering Physicians." *Montana, Magazine of Western History* 21 (October 1971): 2–17.

Williams, J. W. "Military Roads of the 1850s in Central West Texas." *West Texas Historical Association Year Book* 18 (1942): 77–91.

Williams, Mary L. "Care of the Dead (and Lack of It) at 19th Century Posts." *Periodical: Journal of the Council on America's Military Past* 13, no. 1 (1984): 14–30.

———. "Empire Building: Colonel Benjamin H. Grierson at Fort Davis, 1882–1885." *West Texas Historical Association Year Book* 61 (1985): 58–73.

———. "Fort Davis Texas: Key Defense Post on the San Antonio–El Paso Road." *Password* 31 (Winter 1986): 205–10.

Willman, Lillian. "The History of Fort Kearny." *Publications of the Nebraska State Historical Society* 21:213–79. Lincoln: Nebraska State Historical Society, 1930.

Wilson, Frederick T. "Old Fort Pierre and Its Neighbors." Ed. Charles E. De Land. *South Dakota Historical Collections* 1 (1902): 259–440.

Wilson, John P. "Whiskey at Fort Fillmore: A Story of the Civil War." *New Mexico Historical Review* 68 (April 1993): 109–32.

Wooster, Robert. "The Army and the Politics of Expansion: Texas and the Southwestern Borderlands, 1870–1886." *Southwestern Historical Quarterly* 93 (October 1989): 151–67.

———. "'The Whole Company Have Done It': The U.S. Army and the Fort Davis Murder of 1860." *Journal of the West* 32 (April 1993): 19–28.

Wright, Dana. "The Fort Totten–Fort Stevenson Trail, 1867–1872." *North Dakota History* 20 (April 1953): 67–86.

Wright, Muriel H. "A History of Fort Cobb." *Chronicles of Oklahoma* 34 (Spring 1956): 53–71.

Wyman, Walker D. "The Military Phase of Santa Fe Freighting, 1846–1865." *Kansas Historical Quarterly* 1 (November 1932): 415–28.

Young, Otis E. "Military Protection of the Santa Fe Trail and Trade." *Missouri Historical Review* 49 (October 1954): 19–32.

Zimmerman, Jean L. "Colonel Ranald S. Mackenzie at Fort Sill." *Chronicles of Oklahoma* 44 (Spring 1966): 12–21.

Index